PRINCETON SEMINARY

The Majestic Testimony

PRINCETON SEMINARY

David B. Calhoun

Volume 2
The Majestic Testimony
1869–1929

THE BANNER OF TRUTH TRUST

THE BANNER OF TRUTH TRUST
3 Murrayfield Road, Edinburgh EH12 6EL
P.O. Box 621, Carlisle, Pennsylvania 17013, USA

*

© David B. Calhoun 1996
First Published 1996
ISBN 0 85151 695 5

*

Typeset in 11/12pt New Baskerville
at the Banner of Truth Trust, Edinburgh
Printed and bound in the USA

And to Jon

The majestic testimony of the Church
in all time
is that its advances in spiritual life
have always been toward and not away from the Bible,
and in proportion to the reverence for,
and power of realizing in practical life,
the revealed Word.

Caspar Wistar Hodge

CONTENTS

ACKNOWLEDGEMENT

Both author and publisher are indebted to the Rev. William
O. Harris, Librarian for Archives and Special Collections at
Princeton Theological Seminary, for the immense help he has
given in securing and providing so many of the illustrations in
this volume. We could not have had more enthusiastic and
generous support.

[x]

ILLUSTRATIONS

[xi]

ABBREVIATIONS

AP   *American Presbyterians: Journal of Presbyterian*
              History (1985—) (Philadelphia: Presbyterian
              Historical Society)

JPH   *Journal of Presbyterian History (1962–1984)* (Phila-
              delphia: Presbyterian Historical Society)

JPHS   *Journal of the Presbyterian Historical Society* (1901–
              61) (Philadelphia: Presbyterian Historical
              Society)

LCH   *The Life of Charles Hodge, D.D., LL.D., Professor in*
              the Theological Seminary, Princeton, N.J., Archibald
              Alexander Hodge (New York: Charles Scribner's
              Sons), 1880

PSB   *Princeton Seminary Bulletin*

SSW 1, 2   *Selected Shorter Writings of Benjamin B. Warfield,* ed.
              John E. Meeter (Nutley, N.J.: Presbyterian and
              Reformed Publishing Company), 1973

PRINCETON JOURNALS

BR   *Biblical Repertory: A Collection of Tracts in Biblical*
              Literature (1825–28)
              Biblical Repertory: A Journal of Biblical Literature and
              Theological Science (1829)

BRTR   *Biblical Repertory and Theological Review* (1830–36)

BRPR   *Biblical Repertory and Princeton Review* (1837–71)

PQPR   *Presbyterian Quarterly and Princeton Review* (1872–
              77)

PR   *The Presbyterian Review* (1880–89)

PRR   *The Presbyterian and Reformed Review* (1890–1902)

PTR   *The Princeton Theological Review* (1903–29)

FOREWORD

In this second volume of his history of Princeton Seminary Dr. David Calhoun describes the semicentennial of Old Testament Professor William Henry Green, who in May of 1896 could refer to himself as "the only remaining link between the original faculty of the Seminary and its present faculty." Coming about halfway through the six decades covered in this volume, Green's speech on that occasion claimed that Princeton stands,

as it has always stood, for fidelity to the Word of God and the standards of the Presbyterian Church. At the same time it stands for the highest grade of Biblical and theological learning. It welcomes all the light that can be thrown upon the Scriptures from every quarter, and does not shrink from the application of the most rigorous tests to the question of their origin or the nature of their contents. Convinced by the most abundant evidence that these Scriptures are the infallible word of God, and that their teachings are the utterances of divinely sanctioned truth, this Seminary has always maintained that sound learning will ever go hand in hand with implicit faith in this sacred volume.

Praising Princeton's first teachers—Archibald Alexander, Samuel Miller, Charles Hodge, and Addison Alexander— Green said that under these early teachers Princeton theology "gained a definite and well understood meaning, which it is to be hoped, it will never lose; from which may it never swerve."

But swerve it did. Only a generation later, in 1927, New Testament Professor J. Gresham Machen felt constrained to publish *The Attack upon Princeton Seminary: A Plea for Fair Play*, in which he claimed that the Presbyterian Church USA's proposed reorganization of the seminary threatened three major emphases in the Princeton tradition: Princeton's adherence to "the complete truthfulness of the Bible as the Word of God," its commitment to "the Reformed or Calvinistic faith as being the system of doctrine that the Bible contains," and its insistence on a scholarly defense of the Bible and the Westminster Standards. When the reorganization took place in 1929, Machen, Robert Dick Wilson, Oswald T. Allis, and Cornelius Van Til left the faculty of Princeton to form Westminster Theological Seminary, and in 1930 John Murray also left Princeton to join them. Professor Lefferts A. Loetscher conceded in 1980 that the seminary after 1929 was not the same as the Old Princeton tradition.

This story, and much more, is told in lucid fashion by Dr. Calhoun. In his first volume not only the famous earliest professors—Archibald Alexander, Samuel Miller, and Charles Hodge—were vividly portrayed, but also Ashbel Green, James W. Alexander, John Breckinridge, and Joseph Addison Alexander. In this second volume we are shown the intellect and piety not only of Charles Hodge (again), A. A. Hodge, Benjamin Breckinridge Warfield, and J. Gresham Machen, but also that of such figures as James McCosh, William Henry Green, William M. Paxton, Francis Landey Patton, and Geerhardus Vos. To demonstrate that there was no cleavage between piety and learning, Calhoun effectively adds the dimension of human personality to the narrative of Princeton Seminary as an institution. These scholars and preachers were both exemplars of godliness and intellectual giants. As a student said of A. A. Hodge, "he had a powerful brain, a large heart, and the simple faith of a little child."

There are at least three reasons why it is important that this story of Old Princeton be told. One is that it is generally recognized that Old Princeton was a major influence on contemporary evangelicalism in America. By bringing his account down to the watershed date of 1929, Calhoun has brought out fully the consistent combination of scholarship and piety from the seminary's beginnings in 1812. He also keeps before our vision the missionary and evangelistic emphasis that so characterized students and teachers alike. Included in his purview is the role of African Americans at Princeton Seminary. It is beneficial for contemporary evangelicalism to have as full an understanding of the Old Princeton tradition as possible.

Secondly, Calhoun's history provides several correctives to usual interpretations of the Princeton tradition. He counters the claim that it was too rationalistic. Contrary to the views of such scholars as Ernest Sandeen, Jack B. Rogers, and Donald K. McKim, he shows that the doctrine of the inerrancy of Scripture was not a late invention of A. A. Hodge and B. B. Warfield. With regard to the influence of Scottish Common Sense Realism, he builds on George Marsden's point that the Princetonians believed that the same God who created the world created the human mind. Warfield, who stands out in intellect among all the notable scholars of Princeton, is shown to be not only an evidentialist in apologetics, but also one who recognized that believers and unbelievers do not look at the truth in the same way. With regard to Charles Hodge's statement that there were "no new ideas" at Princeton, Calhoun says, "The Princetonians were right in claiming that their theology was not new. When they said new things, or expressed old things in a new way, or advocated new methods, it was always in an effort to conserve the old truth. Their determination to be faithful witnesses enabled them to succeed. The Reformed faith was safe in their hands." In these several instances Calhoun puts common understandings of Princeton in their proper contexts and thus sheds new light. He has mastered the vast corpus of primary materials, and he makes careful use of the secondary literature down to the recent contributions of Bradley Longfield and D. G. Hart.

In the third place, Calhoun's history furnishes important lessons for those of us who in some measure are heirs to the Princeton tradition. In his account of the 1920s he points out that in this "period of siege for Old Princeton," "in its desperate fight for life, attention to some very good things was lessened." Such things as "sturdy biblical exposition, great preaching, and more evangelistic and missionary zeal would have strengthened the Princeton cause" along with its "stalwart defense of the faith." Princeton was not perfect, and we can learn from its occasional imbalances and mistakes. On the other hand, in our delight to maintain some of the distinctives of Old Princeton we should not lose sight of the catholicity of spirit that characterized its theology, particularly that of Charles Hodge. As Calhoun says, "He clearly took more pleasure in citing the consensus of Christendom in opposition to error than in criticizing opinions opposed to Calvinism."

I would add a personal word about the author. For those of us who have had the privilege of knowing him as a schoolmate, a teacher, a colleague, a friend, David Calhoun himself reflects the values of the tradition of which he writes: learning, piety, the human dimension, effective preaching, missionary vision, the aesthetic sensitivity to the appropriate anecdote or illustration to make a well-told story—above all, a love for people whom one senses he looks forward to meeting in the presence of the Lord who is loved most of all.

WILLIAM S. BARKER
Vice President for Academic Affairs
and Professor of Church History
Westminster Theological Seminary,
Philadelphia, August 7, 1995

PREFACE

*Charles Hodge in 1872,
the fiftieth year of his professorship.*

I N 1869 Congress passed the Fifteenth Amendment to the Constitution to ensure black male suffrage in the North and the South. Wyoming became the first state to enfranchise women and give them the right to hold office. On March 4, Civil War hero Ulysses S. Grant was inaugurated president of the United States. On April 7, the first all-professional baseball team, the Cincinnati Red Stockings, opened its season, with the shortstop its highest paid player at $1,400 a year. The transcontinental railroad was completed on May 10 with the help of thousands of Chinese workers—joining by a golden spike in Utah 1,086 miles of track from Omaha with 689 miles across mountains and desert from California. In September the National Prohibition Party formed in Chicago to agitate for temperance. The Suez Canal was opened in November, and on December 8 the Vatican Council began to debate papal primacy and infallibility. In 1869 margarine and celluloid were invented. Claude Monet painted *The Balcony*, Brahms wrote his *Hungarian Dances*, and Wagner completed *The Rhinegold*. R. D. Blackmore's *Lorna Doone* was published, as was Jules Verne's *Twenty Thousand Leagues Under the Sea* and Mark Twain's *Innocents Abroad*. Frank Lloyd Wright was born in Wisconsin, and Mahatma Gandhi in India. In Basel the twenty-four-year-old professor Friedrich Nietzsche brooded his radical thoughts.

Princeton had passed through the bitter years of the Civil War, loyal to the Union but deeply grieved over the tragedy of the national conflict and the breaking of its old ties with the South. In 1869 the College of New Jersey (or Princeton College as it was often called) was one hundred and twenty-three years old, and Princeton Seminary began its fifty-eighth year. The seminary's first two professors, Archibald Alexander and Samuel Miller, "having served their generation," had "fallen asleep in Jesus" in 1850 and 1851. Two of Dr. Alexander's sons, the pastoral James Waddell and the brilliant Joseph Addison, both of whom had taught at the seminary, died in 1859 and 1860. Kind, learned, and beloved, Charles Hodge, now seventy-one years old, had taught at Princeton for almost fifty years. The prodigious William Henry Green joined Hodge on the faculty in 1851, teaching Old Testament and battling the new higher critical views. The versatile Alexander McGill, who came to Princeton in 1854, taught at one time or another pastoral theology, church government, homiletics, and church history. In 1860 Charles Hodge's son Caspar Wistar Hodge reluctantly left the pastorate to accept a place on the faculty as teacher of New Testament. The next year Scottish-born James Clement Moffat became professor of church history.

In 1869 William D. Snodgrass, pastor of the Presbyterian church in Goshen, New York, was president of Princeton Seminary's board of directors. Snodgrass studied at the seminary from 1816 to 1818 (with Charles Hodge and Henry Woodward, Princeton's first foreign missionary). Directors included William Buell Sprague, pastor of the Second Presbyterian Church of Albany, New York; Henry A. Boardman, pastor of Philadelphia's Tenth Presbyterian Church; William M. Paxton, pastor of First Presbyterian Church of New York City; James McCosh, president of Princeton College; Samuel Miller, son of Princeton's second professor; and Levi P. Stone (who endowed the first lectureship in 1878). President of Princeton's board of trustees, which had responsibility for the financial and business arrangements of the seminary, was the Honorable Henry W. Green, an uncle of Professor William Henry Green's. Among those serving with him were James Lenox, generous benefactor of Princeton College and Princeton Seminary; Stephen Colwell; John C. Green, another uncle of William Henry Green's; Lyman Atwater; and Samuel D. Alexander, son of Princeton's first professor.

Hundreds of Presbyterian men and women and members of other churches prayed for the faculty and students and supported the seminary with gifts. Most of their names are not recorded in this history, but their faithfulness to God is a major part of the real story of Princeton Seminary.

The Biblical Repertory and Princeton Review had become, under Charles Hodge's leadership, one of the major journals in the country. "Consistent, judicious, conservative, intelligent . . . literary, often humorous and witty," the *Princeton Review*, for forty-four years, had put forth quarterly Reformed opinion on a large variety of topics and issues.[1]

The two parts of the Presbyterian church in the North came together in 1870 with much celebration—somewhat subdued at Princeton Seminary by Charles Hodge's reluctance to see the Old School Presbyterian Church disappear. With grace, however, Dr. Hodge bowed to the will of the church, while Archibald Alexander Hodge—his professor-son at Western Seminary, soon to be his colleague and then successor at Princeton—rejoiced in the reunion.

In its first half century Princeton Seminary had known theological controversy and ecclesiastical crisis. Firmly and courteously Alexander, Miller, Hodge, and their associates had attempted to guard the faith that had been given to them. United happily and often with other Christians, they were constrained at times to disagree—sometimes in matters of great importance, sometimes in lesser issues. Before long, however, Princeton would find itself fighting the greatest fight of its life—a battle to preserve belief in the Bible as a true book of God, and Christianity in its historic shape as God's way of salvation. The battle would be long and hard and there would be limited success, as the world and even the institutional church viewed success, but the Princetonians, from the days of Charles Hodge and William Henry Green to B. B. Warfield and J. Gresham Machen, contended with courage, scholarship, and faith. Theirs was indeed a *Majestic Testimony*.

DAVID B. CALHOUN
Covenant Theological Seminary
St. Louis, Missouri
September, 1995

1

Faith and Learning

An Old University town ...
Kirk and College keeping time,
Faith and Learning, chime for chime.

Princetoniana

JOHN Maclean had served Princeton College for a half century—as tutor, professor, vice president, and president. Although he was still vigorous and healthy, he believed it was time to submit his resignation. As college trustee Charles Hodge read Maclean's letter to the other members of the board, they listened with deep emotion. Dr. Maclean had built up the college endowment, founded scholarships, elevated entrance requirements, added buildings, and secured better scientific equipment. He had maintained the traditional curriculum and had preserved Princeton's evangelical and Presbyterian orientation. Maclean enjoyed warm, cordial relations with students, parents, and friends of the college and, according to Charles Hodge, was "the most loved man in America."[1] Accepting his resignation, the trustees thanked Dr. Maclean for his faithful, self-sacrificing devotion to the college, his care for the students, and his long service in the cause of Christian education.

Seven of the college's ten faculty members were ministers and all were Calvinists.[2] John Thomas Duffield, graduate of Princeton College and Princeton Seminary, was professor of mathematics and mechanics. Matthew B. Hope, graduate of Princeton Seminary and former missionary in Singapore, was professor of belles-lettres and political economy. Swiss-born Arnold Guyot, professor of geology and physical geography, furthered Princeton's reputation in science. Although he had begun serious preparation for the Christian ministry, Guyot decided on a career in science and studied in Germany with some of the great scientists of his day. He came to America from Switzerland when the Neuchâtel Academy, at which he was professor of history and geography, was suppressed by the revolutionary council of Geneva in 1848. A pioneer in the field of geography as a serious and independent science, Dr. Guyot surveyed and mapped American mountain ranges—engraving "the name of Princeton," a later Princetonian said, "upon this planet." Guyot gave lectures on the harmony of geology and the Bible in New York City in 1852. He repeated the series at the College of New Jersey, Union Theological Seminary, and, for several years in succession, at Princeton Seminary. From 1861 until 1866 he lectured to the seminarians on the "Connection of Revealed Religion and Ethnological Science."[3] Lyman Atwater, a Yale graduate whose English—according to one of his students—would have "delighted the soul of Dr. Johnson," had joined the Princeton faculty in 1854 as professor of moral and mental science. In 1861 Atwater began to lecture at the seminary on the "Connection between Revealed Religion and Metaphysical Science," and for many years he served as an associate editor of the *Biblical Repertory and Princeton Review*. Dr. Atwater was appointed interim president of the college while the trustees looked for a successor to Dr. Maclean.

There was rejoicing among the friends of Princeton when the trustees announced that they had chosen as the new college president Princeton Seminary professor William Henry Green. Joseph Henry—Princeton's famous scientist now directing the Smithsonian Institute—was gratified that the decision had been "so judiciously made" and hastened to write to Dr. Green, urging him to accept. Green, however, quickly and politely turned down the offer and the board was forced to look elsewhere. The trustees saw no other obvious candidate. The story is told of how, in their dilemma, one of them recalled that exactly one hundred years earlier Princeton had turned to Scotland and to John Witherspoon for new leadership. He thought that God might bless the school again in a similar way. Soon the name of James McCosh was brought before the trustees.[4]

In the summer of 1866 James McCosh, professor of logic and metaphysics at Queen's College, Belfast, had come to the

United States on a lecture tour, traveling as far west as St. Louis. Large congregations had gathered to hear him speak. Before a crowded audience at the Fifth Avenue Presbyterian Church in New York City, Dr. McCosh brilliantly defended the truthfulness of the gospels against the attack of Joseph Ernst Renan, who denied the deity and miracles of Christ. McCosh made a special stop at Princeton to see the "famous University and Theological Seminary." Years later he remembered his first view "of the pleasant heights on which the College stands, the highest ground between the two great cities of the Union, looking down on rich country, covered with wheat and corn, with apples and peaches, resembling the south of England as much as one country can be like another." He was impressed also with the Princeton schools and wrote: "Princeton is a remarkable place—we have nothing precisely like it in our own country. It is astonishing to find such a company of eminent professors centered in a small village."[5]

*   *   *

James McCosh was born on April 1, 1811, in a sturdy stone farmhouse—just above the banks of the River Doon—in the village of Patna in southwest Scotland. He was "descended from the old Covenanting stock" and was "brought up in a district where there [were] martyrs' tombs in every church-yard." McCosh studied at the University of Glasgow and at Edinburgh, where he came under the influence of Thomas Chalmers and Sir William Hamilton. From Chalmers he received his earnest evangelical spirit and from Hamilton, his philosophical bent. Ordained to the Christian ministry, McCosh was called to churches at Arbroath and then Brechin, where he and neighboring minister Thomas Guthrie became friends. The two men met often for prayer and discussion. On September 29, 1845, McCosh married Guthrie's niece Isabella, daughter of noted physician Alexander Guthrie. Isabella Guthrie reflected all the energy and vitality of her remarkable family and was a woman of enormous resource-fulness. At the Disruption in 1843 James McCosh established a congregation of the Free Church of Scotland in his old

[5]

parish. He served zealously during the early years of the Free Church—riding long distances on horseback to preach in barns, ballrooms, and fields, raising money, and organizing new congregations and providing them with preachers.[6]

In 1850 James McCosh's *Method of the Divine Government, Physical and Moral*—a book described as a "theistic doctrine of the world"—was published in Edinburgh. According to a later student and colleague, McCosh "was trying to show thinking men who had been trained in religion that a true construction of the facts of mind and nature was a vindication of their Christian faith and that true philosophy strengthened faith in the divine government. It was a book well calculated to stiffen weak backs and strengthen feeble knees." Dr. McCosh's *Divine Government* established him as a philosopher of clear, strong, evangelical views and a writer "at times . . . more hortatory perhaps than the most rigid canons of logic would approve."[7]

Earl Clarendon, Lord Lieutenant of Ireland, sat down to read McCosh's book one Sunday morning and, according to the often-repeated story, became so absorbed in it that he forgot to go to church. He read on till evening without stopping and, soon after, offered McCosh the chair of philosophy in the newly founded Queen's College in Belfast. James McCosh became a successful teacher with a keen personal interest in his students. He published a number of books including *The Intuitions of the Mind, Inductively Investigated,* his "philosophic confession of faith" in which he argued that there are "necessary beliefs" and "immediate knowledge of reality."[8] Dr. McCosh became acquainted with the great universities of Europe, especially Oxford and Cambridge, and formed friendships with distinguished teachers. He was an important leader in the Irish Presbyterian church. He enthusiastically participated in the revival of 1859, helped found the Bible and Colportage Society of Ireland, and conducted regular Bible classes for mill workers in the poorer parts of Belfast.

*   *   *

On April 29, 1868, the Princeton College trustees enthusiastically elected Dr. McCosh president. In the words of a later Princeton historian, McCosh's "views in philosophy were those which had been taught and defended at Princeton College, and his Scottish nationality and his residence in Ulster were an additional recommendation to the college of John Witherspoon and to the church of Francis Makemie."[9] It had taken weeks for the news to reach Witherspoon when he was elected president in 1768; but the invitation to McCosh went by "ocean telegraph," which had been instituted only two years before. In late May the Old School and New School Presbyterian churches were holding their General Assemblies, their main business being the approval of reunion. On the same day that the reunion was accomplished both assemblies paused in the middle of their deliberations to hear their moderators read telegrams informing them of Dr. McCosh's acceptance of the Princeton presidency and to pass resolutions welcoming "the good news."

James McCosh and his family departed from Liverpool in late September 1868, and their ship, the *Tripoli*, arrived at New York on October 20. They went by train to Princeton. Towards three o'clock in the afternoon the students and faculty moved to the little railroad station and welcomed the new president with wild cheering. They escorted the McCoshes to the president's home, which had been thoroughly renovated and prepared for them. McCosh had come, as he himself put it, to devote his "remaining life under God to old Princeton and the religious and literary interests with which it is identified."[10]

Dr. McCosh's inauguration took place on October 27. Special trains from New York and Philadelphia brought "such a concourse of graduates and of learned and distinguished men from different parts of the country as [had] never before been known in the history of the College." Every class for fifty years was represented. Two graduates of the class of 1795 were on the platform to bridge symbolically the years that stretched between the administrations of the Scottish presidents, Witherspoon and McCosh. A member of the senior class gave a welcome address in Latin, interrupted frequently by the vigorous applause of his fellow students. Then Charles Hodge speaking for the college trustees welcomed Dr. McCosh and went on to say: "We would in a single word state what it is we desire. It is that true religion here may be dominant; that a pure gospel may be preached, and taught, and lived; that the students should be made to feel that the eternal is infinitely more important than the temporal, the heavenly than the earthly." Hodge closed his address by commending the new president "to the grace of God, and the guidance of our great God and Saviour, Jesus Christ, for whom this College was founded, and to whom it inalienably belongs."[11]

Dr. McCosh responded by saying, "I have seen enough of the American colleges to become convinced that they are not to be rashly meddled with. . . . Whatever improvements they admit must be built on the old foundations." He added:

In regard to religious truth, there will be no uncertain sound uttered within these walls. What is proclaimed here will be the old truth which has been from the beginning: which was shown in the shadow in the Old Testament; which was exhibited fully in the New Testament as in a glass; which has been retained by the one Catholic Church in the darkest ages; which was long buried, but rose again at the Reformation; which was maintained by the grand old theologians of Germany, Switzerland, England, and Scotland; and is being defended with great logical power in the famous Theological Seminary with which this College is so closely associated.

McCosh then spoke concerning "academic teaching in Europe," drawing on his knowledge of Scottish, Irish, English, and continental universities. He concluded his two-hour discourse by telling his Princeton audience, "And so I devote my life, any gifts which God has given me, my experience as a minister of religion in a great era in the history of Scotland, my experience as a professor in a young and living College, under God to you and your service."[12]

Well over six feet tall, with long white sideburns that extended down half his face, Dr. McCosh was striking in appearance—one student said that he was "the most beautiful human being he ever beheld"—charming in manner, and

[8]

impressive in speech. Woodrow Wilson, who studied at Princeton under McCosh, described his speech as "redolent with the flavor of the Scottish accent that gave piquancy to everything he said. There was always some phrase or turn that seemed wholly his own."[13]

McCosh was convinced that Princeton was destined to become one of the great American universities. "It is the will of God," he said, "and I will do it." He toured the country to gain money and students for his college. He expanded and diversified the faculty. He organized new fellowships for the college's best students, sent some of them to European universities for further study, and brought them back to Princeton as teachers. Under Dr. McCosh the life of the campus was enriched—making "the four long years" more enjoyable. Student publications were established; and the glee club, the dramatic association, and the first eating clubs came into existence. Upon his arrival at Princeton McCosh arranged for the building of a gymnasium, which he welcomed for its potential in "promoting morality and preventing mischief by fully occupying the physical energy of our youth." When he heard that students were gathering at a local billiard hall he ordered three billiard tables for the gym.[14]

The college students played croquet, took part in boxing matches, and played baseball and football. Baseball had been introduced by students from Brooklyn, and in 1862 Princeton became the first school to have an organized college baseball team—meeting teams from the town and the seminary. In the second game on record, played on April 19, 1862, the college defeated the seminary 45 to 13. Football games took place between the different college classes. The class of 1871, which included a Kentucky student by the name of Benjamin Breckinridge Warfield, was the champion team of the college. No other single class would face it; a team had to be made up from the rest of the college to compete against it. But the Warfield team defeated that team twice! On November 6, 1869, a twenty-five-man Princeton team traveled to New Brunswick to meet Rutgers in the first intercollegiate football game played in the United States. Despite President McCosh's enthusiastic cheering, Rutgers won, six goals to four; but a return match at Princeton on November 13 resulted in an eight-to-nothing Princeton victory. The following fall Rutgers was defeated, six to two, and declined to play again that year. The college then played the seminary and won, but the score was not recorded. Enthusiasm for football quickly reached fever pitch. The annual Princeton–Yale game, played in New York City, became a major social event for which the Reverend Henry Ward Beecher and other ministers shortened their Thanksgiving sermons!

*   *   *

In November 1859 British scientist Charles Darwin's 700-page book, *On the Origin of Species by Means of Natural Selection,* appeared. For well over a century the evolutionary idea had been suggested in various forms, but it was Darwin who set forth a theory that captured popular attention. *The Origin of Species* did not go unnoticed at Princeton. Not only the professors at the college but also the theologians at the seminary read it.

The Princetonians were keenly interested in science. In this they followed John Calvin, who encouraged the scientific study of nature, believing that "the elegant structure of the world" served "as a kind of mirror in which we may see God."[15] The Princeton commitment to both science and theology—and their essential unity—resulted in the establishment of a special professorship of science and religion in the college. In 1865 Charles Woodruff Shields, a Princeton College and Princeton Seminary graduate, was appointed to the position. His two-volume *Philosophia Ultima; or, Science of the Sciences* was designed to fulfill what Shields took to be his appointed task, namely, providing "a systematic illustration of the harmony of Biblical and scientific truth involving an argument for the divine authority of the Holy Scriptures and the Christian religion."[16]

Archibald Alexander declared in his inaugural address in 1812:

Indeed, to speak the truth, there is scarcely any science or branch of knowledge which may not be made subservient to Theology. Natural history, chemistry, and geology have sometimes been of important service in assisting the Biblical student to solve difficulties contained in Scripture; or in enabling him to repel the assaults of adversaries which were made under cover of these sciences. A general acquaintance with the whole circle of science is of more consequence to the Theologian than at first sight appears. Not to mention the intimate connexion which subsists between all the parts of truth, in consequence of which important light may often be collected from the remotest quarters; it may be observed that the state of learning in the world requires the advocate of the Bible to attend to many things which may not in themselves be absolutely necessary.[17]

Dr. Alexander expanded these ideas in 1829 in an article in the first issue of the reorganized *Biblical Repertory*, entitled "The Bible, A Key to the Phenomena of the Natural World." Samuel Miller's *Brief Retrospect of the Eighteenth Century* gave ample attention to science. Miller pointed out that "Christian nations . . . have been . . . most remarkable for favoring the advancement of liberal knowledge; [and] literature and science have been most extensively and successfully cultivated." In his sermon "The Teaching Office of the Church" Charles Hodge stated, "Science undermines the pillars of heathenism, and frightens its votaries from its tottering walls." The seminary professors believed that science and theology were allies in establishing the truth. God is the author of both Scripture and creation; so the Bible properly interpreted, they believed and taught, could not conflict with the facts of nature properly understood. Charles Hodge wrote in 1859, "God in nature can never contradict God in the Bible and in the hearts of his people." Hodge was fond of telling the students at the seminary that "the truth has nothing to fear from the truth."[18]

Princeton's Common Sense Philosophy distinguished between facts and theories. As Charles Hodge wrote, "Theory has to be determined by facts, and not facts by theory." Hodge, however, did not limit science to bare facts. In his *Systematic Theology* he made the point that the mere orderly arrangement of facts does not amount to science, which must go beyond isolated facts to exhibit their internal relations and to "understand the laws by which the facts of experience are determined." When science proceeds properly, Hodge argued, we can let it take its course—knowing that "all well-authenticated scientific facts" will prove to be in harmony with the accurate interpretation of the Bible. "Science has in many things taught the Church how to understand the Scriptures," Hodge asserted. He added:

The Bible was for ages understood and explained according to the Ptolemaic system of the universe; it is now explained without doing the least violence to its language, according to the Copernican system. Christians have commonly believed that the earth has existed only a few thousands of years. If geologists finally prove that it has existed for myriads of ages, it will be found that the first chapter of Genesis is in full accord with the facts, and that the last results of science are embodied on the first page of the Bible. It may cost the Church a severe struggle to give up one interpretation and adopt another, as it did in the seventeenth century, but no real evil need be apprehended. The Bible has stood, and still stands in the presence of the whole scientific world with its claims unshaken.

Hodge believed that scientists had achieved much to vindicate and illuminate the biblical record, and for this "the friends of the Bible owe[d] them a debt of gratitude."[19]

As science advanced the knowledge of the universe Charles Hodge demonstrated an openness to a new understanding of what the Bible teaches. For example, Hodge did not insist on the interpretation of the Old Testament genealogies that fixed the age of the earth at about six thousand years. When William Henry Green stated that "the time between the creation of Adam and ourselves might have been, for all we know from the Bible to the contrary, much longer than it seems," Charles Hodge was delighted. A. A. Hodge remembered his father's walking up and down in his study when he heard this, declaring, "What a relief it is to me that he should have said that!"[20]

Furthermore, Hodge was willing to concede that if the idea of a long earth history could be established, the first chapter of Genesis could be interpreted accordingly. Although he never completely surrendered his skeptical attitude toward the conclusions of the geologists, he taught that if they were correct, "we do no force to the Mosaic account by supposing [that] the earth [was] created many ages before the six days' work of creation commenced."[21] At first Hodge favored the "gap," or "interval," theory (that the original creation of the universe recorded in Genesis 1:1 was followed by an indefinitely long interval or gap before the six days described in Genesis 1:3–2:2). By the 1860s Hodge had abandoned that interpretation for the "day-age," or "era," theory (that the six days of Genesis represented six creative eras or ages of indefinite duration)—a view that appeared to be more consistent, he believed, with the fossil evidence.[22]

In 1863 the editor of the *New York Observer* attacked the *Biblical Repertory and Princeton Review* for maintaining that scientists must be free in their investigations and that Christians must remain open to the possibility that Scripture might have to be reinterpreted in the light of scientific evidence. Charles Hodge's reply, which was printed in the March 26 issue of the *Observer,* repeated his view of the harmony between Scripture and science. "Nature is as truly a revelation of God as the Bible," Hodge wrote, "and we only interpret the Word of God by the Word of God when we interpret the Bible by science." According to Hodge, Christians must avoid "a twofold evil"—neither formulating scientific theories that ignore scriptural truth, nor persisting in scriptural interpretations that conflict with well-established scientific truth. Hodge was quite willing for biblical interpretation to proceed under the guidance of proven scientific findings—although he made it abundantly clear that the theologian had every right to demand that alleged "facts" be verified beyond the possibility of doubt in view of the fluctuations in scientific theory from age to age and place to place.

In 1859 and 1862 Charles Hodge wrote articles for the *Biblical Repertory and Princeton Review* opposing the scientific theory of polygenism—the idea that the human races constitute distinct species with separate origins. Most leading naturalists rejected this theory, although a significant minority, including the eminent Louis Agassiz of Harvard, supported it. Hodge pointed to the scientific evidence that opposed polygenism, and to the biblical "facts" that established the unity of the human race. The facts of the Bible, Hodge wrote, "are just as certain and infinitely more important" than the facts of science. Hodge compared one polygenistic scientist to "a specimen of a class of birds which rub their bills against the vast cathedral of Christianity, and think they are overturning its foundations"! In his 1862 article Charles Hodge mentioned Darwin's "interesting work" in a lengthy footnote. Hodge called *The Origin of Species* "a remarkable book from a very high authority," which nonetheless carried "its own refutation in itself in the author's frank admission of the difficulties of his theory, and in the stupendous absurdity of his conclusion."[23]

Charles Hodge referred occasionally to evolution during the 1860s. However, not until he wrote his *Systematic Theology* thirteen years after the first appearance of *The Origin of Species* did he give the matter careful treatment—presenting, according to a modern scholar, "a well-informed review of the Darwinian viewpoint." Demonstrating a firm grasp of the relevant scientific material, Hodge judged that Darwin's theory was "mere hypothesis . . . incapable of proof" and pointed out several of its scientific problems. Hodge noted the absence of experimental evidence proving that an animal of one species, through a series of generations, had given rise to an animal of a distinctly different species. A much more serious problem, however, was Darwin's assertion that the natural causes of change were undirected and hence without design. Hodge could see no room for compromise between a biblical view of providence and a theory of evolution that attributes all development to "blind, unintelligent physical causes." The teachings of the Bible and God's very being as the omnipotent, intelligent, and benevolent creator imply design in his creation, Hodge argued. Although praising Darwin for "his knowledge and his skill in observation and description" as well as for "his frankness and fairness," Hodge forthrightly rejected his views.[24]

Charles Darwin's *Descent of Man,* published in 1871, intensified the debate. With the appearance of this book "evolution became a serious problem," wrote Princeton College professor John Thomas Duffield. The early 1870s, however, marked a point of transition in American attitudes toward Darwin, as more and more scientists—including some conservative Christians—came to accept some version of the theory of evolution.

At the meeting of the Evangelical Alliance in New York City during October 1873 James McCosh presented a paper on "Religious Aspects of the Doctrine of Development." When he had arrived at Princeton in 1868 Dr. McCosh had been hesitant about expressing his views on evolution, but he did so in his classes and in an important series of lectures presented at Union Theological Seminary in New York in 1871. McCosh held to a theory of evolution in which the inheritance of acquired characteristics guided organic progress along paths that God has planned. He told the members of the Evangelical Alliance that instead of simply denouncing evolution, "religious philosophers might be more profitably employed in showing . . . the religious aspects of the doctrine of development." Charles Hodge, who had traveled to New York to deliver one of the keynote addresses, was present to hear his Princeton friend. During the discussion that followed McCosh's paper Hodge rose amid what the *New York Times* called "an immense concourse of people." He addressed a question to the Reverend J. C. Brown of Berwick-upon-Tweed in England, who had declared that he found the developmental hypothesis very helpful:

I don't stand here to make a speech at all. I rise simply to ask Dr. Brown one question. I want him to tell us what development is. [At this point the *Times* recorded "Applause."] That has not been done. The great question which divides theists from atheists—Christians from unbelievers—is this: Is development an intellectual process guided by God, or is it a blind process of unintelligible, unconscious force, which knows no end and adopts no means? In other words, is God the author of all we see, the creator of all the beauty and grandeur of this world, or is unintelligible force, gravity, electricity, and such like? This is a vital question, sir. We can not stand here and hear men talk about development, without telling us what development is.[25]

Charles Hodge returned to Princeton on October 7 and immediately began work to expand his remarks on the topic of evolution. On January 14, 1874, Hodge read "a paper on Darwinism" to an informal meeting of his colleagues in Princeton, and within several months his book *What is Darwinism?* was published. Hodge had doubts about evolution as such and natural selection as a principle of biological descent. However, he argued that "the most important and only distinctive element" of Darwin's theory was not evolution nor natural selection, but "that this natural selection is without design, being conducted by unintelligent physical causes." Although Hodge praised Darwin as "a careful and laborious observer, skillful in his descriptions, and singularly candid in dealing with the difficulties in the way of his peculiar doctrine," he argued that the "grand and fatal objection to Darwinism" was its "denial of design in nature." Hodge wrote:

The conclusion of the whole matter is that the denial of design in nature is virtually the denial of God. Mr. Darwin's theory does deny all design in nature; therefore, his theory is virtually atheistical—his theory, not he himself. He believes in a Creator. But when that Creator, millions on millions of ages ago, did something—called matter and a living germ into existence—and then abandoned the universe to itself to be controlled by chance and necessity, without any purpose on his part as to the result, or any intervention or guidance, then He is virtually consigned, so far as we are concerned, to non-existence. . . . The denial of final causes is the formative idea of Darwin's theory, and therefore no teleologist can be a Darwinian. . . . We have thus arrived at the answer to our question, What is Darwinism? It is Atheism. This does not mean, as before said, that Mr. Darwin himself and all who adopt his views are atheists; but it means that his theory is atheistic, that the exclusion of design from nature is . . . tantamount to atheism.[26]

Significantly, Charles Hodge went on to state that among the last words of David Friedrich Strauss—author of the famous *Life of Jesus* and, to Hodge, the premier representative of post-Christian atheism—were these:

In the enormous machine of the universe, amid the incessant whirl and hiss of its jagged iron wheels, amid the deafening crash of its ponderous stamps and hammers, in the midst of this whole terrific commotion, man, a helpless and defenceless creature, finds himself placed, not secure for a moment that on an imprudent motion a wheel may not seize and rend him, or a hammer crush him to a powder. The sense of abandonment is at first something awful.

[16]

In contrast to the pessimism of atheism, Hodge closed his book by quoting the words that were among the last of the apostle Paul's:

I know whom I have believed, and am persuaded that He is able to keep that which I have committed unto Him against that day. . . . The time of my departure is at hand. I have fought a good fight, I have finished my course, I have kept the faith: henceforth there is laid up for me a crown of righteousness, which the Lord, the righteous judge, shall give me at that day: and not to me only, but unto all them also that love his appearing.[27]

A wide range of denominational journals—including the *Baptist Quarterly*, the Episcopalian *American Church Review*, the *Methodist Quarterly Review*, and even the *Unitarian Review and Religious Magazine*—hailed Hodge's book as a conclusive answer to Darwinism. However, Harvard botanist Asa Gray— probably the most influential defender of Darwin's theory in nineteenth-century America and a conservative Congregationalist—brought out a long rebuttal. "Excellent as the present volume is in motive and tone, and clearly as it shows that Darwinism may bear an atheistic as well as a theistic interpretation," Gray concluded, "we fear that it will not contribute much to the reconcilement of science and religion."[28]

Charles Hodge claimed that God's existence and providence entailed design in living organisms and that Darwinism denied design. Asa Gray argued that Darwin's theory of evolution did not necessitate by definition an atheistic position but could be shown to disclose a previously unrecognized form of natural teleology. Darwin, however, resisted such attempts. He had written to Gray in 1860 that he had "no intention to write atheistically," but that he could not "see as plainly as others do . . . evidence of design and beneficence on all sides of us." "I am inclined to look at everything as resulting from designed laws," he added, "with the details, whether good or bad, left to the working out of what we may call chance." In a letter to Charles Darwin on June 16, 1874, Asa Gray enclosed a copy of his review of Hodge's *What is Darwinism?* and wrote, "You will see what uphill work I have in making a theist of you, 'of good and respectable standing.'" Darwin replied on June 30, "I read with interest your semi-theological review, & have got the book, but I think your review will satisfy me. The more I reflect on this subject, the more perplexed I grow." Both Charles Hodge and Charles Darwin, it seems, agreed that Christianity in its orthodox sense could not be reconciled with Darwin's views of evolution.[29]

Whereas Asa Gray tried to find a place for design within evolution, other Darwinists, such as John Tyndall, were outspokenly opposed to such interpretations. In his presidential address to the British Association for the Advancement of Science, which he gave in Belfast in August 1874, Tyndall attacked those who were incorporating principles of design into Darwin's theory. Robert Watts, a professor of theology at the Presbyterian Assembly's College who had studied at Princeton Seminary in the 1850s, reported Tyndall's speech and the resulting debate to Hodge. Hodge wrote to Watts that he was pleased that the Darwinians, as he put it, "have at last got courage to speak out" in confessing frankly the atheistic direction of their theory. Hodge affirmed that a person "may be an evolutionist without being a Darwinian," holding that evolution could be stated in a theistic as well as in an atheistic manner, but he believed that the theory was speculative and probably false. Louis Agassiz of Harvard had demonstrated that there is no evidence of a direct descent of later-from-earlier species in the geological records, and the only answer of the evolutionists, Hodge stated, was to admit the imperfection of those records. Hodge wrote: "When asked, Where are the immediate predecessors of these new species? they answer, They have disappeared or have not yet been found. When asked, Where are their immediate successors? the answer again is, They have disappeared." More important, Charles Hodge could not see how the theory of evolution could "be reconciled with the declarations of the Scriptures." But he added that "others may see it and be able to reconcile their allegiance to science with their allegiance to the Bible."[30]

James McCosh accepted evolutionary ideas—attempting, though, to surround them with Christian presuppositions. He "did not disagree with Hodge so much in principle as in emphasis. Whereas Hodge judged Darwin's scientific theory by the philosophy that undergirded it, McCosh argued that Darwin's plausible theories about natural mechanisms of development could be separated from his bad philosophy." It was a mistake, McCosh maintained, to regard the theory of evolution as atheistic or hostile to the Bible. He said, "I have regretted for years that certain defenders of religion have been injuring the cause . . . by indiscriminately attacking development, instead of seeking to ascertain what the process is and turning it to religious use. They have acted as injudiciously as those who in Newton's day described the law of gravitation as atheistic." To McCosh, evolution was simply "the method by which God works." If Charles Hodge held that Darwin had "subverted" the idea of design, McCosh "felt that he had expounded it." The Princeton president "set about to prove that the natural origin of species is not inconsistent with intelligent design in nature or with the existence of a personal Creator of the world." He wrote: "As there is evidence of purpose, not only in every organ of the plant, but in the whole plant . . . so there are proofs of design, not merely in the individual plant and individual animal, but in the whole structure of the cosmos and in the manner in which it makes progress from age to age."[31]

Of course, when evolution was held in purely naturalistic terms James McCosh would have agreed with Charles Hodge that it was "atheism." McCosh turned down David Starr Jordan, later president of Stanford University, for a faculty position at Princeton because of his unacceptable views on evolution. Although McCosh viewed evolution as simply the drawing out of potentialities that God built into the original creation, he believed that there were a number of steps in the emergence of the world as we know it—including the origin of life, of intelligence, and of morality—that could be explained only by a direct divine fiat. Furthermore, McCosh insisted that "there has been a special revelation made as to the origins and destiny of Man, and this we must uphold and defend."[32]

The most sustained Princeton treatment of evolution came from George Macloskie. Macloskie had studied with James McCosh at Queen's College in Belfast during the mid-1850s.

When Dr. McCosh assumed the presidency of Princeton College Macloskie followed him as professor of biology. An ordained minister, George Macloskie saw himself in the role of scientific advocate to the theologians and produced a steady stream of articles for Presbyterian journals. In one area Macloskie departed from the revered Princeton tradition—the Baconian ideal, which held that the duty of science was first to observe and register the facts and then to generalize about them. Nature was too complex to be analyzed in this manner, Macloskie argued. Speculation was justified, indeed inevitable. Experience of nature is the jury, he wrote, before which speculations are sent for trial. The Darwinian theory, whatever its problems and irresolutions, Macloskie believed, had reorganized science for the better. It was not "in any way opposed to religion," he stated; "it was only an attempt to show Nature's (or God's) way of doing things." To Professor Macloskie the proper course for Christians was plain: they must judge Darwin's theory on its own merits. Macloskie believed that the Bible contained no errors of any kind, but he stated that the authority of the Bible was not the issue under debate since the Word of God was not "greatly concerned with the fate of evolution."[33]

As the Princeton theologians responded to the challenge of Darwinism, others too were busy analyzing and judging its claims. Unitarian Louis Agassiz, one of the most influential naturalists in the United States, scorned Darwin's theory and became its leading opponent. Agassiz's Harvard colleague Asa Gray, an evangelical Christian who worshiped at Park Street Church in Boston, championed Darwin's cause in America. Attempting to show that natural selection did not exclude design, he pointed out the exquisite adaptations so evident in evolutionary history. George Frederick Wright, a Congregationalist minister, endeavored to construct a Calvinistic idea of design based on Darwin's theories, and James Dwight Dana of Yale came to accept a form of evolution guided by God. Arnold Guyot of Princeton allowed the possibility of some natural development within strict limits, but he insisted that always "God's guiding hand must be discerned."[34]

After Louis Agassiz died in 1873 John William Dawson—

president of McGill University, prominent geologist, and a dedicated Presbyterian layman—became the anti-Darwinian leader. He rejected "the development theory," as he called it, because of its assault on divine design. Dawson visited Charles Hodge in Princeton in December 1874, and Hodge exerted considerable effort in trying to recruit him for the College of New Jersey faculty. In a letter dated April 16, 1878, Dawson spelled out to Hodge his reasons for remaining in Montreal —the main one being to aid Protestants in largely Catholic Quebec. Even though Dawson eventually moved in the direction of developmentalism, holding that evolution could mean something distinct from naturalistic Darwinism, he continued to express his skepticism. The assessment of Darwinism by James McCosh, George Macloskie, and other evangelical evolutionists was quite different from that of Charles Hodge, but they all agreed that the idea of a universe designed by God was absolutely essential to a truly biblical philosophy of science.

*   *   *

As concerned as Dr. McCosh was for a proper harmony of science and theology, he was even more interested in the spiritual state of the Princeton students. He once said that "no student passes through our College without his being addressed from time to time, in the most loving manner, as to the state of his soul." Every morning the college students assembled at seven o'clock for a roll call of their three hundred names and a short service. Each day, including Saturday, ended with prayers at five o'clock. At the ringing of the old college bell lines of students marched across campus, where they could expect to see "Uncle Jimmie" and hear "his broad and not unmelodious Scotch accents" as he poured out "his big, warm heart in prayer." On Sundays students attended chapel at eleven o'clock in the morning and Dr. McCosh's "interesting and valuable" Bible class, on which they were examined, in the afternoon. Many went to the prayer meeting in the early evening and later filled the gallery at First Presbyterian Church. During the week the students received instruction in Bible as part of their regular college course. Freshmen studied the poetical books of the Old Testament and the parables of Christ. Sophomores worked through John's Gospel in Greek. Juniors had courses in Old Testament prophets and Acts. Seniors studied Old Testament history and the book of Romans, the latter taught by Dr. McCosh.[35]

"Religion was a very real and a very pervasive force among us," said Benjamin Warfield, who was a student at the college from 1868 to 1871. Warfield remembered hearing many sermons from visiting preachers, including James H. Brookes, who had spent an unhappy year at Princeton Seminary in 1855. Brookes, said Warfield, preached "with the voice of a lion and the vehemence of an Elijah." "We always heard him gladly," Warfield continued; "and we never heard him without profit to our spiritual life, or without searchings of heart and the fruitage of new endeavors after righteousness." Warfield wrote:

It was said in our time that no class in Princeton College ever passed through its four years without experiencing a religious revival. Our class formed no exception. Our revival came near the end of our junior year. Scarcely anyone in the class was left ungarnered. . . . Princeton College, in the earlier years of the seventies, was found by many an ingenuous youth a "means of grace," as well as a "seminary of learning" and a "school of life."[36]

＊　　＊　　＊

In early May of 1870 the Reverend William Arnot, pastor of the Free High Church, Edinburgh, and a friend visited Princeton. Arnot wrote:

We came to Princeton on Tuesday forenoon. It is a greater college than I expected. Much enlarged since Dr. McCosh came. Fine new class rooms ready to be occupied. We attended worship at five in the chapel—students and professors. Then we were elected members of a certain mysterious literary society, and were duly initiated, both delivering inaugurals. Then the students' own prayer meeting—three hundred in the chapel; both of us addressed them; tender and impressive meeting. Then a mob of ladies and gentlemen in the evening. Much talk all the evening, concluding with ice cream.

Wednesday morning, called and saw Dr. Hodge. Resolved on seeing him, to dress more neatly when I sit in my study.[37]

*　　*　　*

In 1873 there was another revival at the college. Dr. McCosh reported, "Every few weeks we hear of this or that student publicly consecrating himself to Christ." He invited Theodore Cuyler to conduct a service on January 30, 1873— the day of prayer for colleges—as he had done during the 1870 revival. "That visit was followed by the blessed work in which you took an active part," McCosh wrote to Cuyler. "May it be the same this year!"[38]

*　　*　　*

A little earlier that January George MacDonald—the popular Scottish novelist and minister of unorthodox theological views—visited Princeton during his American lecture tour. His wife wrote to their daughter Lily on January 17:

[Papa] got through so well a 3-hours' journey [from New York to Princeton] and lecture in the evening. At a Scotch Presbyterian minister's house—we stayed; very pleasant people, a beautiful white-headed man, with a very nice wife and some sweet Scotch lassie daughters. . . . Papa gave such a glorious lecture on *Macbeth*. He is improving so wonderfully in dramatic power. It's lovely. He really sent us all into the cold shivers last night over the Ghost scene and the sleep walking scenes! He gets so eager and strong on what he has to say that it pours out with great flashes of eloquence that astonish even me. All the divines and the young men, 500 students, listened to him last night. Imagine *Macbeth* in a Presbyterian Church! This is quite the hot bed of the old Theology too, and yet they came out to hear him! And this old Dr. McCosh *asked Papa to preach!*[39]

*　　*　　*

Early in 1876 the college experienced another revival, originating mainly with the students themselves but greatly encouraged by President McCosh. Christians worked earnestly to witness to their fellow students. Prayer sessions in

[23]

dormitory rooms lasted into the late night and early morning hours. Theodore Cuyler and other ministers preached in Princeton with good results. In February evangelist D. L. Moody and his associate, Ira Sankey, came to Princeton at the invitation of McCosh, Charles Hodge, and the students. College and seminary students and professors, as well as townspeople, crowded the four meetings on Saturday night and Sunday. Sankey led the congregational singing from a portable organ and sang "The Ninety and Nine," "Jesus of Nazareth Passeth By," and other gospel songs for which he was known. Moody preached in his usual anecdotal and moving style. The *Observer* reported that on Sunday evening "the impression was so decisive that one hundred arose to ask for prayers." Moody himself was greatly impressed by his brief visit to Princeton. He wrote:

I saw more zeal when I was in Princeton last Sunday than I have in many a year. I was talking to the students there about their souls, and after I had been talking for some time, quite a group of young men gathered around me, and the moment one of them made a surrender and said, "Well, I will accept Christ," it seemed as if there were twenty-five hands pressed right down to shake hands with him. That is what we want—men that will rejoice to hear of the conversion of men.

A few days later a college student wrote:

God's spirit is still doing wondrous things for us. Almost every one is awakened. Our prayer-meetings are filled to overflowing, and are characterized by great earnestness and power. Those who have lately found Christ are very earnest in leading their associates to seek Him. We hope and pray that not a single one will be left out of the fold. The visit of Messrs. Moody and Sankey has been blessed to us all.[40]

Princeton—which had so strongly opposed the theology and revival practices of Charles Finney—gladly supported D. L. Moody. Although influenced by the Arminian theology characteristic of much of American evangelicalism of the time, Moody's views, unlike Finney's, were tempered by Calvinism. Moody "emphasized the sinful condition of man

[24]

and the sole activity of God in regeneration" and stressed that "the believer's salvation is certain and irrevocable." He stated that he accepted the doctrine of election but added, "I have no business to preach [it] to the world at large." Moody, who was converted during the revival of 1857–58, was not greatly influenced by the techniques of Charles Finney. He did not believe that a revival could be created by human means. "We cannot tell whether we are going to have a revival or not," Moody said; "that depends upon whether God comes." He avoided high-pressure tactics to manipulate audiences, although his preaching style—with its stream of stories in which "he drew artlessly on powerful themes of Christian sentiment"—and the popular and moving gospel hymns of Ira Sankey did produce emotional responses. Moody did not use Finney's "anxious bench" but took a step in the same direction with an "inquiry room," although he warned that caution was needed in public meetings lest people be led by an enthusiastic mood rather than by the Spirit of God. He refused to keep a record of "converts," saying that he did the best he could and left "the results with God." Some evangelical friends worried that Moody, in his desire to avoid divisive issues and to extend his ministry as widely as possible, was too ready to accept the support of those who made too many accommodations to modern religious thought. Moody, however, never deviated from a simple, conservative Bible message. He insisted on agreement "as to the nature of the Gospel, and even counselled believers to leave churches that were not true to the Gospel."[41]

Princeton appreciated the simplicity and humility of D. L. Moody, the biblical aspects of his preaching, and the good results of his meetings. With their long commitment to genuine revivals and their concern to stand with those who truly believed the Bible and preached the supernatural salvation of sinners, the Princetonians, like their fellow Calvinists Charles Spurgeon in England and Andrew and Horatius Bonar in Scotland, warmly supported Moody. Lyman Atwater reviewed the "Revivals of the Century" in the *Presbyterian Quarterly and Princeton Review* in October 1876, just after Moody and Sankey had visited Princeton. He ended his historical survey with comments on the "great revivals of

1875–6" and their "most conspicuous agents"—D. L. Moody and Ira Sankey. Their work, he wrote, "did not interfere with, it only assisted, genuine work . . . in particular congregations, while it, more largely than ordinary agencies, reached the unevangelized." "The teaching and tone of Mr. Moody," Atwater judged, "have been singularly scriptural and sound, his spirit earnest and loving, his attitude toward the stated ministry always brotherly and helpful, never harsh or injurious; his measures and methods, with rare exceptions, judicious and safe."[42]

2

Jubilee!

I have seldom seen a man more genial and attractive than this representative of the American Presbyterians. Clear light did not interfere with warm love in good old Dr. Hodge; and I remember his parlour-study as one of the cheeriest glimpses I had of an American interior.

Editor of *Sunday at Home*

Seminary professors Charles Hodge, William Henry Green, Alexander McGill, Caspar Wistar Hodge, and James C. Moffat were joined in 1871 by Charles A. Aiken. Aiken, a New Englander and graduate of Dartmouth College and Andover Seminary, served as a pastor in Maine for five years. He was called to his college *alma mater* in 1859 as professor of Latin language and literature. When the Princeton College trustees elected Aiken to their faculty in 1866 President Maclean argued against his appointment because he was not a Presbyterian but a "Congregationalist from New England," and so would be distasteful to many graduates. Before taking final action, the trustees sent a representative to investigate the new professor. At Portland the Princeton trustee asked a friend, "Can we make a good Presbyterian of him?" "No doubt of it, sir! No doubt of it!" was the emphatic reply. Wherever he went the trustee had good reports of Aiken's "scholarship, gentlemanly and affable manners and his theological soundness." "Nor is there any reason to fear in regard to his substantial accord with Princeton in theological sentiment," he wrote Maclean. "He is by inheritance a Presbyterian, his connection with the Congregational Church being purely accidental. His father and mother are both descendants from the Scotch-Irish, who left the north of Ireland in the Londonderry troubles and established the Presbyterian Church in New Hampshire." Satisfied, President Maclean wrote to Aiken assuring him of a warm welcome.

[29]

Charles Aiken left Princeton College in 1869 to become president of Union College in Schenectady, New York, but he returned to Princeton two years later to join the seminary faculty as the Archibald Alexander Professor of Christian Ethics and Apologetics—the first chair of Christian ethics to be established in a theological seminary. The moving spirit in the creation of the new chair was Stephen Colwell, trustee of Princeton Seminary from 1854 to 1871. Colwell—a lawyer, successful iron merchant, and notable Presbyterian layman— was outspoken about the church's failure to deal with the social problems of the time. In his book, *New Themes for the Protestant Clergy*, published in 1851, Colwell argued that whereas the Reformation had rightly saved Christian doctrine from the perversions of Roman Catholicism, Protestantism had often overlooked the needs of the poor. "The success of the Reformers," Colwell wrote, "was remarkable; but they were far from seizing and presenting the whole scope and spirit of Christianity. . . . It has been the duty of Protestants ever since, not only to vindicate constantly the great truths brought out at the Reformation, but constantly to extend and purify their knowledge; and whilst thus holding up the truth, to aim at a better fulfillment of the duties of Christianity."[1] Unfortunately, Protestantism, Colwell claimed, looked increasingly like any other prosperous business venture and was in danger of losing its true Christian identity. Although Colwell did not address the slavery issue (he was opposed to the abolitionist movement), he did focus on problems in the North, especially "wage slavery," industrialism, and a complacent Christianity. *New Themes for the Protestant Clergy* generated such interest that a second edition was published a year later.

Mr. Colwell's vision for a socially active Protestant church and his financial support led to the establishment of the new chair at Princeton. The faculty statement declared that the design of the chair

was to treat of the Religion of Christ, in its bearing upon human society and the welfare of man in general, and, particularly, by developing the gospel law of charity or mutual love, to expound the duties which men owe to their fellow men, not only in their individual capacity, but organized and associated as churches, communities and nations. This subject was to be presented not only didactically but historically, by showing what the gospel has done to change the face of society and ameliorate the condition of man since its first introduction into the world.[2]

In his inaugural address on September 27, 1871, Charles Aiken defined his task. There are three great questions to be asked, he said: "Is the co-existence and co-working of the supernatural and the natural in this world of ours conceivable and possible? Can such an active co-existence be proved to the satisfaction of a rational mind? Is the supernatural present and working in, with, and for Christianity?" He answered:

Following our deepest judgment and our warmest impulse we, fulfilling the true office of the Christian Apologist, seeking that Christianity may justify itself, would answer the last of the three inquiries first. We would hold up Christianity that men may see the supernatural there present and working; Christianity in the person of its founder; Christianity in the history and life of his Church; Christianity in the experience of any one believer. In each of these [we] behold the supernatural. . . . But the Christian Apologist need not fear to take the earlier queries by themselves, and maintain that God has neither shut himself out from his own world, nor from the minds whose laws of belief he fashioned.

Aiken described the way in which the other departments in the seminary also imparted apologetical teaching.

The development of Didactic and Polemic Theology must be and is (must be and is do not always go together) full of strong pleas for the divinity of Christianity. Both departments of Biblical Literature, and that of Church History, would not and cannot be cut off from the earnest and telling presentation of the credentials of our faith, supplied by its records and its living products.

Aiken then paid tribute to Stephen Colwell, "whose earnest thinking and liberal purpose gave the first impulse to this organization and endowment," and to Archibald Alexander, "whose presence and whose spirit have been from the first so great a power here." He closed his address by saying that in the apologetical work of the seminary "our trust is in the

Lord our God, and in this blessed faith of his Gospel, which has not stood all the tests of the past to be found in the utmost future trial, a spider's web to trusting simplicity."[3]

*   *   *

In 1868 Lyman Atwater became coeditor of the *Biblical Repertory and Princeton Review*. Charles Hodge had managed the journal for over forty years—"a ball-and-chain," he wrote in 1865, borne "with scarcely any other compensation than the high privilege and honour of making it an organ for upholding sound Presbyterianism, the cause of the country, and the honour of our common Redeemer." Atwater, a transplanted New Englander who had been both a parishioner and student of Nathaniel W. Taylor, had shouldered the major burden of replying to the theological errors that the Princetonians perceived in New England theology.[4] When Charles Hodge fully retired from the editorship in 1871 the *Biblical Repertory* was the second oldest quarterly in the United States. It was, according to John Oliver Nelson, "consistent, judicious, conservative, intelligent," always "literary, often humorous and witty." A year's subscription was still three dollars, as it had been in 1828. Dr. Hodge had personally contributed 142 articles—a total of 5,000 pages.[5] During his four decades as editor Hodge wrote some 6,000 letters addressed to more than 700 different persons, including a letter in 1869 to Pope Pius IX explaining why the Presbyterian church was declining an invitation to send a representative to the Vatican Council of 1870.

Charles Hodge, now in his seventies, was busily writing his *Systematic Theology* with a dilapidated gold pen that he alone could get to work. In 1845 he had changed his classroom method from student recitations on Turretin's text to his own lectures on theological topics. Later he commented on the problems created by repeating his lectures year after year.

First, the students taking notes of the lectures have come, in a succession of years, to have almost complete copies of them. I am subjected, therefore, to the embarrassment of reading lectures, copies of which many members of the class hold in their hands. This I find a great bore. Secondly, the students, instead of writing answers to the questions given to them, after studying and reflecting for themselves, in most cases simply transcribe the copies of the lectures which are handed down to them by the preceding classes. The result is that the interest in the lectures and in the written exercise has greatly decreased, while that in the oral questioning remains. For several years no one has come to the lecture who could help it; whereas the room is commonly crowded at the oral examination. I am at a loss how to get over this difficulty.[6]

The students were glad to provide an answer to Dr. Hodge's problem. For years they urged him to publish his material so that they could avoid the tedious work of copying the lectures. "These manuscript copies present to our mind several objectional features," explained the class representatives in a petition to Hodge in 1853. "Copied by students, the manual labor is injurious to health and eyesight, and consumes important time that should be given to study and investigation. Transcribed by copyists, the expense places them beyond the reach of the great majority of the students." The students made a good case; but Dr. Hodge delayed, influenced by the fear of some of the directors that if his lectures were published there would be a loss of students to the seminary. The students finally produced a printed syllabus in 1865; the volume was entitled *Systematic Theology: A Series of Questions Upon the Lectures Delivered to the Students in Princeton Theological Seminary, by the Rev. Charles Hodge, D.D., edited by A Member of the Senior Class and Printed for the Use of the Students*. The editor noted in the preface that "at present Dr. Hodge is engaged in rewriting his entire course of lectures, and has progressed as far as the subject of Original Sin."[7] Hodge's revision continued slowly, but in 1872 the task was complete. The result was a fresh statement of his views, based on years of teaching and study and enriched with a great amount of special reading and reflection. Hodge's *Systematic Theology*—2,000 pages and three volumes in English—now replaced Turretin's 2,000 pages and three volumes in Latin as the major theology textbook at Princeton. With his book in print Hodge felt "as if set free" and returned to his favorite method of teaching—questioning students on the basis of their reading, thus encouraging them to think through the material for themselves.

* * *

Both Charles Hodge's lectures and his Systematic Theology followed a "straightforward ordering," which helps account for their "original and continued appeal." He reduced the numerous divisions in Turretin to four: method of theology, theology proper (the doctrine of God), anthropology, and soteriology. Two central ideas set the tone: the inspiration and authority of the Bible and a careful inductive theological method. Hodge set forth three possible methods of studying theology: the speculative, the mystical, and the inductive or scriptural. The speculative method assumes certain rational principles and from these undertakes to determine what is true. It has produced deism, scholasticism, and transcendentalism. The mystical method, which found its most influential advocate in Schleiermacher, teaches that feelings, not reason, are to be relied upon in the sphere of religion. The Christian consciousness is the source of religious knowledge. The inductive method, according to Hodge, is the only valid approach to theology. The theologian works with truths revealed in the external works of God, the constitution of human nature, the religious experience of believers, and primarily the Bible. Truths from the other sources, Hodge believed, are contained and authenticated in Scripture, which is therefore *the* source of all true theology. Hodge described the task of the theologian as a careful, inductive, scientific enterprise. He wrote:

The true method of theology is, therefore, the inductive, which assumes that the Bible contains all the facts or truths which form the contents of theology, just as the facts of nature are the contents of the natural sciences. It is also assumed that the relation of these Biblical facts to each other, the principles involved in them, the laws which determine them, are in the facts themselves, and are to be deduced from them, just as the laws of nature are deduced from the facts of nature.

Hodge was so successful in following this principle that a critic censuring his volumes of theology said, "It is enough for Dr. Hodge to believe a thing to be true that he finds it in the Bible"![8]

In his *Systematic Theology* Charles Hodge especially stressed
the issues about which he continually studied and wrote
during the Old School–New School controversy—the
doctrines of imputation, depravity, regeneration, and
the atonement. Hodge's theology was "polemic" as well as
"didactic" and set forth firmly his Reformed viewpoint; but it
also revealed the catholicity of spirit that so truly characterized him. He took more pleasure in citing the consensus
of Christendom in opposition to error than in criticizing
opinions opposed to Calvinism.

Charles Hodge's "three volumes" quickly became the
standard conservative theology among English-speaking
Reformed Christians. Francis L. Patton, a student of Hodge's
and later president of both Princeton College and Princeton
Seminary, considered Dr. Hodge's work "the greatest treatise
on Systematic Theology in the English language" and praised
its "comprehensiveness and completeness," its "freedom
from questionable philosophical commitments," and its
"loyal devotion to the words of Scripture." In Presbyterian
Scotland it was well received—finding "its way into not a few
Free Church manses" as gift-copies from Alexander Whyte,
pastor of Free St. George's in Edinburgh.[9] In England,
Charles Spurgeon's *Sword and Trowel* welcomed Hodge's
work:

It is truly reviving to see the old theology rising in its wonted
majesty, and clothed with its own verdure and fruitfulness, into
prominence in modern times. . . . Such a work is peculiarly season-
able on both sides of the Atlantic, and we hail its publication in this
country as a token for good. The introduction is particularly
valuable for its defence of systematic theology against the many
attempts to bring it into disrepute, and to substitute a more
unrestrained method of interpretation in its place.[10]

A modern historian describes the theology of Charles
Hodge as "stout and persistent" and adds what surely would
have pleased Hodge most: "We find in his work an almost
classic realization of the kneeling, as opposed to sitting,
theologian. He had seen the grace and glory of God, and in
his *Systematic Theology* he turns to the world to explain his
vision."[11]

Charles Hodge's *Systematic Theology* did not include the doctrine of the church, of which he was eminently qualified to write. From 1835 to 1868 (with the probable exception of 1841) he produced a series of annual reports in review of the actions of each General Assembly (Old School from 1838 on). They contained, according to A. A. Hodge, "an exposition of his views underlying the constitution of the Church and its administration, and of the practical application of these principles to the various historical conditions experienced by the American Presbyterian Church during that long period." In 1845 Charles Hodge began to lecture to his seminary classes on ecclesiology and, between 1846 and 1857, wrote a number of articles on this topic for the *Biblical Repertory and Princeton Review*. After the publication of his *Systematic Theology* he often expressed a desire to complete that work with a fourth volume on ecclesiology. A student who was a member of Dr. Hodge's last class commented that Hodge would have written a fourth volume "but for the infirmities of age." One of Charles Hodge's students, William Durant, selected and arranged material from Hodge's articles on the church to create a "valuable discussion of Church principles and their practical applications." A. A. Hodge reviewed the work and wrote that it contained "a fair and, as far as the circumstances admit, an adequate exposition" of his father's views. It was published in 1879 as *The Church and its Polity*.[12]

*　　*　　*

In 1872 Princeton celebrated the fiftieth year of Charles Hodge's professorship, an event at that time without precedent in American academic life. The "jubilee" was planned by Hodge's colleague William Henry Green, assisted by the board of directors and a committee of seventy alumni. On April 24 the shops in Princeton were closed and people came from far and near to fill the First Presbyterian Church. Charles Hodge's wife, Mary, his eight children, his beloved brother, Hugh—now blind—and the great company of Hodge grandchildren were there. Also present were four hundred former students from almost every year of the seminary's history. There were presidents and faculty representatives from many colleges and seminaries and delegates from American and European churches: Lutherans, Methodists, Episcopalians, Baptists, and Independents, as well as Presbyterians. According to Henry B. Smith, who represented Union Theological Seminary in New York, it was "a noble occasion."[13]

Henry Boardman spoke for the trustees. He noted that celebrations for heroes, statesmen, and authors were not unusual, but that here was "the spontaneous homage paid to a simple teacher of God's Word, and defender of his truth, by a vast assemblage." He addressed Dr. Hodge:

But what honor, beloved Brother, has God put upon you! For fifty years you have been training men to preach the glorious gospel of the grace of God to their fellow-sinners. The teacher of teachers, your pupils have become professors in numerous Colleges and Seminaries at home and abroad. Not to speak of one or two thousand pastors, who are exerting an ameliorating influence upon this nation more potent than that of an equal number of men belonging to any other calling, you are helping, through your students, to educate a great body of Christian ministers, not a few of whom are to be employed in laying the foundations of Christianity in pagan lands.

Charles Hodge had taught 2,700 students—more than had attended any other seminary in the country. Now scattered across America and around the world, these men honor him, said Boardman, for the great mind God has given him and "love him for his still greater heart."[14]

Fifteen speeches followed Boardman's, and, according to Henry B. Smith, "at least five hundred speeches" were not delivered! The words spoken by Charles P. Krauth, earnest champion of Lutheranism in America, Charles Hodge remembered afterwards with particular satisfaction. Krauth paid tribute to the Princeton theologian as a man who "had always treated the doctrines of Churches and parties differing from his own with candor, love of truth, and perfect fairness."[15]

Out of sight, reclining on a sofa at the back of an enlarged stage, the seventy-five-year-old Charles Hodge listened to these congratulatory addresses. He rose to embrace his old friend Theodore Woolsey, former president of Yale, who spoke tenderly of the affection he had cherished for Charles Hodge ever since 1828, when Hodge had spoken words of Christian "cheer, comfort and of strength" to his heart.

As Dr. Hodge came to the platform to reply to the addresses of the morning the audience rose to welcome him, and many remained standing while he spoke. Hodge said:

A man is to be commiserated who is called upon to attempt the impossible. The certainty of failure does not free him from the necessity of effort. It is impossible that I should make you understand the feelings which swell my heart almost to bursting. Language is an imperfect vehicle of thought; as an expression of emotion it is utterly inadequate. We say, "I thank you," to a servant who hands us a glass of water; and we thank God for our salvation. The same word must answer these widely different purposes; yet there is no other. When I say thank you for all your respect, confidence, and love, I say nothing, I am powerless. I can only bow down before you with tearful gratitude, and call on God to bless you, and to reward you a hundredfold for all your goodness.

Charles Hodge then praised Archibald Alexander and Samuel Miller and their Christ-centered teaching and piety for making Princeton Seminary "what it is" and, Hodge added, "what I trust it will ever continue to be."[16]

There was a public dinner and an afternoon meeting at the Presbyterian church for the reading of letters of congratulations from friends not present. Afterwards Henry Boardman said to Dr. Hodge, "How did you stand all that?" "Why," Hodge replied smiling, "very quietly. It didn't seem at all to be me they were talking about. I heard it all as of some other man." The seminary alumni provided $45,000 to endow Hodge's chair of systematic theology and gave him a gift of over $15,000. In the evening friends crowded into Dr. Hodge's house for a reception in his honor. Over the doors were the significant dates *1822–1872*. The seminary building next door was brightly lit. That night Charles Hodge wrote in his journal:

April 24th. The apex of my life. The Semi-centenary Anniversary of my connection with the Seminary as Professor. The day, by the blessing of God, was fine, and the celebration a wonderful success.

[38]

The attendance of Alumni very large; delegations of other institutions numerous, and of the highest character; the congratulations from all at home and abroad of the most gratifying kind, altogether affording an imposing and most affecting testimony of the unity of the faith, and of common love to the same gospel, and to our common God and Saviour Jesus Christ.[17]

*   *   *

Theodore Woolsey, at the semicentennial, wished for Charles Hodge "a sweet old age." Hodge looked the part of a patriarch—having a pale complexion and curling hair, dignified bearing, and kind, calm gaze. He lectured to the seminary students with his cane resting by his chair, his eyes often closed, and his fragile gold-rimmed glasses thrust up above his forehead. B. B. Warfield, who entered Princeton Seminary in 1873, described Dr. Hodge:

Infirm as he was, he was not bent by extreme age or infirmity; his carriage was erect and graceful, and his step always firm. The mantle that hung from his shoulders during the cooler months heightened the effect of graceful movement. I well remember that when he stepped into the aisle of the First Church to welcome Drs. Dorner and Christlieb on their visit to Princeton, in the autumn of '73, I thought I had never witnessed a finer spectacle of strength and grace combined. And yet it was but an example of his ordinary bearing; he gave me the same impression every time he entered the recitation room.[18]

Except for a year in Philadelphia and two years in Europe, Charles Hodge had lived in Princeton since his college days. He loved the town—its seminary, its college, and its people. He preferred to follow old familiar patterns, using one study chair and patronizing the same tailoring shop despite a succession of good and bad proprietors and the complaints of the younger Hodges. His son wrote that "there was no element of his nature inclined to new measures, any more than to new doctrines." For over forty years he had recorded the daily temperature, wind direction, and cloud cover in Princeton—constituting, according to Joseph Henry, the only persistent meteorological record in Princeton during those years.

Visiting his patients late in the night of February 24, 1873, Charles Hodge's brother, Hugh, suffered a heart attack and died the next day. Charles sadly wrote the news to his old friend Episcopal bishop John Johns, adding, "we are left like two old trees standing almost alone." In May Charles Hodge was in Washington visiting with his brother-in-law, General David Hunter. The General Assembly, meeting in Baltimore, adjourned in a body "to wait upon Dr. Hodge" at Willard's Hotel in Washington. The old man dissolved in tears as the commissioners presented themselves to do him honor.[19]

In early October 1873 Charles Hodge, James McCosh, and others from Princeton were in New York City for the Sixth General Conference of the Evangelical Alliance. One observer described Hodge as "the most impressive personality of the Alliance," a picture of "strength lying in repose," with a face both "radiant" and "serene." He carried a gold headed ebony cane and leaned on it as he spoke with his many friends. Dr. Hodge gave the opening prayer, saying in a voice softened by old age:

Come, Holy Spirit, come! Descend in all Thy plentitude of grace. Come as the Spirit of reverence and love. Aid us, O God, in the discharge of the duties on which we are about to enter. We have assembled here from almost all parts of the world. We have come to confess Thee before men; to avow our faith that God is, and that He is the Creator, Preserver, and Governor of the World. We are here to acknowledge that the God of Abraham and Isaac, and of Jacob is our God. We are here to confess Christ as God manifest in the flesh, and as our only and all-sufficient Savior, who for us sinners died upon the cross, to reconcile us unto God, and to make expiation for the sins of men; and who, having died for our offenses, has risen again for our justification. We acknowledge Him as now seated at the right hand of the Majesty on high, all power in heaven and on earth having been committed to His hands. Thanks be to God, thanks be to God, that He has put on us, unworthy as we are, the honor to make this confession, and to bear this testimony to God and to His Son. O God, look down from heaven upon us. Shed abroad in our hearts the Holy Spirit, that we may be truly one in Christ Jesus.

O Thou blessed Spirit of the living God, without whom the universe were dead, Thou art the source of all life, of all holiness, of all power. O Thou perfect Spirit, Thou precious gift of God, come, we pray, and dwell in every heart, and touch every lip. We invoke the blessing of Father, Son and Holy Ghost on this Evangelical Alliance. We spread abroad our banner, in the sight of all men, with the confession which Thou has put on our lips—the confession of all Christendom. We confess God the Father to be our Father; Jesus Christ His Son, to be our Savior; and the Holy Ghost to be our Sanctifier; and His Word to be the infallible rule of faith and practice. Grant, O Lord, that whatever human words are uttered, this confession may be the language of every heart. And to the Father, Son and Holy Ghost be glory, now and evermore. Amen.[20]

Later in the conference Charles Hodge addressed the delegates on the "Unity of the Church Based on Personal Union with Christ"—a moving call to Christians and churches to manifest real unity in spite of their differences. Dr. Hodge said:

The idea of the Church . . . as presented in the Bible, is that believers scattered over the world are a band of brethren, children of the same Father, subjects of the same Lord, forming one body by the indwelling of the Holy Ghost, uniting all to Christ as their living head. This indwelling of the Spirit makes all believers one in faith, one in their religious life, one in love. Hence they acknowledge each other as brethren and are ready to bear each other's burdens.

Therefore, said Hodge, as we are not at liberty to give any definition of a Christian that shall exclude any of the true followers of Christ, so we are not at liberty to give any definition of a church that shall exclude any body that Christ recognizes as a church by his presence. Speaking with intense emotion, Dr. Hodge said:

If all Christians really believed that they constitute the mystical body of Christ on earth, they would sympathize with each other as readily as the hands sympathize with the feet, or the feet with the hands. If all churches, whether local or denominational, believed that they too are one body in Christ Jesus, then instead of conflict we should have concord; instead of mutual criminations we should have mutual respect and confidence; instead of rivalry and opposition we should have cordial cooperation. The whole visible Church would then present an undivided front against infidelity and every form of Anti-Christian error, and the sacramental host of God, though divided into different corps, would constitute one army glorious and invincible.[21]

A few days later, on October 13, 275 members of the Evangelical Alliance—*en route* to Washington to hold a brief service at the Capitol and meet with President Grant at the White House—stopped in Princeton especially to honor Charles Hodge.

In 1874 the seminary chapel was remodeled— "Victorianized" with stained glass windows, carpeting, and upholstered pews—through the gift of trustee John C. Green, a generous benefactor of the seminary who died the following year. At the seminary's opening in September Charles Hodge gave the sermon. Hodge noted that over 3,000 ministers of the gospel had been trained at Princeton. "With rare exceptions," he said, "they have been faithful men. They have labored in every part of our own land and in almost every missionary field." He told the present students that they had assumed "grave responsibilities in coming to this place." "Your first duty," he said, "is to make your calling and election sure." It is important that you seek the ministry, he told them, with pure and honest motives—"love to Christ, zeal for his glory, and a desire to save your fellow men." "Your second duty," Hodge said, "is to throw your whole heart into the work and, while here, into the work of preparation and into the life of the Seminary, whether in the classroom, the chapel, the conference, or prayer meeting." Finally, in the name of his colleagues Hodge made a request of everyone.

It is a small matter to you, but a great matter to us. We beg that each of you, as long as he lives, would daily pray that the officers and students of this Seminary may be full of faith and of the Holy Ghost. Let others believe and say what they please, we believe and know that God is the hearer of prayer. If each of the two thousand surviving alumni of this Institution would daily offer that prayer, what a place Princeton would be![22]

*   *   *

Alexander and Robert Stuart, sons of a Scottish immigrant who made a fortune in sugar and candy, purchased land to add a new classroom building to the seminary campus. They engaged William A. Potter, later United States Supervising Architect, and contributed over $100,000 for construction.

Completed in 1876, the grand three-story Venetian-Gothic building with a bell tower contrasted sharply with the old seminary building, the chapel, and Brown Hall. The "massive, beautiful and imposing" Stuart Hall was much admired by townspeople and praised by the seminary as "the finest hall for recitations possessed by an educational institution in the land." The deed gave the new classroom building to Princeton Seminary with the condition that the seminary remain under the control of the Presbyterian church and that the Old School Presbyterian interpretation of the doctrines of the Westminster Standards continue "to be taught and inculcated."[23]

In 1879 a red brick library was completed—the gift of James Lenox, who thirty-six years earlier had given Princeton Seminary its first library. The new building, facing Stockton Street, stood behind the old Lenox Library, which continued to provide reference services. The new Lenox Library, which housed the circulating books, was flanked by two large red brick houses for professors, also provided by Mr. Lenox. The library displayed impressive woodwork and furnishings of rich golden oak. Light flooded the building from windows in the clerestory.[24] William Henry Green had succeeded Archibald Alexander as librarian in 1851 and served for twenty years. Charles Aiken was librarian from 1871 to 1877, when William H. Roberts became the seminary's first full-time librarian.

3

The Hodges: Father and Sons

We have had, of later years, no abler theologians than the Hodges, and we fear it will be many a day before we see their like. . . . We value every morsel about the Princeton worthies; may their influence long endure. Even apart from his theological excellence, the sayings of the younger Hodge are full of Scripture and salt, weight and wit. The modern school thinks us fools, but certainly we were taught by wise men. . . . Finer minds than those of the Princeton tutors have seldom dwelt among the sons of men. We count it a precious memory that we once spent a day with the younger Hodge. No better textbook of theology for college and private use is now extant than the old edition of "Hodge's Outlines."

CHARLES HADDON SPURGEON

IN 1873 the directors had proposed that Archibald Alexander Hodge, professor of systematic theology at Western Theological Seminary, be appointed assistant to his father at Princeton. Charles Hodge thought the move unnecessary and no further steps were taken until 1877, when Dr. Hodge notified the directors that it was time for him to give up, or at least reduce, his teaching. Again the name of A. A. Hodge was put forward. Charles Hodge wrote to his son:

My Dear Alexander:
You say I told you to go to Allegheny [Western Seminary]; your memory may be better than mine, but I have no recollection of having been so unwise. At any rate, in the event of your being called to Princeton, I shall not assume the responsibility of deciding whether you ought to come. . . .

The view I take of the matter is simply this:

1. Our Board is bound to take that course which it thinks will best promote the interests of this Seminary and the general interests of this Church.

2. If our Directors think there is any other man available, as well qualified to fill the position as you, they ought to leave you where you are.

3. But if they are satisfied that you are the best man to keep up the character of this Institution for fidelity to our doctrinal standards, I, if a Director, although your Father, would vote for your election.

4. I would do this, because I think that this Seminary, not

[47]

because of any superiority of its faculty, but simply because of providential circumstances, is at present at least, of special importance. It, therefore, should be specially considered.

5. All such considerations, as delicacy, your personal wishes, cheapness of living here or there, are not of any serious weight.

6. The question whether you are the best available man to fill the place here, is for our Directors to decide. Their decision, however, is subject to a veto from your "inner consciousness," if your conscience constrains you to exercise it. "Commit your way unto the Lord, and He will direct your steps."[1]

The directors elected A. A. Hodge associate professor of didactic theology, and he accepted and was inaugurated on November 8, 1877, in the First Presbyterian Church in Princeton. William M. Paxton, pastor of the First Presbyterian Church of New York City, spoke for the board of directors. Princeton, he said, is a "school of learning" and a "cradle of piety." "It is a place where educated young men are imbued with the doctrine of the Cross, and with this truth as a burning power in their hearts, they go out into the world to kindle and fire the hearts of others." Your work is not done, Paxton reminded Hodge, "when you have demonstrated a truth or deposited an intellectual dogma in the memory of a student." "No, no," he added, "your responsibility continues until you have sent that truth as a lighted torch into his soul to kindle there its light and to warm his whole being as with fire." "Give them Theology, give them orthodoxy, give them exposition, proof, demonstration, give them learning," Paxton told the new professor, "but give it to them *warm*." He continued:

This quickening power must come from the presence of the Divine Spirit. . . . A lecture upon Theology must be conceived by help of the Holy Ghost, delivered under his melting influence, and received by the student under his blessed illumination. Hence the Professor's study must be a Bethel in direct communication with Heaven; and a Theological Seminary must be a Bochim, from which strong cries for help are constantly going up.

"You, my Brother, stand in a historic situation," Paxton told the son of Charles Hodge.

The name of this Seminary is known in all the world. Its chief distinction is its Biblical teaching. The ground of its faith is the *Bible*. Its only question is, "What has God said?" Its only proof is God's Word. Its professors have never reached the point of thinking that they knew more than the Bible. This Seminary has always taught that there are but two questions to be considered. First. Is this the Word of God? Secondly. What does it mean? and this ascertained, there is nothing left but to believe and adore. The preaching which has always been taught in this seminary and illustrated in the pulpits of its graduates has been simple Biblical preaching. . . . The Princeton student has always been known by the honor which he puts upon the Divine Word.

"My dear Brother," Paxton concluded, "I need only to say to you *'continue in these things.'"*[2]

A. A. Hodge then gave his inaugural address on "Dogmatic Christianity, the Essential Ground of Practical Christianity." He affirmed his belief that "the Scriptures of the Old and New Testaments in their integrity *are* the Word of God" and—"not as a professional propriety, but as a personal conviction"—that "the Confession and Catechisms of the Westminster Assembly contain the system taught in the Holy Scriptures." Hodge protested against the modern tendency to oppose "creed and morals, faith and character" and proclaimed "the opposite principle as fundamental—that truth is in order to holiness, and that knowledge of the truth is an essential to right character and action." Hodge acknowledged that "one of the sins most easily besetting theologians has been a tendency to over-refinement in speculation, over-formality of definition, and an excess of rigidity of system." "Logical notions," he said, "creatures of the understanding, have too often been substituted for the concrete form of spiritual truth presented by the Holy Ghost to faith." Furthermore, Hodge added, "zeal for doctrine has in too many instances been narrow and prejudiced, mingled with the infirmities of personal pride and party spirit, and has hence led to the unnecessary divisions and alienations of those who were in reality one in faith, and to the conditioning of communion, and even of salvation, upon unessential points." Some theologians, he said, have "betrayed their want of perfect confidence in the foundations on which they have builded by a disposition to discourage the fearless investigations of new truth in all directions, and to put an ungenerous interpretation upon all opinions to which their own minds were unaccustomed." "Truth," however, "once adequately established," Hodge asserted, "must be held fast forever"; and it is just that truth—"revealed in the Scriptures, and embraced in what evangelical Christians style Christian dogma"—which is "the great God-appointed means of producing in men a holy character and life." "Dogmatic Christianity," Hodge stated again, is "the essential ground of practical Christianity." In conclusion, A. A. Hodge considered the modern situation and made a promise:

In the face of the deluge of aggressive unbelief, we are invited by not a few sentimental friends to disembarrass ourselves of the incumbrance of system in order that each of us may escape with some dislocated fragment in his grasp. . . . Whether this policy of preserving the truth by means of its disintegration be urged upon us by subtle enemies or by silly friends, we intend to refuse it utterly. We will maintain the whole truth to be the only pure truth, and the whole truth to be the truth as a whole—a complete system divinely revealed in all its parts, and invincible through the comprehension of all the parts in the whole.

The new professor closed his address with the words:

Fathers and brethren of the Board of Directors, your representative in his charge has reminded me that the chair to which I am called is historical, having for sixty-five years from the beginning been occupied only by Archibald Alexander and Charles Hodge. Alas, sirs, when I think of myself, I often cry—Woe is me, that such a one as I should be called to inherit the responsibilities descending in such a line! And when I think of the Church, I cry with a far sorer wonder—What times are these, when such a man as I should be made to stand in such a place? But God has done it. He has chosen a vessel, earthen indeed, that the excellency of the power may be the more conspicuously shown forth to be His alone. Directors, since your responsibilities in the matter are at least equal to my own, I can surely claim your prayers, that in this service, today inaugurated, *God's* strength may be made perfect in weakness.[3]

During the impressive service Dr. Charles Hodge sat somewhat apart in the corner of the church. He must have remembered when he, as a boy, attended the inauguration of Archibald Alexander to the same office. From August 12, 1812, until November 8, 1877—for more than sixty-five years—there had been only two professors of systematic theology in Princeton; and "Dr. Hodge received the office from a man he delighted to call father, and now transmitted it to his son."[4]

*   *   *

In addition to his famous name, Archibald Alexander Hodge brought experience as a missionary, pastor, and teacher to his task at Princeton. A. A. Hodge and his wife, the former Elizabeth B. Holliday of Winchester, Virginia, had served at the Presbyterian mission in Allahabad, India, for nearly three years, until serious physical problems forced them— with their two children—to return to the United States in 1850. He became "a living missionary force" at the seminary. According to Francis L. Patton:

His experience in the mission field enhanced his zeal for the mission cause, gave him a grasp of the missionary problem, and an interest in missionaries that made him always the trusted counsellor of all those among his pupils who contemplated a missionary career. If the students wished advice, they went to him; if the Sunday evening missionary meeting was to be addressed, he was called upon; if, at the Monthly Concert, the expected speaker failed to arrive, he was called upon; if the son of a converted Brahmin was sent here to be educated, he was his guardian; if a penniless Oriental, bent on knowledge, and seeking it, that he might carry the gospel back to his countrymen, sought premature admission to the Seminary, he found an eager advocate in Dr. Hodge, if anything could be said in his behalf; and if, as sometimes happened, it was necessary to let him know that his coming had been a mistake, kind words from Dr. Hodge, and not infrequently a draft upon his exchequer, sent him away in peace; if the Inter-Seminary Missionary Conference held its meetings at Hartford, Dr. Hodge must make an address; if it met in Princeton, Dr. Hodge at least must pray.[5]

From 1851 until 1864 A. A. Hodge served churches in Maryland, Virginia, and Pennsylvania. He settled first in Lower West Nottingham, Maryland—a rural charge with a small salary. In 1855 he went to Fredericksburg, Virginia, where he developed his gift for popular exposition of theology. His first book, *Outlines of Theology,* was the result of theological sermons preached to his congregation on Sunday evenings. He followed a list of questions given by Charles Hodge to his classes of 1845 and 1846 and his own class notes —written "copiously, and after frequent oral communication with [his] father, both in public and private," A. A. Hodge explained in the preface to his book. A later Princetonian remarked, "It is said, sometimes, that we cannot preach theology. Here is a theology, however, every word of which was preached, and not only preached, but listened to with eagerness." In 1861 Hodge was called to the Presbyterian church in Wilkes-Barre, Pennsylvania.[6]

After thirteen years as a pastor Archibald Alexander Hodge spent another thirteen years as professor of theology at Western Seminary. He not only taught theology at the seminary but supplied the First Presbyterian Church of Pittsburgh for a year, then became pastor of the North Presbyterian Church—fulfilling a double ministry as pastor and professor.[7] He wrote a book on the *Atonement* in 1867 and two years later published his *Commentary on the Confession of Faith.* In Allegheny, Hodge's wife, Elizabeth, died. He was married again on December 20, 1869, to Margaret McLaren Woods of Detroit.

In 1877 he came home to Princeton. A. A. Hodge was "emphatically a Princeton man. He was born there. It was his father's home, and he was bound to it by a network of domestic relationships. He was loyal beyond measure to the ideas with which Princeton is identified, and loved to refer to her traditions. His large heart embraced the world, but no one could mistake the special place that Princeton had in his affections."[8] For one session father and son shared the teaching of theology at Princeton, and then Charles Hodge turned over to A. A. Hodge the entire work of the department.

* * *

At one time there had been three Alexanders at Princeton Seminary—father and two sons; there were now three

Hodges. Since 1860 New Testament Greek and literature had been taught by Caspar Wistar Hodge. A large, finely built man, Hodge, according to a colleague, "had the air of a man who is dignified without being pompous, and who, without being careless of personal appearance, is at the same time not thinking of himself." Caspar Wistar Hodge was not made for leadership and did not like it. He had no zeal for controversy. "He seemed to be without love of fame, and indifferent to the world's honors." For years Princetonians watched him slowly sauntering down the street, or walking more quickly from the seminary classrooms toward his study door with his books under his arm.[9]

With painstaking care Dr. Hodge prepared and taught his classes in New Testament Canon, the Life of Christ, the History and Literature of the Apostolic Church, and New Testament books—John, Romans, I Corinthians, Galatians, Ephesians, Philippians, Colossians, and Hebrews. According to George Purves, his student and successor, "he especially loved the fourth gospel, because of his profound interest in the person of Christ." Another of his students said that Hodge had "inherited in a marked degree his father's gift of prompt analytical insight, with a more practised skill in dealing with the details of exegesis, and undeniably more patience and tact in handling questions of textual criticism."[10]

Caspar Wistar Hodge, like his father and brother, strongly defended "the plenary inspiration of the Scriptures." At the same time he urged careful study of its human history and language. Hodge wrote that if the Bible "be God's Word given under historic conditions and through living human agents, then every phase of its thought, every turn of its expression, every grammatical form, becomes worthy of study." He did not ignore the critical attacks upon the Bible, but "he acted upon the manly plan of meeting false criticism by true criticism, and of showing that a true inductive method does not lead to the barren conclusions that the critics claim." Caspar Wistar Hodge was a "Calvinist of a type perhaps a little higher than his father," said Francis Patton.[11]

Dr. Hodge was not a skillful teacher; he often read his lectures. He believed that students were old enough to know what they wanted, so he did not try to compel their attention.

[53]

According to one of his students, however, Dr. Hodge "awakened our minds to the possibilities of Bible study." He "taught us to study with boldness and critical acuteness and yet with faith and love." Another student remembered "the incomparable Hodges, Dr. Archie Hodge and his younger brother. We never knew which we loved the most. The fact is we had place in our hearts for both because they were so different, and yet each one so splendid in his way." John Macmillan, who studied at Princeton from 1876 to 1878, remembered Caspar Wistar Hodge's lectures, which "hushed his class and frequently made it resemble more a company of boys gathered round a communion table than aught else." With modesty and reserve, but with conviction and power, Dr. Hodge "made the New Testament new" to successive classes of Princeton students.[12]

* * *

One of the students who studied with all three Hodges was Francis James Grimké, a young African American who turned from law to the ministry and entered Princeton Seminary. A year after Grimké's graduation in 1878 James McCosh wrote that "the late Dr. [Charles] Hodge reckoned him equal to the ablest of his students." Since the admission of Theodore Wright in 1825 Princeton Seminary had trained a sprinkling of African-American students, a number of whom passed through the seminary in the late 1870s. Matthew Anderson graduated in 1877 and became pastor of the Berean Church in Philadelphia. Grimké, who finished his work a year later, became the distinguished pastor of the Fifteenth Street Presbyterian Church in Washington, D.C. Hugh M. Browne, who was in Grimké's class, became a teacher and director of Cheyney State University. The next year Daniel W. Culp graduated and served as a pastor in South Carolina, Florida, Alabama, and Tennessee before studying medicine. Thomas M. Stewart finished his studies in 1881 and became a minister of the African Methodist Episcopal Church. After serving a number of churches in the United States, he became a teacher and attorney, eventually settling in Liberia.

Princeton was attracting a growing student body. Robert

Lewis Dabney fretted that Union Seminary in Virginia was declining because the students were "going off to Princeton." A number of students from other countries, mainly from the British Isles and Canada, studied at Princeton Seminary. Like their American colleagues they admired the faculty and appreciated each other. John Macmillan from Ireland described his fellow students: "their devotion to study, their brotherly kindness, their regularity at morning and evening prayer, their uniform courtesy to the members of the Faculty and to one another, and the harmony which characterized the life of our community."[13]

*   *   *

Charles Hodge taught his four classes each week during the winter and spring of 1877–78. He reread Darwin's *Voyage of the Beagle* and, as his grandson remembered, commented, "That is a very remarkable and delightful book."[14] On April 14 he spoke at the Sabbath Afternoon Conference in the old oratory in Alexander Hall. His topic was "Fight the Good Fight of Faith" (I Timothy 6:12). "The first necessary condition of contention for the faith," Dr. Hodge told the students, "is the firm conviction that the Bible is the infallible rule of faith." The second condition is "a firm conviction of the importance of the things" revealed in the Scriptures. The third is "an inward experience of the power of the truth." The "way to contend for the truth," Hodge said, is, first, "to confess it, to proclaim it"; second, "to answer misrepresentations"; and, third, to do this "with meekness, speaking the truth in love, remembering that Paul may plant and Apollos water, but it is God who gives the increase." A week later he preached in the seminary chapel at the communion service for the graduating class. The Lord's Supper, he said, is a commemoration, a communion, and a consecration by covenant. "We cannot commemorate Christ as Saviour without thereby acknowledging ourselves to be his, the purchase of his blood and devoted to his service," Dr. Hodge told the seminary seniors.[15] In May he went to Washington for his annual visit with his brother-in-law. There, on May 16, he attended church for the last time, leading in prayer at the funeral of his old friend Professor Joseph Henry of the Smithsonian Institute.

Charles Hodge returned home to Princeton and began rapidly to decline in strength. He sat in his beloved chair in his study, talking about the grandchildren, whose tiniest concerns he cherished, and about the General Assembly, the Berlin Conference, the affairs of the town that had been his home since boyhood, and especially about the seminary in which he had taught for over fifty years. To a relative he said, "To be absent from the body is to be present with the Lord; to be present with the Lord is to see Him; to see Him is to be like Him." To the loving inquiry of his wife he answered, "Yes, my love, my Saviour is with me every step of the way, but I am too weak to talk about it." He died on June 19, repeating to himself the hymn,

> Jesus, I am never weary, when upon this bed of pain;
> If thy presence only cheer me, all my loss I count but gain
> —ever near me, ever near me, Lord, remain![16]

The funeral was on June 22, 1878, at the end of the college's commencement week. It was a beautiful afternoon in the little town. All the stores were closed and all business suspended. The procession formed at the seminary—sons and relatives followed by members of the Presbytery of New Brunswick, the directors and trustees of the seminary, the officials of the college, clergymen, students, and friends. William Paxton gave the funeral address, paying heartfelt tribute to their teacher and friend. "To sum up all," he said,

When due allowance is made for his intellect and his learning, after all his chief power was in his goodness. Christ enshrined in his heart was the centre of his theology and his life. The world will write upon his monument GREAT; but we, his students, will write upon it GOOD.

After the service at the First Presbyterian Church, in which Charles Hodge had worshiped for sixty-three years, the procession formed again and moved slowly down Witherspoon Street to the cemetery. Francis Patton later described the scene:

His own sons carried him to the grave. They laid him beside the wife of his youth; and, reading in the light of the setting sun the graven words that years ago had given expression to a sorrowing husband's heart, they doubtless said once more: *"We Lay You Gently Here, Our Best Beloved, To Gather Strength And Beauty For The Coming Of The Lord."*[17]

*   *   *

For over a half century Charles Hodge held fast the old Calvinism "at all cost as the truth of God, from loyalty to Christ, and love for human souls." His understanding of Christianity had come from his boyhood study of the Shorter Catechism, the revival in Nassau Hall during his college days, and "the Alexandrine theology" of the seminary's first professor. On August 24, 1857, Hodge had written to William Cunningham:

I have had but one object in my professional career and as a writer, and that is to state and to vindicate the doctrines of the Reformed Church. I have never advanced a new idea, and have never aimed to improve on the doctrines of our fathers. Having become satisfied that the system of doctrines taught in the symbols of the Reformed Churches is taught in the Bible, I have endeavored to sustain it, and am willing to believe even where I cannot understand.[18]

Hundreds of students heard his lectures at the seminary, thousands heard his sermons, and tens of thousands read his writings—5,000 pages in the *Biblical Repertory and Princeton Review* and an equal amount in other articles and books. Lyman Atwater summarized Hodge's contribution to the Princeton journal:

Among the topics upon which he cast a powerful light in this *Review* were the relation of the Church to Slavery, on which he took ground equi-distant from Pro-slaveryism on the one hand, and those who maintained that slaveholders as such should be excluded from the church on the other; on Temperance, favoring Total Abstinence as a matter of expediency, but insisting that it could not be made a test of Christian character or a term of communion; in regard to voluntary societies, opposing alike those who would commit to them the evangelistic work of the church, in preference to church boards, and those who would discountenance all voluntary associations for any purpose whatsoever; in regard to the Scriptural idea of the church, showing that to the church invisible, consisting of all the redeemed, the scriptural definitions, promises and prerogatives pertain, while they pertain to the church visible, or to any organized church, just and only so far as it includes and manifests, makes the profession and has visibly the marks of the "sanctified in Christ Jesus, called to be saints"; in regard to Scriptural exegesis, accepting all true corrections of the received version and its interpretation which Germany could afford, but repudiating the extravagances and destructive rationalism which so many were eagerly importing from that country. In regard to theology, he repelled Pelagian, Sabellian, Socinian, and other rationalistic assaults upon the standards of his church, while guarding against the hyper-Calvinism that sometimes provoked or palliated them. The field of politics he entered only at its points of contact with ethical and scriptural doctrine, as Sabbath observance, marriage, divorce, and especially the attempt to sever the country by force of arms.[19]

Charles Hodge's theology, according to the Lutheran Charles Krauth, was "a Calvinism so gentle in its spirit toward other forms of evangelical Christianity." William Paxton wrote that Hodge presented Calvinism in its "attractive garb." "There is not one point of the Calvinistic system that he obscures," Paxton added, "but he lets in upon it the full light of God's love and mercy." A. A. Hodge described his father as both "conservative" and "moderate." He wrote:

He was conservative because the truth he held was not the discovery of the progressive reason of man, but the very word of God once delivered to the saints, and therefore authoritative and irreformable; and because reverence for that word repressed in him all ambition for distinction as the discoverer of new opinions, or as the improver of the faith of the Church. . . . He was always moderate also, because his loyalty to the Master made party spirit impossible, and because the amount of his knowledge and force of his logic caused him to see things in all their relations in all directions, by the aid of the sidelights as well as by the aid of those shining in the line of his direct vision.[20]

Charles Hodge was almost always generous in his treatment of theological opponents, and he usually sought to find the largest amount of common ground between his position and that of those with whom he differed. He was praised not only by those closest to him but also by many who took other theological positions. Charles Krauth said of him:

Next to having Dr. Hodge on one's side is the pleasure of having him as an antagonist; for where conscientious men must discuss a subject, who can express the comfort of honorable, magnanimous dealing on both sides—the feeling that in battling with each other they are also battling for each other, in that grand warfare whose final issue will be what all good men desire, the establishment of truth?

Stating that "we differ widely with him in many things," a Methodist theologian and editor of the *National Repository* described Charles Hodge as *"par excellence* the Calvinistic theologian of America" and praised his "beautifully adorned life."[21]

Although at times courteously disagreeing, Hodge praised the work of his German friends who stood on the broadly conservative side of the continental theological scene. Hodge's writings against the Mercersburg and the New England theologians, however, were sometimes quite sharp in tone. Hodge, no doubt, saw these friends as having in some sense betrayed their own Reformed tradition, and his disappointment was strongly expressed. Hodge firmly opposed Charles Finney's theology and revival methods but respected the man. When, a few weeks before Hodge's death, Theodore L. Cuyler told him that Finney had written to Cuyler inviting him to be his successor in the college pulpit at Oberlin, Hodge simply remarked that "his Brother Finney had become very sweet and mellow in his later years."[22]

Charles Hodge had weaknesses. He was not a great preacher. His voice was not strong, and his sermons often suited the classroom better than the pulpit. Although he excelled in setting forth the general meaning of a passage of Scripture, he was not a careful linguist nor always an exact exegete. He was not at his best in history. According to A. A. Hodge, "he was apt sometimes, as his critics have successfully pointed out, to go beyond the warrant of historical fact, in asserting that the Church had everywhere and always held as he held as to secondary matters." Charles Hodge was not bothered by hostile criticism of his work. He read such replies calmly or sometimes simply ignored them. His son wrote that "he certainly missed much improving discipline, which his antagonists . . . laboriously prepared for his good!"[23]

For fifty-eight years at Princeton Seminary Charles Hodge had taught the Bible and its doctrines. In a meeting in the seminary chapel immediately before his funeral a statement prepared by Lyman Atwater was adopted in honor of the seminary's greatest teacher. It began with the words "Mighty in the Scriptures, and in maintaining their plenary inspiration and infallible authority, he was mighty also as a defender and expounder of the truths they teach." Hodge set forth faithfully the doctrines of the Reformed faith—perhaps not so totally without change as he himself imagined, but substantially the theology of Calvin, the Westminster Confession, and the great Reformed teachers of the seventeenth century. William Shedd of Union Seminary in New York said that "Dr. Hodge [had] done more for Calvinism than any other man in America." The *British Quarterly Review,* in an article on the American press, reported that Charles Hodge's *Biblical Repertory and Princeton Review* was "the greatest purely theological Review that has ever been published in the English tongue, and has waged war in defence of the Westminster standards for a period of forty years, with a polemic vigour and unity of design without any parallel in the history of religious journalism." The British journal continued, "If we were called to name any living writer who, to Calvin's exegetical tact, unites a large measure of Calvin's grasp of mind and transcendent clearness in the department of systematic theology, we would point to this Princeton Professor."[24]

African Methodist Episcopal Church leader Bishop Daniel Payne, who studied at the Lutheran Gettysburg Seminary under Princeton Seminary graduate Samuel S. Schmucker, described Charles Hodge as "the greatest theologian . . . America has yet produced." Sir William Nicoll, a sound judge of literary quality, believed that Charles Hodge was "surely the most luminous of all theological writers." John Kennedy, pastor of the Free church in Dingwall, Scotland, visited the United States in 1873. On his return home he is reported to have said that there were two things he saw in America that exceeded his expectation—Niagara Falls and Dr. Hodge! A modern historian says that Charles Hodge remains "the great representative of conservative Calvinism in the nation's last two hundred years." Another historian states that "Hodge was as well-informed a thinker as American Presbyterianism possessed in the mid-nineteenth century, and his erudition ranged widely over the fields of Biblical scholarship, the history of doctrine, and philosophical theology. Probably nobody in the country was so generally well-versed in all the sciences of theology."[25]

Charles Hodge taught generations of Princeton Seminary students, many of whom became pastors, missionaries, and church leaders. They valued Hodge's teaching of the Reformed faith and they loved him for his Christian life and example. A. A. Hodge wrote:

From about 1868 to the year of his death, each graduating class at the very last took a special, personal farewell of Dr. Hodge. After receiving their diplomas, and the valedictory charge, and benediction of the representative of the Board of Directors, the class formed a circle with Dr. Hodge at the centre, in the middle of the front campus. They sang [in 1869] several verses of the hymn, "All hail the power of Jesus' name," and the verse of the missionary hymn beginning, "Shall we whose souls are lighted, etc." Then making a close ring, each one crossing his arms, they held hand by hand, and sang "Blest be the tie that binds," and then the Long Metre Doxology. After that Dr. Hodge pronounced the Benediction. He then shook hands with each student, and each student shook hands with all the others, and they separated.[26]

The Princeton students and faculty were lavish in their praise of their beloved teacher and friend. James P. Boyce said, "He is one of the most excellent of men; so modest and yet so wise, so kind and fatherly in his manner, and yet so giant an intellect, he is a man who deserves a world of praise." William Paxton said, "His was not a dead theology. . . . What he gave us was bread from our Father's table." John Macmillan remembered "the marvelous manner in which he brought [God's] love and life down into our lives." Charles Aiken told the Princeton students, "To him more than to any other man I ever knew had the grace been given not only to 'bring into captivity every thought to the obedience of Christ,' but to draw the motives of life from Christ, and to find the daily strength and joy of life in Christ." Francis Patton summarized Dr. Hodge's contribution to the church: "He had no ambition to be epoch-making by marking the era of a new departure. But he earned a higher title to fame in that he was the champion of his Church's faith during a long and active life, her trusted leader in time of trial, and for more than half a century the most conspicuous teacher of her ministry."[27]

Despite the praise and acclaim he received as a great theologian and churchman, Charles Hodge was humble. About a year before his death Dr. Boardman said to him, "You ought to be a very happy man. Consider what you have accomplished, and the universal feelings toward you—" "Now, stop!" said Hodge, with a wave of his hand. "All that can be said is, that God has been pleased to take up a *poor little stick* and do something with it. What I have done is as nothing compared with what is done by a man who goes to Africa, and labors among a heathen tribe, and reduces their language to writing. I am not worthy to stoop down and *unloose the shoes* of such a man."[28]

Mary Hunter Hodge survived her husband by twenty months. She "presid[ed] in his place in the large family circle," A. A. Hodge wrote, "preserving with us the traditions and associations sacred to his memory, the object of the affection and gratitude of all their children. Left by his death as a stricken deer, she had no desire to live. Through much pain, yet with unwavering faith, she went to rejoin him on the early morning of February 28th, 1880."[29]

4

Thy Word is Truth

I would pray and labour that in gaining breadth we may not lose height, and in gaining peace and love we may not lose purity and truth.

ARCHIBALD ALEXANDER HODGE

O N the last New Year's day of Charles Hodge's life a
seminary student visited him in his study and asked
for a motto. The old man wrote in a firm hand "Thy
word is truth." This was the strength of Charles Hodge's
theology and his bequest to the next generation. On September 6, 1878, as the seminary began its first academic year
without Dr. Hodge, Charles Aiken told the students and
faculty, "We gird ourselves for new tasks. His lips and his life
have taught us to whom to look both for large consolation
and for adequate supplies of grace."[1]

         *   *   *

The late nineteenth century was marked by expansion,
development, and progress in America—and by profound
social change. The United States faced the practical and moral
dilemmas of industrialism, urbanization, and immigration.
There were also indications of pervasive shifts in moral
attitudes and religious views. For many Americans, self-sufficiency replaced the old Calvinistic doctrines of
human depravity and moral inability. Intellectual questions
provoked by scientific discoveries and modern scholarship
created a growing skepticism about traditional Christianity.
Eighteenth-century rationalism, beginning in Germany
and slowly making its way to Britain and North America, had
opened the door to higher critical views of the Bible. These
new ideas challenged the accuracy and authority of Scripture

[65]

by stressing its human origin and claiming that it was marred by historical errors. The study of comparative religions—leading to the view that world religions were merely different expressions of a common, evolving human religious experience—challenged the uniqueness of Christianity. Evolution became not only an explanation of physical life but a universal principle—subjecting all absolutes, including religious and ethical ones, to natural and immanent development. The effect of these great forces at work in Western culture was the questioning of orthodox Christian convictions about God, humanity, the Bible, miracles, providence, and salvation.

American Christianity seemed as strong as ever, with great stone churches in the cities and large congregations everywhere; but a serious rift began within Protestantism. Evangelical Christianity presented its message of sin and salvation and promoted the revivals of D. L. Moody, crusades for temperance, and foreign missions. Liberal theology attempted to mediate between Christianity and the radically altered scientific and cultural outlook, leading to its persistent emphasis on the immanence of God, the goodness of humanity, and the importance of experience, feeling, and ethics in religion.

The recently reunited American Presbyterian church faced these troubled times of social and theological change. Early in 1873 Francis Landey Patton—young professor of theology at the Presbyterian Seminary of the Northwest in Chicago—warned against "broad churchism" and predicted that the day was coming when the Presbyterian church would have to fight to save its Reformed theology. It was Francis Patton who, the next year, presented formal charges of heresy against David Swing, popular and poetic preacher of Chicago's Fourth Presbyterian Church—accusing him of violating his ordination vows by not sincerely receiving and adopting the Confession of Faith of the Presbyterian church and by failing to zealously and faithfully maintain the truths of the gospel. Patton offered specifics:

He omits to preach or teach one or more of the doctrines indicated in the following statements of Scripture, namely: that Christ is a "propitiation for our sins," that we have "redemption through his blood," that we are "justified by faith," that "there is no other name . . . whereby we may be saved,". . . that "all Scripture is given by inspiration of God," and that "the wicked shall go away into everlasting punishment."

In his formal plea of "not guilty," Dr. Swing repudiated Patton's charges, saying that if his ordination vows imposed upon him the necessity of living "a life of ignorance and stupidity," the sooner he was relieved of those vows "the better." Swing emphasized the historical and relative character of all creeds. "A creed is only the highest wisdom of a particular time and place," he said. "As in states, there is always a quiet slipping away from old laws without any waiting for a formal repeal . . . so in all formulated creeds, Catholic or Protestant, there is a gradual, but constant, decay of some article or word which was once promulgated amid great pomp and circumstance." Swing criticized the "dark fatalism" of Presbyterianism, its "overstatement of the idea of salvation by faith alone," and "its terrific doctrine of hell." "Not one of you, my brethren," Swing told his fellow presbyters, "has preached the dark theology of Jonathan Edwards in your whole life." Swing argued that the doctrine of eternal punishment was unpalatable for the modern mind and therefore unacceptable. Dr. Patton replied, "I cannot help it if that is a doctrine which is unpleasant to the feelings. It is in the Confession of Faith." When the presbytery acquitted Swing by a vote of 48 to 13, Patton at once announced that he would appeal the case. Five days later Dr. Swing withdrew from the Presbyterian church and founded the independent Central Church in Chicago.[2]

*   *   *

In 1880 Union Seminary in New York City had 144 students, Western had 136, and Andover, 126. Princeton was the largest American seminary, even though its enrollment in 1880 was only 172—the same as it had been twenty years earlier. The Princeton faculty was committed to the task of preparing its students to stand for the faith. A. A. Hodge, who knew seasickness firsthand from his voyages to and from India, told the seminarians, "There is a great deal of seasickness in theology, till you get your sea legs on—sky, and land, and water all mixed!"[3]

In their theology classes the students "recited" on the assigned section of Charles Hodge's *Systematic Theology*, and A. A. Hodge lectured on each topic. His lectures were enlivened by his exuberant speech, witty sayings, and apt analogies. When his students failed to understand, "he swept the universe for illustrations, and poured them out so copiously and with such manifest spontaneity, that [the students] overwhelmed him with their applause."[4]

A. A. Hodge maintained that the Bible is the authoritative source of all Christian doctrine. "We accept [the Scriptures] as the infallible rule of faith because they are the very Word of God," he said. "They were designed to furnish us all the information which is needed by us, and all that God intends us to have." He added:

We must come to the study of this Word in a teachable spirit, with a mind open to receive all that it has to convey to us, with simplicity and godly sincerity, without prejudice. What we need above all things is, not what we think or what other men think ought to be, but what is, in fact, the real, plain meaning of God's declaration. . . . The question is not, What can we, with skillful exegetical management, get out of the Bible . . . by breaking up the text and bringing the stress of our strong wills to bear against the natural sense of each separate clause?—the question is not, What may the several passages possibly mean in the way we wish? but, What, upon the whole and along the entire line of Scripture, did God the Holy Ghost intend us to believe, what impression did he intend to make upon us, as to these stupendous subjects by the language he has chosen, by the general method in which he has conducted the argument?[5]

"It is one thing to stand faithfully by what God says," A. A. Hodge told the students; "it is another thing to draw inferences from what God says. Our principles as Protestants make us deal with the Bible alone, and not with systems of divinity, and not with inferences from what the Bible says." Hodge confessed that he was "never absolutely convinced by one text." "I do not believe God ever meant us to believe in a great doctrine upon a single text," he said. Concerned about the possibility of an error in transcription or interpretation, he sought to base his theology on scriptural teaching "interwoven in the whole scheme of redemption."[6]

Dr. Hodge believed that the constructing of a true theology from the Bible was far from a simple matter. "Truth is many sided," Hodge said, "and it radiates from above and beneath, from north, south, east, and west. It is not a line, but to be compared rather to a surface or a solid." There was a sense in which it was well, he told the students, to be "broad church" and "catholic"—though "not the popular sense," he added. "All truth is catholic," Hodge insisted; "it embraces many elements, wide horizons, and therefore involves endless difficulties and apparent inconsistencies. The mind of man seeks for unity, and tends prematurely to force a unity in the sphere of his imperfect knowledge by sacrificing one element of the truth or other to the rest." Hodge added, "Almost all heresies are partial truths—true in what they affirm, but false in what they deny." "Definitions are made for man," Hodge liked to repeat, "not man for definitions. They are like ring-fences out on the prairies. They are useful, and I am fond of them. But they have to be learned and unlearned." Hodge maintained that "the doctrines of the Bible are not isolated, but interlaced; and the view of one doctrine must necessarily affect the view taken of another." "Beginning with a diagnosis of the nature of the disease," he said to the seminarians, "you may infer the kind of treatment and the sort of physician necessary. Or, if you find a certain physician applying a certain remedy, you may infer the nature and gravity of the disease."[7]

Dr. Hodge made the point that "the amount of the highest talent and learning consecrated within the Christian Church to the defence and elucidation of the sacred Scriptures would infinitely surprise the shallow critics who are vociferously claiming that its pretensions have been disproved." He reminded his students "that a few frogs in a swamp make incomparably more noise than all the herds of cattle browsing upon a hundred hills." "Yet none are deceived," he added, "except the frogs themselves."[8]

In his discussion of the doctrine of God, A. A. Hodge attempted to "comprehend all the half-truths or heresies which have divided the schools." God, he said, is "always beyond us, hid in the light which is impenetrable." He is "always above us, enthroned in heaven, commanding, revealing, ruling, showering myriad blessings from above." He is "before us, looking upon us and speaking to us face to face. He is our heavenly Father." This same God is "ever within us, the ultimate ground of our being and the unfailing source of our life."[9]

Dealing with the doctrine of the trinity, Hodge showed how "all of the straggling and apparently conflicting rays of light" preserved in human systems of false religions— deism, pantheism, polytheism—are comprehended "in a harmonious and pure form" in the Bible and the early creeds. Furthermore, Hodge asserted, the doctrine of the trinity makes the nature of God "infinitely more intelligible to us." "The condition of our knowing God at all," he said, "is wholly that we were created in his image."

We are spirits, persons, and causes; therefore we know God to be a personal spirit and first cause. But we are no less essentially social beings, and to us all life and character, intellect, moral or practical, is conceivable only under social conditions. A unitarian, one-personed God might possibly have existed, and if revealed as such it would have been our duty to have acknowledged his lordship. But, nevertheless, he would have always remained utterly inconceivable to us—one lone, fellowless, conscious being; subject without object; conscious person without environment; righteous being without fellowship or moral relation or sphere of right action. Where would there be to him a sphere of love, truth, trust; of sympathetic feeling? Before creation, eternal darkness; after creation, only an endless game of solitaire, with worlds for pawns. But the Scriptures declare that love is not only a possibility to God, or an occasional mood, but his very essence. If love be of the essence of God, he must always love; and, being eternal, he must have possessed an eternal object of love; and, being infinite, he must have eternally possessed an infinite object of love. This of course the eternal Persons find mutually in each other.[10]

Discussing the doctrine of divine providence, A. A. Hodge told a story about "the great Dr. Witherspoon" who "lived at a country-seat called Tusculum, on Rocky Hill, two miles north of Princeton."

One day a man rushed into his presence, crying, "Dr. Witherspoon, help me to thank God for his wonderful providence! My horse ran away, my buggy was dashed to pieces on the rocks, and behold! I am unharmed." The good doctor laughed benevolently at the inconsistent, half-way character of the man's religion. "Why," he answered, "I know a providence a thousand times better than that of yours. I have driven down that rocky road to Princeton hundreds of times, and my horse never ran away and my buggy was never dashed to pieces."

"Undoubtedly, the deliverance was providential," Hodge said, "but just as much so also were the uneventful rides of the college president."[11]

Hodge quoted John Stuart Mill, who said, "I have never seen any providence." "But this is nothing wonderful," countered the Princeton professor. "I have never seen the world revolve, though I have lived upon it more than fifty years. The broad current carries the ship with it though you do not mark the track. And the providence of God encircles you, and your vessel, and your ocean too; and while you may take your own little path upon that ocean, the ocean, ship, and passenger are being made subservient to a Higher Will."[12]

In arguing for the reality of the biblical miracles against those who say that "the proof of which moral and spiritual truths are susceptible is their own inherent self-evidencing light," Hodge stated that since "the gospel is not a disclosure of abstract moral or spiritual truths, but rather a series of objective facts constituting the stupendous history of redemption," miracles are appropriate and valuable evidences of God's revelation. "Given a supernatural crisis, a supernatural teacher, and a supernatural doctrine," Hodge said, "miracles are found to be in place like jewels on the state robes of a king." He added, "All the great miracles recorded in Scripture gather around two great foci in the history of redemption—the giving of the law through Moses, and the life and death of the incarnate God. Miracles in such connections are inevitable, and in the highest sense congruous. Their absence would have been unaccountable." But he would not believe "a sporadic miracle," Hodge told the students. "Though old Dr. John McLean even were to take us all down to the graveyard and raise up a man who looked like

Jonathan Edwards, it would weigh nothing with me. A purposeless, isolated miracle proves nothing. The miracles of Scripture are not mere addenda to revelation, but are themselves media of the communication of truth."[13]

In illustrating the conviction of "evangelical Christians of the school of Augustine and Calvin" that even the sinful actions of human beings originate in God as to their matter, and that as to their form or moral quality they originate in the creature alone, Hodge depicted a great artist handling "an instrument out of tune." "The sound that issues," he said, "is due to the artist, but the discord which deforms it issues only from the unbalanced organism of the instrument, the unstrung cords or the unadjusted pipes."[14]

In discussing the doctrine of original sin, Hodge said that "if dice, being thrown 1,000 times, always turn up sixes, you say the dice are loaded. So with babies. They come into the world as thick as those flakes of snow today: and they always come 'sin up.'" "How do you explain it?" he asked. "The dice are loaded." Dr. Hodge contrasted three views of "man's state and need": "the Pelagian says—Man is well, and simply needs teaching. The Semi-Pelagian—Man is sick, and needs medicine. The Augustinian—Man is dead, and needs a new creation." Hodge compared the difference between "hearers of the same gospel." "A" became a Christian, and "B" did not. Why? Hodge answered:

The Pelagian says—"A's purpose was sufficient: he willed it, and he became a Christian."

The Semi-Pelagian says—"A did his best, and God helped him."

The Arminian says—"A used the gracious ability, the prevenient grace, given by God to all, while B did not."

The Lutheran says—"A and B both needed prevenient and co-operating grace. Neither could cooperate, but either might resist. B did resist, while A did not. Hence the difference."

The Calvinist says—"A was regenerated by the grace of Almighty God."[15]

A. A. Hodge taught that Calvinism "glorifies the free and sovereign grace of God by attributing to it alone all the efficiency in saving the believing sinner." The truth that "we did not first choose [God], but he first chose us," Hodge said, "enters into all genuine Christian experience." "In the theology of the heart," he stated, "all Christians are Calvinists—that is, all Christians ascribe all their salvation unto God. And this is the only form in which the doctrine of sovereign predestination should be insisted upon as of vital religious interest."[16]

In a lecture on "Predestination" to his Philadelphia Bible class Hodge said:

Here, as everywhere else, there is essential truth on both sides of every controversy, and the real truth is the whole truth, its entire catholic body. Arminianism in the abstract as an historical scheme is a heresy, holding half the truth. Calvinism is an historical scheme which in its best representatives comprehends the whole truth with considerable completeness. But the case is essentially different when we come to consider the great co-existing bodies of Christian people calling themselves respectively Calvinists and Arminians. Each of these parties holds all essential truth, and therefore they hold actually very much the same truth. The Arminians think and speak very much like Calvinists when they come to talk with God in either the confession of sin or the supplication for grace. They both alike in that attitude recognize the sovereignty of God and the guilt and helplessness of men. Indeed, how could it be otherwise? What room is there for anything other than essential Calvinism on one's knees? On the other hand, the Calvinist thinks and speaks like the better class of Arminians when he addresses the consciences of men, and pleads with them, as free, responsible agents, to repent and believe in Christ. The difference between the best of either class is one of emphasis rather than of essential principle. Each is the complement of the other. Each is necessary to restrain, correct, and supply the one-sided strain of the other. They together give origin to the blended strain from which issues the perfect music which utters the perfect truth.[17]

Hodge illustrated for the students the difference between irresistible grace and coercion by a reference to Aesop's fables. "When the wind beat upon the man," he said, "it made him only draw his cloak the closer round him. But when the sun made him hot, he by his own will threw off the cloak, which the storm without had not torn from him." "You might be got out of this room in two ways," he continued. "A strong man might come and thrust you out, or a beautiful lady might invite and thereby draw you!" Hodge concluded:

"Now, it is an utter misconception to suppose that by 'irresistible grace' is meant an *ab extra* coercing influence. Grace acts from within, through the will. The man becomes willing: and so there is no resistance or desire to offer it. To be 'made willing in the day of God's power' is the highest liberty."[18]

In discussing sanctification, A. A. Hodge argued that those who say "We have already attained and are already perfect" lower the standard. "Instead of sanctification," he said, "it is pollution; instead of a higher life, it is a lower life." He illustrated the true biblical nature of sanctification by comparing it with the ripening of a pear.

There is a ripening which goes on in the autumn of the year which is perfect; and perfectly ripe fruit is one of the most perfect and beautiful things in nature. It is a gradual process from the blossom through all the different stages. You could not hasten it. It is growing on in the sunshine and when the dews of heaven descend upon it. The ripening is perfect; and when you take the pear from the limb, you say, "Thank God, this is perfect! It has run through all the stages, it has omitted none; it has come to the end, it is finished." But you go sometimes and you find pears early ripe, and they have a sweet and luscious self-consciousness of it; and they fall down flat on the earth and are soft because there is a worm at the core. My good grandmother used to say, and I think now it is worth repeating, "I do hate the early-ripes."[19]

In answer to the question "How is the soul made fit for heaven?" Hodge said:

Perfectionists say that the soul is made fit in this life for heaven, and that the perfecting work may be done early, through the believer's act of faith in Christ. Romanists postpone the completion of the work, in the case of all, till after death; and hence they provide purgatory for good Catholics. We say that, though there is nothing in death itself that sanctifies, Christians are at death made perfect in holiness by Divine and gracious power. Without such a provision, what would become of Christians who are hardly fit to go to prayer meeting on earth, not to speak of being fit to enter Heaven![20]

A. A. Hodge often discussed missions with the students. "Millenarian missionaries have a style of their own," he said. "Their theory affects their work in the way of making them seek exclusively, or chiefly, the conversion of individual souls." He added, "The true and efficient missionary method is to aim directly, indeed, at soul winning, but at the same time to plant Christian institutions in heathen lands, which will, in time, develop according to the genius of the nationalities."[21]

At the closing lecture of his first term's teaching at Princeton, A. A. Hodge began by saying, "Now gentlemen, we might as well come to 'the end of the world.' Mr. Rubinkam, will you please recite: we have very little time, sir!" Hodge objected to the common arrangement of systematic theology that ended with "hell" and "eternal punishment"—"as if these were the climacteric categories in which the study of the nature, purposes, and works of the Lord must find its final and characteristic goal." In his teaching he purposely reversed the usual order so as to complete his theology classes with a study of "the endless blessedness of the redeemed." "It is the presence of God as unreconciled that constitutes hell," Hodge said; "it is the presence of God, as reconciled in Christ, that makes heaven."[22]

A. A. Hodge "was always reasoning on the relations of doctrines to each other, and to the great scheme of grace." His ability in this area—as well as the practical thrust of all his theological writings—is illustrated by his article "The Ordo Salutis: or, Relation in the Order of Nature of Holy Character and Divine Favor." In his *Outlines of Theology* A. A. Hodge set forth the four great concerns of his teaching:

The point of view adopted in this book is the evangelical and specifically the Calvinistic or Augustinian one, assuming the following fundamental principles: 1st. The inspired Scriptures are the sole, and an infallible standard of all religious knowledge. 2d. Christ and his work is the centre around which all Christian theology is brought into order. 3d. The salvation brought to light in the gospel is supernatural and of *free grace*. 4th. All religious knowledge has a *practical end*. The theological sciences, instead of being absolute ends in themselves, find their noblest purpose and effect in the advancement of personal holiness, the more efficient service of our fellow men, and *the greater glory of God*.[23]

A. A. Hodge was a Presbyterian by inheritance and by conviction; but he believed that Christ and the apostles "never intended to impose upon the Church as a whole any particular form of organization." They never went "beyond the suggestion of general principles and actual inauguration of a few rudimentary forms," Hodge said. Hodge greatly appreciated the historic continuity of the Christian church through all the centuries and loved the "Christian year" and the great liturgical formulas of the different churches. Although he had supported the Presbyterian Old School–New School reunion, he was not an enthusiast for general church union. "Unless touched by the spirit of schism," the denominations, he believed, are "not detrimental to the Church," which in its essence is "a great spiritual body, constituted by the indwelling of the Holy Ghost through all the ages and nations, uniting all to Christ." Denominations, Hodge believed, "represent great ideas . . . which God commits to them, in order to have them act upon them." It is their duty to maintain their "true inheritance." The best way for denominations to work together, Hodge asserted, is not by uniting the different denominations but "by the unity of the Spirit; it is not by working from without, but from within outward; by taking on more of Christ, more of the Spirit." "In God's good time," organic unity of the different denominations would come, Hodge believed, "as an incidental effect of the ripening of all churches in knowledge and love and in all the graces, and especially of a whole-souled, self-forgetful consecration of all to the service and glory of their common Lord."[24]

5

Evolution and Inspiration

There is no escape from the position that the Church is bound to confess all that God has lovingly revealed to her as His truth. What the Bible teaches, not what is convenient, undisputed, or likely to put us to the trouble of defending, is the proper measure of the contents of our *credo*.

BENJAMIN BRECKENRIDGE WARFIELD

L IKE his Princeton predecessors, A. A. Hodge—who had studied science with Joseph Henry at Princeton College before devoting his energies to theology— believed that scientific and religious truths were not "mutually contradictory, but supplementary." "Standing upon the rock of divine truth," he wrote, "Christians need not fear, and can well afford to await the result. Perfect faith, as well as perfect love, casteth out all fear. All things are ours, whether the natural or the supernatural, whether science or revelation." Hodge warned, however, that "science is only the human interpretation of God's works, it is always imperfect and makes many mistakes. Biblical interpreters are also liable to mistakes and should never assert the absolute identity of their interpretations of the Bible with the mind of God."[1]

In his discussion of the statement of the Confession of Faith that God created the universe "in the space of six days," Hodge judged that no adjustment had thus far been found that perfectly harmonized the biblical text with geological discoveries of the various conditions through which the world had passed before its present order. He was confident, however, that "the book of revelation and the book of nature are both from God, and will be found, when both are adequately interpreted, to coincide perfectly." Since the laws of nature are "the methods self-ordained of a personal Agent," Hodge asserted, "the true scientists are the sons of God, who were not created for the laws of nature, but the laws of nature for them."[2]

A. A. Hodge agreed with his father that any theory of evolution in which "the universe and its order is referred to chance" is atheistic. But there are two kinds of evolution, Hodge told the seminarians.

When Christian people say, "Evolution means Atheism," a distinction should be observed. If it is Darwinianism they mean, they are right to demonstration. But evolution in the Duke of Argyll's *Reign of Law* sense may be admitted consistently with Christianity; so that, when other Christian people are found saying, "Evolution does *not* mean Atheism," they too may be right.[3]

A. A. Hodge stated that "the natural theologian" has "only the most friendly interest" in those theories of evolution that "neither deny nor obscure the evidence which the order and adaptation observed in nature afford to the existence of God, and his immanence in and providential control of his works." In his review of Asa Gray's *Natural Science and Religion,* Hodge came to see a "more comprehensive and ultimate teleology" in the ideas of "continuity of causation throughout the universe." If the universe is the manifestation of a coherent plan of God, he wrote, the concept of "an ideal evolution, a providential unfolding of a general plan, in which general designs and methods converge in all directions to the ultimate end of the whole," is far from incompatible with Christian theism. Although Hodge felt that "the doctrine of the descent of species from species" could be held by Christians (if man were excluded from the process), he believed that such descent had not been proven. Even this process, however, would require the engrafting on earlier organisms of "new and higher powers" by direct acts of God's will. Such a combination of process and divine intervention, he stated, should not be called "evolution" but "mediate creation."[4]

A. A. Hodge made a distinction between evolution "as a working hypothesis of science" and evolution "as a philosophy." Christians need not be afraid of the doctrine of evolution when it is confined to a scientific theory, Hodge told his students. "It cannot affect any of the questions of religion; it cannot affect any questions of revelation." But there was the danger that the theory of evolution would be enlarged to a comprehensive philosophy of evolution—

"evolution run wild . . . the general talk of the people."
"Philosophy," Hodge said, "is different from science. Science
is applied to facts, philosophy has to do with causes."
Christians need not fear "evolution in the department of
science," but they must "fear and oppose evolution with all
[their] might when it is given . . . as a philosophy." Hodge
said that after the Charleston, South Carolina, earthquake of
1886 (which killed ninety-two people) scientists had scoffed
at Christian preachers who were putting before their hearers
"the scriptural lessons of the event viewed as a divine dispensation." "These men of mere science," Hodge asserted, "may
have been able and useful in their narrow specialty, but they
were certainly very absurd philosophers." He added, "They
were perfectly right in confining their own investigations to
the scientific aspects of the phenomena, [but] the preachers
had an equal authority in calling the attention of the
Christian people to the aspect which the light of the inspired
Scriptures, when thrown upon the providential facts, presented."[5]

When the friends of James Woodrow of Columbia Seminary used A. A. Hodge's writings—along with those of James
McCosh and Francis Patton—to support Woodrow's views on
evolution, Hodge explained his position in a letter to the
Memphis Appeal on March 29, 1886. He stated that "evolution
as a working hypothesis of scientific men lies beyond the
sphere of our criticism, and threatens no interest with which
we are concerned." But that sphere is quite limited, Hodge
stated; it has to do with phenomena and cannot include
speculation "as to causes and final ends." There is no evidence, Hodge continued, "to prove that man was originally
generated from non-human ancestors." Even if God used
"specific variation by descent" to bring into existence the
"successive orders of the lower animals," the immense
probability in the case of man, Hodge believed, is "that God's
own image was brought into existence by an immediate act of
God himself."[6]

A. A. Hodge attempted to follow and monitor scientific
developments, setting forth those areas in which he found
compatibility with Christian theism. He warned against
non-Christian presuppositions and conclusions. Although he

[81]

took a more positive view of the possibilities of evolution than did his father, the younger Hodge did not accept the theory as fact. He was willing to grant that Christian theism has no essential objection to the idea that all plants and animals have been produced by descent from earlier, more simple, forms of life—provided that a series of definite divine interventions be allowed to introduce higher powers into the process. Hodge stated in his introduction to Joseph Van Dyke's *Theism and Evolution* that "evolution considered as the plan of an infinitely wise Person and executed under the control of His everywhere-present energies can never be irreligious; can never exclude design, providence, grace or miracles." He did not accept the view, however, that the body of man had a genetic connection with some lower animal, because "of the specific assertions of Scripture." Hodge summarized his views on the origin of man by telling a Philadelphia audience in 1886 that he believed "that the body of man was made out of pre-existing materials; that the soul of man was created by the mighty power of God; and that Eve was made from Adam by the miraculous power of God."[7]

*   *   *

Essays and Reviews—published in England four months after Darwin's *Origin of Species*—sought to bring the views of continental critical biblical scholarship to the English-speaking world. The common theme of the book was the assertion of naturalistic development in religion, similar to evolution in biology. The authors—six of the seven were clergymen—argued that all social institutions, including Christianity itself, were to be understood and evaluated through the study of their historical origins and development; and all notions of truth and value, including Christian teaching, were to be seen as "products forged within the historical process." Since the Bible and the Christian faith are products of their cultural milieu, they must be "open to critical study and analysis." *Essays and Reviews* received much more immediate attention in the press than Darwin's book and convinced "evangelicals on both sides of the Atlantic that the time had arrived for addressing the new critical challenge."[8]

After Charles Hodge's retirement as editor of the *Biblical Repertory and Princeton Review* in 1871, the journal merged the following year with the *American Presbyterian Review* (which began as a New School Presbyterian Church publication) and became the *Presbyterian Quarterly and Princeton Review*. It was edited by Lyman Atwater of Princeton College and Henry B. Smith of Union Seminary in New York. In 1878 it was succeeded by *The Princeton Review,* the cover of which featured the words "By Whom, all things; for Whom, all things."[9] Since *The Princeton Review* was devoted chiefly to philosophy, science, and literature, there was a need for a new theological journal to represent the reunited Presbyterian church, and *The Presbyterian Review* was inaugurated in 1880. A. A. Hodge of Princeton and Charles A. Briggs of Union Seminary in New York were chosen by their respective faculties as coeditors; and the other Presbyterian seminaries—Auburn, Western, Lane, and McCormick—were represented by associate editors.

Charles Briggs, the son of a wealthy merchant, was born in New York City in 1841. He studied at the University of Virginia, where he was converted during the revival of 1858 and decided to enter the ministry. His uncle Marvin Briggs, a graduate of Princeton Seminary, wrote to his nephew in Charlottesville encouraging him to attend an "Old School" seminary. He added, "You will agree that you won't find a superior to Dr. [Charles] Hodge." But Charles Briggs went to Union Theological Seminary in New York and then spent three years in Germany, where he experienced "a new divine light" (as he described it) from the study of the methods of historical criticism. In 1874, upon Henry B. Smith's retirement, Charles Briggs—strongly recommended by Smith and Philip Schaff—became Union's professor of Hebrew and cognate languages. It was at Briggs's urging that President William Adams of Union wrote to "Brother" A. A. Hodge of Princeton, suggesting the need of a theological journal for Presbyterians that would demonstrate the strength and vitality of their now-united church. Less than a week later Hodge replied that it seemed to him "very plain that it is both the right and the interest of the Presbyterian Church to be represented by a theological review," and "that it is best that

Union and Princeton, representing the two great halves of the past, should cooperate in the management of such a review." For the first three issues of 1880 Charles Aiken served as the Princeton editor while A. A. Hodge completed the biography of his father, and then Hodge became co-editor with Briggs.[10]

On the afternoon of January 11, 1880, the first number of *The Presbyterian Review* was sent out by a New York publishing company to several hundred subscribers. It described itself— in an announcement written by Charles Briggs but signed as well by A. A. Hodge—as an enterprise that would seek "to combine all the varied interests and sections of our church. It will be the aim of the *Review* to treat all subjects in a broad and catholic spirit, comprehending those historical phases of Calvinism which combined in the Presbyterian Church at the reunion."[11]

*   *   *

For the October 1880 issue of the *The Presbyterian Review* Charles Briggs submitted a "historical account" of the William Robertson Smith trial in Scotland. For some time Dr. Smith, professor of Old Testament studies in the Free Church College at Aberdeen, had been the center of controversy for his higher critical views of the Bible. A year after he had been appointed to his post at Aberdeen he wrote to his publisher, "I glanced over the standard religious authority—[Charles] Hodge—a few days ago. He has no conception of the modern form of the problem, and proves nothing. I fear it is so with all our 'orthodox' men."

Smith was deeply influenced by the Graf-Wellhausen views during the early 1870s and expressed his own ideas in a series of articles that he wrote for the ninth edition of the *Encyclopedia Britannica*. His article on the Bible—which appeared in the third volume of the encyclopedia on December 7, 1875— began a five-year controversy in the Free Church. The proceedings in presbytery and at General Assembly were followed and discussed in classrooms, railway cars, and work-shops in Scotland and read by Americans in the pages of the *New York Times*. Charles Briggs's account of the trial in *The Presbyterian Review* appeared to dismiss "the competency of church courts to judge the veracity of the complicated new critical theories" and described Smith's theological positions as "legitimate differences" that might be accepted within a broadly evangelical Presbyterian church. Briggs was informed from Princeton—"in a note that was itself a model of studied understatement"—that what he had appended to his account of the trial seemed "to go beyond our understanding." The Smith case, stated A. A. Hodge, involved "many delicate and vexed questions on which we have all along known that we [were] divided." Briggs stubbornly refused to revise or withdraw the notice; and Hodge, "with his wonted good sense," recognized at once that quibbling with Briggs over it would be fruitless. The notice was printed with a statement from Hodge calling for a "full, free and frank" discussion of the issue that had so disturbed the Scottish church.[12]

Briggs and Hodge agreed upon a plan whereby *The Presbyterian Review* would publish a series of eight articles, to begin in April 1881 after the Free Church had decided on the fate of Robertson Smith.[13] The bounds of the debate were set by Hodge in a letter to Briggs on February 15, 1881. "Neither side is to go beyond the positions occupied by you and me," Hodge explained; "none shall exceed in conservativism the positions laid down in my article on inspiration, and no relaxation of doctrine shall be admitted beyond the views held and stated by you."[14] Dr. Hodge was to open and close the series, and both Briggs and Hodge were to choose two other scholars to take part in the discussion.

For the first article in the series—entitled "Inspiration"— Dr. Hodge invited B. B. Warfield, a brilliant young professor of New Testament literature and exegesis at Western Theological Seminary, to join with him by handling the "critical" matters. Hodge wrote: "Briggs has for many months insisted that early in this second year of the history of *The Presbyterian Review* an article should appear on the subject of 'Inspiration' over my name. That I should appear in it is insisted upon, because I am presumed to represent in some way, the old orthodoxy. They will make that article a starting point for discussions more or less general on the new attitude of the question of Biblical interpretation resulting from the latest attitude of Biblical criticism." In the article Hodge set forth the doctrine of inspiration, whereas Warfield dealt with textual critical issues and alleged inaccuracies or contradictions in the Bible. They stated that "the Scriptures not only contain, but *are the Word of God,* and hence that all their elements and all their affirmations are absolutely errorless, and binding the faith and obedience of men." Hodge and Warfield insisted that although errors could and did appear in the current texts of Scripture, the "original autographs" were inerrant. "The errorless infallibility of the Word," they maintained, was the view of Christ, the apostles, and the "great historic churches." They wrote:

This is everywhere shown by the way in which all the great bodies of Protestant theologians have handled Scripture in their commentaries, systems of theology, catechisms, and sermons. And this has always been pre-eminently characteristic of epochs and agents of reformation and revival. All the great world-moving men, [such] as Luther, Calvin, Knox, Wesley, Whitefield and Chalmers . . . have so handled the divine word. Even if the more lax doctrine has the suffrage of many scholars, or even if it be true, it is nevertheless certain that hitherto in nineteen centuries it has never been held by men who also possessed the secret of using the word of God like a hammer or like a fire.

Therefore, stated the authors, "we rest in the joyful and unshaken certainty that we possess a Bible written by the hands of men indeed, but also graven with the finger of God." A. A. Hodge and B. B. Warfield "represented, in a comparatively brief space of thirty-five pages, the culmination of a half-century of Princeton theology" concerning the inspiration of the Bible.[15]

Charles Briggs replied to Hodge and Warfield in an article entitled "The Critical Theories of the Sacred Scriptures in Relation to their Inspiration: The Right, Duty, and Limits of Biblical Criticism." Briggs held that inspiration and infallibility extended only to the inward, spiritual sense of Scripture and not to its external words and meanings, which were subject to errors and inconsistencies. This approach to the Bible, Briggs argued, offered a better tool for dealing with modern science, which had, in fact, he claimed, found numerous errors in the Bible. He denied the Hodge-Warfield assertion that the doctrine of "verbal inspiration" was the historic teaching of the church and attacked "scholastic theology," which, he stated, was the real source of the theory of verbal inspiration. He appealed to the Reformers and to the Bible itself against the Reformed dogmaticians of the seventeenth century and their modern disciples at Princeton. Briggs argued that each age has its own spiritual needs and so must translate anew, in its own language and to its own understanding, the truths of the Bible, which changed of necessity precisely because they took shape in history. He attempted by "a skillful and politically astute attempt to baptize historical criticism into the evangelical cause by claiming that criticism as an intrinsic part of the evangelical Calvinist tradition." But he failed "to address the fact that Hodge and Warfield had presented the literal understanding of biblical infallibility held by most English-speaking evangelicals."[16]

In a letter to A. A. Hodge, Caspar Wistar Hodge, professor of New Testament at Princeton, responded immediately to Briggs's article. He disputed the Union Seminary professor's contention that only biblical theology—and not systematic theology—had proper critical foundation or concern for biblical teaching. He regretted Briggs's minimizing of the Bible's witness to itself and rejected his conception of the Bible's inspiration in its contents apart from its words. He countered Briggs's effort to enlist the Westminster divines on the side of the critical use of the Bible by his shrewd comment, "The very characteristic of [the Westminster theologians'] writing and preaching was extreme literalness, showing that the words and forms of expression were to them authoritative." What was "worst of all" in Dr. Briggs's article, according to Caspar Wistar Hodge, was the author's idea that "the canon is determined subjectively by the Christian feeling of the Church, and not by history, and that it is illogical to prove first canonicity, and then inspiration." If this be accepted, Hodge argued, "you have given away the whole historical side of the argument for the Apostolic origin of the Books and of Christianity itself."[17]

The third article in *The Presbyterian Review* series was by Princeton's William Henry Green, the foremost defender of the integrity of the Pentateuch and the authenticity of biblical history. Green knew that "the battle" was now on "as never before" but believed that "the old faith" was "too solid and too thoroughly dovetailed to be set aside." With scholarship and analytical keenness, he attacked the radical reconstruction of Israel's history as proposed by Julius Wellhausen and supported by William Robertson Smith. Dr. Green did "not shrink from the application of the most rigorous tests" to the question of the origin and contents of the Scriptures—to use his own words—but remained convinced "by the most abundant evidence that these Scriptures are the infallible Word of God." Even Robertson Smith respected the learning of William Henry Green and called him "the most scholarly by far of my assailants."[18]

In the fourth article, which appeared in April 1882, Henry Preserved Smith of Lane Seminary wrote on the "Critical Theories of Julius Wellhausen." Smith conceded that differences in biblical style implied differences in authorship and exhorted his readers to open-mindedness and tolerance in the whole matter. The fifth article of the series, from Samuel I. Curtiss of the Congregational Theological Seminary in Chicago, presented a cautiously positive report on the pentateuchal criticism of Franz Delitzsch. In the sixth article Willis J. Beecher of Auburn Theological Seminary criticized the views of the Dutch critic Abraham Kuenen, although praising the thorough nature of his scholarship. In the seventh article, "A Critical Study of the History of Higher Criticism with Special Reference to the Pentateuch," Charles Briggs clearly stated his acceptance of the view that separate, contradictory Pentateuchal documents existed and indicated various stages in the development of Israel's religion.

In the eighth and "summation" article, "The Dogmatic Aspect of Pentateuchal Criticism," Francis L. Patton now of Princeton Seminary insisted that though Presbyterians were free to investigate the higher critical proposals, they were not free "to teach contrary to the Confession of Faith." Patton demonstrated that the church's historic belief was in the complete accuracy of the Bible and answered Briggs's contention that the Westminster Confession did not support full biblical inspiration. Patton criticized the uncritical attitudes of the critics. It was "naturalistic postulates," he claimed, and not the weight of evidence that led scholars to discredit the Mosaic authorship of the Pentateuch. Dr. Patton's final words concluded the series of eight articles:

We believe that the Law was given to Moses by Jehovah and not imputed to him by "legal fiction." We believe that the Pentateuchal codes were meant for the immediate use of the Israelites in the wilderness and that they were not merely "prophetic ideals." We put the words of Jesus above the inductions of the critics, and are sure that the responsibility of Moses for the books that are called by his name must be understood according to the plain implication of the passage which speaks of them as "his writings." We do not believe in the composite character of the Pentateuch; and if we did we should have no confidence in the critical omniscience that pretends to determine within "fractions of a verse" what part was written by the Jehovist, what by the Elohist and the Deuteronomist, and where the handiwork of the Redactor is visible. We believe that Moses wrote substantially the whole Pentateuch. This view is in harmony with antecedent probability, with the presumptions of tradition, with the internal testimony of the books, with the unvarying voice of Inspiration, with the words of Christ. And after all that has been said, the leading reason in support of the contrary idea seems to be founded on the deep conviction that God cannot work miracles and critics can.[19]

The Presbyterian Review series ended, but Charles Briggs continued to press for larger critical and theological freedom in the church and denounced his orthodox opponents, centered at Princeton Seminary, as "scholastics." His *Biblical Study: Its Principles, Methods and History*, which appeared in 1883, was described by A. B. Bruce—professor at the Free Church Divinity Hall in Glasgow—as Briggs's "polemic with the *Rabbis* of Princeton."

6

A Sacred Trust

Archibald Alexander Hodge held "the Reformed faith as a sacred trust, and also as a personal possession; he was not simply a theological professor, he was a great spiritual force."

FRANCIS LANDEY PATTON

FROM September 23 to October 2, 1880, the Second General Council of the Presbyterian Alliance met at the Academy of Music and adjoining Horticultural Hall in Philadelphia. Philadelphia was the site of the first American presbytery and now home to 120 Presbyterian congregations. Philadelphia's senior Presbyterian pastor, Henry A. Boardman, a director of Princeton Seminary since 1835, died shortly before the meeting convened. William Pratt Breed, Princeton graduate and pastor of the West Spruce Street Church in Philadelphia, took Dr. Boardman's place in welcoming the delegates, local and visiting Presbyterian ministers, and the congregation of 4,000 people. William M. Paxton, pastor of the First Presbyterian Church of New York (and later professor at Princeton Seminary), preached the opening sermon on Matthew 8:11—"And I say unto you, That many shall come from the East and West, and shall sit down with Abraham, and Isaac, and Jacob, in the kingdom of heaven." During the third day's session James McCosh, who was one of the leaders in the movement that led to the formation of the Presbyterian Alliance in London in 1875, spoke on "How to Deal with Young Men Trained in Science in This Age of Unsettled Opinion." On the fourth day Lyman Atwater of Princeton College addressed the delegates on "Religion and Politics"; the next day A. A. Hodge read a paper on the "Vicarious Sacrifice of Christ, as Understood by the Presbyterian Churches Represented in This Council." As Hodge came forward to speak, Dr. J. M. Lang of Glasgow, who was presiding, took Dr. Hodge by the hand and said to the council:

Brethren, may I for a moment be allowed to depart from the reticence usually observed by the presiding officer? A Scotchman, by your favor, occupies the chair today; and I think I speak in the name of all my co-delegates from the other side of the ocean, when I express the reverence, the admiration, the gratitude with which we receive, to enshrine in our heart of hearts, the honored name borne by the distinguished Professor whose hand I hold?[1]

On the Monday after adjournment members of the Presbyterian Alliance came to Princeton in a chartered train. Dr. McGill welcomed the guests in the seminary chapel, and Dr. McCosh addressed them in the First Presbyterian Church.

*   *   *

In 1881 Francis Patton, who had gained wide attention as an able advocate for conservative theology in the David Swing heresy trial, was called to Princeton Seminary to the Chair of the Relations of Philosophy and Science to the Christian Religion, endowed for Dr. Patton by Robert L. Stuart.

Francis Patton was born in Warwick, Bermuda, in 1843 and was baptized there at the Church of Scotland's Christ Church, founded in 1719. He studied at Warwick Academy, a little schoolhouse just over the hill from where he lived; Knox College of the University of Toronto; and Princeton Seminary, graduating with the class of 1865. That same year he was ordained and served churches in New York City, Nyack, and Brooklyn. His *Inspiration of Scripture,* published in 1869, with its defense of the inerrancy of the original manuscripts of the Bible, established Patton as an able spokesman for orthodox theology.[2] In 1872 he was persuaded by Cyrus H. McCormick to come to the Presbyterian Theological Seminary of the Northwest in Chicago as professor of theology. McCormick, a stalwart of the former Old School Presbyterian Church who had made a fortune in farm machinery, hoped that Patton would provide an articulate voice for classic Calvinism against the liberal theological trends in the seminary and presbytery. In his inaugural address, "Christian Theology and Current

Thought," Dr. Patton made clear his commitment to orthodox Christianity. He used as the text in his theology classes Charles Hodge's *Systematic Theology*. Patton served as editor of the Presbyterian weekly called *The Interior* and was pastor of a Chicago church in addition to his teaching at the seminary.

In 1878 the thirty-five-year-old Patton was elected moderator of the General Assembly. Later that year his powerfully orthodox sermons at the meeting of the Pan-Presbyterian Council at Edinburgh made such an impression that the Presbyterian Theological College in London offered him a professorship. Patton, a British subject, considered the move, but Cyrus McCormick persuaded him to stay in Chicago. Princeton's invitation to Patton three years later dismayed McCormick, who warned that his departure would bring "temporary ruin" to Presbyterianism in the West. Patton, however, upon the urging of men such as A. A. Hodge, decided to go to Princeton. Hodge wrote, "Surely, in the next thirty years, Princeton, with its endowments and connections, with its widespread influence all over the South as well as the North, ought to have the ablest Old-School theologians in the Church. We need you very much."[3]

At Princeton Dr. Patton taught apologetics at the seminary and, in 1884, became Lyman Atwater's successor as teacher of ethics at the college. When Patton came to the seminary Charles Aiken taught Christian ethics and added Old Testament literature, which he had wanted to teach. William B. Greene, who was one of Dr. Aiken's students and later his successor, said that Aiken's courses in apologetics and ethics were marked "by the accurate learning, the elegant culture, and the beautiful spirit which characterized all his work."[4]

*　　　*　　　*

In 1883 William Miller Paxton succeeded Alexander T. McGill in the chair of ecclesiastical, homiletical, and pastoral theology. Dr. McGill had taught practical theology since 1854. The catalog for 1869–70 stated that "the weekly preaching of the senior class" was under the direction of McGill, "who also has exercises with all the classes in extempore speaking, in writing sermons, and in preparing written criticism upon the sermons of others." Dr. McGill assumed a large amount of the administration of the seminary—"not so much by positive arrangement," according to his colleague William Henry Green, as "by a sort of spontaneous necessity." McGill was elected moderator of the General Assembly (Old School) in 1848. He served for twelve years as the permanent clerk and for eight years as the stated clerk of the denomination. His first wife died in 1873; two years later he married Catherine Bache Hodge, the daughter of Charles Hodge.[5]

The "substance" of Dr. McGill's lectures on church government was published in 1888—as "a tardy compliance with the formal petitions of successive classes." "All may discern," he wrote in the preface, "that there has been no change of principles in the granite foundation of my own convictions, laid by the Bible as interpreted by Westminster literature of the seventeenth century, and the reproduction thereof, with lucid and masterly exposition, by Drs. John M. Mason and Samuel Miller, in the first half of this century." McGill stated that he wrote "as a teacher more than as an author." He added, "The intelligent reader will see that the man who stands by his standards in attempting to teach 'the generation following' must give what he has received rather than what he has contrived." Alexander McGill indicated one area of special emphasis in his book: "My readers will see throughout the volume that ruling elders, whether learned or unlearned, are a leading order, in the writer's judgment, to be understood, instructed and animated with ever-increasing concern."[6]

Princeton's new professor William Paxton cherished his Scotch-Irish and Pennsylvanian ancestry. Born in 1824, Paxton grew up at Gettysburg and studied at the Lutheran Pennsylvania College (later called Gettysburg College). He graduated in 1843 with a reputation for oratorical ability. In the spring of 1845, after two years of law study, he became convinced that he was called to the ministry of the church; in the fall he entered Princeton Seminary. B. B. Warfield later wrote, "It would appear . . . that when he gave himself to his Lord he gave himself completely, holding nothing back."[7] Paxton was the last member of the seminary faculty to study under the first two professors, Archibald Alexander and Samuel Miller. Because he began to study theology within three months of the death of his own grandfather, their combined ministries, he liked to say, lasted for more than one hundred years.

William Paxton wanted to be a doctrinal preacher, a preacher who could preach doctrine, as he put it, "all ablaze"—who could "put the light of his own living experience inside" the doctrine and "make it a spiritual transparency" that would "interest and attract." After graduation from Princeton, the friendly, handsome young preacher received a call to the Presbyterian church in Greencastle, Pennsylvania. There he prepared his sermons by "walking them out"—mentally composing them as he paced back and forth in his study, wearing a path in the carpet. He arranged his points, gathered illustrations, reviewed words and sentences without a book except the Bible, without a scrap of paper, without pen or pencil. The first sentences of his sermons were always, as he later explained to his students, "a centre shot at a target" and attracted attention that was never lost.

Late in 1850 William Paxton was called to the First Presbyterian Church of Pittsburgh, where he established a reputation as a model preacher in both content and delivery. While he served as pastor he taught preaching at Western Seminary. He told his students that the secret for success in preaching was "Work! Work! Work!" The young men sat in his classes during the week and then flocked to hear him preach on Sundays. The pulpit area in the new First Presbyterian Church building gave him a space of fifteen feet, along which he would walk back and forth addressing the people in every part of the large congregation during his hour-long sermons. One hearer said:

He set his sermon squarely on his text as a tree stands on its tap-root: sent out smaller roots all through the context: the trunk was short and stocky; then he threw out the great branches, following each to its smaller limbs and even twigs, until his sermon stood complete and symmetrical and stately like one of the great live-oaks of California.[8]

Some of Dr. Paxton's seminary students felt at first that he was too formal and distant, but they soon found him a sympathetic teacher. He always began his course with a series of

[97]

lectures on the preachers of the Bible, from Enoch to Christ and the apostles—instilling in the students a sense of the holiness and importance of the preacher's task. After his treatment of the biblical history of preaching Paxton lectured on the construction of sermons. He told the seminarians how they should study their prayerfully chosen texts, tossing them "as balls before their minds," and grasping them "with an unfaltering faith in God"—holding on to them "until, with the help of the good Spirit, they were clad in plain and simple language for their hearers." He presented a variety of methods of dealing with a text and stressed natural divisions in creating an outline. Dr. Paxton's primary stress was on substance and purpose in preaching; and, when he told his students that "the object of preaching is nothing else but to make clear what the Lord has taught," he sounded the key-note of his entire homiletical system. His own sermons were well crafted and clearly presented with memorable outlines. It always appeared to his students that his treatment of a passage was the only right one. A young preacher came to Dr. Paxton for help with the text that had been assigned to him by presbytery for his trial sermon, Mark 3:35—"For whoso-ever shall do the will of God, the same is my brother, and my sister, and mother." The student later wrote:

[Dr. Paxton] opened his study Bible at the place, and said, "I have nothing on that text." He rose and paced the floor for two or three minutes, and then standing before me said: "The theme of this text is spiritual relationship to Christ. I. Its superiority to earthly relationship ('brother, sister, mother'). It is (1) more intimate, (2) more blessed, (3) more enduring. II. Its condition is obedience ('doing the will of God'). This obedience should be (1) entire, (2) cordial, (3) persevering." I went out of the study wondering why I could not have thought of that, it seemed so natural and easy.

In 1865 William Paxton accepted a call to the First Presbyterian Church in New York City. He served on the boards of Princeton College and Princeton Seminary and, from 1872 to 1875, taught homiletics at Union Theological Seminary. In 1880 he was elected moderator of the General Assembly by acclamation. In 1883 he came to Princeton Seminary. It was hard for him to give up the pastorate for the classroom, but he felt that the training of preachers was the best service he could provide the church. Dr. Paxton was, as one of his students said, "a pastor in the pastoral chair." His teaching was "concrete, and was apt to be illustrated by stories of Christian experience and personal work." He "aimed to make the homiletical classroom the 'assembling-room,' gathering together the work of all the classrooms; the fusing of the rays of scholarship and workaday life into the white light of the ministry." In addition to homiletics Dr. Paxton taught church government and practical theology. In these classes his students appreciated his skill, his knowledge, and his spirit. He was an experienced pastor and a convinced Presbyterian who loved the church. In 1885, after hearing D. L. Moody preach in Princeton, he told his students that he was "home-sick for the pastorate."[9]

James Frederick McCurdy graduated from Princeton Seminary in 1871 and was appointed Dr. Green's assistant. A gifted language teacher, McCurdy served from 1873 to 1877 as the L. P. Stone Tutor of Hebrew, and from 1877 to 1882 as the J. C. Green Instructor in Hebrew and other Oriental Languages. He worked as the assistant librarian at the seminary and taught Sanskrit at Princeton College, from which he received an honorary doctorate in 1878. Despite William Henry Green's persistent urging that McCurdy stay at the seminary, he resigned in 1882 to spend several years in Germany for advanced study in Assyriology and Semitic philology.[10]

Dr. McCurdy's place at the seminary was taken by John D. Davis. After graduating from Princeton College in 1879 with highest academic honors and a fellowship in classics, Davis studied at the University of Bonn in Germany. He then completed his theological studies at Princeton Seminary in two years (winning the George S. Green Fellowship in Hebrew) and taught Hebrew at the seminary for a year. He did further study at the University of Leipzig, where he concentrated on the new field of Assyriology. In 1886, when Davis came back to teach at Princeton Seminary, he was one of the best equipped professors of Old Testament in the United States. He was awarded his doctorate from the College of New Jersey primarily on the basis of his graduate work in Leipzig. Dr.

Davis was a gifted language teacher. He held high standards but freely conceded that in the learning of Hebrew there was occasion to remember the text "Even the youths shall faint and be weary"! In 1888 Davis was appointed professor of Hebrew and cognate languages, and four years later, when his teaching responsibilities had expanded, he became professor of Semitic philology and Old Testament history.

*　　*　　*

In 1886 the seminary faculty was made up of seven teachers: William Henry Green, Caspar Wistar Hodge, James C. Moffat, Charles A. Aiken, Archibald Alexander Hodge, Francis L. Patton, and William M. Paxton. John D. Davis was instructor in Hebrew, and the seminary librarian was Joseph H. Dulles, a graduate of Princeton College and Princeton Seminary.

Although he was not the senior professor, the real power at Princeton Seminary was Archibald Alexander Hodge. Charles Hodge's son and successor was known as a theologian who could preach and a preacher who could teach theology. During his first year at Princeton College Robert Speer went to the old beer hall on Nassau Street to evangelistic meetings conducted by professors of the seminary. He never forgot the sermon by "the little round, redheaded man who preached with tears coursing down his cheeks." Years later Speer said, "I can still hear the message Dr. Archie Hodge gave on that platform. If ever there was a man who could plead for Christ with a clear and intellectual presentation of the Gospel, but with all the fervor and tenderness of a Christian apostle, it was Archie Hodge."[11]

Although A. A. Hodge's voice was weak and his speech often labored, Francis Patton declared that "to hear him when he was at his best was something never to be forgotten." Patton, himself a gifted speaker, thought that A. A. Hodge was "one of the greatest preachers" in America. Hodge's sermons, though never written, were repeated often but always freshly reworked. People remembered his sermons— on the immanence of God, the person of Christ, the miracles, the resurrection, the *koinonia,* and especially "the sermon that he loved to preach so well, that [was] listened to by so many congregations, that was preached in the Seminary Chapel and the College Chapel in Princeton, that was preached in Philadelphia, and New York, and Washington and Edinburgh: the sermon on 'My Father's House of Many Mansions.'"[12]

Although he was not so broad in learning as his father, A. A. Hodge impressed his students with his clarity and fervor. They praised him for the way he applied the doctrines he taught to their Christian lives. "Dr. Hodge made theology to us supremely a thing of life," one student commented. "It thrilled us as we learned it. It changed us as we appropriated it to ourselves."

A. A. Hodge's books spread his name far beyond Princeton: *Outlines of Theology* (1860), *Atonement* (1867), *A Commentary on the Confession of Faith* (1869), *Questions on the Text of the Systematic Theology of Dr. Charles Hodge* (1885), and *Popular Lectures on Theological Themes* (1887). Hodge's *Outlines of Theology*, expanded in 1879, was reprinted in Great Britain in 1880 and translated into Welsh, Greek, Hindustani, Malagasy, and other languages. Princeton graduate Ashbel Green Simonton urged the translation of *Outlines of Theology*, which he felt was needed for the Brazilian seminary that he had founded in 1867.[13]

Two of A. A. Hodge's articles are of special importance. His 1881 essay on "Inspiration" (written with B. B. Warfield) became a classic statement of the Christian doctrine of Scripture. Hodge believed that the most important issue of his time was the defense of historic Christianity and especially of the doctrine of the inspiration of the Bible. In all his later writings he affirmed "with ever increasing warmth" that the Scriptures are "the very word of God, and the only infallible rule of faith and practice." In "The Consensus of the Reformed Confessions," Dr. Hodge showed (against Charles Briggs and others) that the Reformed confessions agreed with the predestinarian teaching of the Westminster Confession of Faith. Hodge claimed that the sudden interest in and appeal to the development of the Reformed creeds—"ostensibly for the sake of Presbyterian unity and evangelical truth"— actually masked heterodox impulses desiring to be "relieved from the pressure of the old creeds" and evinced a cowardly "restlessness under the obligation of subscription." In his brief outline of the confessional history of the Reformed churches Hodge showed that there was not an evolving, developmental pattern, as Briggs had argued, but an impressive identity or "consensus."[14]

The last of A. A. Hodge's books, *Popular Lectures on Theological Themes,* comprised nineteen lectures, given first to a class of women in Princeton and later repeated in Philadelphia. Printed serially in *The Presbyterian,* Hodge's lectures were published later as a book. At the time of his death Dr. Hodge was working on a brief exposition of the Shorter Catechism. He completed part one, setting forth "what man is to believe concerning God"; his cousin J. Aspinwall Hodge, pastor of the First Presbyterian Church of Hartford, Connecticut, prepared part two, "what duty God requires of man."[15] The book was published in 1888 as *The System of Theology contained in the Westminster Shorter Catechism Opened and Explained.*

On May 30, 1886, Dr. Hodge concluded his last lecture to the large audience that had gathered in Philadelphia to hear him:

And now these lectures are ended. We shall not meet together here any more. Let us pledge one another, as we part, to reassemble in heaven. We are now parting from one another, as pilgrims part upon the road. Let us turn our steps homeward, for if we do we shall soon—some of us now very soon—"be at home with the Lord." Adieu![16]

A shock of personal bereavement was felt by everyone in Princeton when word went out on the morning of November 12, 1886, that Dr. Archibald Alexander Hodge was dead. "His death was sudden," wrote Francis Patton,

but never was one more ready for it. He preached with great power and persuasiveness in the college chapel on Sunday morning; participated in the usual conference services in the Seminary in the afternoon; was taken ill on Sunday night and after a period of great suffering found rest in the sleep of death about midnight on Thursday.

On November 15, the day of Hodge's funeral, all the shops in Princeton were closed. A long procession of townspeople and friends followed the seminary faculty and students, who, according to Dr. Patton, carried him "along the rugged street that leads to the place which from time to time has claimed the best that Princeton had to give—Edwards, the Alexanders, Charles Hodge—men who have given Princeton a name in all the earth." Dr. Paxton, who had given the charge to Dr. Hodge when he came to Princeton Seminary in 1877, preached the funeral sermon. He referred to a "transcendent something" in A. A. Hodge's life that "those who really knew him" could not fail to recognize. Paxton described the honesty, the sympathy, and the simplicity of Dr. Hodge's faith. "His heart, like his intellect, moved in vast circles, and encompassed the world," Paxton said. "While God had created him with a giant intellect, grace had made him a child, in the simple, sincere, undoubting exercises of piety." He was, said Dr. Paxton, "Christian–Philosopher– Theologian–Orator–Poet–Child."[17]

A. A. Hodge was sixty-three years old when he died; only seven years earlier he had taken over the chair of theology from his father. B. B. Warfield, who would soon join the Princeton faculty as Hodge's successor, wrote, "Nothing can give the faintest conception of the beauty of his Christian character, or of the astounding greatness of his ordinary conversation. His intimate acquaintances feel that a great light has gone from their lives in his departure. No one can enter in where he entered into our hearts, and no one can rule as he ruled by our firesides and at our tables." William Shedd, professor at Union Seminary in New York, said, "I was struck with his great directness and sincerity, intellectually as well as morally. His mind, like his heart, worked without ambiguity or drawback. Hence his energy in the perception and statement of truth." "He had the confidence of the Church as few men have," Francis Patton wrote; "the North loved him; the South honored him. In Canada, in Great Britain, and over the wide missionary area, his judgments on theological matters were deferred to and quoted with respect." In far-off Scotland John Cairns declared, "The whole evangelical Church has lost in him a powerful and intrepid defender of its best and dearest beliefs."[18]

On December 21, 1886, Francis Patton gave a memorial

address for A. A. Hodge in response to an invitation from the Philadelphia Presbyterian Ministerial Association. Speaking in the Chambers Presbyterian Church in Philadelphia—"city of [Dr. Hodge's] forefathers, the city that he loved above all others"—Dr. Patton said, "I do not know what his epitaph will be; but I venture to say, that no words will so well convey the idea of what he would regard as a rounded life of realized desire as those which state the simple fact that he was Third Professor of Theology in Princeton Seminary." Another Princetonian said that "by the flame of his genius [he] made even the darkest theology glow with an almost supernatural light." One of his students remembered him this way: "He had a powerful brain, a large heart, and the simple faith of a little child."[19]

*　　*　　*

Charles Hodge wrote a little while before he died, "I am fully persuaded that the vast majority of the human race will share in the beatitudes and glories of our Lord's redemption." A. A. Hodge believed that "the infinite provision made for human salvation . . . and the intense love for human sinners therein exhibited" is such "that the multitude of the redeemed will be incomparably greater than the number of the lost." He wrote:

In all the growing of the seeds and all the blowing of the winds; in every event, even the least significant, which has advanced the interests of the human family either in respect to their bodies or their souls, and thus made their lives better or worthier; in all the breaking of fetters; in all the bringing in of light; in the noiseless triumphs of peace; in the dying out of barbarisms; and in the colonization of great continents with new populations and free states—the kingdom is coming. Above all, in the multiplication of the myriad centres of Christian missions and of the myriad hosts of Christian workers, each in the spirit of the King seeking the very lowest and most degraded, everywhere lifting upward what Satan's kingdom has borne down, the kingdom is coming.[20]

When A. A. Hodge died in 1886 world missions was again capturing the allegiance of many young American Christians.

One of the major centers for the Society of Inquiry on Missions—the most important student missionary organization during the first half of the nineteenth century—had been Princeton Seminary. By the middle of the century there were over one hundred missionary organizations—modeled on the Andover-Princeton Society of Inquiry plan—in the colleges and seminaries of the United States. The YMCA, with local organizations in towns and cities and on college campuses, inspired missionary commitment. A college division of the YMCA was created in 1877; Luther Wishard, who had been active in YMCA work at Hanover College and at Princeton, was its corresponding secretary. Wishard's goal was the conversion of students to Christ and their commitment to active Christian service, especially foreign missions. When he heard of the famous Haystack Prayer Meeting that had taken place at Williams College in 1806, he saw at once that the same spirit of missions was being renewed in his day. "What they had done was ours to complete," he said.

One of the students at Andover Seminary who had been influenced by the Society of Inquiry in the 1840s was Royal G. Wilder. Wilder went to India with the American Board of Commissioners for Foreign Missions and served there for thirty years. When he returned to the United States in 1877 he settled in Princeton, where he founded and edited *The Missionary Review of the World*. His son Robert P. Wilder, who was born in India in 1863, became a brilliant student in Greek and philosophy at Princeton College. In the autumn of 1883, Robert Wilder and two of his friends attended a conference of the Inter-Seminary Alliance in Hartford, Connecticut. There they heard the powerful missionary messages of Dr. A. J. Gordon, pastor of Boston's Clarendon Street Baptist Church. Wilder later wrote:

We three college students returned to Princeton inspired with the desire to accomplish two things: First, to pray and work for a revival in our college, and, second, to stir up missionary interest. We prevailed on like-minded students to form groups, usually consisting of three or four, who met daily at the noon hour. Afterwards we did personal work with those for whom we had prayed.

In the fall of 1883, Robert Wilder and his friends formed

the Princeton Foreign Missionary Society at Princeton College. The constitution stated:

The object of this Society shall be the cultivation of a missionary spirit among the students of the College, the information of its members in all subjects of missionary interest, and especially the leading of men to consecrate themselves to foreign missionary work. . . . Any student of the College who is a professing Christian may become a member by subscribing to the following covenant: We, the undersigned, declare ourselves willing and desirous, God permitting, to go to the unevangelized portions of the world.

The Princeton society met on Sunday afternoons in the Wilder home for prayer and discussion of missions. Robert and his sister Grace earnestly prayed for a widespread missionary movement in the colleges and universities of America; they prayed that "ultimately one thousand volunteers might be secured to labor in foreign fields."[21]

By securing thousands of signatures from students, Luther Wishard persuaded a reluctant D. L. Moody to include colleges in his preaching schedule. Moody went to Princeton, Dartmouth, and Yale in 1885 and the next summer invited students to a month-long Bible conference at Mount Hermon in Northfield, Massachusetts. Two hundred and fifty-one students from eighty-nine colleges and universities of the United States and Canada attended, including Robert Wilder and John Forman from Princeton College and Princeton Seminary, and John R. Mott from Cornell. As the conference opened, Moody announced that there would be informal Bible studies and times of worship and singing. There was at first no definite missionary emphasis; but Robert Wilder and a few others met regularly to pray that God would raise up missionary volunteers. One by one, students declared that they were willing to go to "the unevangelized portions of the world." On July 16 the students asked Dr. A. T. Pierson, Presbyterian minister of the nondenominational Bethany Tabernacle in Philadelphia, to address them on "God's Providence in Modern Missions." Dr. Pierson stressed that "all should go, and go to all." On July 24, ten students told why they hoped to become foreign missionaries. By the time the conference ended one hundred students—"the Mount

Hermon Hundred"—had signed a statement definitely committing themselves to foreign missions.

Like the famous Cambridge Band, who had made a memorable tour of the British universities before going to China, the Princeton representatives Robert Wilder and John Forman were chosen to spread the missionary vision to North American campuses. During the academic year 1886–87 they visited 162 schools in the United States and Canada and saw 2,106 students, including 500 women, sign the declaration. Princeton tersely reported, "Princeton now stands: Seminary 27, College 22 for missions." In the summer of 1887 John Forman sailed for India under the Presbyterian board, generously supported by his fellow Princeton students.

By the end of 1888 the Student Volunteer Movement for Foreign Missions was organized under the leadership of Robert Wilder and John R. Mott. With its famous watchword, "The evangelization of the world in this generation," the Student Volunteer Movement led hundreds of young Americans to missionary commitment. During the 1889–90 school year Robert E. Speer of Princeton visited 110 colleges and universities, enlisting 1,100 undergraduates for foreign missions. By 1892 over 500 volunteers had already gone to foreign mission fields and another 100 were under appointment. President McCosh asked, "Has any such offering of living young men and women been presented in our age, in our country, in any age, or in any country, since the day of Pentecost?"[22]

After his time of service with the Student Volunteer Movement Robert Speer entered Princeton Seminary in 1890. Speer, a tackle on the college football team for three years, continued on the team during his seminary studies—as allowed by the rules in the 1890s. One afternoon, when Speer was a seminary middler, a representative of the Presbyterian Board of Foreign Missions came to Princeton to offer the young missionary enthusiast a position as secretary of the board. Not finding him in the dormitory or classrooms, the visitor went to the football field where Speer was scrimmaging with the varsity eleven against the second team. Speer was excused from practice and came to the sidelines. The two men made a striking picture as they walked back and forth in earnest conversation. After consulting friends, Robert Speer accepted the invitation and left the seminary for a distinguished career as a missionary leader.[23]

Beginning in 1892–93, Princeton Seminary students planned and largely financed the "Students' Lectures on Missions." The first lecturer, James S. Dennis, spoke on "Foreign Missions after a Century." Annual lectures followed on "The Work of the Presbyterian and Reformed Churches in Japan" (1893–94), "Apostolic and Modern Missions" (1894–95), "Christian Missions and Social Progress" (1895–96), and "China as a Mission Field" (1896–97). Robert Speer came during the 1897–98 school year to speak on the "Present Missionary Situation in Asia."

While a new generation of students directed their attention and resources to the evangelization of the world, many from Princeton were already working for that same goal. Over a thousand home and foreign missionaries had gone out from the seminary. The largest number of Princeton missionaries serving overseas was in India, the next largest in China, then in Africa. John Nevius had developed a strategy of missions in China that when transplanted to Korea contributed to the fastest growing Presbyterian church in the world. Since 1858 Daniel McGilvary and his classmate Jonathan Wilson had worked with the Lao people in Siam, where they founded churches, schools, and medical clinics. In Africa Robert Nassau, the missionary-doctor, was busy preaching, teaching, healing the sick, and translating portions of the Bible into the two dialects of the Bantu-Benga language. Sheldon Jackson, "the missionary with the flying coattails," traveled a million miles in stagecoaches and buckboards, in ox-carts and reindeer sledges, and established a hundred churches and many more Sunday schools "on the distant edges of things" in the far West and Alaska.

* * *

On May 24, 1888, Princetonians gathered with other Presbyterians and friends at the Academy of Music in Philadelphia to celebrate the centennial of the General Assembly of the Presbyterian Church. The "Historical Address" was given by

Theodore Cuyler, pastor of the Lafayette Avenue Presbyterian Church of Brooklyn, New York. Cuyler, who studied at both Princeton College and Princeton Seminary, traced the march of "hard-headed, long-winded, stout-hearted Presbyterianism" down through the centuries. He paid tribute to William Tennent's Log College—"twenty feet square and chinked with mud"—which "contained in its rude husk the seeds of Princeton College, and Theological Seminary, and all the great training-schools of our Faith on the continent." He noted the founding of Princeton College in 1746 and Princeton Seminary on August 12, 1812, when "that sunny-souled patriarch who combined the wisdom of a seer with the simplicity of a child, Dr. Archibald Alexander, was inducted into its chair of theology." In his retrospect of the past century Cuyler found "abundant cause for devout thanksgiving." He said:

We may well be thankful that the Presbyterian Church has so largely escaped the prevailing . . . doubt and dissatisfaction with the ancient faith delivered to the saints. From the old bed-rock we have taken no 'new departures.' It was the honest boast of the greatest of our theologians, Dr. Charles Hodge, that Presbyterianism has made no new discoveries in Bible theology. . . . Thank God! the *past* of American Presbyterianism is secure.[24]

7

The Majestic Testimony

Your future ministry is cast in times of great theological unrest. Foundations are broken up; truths long accepted are brought anew into question; the very principles upon which the certitude of belief is to rest are under debate. There is no use in these days for men of a light and easy temper, who make up their judgment hastily on the most vital questions, or who like to be in the advance of all changes, and easily renounce the most sacred of heritages. Men should be sober and thoughtful; they should be students of history; they should be prayerful students of the Bible. Change is not necessarily advance. The majestic testimony of the Church in all time is that its advances in spiritual life have always been toward and not away from the Bible, and in proportion to the reverence for, and power of realizing in practical life, the revealed Word.

CASPAR WISTAR HODGE

I N 1887 Benjamin Breckinridge Warfield was called from Western Seminary to Princeton to succeed Archibald Alexander Hodge as the Charles Hodge Professor of Didactic and Polemic Theology. The thirty-six-year-old Warfield had established a solid reputation as a careful biblical scholar. His writings for *The Presbyterian Review*, especially his collaboration with A. A. Hodge in their article "Inspiration," were widely appreciated. Warfield also had demonstrated considerable expertise in historical theology with his "Introductory Essay on Augustine and the Pelagian Controversy" solicited by Philip Schaff for the prestigious *Nicene and Post-Nicene Fathers* series.[1]

Soon after the critical Greek text of Westcott and Hort appeared in 1881, B. B. Warfield discussed it in *The Presbyterian Review*. Philip Schaff, himself an accomplished textual scholar, was so impressed with Warfield's article that he invited him to explain the textual principles of Westcott and Hort in Schaff's own *Companion to the Greek Testament and English Version*. Warfield's *Introduction to the Textual Criticism of the New Testament*, the first primer on the practice of New Testament textual criticism by an American, was published in England in 1886. The very process of scrutiny of the text assures us, Warfield stated, that the New Testament has been transmitted without substantial variation from the original. He maintained that "no important doctrine was in doubt and that all significant variants together would constitute only half a page of the New Testament." Furthermore, he claimed, the proper use of textual criticism would establish a text even nearer to the original. Warfield's *Introduction to the Textual Criticism of the New Testament* was recognized as a masterful, scholarly treatment of the subject. His positive attitude toward textual criticism influenced many to appreciate the science and to value the new translations of the Bible based upon its work.[2]

Some of B. B. Warfield's friends questioned the wisdom of his moving from New Testament to theology, but, remembering that Charles Hodge had followed the same path, he decided to accept the call to Princeton. Caspar Wistar Hodge welcomed him to the chair that Hodge's father and brother had successively held. In his inaugural address Warfield said, "Though the power of Charles Hodge may not be upon me, the theology of Charles Hodge is within me . . . and this is the theology . . . I have . . . in my heart to teach. . . . Oh, that the mantle of my Elijah might fall upon my shoulders; at least the message that was given him is set within my lips."[3]

*   *   *

Benjamin Breckinridge Warfield was born at "Grasmere," his family's estate near Lexington, Kentucky, on November 5, 1851. His father, William Warfield, was a descendant of English Puritans who had settled in Virginia before being expelled by Governor Berkeley for refusing to accept his proclamation of Charles II as king. The Warfields moved to the colony of Maryland and some of them later to Kentucky, where William became a prosperous gentleman-farmer and an authority on the breeding of horses and cattle.[4] Benjamin's mother, Mary Cabell Breckinridge Warfield, was descended from Scotch-Irish families who first settled in the Cumberland Valley of Pennsylvania during colonial times. Mary's grandfather John Breckinridge was a United States senator and attorney general under Thomas Jefferson. Her father, Robert Jefferson Breckinridge, practiced law and served in the Kentucky legislature before entering the ministry of the Presbyterian church. He studied at Princeton Seminary in 1832, a few years before his brother John, son-in-law of Samuel Miller, became professor of missions there.

Robert's seminary work was shortened when he was called to the Second Presbyterian Church in Baltimore in 1832. In 1845 he became president of Jefferson College in Pennsylvania, and two years later he went as pastor to the First Presbyterian Church of Lexington, Kentucky. In 1853 he founded the Presbyterian seminary in Danville, Kentucky, where he taught theology for the rest of his career. Dr. Breckinridge was elected moderator of the General Assembly (Old School) in 1841. He edited two journals, the *Spirit of the Nineteenth Century* and the *Danville Review,* and published a two-volume systematic theology entitled *The Knowledge of God Objectively and Subjectively Considered.*[5]

Young Benjamin Warfield inherited the intellectual gifts of his mother's family and his father's quiet disposition. In his Presbyterian home he memorized the Shorter Catechism by the time he was six, then learned the Scripture proofs before going on to the Larger Catechism. At sixteen he made a profession of faith and joined the Second Presbyterian Church in Lexington, whose minister was Robert Garland Brank, a Kentuckian and Princeton Seminary graduate.[6] Benjamin went to private schools in Lexington, where he studied with two young college graduates, Lewis Barbour and James Kennedy Patterson (who later became president of the state college). He loved to tramp the fields and wander through the woods of the Kentucky countryside collecting birds' eggs, butterflies, moths, and rocks. As a boy he eagerly read Darwin's books on evolution and treasured his copies of Audubon's works on American birds and mammals. He was so interested in science and set on a career in that field that he strenuously, but futilely, objected to studying Greek.

In August 1868 Benjamin and his father traveled to New Jersey for young Warfield to take his entrance exams at Princeton College. The students had not arrived for the fall term, but the village streets were filled with fine setter dogs. Mr. Warfield, who observed that the dogs were well bred and well trained, was pleased. "All his reluctance to leaving me in Princeton vanished," wrote Benjamin; "he felt sure that where there were so many good dogs there must be some good fellows"![7]

Benjamin was admitted to the sophomore class. He found

a room near the seminary and soon was slushing through cow lots and climbing three fences to reach the college campus. He attended classes in the dark, damp basement of Geological Hall and worshiped in the small chapel that stood a little east of Nassau Hall. With the other students he jammed into the town post office to wait for the mail to be distributed. He loafed in the early evenings at Stelle's bookstore or, occasionally, at Streeper's tobacco shop. His fellow students called him "Wo-field," probably an imitation of his soft, Kentucky accent. Like almost every college student Benjamin joined one of the literary societies. "The rare student who was a member of neither [Whig nor Clio]," he wrote, "was looked upon as some stray beast might have been, which had wandered into the wrong pasture."[8] Benjamin was an editor of the *Nassau Literary Magazine,* which instructed the students upon such matters as "The Mission of the Beautiful" and "National Credit among the Nations of Europe" and set forth a variety of editorial opinions with vigor and cheerfulness. Warfield's own contributions included poems ("The Jewish Thermopylae," "The Taking of the Suburbs," and "Despise Not Wrinkles") and essays on "Milton's Satan," "Woman's Mission," and "Poetic Genius of Poe."

The professors and tutors were able, cultured men and skillful teachers. Warfield found Dr. Atwater "a solid lecturer and a fine drill-master." "Nothing could be more lucid than Dr. Duffield's mathematical expositions," he wrote. Dr. Guyot "knew how to present his material interestingly," and Dr. Schanck "was that rare chemist whose experiments never failed." Dr. Aiken "was an exceptionally good teacher of language," and Dr. Shields "was at the moment the most admired preacher in Princeton." James McCosh, the new president, arrived from Scotland the same year Benjamin Warfield entered Princeton. Dr. McCosh was "distinctly the most inspiring force" that came into Benjamin Warfield's life during his college days. Every two or three weeks the young collegian visited the retired president, Dr. Maclean, "to take tea with him" and "eat his coriander-seed cookies and listen to his grave, wise talk, learning to love him as everybody who knew him learned to love him."[9]

Benjamin Warfield's greatest academic interests were in

mathematics and physics, in which studies he obtained perfect marks. He graduated in 1871 at the age of nineteen, having won highest honors, prizes for essay and debate, and a fellowship in science for further study in Europe. His father, however, encouraged him to turn down the fellowship, so that he would have the freedom to follow his interests as they developed during his time in Europe. Benjamin sailed in February 1872 and, after a short time in Edinburgh, moved on to the continent.

Writing from Heidelberg in midsummer, Benjamin surprised his parents and friends by announcing that he intended to study for the ministry. His mother was delighted; she had long hoped that her sons would become ministers of the gospel.[10] After his time in Europe Benjamin returned to his Kentucky home and served as livestock editor of the Lexington *Farmer's Home Journal* until he entered Princeton Seminary in September 1873.[11] Years later Charles Barrett, a close college friend and companion in Europe who was also beginning seminary study, remembered their first Sunday evening at the seminary:

We were seated together before an open window in Brown Hall. We drew our chairs close together and we sat there in the calm of a September evening. Our souls seemed to draw near together. A close friendship had been established when we were fellow students over in Princeton College, where he led the class. This friendship had been cemented by a year of travel abroad. Together we had visited the largest cities. We had wandered through quaint old towns. [And]. . . on foot among the Alps—I suppose we wandered for a thousand miles together. . . . [Now] we sat together there in old Brown Hall, with reminiscences in our hearts. At last I turned to him and said, "What was it that decided you to enter the ministry?" I can see his face, the tender look that came into his face. He was very near to me just at that moment, now forty-three years ago. . . . I can hear the very tone of his voice. He turned to me and said, "Because I think that in the work of the ministry I can do the most to repay the Lord for what he has done for me."[12]

B. B. Warfield supplied the Presbyterian church at Concord, Kentucky, during the summer of 1875. He graduated from seminary in May 1876 and served for several months as stated supply at the First Presbyterian Church of Dayton,

Ohio. On August 3 he married Annie Pearce Kinkead, daughter of a prominent Lexington lawyer (who had represented Abraham Lincoln in trial in 1853) and descendant of the American explorer George Rogers Clark. Warfield declined a call to the Dayton church so that he could go abroad for further study, and he and Annie sailed for Europe. On the advice of Caspar Wistar Hodge and with a letter of introduction from Philip Schaff, Benjamin went to the University of Leipzig. When he found that Heinrich Merkel (with whom he had hoped to study) had died a few months earlier, the young American turned instead to Cristoph Ernst Luthardt and Franz Delitszch.[13] Late in the summer of 1877 the Warfields returned to the United States by way of Edinburgh, where they attended meetings of the Pan-Presbyterian Alliance. *En route* to Kentucky they lost all their luggage in a riot in Pittsburgh—including a large collection of German books for which they had paid $1,000!

Benjamin Warfield served as assistant pastor at the First Presbyterian Church of Baltimore from November 1877 to March 1878. He turned down an appointment to the Old Testament department at Western Theological Seminary, having decided—despite his early antipathy to Greek— to concentrate in New Testament studies. When Western Seminary then offered him a position as instructor of New Testament language and literature, he accepted. The next year he was appointed professor. Warfield began his inaugural address with a "personal statement":

Fathers and Brothers: It is without doubt a very wise provision by which, in institutions such as this, an inaugural address is made a part of the ceremony of induction into the professorship. Only by the adoption of some such method could it be possible for you, as the guardians of this institution, responsible for the principles here inculcated, to give to each newly called teacher an opportunity to publicly declare the sense in which he accepts your faith and signs your standards. Eminently desirable at all times, this seems particularly so now, when a certain looseness of belief (inevitable parent of looseness of practice) seems to have invaded portions of the Church of Christ—not leaving even its ministry unaffected— when there may be some reason to fear that "enlightened clerical gentlemen may sometimes fail to look upon subscription to creeds as our covenanting forefathers looked upon the act of putting their names to theological documents, and as mercantile gentlemen still look upon endorsement of bills." And how much more forcibly can all this be pled when he who appears before you at your call is young, untried and unknown. I wish, therefore, to declare that I sign these standards not as a necessary form which must be submitted to, but gladly and willingly as the expression of a personal and cherished conviction; and, further, that the system taught in these symbols is the system which will be drawn out of the Scriptures in the prosecution of the teaching to which you have called me—not, indeed, because commencing with that system the Scriptures can be made to teach it, but because commencing with the Scriptures I cannot make them teach anything else.[14]

Warfield then announced his topic. "In casting about for a subject on which I might address you," he said, "I have thought I could not do better than to take up one of our precious old doctrines, much attacked of late, and ask the simple question: What seems the result of the attack? The doctrine I have chosen is that of 'Verbal Inspiration.'" After taking his hearers through an extensive investigation of the topic Warfield summarized his findings. "If the sacred writers clearly claim verbal inspiration and every phenomenon supports that claim, and all critical objections break down by their own weight," he asked, "how can we escape admitting its truth? What further proof do we need?" The young professor closed his address with the words "Let us bless God, then, for His inspired word! And may He grant that we may always cherish, love, and venerate it, and conform all our life and thinking to it! So may we find safety for our feet, and peaceful security for our souls."[15]

Benjamin Warfield's conviction and ability soon attracted the attention of many—including the trustees and faculty of his *alma mater*, Princeton College, which, in 1880, conferred upon him the doctor of divinity degree. In 1881 he declined a call to teach theology at the Theological Seminary of the Northwest in Chicago. But, after nine years at Western, he came to Princeton Seminary in 1887 to occupy the chair of theology made famous by Archibald Alexander and the two Hodges. Annie and Benjamin Warfield moved into a seminary house next to Alexander Hall.[16] They were glad to be in Princeton. Dr. Warfield loved "with an enthusiastic devotion the University and the Seminary, which he counted in very truth his *almae matres.*" His brother wrote:

He venerated as only a pure and unselfish spirit can the great men and hallowed memories which have made Princeton one of the notable seats of theological scholarship. His reverence for those who had taught him was equalled by his admiration of his colleagues, and the love which he delighted to express for those who had taught him was constantly reproduced in his affection for his younger colleagues and the successive classes of students who thronged his classrooms.[17]

*   *   *

When Dr. Patton resigned as coeditor of *The Presbyterian Review* in 1888, the Princeton faculty elected Dr. Warfield as his successor. As a young New Testament professor at Western Seminary, Warfield had opposed the founding of the journal, begging that no such compromise measure be taken. Although Warfield had loyally supported *The Presbyterian Review,* he realized soon that his earlier misgivings were not without foundation.

The First General Council of the new Alliance of Reformed Churches Throughout the World Holding the Presbyterian System, which met in Edinburgh under Free Church auspices in 1877, revealed that most of the European Presbyterian and Reformed churches had already revised their confessions. Many American Presbyterians were anxious to do the same. They were unhappy particularly with the Westminster Confession's chapters on "God's eternal decree" and "Effectual calling" and wanted statements that placed more emphasis on God's love and on human responsibility. The 1889 General Assembly, meeting in Philadelphia, voted by an overwhelming majority to submit two questions to the 209 presbyteries of the church: "Do you desire a revision of the Confession of Faith? If so, in what respects, and to what extent?" This action set off "a paper war" that was "unrivalled in American Presbyterian (and perhaps evangelical) history" and made "Warfield, Briggs, Patton, and Henry Van Dyke household names across the nation."[18]

In his *American Presbyterianism: Its Origin and Early History* Charles Briggs had argued that the "true American party"— of Francis Makemie, the Tennents, and Jonathan Dickinson —had opposed the "strict subscription" to the Westminster Confession of Faith that was favored by the staunchly orthodox Scotch-Irish. In September 1889 Briggs published *Whither? A Theological Question for the Times,* in which he called for a new direction in theological thought and strongly attacked his opponents. He identified by name those he called the "betrayers" of the Reformed tradition—the Princeton professors, Robert L. Dabney, and his own Union Seminary colleague William G. T. Shedd. "It is the theology of the elder and younger Hodge," Briggs wrote, "that has in fact usurped the place of the Westminster theology in the minds of a large portion of the ministry of the Presbyterian Churches, and now stands in the way of progress in theology and of true Christian orthodoxy; and there is no other way of advancing in truth except by removing the errors that obstruct our path." He claimed that the Princetonians and their supporters were not champions of orthodoxy at all but of what he called "orthodoxism." He described it harshly: "Orthodoxism assumes to know the truth and is unwilling to learn; it is haughty and arrogant, assuming the divine prerogatives of infallibility and inerrancy; it hates all truth that is unfamiliar to it, and persecutes it to the uttermost . . . preferring the traditions of man to the truth of God."[19]

The October 1889 issue of *The Presbyterian Review* contained two articles on confessional revision. Philip Schaff of Union, supporting revision, concluded his argument with these words:

We need a theology and a confession that is more human than Calvinism, more divine than Arminianism, and more Christian and catholic than either; a confession as broad and deep as God's love, and as strict and severe as God's justice. We need a theology and a confession that will not only bind the members of one denomination together, but be also a bond of union between the various folds of the one flock of Christ, and attract the ungodly world, that it may be converted by the regenerating and sanctifying power of the everlasting gospel.[20]

John DeWitt of McCormick Theological Seminary set forth the arguments against revision. Concerning the suggested changes he asked:

Will they remove great evils? Will they secure great benefits? Are they sufficiently valuable to overbear the strong presumption against the amendment of this most beneficent document, which, ancient as it is, is still instinct with a vitality so commanding? These, after all, are the important and determining questions. Deeply impressed by the considerations, which I have inadequately set forth in this paper, I expect to cast my vote in behalf of the Confession as it is.[21]

Dr. Warfield objected to the content and tone of Dr. Briggs's notice of the 1889 General Assembly for *The Presbyterian Review* and notified him that the editorial arrangement, by which a report on the assembly had been exchanged between the editors, would have to be discontinued. The October 1889 issue of the review did carry Briggs's General Assembly article, but increased tensions between the two editors. Warfield resigned as Princeton editor, and the Princeton faculty elected Charles Aiken to succeed him. When Briggs also resigned, the Union Seminary faculty recommended that the journal be discontinued. A few days later the Princeton faculty agreed. In January 1890 a new theological journal was begun—*The Presbyterian and Reformed Review*—under the editorship of Dr. Warfield, with an "associate editor" appointed from each of the seminaries represented in the old review.

Many church leaders had become active in the revision debate. The recently retired James McCosh produced the whimsically titled *Whither? O Whither? Tell Me Where*—a sophisticated and masterful answer to Briggs. Although Dr. McCosh would allow minor revisions in the Confession, he was solidly on the side of the Princeton theologians on the central issues. Union Seminary professor William G. T. Shedd attacked Briggs's views and the revisionist movement in his *Proposed Revision of the Westminster Standards*. Shedd noted that the fact that the spirit of revision was "in the air" was given as a reason it should be "stimulated and strengthened." "This would also be a reason for the increase of malaria," he wrote.

He warned that if the desire to "revise the Calvinistic creed" continued to increase, there could "be little doubt that the historical Calvinism will be considerably modified; and doctrinal modification is an inclined plane." He added:

In an age of materialism in philosophy, and universalism in religion, when the Calvinistic type of doctrine is more violently opposed than any other of the evangelical creeds, because of its firm and uncompromising nature, the Presbyterian Church should not revise the creed from which it has derived its past solidarity and power, but should *reaffirm* it; and non-revision is reaffirmation.[22]

Philip Schaff's book on *Creed Revision in the Presbyterian Churches,* published in 1890, enthusiastically supported revision as a first step toward "the reunion of Christendom in the Creed of Christ." Dr. Schaff believed that the Westminster Confession—"the product of the most polemical and most intolerant age of Christendom"—overstated God's sovereignty and ignored the general love of God for all people. "It is a Confession for the exclusive benefit of the elect," he wrote. "To this small inside circle all is bright and hopeful; but outside of it all is dark as midnight."[23]

Charles Briggs began to advocate "a simple, devotional statement of our faith" to stand beside the Confession expressing "the faith, life, and devotion of the present time, born of our experience and needs." Henry Van Dyke presented suggestions for revisions of the Confession. In a series of papers—published as a book entitled *Ought the Confession of Faith Be Revised?* —John DeWitt of McCormick Seminary, W. G. T. Shedd of Union in New York, and B. B. Warfield of Princeton responded. They argued that to amend the Confession as Henry Van Dyke proposed would actually narrow its position, for as written it allowed for various views within Calvinism. Warfield pointed out that the Confession sets forth the character of the God of love and of infinite compassion for sinners. He commented that Van Dyke "appears to set God's sovereignty and His love unduly over against one another," so that God's election in grace becomes a limitation of God's love rather than the expression of it.[24]

On June 25, 1889, New Brunswick Presbytery—which

included the faculty of Princeton Seminary—voted against the revision overture sent to the presbyteries after the General Assembly in May. Presbytery adopted a paper written by B. B. Warfield in which he set forth the reasons he was opposed to revision. The Confession, Warfield stated, "expressed the general and common faith" of the whole church and the terms of subscription made it unnecessary for each person "to conform to the Confession in all its propositions." Furthermore, in Dr. Warfield's view "the Westminster Confession is the best, safest and most acceptable statement of the truths and the system which we most surely believe . . . has ever been formulated; and we despair of making any substantial improvements upon its forms of sound words."[25]

The Confession of Faith, Dr. Warfield liked to say, "suited him down to the ground." Despite his strong sentiments, Warfield was not opposed in principle to revision of the Confession. "If there is a call for revision at all," he wrote, "it is obviously for even clearer and more precise definition, for even higher and more finished construction, than the Westminster divines have given us in their noble formulation of the truth." Warfield feared, however, that the Presbyterian church was rejecting the demands made on it "for progress in the doctrinal statement of our orthodox truth in relation to our present-day needs" and was being tempted "to lower its voice in telling the world the truth!" "It is not a time in which to whisper the truth in doubtful phrases," he wrote, "but to shout it from the housetops in the clearest and sharpest language in which it can be framed."[26]

By the time of the 1890 General Assembly, which met in Saratoga, New York, 134 presbyteries had voted for a revision of the Confession of Faith. Twenty-five presbyteries proposed models of a new and simpler "consensus creed." Victory for Charles Briggs and the revisionists appeared certain, but before the final decision at the 1893 General Assembly momentous issues would affect the outcome of that vote.

*   *   *

As the Presbyterian church debated revision of its Confession, it considered also the role of women in the work of the

[124]

church. A. A. Hodge, B. B. Warfield, and Alexander McGill all supported the deaconess movement as a means of using the ministries of women. The first issue of *The Presbyterian Review* in 1880 contained an article by Dr. McGill proposing that deaconesses be organized into a series of boards corresponding to presbyteries, synods, and the General Assembly—under the control and supervision of judicatories composed of ministers and elders. Referring to McGill's article, the editor of *The Presbyterian* predicted that the proposal "was a foreshadowing of the elevation of women which may be at hand." He added, "And if there is any place where pious and zealous women should be honored, it is in the Church of God."

After receiving a number of overtures requesting denominational sanction of deaconesses, the General Assembly of 1889 appointed a special committee led by B. B. Warfield to present recommendations the following year. The committee thought that "the time was ripe for the reconstitution of the office of deaconess in the Church" but was reluctant to recommend legislation regarding structure and duties of the new order, assuming that such details would evolve gradually over time. With Warfield's endorsement the 1890 General Assembly sent down an overture that recognized the apostolic origins of deaconesses and specified their "election" (but not ordination) "in a manner similar to that appointed for deacons, and set apart by prayer." Strong opposition, however, brought the measure down to defeat. A similar overture in 1892, which omitted the question of apostolic origin of deaconesses and provided for sessional appointment of "godly and competent women . . . for the care of the poor and sick, and especially of poor widows and orphans," was approved.[27]

*   *   *

James Moffat, Princeton's much-loved professor of church history from 1861 to 1888, died on June 7, 1890. The funeral service on June 11, the college's commencement day, was held at the Second Presbyterian Church. The sermon was given by William Henry Green, the senior professor at the seminary. He described Moffat's love for his Scottish home-land:

Dr. Moffat ever felt an honest pride in claiming Scotland as the place of his birth—the land of John Knox and of Robert Burns. He brought from it his vigorous constitution, the ineffaceable Scotch tone of his voice, an enthusiastic admiration for the scenery, the history, the literature, and the institutions of his native land. When, some years since, he revisited the scenes of his childhood, after a long period of absence, it was with untold delight that he retraced the objects familiar in his early youth—the mountain slopes on which he had pastured his flocks as a shepherd boy, the lake that reposed at their foot, and the scattered habitations of kindred and neighborly households—and sought out the few remaining survivors among the friends of long ago. He never spoke of this visit but in glowing terms. He could never hear or utter the Scotch dialect without kindling into fervor. The simple-hearted piety learned at his godly mother's knee was inwrought into every fiber of his being. He was inborn and ingrained a true Scotch Presbyterian, not in any bigoted or prejudiced sense, but with a thorough, honest conviction.[28]

In 1891 Caspar Wistar Hodge died after teaching New Testament literature and exegesis for thirty-one years. All his life, except for the seven years he was a pastor in New York and Pennsylvania, was spent in Princeton. "His life was singularly uneventful," said Francis Patton, "and there is something almost pathetic in its quiet, even flow." Dr. Patton, who called Caspar Wistar Hodge "the grandest man I ever knew," preached the funeral sermon. He took for his text the words of Luke 24:32—"He opened to us the scriptures." These words were spelled out in flowers upon Dr. Hodge's coffin—a final tribute from his students. Dr. Patton told the congregation: "This is your answer to the question, What did he do? It is a sufficient answer. He wrote no books, his voice was seldom heard beyond his native town, he took no active part in public affairs, and he shrank from the public gaze; but he opened to us the Scriptures."[29]

George Tybout Purves came to Princeton Seminary from the First Presbyterian Church in Pittsburgh to succeed his beloved teacher. The quiet, winsome Philadelphian had entered Princeton as a student in the fall of 1873. He was the best preacher in his class and a zealous New Testament scholar. He graduated in 1876 but remained at the seminary for an additional year of study with professors Hodge and Green. Purves then served the Presbyterian church in Wayne, Pennsylvania, the Broadway Avenue Church in Baltimore, and in 1883 was called to Pittsburgh's First Presbyterian Church. There he combined deep commitment to the pastoral ministry with continued scholarship. In 1888 he gave the Stone Lectures—from 1878 an annual series at Princeton Seminary—on the "Testimony of Justin Martyr to Early Christianity." Seminaries sought to add Purves to their faculties. Princeton tried to recruit him for church history; Western and McCormick wanted him for theology. But his heart was fixed on New Testament, and when Dr. Hodge died Purves came to Princeton. According to B. B. Warfield, he brought with him "an unbounded energy and zeal, and a depth of religious sentiment which rendered every word of the New Testament precious to him, and made its exposition and enforcement his greatest delight."[30]

Dr. Purves's inaugural address as professor of New Testament literature and exegesis, entitled "St. Paul and Inspiration," concluded with the words:

Some one will say, perhaps, that in entering on my professorial work, I ought to have emphasized the human side of Scripture rather than the divine side—since the examination of the Bible on its human side has in modern times proved so rich a blessing to the Bible-using Church. I have no intention of forgetting this. But there is now no danger, as once there was, of our undervaluing the human side. The danger lies in our failing to perceive the definite claims which the Bible makes for itself; in our failing to perceive that, even though human, it is also divine, and this not in a vague, indefinable way but in the distinct sense that, as a literary product, and in all the parts thereof, it is animated by the thought and moulded by the intention of the Divine Spirit. . . . As divine has the Bible been bequeathed to us by the apostles. As such, it is more worthy of lifelong study than on any other supposition it could possibly be. As such, its humanity, if I may so speak, becomes the priceless treasure that it is. As such, it occupies the place it does, alike in theological discipline, in the Church, and in human history. As such, and only as such, does it provide that which nothing else provides—a rock, on which man's feet may stand amid

the shifting sands of thought and while the mist of ignorance—
dimly lit by guesses, hopes, and fears—still hides the sun.[31]

The Alexanders and the Hodges were no longer at
Princeton, nor was Samuel Miller; but professors William
Henry Green, B. B. Warfield, George Purves, and their colleagues taught the old truths that were the foundation of the
seminary. The Bible, the inerrant Word of God, was the rock
on which Princeton continued to stand "amid the shifting
sands of thought." The Reformed faith, as set forth in the
Westminster Confession, united the faculty and guarded
their teaching.

8

Cloud of Witnesses

May God by His Spirit maintain among us, and through our own instrumentality revive around us, that truly evangelical type of piety which not merely tolerates facts and doctrines, but draws from them its strength and inspiration in life and service, its only comfort and hope in the hour of death.

GEERHARDUS VOS

CHARLES Briggs was again the center of controversy in the Presbyterian church. In November 1890 the Union Seminary board of directors transferred Briggs to the newly endowed Edward Robinson Chair of Biblical Studies—named for Union's first Bible professor. On the evening of January 20, 1891, after solemnly declaring his acceptance of the Scriptures as the "only infallible rule of faith and practice" and of the Westminster Confession as containing the "system of doctrine taught in Holy Scripture," Dr. Briggs delivered an almost-two-hour inaugural address on the "Authority of Holy Scripture." He stated that there are three great fountains of divine authority—"the Bible, the Church, and the Reason." Against each of these "three ways of access to God" obstructions have been raised, he said, "by the folly of men." When Briggs criticized "the breastworks of traditional dogmatism and the barriers of ecclesiasticism" that have prevented free access to the Bible, it was obvious to many that his description "bore a striking resemblance to the Princeton theology." Against the Princeton view, Briggs insisted that "there are errors in the Scriptures that no one has been able to explain away; and the theory that they were not in the original text is sheer assumption." He went on to deny the Mosaic authorship of the Pentateuch, the single authorship of Isaiah, and the conception of predictive prophecy. The morning edition of the *New York Tribune* for January 21 included a long article summarizing Charles Briggs's manifesto and two extended "letters of regret" from William Henry Green and James McCosh.[1]

Many in the church were disturbed by Dr. Briggs's address. New York Presbytery—after an unprecedented three-day debate—voted to bring him to trial. Presbytery acquitted Briggs, and five days later the 104th General Assembly of the Presbyterian Church convened in Detroit. William Henry Green was elected moderator, and he appointed Francis Patton chairman of the strategic committee on theological seminaries, which was assigned the responsibility of examining the Briggs issue. Dr. Green remanded the creedal revision question remaining from the previous assembly to a special committee for further consideration and turned the floor over to Dr. Patton. Patton reported that his committee had received overtures from sixty-three presbyteries calling for some action in the matter of Dr. Briggs's inaugural address. In the light of such widespread concern, Patton announced, his committee recommended that the assembly veto Briggs's appointment to the new chair at Union Seminary.[2] On May 27 debate began; Judge S. M. Breckenridge of St. Louis died dramatically the following day as he argued in favor of the committee's report. On May 29 the General Assembly denied Briggs's appointment with a vote of 440 to 60 and returned the case to New York Presbytery for a new trial. In November an overwhelming majority of the presbytery, after a motion from Henry Van Dyke, again dismissed the case "in the name of the peace and unity of the church."[3] The prosecuting committee, however, filed a formal appeal, not to the Synod of New York—the normal procedure—but rather to the next General Assembly.

The opposition to Dr. Briggs was depicted by his supporters as a "Princeton conspiracy" and a "heresy hunt." Dr. Green, however, stated that he and his colleagues opposed Dr. Briggs for the sake of the church and not for personal reasons. Green asked, "Are there those who reluctantly undertook the unwelcome and unpopular task assigned them in this matter, and have borne the brunt of calumny from the public press, and private circles, in a dignified and honorable manner, with no personal unfriendliness to Dr. Briggs, but a conscientious regard for the truth of God and the welfare of the Church—are they to be branded as heresy hunters, and held up to scorn and reprobation?"[4]

*   *   *

On the first Sunday of 1892 Professor William Paxton preached in chapel on Psalm 90:9—"How We Spend Our Years." A few days later Charles Aiken died—the third member of the faculty to die within a year. The students and faculty loved Dr. Aiken. Charles Hodge had once said that Charles Aiken was as attentive and kind to him in his old age as one of his sons could be. William Brenton Greene, a former student and Aiken's successor at Princeton Seminary, said that Dr. Aiken was his "ideal of the equal union of the scholar, the gentleman, and the Christian." Charles Aiken had served the seminary for twenty years—teaching apologetics, Christian ethics, Hebrew and cognate languages, and Old Testament history. For six years he had been librarian. Dr. Aiken was remembered as a preacher of considerable ability and a man who bore the students, both past and present, on his heart. Dr. Warfield said, "He knew everything that was going on; he knew not only all about every student in the Seminary, but all about his past history and antecedents; and he knew accurately the history of every former student. Of course it was his heart that lay at the bottom of this vast body of information, which was an unfailing source of wonder and envy to the rest of us." The Sunday after Dr. Aiken's death, January 17, Warfield preached at the seminary chapel on the "Christian's Attitude toward Death" from II Corinthians 5:1–10—a passage in which "Paul's whole heart is now before us," Warfield told the grieving Princeton community. "It is the model of the Christian's attitude toward life and death and the life that lies beyond death. Let us seek to make it such for our bruised hearts today."[5]

In 1892 the seminary directors elected the handsome, courtly John DeWitt to the chair of church history, which had been vacant since Dr. Moffat's resignation in 1888. The fifty-year-old DeWitt, a graduate of Princeton College and Princeton Seminary, had already served three pastorates and had taught at three theological seminaries. He was pastor of the Presbyterian church (New School) of Irvington, New York; the Central Congregational Church of Boston; and the

Tenth Presbyterian Church of Philadelphia, which, under the long tenure of Henry Boardman, had become one of the most important churches in the denomination. Dr. DeWitt's ministry at Tenth was characterized by impressive sermons on Reformed doctrine and popular Sunday afternoon lectures in church history.

In 1883 Dr. DeWitt became professor of biblical and ecclesiastical history at Lane Theological Seminary in Cincinnati, where, according to one student, "he made church history the livest subject in the curriculum." In 1888 he went to McCormick Seminary in Chicago as professor of apologetics and missions. There he played a prominent part in the controversy concerning the revision of the Westminster Confession of Faith, urging that the standards be left unchanged. In 1892 he became the sixth professor of church history at Princeton—following Samuel Miller, J. W. Alexander, J. A. Alexander, Alexander McGill, and James Moffat. Like his predecessors in this chair Dr. DeWitt was both a preacher and a teacher.[6]

The third new professor to join the seminary faculty in 1892 was William Brenton Greene, who became professor of the Relations of Philosophy and Science to the Christian Religion—following Francis Patton and Charles Aiken in that position. Born in Providence, Rhode Island, in 1854, Greene studied at Princeton College and Princeton Seminary. He served as pastor of First Presbyterian Church in Boston before becoming John DeWitt's successor at Tenth Presbyterian Church in Philadelphia in 1883. When Greene came to Princeton Seminary only William Henry Green—one of the seven men who had taught him sixteen years earlier—was still there. "After consulting many and more ambitious books" on apologetics, Greene found Dr. Aiken's old syllabus the best. Dr. Patton, now president of Princeton College, continued to lecture on theism; and Dr. Greene had the responsibility of "vindicating the Bible as a divine revelation, and . . . showing the defensible character of Christianity against the assaults of all who would deny its supernatural origin."

William Brenton Greene's inaugural address, "The Function of Reason in Christianity," was given on September

22, 1893. He insisted that Christians must give a reasonable defense of their faith but also stated, as had the Princetonians before him, that reason is both finite and marred by sin. He added:

Were human reason both unimpaired and infinite, it still would not be fitted to solve the deepest problems of religion, or to answer the most pressing questions of human life. For, after all, the one inquiry which will not be suppressed is not, What is God? or What is man? but it is, How can man be just with God? The consciousness of guilt is universal; all religions testify to it. But further than the consciousness of guilt, reason, unaided, cannot go.

Dr. Greene told about the Mohican chief who came to the Moravians to ask for a missionary for his people. He said, "Do not send us a man to tell us that there is a God—we all know that; or that we are sinners—we all know that; but send one to tell us about salvation." "In a word," William Brenton Greene said, "the entire course of study should so set forth man's need of redemption and the inability of reason unaided to provide or discover it, that it shall be felt that the only rational attitude for anyone in religion is that of humble, reverent, adoring inquiry before the cross of Him in whom 'the wisdom and the power and the grace of God' are 'reconciling the world unto Himself.'"[7]

*   *   *

The 1892 General Assembly met in Portland, Oregon. Although Charles Briggs declared his orthodoxy in all the doctrines involved in the charges against him, the majority of the commissioners were unconvinced and voted to send the case back to the Presbytery of New York for a new trial. Before adjourning, the assembly passed what came to be known as the "Portland Deliverance," when it reminded "all under its care that it is a fundamental doctrine of this Church that the Old and New Testaments are the inspired and infallible Word of God" and that "the inspired Word, as it came from God, is without error." On October 13, 1892, the Board of Directors of Union Seminary announced that "the agreement [of 1870] between the Union Theological Seminary and the General Assembly of the Presbyterian Church should be, and hereby is, terminated."[8] Dr. Briggs's case was retried by the largely sympathetic New York Presbytery, and on December 31, 1892, he was acquitted again on all counts. On January 13, 1893, the prosecuting committee filed yet another official appeal to the General Assembly.

The 1893 General Assembly, meeting in Washington, D.C., voted by a decisive 41–to–145 majority to try the Briggs case on appeal. Many in the church were tired of the "gentlemanly" tactics of Princeton Seminary and wanted a more aggressive approach to the "Briggs problem." After five days of debate, during which even standing room in the gallery of the New York Avenue Presbyterian Church was filled, the General Assembly, late in the day on May 31, came to a roll-call vote. Each commissioner, in delivering his vote, was allowed three minutes to speak. During the four hours that it took to complete the vote "an almost painful stillness prevailed throughout the Assembly Hall." When it was all over, 295 commissioners had voted to sustain the appeal of the prosecutors as a whole, 84 to sustain the appeal in part, and 116 voted against the appeal. The official statement released to the press the next day stated that Charles Briggs was suspended from the office of minister for teaching "views, doctrines and teachings . . . contrary to the essential doctrine of Holy Scripture and the Standards" until "such time as he shall give satisfactory evidence of repentance to the General Assembly of the violation by him of [his] ordination vow."[9] When the assembly refused to hear Dr. Briggs's appeal a group of commissioners issued a written protest. A committee of five—including B. B. Warfield's brother, Ethelbert Warfield, and James H. Brookes, pastor in St. Louis—wrote a response, sustained by the assembly. The statement reaffirmed the "Portland Deliverance" of the preceding year—that the church held and had always held that "the Bible as we now have it, in its various translations and versions, when freed from all errors and mistakes of translators, copyists, and printers, is the very word of God, and consequently wholly without error." In no uncertain terms the Presbyterian church had placed itself squarely on the side of biblical inerrancy—the position that Princeton Seminary had stoutly maintained.

*　　*　　*

Princeton Seminary was famous for its emphasis on systematic theology—didactic and polemic theology as it was called—with a great succession of teachers: Archibald Alexander, Charles Hodge, A. A. Hodge, and B. B. Warfield. Early on, the Princetonians had also emphasized the importance of what came to be known as biblical theology. Charles Hodge "anticipated and preserved in his system much of the results of the deservedly vaunted discipline of Biblical Theology," wrote A. A. Hodge, "having, as a matter of actual history, as well as of intention, so immediately drawn his material [for his theology] from a continuous study of the sacred text." In his inaugural address in 1851 William Henry Green stated that each truth of the Bible must be studied separately in its own order, "considering the time of its unfolding and the place it holds in the gradual advance." Studying "the lively oracles in the precise form given to them by the inspired writers," Green said, will lead to a proper appreciation of the diversities in Scripture and to an understanding of "the gradual communication of divine truth." With this approach to the study of Scripture, Dr. Green said, "the whole of the contents of the inspired volume are most likely to be brought out, and all in their due proportion." In his introductory lecture of 1883, Caspar Wistar Hodge described the value and importance of the study of biblical theology and argued that the best way to protect the church against its misuse would be to establish a chair of biblical theology at Princeton Seminary.[10]

Some conservatives were reluctant to accept the new discipline of biblical theology because, as B. B. Warfield noted, it "came to us wrapped in the swaddling clothes of rationalism, and it was rocked in the cradle of the Hegelian recasting of Christianity." Warfield believed, however, that "it was born to better things." He said:

And now as it grows to a more mature form and begins to overtake the tasks that belong to its adulthood, it bids fair to mark a new era in theological investigation by making known to us the revelation of God genetically—that is, by laying it before us in the stages of its growth and its several stadia of development. If men have hitherto been content to contemplate the counsel of the Most High only in its final state—laid out before them, as it were, in a map—hereafter it seems that they are to consider it by preference in its stages, in its vital processes of growth and maturing. Obviously a much higher form of knowledge is thus laid open to us; and were this discipline the sole gift of the nineteenth century to the Christian student, she would by it alone have made good a claim on his permanent gratitude.[11]

In 1891 the Princeton faculty requested that the board of directors establish a professorship of biblical theology. The directors agreed and immediately attempted to recruit Geerhardus Vos, a brilliant young theologian who was teaching in the Theological School of the Christian Reformed Church in Grand Rapids, Michigan. After Vos declined an invitation for the fall of 1892 William Henry Green, who had been Vos's Old Testament teacher at Princeton, wrote urging him to accept the call. Dr. Green compared Vos to an engineer at work on a minor job in the interior when his services were needed at the coast where a major break in the dykes threatened the entire country with devastating flood waters! He concluded his letter with these words, "Remember that the Master, under whose orders you serve, rules the whole field of battle, and not one corner of it merely. Is he not calling you to a point where you can do his work more effectively, and where there is a more pressing need than where you are now?"[12] It was a strong appeal and this time the young Dutchman accepted—although not primarily because of Princeton's larger student body nor its strategic importance on the American theological scene, but because of the opportunity to concentrate his efforts in the field of biblical theology and to serve with Princeton's outstanding faculty.

Geerhardus Vos was born in Heerenveen in the Netherlands on March 14, 1862. His parents—descendants of French Huguenots named Vosse who fled to Germany to escape persecution—had moved from Germany to the Netherlands. His father became a pastor in the Christian Reformed Church, a denomination dating from 1834 when Christians holding to the doctrine of the Synod of Dort broke with the prevailing rationalism and liberalism of the state church. Geerhardus graduated with honors from the gymnasium in Amsterdam and then moved with his family to Grand Rapids, Michigan, where his father accepted a call to a Christian Reformed church. Vos studied at his denomination's theological school in Grand Rapids and at Princeton Seminary. At Princeton he won the Hebrew Fellowship for his thesis, entitled "The Mosaic Origin of the Pentateuchal Codes" (published in London in 1886 with an introduction by William Henry Green). Vos continued his study in Europe —one year at Berlin and two in Strasbourg—and in 1888, at the age of twenty-six, received the doctor of philosophy degree in Arabic studies. He regretfully declined an appointment to the faculty of the Free University of Amsterdam, which had been founded in 1880 by Abraham Kuyper. Vos wrote to Kuyper that "the impulse of an undivided sympathy with the glorious principle that your Institution represents and seeks to propagate, drives me, as it were, within its walls." He was, however, constrained by the wishes of his parents to return to the United States to teach at the Theological School of the Christian Reformed Church in Grand Rapids. For the next five years the talented young professor taught twenty-five hours a week in various subjects, from Greek grammar to systematic theology, and completed several major writing projects.[13]

In 1894 Geerhardus Vos was married to Catherine Francis Smith. In April of that year he was received from Classis Holland of the Christian Reformed Church by the Presbytery of New Brunswick and ordained April 24. On May 8 he was installed as professor of biblical theology at Princeton Seminary. Speaking in the First Presbyterian Church of Princeton, Vos recalled "the names of those illustrious men through whom God has glorified Himself in this institution." Some of those teachers, he said, "at whose feet I used to sit while a student here, are fallen asleep, a smaller number remain until now. There is something in these associations that might well fill me with misgivings at this moment, but I shall not endeavor to conceal on the other hand [that] they are to me a source of inspiration. In view of my own insufficiency I rejoice all the more in having behind and around me this cloud of witnesses. I am thoroughly convinced that in no other place or environment could the sacred influences of the past be brought to bear upon me with a purer and mightier impulse to strengthen and inspire me than here."

In his inaugural address, "The Idea of Biblical Theology as a Science and as a Theological Discipline," Dr. Vos provided a clear, fully developed discussion of the idea of biblical theology and its place among the other theological disciplines. "It is certainly not without significance that God has embodied the contents of revelation, not in a dogmatic system," Vos said, "but in a book of history, the parallel to which in dramatic interest and simple eloquence is nowhere to be found."[14]

Geerhardus Vos believed that Reformed theology had "from the beginning shown itself possessed of a true historic sense in the apprehension of the progressive character of the deliverance of truth. Its doctrine of the covenants on its historical side represents the first attempt at constructing a history of revelation and may justly be considered the precursor of what is at present called Biblical Theology." Biblical theology, a part of exegetical theology applies "no other method of grouping and arranging" the contents of the Bible than is given in "the divine economy of revelation itself." Systematic theology is concerned with the contents of this same revelation but as materials "for the human work of classifying and systematizing according to logical principles." Both are essential and can be truly biblical, the Princeton professor maintained. Biblical theology sets forth the inherent organic structure of the history of redemption revealed in the Scriptures, whereas systematic theology presents the redemptive and revelatory activity of God as a completed project. As Vos put it, "biblical theology draws a *line* of development. Systematic theology draws a *circle*." Vos urged Christians to learn from the critical school to place greater emphasis on the historical development of the Scripture without making the mistakes that the critics had. He said, "Biblical Theology, which can only rest on the basis of revelation, began with a denial of this basis; and a science, whose task it is to set forth the historic principles of revelation, was trained up in a school notorious for its lack of

historical sense." Vos believed, however, that a proper understanding of biblical theology would provide "a most effective
antidote to the destructive critical views now prevailing,"
enable the seminary students to become "in the highest sense
householders bringing out treasured things new and old,"
prepare them for the study of systematic theology, and finally
grant them a greater vision of the glory of God. At Princeton
the new professor of biblical theology added his fresh insights
into Scripture to B. B. Warfield's great doctrinal and historical
emphases and William Henry Green's learned defenses of
the Bible.[15]

*   *   *

In 1886 the faculty at Andover Seminary published a volume
entitled *Progressive Orthodoxy*. It suggested that theology could
no longer be viewed as a fixed body of eternally valid truths
but should adjust to the standards and needs of modern
culture. What once had been assumed as settled in American
Calvinism—the doctrine of the inspiration and authority of
the Bible—was now a matter of debate.

In "a series of carefully crafted essays," B. B. Warfield, who
had written with A. A. Hodge the famous 1881 article on
"Inspiration," clarified and defended the Princeton position
on Scripture. Again and again Dr. Warfield explained that
the historical doctrine of "the plenary inspiration of the
Bible" held that "the Bible is inspired not *in part* but *fully*"—
in matters of history and science as well as of faith and
practice, in words as well as thoughts. Rejecting a mechanical
dictation view, the Princeton professor argued that "justice is
done to neither factor of inspiration and to neither element
in the Bible, the human or the divine, by any other conception of the mode of inspiration except that of *concursus,* or
by any other conception of the Bible except that which
conceives of it as a divine-human book, in which every word is
at once divine and human." The Scriptures, therefore, are
the joint product of divine and human activities, "both of
which penetrate them at every point, working harmoniously
together to the production of a writing which is not divine
here and human there, but at once divine and human in
every part, every word and every particular."[16]

In January 1894 Dr. Warfield produced a review of the opinions of Henry Preserved Smith, professor at Lane Theological Seminary, who had espoused the views of Dr. Briggs and had been suspended from the ministry by the Presbytery of Cincinnati in 1892. Warfield showed that Smith's concept of "limited inspiration"—that the Scriptures are infallible only in matters of faith and practice—was opposed to the teaching of the Scripture and the Westminster Confession of Faith, both of which set forth the doctrine of a fully inspired and inerrant Bible. Dr. Warfield wrote that "the new critical theories are consciously inconsistent with the old doctrine of inspiration" and asserted that "it is clear that one or the other must go to the wall."[17]

Warfield admitted that "the phrase 'the inerrancy of the original autographs' [was] not an altogether happy one to express the doctrine of the Scriptures and of the Westminster Confession as to the entire truthfulness of the Scriptures as given by God." He believed, however, that the phrase was intended to express the doctrine of the Bible and the Confession and that it did, "in its own way, sharply affirm it." "The strenuous opposition to it," he stated, had "its roots in doubt or denial of this Scriptural and Confessional doctrine." Warfield answered the objection that "since we do not have any of the original autographs we do not possess an inerrant Scripture" by asserting that "God has not permitted the Bible to become so hopelessly corrupt that its restoration to its original text is impossible." As a matter of fact, Warfield claimed, practically the whole of the Bible is "in its autographic text in the best texts in circulation; and he who will may today read the autographic text in large stretches of Scripture without legitimate doubt."[18]

In three notable articles written at the turn of the century Dr. Warfield continued his defense of the Bible as the divinely inspired Word of God. In "God-Inspired Scripture," Warfield thoroughly re-examined the word *theopneustos* (II Timothy 3:16) in the light of the new critical definition of "inspiring." Investigating every possible occurrence and reference to this key word, Warfield defended the traditional orthodox understanding of its meaning as "God-inspired" or "God-breathed." His study entitled "It Says: Scripture Says:

God Says" concluded that "we may well be content in the New Testament as in Philo to translate the phrase, wherever it occurs, 'It says'—with the implication that *this* 'It says' is the same as 'Scripture says,' and that this 'Scripture says' is the same as 'God says.'" In the "Oracles of God" Warfield showed that the true meaning of the word *logia* is "oracle"—a heavenly authoritative utterance—against the modern enfeebled sense of "sayings."[19]

Not only did the Scripture itself teach plenary, verbal inspiration, but, Dr. Warfield maintained, it was held by the church of all ages until recent times—"the assured persuasion of the people of God from the first planting until today." This historic view of the Bible found its most lucid and classic expression, Warfield believed, in the first chapter of the Westminster Confession of Faith. In weighty studies on the "Westminster Doctrine of Holy Scripture" and the "Doctrine of Inspiration of the Westminster Divines," Dr. Warfield showed that the Confession of Faith taught that the vernacular translations competently transmitted the Word of God for all practical purposes; that the transmitted text has been kept so pure as to retain full authoritativeness in all controversies of religion; and that the original text was "immediately inspired of God"—a technical expression in common theological use at the time of the Westminster divines, by which the idea of divine authorship, in the highest sense of the word, was conveyed. Warfield argued that the Westminster Confession of Faith taught "precisely the doctrine which is taught in the private writings of its framers, which was also the general Protestant doctrine of the time, and not of that time only or of the Protestants only; for, despite the contrary assertion that has recently become tolerably current, essentially this doctrine of inspiration has been the doctrine of the church of all ages and of all names."[20]

Through careful investigation of the views of the men who wrote the Confession, Dr. Warfield showed that although they did not use the same terms, they possessed the same convictions as those who now were defending the inerrancy of the original autographs. In an extensive survey of the writings on Scripture by John Lightfoot—"probably the greatest

[143]

Biblical scholar that took any large part in the discussions of the Assembly"—Warfield concluded that

it is perfectly evident that [Lightfoot's] fundamental conception of Scripture was that it is the Book of God, the "dictates of the Holy Spirit," every part and every element of which—its words and its very letters—God is Himself the responsible author. It is perfectly evident that he would have considered it blasphemy to say that there is anything in it—in the way of falseness of statement, or error of inadvertence—which would be unworthy of God, its Author, who as Truth itself, lacks neither truthfulness nor knowledge. It is perfectly evident, in a word, that he shared the common doctrine of Scripture of the Reformed dogmaticians of the middle of the seventeenth century. It is perfectly evident also, we may add, that his doctrine of Scripture is generally that of the Westminster Confession; and that he could freely and with a good conscience vote for every clause of that admirable—the most admirable extant—statement of the Reformed doctrine of Holy Scripture. It is a desperate cause indeed, which begins by misinterpreting that statement, and then seeks to bolster this obvious misinterpretation by asserting that men like Lightfoot, and Rutherford, and Lyford, and Capel, and Ball, and Baxter, did not believe in the doctrines of verbal inspiration and the inerrancy of Scripture. If they did not believe in these doctrines, human language is incapable of expressing belief in doctrines. Is it not a pity that men are not content with corrupting our doctrines, but must also corrupt our history?[21]

B. B. Warfield fought to preserve for the church the doctrine of the plenary, verbal inspiration of the Bible because of what he saw at stake. If we do not accept this doctrine, Warfield believed, we can hardly accept the teaching of Jesus and the authors of the Bible as a trustworthy guide in anything, since they clearly present such a view of Scripture. Furthermore, "he who no longer holds to the Bible of Jesus—the word of which cannot be broken—will be found on examination no longer to hold to the Jesus of the Bible." Dr. Warfield insisted that it was not biblical criticism that had "destroyed" the old doctrine of verbal inspiration, but the "scholastic theories" of the critics that had drawn them away from "the pure deliverances of Biblical theology." Even the opponents of the orthodox view must admit that Christ and the apostles held to an inerrant Bible, Warfield maintained, so that the "real problem of inspiration" was whether to believe *them* or not. He wrote, "Stated plainly it is just this: Are the New Testament writers trustworthy guides in doctrine? Or are we at liberty to reject their authority and frame contrary doctrines for ourselves?" "The present controversy," Warfield stated, "concerns something much more vital than the bare 'inerrancy' of the Scriptures, whether in the copies or the 'autographs.'"

It concerns the trustworthiness of the Bible in its express declarations, and in the fundamental conceptions of its writers as to the course of the history of God's dealings with his people. It concerns, in a word, the authority of the Biblical representations concerning the nature of revealed religion, and the mode and course of its revelation. The issue raised is whether we are to look upon the Bible as containing a divinely guaranteed and wholly trustworthy account of God's redemptive revelation, and the course of his gracious dealings with his people; or as merely a mass of more or less trustworthy materials, out of which we are to sift the facts in order to put together a trustworthy account of God's redemptive revelation and the course of his dealings with his people. It is of the greatest importance that the Presbyterian Church should not permit its attention to be distracted from this serious issue.[22]

Tirelessly Dr. Warfield carefully defined the issue of biblical inspiration, showed its biblical basis, and set forth its historic position in Christian history. Francis Patton said that Warfield "made no abatement of his belief in the Bible's inspiration, and like a wise general he knew that the surest way to save the citadel is to protect the outposts. He believed in the supernatural contents of Scripture, but he believed also in the supernatural structure of Scripture." "In this he was rendering a great service to multitudes of faithful ministers who for lack of adequate learning were themselves unable to vindicate their faith in the Word of God," Patton added. "His fearless belief was a buttress to men as he stood foursquare to every wind that blows in his unshaken confidence in the oracles of God." Dr. Warfield's articles on the Bible gathered in book form—*Revelation and Inspiration*—constitute the ablest defense of the Bible as "the Word of God, the only infallible rule of faith and practice," that has yet appeared in the English language.[23]

9

The Seminary and the College

It is required of [Christians] that they be strong in faith, with a firm grasp upon the promises, doing all things, daring all things, enduring all things for Christ's sake. There is no room for cowardice and vacillation and shrinking from what is difficult and toilsome. Christ must be followed through evil and through good report; his commands must be obeyed at all hazards; the burdens which he lays upon you must be borne without faint-heartedness.

WILLIAM HENRY GREEN

D URING the years 1887 to 1893 six professors were inaugurated at Princeton Seminary, two of them to newly established chairs. Five of them were in their thirties and the sixth in his forties. All had received their training under the teachers whom they succeeded and whose doctrine and spirit they had absorbed. Enthusiastically they joined William Henry Green, the last living link at Princeton Seminary with Archibald Alexander, Samuel Miller, and Charles Hodge.

Archibald Alexander and Samuel Miller taught at Princeton for nearly forty years; J. A. Alexander for twenty-seven years; Alexander McGill for thirty-five years; Caspar Wistar Hodge for thirty-one years; and James Clement Moffat for twenty-nine years. But only Charles Hodge, whose career spanned fifty-eight years, taught longer than did William Henry Green. Green began in 1846 as tutor in Hebrew, becoming in 1851 professor of Oriental and Old Testament literature. As Old Testament professor, he followed Archibald Alexander, Charles Hodge, and J. A. Alexander. Archibald Alexander taught Old Testament and almost everything else during the early years of the seminary's existence. Charles Hodge, one of "the most qualified Hebrew teachers in early nineteenth-century America," came back from his European studies "in a position to become one of America's finest Old Testament scholars." But after teaching the Old and New Testaments for eighteen years, Hodge became Dr. Alexander's successor in systematic theology. It was J. A. Alexander, "the

[149]

first of the Princetonians to have exegesis as the great passion of his life," who established Princeton's reputation as a center for Old Testament study.[1]

Laboring steadily, wisely, and effectively, William Henry Green had built on that tradition. He was a masterful teacher of Hebrew. One of his students commented that in his Hebrew classes there was "linguistic study ministering not merely to taste and judgment, but to the imagination and the heart." Dr. Green's *Grammar of the Hebrew Language* represented "a major contribution to the field of Hebrew studies in America." Green also taught courses in the Old Testament prophets and in various Old Testament books. He offered classes in comparative philology, archaeology, and ancient Near Eastern history and in Aramaic, Syriac, Arabic, and Sanskrit.[2]

Dr. Green's students appreciated the way he related the study of the Old Testament to the practical aspects of their ministry, and they caught his "love and enchantment with the biblical texts." In his lectures on the book of Job Dr. Green presented the book as both a record of actual events and a work of art. "While we humbly receive its inspired lessons," he said, "there is no reason why we should be insensible to its gracious beauty, or refuse to recognize its other attractions." He drew forth the book's timeless lessons and emphasized its place "in the scheme of Holy Scripture." "The history of Job," he told the students, "is one among a great body of signal facts illustrative of God's ways with men and of His plan of grace." These lessons of Job, however, do not in any case "pass the bounds imposed on the knowledge of God's grace for the time then present, nor do they ever anticipate in its fulness what was reserved for a brighter future. Piety was still, as it is prevailingly characterized in the Old Testament, 'the fear of the Lord.' The love of God, springing from the knowledge and belief of the love that God hath to us, had not yet been made perfect."[3]

Although critical views had circulated in Europe's scholarly circles for some time, Dr. Green named 1878—the year in which Julius Wellhausen published his presentation of the documentary hypothesis—as the year of "The Sudden Revolution." Green did not lightly dismiss the new views. "I am not insensible to the great value of German scholarship and researches," he wrote to Charles Briggs in 1882, although he added, "we would doubtless differ in some instances as to what was to be considered chaff and what was genuine grain." To Dr. Green there was not only chaff in the teaching of the critics but a "far subtler and bolder form of attack" on Christianity than the Christian church had yet faced. It comes not from "professed foes outside the church, but from men who call themselves Christians" and who are "fortified by their position in the church, by their extensive research and their unquestioned ability." These critics direct their assaults "not merely at the external evidences of revealed religion" nor "at particular doctrines of the Word of God," but undertake "to explode all that has been most surely believed from the days of the prophets and apostles." The critical challenge to the Bible was "but the providential method of compelling the lovers of God's word to a deeper and more careful study of its contents. They must take the learning of their foes and their results elaborated with hostile intent, and build them into secure defenses, or gather from them what shall contribute to a more complete elucidation or a more vivid presentation of heavenly truth."[4] With courage, hard work, and great persistence, Dr. Green gave himself to the enormous task of mastering and answering the writings of the higher critics.

In spite of his first thought that the "faultfinding" of John William Colenso's book on the Pentateuch was "too childish to merit a serious reply," Dr. Green prepared a response entitled *The Pentateuch Vindicated from the Aspersions of Bishop Colenso.* Colenso, the Anglican bishop of Natal in South Africa, was an evangelical missionary who, in his attempts to communicate the gospel to the Zulus, "gave way, first discarding the fundamentals of evangelical religion, and then his belief in the Bible as the infallible Word of God; and thus became the protagonist of critical rationalism on English ground." Dr. Green stated that "the Pentateuch has borne assaults before unscathed, and it will not be damaged by his, even if he is a missionary bishop; nor by the *Essays and Reviews* which he holds in such esteem." Green reviewed the traditional proofs of the Pentateuch's divine character and authority, stressing Jesus' words in John 5:46—"Moses wrote

[151]

of me." He commented that "all who have any reverence and love for this heavenly Teacher will undoubtingly receive his testimony. The utter want of confidence in Jesus and reverence for his words, which Colenso displays, . . . is among the most painful things in his book."[5]

In 1875 Abraham Kuenen of the University of Leiden applied advanced historical-critical methods to the reconstruction of Israel's history in his book *Prophets and Prophecy in Israel.* He asserted that the prophets possessed no certain insight into the future and that the Old Testament contained no specific prediction of Jesus. Dr. Green's *Moses and the Prophets*—published in 1882—answered Kuenen's "ultracritical" theories and attacked his "absolute anti-supernaturalism." Green read Robertson Smith's book on *The Prophets of Israel*— also published in 1882—"with disappointment and pain," since he had not anticipated "the extremely low estimate" that the Scottish scholar "put upon the religion of Israel and the teaching of the Prophets."[6]

In 1888 Dr. Green and William Rainey Harper, a noted philologist and Old Testament scholar at Yale, debated the higher critical issues in the pages of the journal *Hebraica,* of which Dr. Harper was editor. Harper presented "the facts and considerations" in favor of the documentary partition of the Pentateuch; and Green—whom he chose for the task— presented "the counter-statement or criticism." The long and polite debate, in the view of one reader, required "a vast amount of patience and toil" on the part of the two scholars and "very much . . . patience and toil on the part of a reader to follow the discussion through." Dr. Green stated that he began his work on the documentary theory "convinced at the outset of the unsoundness in the main of the arguments urged on behalf of the critical partition of the Pentateuch," but fearing that "there might be some fire where there is so much smoke, some positive foundation for the positive assertions in which the critics are so prone to indulge." As he studied the issue, Dr. Green claimed, he became more and more convinced that the assumption of pre-existing documents was unreasonable and the "discovery" that led to their creation was no discovery at all, "but an *ignis fatuus* which has misled critics ever since into a long and weary and fruitless search through fog and mire, that might better be abandoned for a forward march on *terra firma.*" He resolutely defended the Mosaic Pentateuch, arguing that no evidence existed to prove that the alleged documents contradicted one another. The critical hypothesis not only divided the text, he said, but impugned divine revelation, miracles, prophecy, and the spiritual value of the Old Testament. Dr. Green's books on *The Higher Criticism of the Pentateuch* and *The Unity of the Book of Genesis* flowed out of his debate with William Rainey Harper. With a vast amount of patience and toil he exposed the weaknesses of the critical hypothesis of diverse authorship and reasserted the validity of the old views—not because they were old but, as Dr. Green claimed, because they were right.[7]

In a lecture series on the "Hebrew Feasts," given in 1895 at Newton Theological Institute in Massachusetts, Dr. Green presented fuller answers to the Graf-Wellhausen theories. He maintained that the critics used scholarly methods as a guise of scientific inquiry, whereas in reality they manipulated the Old Testament text so that it fitted their hypotheses. In his lectures Dr. Green presented detailed, complex answers to the critics. At the end of "the long and weary road" that they had traveled together he told his patient audience that he had "not knowingly shunned any point that our antagonists have raised."[8]

Dr. Green warned Christians that Wellhausen's views impugned "the truthfulness of the Scriptures" at every step. "If the hypothesis be true," he wrote, "the Scriptures are not what they represent themselves to be; the facts of the history are altogether different from that which they declare; their testimony is unreliable and untrustworthy." The Princeton professor insisted that "the Bible's own account of itself satisfies the actual phenomena involved better . . . than does any other theory," that "it is further supported by unbroken and unanimous testimony reaching back from Christ and His apostles into the earliest literature," and that "it alone requires no rejection and no minimizing of well-ascertained truths." Dr. Green urged those who had been influenced by the higher critical views to "revise their own ill-judged alliance with the enemies of evangelical truth" and reconsider whether "Christ's view of the Old Testament may not, after all, be the true view."[9]

In his classes at Princeton Dr. Green changed "neither his approach to the literature nor his views about the integrity, structure, dating and authorship of the various Old Testament books." With his students he scrutinized the book of Genesis to prove that it was "not a compilation from different documents, but . . . the continuous work of a single writer." He always began his course in the Old Testament prophets by defining a prophet as "an authoritative and infallible expounder of the will of God." In 1881, in his opening lecture of the fall semester at Princeton, Dr. Green expressed his deep concern for the future of orthodoxy as it faced what he described as "the eve of an agitation upon the vital and fundamental question of the inspiration and infallibility of the Bible, such as it had never known before." "There is a demand now, as never before, for high Biblical scholarship," he told the students, "for well-trained exegetes and critics— for men well versed in the critical and speculative attacks made upon the Word of God, and who are well prepared to defend it." Dr. Green's great vision was for a company of believing scholars who would equal the critics in "learning, ingenuity, and patient toil" and who would have "some reverence for what is sacred, some respect for historical testimony, and some regard for the dictates of common sense."[10]

William Henry Green was recognized on both sides of the Atlantic as the champion of orthodoxy in Old Testament matters, the leader of "the reverent and conservative school of higher criticism."[11] Conservatives were heartened by his meticulous scholarship, and his opponents respected him for his fairness. Dr. Green's name appeared not only in American and English reviews but also in the German theological journals, in which he came to be known as "the American Hengstenberg." Adolph Zahn called Green and Warfield "two of the greatest experts on Calvinism."

Dr. Green was a popular preacher—well received by churches, the seminary community, the Bible conference movement, and children's groups. He contributed to a manual for Sunday school teachers and wrote an extended series of Old Testament lessons for the *Sunday School Times* as part of the International Sunday School Lesson Plan. When questions arose concerning the propriety of including the Old Testament in the Sunday school curriculum, Green insisted that the Old Testament was an integral part of the Christian's Bible. As chairman of the Old Testament Division of the American Bible Revision Committee, Green labored to present to the Bible-reading public a more accurate translation of the Scriptures. He campaigned for the acceptance of the new translation, especially among those conservatives who clung to the wording and sometimes even the punctuation of the Authorized Version.

On Tuesday morning, May 5, 1896, the closing exercises of the seminary were held in Miller Chapel. After the address and granting of diplomas the seventy-eight members of the graduating class remained standing in front of the platform while Dr. William Miller Paxton addressed them on behalf of the faculty. Stressing that the life of the minister is largely his sermon, Paxton passed on to the students the advice Samuel Miller had given him when he had graduated from Princeton Seminary in 1848—to keep near the throne of grace and to care for the children of his congregation.

The graduation exercises began earlier that year and were briefer than usual so that most of the day could be given to the celebration honoring William Henry Green's fifty years as a teacher at Princeton Seminary. Special trains had brought to Princeton a large number of alumni, distinguished scholars from many universities and theological seminaries, colleagues of Dr. Green from the American Bible Revision Committee, and many friends. When the graduation service was over the crowd of about two thousand marched, double-file, "at a slow and dignified pace" ("as though mindful of the Princeton principle to make speed slowly," commented the *New York Observer*) to Alexander Hall on the college campus. In the long line there was an abundance of black gowns and mortarboard caps, and here and there a doctor's hood of buff or scarlet. When Dr. Green entered Alexander Hall and slowly made his way to the chair in the front, the whole assembly rose cheering. After the hymn "I love thy kingdom, Lord" and prayer, speeches were given concerning various aspects of Dr. Green's long ministry.

Abraham Gosman, pastor of the Presbyterian church in Lawrenceville, New Jersey, spoke of William Henry Green's service to the seminary and expressed the abiding love of the directors and trustees for him and their strong confidence in him. He concluded his tribute with the words "Thanks, beloved teacher and friend!" Francis Patton—who told the large audience that he venerated Dr. Green as he venerated "no other living man"—spoke about Dr. Green's services to the church at large and praised the Princeton professor because "he has not read the Bible with a shake of the head or a shrug of the shoulders." Charles M. Mead of Hartford Theological Seminary reviewed Dr. Green's contribution to biblical studies. He is learned in the languages, the history, and the archaeology of the Bible, Mead said,

and with all, and above all, he has faith in revealed truth and a comprehensive view of its relation to the purposes of God in human history, such as serve to give balance and steadiness to his critical judgments. Some men say that he is prejudiced. Yes, he is prejudiced in favor of the belief that God has revealed His will and purposes to men; in favor of the reality of the redemptive work of God begun in Israel and finished in Jesus Christ; in favor of the credibility of the sacred books which have been handed down as the record of that work and as the oracles of God to guide men to eternal life.[12]

Princeton graduate J. F. McCurdy of the University of Toronto called Dr. Green "the most influential Hebrew teacher of his time" in the English-speaking world and described Green's contribution to Semitic scholarship. He said, "It is a great thing to have been a teacher fifty years, it is greater to have been a teacher in Princeton Seminary for so long a time, and it is greater still to have been a teacher of Hebrew. For Hebrew lies at the bottom of things—at least, of the things which are worth most at Princeton." In Dr. Green's teaching, McCurdy added, one could see "the vindication of the Princetonian tradition of thoroughness and fidelity" to the written Word of God. McCurdy said that Dr. Green regarded all his philological study as a preparatory discipline —as an aid to the understanding of the Scripture. "With Professor Green," Dr. McCurdy said, "'philology' meant always not the love of words, but the love of the Word."[13]

[156]

Dr. Green replied in a short speech to the addresses of the morning. Princeton Seminary stands, he said,

as it has always stood, for fidelity to the Word of God and the standards of the Presbyterian Church. At the same time it stands for the highest grade of Biblical and theological learning. It welcomes all the light that can be thrown upon the Scriptures from every quarter, and does not shrink from the application of the most rigorous tests to the question of their origin or the nature of their contents. Convinced by the most abundant evidence that these Scriptures are the infallible word of God, and that their teachings are the utterances of divinely sanctioned truth, this Seminary has always maintained that sound learning will ever go hand in hand with implicit faith in this sacred volume.[14]

Dr. Green praised Princeton's first teachers—Archibald Alexander, Samuel Miller, Charles Hodge, and Addison Alexander—that "splendid quaternion" who gave Princeton "its reputation before the church and the world." It was under them, he said, that the Princeton theology "gained a definite and well understood meaning, which, it is to be hoped, it will never lose; from which may it never swerve." All the professors who followed them "have cordially and earnestly taken the same attitude toward the Scriptures that was so steadfastly held by their predecessors," Dr. Green added. Furthermore, he claimed that

the great body of those who have gone forth from [Princeton Seminary] to preach the everlasting Gospel of the grace of God in this and other lands have stood firmly by the instructions which they here received on this fundamental matter, and that they have not weakened the power of that divine message which they were charged to bear to immortal men by entertaining or suggesting doubts as to the genuineness of the books of the Bible, or the truth and authority of its contents.

Dr. Green expressed his conviction that the faculties of nearly every theological seminary in the various branches of the American Presbyterian church maintained "the trustworthiness, the genuineness, and the infallible inspiration of the books of Holy Scripture" exactly as held by Princeton. "We have nothing to boast of in this respect," he said, "which has not been the common faith of Christendom from the beginning; and so long as the Spirit of God rules in the hearts of men His revealed Word will be held in high honor." Looking around the great gathering, Dr. Green closed his remarks with the words "May the Word of God, my dear friends, abide in you, and crown you all with its richest blessing."[15]

Speeches of congratulation followed. Robert Russell Booth, moderator of the General Assembly of the Presbyterian Church in the United States of America, said that in the great controversy concerning the authenticity and truthfulness of the Old Testament, the "believing Church of God" had seen in Dr. Green "its standard-bearer and had realized that, as it was in the Arian controversy of the olden time, so in this great debate," Dr. Green had been an "Athanasius against the world." "And so today this Church of ours," he continued, "out of its loving heart, sends forth a greeting to the man who has strengthened her hold upon the Bible and has thus given validity to her immortal hope and to her mission of salvation in the name of Christ."[16] William M. McPheeters of Columbia Theological Seminary spoke on behalf of sister churches, and Willis J. Beecher of Auburn Seminary for sister seminaries. President Ethelbert Warfield of Lafayette College spoke for Princeton College, Green's *alma mater*, and Henry M. Alexander, the son of Archibald Alexander, represented the trustees of Princeton College. Howard Osgood of Rochester Theological Seminary spoke for the members of the Old Testament Revision Committee, of which Dr. Green was chairman.

On a table at the front of the hall was a pile—about two feet high—of letters from institutions and individuals in America and Europe. The Princeton Seminary faculty expressed their "profound respect and warm affection" for their colleague. The students wrote of Dr. Green's "warm personal interest" in them and "his simple, right life, his humble piety and Christian walk." The faculty of Princeton College praised his eminent scholarship and "his intelligent reverence for the Holy Scriptures." The result, they said, was that he had not "disturbed the faith of the unlearned, while commanding the respect of scholars." New College, Edinburgh, which more than ten years earlier at its tercentenary had conferred on Green the doctorate in divinity, wrote of his "exact learning, devout spirit, and courtesy as a controversialist."

During lunch at the University Hotel there were toasts to Dr. Green and more speeches—describing his boyhood and youth, his life as a seminary student, and his career as a young professor, an established teacher, a learned doctor, and the head of the faculty. Then, rising, the great crowd received the benediction from Arthur J. Mason, professor of divinity from the University of Cambridge, England. The *New York Observer* stated that Princeton's celebration for Dr. Green was an expression "of the faith of the Church that the Bible is the Word of God." "The occasion was great," it said, "the man was greater, but the Bible was the greatest."[17]

* * *

James McCosh resigned as president of Princeton College in the spring of 1888. During his administration the student body had increased from 281 to 603 and the faculty expanded from 17 to 40. McCosh "aggressively recruited" new faculty "from outside Princeton, Presbyterianism, and even the country." He recommended that the board of trustees "take at times an instructor belonging to another evangelical denomination, provided he is very eminent in his department. This will not impair but rather strengthen our Presbyterianism," he said. The cautious trustees countered with a preference for alumni, for teaching ability, and, as far as possible, for "members of the Presbyterian Church, or of those denominations closely allied to it, the Reformed Dutch and the Congregational." Thirteen of the seventeen faculty appointments made between 1868 and 1880 had no previous affiliation with Princeton College or Princeton Seminary, and several were not Presbyterian. Fifteen of McCosh's last twenty-three appointments, however, were alumni of the college. McCosh introduced new courses at Princeton and a limited elective system. Beginning with the academic year 1869–70, four subjects—modern languages, Latin, mathematics, and Greek—were offered, of which the students could choose two. He strengthened the science department, adding advanced laboratory sessions in chemistry and museum work in biology and paleontology. In 1873 he established the Green School of Science. Its three-year bachelor of science degree concentrated in science and mathematics but also included English, history, French, and German. To encourage academic excellence McCosh created numerous prizes and competitive fellowships.[18]

During Dr. McCosh's presidency fourteen new buildings were added to the campus. McCosh, it was said, "found Princeton brick, and left it marble." Ornate towers, steep roofs set off by varicolored slate, and Romanesque doors and windows joined the Early American architectural traditions of Nassau Hall and other older buildings. Included among the new buildings was a gymnasium and a well-lighted and well-heated classroom building, Dickinson Hall. McCosh often said, "I never ask anyone for a gift for my college. I just take him out and, pointing, say 'That is the place for a new building,' and somehow it comes." On more than one occasion, however, he needed help from his wife. A story is told that she and her husband went to Princeton Junction to meet the train bringing Andrew Carnegie to the campus. Carnegie greeted the president, "Dr. McCosh, for a long time I've been much interested in Princeton." Isabella answered, "Indeed, Mr. Carnegie, thus far we have seen no financial evidence of it."[19]

Dr. and Mrs. McCosh lived in "Prospect," the Florentine-style campus mansion completed in 1849. They launched an ambitious program of planting that created the beautiful grounds around the president's house, which McCosh compared to Eden. Every year the McCoshes entertained each of the undergraduate classes and a host of visitors. On these occasions McCosh "survived while Isabella shone." He would greet the students at the door saying, "Glad to see you, sir; hope you're well, sir. There's Mrs. McCosh."[20]

Dr. McCosh always shared credit for his many accomplishments with Mrs. McCosh. "She advised and assisted me in all my work," he said. Isabella McCosh brought to Princeton the skills learned from her illustrious father-physician. She was Princeton's unofficial nurse, the only "medical presence" on the campus. No student went through Princeton without the benefit of her kindness and care. Each morning she received from the proctor's office the names of sick students, and soon there would be a gentle knock on their door and a kind "May I come in?"[21]

James McCosh's quick temper and immense pride were checked by Isabella's wit and wisdom. When he saw his way to a course of action he stubbornly claimed that "it's the will of God." To which she sometimes replied, "Indeed, I'll be thinking it's the will of James McCosh." Once, when McCosh was late in years, he expressed disappointment in a recently completed portrait of him. He scoffed at the picture, saying, "It makes me look as though I had no teeth." Isabella answered, "James, you hae non an' it's a fine picture."[22]

"The best thing that Dr. McCosh brought to Princeton was himself," wrote one of the college students; "he had an inspiring personality and was a great teacher." He was "perfectly helpless in the face of disorder" and lacked a sense of humor, the student added, but everyone had a genuine appreciation for "his real greatness." When the senior class heard of Dr. McCosh's plans to resign they petitioned the trustees to extend the date of his administration to their graduation so that his signature might appear on their diplomas. Dr. McCosh's colleagues respected and admired him. "He knew what he believed and why he believed it," one wrote, "and he taught it with a moral earnestness that enforced attention. He was so honest, so unselfish, so anxious to see the truth and have others see it, that men had to listen."[23]

Dr. McCosh's 1882 article on the "Scottish Philosophy, as Contrasted with the German" began with a paragraph describing the typical Scot—and undoubtedly Dr. McCosh himself!

It is not very difficult to recognize a Scotchman wherever you happen to meet with him. He has stout, bony limbs, and stands well upon his feet; he is canny, that is, cautious, otherwise he would not be a Scotchman; but he is considerably independent, and can resist attack, his motto being *Nemo me impune lacessit* (no one provokes me with impunity); he is firm, not to say obstinate, especially if he is from the Highlands, whose rocks and mountains he takes as models; he boasts that his ancestors could not be conquered even by the Romans, when they subdued all other people of Europe and western Asia—except the Arabs. He is naturally quiet and submissive to circumstances, but is capable of being roused, like the

Yankee, whom he somewhat resembles, into intense enthusiasm, as has been shown in his contests with England, and generally in his fights for the independence of his country and of his church. He uses a softer, broader speech than the English, coming more from the mouth and less from the throat; and he can make his meaning clear and carry it into practical effect. I mention these things because no man can understand the Scottish philosophy without knowing the Scottish character, of which it is a reflection and a picture.[24]

Dr. McCosh, "probably the most distinguished philosopher of his generation in America," championed the old Scottish Common Sense Realism. His last major philosophical work, published in 1889 as *First and Fundamental Truths,* reiterated the basic principles of the Scottish philosophy at a time when American academics were abandoning it for evolutionary, developmental, and historicist ideas. But McCosh "maintained that we have immediate knowledge of the not-self; and was a pronounced believer in mind and matter," one of his colleagues said. "He rejected all relativity of knowledge, no matter how disguised, as being the prolific mother of agnosticism." He had "a kind of *phobia* for all idealistic or phenomenalistic theories," another colleague said, "and was wont to huddle them together and smite them all with a somewhat indiscriminate slaughter." The possibility of careful thought leading to valid truth, to James McCosh, was the foundation for everything. "The function of mind is to know things," McCosh insisted, "and to know them as they are." One of his recurring phrases was that "the human mind is so constituted"—that is, there are "regulative laws and principles guiding the mind." The mind is, therefore, designed to know truth, and the objective world is real and available to the mind through the senses. Dr. McCosh, of course, recognized that human knowledge was limited and imperfect, but he believed that it could be correct "so far as it goes." The last time he stood in the chapel pulpit he opened the Bible to a favorite passage, I Corinthians 13. As he reached the sentence "We know in part," he paused. His face brightened as he condensed his entire philosophy into a single characteristic utterance. "We know in part," he said, *"but we know!"*[25]

While Dr. McCosh worked energetically to increase the academic reputation of Princeton College he also endeavored to maintain its evangelical Christianity. He wrote to William Scott, a Princeton graduate whom he had encouraged to study at Heidelberg University, about the possibility of Scott's returning to Princeton to teach: "You are aware that the Trustees and all your friends here are resolute in keeping the College a religious one. You have passed through various scenes since you left us. . . . If a man has the root in him he will only be strengthened in the faith by such an experience. It will be profitable to me to find how you have stood all this."[26]

Dr. McCosh prayed for the students, helped them in their Christian walk, and encouraged the revivals that, to his great delight, came from time to time to the campus. Students were required to attend church services and prayer meetings, although Dr. McCosh moved the morning prayers to 8:15— after breakfast! Proud of having taken a costly stand on doctrine at the Disruption of the Scottish church in 1843, the Princeton president insisted that definite Christian theology should undergird the teaching of the college. Although he believed that a properly stated and limited view of evolution was scriptural and therefore permissible, he took a strong stand against the higher critical views of the Bible.

In 1885 Dr. McCosh met President Charles Eliot of Harvard in a gentlemanly debate in New York City concerning the future of America's colleges. Eliot argued for virtually total curricular freedom for undergraduates, and McCosh—who had himself introduced the elective idea at Princeton—countered that freedom must always exist within limits. McCosh was particularly alarmed that the extreme application of the new approach could lead to a student's earning a degree without any study of ethics and religion. He ended his presentation by suggesting that a second debate be held about the place of religion in colleges. On a stormy evening in February 1886 the two presidents met again before a large crowd including many newspaper reporters. Dr. Eliot argued for a nonsectarian approach to education that would unite all people against materialism and hedonism. Dr. McCosh countered that it did not make sense to say that because of alleged sectarianism one of the greatest forces in the shaping of modern civilization should be excluded from higher education. He suggested that at places like Harvard the motto over the gates should read "All knowledge imparted here except religious." Religion that is merely tolerated will soon come to be regarded as antiquated superstition, McCosh asserted, and agnosticism will flourish. Students needed religious answers to their questions—especially the question "Is life worth living?"—and Harvard students were wrestling with such questions, McCosh suggested, whether their president knew it or not. Eliot responded by stating that he too believed that religion should be inculcated in a college setting, but a "cosmic religion" found in the phrases "In him we live and move and have our being" and "Beneath are the everlasting arms." Dr. McCosh objected that such a religion was far too vague and ineffective to assist college students in the most important search of their lives.

Dr. McCosh, an impressive president who had the respect of his students and faculty, was able to keep things in line at Princeton by his personal views and oversight. But the days of such control were numbered. Most other major American colleges—like Princeton founded with strong Protestant Christian commitments—had moved more rapidly toward secularization. Specialization replaced the classical curriculum, and academic freedom replaced the constraints of doctrinal creeds. State governments and wealthy industrialists now far outpaced the churches as major contributors to higher education.[27]

McCosh's Princeton did not escape these pressures, and signs of change were evident. A later student, novelist F. Scott Fitzgerald, would write that the Princeton University he "knew and belonged to grew up from President McCosh's great shadow in the seventies." It is to Dr. McCosh, the *New York Tribune* stated, "more than any other man in its history," that Princeton "owes the reputation which it has today as a broad, unsectarian, progressive institution of learning." To James McCosh this would have been a bittersweet compliment. He would have rejoiced in the advance of Princeton's reputation in the world of learning, but he would have mourned deeply the eventual passing of its old heritage of evangelical Christianity.[28]

*   *   *

When McCosh retired, the more conservative trustees of the college promoted Princeton Seminary's Francis Landey Patton to be the next president. Others—who wanted to end the succession of Presbyterian ministers as presidents and create a "new" Princeton—opposed Patton. Some students feared that they would be "admonished, sermonized, disciplined after John Knox fashion." Some of the alumni considered Patton—the chief prosecutor in the David Swing heresy trial—a "narrow-minded bigot." Others preferred an experienced administrator to a preacher-teacher. Still others objected that Patton had not been born in the United States. Dr. Patton soon won many of his opponents by his charm and marvelous ability as a speaker, to which his rasping delivery somehow added force. On March 15, 1888, he addressed the New York alumni in an atmosphere of cold hostility. Taking up their objections one by one without appearing to do so, he answered them skillfully. "When I think of Witherspoon and McCosh," he said, "I am compelled to believe that there is more joy among the alumni over the one president who is naturalized than over the ninety and nine who need no naturalization." Before Dr. Patton had finished he had captured the gathering, and even his greatest critics were standing on tables waving napkins and yelling in a frenzy of enthusiasm.[29]

Already a familiar sight on the campus—with his poke collar, white lawn tie, and black frock coat—the new president committed himself to the Princeton ideal of science and religion. "We shall not be afraid to open our eyes in the presence of nature," he said, "nor ashamed to close them in the presence of God." He was determined to keep Princeton "a Christian college." This meant, Patton said, that if a student "went to his church on Sunday, on Monday he would not be taught a philosophy which would undermine his faith."[30]

*   *   *

After his retirement James McCosh continued to live in Princeton. His successor said that Dr. McCosh "was more

[165]

than a model President. He was a model ex-President." He taught some classes and maintained a lively interest in the college, but he never interfered with the new administration. McCosh loved to walk—in the town, out in the country, and especially on the campus under the elms and along the path that soon became known as McCosh Walk. The students watched as the grand old man would stop and stand for a long time; they concluded that he was lost in thought, trying to unravel some difficult philosophical problem. Then McCosh would strike his cane on the ground and move on, and they knew that the problem was solved! Well into his seventies, he walked as much as ten miles a day; but gradually the distance shortened. Dr. McCosh dearly loved Princeton. He wrote, near his death, that if he were permitted to come back from the other world to this he would want to visit "these scenes" so dear to him and once again see "the tribes on a morning go up to the house of God in companies." He died on November 16, 1894. The news quickly swept the campus, "and the students whom he never taught, but who loved him, rang the bell at Nassau Hall to tell Princeton that Dr. McCosh was dead."[31]

Dr. Patton gave the college's baccalaureate sermon in Marquand Chapel on June 9, 1895. It was a tribute to James McCosh. "He was a great man: and he was a good man," Patton said:

Eager as he was for the material and intellectual advancement of the college, he thought even more of its moral and religious tone. He was an earnest and able preacher: and his trumpet gave no uncertain sound. Alike in speculative philosophy and in practical morals he was always on the Christian side. He never stood in a doubtful attitude towards the Gospel and never spoke a word that would compromise its truths. So that when I think of his long career and what he did and how he lived, I am reminded of the apostle who was so consciously devoted to the service of the Gospel that he could not conceive himself as under any circumstances doing anything that would hinder it; and who said in the words that I have placed at the beginning of this discourse: "We can do nothing against the truth, but for the truth" (*II Cor.* 13:8).[32]

The seminary respected and honored Dr. McCosh and claimed him as a friend and ally. Although the college and seminary had always been separate institutions, they "were joined in spirit . . . through interlocking boards, shared concerns, and their common location." John DeWitt, Princeton Seminary's professor of church history, wrote that Dr. McCosh's administration, although "loyal to the foundation and history of the college," was "the most successful, and in important respects the greatest administration the college has enjoyed." Theodore Cuyler, Princeton Seminary graduate and Brooklyn pastor, praised McCosh as "a complete combination of philosopher, theologian, preacher, scholar, and college president all rolled into one!" "The best qualities of his predecessors were combined in him," Cuyler added—the "metaphysical acumen" of Jonathan Edwards, the "fervor" of Samuel Davies, and the "kindness of heart" of John Maclean. B. B. Warfield wrote that Dr. McCosh was "a devoted pastor, a preacher of simplicity and power, an impressive teacher, a college president great in all the qualities requisite to success in that complicated sphere, a writer of a strikingly attractive English style: but he was above all things a great religious philosopher."[33]

In a memorial note in *The Presbyterian and Reformed Review* Dr. Warfield paid tribute to McCosh, who died at Princeton on the evening of Friday, November 16, and to William Shedd, who died a few hours later on Saturday morning in New York City. "Thus nearly together," Warfield wrote, "passed into their reward two of the greatest Presbyterians of our generation. Each had been given a message to deliver, and had delivered it. Each had had committed to him a charge to keep, and had kept it. Each had been called upon to champion the cause of truth against serious odds, and had not shunned the task." Warfield added: "There is a realm of truth, and these men set themselves for its defense; and it is in part due to them that we still possess it as our heritage. We can never estimate the greatness of this possession; but at least

'We have a voice, with which to pay the debt
Of boundless love and reverence and regret
To those great men who fought, and kept it ours—
And keep it ours, O God!'"[34]

[167]

*   *   *

In the summer of 1896 four members of the Princeton College track team, the first college athletes to represent the United States abroad, sailed for Athens to take part in the revival of the ancient Olympic games. That October, during the soft days of an Indian summer, Princeton College—still officially the College of New Jersey—celebrated its sesqui-centennial. The lovely campus trees—gentle elms, tall tulip trees, and scarlet maples—were at their best, and Virginia creepers clothed the old walls with festive purple. For a week distinguished professors from Dublin, Göttingen, Cambridge, Leipzig, Utrecht, Edinburgh, and other European universities gave lectures in Alexander Hall on the college campus.

At dawn on the morning of Tuesday, October 20, the college and town were alive with excitement. Every store on Nassau Street was decorated. The American flag waved beside pennants of orange and black; the horses wore orange ribbons in their manes. Spanning the street at one end was an arch with the inscription "From the Town to the University." At 10:30 in the morning an academic procession left Marquand Chapel and marched across the campus to Alexander Hall. Leading were President Patton and Charles E. Green of the board of trustees. Delegates, trustees, and faculty followed—crimson, orange, green, white, and purple of academic dress glistening in the sunlight. When all had been seated Dr. Patton delivered the sermon, "Religion and the University." He reminded his audience—one of the most distinguished, people said, ever assembled in America—that "the fathers" of Princeton College had "laid the foundations deep and strong." "It is ours to build thereon," he added. "Let us take heed how we build. Let us especially be careful not to undo the work already done: for other foundation can no man lay than that is laid, which is Jesus Christ."[35]

In the afternoon, after a welcome address to the visiting delegates, President Eliot of Harvard responded for the American universities and Professor J. J. Thomson of

Cambridge, for the European universities. There were scores of congratulatory letters from colleges and universities around the world, including one from the University of Edinburgh that read: "We have ever fondly regarded the College of New Jersey as a near Scottish cousin." In the evening, a concert orchestra played Schubert's *Unfinished Symphony* and Brahms's *Academic Festival Overture.*

The next morning Henry Van Dyke, the literary-minded pastor of Brick Presbyterian Church of New York City, delivered his anniversary ode, *The Builders.* The long poem composed for the occasion included these lines:

> Fair Harvard's earliest beacon tower had shone;
> Then Yale was lighted, and an answering ray
> Flashed from the meadows by New Haven Bay.
> But deeper spread the forest, and more dark,
> Where first Neshaminy received the spark
> Of sacred learning to its frail abode,
> And nursed the holy fire until it glowed.
> Thine was the courage, thine the larger look
> That raised yon taper from its humble nook.
> Thine was the hope and thine the stronger will
> That built the beacon here on Princeton hill.

The reading of the poem was followed by an eloquent speech, "Princeton in the Nation's Service," by Professor Woodrow Wilson. In the afternoon the Princeton football team defeated the University of Virginia 48 to 0. The Virginia team, it was reported, "played a manful game and were roundly applauded." That evening a torchlight procession began at the cannon. Nassau Hall was outlined in hundreds of electric lights, and the entire campus was decorated with orange-colored Chinese lanterns.

The third day of the celebration, October 22, was the 150th birthday of the college. An excited, expectant crowd filled Alexander Hall, where the president of the United States sat on the platform surrounded by a group of important guests. There was deep silence as President Patton rose. "It is my pleasure," he said, "for expression of which I have no equivalent in words, to say that the wishes of the alumni have at last been fully realized; to say that the faculty, trustees and alumni stand together, and, as with the voice of one man, give hearty approval. . . . It is my great pleasure to say that from this moment what heretofore for one hundred and fifty years has been known as the College of New Jersey shall in all future time be known as Princeton University." This announcement was received with uproarious applause interspersed with cheers for "Princeton University!"

10

Princeton *Contra Mundum*

I may be wrong; but it seems to me that American Christianity is about to pass through a severe ordeal. It may be a ten years' conflict, it may be a thirty years' war; but it is a conflict in which all Christian churches are concerned. The war will come. The Presbyterian Church must take part in it; and Princeton, unless her glory is departed, must lead the van in the great fight for fundamental Christianity.

FRANCIS LANDEY PATTON

DURING the 1890s Mercer Street, which bisected the seminary campus, was graded and paved for the first time. Electricity replaced gas lighting, and the first telephone on the campus was installed in the library. A four-story brownstone dormitory—designed so that each suite of rooms received sunlight during some part of the day—was built on the site of an old wooden gymnasium at the seminary. Construction costs, amounting to $106,200, came from the $300,000 bequest of Mrs. Robert L. Stuart.[1] The new dormitory was named Hodge Hall, the old seminary building was now called Alexander Hall, and the chapel, Miller Chapel—appropriate honors to the first three Princeton professors. By the end of the century the assets of the seminary totaled over $2 million, with a yearly income from endowment of $80,000. Funds had been established to benefit the library, to finance one hundred scholarships, to endow the first lectureship—initially financed by and named for Levi P. Stone (a director from 1869 to 1884 and trustee from 1875 to 1884)—and to begin the Students' Lectureship on Missions.

Students were attracted by Princeton's great history and strong faculty, as enrollment increased from 140 in 1885 to 250 in 1895. The 97 members of the class of 1894 came from twenty states and ten foreign countries. Twenty students were from Pennsylvania; others came from New Hampshire, Georgia, Texas, California, and other states. Eleven students were from Ireland and seven from Canada, with England,

[173]

Scotland, India, Persia, Australia, Italy, Japan, and Turkey also represented. William Alfred Byrd of Winnsboro, South Carolina, the one African American of the class of 1894, became an honor student and treasurer of his class.[2]

During the early period of the seminary's history the academic progress of the students was determined by their attendance records and oral examinations—conducted by a committee of the directors. As enrollment increased, written examinations were introduced and, by the 1890s, had completely replaced the oral presentations. By 1894, however, the number of written examinations overwhelmed the directors, and they requested a review of only those that the faculty considered unsatisfactory.

For many years those students who completed the three-year program and successfully passed the examinations received a certificate signed by the professors. Following approval by the New Jersey legislature in 1897 for seminaries to grant degrees, Princeton began to award the bachelor of divinity degree. Students left the seminary not only with a certificate or, later, a degree and the professors' blessing, but also with a "suit of broadcloth, called a preacher's suit"— provided by the generosity of the women of the Fifth Avenue Presbyterian Church in New York City.[3]

*   *   *

At the beginning of the term in September 1896 B. B. Warfield addressed the seminary community on "Christian Supernaturalism." The starting point of the liberals, Warfield asserted, was unbelief in the supernatural, and their goal was the creation of a naturalistic development of biblical religion in both the Old and New Testaments. These theologians no longer constructed doctrines on the basis of what the Scriptures teach, Warfield said, but according to what it is reasonable to suppose. Dr. Warfield insisted that Christians must hold to "supernaturalism" and described five areas in which it was particularly essential: "the supernatural fact" that God is; "the supernatural act" of God's creation; "the supernatural redemption" of the Divine Redeemer, the God-Man; "the supernatural revelation" of God's setting forth the

[174]

meaning of the "great series of redemptive acts" in the Bible; and "the supernatural salvation" in which redemption is applied by the Holy Spirit.[4]

On November 8, 1897, Dr. Warfield made one of his rare trips from Princeton to speak to the Presbytery of New York on the occasion of the celebration of the 250th anniversary of the completion of the Westminster Standards. He told the presbyters:

These precious documents appeal to us as but the embodiment in fitly chosen language of the pure gospel of the grace of God [and] in these forms of words we possess the most complete, the most fully elaborated and carefully guarded, the most perfect, the most vital expression that has ever been framed by the hand of men, of all that enters into what we call evangelical religion, and of all that must be safeguarded if evangelical religion is to persist in the world.

Warfield said that the Puritan divines who drew up the Westminster documents—taught by 150 years of Reformation thinking and "purified and refined" by faithfulness in suffering—embodied "the gospel of the grace of God with a carefulness, a purity, and an exactness never elsewhere achieved." We can never hope to surpass their work, Warfield told the presbytery that five years earlier had acquitted Dr. Briggs; and we will "lightly lose or rashly cast" it from us only when "our grasp upon evangelical religion becomes weak or our love for it grows cold." "To read over a chapter or two of the Westminster Confession," he told the presbyters, "gives one fresh from the obscurities and confusions of much modern theological discussion a mental feeling very nearly akin to the physical sensation of washing one's hands and face after a hot hour's work." The statements of the Westminster divines were not speculative theology, Dr. Warfield stated, but "the pulsations of great hearts heaving in emotion." Like all the creeds, they were given to the church "not by philosophers but by the shepherds of the flocks, who loved the sheep." These "shepherds" not only "[knew] what God is; they [knew] God," the Princeton professor added, "and they make their readers know Him."[5]

*   *   *

In 1898 Princeton University invited Abraham Kuyper—the famous Dutch Calvinist theologian, writer, editor, educator, and political leader—to come to America to receive an honorary doctor of laws degree.

Kuyper was born in Massluis, Netherlands, in 1837. He graduated from Leiden University, from which he also received his doctorate in theology in 1863. "I entered the university a young man of orthodox faith," he later wrote, "but I had not been in the school more than a year and a half before my thought processes had been transformed into the starkest intellectual rationalism." But before long another change came. It was not the result of a momentary crisis or the conclusion of long, painstaking intellectual research, but through "a chain of gripping life experiences." It was the finding of some lost books, the reading of a novel, and the teaching of simple Christian people that turned Kuyper's life in another direction. The books were scarce copies of the works of John a Lasco, the great Polish reformer of the sixteenth century. For a prize offered by the University of Groningen, Kuyper planned to write an essay comparing John Calvin's and John a Lasco's views of the church. When he despaired of locating the books he needed, Kuyper was sent to a minister in Haarlem who, unknown to himself, had among his own books "a collection of Lasciana richer than any library of Europe possessed." This made a profound and lasting impression on Kuyper; he could no longer deny that there was such a thing as "the finger of God." The 1853 novel *The Heir of Redclyffe* by the English writer Charlotte M. Yonge further altered Kuyper's outlook. "What I lived through in my soul in that moment I fully understood only later," Kuyper wrote, "yet from that hour, after that moment, I scorned what I formerly esteemed, and I sought what I once dared to despise." Kuyper served for several years as a minister of a church in the small fishing village of Beesd where the people clung tenaciously to their Reformed convictions. Their pastor soon felt in his soul that he had to choose. He must set himself sharply against them, or he must go with them all the way until "full sovereign grace," as they expressed it, was acknowledged in his life. He wrote that the faithful loyalty of the people became "a blessing to my heart, the rise of the morning star of my life. I had been apprehended, but I had not yet found the Word of reconciliation. In their simple language they brought me this in the absolute form in which alone my soul can rest. I discovered that the Holy Scripture does not only cause us to find justification by faith, but also discloses the foundation of all human life, the holy ordinances which must govern all human existence in Society and State."

In 1870 Abraham Kuyper moved to a popular pulpit in Amsterdam and gained a national forum in the daily newspaper *De Standaard,* which he edited. He established a political party, founded the Free University in Amsterdam, and led a movement from the state church in 1886 into the independent Gereformeerde Kerken. Claiming that he too had "dreamed the dream of modernism," Kuyper fought against religious and secular liberalism, which were, he insisted, "corrosive of justice and equity as much as of Christian faith." Princeton had followed Kuyper's work with interest and appreciation. Dr. Warfield wrote, "Our own days have seen a new exhibition" of Calvinism's power "to awake to new life in Holland, through the steady testimony of the Christian Reformed Church and the great leadership of Dr. Kuyper."[6]

While he was in Princeton in October 1898 Abraham Kuyper delivered the L. P. Stone Lectures in the seminary chapel. Faculty, students, and visitors watched with great interest as Dr. Kuyper rose to speak. They saw a remarkably handsome man in his early sixties, with slightly graying hair and penetrating eyes beneath thick, shaggy brows. He spoke in a decisive and authoritative tone—his voice resonant and clear, his eyes glowing at times with flashes of burning energy. Kuyper told the Princetonians that "a traveler from the old European Continent, disembarking on the shore of this New World, feels as the Psalmist says, that 'his thoughts crowd upon him like a multitude.'" He compared the "many divine potencies" of America with the "longer historical past" of Europe. "You are yet in your Springtide," he said; "we are passing through our Fall—and has not the harvest of Autumn an enchantment of its own?" The old world and the new are linked, Kuyper added, "by virtue of our common origin" and even more by our "Christian name." "That crown is our common heritage," he said.

It was not from Greece or Rome that the regeneration of human life came forth—that mighty metamorphosis dates from Bethlehem and Golgotha; and if the Reformation, in a still more special sense, claims the love of our hearts, it is because it has dispelled the clouds of sacerdotalism, and has unveiled again to fullest view the glories of the Cross. But, in deadly opposition to this Christian element, against the very Christian name, and against its salutiferous influence in every sphere of life, the storm of Modernism has now arisen with violent intensity.

Abraham Kuyper went on to describe how "two *life systems* are wrestling with one another, in mortal combat."

Modernism is bound to build a world of its own from the data of the natural man, and to construct man himself from the data of nature; while, on the other hand, all those who reverently bend the knee to Christ and worship Him as the Son of the living God, and God himself, are bent upon saving the "Christian heritage." This is *the* struggle in Europe, this is *the* struggle in America, and this also, is the struggle for principles in which my own country is engaged, and in which I myself have been spending all my energy for nearly forty years.

Opposed to "the vast energy" of the "all-embracing life-system" of "Modernism," Kuyper proposed to take his stand in a "life-system of equally comprehensive and far-reaching power"—Calvinism. "In Calvinism my heart has found rest," he told the Princetonians.

From Calvinism have I drawn the inspiration, firmly and resolutely to take my stand in the thick of this great conflict of principles. And therefore, when I was invited most honorably by your Faculty to give the Stone-Lectures here this year, I could not hesitate a moment as to my choice of subject. Calvinism, as the only decisive, lawful, and consistent defense for Protestant nations against encroaching, and overwhelming Modernism—this of itself was bound to be my theme.

Dr. Kuyper's first lecture on "Calvinism as a Life-System" was followed by lectures on Calvinism and religion, politics, science, and art. He ended his last lecture, "Calvinism and the Future," with the words:

Now the period in which we are living at present is surely at a low ebb religiously. Unless God send forth His Spirit, there will be no turn, and fearfully rapid will be the descent of the waters. But you remember the Aeolian Harp, which men were wont to place outside their casement, that the breeze might wake its music into life. Until the wind blew, the harp remained silent, while, again even though the wind rose, if the harp did not lie in readiness, a rustling of the breeze might be heard, but not a single note of ethereal music delighted the ear. Now, let Calvinism be nothing but such an Aeolian Harp—absolutely powerless, as it is, without the quickening Spirit of God—still we feel it our God-given duty to keep our harp, its strings tuned aright, ready in the window of God's Holy Zion, awaiting the breath of the Spirit.[7]

B. B. Warfield wrote that Abraham Kuyper was "one of our own prophets to whose message we have a certain right" and a "dear friend charged in a sense with care for our welfare." Warfield read the works of Kuyper in Dutch and provided reviews of them for American readers. In his introduction to the English translation of Kuyper's *Encyclopedia of Sacred Theology*, Warfield praised "the depth of [Dr. Kuyper's] insight, the breadth of his outlook, the thoroughness of his method, the comprehensiveness of his survey, the intensity of his conviction, the eloquence of his language, the directness of his style, the pith and wealth of his illustrations, the force, completeness, winningness of his presentation." In an introductory note to the English translation of Kuyper's *Work of the Holy Spirit*, Warfield stated that the author brought together the different aspects of the doctrine of the Holy Spirit "with a systematizing genius that is very rare," and presented it "with a penetrating appreciation of its meaning and a richness of apprehension of its relations that is exceedingly illuminating."[8]

Abraham Kuyper's emphasis on a world view infused with his "vision of reforming all culture" under Christ impressed and pleased Princeton. "In the total expanse of human life," Kuyper often said, "there is not a single square inch of which Christ, who alone is sovereign, does not declare, 'That is mine!'" Warfield praised Kuyper and his colleague Herman Bavinck for their "wide-minded conception of the mission of Christianity in the world." Warfield too taught that the Reformed world view was one that centers in the vision of God in his glory and determines to render to God his rights in every sphere of human life. He urged Christians to work toward "the reformation of the world after the plan of God and its gradual transmutation into his Kingdom in which his will shall be done even as in heaven." God was, Warfield insisted, "saving the world and not merely one individual here and there out of the world." He agreed with Kuyper that neither art, science, literature, or politics fell outside the concern of Christian influence. Rather, Christians were called to consecrate all of life to the cause of Christ. William Brenton Greene stressed the same theme when he wrote, "Christ's kingdom means his dominion in all spheres and over all relationships. He 'shall reign until he has put all things under his feet' (*I Cor.* 15:27). 'Every thought even must be brought into captivity to the obedience of him' (*II Cor.* 10:5). Therefore, his followers must live in the world and come into relation to its interests and take part in its business that Christ may be recognized as 'Lord of all.' It is for a mission which is as broad and as comprehensive as the world that he has called them out of the world."[9]

B. B. Warfield and the Princetonians, however, were baffled by Dr. Kuyper's apologetical method. Kuyper held that an absolute antithesis exists in all of life between the believer and unbeliever—an antithesis between Christian thought, which recognizes God's sovereignty over all creation, and non-Christian thought, which proceeds on the basis of human autonomy. Working from differing starting points and holding differing assumptions, Christians and non-Christians, Dr. Kuyper believed, were not working on different parts of the same building but on different buildings. Just as there are "two kinds of people," Kuyper maintained, there are "two kinds of science." He therefore called for an approach that would array "*principle . . .* against *principle.*" Dr. Kuyper, in his first lecture at Princeton, asserted that in the great battle with modernism, apologetics had not advanced the Christian cause "one single step." Dr. Warfield expected a lack of concern for apologetics from rationalists and mystics, but he was dismayed when he heard similar ideas from "heroes of the faith" like Abraham Kuyper, "who depreciate apologetics because they feel no need of 'reason' to ground a faith which they are sure they have received immediately from God." Dr. Kuyper, Warfield admitted, did not "abolish apologetics altogether," but one has to search for it before he finds it in Kuyper's *Principles of Sacred Theology.* "And when he finds it, he discovers that its function is confined closely, we might almost say jealously, to the narrow task of defending developed Christianity against philosophy, falsely so called."[10]

Caspar Wistar Hodge Jr., who as a seminary student heard Dr. Kuyper's Stone Lectures, later summarized the Princeton understanding of the apologetic of Abraham Kuyper and Herman Bavinck. Their view, Hodge stated,

is rooted in the deeply evangelical spirit and thorough super-naturalism characteristic of Calvin and all the Reformed theologians. It is due to a deep sense of the effects of sin and of the power of God's grace. They argue that, because saving faith is due to the Witness of the Spirit, and because arguments do not produce the conviction of the Christian, therefore rational grounds of faith may be dispensed with. Apologetics has a secondary place, and is the "fruit" of faith. Bavinck seeks to show that Christian certitude is not the result of Christian experience which really grows out of it, nor of arguments which cannot give absolute certitude or true faith, but that it simply flows from faith itself which springs up in a renewed heart in contact with Christ. Kuyper has fully worked out these principles in his profound discussion of the effects of sin and of regeneration upon our knowledge and upon science. The un-regenerate and the regenerate form two classes, distinct in kind and hence totally removed the one from the other in their intellectual processes and products. The one class is working out a science under the obscuring effects of sin, the other under the illumination of the Spirit in regeneration. No argument can lead from one sphere to the other, hence no arguments for the science of the regenerate can be regarded as universally valid. Apologetics is of secondary importance. It is for the benefit of the Christian and for the purpose of defending Christian faith, and not for the purpose of grounding it or serving under the Spirit's power to produce faith.[11]

In his inaugural address at Princeton B. B. Warfield stated

that "apologetical theology prepares the way for all theology by establishing its necessary presuppositions without which no theology is possible—the existence and essential nature of God, the religious nature of man which enables him to receive a revelation from God, the possibility of a revelation and its actual realization in the Scriptures." Warfield frequently asserted that the Christian faith is a reasonable faith based on good and sufficient evidence, not a "blind and ungrounded faith." In 1903, in an "Introductory Note" to Francis R. Beattie's *Apologetics or the Rational Vindication of Christianity*, Warfield argued that apologetics was vital, since faith is "a form of conviction, and is, therefore, necessarily grounded in evidence." He wrote:

It is the distinction of Christianity that it has come into the world clothed with the mission to *reason* its way to its dominion. Other religions may appeal to the sword, or seek some other way to propagate themselves. Christianity makes its appeal to right reason, and stands out among all religions, therefore, as distinctively "the Apologetic religion." It is solely by reasoning that it has come thus far on its way to its kingship. And it is solely by reasoning that it will put all its enemies under its feet.[12]

Apologetics does not have in itself "the power to make a man a Christian or to conquer the world to Christ," Dr. Warfield acknowledged. "Only the Spirit of Life can communicate life to a dead soul, or can convict the world in respect of sin, and of righteousness, and of judgment." Christians, however, must present the evidence for the truthfulness of Christianity, which to Dr. Warfield was part of the task of preaching the gospel. "For the birth of faith in the soul, it is just as essential that grounds of faith should be present to the mind as that the Giver of faith should act creatively upon the heart," he maintained.[13]

*   *   *

During the last three decades of the nineteenth century there was growing interest among conservative Protestants in the belief that Jesus Christ would return and set up his kingdom before the millennium, or thousand-year period of peace mentioned in Revelation 20. The Princeton theologians were all postmillennialists, holding that Christ would return after the millennium. Charles Hodge set forth in his *Systematic Theology* what he called "the common church doctrine." The "universal diffusion of the Gospel" would lead into a thousand-year period in which Christian truth would dominate the world. Toward the end of the millennium many Jews would be converted to Christ, followed by the appearance of Antichrist and, shortly thereafter, by the personal, visible return of Christ. A. A. Hodge wrote that before the return of Christ the gospel would "exercise an influence over all branches of the human family, immeasurably more extensive and more thoroughly transforming than any it has ever realized in time past. This end is to be gradually attained through the spiritual presence of Christ in the ordinary dispensation of Providence, and ministrations of his church." B. B. Warfield interpreted the apocalyptic biblical prophecies of warfare as pertaining to the battles and victories of the truth of God. Taking the "hint" of Revelation 19 that the sword of victory proceeds "out of the mouth of the conqueror," he concluded that "the conquest is wrought by the spoken word—in short, by the preaching of the Gospel. The day is certainly to come," wrote Warfield, "when the whole world—inclusive of all the Jews and Gentiles alike, then dwelling on the globe—shall know and serve the Lord."[14]

The Princeton professors' attitude toward premillennialism has been described as one of "tolerant dissatisfaction." They criticized the literalism of premillennial interpretation of biblical prophecy. Charles Hodge held that prophecy "makes a general impression with regard to future events . . . while the details remain in obscurity." He believed that premillennialism was a "Jewish doctrine" because it expected a literal earthly kingdom such as the Jews looked for at the time of the first advent. B. B. Warfield asserted that premillennialists "invent a whole unscriptural history of the last things" from the one "obscure passage" of Revelation 20:1–7. The Princetonians believed, however, that eschatological theories were not essential to the system of doctrine of the Westminster Standards—which were, in fact, silent as to the relation of the second coming of Christ to the millennium. Several prominent teachers of premillennialism had some connection with Princeton. The Princeton-trained missionary, seminary professor, and pastor, Samuel H. Kellogg, presented the premillennialist position in the pages of *The Presbyterian Review.* James H. Brookes, who spent a short time as a student at Princeton, published the premillennialist magazine *The Truth.* The Princetonians and the premillennialists shared basic convictions about the truthfulness of the Bible and the dangers of liberalism to the Christian church. As the nineteenth century drew to a close the theologians at Princeton and the popular preachers of the premillennialist movement found themselves allies on the same side of "the dawning theological chasm."[15]

*　　*　　*

William Henry Green died on February 10, 1900. For fifty-three years he had taught at Princeton, seventeen years as the senior professor. One member of the faculty—William Paxton—had been a fellow student with Green at the seminary; the others were his pupils. John D. Davis, who had worked with Dr. Green in the Old Testament department, gave a commemorative address in the seminary chapel on March 27. Dr. Davis said that to William Henry Green fell tие "arduous duty of entering the arenas of higher criticism and religious philosophy, and with the keen weapons of exact scholarship contest[ing] the field in high debate on Biblical literature, history and prophecy." Davis stated that in answer to the critics—who "went over the whole Bible adjusting text and exegesis to the theory"—Dr. Green "introduced no novelty and he founded no school, but he constructed a system out of the Biblical representation." Davis explained:

To the theory of natural development he opposed the conception of an organic revelation. He first of all pointed out the evidence of an organic structure afforded by the harmonious unity which pervades all the parts of Scripture, the definite and intelligible relation in which they stand to each other, and the grand design of the whole. He was able to show that, starting with the law of Moses as the basis, the whole structure of the Old Testament unfolds itself symmetrically along certain lines of development; or, starting with Christ as the end, these lines of development converge in Him, and it now appears that from the beginning Christ was the controlling, forming principle of all.[16]

John Davis claimed that during the last quarter of the nineteenth century "Dr. Green did more than any one man of his time to rally and steady and inspirit the Church under the shock of a sudden and mighty assault on the trustworthiness of the Scriptures." Noting that William Henry Green has been "justly called a great scholar," Dr. Davis added, "We wish to insert one word in that title and shift the emphasis. Dr. Green was a great *Christian* scholar. He who defended the Church's doctrine of the Bible exemplified the Bible's standard of conduct. He made the Church glad. He maintained her doctrines by his scholarship and adorned them by his life." The published booklet containing Davis's tribute included the verse that the Princetonians felt summarized the life and work of their beloved colleague—He "set his heart to seek the law of the Lord, and to do it, and to teach in Israel statutes and judgments."[17]

In 1900 Dr. Davis succeeded his teacher as Helena Professor of Oriental and Old Testament Literature, and James Oscar Boyd, a Green Fellow in Old Testament Literature, was appointed instructor in Old Testament. A graduate of New York University, Boyd studied further at the University of Erlangen in Germany and then at Princeton Seminary.

Also in 1900 George Purves, the Princeton preacher-scholar, resigned his professorship in New Testament to return to the pastorate. When he was a pastor Dr. Purves was sought by the seminaries, and when he became a professor he was besieged by the churches. B. B. Warfield said of him, "He was never more the profoundly instructed scholar than when he stood in the pulpit: he was never more the preacher of righteousness than when he sat in the classroom." During his eight years in Princeton Dr. Purves taught New Testament and preached regularly, serving for a time as pastor of the First Presbyterian Church in Princeton. During 1897 the church experienced "a year of prosperity greater than at any previous time" in its history and credited this to "the very faithful and efficient labors of Dr. Purves." Finally Dr. Purves accepted a call to the Fifth Avenue Presbyterian Church in New York City (once served by James W. Alexander). After a short ministry there of eighteen months he died in 1901, at the age of forty-nine.[18]

Princeton greatly missed Dr. Purves. "He was wont, as was his and our Master and Exemplar," William Brenton Greene said, "so to preach even 'the deep things of God' that 'the common people would hear him gladly.'" Reflecting on the fact that Purves wrote few books, B. B. Warfield commented, "We are, perhaps, prone to overestimate the relative importance of books: *Litera scripta manet.* But the 'winged word' of speech moves the world; and it is better, after all, to form characters than to compile volumes." Warfield said that "for many years to come the Church will be richer in men who know and love the New Testament" because of Dr. Purves's work in the seminary.[19]

During the long illness of William Henry Green, William Paxton had carried many of the duties of senior professor; and after Dr. Green died he fully assumed that role. Dr. Paxton, the only remaining faculty member who had been a student in the seminary during the days of Archibald Alexander and Samuel Miller, taught church government, pastoral theology, and homiletics. He often stressed the necessity for practical spiritual training and was the faculty voice that constantly warned against "scholasticism." He was led, now and again, according to Dr. Warfield, into judgments and expressions that were somewhat extreme; but "what he took his real stand upon was the perfectly sound position that our theological seminaries are primarily training-schools for ministers, and must be kept fundamentally true to this their proper work." The dignified and courtly Paxton was loved and appreciated for his "devotional spirituality." His sermons, his conference talks, and his prayers were effective and often deeply moving. Warfield said, "If there ever was a preacher in the chair of preaching it was Dr. Paxton."[20]

Dr. Paxton retired from active teaching in 1902 but continued to be part of the seminary community. "And so," spoke Dr. Warfield for Princeton, "as he went back and forth to the devotional exercises of the seminary, of which he was a faithful and devout attendant to the end, and as he walked daily through the streets, though his voice was no longer heard in the classroom or pulpit, he was still our teacher and our preacher." On June 4, 1904, Dr. Paxton's eightieth birthday, his seminary colleagues wrote to congratulate him:

You have reached age and distinction in health and strength, and at fourscore years you still stand among us with the harness on. Your kindly face, your courteous manner, your helpful Christian life, together with the gentle presence of the quiet, efficient, godly lady at your side, have been a blessed influence at Princeton; and we are grateful to our Father in heaven that He gave both of you to us.

Dr. Paxton suffered a stroke in November and died two weeks later.[21]

*   *   *

At the turn of the century a new attempt to revise the Westminster Confession of Faith arose suddenly in the Presbyterian church. The 1900 General Assembly appointed a "Committee of Fifteen" to draft amendments to the Confession and to draw up a brief, nontechnical statement of the Reformed faith. B. B. Warfield, who declined an invitation to serve on the committee, wrote, "It is an inexpressible grief" to me to see the church "spending its energies in a vain attempt to lower its testimony to suit the ever-changing sentiment of the world about it."[22]

Once again much of the debate centered around the Confession's third chapter, "Of the Decree of God." In May 1900 Dr. Warfield addressed the issue in *The Presbyterian Banner* with two articles on "The Significance of the Confessional Doctrine of the Decree." He began with the forthright declaration that "the fundamental postulate of what we know as the Calvinistic system is that God is a person, and, as a person, acts in all things purposively." Warfield went on to state that "no . . . Christians possess a clearer or more pervading appreciation of all that enters into the idea of God's character as righteous and holy and good, faithful and loving and gracious than those that bear the name of Calvinists."

[187]

Chapter three of the Confession was necessary, Warfield argued, "to guard the purity of our theism and the surety of our hope of salvation." Warfield's 1901 article "Predestination in the Reformed Confessions" demonstrated how vitally important the doctrine of predestination was to the whole Reformation theology. The great reformers held to predestination, he asserted, because they taught "salvation by the free grace of God alone." When "you teach free grace, absolutely free grace, and mean it," Warfield wrote, "you are a predestinarian."[23]

John DeWitt, Princeton's professor of church history, asserted that successful creed-making periods were ages of faith, whereas the present, he said, was an age of doubt. Francis Patton expressed his mind on the matter when he often said, "If the Presbyterian Church is a Calvinistic Church, as I believe it is, there is no need of revising the Confession of Faith." Geerhardus Vos argued that one of the gravest symptoms of the revision movement was its lack of serious appeal to scriptural authority for the confessional changes it advocated. Dr. Vos had the revision movement in mind when he chose for his address at the opening of the seminary in the fall of 1901 the topic "The Scriptural Doctrine of the Love of God." He warned that the new ideas would lead to "extravagant, un-Calvinistic, unscriptural notions on the subject" and a confusion between God's "general benevolence" and his "special affection" for his people. "The divine love for the elect is different not only in degree but specifically from all the other forms of love," Vos claimed, "because it involves a purpose to save." Whereas in the period of its supremacy orthodoxy did not stress the love of God exclusively as was now the tendency, it did, Vos asserted, in those days appreciate more fully "the infinite complexity and richness of the life of God." Even though "the music of [the older] theology may not always please modern ears, because it seems lacking in sweetness, . . . it ranged over a wider scale and made better harmonies than the popular strains of today."[24]

The General Assembly of 1902—concerned that long doctrinal disputes not be allowed to impede the work of the church—quickly approved and transmitted to the presbyteries eleven overtures dealing with confessional revision—two new chapters entitled "Of the Holy Spirit" and "Of the Love of God and Missions"; a declaratory statement that explained that chapter 3, "Of God's Eternal Decree," was to be interpreted in harmony with the belief that God loves all mankind, and that chapter 10, section 3, which speaks of "elect infants," is not to be regarded as teaching that any who die in infancy are lost; and a number of textual modifications, such as dropping from chapter 25, section 6, the statement that "the Pope of Rome" is "antichrist." All eleven overtures were approved by well over the necessary two-thirds majority of the presbyteries.

Although some saw the revisions of 1903 as "a definite toning down of the Calvinistic emphasis of the Confession of Faith," Dr. Warfield—who had remained in opposition to confessional revision to the end—was surprisingly positive in his judgment of the "revision material."[25] The "Declaratory Statement," in Warfield's opinion, "reaffirmed" while it "explained" the third chapter. It was, he wrote, "the common Calvinistic response" to Arminian attacks on the doctrine of God's decree and defended it with quotations from Calvin, Turretin, Edwards, the Puritans, the Hodges, Shedd, and Southern Presbyterian theologians. In its interpretation of chapter 10, section 3, the "Declaratory Statement" read that it "is not to be regarded as teaching that any who die in infancy are lost. We believe that all dying in infancy are included in the election of grace." Dr. Warfield believed that this statement went beyond the teaching of the Confession, which confined itself "strictly to the way in which dying infants are saved, without any implication whatever as to the number of them that are saved." However, the "Declaratory Statement" Warfield believed to be "logically altogether hospitable" to Calvinism. It had been the teaching, he claimed, of "some of the best of Calvinists, and for the last hundred years by practically all Calvinists."[26]

Two new chapters were added to the Confession of Faith— chapter 34 ("Of the Holy Spirit") and chapter 35 ("Of the Love of God, and Missions"). Chapter 34, Warfield commented, is "a compact summary of the ordinary Calvinistic doctrine of the Holy Spirit and his work." The first section "merely repeats what the Confession has already said," but section two is largely new and gives "a comprehensive statement of [the] great and distinctively Calvinistic doctrine" of common grace. The third section of the new chapter "evinces no great firmness or precision of touch" but manages, "even in its somewhat bungling way, to set forth . . . a very tolerable account of the progressive stages through which (in the Calvinistic view) a sinner passes as he is brought into the experience of salvation by the Holy Spirit." Although the fourth section of the new chapter mainly repeated statements already found in the Confession, Warfield believed that "the doctrine of the work of the Holy Spirit in the Church" was stated in it "comprehensively, and not without point." He criticized the title of chapter 35—"Of the Love of God and Missions"—"as not perfectly appropriate to its contents. It is a development of the doctrine of 'the Gospel,'" he wrote, "which it very properly represents as originating in and proclaiming the love of God, and as issuing in missions." The new chapter 35, in Warfield's opinion, made "a substantial addition to the doctrinal definitions of the Confession" by incorporating into the Confession "a rather full exposition of the doctrine of the External Call, sufficiently clear, calmly stated, and thoroughly sound."[27]

Dr. Warfield believed that the omission in chapter 22, section 3 (of the single sentence "Yet it is a sin to refuse an oath touching anything that is good and just, being imposed by lawful authority") did not deny what the Confession had stated, but simply left it an open matter. Chapter 25, section 6 was rewritten to avoid calling the pope of Rome "that antichrist, that man of sin, and son of perdition, that exalteth himself in the Church against Christ and all that is called God"—"which does seem rather strong language," Dr. Warfield wrote. The "remodeling" of chapter 16, section 7— the section in the chapter on "Good Works" that treats the works of the unregenerate—Dr. Warfield believed to be "a positively bad piece of work." The new section was neither "untrue" nor "unsound" but created the suspicion that the determining motive for the change may have been to avoid affirming that works done by unregenerate men "are sinful and cannot please God."[28]

Dr. Warfield summarized his views of the revision:

> Certainly new doctrines [common grace, the external call, infant salvation, and the work of the Holy Spirit in the church] have been inserted into the Confession by the Revision of 1903; and we have no disposition to minimize the importance of these new doctrines. But there is something else that must be said about them also. These new doctrines are true doctrines—good, sound, Calvinistic doctrines, which, taking their places in a statement of the Calvinistic system, simply expand it into greater completeness of treatment, and in no sense modify either it or any of the doctrines that enter into it.[29]

Conservatives took comfort that the matter of confessional revision was settled and that "no doctrine has been touched, so the church stands just where it did before." *The Presbyterian Journal* noted Warfield's minor criticisms—mainly of style rather than substance—and commented, "If Professor Warfield's microscope reveals no more flies than those mentioned, then the revision ointment is about as pure as human ingenuity can make it."[30]

There were apparently many reasons for Princeton Seminary to be encouraged. The "Portland Deliverance" of 1892—in which the church stated its belief in the inerrancy of the Bible—had been reaffirmed by the General Assemblies of 1893, 1894, and 1899. Charles Briggs had been removed from the Presbyterian ministry for heresy in 1893, and Henry Preserved Smith in 1894. A. C. McGiffert resigned from the Presbyterian ministry in 1900 after having been charged with departure from the Westminster Confession, particularly concerning his views of the authority of the Bible. But there were alarming weaknesses in American Protestant Christianity and in the Presbyterian church. William Henry Green had observed in 1883 a general tendency toward "doctrinal indifferentism" and "a weakening of the strict religious sentiment," which were preparing many American Christians to receive the critical views of the Bible and liberal theology with interest and considerable openness. There had indeed been some notable conservative victories, but the greater battle was yet to come—"the most fundamental controversy to wrack the churches since the age of the Reformation."[31]

By the opening of the new century younger scholars—such as Walter Rauschenbusch, William Newton Clarke, Arthur Cushman McGiffert, and William Adams Brown—were constructing a modernist gospel far more radical than anything Dr. Briggs and his generation had envisioned. McGiffert referred to the great doctrines of the church as "theological tyranny" and stated that modern people "have learned to think for ourselves in religion, instead of simply repeating the thoughts of other generations." The doctrine of the Virgin Birth was seen by many as a later, mythical interpretation of Jesus' origin. The sacrament of the Lord's Supper was believed to be a product of the evolving communal life of the primitive church. The doctrine of Jesus' physical resurrection was denied on "scientific" grounds. Creeds and dogmas were believed to be "human constructions" subject to evolutionary development and interpretation. McGiffert spoke for many liberals when he wrote that "the modern recognition of experience" was "the only legitimate basis of theology." This enabled the liberals, he stated, to give their attention "to other things of more immediate and practical concern." In 1899 the Scottish Old Testament scholar George Adam Smith declared at a Yale lecture that modern scientific criticism had won its war against traditional orthodoxy. The only task remaining, he asserted, was "to fix the amount of the indemnity."[32]

In 1902 *The Presbyterian and Reformed Review* was taken over by the faculty of Princeton Seminary and the title changed to *The Princeton Theological Review*. The publication continued its course with little apparent change, but there was a real significance in the new arrangement. The defense and propagation of orthodox Christianity and biblical Calvinism had been the task of the Presbyterian church as a whole. It was becoming clear, however, that bold adherence to the theology of the Westminster Standards was giving way to a view in which critical openness and religious sincerity were seen as more important than careful doctrinal formulations. *The Princeton Theological Review* emphasized the commitment of Princeton Seminary to champion historic Christianity and to uphold faithfully the Reformed faith.

William Hutchison notes that as liberalism gained a

dominant position in American academia and among the clergy of the mainline churches, opposition—such as expressed in the major theological journals—was weak and unimpressive. The one exception, he states, was *The Princeton Theological Review* (and its predecessors). "The inspired obstinancy of the Hodges, Patton, and Warfield, and later of John Gresham Machen, shone in marked, self-conscious contrast with all such flickering lights." Hutchison continues:

Book reviews offer a limited picture of Princeton's reaction to liberalism, but it is a revealing one. The editors seem to have been able to call upon a stable of orthodox reviewers of very marked theological and literary abilities, chiefly from outside the seminary faculty; and their lengthy, courteous, anti-liberal essays poured out, through these years, as mighty waves of sound from the same well-planned orchestration. Their central theme was one that would reach a culmination and gain greater popular expression some years later in Machen's *Christianity and Liberalism*. The realistic, if sometimes disingenuous, message of Princeton was that liberalism and modernism were attractive, perfectly respectable religious systems that good men might choose [but] they were also systems that should stop claiming the name and sanction . . . of Christianity.[33]

With many American seminaries and most of the great urban pulpits now in the hands of liberals, Princeton Seminary was more important than ever—"not only for Presbyterianism, but for all the denominations that honored the Reformed tradition, and even for some that did not." Southern Presbyterians, for the most part, held to the theology long championed by Princeton. Union Seminary in Virginia—which was founded, as John Holt Rice wrote to Archibald Alexander in 1823, with "Princeton as our model"—remained a seminary of orthodox Calvinism, as did the Presbyterian seminaries in Columbia, South Carolina, and Louisville, Kentucky. Throughout Southern Presbyterianism Princeton was recognized as the best school for graduate theological study, and "admiration for Dr. B. B. Warfield reached such a point that the initials 'BBW' became almost the last word on a question." Among orthodox Calvinists around the world Princeton remained the center and stronghold of historic Reformed Theology. And Bible-believing people of other churches looked to Princeton for a conservative and scholarly defense of the faith.[34]

Despite continuing support in these circles the Princeton view, once dominant in American Presbyterianism and influential in American Protestantism, now appeared to many to be a stubborn conservatism, resistant to newer and better ideas. "Almost alone among the earlier centers of conservative scholarship, Princeton Theological Seminary continued to engage the modern questions through vigorous academic inquiry," Mark Noll has written. "Yet even as an exception, the Princeton scholars were becoming increasingly isolated. Because their work was so forthrightly conservative, it no longer had much of a place in the larger academic world." At his death in 1900 *The Congregationalist* stated that William Henry Green was "one of the last of the active professors of Old Testament literature in American universities who held the views concerning the authorship and inspiration of the Bible which were generally adopted by evangelical leaders a generation ago." It seemed that more and more Princeton Seminary was becoming "Princeton *contra mundum.*"[35]

11

The Faculty of 1902

In 1902 Princeton Seminary, within a decade of rounding out the first century of its life, enjoyed the reputation of being a Gibraltar of orthodoxy and a school of eminent scholarship.

NED B. STONEHOUSE

I N 1902 Princeton Seminary was being served by seven professors—Francis Landey Patton, Benjamin Breckinridge Warfield, Geerhardus Vos, John D. Davis, Robert Dick Wilson, John DeWitt, and William Brenton Greene.

* * *

Dr. Patton ended his fourteen-year administration at Princeton College in 1902.[1] During his presidency the college had become a university, and the faculty and student body had doubled in size. Patton greatly extended the electives permitted under McCosh; by 1900 only one third of the junior courses and none of the senior courses were required. The proportion of students in the Green School of Science doubled from one sixth to about one third.

New buildings had been erected, including the first of Princeton's Gothic buildings, the impressive Blair Hall— complete with battlements, pointed arches, leaded glass, and bay windows. Through the years the campus—beautiful with great trees, vines, and shrubs—had become an architectural hodgepodge. The Florentine Prospect, the Romanesque Alexander Hall (named for Charles B. Alexander, the grandson of Archibald Alexander), and the Grecian Whig and Clio contrasted with the elegant simplicity of Colonial Nassau Hall. Professor Andrew Fleming West won Princeton over to Tudor Gothic. The new buildings of gray foxcroft and limestone were embellished with gargoyles—eloquent reminders of medieval fondness for handmade detail. Woodrow Wilson declared that the adoption of Gothic architecture added "a thousand years" to the history of Princeton.

Dr. Patton was committed to keeping Princeton Christian. He had stated at his inauguration that "there should be a distinct, earnest, purposeful effort to show every man who enters our College Halls the grounds for entertaining those fundamental religious beliefs that are the common heritage of the Christian World." In his baccalaureate sermon in memory of James McCosh on June 9, 1895, Patton said that "it is not the college with largest endowments, or most brilliant faculty, or most varied curriculum that most fulfills the end of its existence; it is the college which, in connection with all this, stands most conspicuously for the great ideas of truth and duty, and faith in God and the religion of Christ." Dr. Patton realized that the accomplishment of this goal rested largely with the university's professors. When Woodrow Wilson was elected to the faculty Patton wrote to congratulate him but went on to urge him to express a more distinctively Christian approach in his teaching. In your writings, he told Wilson, "you minimize the supernatural and make such unqualified application of the doctrine of naturalistic evolution . . . as to leave the reader of your pages in a state of uncertainty as to your position and the place you give to Divine Providence." Patton added that at Princeton Wilson would be expected to approach his subject of political science "under theistic and Christian presuppositions." Despite this rebuke, Wilson wrote to a friend that Patton was "a man of most liberal outlook in his whole mental attitude, outside of church battles."[2]

Dr. Patton meant to keep Princeton "on the old grounds of loyalty to the Christian religion," but he did not attempt to make it conform in every aspect to conservative views. One of the faculty members, James Mark Baldwin, professor of philosophy and psychology, recalled that Patton encouraged him to continue his investigations in the evolutionary development of the mind. He added that he saw two Pattons—"a Calvinist of the most thorough stripe in the pulpit, but a person of immense charity among the 'sinners' of the world the rest of the week." When in 1897 the Princeton academic community came under sharp attack from some Presbyterians who were angered that members of the faculty had supported a petition to grant a liquor license to the Princeton Inn so that wine and beer could be served, Dr. Patton promised, as he stated, to do all he could "to keep the hand of ecclesiasticism from resting on Princeton University."[3]

Under President Patton students attended daily chapel, evening vespers, and Sunday morning and evening services. Bible instruction continued to be part of the required curriculum. Dr. Patton himself taught three semesters of New Testament studies to the underclassmen and the course in ethics and apologetics for the seniors. One graduate recalled that "the fundamentals of the Christian religion were defended by him as a high-minded man would defend his personal honor." Some faculty members, however, thought that Patton was too direct in his preaching. Woodrow Wilson once told him, "You engender the spirit of doubt by stating a thing dogmatically."[4]

When Patton, Andrew West, and the trustees blocked Woodrow Wilson's recommendation that historian Frederick Jackson Turner, a Unitarian, be added to the faculty for a new professorship of American history, Wilson was "chagrined and mortified." Turner had asked about possible religious tests at Princeton, and Wilson had replied, "I think I can say without qualification that no religious tests are applied here. The president and trustees are very anxious that every man they choose should be earnestly religious, but there are no doctrinal standards among us." However, the Princeton board hesitated and then turned down Turner's appointment—stating that the school could not afford to create a separate professorship in American history. Embarrassed, Woodrow Wilson's wife, Ellen, wrote, "We can't hope to be anything but a respectable, old-fashioned Presbyterian College; before [the sesquicentennial] we were that simply and without pretense; now we have merely made ourselves ridiculous before the whole academic world by making big promises that we have neither the will nor the power to carry out."[5]

Many Princetonians appreciated and loved Dr. Patton. Students of the 1890s, after becoming alumni, built Patton

Hall as a tribute to him and sang his praises in their first faculty song:

> Here's to Patton, our President
> In Princeton College he pitched his tent
> And now he's boss of this wonderful show
> Here's to Francis Landey O!

Patton was not only a man of considerable personal charm and ability; he was a good teacher and a popular preacher. He possessed "a strong and consistent conviction and a vigorous and agile mind," and Princeton student and later professor James Mark Baldwin declared that his lectures were "a revelation and enchantment." Woodrow Wilson believed that Patton was "the ablest man on his feet" that he had ever heard. When he spoke in chapel one alumnus said that even "the most indifferent loafers slouched over to hear him."[6]

Stories about the president's wit and wisdom circulated around the campus and the town. When an anxious mother asked if her freshman son would receive a good education at Princeton College, Patton replied, "Yes, madam, satisfaction guaranteed, or the product will be returned." One day when students began to close their books and shuffle their feet, anticipating the end of the class hour, Dr. Patton said, with a twinkle in his eye, "Please restrain your impatience, gentlemen. I have still a few more pearls to cast!" After one of his public lectures a woman asked Patton to give her the strongest argument against theosophy. "Madam," said Dr. Patton, "the strongest argument against theosophy is that there is no argument for it."

Despite the best intentions of Presidents McCosh and Patton, a new secularism had begun to replace the earlier evangelicalism of Princeton. Old Nassau Hall had become the famous and fashionable Princeton University. Although the school continued its commitment to undergraduate training for future ministers, their numbers were few compared with those preparing for other careers. The proportion of Presbyterians, about three fourths of the students in the 1870s, declined to about half by the turn of the century.[7] Princeton gained the reputation of a "rich man's school." Many students were more interested in making friends and playing football than in serious studies. Dr. McCosh, who had encouraged collegiate sports, discovered to his dismay that "emphasis on athletics, rather than promoting a gentlemanly balance of mind and body, was beginning to produce specialist athletes who did not concentrate on anything else." Dr. Patton was well aware of what was happening at Princeton University and, it was said, once remarked that he presided over the finest country club in America. He apparently did not worry overmuch about rigorous student discipline. He believed that only a small group of students would be truly serious about academic matters; but he wanted Princeton to be a school in which all would profit from the social and spiritual benefits of life together. He openly stated in faculty meetings that "it was good for a young man to come to college, even if he did no more than rub his shoulders against the buildings."[8]

Dr. Patton was not an effective president. Many trustees and younger faculty members believed that he simply left things to drift and that—despite the new buildings and larger faculty and student body—Princeton was falling behind in the academic world. One colleague put it gently when he said that Patton was "a wonderfully poor administrator." Dr. Patton was not "lazy," as some of his critics claimed, but approached the leadership of Princeton as a pastor rather than an administrator. He believed that the university, being composed of free and mature individuals, should run itself without much presidential interference or systematic planning. He had a "study" rather than an "office" and carried on his extensive correspondence without a secretary—answering most of his letters by hand and, "in true gentlemanly manner," responding to even the most trivial inquiries. His meetings with the board of trustees included scripture reading, prayer, and a sermon, but his reports were brief and incomplete. Patton's outdated style of leadership could not cope with Princeton's rapid growth. His failure to reform the undergraduate program allowed lax requirements that lazy students exploited. In 1891 Patton missed an opportunity to found a law school at Princeton. Professor Andrew West maneuvered the trustees to by-pass Patton in the establishment of the graduate school. Woodrow Wilson complained that Patton could "not be depended on for anything at all."[9]

A small group of faculty members, including Woodrow Wilson, suggested to the trustees that Dr. Patton continue as the nominal head but that three professors and two trustees be appointed as an executive committee to administer the affairs of the university. Patton decided, however, just before the commencement exercises of 1902, that it would be in the best interests of Princeton if he resigned. Always the gentleman, he immediately suggested Woodrow Wilson to be his successor. John A. Stewart, who had nominated James McCosh to the presidency thirty-four years before, put the name of Wilson before the trustees. The twenty-six trustees—reputed to have never before agreed immediately on anything—were of one mind, and, on June 9, 1902, Wilson was unanimously elected. Students, faculty, townspeople, and the press praised the trustees' choice.[10]

*   *   *

Thomas Woodrow Wilson was the first layman to become president of the 156-year-old college. The son of Southern Presbyterian pastor and seminary professor Joseph Ruggles Wilson and his wife, Janet, Tommy "grew up on family worship, Bible reading, study of the *Shorter Catechism,* and stories of Scottish Covenanters" in Presbyterian manses in Virginia, Georgia, and the Carolinas. After a year at Davidson College and graduation from Princeton in 1879 Wilson studied law at the University of Virginia and practiced briefly in Atlanta. Disillusioned by the tedium and materialism of legal damage suits, he returned to the academic world for doctoral studies in political science and history at Johns Hopkins University. He taught at Bryn Mawr College and Wesleyan University and in 1890 came to Princeton as professor of jurisprudence and political economy. He wrote two best-selling books and became widely known as an effective lecturer. Woodrow Wilson was determined to develop a university with a prestigious faculty and high academic standards. He began to plan for added endowment, new buildings, revision of the curriculum, reform of the system of classroom instruction, and the addition of distinguished professors.[11]

Faculty of 1875, (left to right): *standing*—James C. Moffat, Caspar Wistar Hodge, Charles A. Aiken, William H. Green; *seated*—Alexander T. McGill, Charles Hodge

Faculty of 1885, (left to right): *standing*—Francis L. Patton, Charles A. Aiken, C. W. Hodge; *seated*—A. A. Hodge, James C. Moffat, William H. Green, William M. Paxton

William Henry Green, 1885

Dr. Green's Study

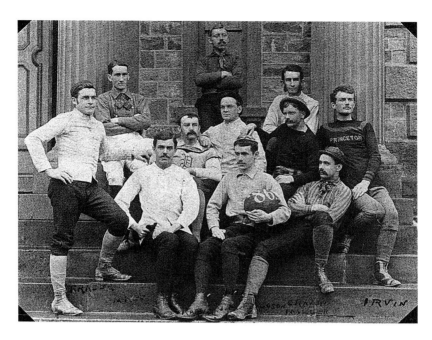

Princeton Seminary Football Team, 1886

Faculty of 1888 (left to right): *standing*—C. W. Hodge, William B. Greene, B.B. Warfield, John Davis; *seated*—James C. Moffat, Francis L. Patton, W. H. Green, William M. Paxton

*   *   *

When someone once asked Dr. Patton what position he had held at the university he cheerfully replied, "President, once removed." After serving as the university's president for fourteen years, Dr. Patton became in 1902 Princeton Seminary's first president. For ninety years the senior seminary professors—Archibald Alexander, Charles Hodge, and William Henry Green—had presided over faculty meetings and other official events; but in 1902 a Joint Committee on Administration (consisting of three members each from the board of directors, the board of trustees, and the faculty) recommended to the General Assembly that the "Plan" of the seminary be amended to provide for a president. The office was created to establish stronger contact with the church and improve administrative efficiency—and to honor Dr. Patton. Dr. Patton moved into the Victorian "Springdale" at 86 Mercer Street—built for Richard Stockton in 1846 and now provided for the seminary's president—and soon came to enjoy greatly his role as president of the seminary, where he saw himself as "first among equals."

Dr. Patton, in his inaugural address as Princeton Seminary's first president, declared that "the crisis in which we are today is the greatest war of the intellect that has ever been waged since the birth of the Nazarene." If battle with modern thought could not be joined fully at the university, it certainly could be, Patton thought, at the seminary. Some seminary students found their new president a rather formidable figure and his lectures on theism, "soliloquies"; and "yet, somehow, he radiated a personal influence that was persuasive." In an informal gathering with one class, a student recalled, "he pleased and teased us with pawkily humorous asides, and won our hearts by describing himself as 'a hardened old sinner.' One bit of advice that he gave us [was that] we should not overload our sermons with lengthy quotations from the poets. A line or two was enough. Among the Swiss Alps the merest bell-tinkle, floating down to the valleys, was signal enough that the herd-leader had been grazing in high pastures."[12]

[203]

*   *   *

The best-known teacher at Princeton Seminary at the turn of the century was B. B. Warfield. Fifty years old in 1902, Dr. Warfield was in his prime. Student O. T. Allis described Warfield as "a tall, dignified, and impressive figure, [with] ruddy cheeks, hair parted in the middle, sparkling eyes, and a graying full beard." With "singular grace and courtesy of demeanor," he "bore the marks of a gentleman to his finger-tips." Dr. Warfield presided at the opening exercises for the 1902 school year. In an easy, charming manner and soft southern accent he welcomed old and new students cordially. He announced that the faculty would no longer sit in the central block of seats in the chapel and so leave them free for students, and he expressed the hope that the students would respond by faithfully filling them.[13]

Dr. Warfield's students were impressed with his range of knowledge—his exacting use of New Testament criticism, his skilled linguistic ability, and his thorough knowledge of Bible, theology, and history. The students came to realize that they were hearing "one of the greatest masters in the field of the history of doctrine." Warfield knew the early church fathers—and placed special emphasis on Tertullian and Augustine—and the medieval period. The Reformation, however, was for him the major epoch in theology—beginning dramatically with Luther's theses, coming to its greater statement in John Calvin, and advancing further in the work of the British Puritans. Dr. Warfield inspired the students with a sense of the greatness of the task of systematic theology. It is an "attempt," he told them, "to reflect in the mirror of the human consciousness the God who reveals Himself in His works and word"; and it is "a progressive science" that will "be perfected only in the minds and hearts of the perfected saints who at the end, being at last like God, shall see Him as He is."[14]

Dr. Warfield's theology classes read Charles Hodge's *Systematic Theology.* Sometimes Warfield gave formal lectures, but more often he talked informally about a subject and then engaged one of the students in animated discussion about it.

The students appreciated Warfield's use of questions and answers "in unfolding the truth, so as to encourage young men to think for themselves." George L. Robinson, who graduated from Princeton Seminary in 1903 and then studied at Berlin and Leipzig, wrote:

Dr. Warfield was the best teacher I ever had either in America or Germany. I took notes under him assiduously; and the notes I took I have used more than those of all other professors together. He taught us with rare clarity and persuasiveness. He combined quizzing and lecturing in a most marvelous way. He kept a man on his feet from twenty to thirty minutes, interrogating him and in Socratic style informing him.[15]

Andrew Blackwood, who studied at Princeton during 1905 and 1906, said that Warfield quickly became one of the most "formative influences" in his life. From a conservative Covenanter-Seceder Presbyterian home, Blackwood went to Harvard, where his interest in modern theology grew under the teaching of Francis G. Peabody and other followers of William E. Channing. After Harvard Blackwood—now clearly liberal in his views—took classes at Princeton Seminary to see "what the other side had to say." He enrolled in B. B. Warfield's elective course on the deity of Christ. Blackwood was impressed that Dr. Warfield was "kind to those who differed from him" and called the Princeton professor a "charming gentleman" and a "good crusader." Furthermore, he saw Warfield—and Geerhardus Vos—as "intellectually the equals" of his ablest professors at Harvard. Blackwood later wrote, "Looking back now, many of us are conscious that we owe to [Dr. Warfield], and to a few other teachers, more than words can tell, and we must confess that we never even thanked them; we were like the nine lepers whom the Master healed."[16]

The students did appreciate Dr. Warfield, to whom they referred affectionately but privately as "Benny." "In wonderfully generous fashion," one of them wrote, he would "go out of his way to give a word of encouragement to a younger man." Dr. Warfield arranged that student C. D. Brokenshire would research articles on John Calvin in American magazines and journals (for Warfield's friend Émile Doumergue, dean of the Free Theological Faculty of Montauban). Brokenshire remembered that "the Doctor asked if the pay was enough. I told him I thought it was even generous," Brokenshire said; "He was anxious to be kind and just in the affair." Dr. Warfield was known for his quiet sense of humor. One day as Francis Patton was standing with Warfield outside his house on Mercer Street, they saw a woman approaching. Dr. Patton, who was very nearsighted, asked Warfield whether he should greet the woman. "I think I would if I were you," Warfield answered; "it is Mrs. Patton."[17]

Dr. Warfield's classes sparkled with apt quotations and vivid illustrations. During a class dealing with the subject of miracles Warfield noted that the questions and answers indicated some confusion or doubt. He stopped and remarked with a twinkle in his eye, "Gentleman, I like the supernatural!"[18] In discussing the charge of some that the perfection of Scripture was distorted by its fallible human writers, Warfield described a stained-glass window through which the light, as it passed, was colored by the pieces of brittle glass of varying tint and shape that embodied the artist's design. "And wasn't this precisely what the artist had intended?" he asked.

And wasn't every bit of tinted glass specifically chosen and prepared to fulfil that design and make up the many-colored picture? When, therefore, God, designed his window of revelation through which the eternal light of truth was to pass, were we to suppose that he overlooked the coloring media of the fallible human minds that went to the fashioning of that window? Did he not foreknow and choose each tint and type to subserve his own infallible purpose and make his window perfect and complete?[19]

Students long remembered Dr. Warfield's illustrating the difference between God and fate by telling the story of a little Dutch boy.

This little boy's home was on a dyke in Holland, near a great windmill, whose long arms swept so close to the ground as to endanger those who carelessly strayed under them. But he was very fond of playing precisely under this mill. His anxious parents had forbidden him to go near it; and, when his stubborn will did not

[206]

give way, had sought to frighten him away from it by arousing his imagination to the terror of being struck by the arms and carried up into the air to have life beaten out of him by their ceaseless strokes. One day, heedless of their warning, he strayed again under the dangerous arms, and was soon absorbed in his play there— forgetful of everything but his present pleasures. Perhaps, he was half conscious of a breeze springing up; and somewhere in the depth of his soul, he may have been obscurely aware of the danger with which he had been threatened. At any rate, suddenly, as he played, he was violently smitten from behind, and found himself swung all at once, with head downward, up into the air; and then the blows came, swift and hard! O what a sinking of the heart! O what a horror of great darkness! It had come then! And he was gone! In his terrified writhing, he twisted himself about, and look-ing up, saw not the immeasurable expanse of the brazen heavens above him, but his father's face. At once, he realized, with a great revulsion, that he was not caught in the mill, but was only receiving the threatened punishment of his disobedience. He melted into tears, not of pain, but of relief and joy. In that moment, he under-stood the difference between falling into the grinding power of a machine and into the loving hands of a father.

"That is the difference between Fate and Predestination," Warfield said with great emphasis. "And all the language of men cannot tell the immensity of the difference."[20]

Dr. Warfield illustrated the "indelible mark" of the Shorter Catechism by telling a story about an officer of the United States army who was in a western city at a time of violent riot-ing. The streets constantly were overrun with a dangerous crowd. One day a man whose calm and firm demeanor inspired confidence walked toward the officer. So impressed was the officer with the man's bearing in the midst of the surrounding uproar that when the man had passed, he turned to look back at him—only to find that the stranger had done the same. The man at once came back, touched his chest with his forefinger, and demanded without preface, "What is the chief end of man?" On receiving the correct answer—"Man's chief end is to glorify God and to enjoy him forever"—the stranger said, "Ah! I knew you were a Shorter Catechism boy by your looks!" The officer replied, "Why, that was just what I was thinking of you." "It is worthwhile to be a Shorter Catechism boy," Dr. Warfield told the students.

[207]

"They grow up to be men. And better than that, they are exceedingly apt to grow up to be men of God."[21]

*   *   *

Professor of biblical theology Geerhardus Vos taught the two required courses in Old Testament and New Testament theology, as well as courses on the eighth-century prophets, the epistle to the Hebrews, and Pauline studies. In his classes he sought to counter the destructive influences of higher criticism and comparative religion. Christology was one decisive battleground because, as he said, with it "the Christian religion stands or falls." The major issue was "whether Jesus believed and claimed to be the Messiah." Vos argued that we must accept him "at the face value of his central self-estimate" and stated that "no one can take a Savior to his heart in that absolutely unqualified sense which constitutes the glory of religious trust if there persists in the background of his mind the thought that this Savior failed to understand himself." Jesus was the founder of no new religion, Dr. Vos contended; there is a historic unity between his teaching and the revelation of the Old Testament regarding the kingdom. "The Church is a form which the kingdom assumes in result of the new stage upon which the Messiahship of Jesus enters with His death and resurrection."

Dr. Vos's presentation of a comprehensive, orthodox, and distinctly Reformed biblical-theological approach to the Holy Scriptures was his most important contribution to the seminary curriculum. In his teaching he stressed the progress found within biblical revelation but always insisted that this progress has objective, and not merely subjective, religious and theological validity. It is God who has revealed himself in the biblical events and in the Bible's interpretation of those events. True biblical theology, Vos told the students, permits "Scripture to set its own agenda. Theology, in its content and form, ought to be what the Scripture irresistibly demands."[22]

Because of the weightiness of his lectures and his patient, methodical style of scholarship, the enrollment in Dr. Vos's elective classes was often sparse. He was a patient teacher, however, and when a student was unable to recite satisfactorily Dr. Vos would continue to frame his questions in such a way as virtually to provide the answers. He had a refreshing and, at times, almost irrepressible sense of humor. On an occasion when the pet dog of a student followed him into the classroom, Dr. Vos—speaking with his decided Dutch accent—commented, "Please close the door; we must draw the line somewhere!"[23] Dr. Vos impressed the students as a "many-sided" man. He was widely read, loved painting, and wrote poetry. Six collections of his poetry were published, four in Dutch and two in English—including the following lines:

> Our Easter should have flowers
> From fields where nothing dies,
> Transplanted from the life-streams
> Of God's new paradise.
> Thou sayest: this were a wonder
> Such as no memory knows;
> Was it a lesser wonder
> That Christ from Hades rose?

The students respected Dr. Vos for his piety. One of them wrote about a sermon he had heard Dr. Vos preach in the seminary chapel:

We had this morning one of the finest expository sermons I ever heard. It was preached by Dr. Vos, professor of Biblical Theology . . . and rather surprised me. He is usually too severely theological for Sunday morning. Today he was nothing less than inspiring. His subject was Christ's appearance to Mary after the resurrection. Dr. Vos differs from some theological professors in having a better-developed bump of reverence.

Vos ended that sermon with these words:

Let us not linger at the tomb, but turn our faces and stretch our hands upwards into heaven, where our life is hid with Him in God, and whence He shall also come again to show Himself to us as He did to Mary, to make us speak the last great "Rabboni" which will spring to the lips of all the redeemed, when they meet their Savior in the early dawn of that eternal Sabbath that awaits the people of God.[24]

Dr. Vos's fine features, slightly stooped figure, and quiet dignity were a familiar sight to his fellow Princetonians. For years they saw him and Dr. Warfield walking together almost every day about noon, up and down Mercer Street. Gentle and naturally retiring, Vos avoided active participation in public life and controversy and lived the life of a scholar and mystic—as he sometimes styled himself. Guests in the Vos home were always invited to family prayers, in which Catherine Vos (who wrote the well-known *Child's Story Bible*) read the Scriptures with vivid running comments for the children. Her husband led in the prayer.[25]

*   *   *

Since 1886 John D. Davis had taught Old Testament at Princeton, for two years as instructor in Hebrew and then professor of Hebrew and cognate languages. In 1892 his title was changed to Professor of Semitic Philology and Old Testament History, and in 1900 he succeeded William Henry Green as the Helena Professor of Oriental and Old Testament Literature. Dr. Davis was recognized as one of the foremost Hebraists in America and, after the death of William Henry Green, the most influential defender of the authenticity of biblical history, the unity of Genesis, and the Mosaic authorship of the Pentateuch. His book on *Genesis and Semitic Tradition* demonstrated his ability to use comparative Near Eastern sources to elucidate and verify the biblical texts. When the first edition of Davis's acclaimed *Dictionary of the Bible* appeared in 1898, William Henry Green praised it "as embodying the fruits of the most recent and reliable researches" with "a reverent and believing attitude" toward "Holy Scripture."[26]

Dr. Davis was a cautious scholar who refused to dismiss lightly the views of his rationalistic opponents. The students often heard him utter his favorite phrase, "We must wait for further light." Modest and reserved almost to the point of shyness, Dr. Davis was nonetheless a good classroom teacher. He presented the Old Testament homiletically and practically. In his course on the prophets—as in his other classes—he stressed right principles of interpretation and inspired the students to develop worthy habits of Bible study. Professor and class worked together on a selected number of passages in the prophets that had especially challenged commentators throughout the history of the church.

*   *   *

Robert Dick Wilson taught with Dr. Davis in the Old Testament department. Wilson, the first professor who was not a graduate of Princeton Seminary since Charles Aiken had arrived in 1871, studied at Princeton College, Western Theological Seminary, and the University of Berlin. He returned to Western Seminary in 1883 to teach Old Testament and came to Princeton in 1900 as the William Henry Green Professor of Semitic Philology and Old Testament Introduction. One student wrote that Dr. Wilson "held the chair in Hebrew. Certainly no chair could hold *him*. As he warmed to his subject (say, linguistic clues to the date of the Book of Daniel) he would spring from his chair, pace up and down, and then, leaving the platform, drive home his point by pounding the desks of one and another of the students who caught his eye. 'Dr. Dick's' linguistic and textual erudition was fabulous, and to watch and hear him pulverizing the higher critics was a memorable experience." Despite his great learning, however, Dr. Wilson "had nothing of the aloofness which sometimes characterizes the scholar and pedagogue," the student continued. "He was (in the British sense of the word) homely and accessible and liked to dine with us at our clubs and regale us with his stories and shrewd counsel."[27]

Dr. Wilson believed that the controversy concerning the Scriptures dealt with the most important theological issue in all of Christian history. He used his expertise in biblical and extrabiblical sources and languages to defend the historicity and Mosaic authorship of the Pentateuch ("though it may have been revised and edited by later inspired redactors") and the traditional dating of other Old Testament books. He followed what he called the "evidential method of inquiry" —that is, "the laws of evidence as applied to documents admitted in our courts of law"—to demonstrate that it is reasonable to believe "that the text of the Old Testament which we have is substantially correct and that, in its true and obvious meaning, it has a right to be considered a part of the 'infallible rule of faith and practice' that we have in the Holy Scriptures." Wilson's insistence that the students follow a strictly objective study of the biblical texts, without subjective presuppositions, stood firmly within the Princeton tradition of Scottish Common Sense Realism, which stressed scientific and objective research. At the same time he exemplified the Princeton practice of simple piety and trust in God and his Word. Students heard him say:

Boys, I must admit there are questions that sometimes bother me when I read the Bible. This I can understand because I'm a sinner and my understanding is limited, so I'm not going to charge God with not being clear. I'm going to lay it to my own ignorance. But I will say this: after studying God's Word for over fifty years I have come to the conclusion that no man on earth knows enough to claim there is a single inaccuracy in the original Scriptures of the Old and New Testaments.[28]

Dr. Wilson made a particular study of the attacks directed against the miracles, prophecies, and history of the book of Daniel. He told the students that if they could keep straight on Daniel they would keep straight on the rest. Many critics had assigned to Daniel a late dating, so that its statements could be understood as history written after the event rather than prophecy given by revelation of God. Wilson carefully examined their claims, answered them one by one, and defended the traditional dating through the use of "new data and finely honed arguments." It was his conviction, he told the students, that if the book of Daniel was not written by Daniel, it was written by another man who had the same name and who lived at the same time and had the same experiences as Daniel! S. R. Driver and H. H. Rowley—primary creators and defenders of a late dating for Daniel—rather grudgingly acknowledged Wilson's "considerable evidence and well-framed arguments" but were openly disdainful of his conservatism, which in their view invalidated his scholarship.[29]

*　　*　　*

In 1900, after teaching New Testament for eight years, George Purves returned to the pastorate, and William Park Armstrong, instructor in New Testament literature, was placed in charge of the department. A native of Selma, Alabama, Armstrong graduated from Princeton College and Princeton Seminary. He pursued New Testament studies in Germany—with Jülicher at Marburg, Harnack at Berlin, and Zahn at Erlangen. He returned to Princeton Seminary in 1899 as Dr. Purves's assistant and was chosen professor of New Testament literature and exegesis in 1903, when he was only twenty-nine years old. The next year he married Rebekah Purves, the daughter of his admired teacher. A seminary student described Princeton's New Testament professor:

One of Armstrong's strongest points is that he combines detailed knowledge of critical and historical questions with an understanding of great underlying principles. His wide reading in philosophy enables him to show the connection between schools of New Testament criticism and various schools of modern philosophy; but, above all, he is able to exhibit the connection between the supernaturalistic view of the New Testament and the theistic view of God and the world upon which the Christian religion depends.[30]

Caspar Wistar Hodge Jr. (the grandson of Charles Hodge, the son of Caspar Wistar Hodge, and the nephew of Archibald Alexander Hodge) joined William Park Armstrong as instructor in New Testament in 1901. Ten years had passed since the death of his father in 1891—the only period since 1820 without a Hodge teaching at Princeton. He had studied at Princeton College, Princeton Seminary, and in Europe at Heidelberg and Berlin. He then taught philosophy at Princeton College for three years and ethics at Lafayette College for two years. Recognized for his deeply Christian spirit and his breadth of learning and exacting scholarship, Wistar Hodge was well prepared to teach at Princeton Seminary.

*   *   *

Beginning in 1892, John DeWitt was Princeton's professor of church history. One of Dr. DeWitt's students said that "he taught church history with a twinkle in his eye. The subject could have been made a very dry one, but he made it a very tasty one." At times DeWitt laid aside his notes to give remarks on a great variety of themes—mostly connected with the topic of his lecture but often suggested by some student question or news in the daily papers. Rising from his chair and walking up and down the full length of the platform as he talked, he enjoyed these times as much as the students did. Dr. DeWitt, who had served as a pastor for seventeen years, always ended his course with a brief talk on the importance and value of continued study of church history for the minister of the gospel. Then he would read one of his own historical sermons. Frederick W. Loetscher, who graduated in 1900, wrote, "In my senior year . . . the subject presented was 'Athanasius,' and to this day I retain a vivid recollection of the inspiring and instructive character of this discourse, and of the deep religious impression it made upon us all." In 1903 Frederick Loetscher became instructor in church history—the position having been established by Dr. DeWitt himself (with $1,500 from his own salary of $3,700). Clarence Macartney, who studied at Princeton from 1902 to 1905, said that Dr. Loetscher "did more than any other to open for [him] the thrill, romance and majesty of the long history of the Christian Church." "This proved to be of the highest importance for me in my work as a minister," Macartney added.[31]

*　　*　　*

William Brenton Greene taught apologetics and sociology as the Stuart Professor of the Relations of Philosophy and Science to the Christian Religion. Dr. Greene labored quietly under the shadow of the popular Francis Patton, whose lecture topics often overlapped his own, and the gifted B. B. Warfield, who frequently commented on apologetics in his theology classes and in his writings. Although he wrote few books, the hard-working Greene read widely in his field and reviewed hundreds of books in *The Princeton Theological Review* and other journals.[32] Among the students Dr. Greene's lectures were notorious for "their analytical divisions, subdivisions, and sub-sub-divisions." It was said that "his ordinary gesture was a slight inclination of the right forefinger at the top joint. On the rare occasion of more violent emphasis, the finger would be bent at the second joint!" "But his lectures," student Gwilym O. Griffith stated, "were models of logical coherence and lucidity, and I can still hear that familiar high-pitched voice ending a dialectical passage with the satisfying conclusion, 'All arguments to the contrary serve only to strengthen our position.'"[33]

"Brenny" Greene, as the students affectionately called him, was a man of "extraordinary meekness and gentleness" with "a bland and rather subtle innocence." Gwilym Griffith, who came to Princeton from Wales in 1906, described Greene as a "rather tall spare figure" with "guileless blue eyes, his mild countenance elongated by a drooping beard." "In those days the Seminary allowed generous grants to students from overseas," Griffith explained, "and Dr. Greene passed me the usual application form for my signature. I noticed that I was required to subscribe a declaration that the grant was necessary to me. Rather priggishly, I objected that, in my own case, the word 'necessary' conveyed an overstatement." Dr. Greene replied, "Mr. Griffith, the word 'necessary' has more than one connotation. If you sign this form, we shall not understand you to have stated that if you are not allowed the grant you will die."[34]

*   *   *

William Miller Paxton retired in 1902 after teaching homiletics in three seminaries—for twenty years at Princeton. Dr. David J. Burrell, at the height of his fame as minister of the Marble Collegiate Church of New York City, came to Princeton every Monday to lecture and hear the students preach. Two things he stressed—first, have a clear outline; second, preach without notes. Andrew Blackwood remembered him as "an able New York pulpit master, who did not excel as a teacher." His lectures were "brilliant" but "mechanical." Blackwood later wrote: "A sermon is not made. It grows. It is living like a poem. But homiletics, as I was taught, was like making a form out of wood, filling it up with broken stone and cement mixed with water, and then letting it harden. It seemed almost as mechanical as the work of a brick layer." The teaching of homiletics at Princeton took the form of lectures and of asking questions about the textbook, John Broadus's *Preparation and Delivery of Sermons,* without the innovations in methodology—such as case method and work-shop techniques—that were being used in some American schools. Since 1878 Henry W. Smith, who studied and taught at the Boston University School of Oratory, had taught speech at the seminary. He was joined in 1902 by Edmon Morris, instructor in vocal music.[35]

Practical theology was Princeton's weakest area. It was difficult to find the scholar-pastor-preacher combination to fill the need, and there was apparently some reluctance on the part of the faculty to develop this department fully, fearing that it would detract from the more "academic" work of the seminary. Princeton, however, regularly invited pastors to give lectures on pastoral theology. A student (from the late 1870s) wrote that "a number of the leading preachers of Philadelphia and New York . . . visit Princeton during the session—to listen to whom is itself no mean educational advantage for a future preacher." Princeton Seminary, which claimed that it was geographically nearer a larger number of Presbyterian churches than any other seminary, encouraged its students to accept preaching assignments—but only insofar as this did not interfere "with the more important work of preparation for preaching." Pastoral theology would continue to be a problem for Princeton, leading eventually to student unrest and faculty disagreement.[36]

*　　*　　*

Despite an ever-increasing annual deficit in the 1890s (it rose as high as $17,000), the board of directors saw the importance of strengthening Princeton Seminary's program. The number of extracurricular courses—graduate classes and honors classes for undergraduates—rose to thirty-two by the academic year 1902–3. The expanded curriculum necessitated the addition of a corps of instructors—capable young men who worked under the supervision of the professors. Instructors had been part of the seminary since 1820, when Charles Hodge was appointed "assistant teacher of the Oriental languages of Scripture." From that time there was almost continuously an instructor in Hebrew. Later regular instructorships were added in elocution (1878), Old Testament (1892), New Testament (1899), theology (1901), and church history (1902).

In 1903 a special meeting of the trustees was convened to consider the largest bequest ever received by Princeton Seminary. Mary J. Winthrop of New York City left part of her estate to the seminary to establish the Gelston-Winthrop Fund, named for her sister and herself. When the will was settled the seminary's portion came to over $1.6 million. In 1904 the Charles T. Haley professorship was established by a gift of $90,000 from Haley's sister. These gifts enabled the seminary to stabilize financially and to develop and expand its program. In the fall of 1905 the directors proposed that the yearly salaries of all professors be raised from $3,700 to $5,000—although further consideration resulted in a compromise of $4,500. The chair of ecclesiastical, homiletical, and pastoral theology was divided into two positions—homiletics and practical theology. Each of the remaining chairs now had an instructorship attached—except apologetics, which had the help of Dr. Patton. For the first time a registrar—Paul Martin, graduate of 1886—was added to keep up with Princeton's larger and more complicated program. About forty extracurricular courses were attracting to the seminary a large number of "graduate students." According to Dr. Warfield, the presence of these men—with some years of experience in the pastorate or on the mission field—contributed greatly to an "increase of consecration" in the student body and "a sane and hopeful outlook upon the practical work" of ministry. The seminary considered the possibility of new courses for lay workers. Princeton existed, said Warfield, "to form men for the Gospel ministry"; but by also training Bible teachers in schools and colleges, and missionary agents, it could "widen the area of its impact on the religious life of the times."[37]

Despite the storm clouds—and the storms—of the past several decades, Princeton Seminary's outlook, as the new century began, was bright. Few, if any, expected the turmoil and trauma soon to come.

12

J. Gresham Machen

The greatest opportunity the world has ever offered to the pulpit is with us now. Without the infusion of a spiritual vitality into really intellectual preaching, I do not know what is to become of our nation. . . . This generation has almost ceased to be Christian; it would not be surprising if the next generation were godless.

ARTHUR MACHEN
to his son Gresham
August 19, 1903

THE entering class of 1902 included J. Gresham
Machen of Baltimore. Gresham's father, Arthur
Webster Machen, was a highly successful Harvard-
trained lawyer from Virginia. He had declined the position of
attorney general of Maryland during the Civil War lest he
have to prosecute Confederate sympathizers. Arthur's father,
Lewis Machen, had been a man of strong convictions who
had left the Fourth Presbyterian Church in Washington,
where he was a ruling elder, when that church cast its lot with
the New School in 1837. He wished to join, he said, a church
that maintained without dilution the Calvinistic doctrines of
the Westminster Confession of Faith.

In 1873 the forty-five-year-old Arthur Machen married
twenty-four-year-old Mary, or Minnie as she came to be
called, Gresham of Macon, Georgia. Mary's father, John
Jones Gresham, was twice mayor of Macon, for forty-four
years a ruling elder in the First Presbyterian Church, and a
director of Columbia Theological Seminary. Educated at
Macon's Wesleyan College, Mary Gresham enjoyed the social
and literary life of the thriving Georgia city. Among her
close friends were Gertrude Lanier, the sister of poet
Sidney Lanier, and Mary Day, who became Sidney's wife.[1] In
Baltimore Arthur and Mary Machen were members of the
Franklin Street Presbyterian Church, a congregation that
under the leadership of Dr. J. J. Bullock, a staunch supporter
of the Confederacy, had united with the Southern Presbyterian Church in 1866.

[221]

Arthur Machen loved and avidly collected books, always looking for the finest and most beautifully printed and bound volumes, especially rare editions of classical authors. He took pleasure in the works of Horace, Thucydides, and Caesar and found personal inspiration in the Septuagint and Greek New Testament. He dabbled in writing, publishing several detective stories and short novels. Mary Gresham Machen enjoyed the theater and opera, read widely in French and English fiction and prose, and studied Victorian poetry. In 1903 she published a book entitled *The Bible in Browning*. Gresham wrote of his mother:

Her most marked intellectual characteristic, perhaps, was the catholicity of her tastes. She loved poetry with a deep and discriminating love, but she loved with equal ardour the wonders and beauties of nature. . . . She was a student of botany and also a student of the stars in their courses. I shall never forget the eager delight with which she used to stand with me, when I was very young, upon a ridge in the White Mountains and watch the long shadows creep upward upon the opposite heights. She loved nature in its more majestic aspects, and she also loved the infinite sweetness of the woods and fields.[2]

It was into this cultured Baltimore home that John Gresham Machen, the second of three sons, was born on July 28, 1881. As a child he often journeyed to Macon with his mother to visit his grandparents in their mansion on College Street. The house was "built of wood in the colonial style," Machen wrote. In front, supporting the roof, stood "four tall fluted hollow pillars," which were used during the Civil War "to hide the family silver from the Yankees." All his life Gresham remembered the "spaciousness and simplicity" of his mother's Georgia home, surrounded by great magnolia trees and splendid rose bushes. He mourned the passing of that "by-gone age" as the departing of "something precious . . . from human life." In the summers he accompanied his parents to New England, where he developed a love for the outdoors and for mountain climbing. At home he cheered the Baltimore Orioles, who won three pennants in succession during the years 1894, 1895, and 1896.[3]

From his parents Gresham Machen learned "what Christianity is" and that it can go "hand in hand with a broad out-look upon life and with the pursuit of learning." Gresham greatly respected his mother's faith. Beneath her love of nature and beneath her love of poetry, he wrote, "there lay her profound reverence for the Author of all beauty and all truth. To her, God was all and in all, and her access to God she found only through the new and living way that the Scriptures point out." He described his father as a "profoundly Christian man" whose "Christian experience . . . was a quiet stream whose waters ran deep."

He did not adopt that "Touch not, taste not, handle not" attitude toward the good things or the wonders of God's world which too often today causes earnest Christian people to consecrate to God only an impoverished man, but in his case true learning and true piety went hand in hand. Every Sunday morning and Sunday night, and on Wednesday night, he was in his place in Church, and a similar faithfulness characterized all his service as an elder in the Presbyterian Church.[4]

Gresham Machen grew up with an early knowledge of the Bible and the Westminster Shorter Catechism. He did not get his "knowledge of the Bible from Sunday School or from any other school," he once said, "but I got it on Sunday after-noons with my mother at home." His childhood comment on the catechism—"I like it very much and do it very much"—may indicate more tedium than pleasure, but he came to appreciate greatly this early training. With his parents he worshiped at the Franklin Street Presbyterian Church, which he joined in 1896 at the age of fourteen. "I shall never forget the pastor of the church in which I grew up," he later wrote. Harris E. Kirk "was a good preacher in many ways, but his most marked characteristic was the plainness and definite-ness with which he told the people what a man should do to be saved."[5]

Machen attended a private school in Baltimore, then had a brilliant career as a student at Johns Hopkins University, which was located just a few blocks from his home. He was guided in his studies by Basil L. Gildersleeve, the leading classical scholar in the country and an elder in the Franklin Street church. Gresham long remembered the seminars with

Gildersleeve, whom President Daniel Coit Gilman had recruited from the University of Virginia. Gilman, it was said, put Gildersleeve in an empty classroom and told him to "radiate." Gildersleeve, "with a magisterial disregard of anything like system," Machen recalled, would begin with Greek syntax and then allow his comments "to range over the literature of the world." At Johns Hopkins Machen studied Greek, Latin, French, German, history, and philosophy. He loved classics and acquired a lifelong habit of always carrying a small volume of the Loeb Classical Library to read in spare moments. In the summers he attended the Christian conferences at Northfield, Massachusetts, founded by D. L. Moody. In 1901 Machen delivered the class valedictory and graduated with highest honors. He toured Europe with his older brother and cousin, returned to Johns Hopkins for a year of graduate study under Gildersleeve, and then took summer courses in banking and international law at the University of Chicago. He found Chicago "the best summer resort," with its theaters, bookstores, and flat terrain for bicycle rides, but he was totally perplexed about what he should do next. He gave some thought to studying economics at Columbia University. By late summer, however, he accepted his minister's advice and decided to go to Princeton Seminary for one year—although he wrote to his mother that he wished he could do it "with more faith and more assurance that it is the right thing."[6]

Gresham Machen did not take great interest in his seminary subjects—mainly Old Testament and homiletics—during his first semester. He complained about compulsory class attendance and abhorred afternoon classes—"that evil invention," he called them. He remained at Princeton a second year but was still "chiefly afflicted by the boredom of the thing." He found some diversion, however, by attending classes at the university—Alexander T. Ormond's seminar in German philosophy, Henry Van Dyke's class in English poetry, Francis Patton's course in ethics, and (along with many other seminary students) Woodrow Wilson's lectures on American constitutional history. During his time at the seminary Machen did sufficient studies at the university to earn a master's degree. Woodrow and Ellen Wilson had often visited Machen's home in Baltimore, and from time to time they invited the young seminarian to their Princeton home for a meal.[7]

Machen lived in room 39 in Alexander Hall and took his meals at the Benham Club. The refectory, built in 1847, had gradually lost favor and was closed in 1899. The students preferred nearby boarding houses, from which evolved the seminary eating clubs. The oldest, Benham, began in 1879 at the home of the widowed Mrs. Anna Amelia Benham. Her "beautiful provisions for our gastronomic demands were noised about," her enthusiastic boarders declared, "and our table would scarce accommodate the number who sought entrance." The Friars Club was organized on January 21, 1892, by a group of seven men who "joined heart and hand in solemn conclave within the walls of 21 Brown Hall." Calvin Club was founded in about 1903. The Seminary Club became the fourth eating club. For meals members gathered in a dining room around one or two large tables. Sometimes guests were invited; on at least one occasion Woodrow Wilson enjoyed an evening with the Friars Club. Machen joined Benham—whose diners were prohibited from talking about theology and women—and, although he was at first shocked to find that the seminary students were so much like "ordinary college fellows," soon became an enthusiastic and loyal member. Each club had a social room where "stunting" —relating humorous tales in an exaggerated and boisterous manner—was practiced. Dinnertime strollers along Mercer, Alexander, and Dickinson streets were treated to snatches of stories or orations. At Christmastime the tinkling of "Jingle Bells" on water glasses and the sound of booming carol renditions emerged from the clubs.[8]

Despite his initial lack of enthusiasm for his seminary classes Machen enjoyed life at Princeton. There were bike rides to Swarthmore to watch the Johns Hopkins lacrosse team play. Football, however, was his "chief pleasure." He skipped a late afternoon Hebrew class to attend a game between Princeton University and the University of Maryland. He complained about the poor condition of the seminary's tennis courts, but in the winter there was ice skating on the Delaware Canal. Occasionally he traveled to New York to browse in secondhand bookstores and take in performances of classical and current plays. Machen, called by his nickname "Das" (suggested by the German *Das Mädchen*), was known by his fellow students for liveliness and good humor. He quickly developed a reputation for being one of the greatest "stunters" of Benham. He began a "Checkers Club" in his room in Alexander Hall, always providing for his guests an ample supply of fruit, nuts, and cigars. When the games of checkers and chess began Machen would work for a while and then, putting away his books, join in the fun.

Princeton Seminary began to make a more serious impression on the young student. He joined in the weekly worship services, the Sunday Afternoon Conference, the daily prayer meetings, and the monthly prayer meeting for missions. Dr. Patton's hospitality and sympathy encouraged and stabilized him. Machen wrote, "With infinite patience he brought me through my doubts and helped me in my difficulties. Never did a doubter and a struggler have a better friend that I had in this wonderfully eloquent and brilliant man." An even more profound impact upon Machen's thought was made by Dr. Warfield, as Machen came to appreciate the extent of his scholarship and the clarity of his understanding with regard to the doctrinal and ecclesiastical issues of the day. Machen later wrote:

When I was a student at Princeton I admired Warfield, as we all did; but I was far from understanding fully his greatness both as a scholar and as a thinker. I was still playing with the notion that a minimizing apologetic may serve the needs of the Church, and that we may perhaps fall back upon a Biblical Christianity which relinquishes the real or supposed rigidities of the Reformed system. Subsequent investigation and meditation have shown me, as over against such youthful folly, that Warfield was entirely right; I have come to see with greater and greater clearness that consistent Christianity is the easiest Christianity to defend, and that consistent Christianity—the only thoroughly Biblical Christianity—is found in the Reformed Faith.

Machen was amazed at Warfield's prodigious learning. He found that he could consult him on the most out-of-the-way topics and find that he had the "literature" of each "at his tongue's end and [was] able to give you just the guidance of which you had need."[9]

At first Machen was disappointed in the "rather dry theological lecture style" of William Park Armstrong, especially since Armstrong was "a Southerner and a very bright man"; but he soon came to appreciate him as "imbued with 'university' spirit in its best form." Before long Armstrong had become Machen's closest friend and mentor. Under his guidance and inspiration Machen took more seriously his work in New Testament and began to see how he could use his training in philology and the classics to ground orthodox belief in sound scholarship. He won the middler prize in New Testament for the best paper on John 1:1–18. At the beginning of his senior year Machen mentioned to Kerr Duncan Macmillan, instructor in Semitic philology, that he was undecided as to whether to do general reading or compete for the New Testament fellowship, the Maitland Prize, during his senior year. Macmillan told him that he could do general reading at any time in his life, but the opportunity to do that piece of detailed research would be his then and then only. Machen acted upon that "excellent advice" and wrote a forceful thesis on "The New Testament Account of the Birth of Jesus." He won the fellowship and had the rare distinction of seeing his work published in *The Princeton Theological Review.* Looking back later on his seminary days, Machen commented, "The old Princeton was an environment in which a man felt encouraged to do his very best."[10]

After graduation in 1905 Machen sadly left the seminary and "old 39" in Alexander Hall and the "old 39 crowd." He often said that his idea of a delightful time was "a Princeton room full of fellows smoking." When he thought "what a wonderful aid tobacco is to friendship," he sometimes regretted that he never took it up. After a summer bicycling in Germany and mountain-climbing in Austria, Machen hurried to Marburg, where he planned to spend the winter term studying under Adolph Jülicher, Johannes Weiss, and other scholars there. He sorely missed the kind of fellowship that had warmed his heart at Princeton—and the football games. He wrote to his parents urgently requesting that they send him the scores, adding, "When I see a vacant field on one of these autumn days, my mind is filled with wonder at this benighted people which does not seem to hear the voice of nature when she commands every human being to play football or watch it being played." The sociable Gresham Machen soon joined one of the German student societies, which, according to his estimate, required six hours of activity each day. Members, he explained to his brother, ate large quantities of food, drank beer, played tennis, fenced, and, when women were present, danced. On one occasion Machen joined a hastily organized *Nachtbummel,* which took him with a crowd of his German fellow students on an expedition through the surrounding country that lasted from midnight until seven o'clock, causing him to miss his morning lecture.[11]

Although Machen was not at first impressed with Johannes Weiss, he admired Adolf Jülicher despite his very different approach to the New Testament from that at Princeton. When Machen heard Rudolf Knopf's lectures on New Testament introduction he was delighted to realize that Armstrong's classes at Princeton had placed the real questions before him in a thoroughly fair and comprehensive way. "The conclusions arrived at in the two cases were very different," Machen later wrote, "but at least my Princeton teacher had not concealed from me either the position of the opponents or the evidence upon which their contentions were based." Machen described Walter Bauer's lectures on the Gospel of John:

The course, which came at eight o'clock on the dark winter mornings, was attended by four students—two Germans, one Englishman, and myself. On a number of occasions the two Germans were absent; and once, I remember, the Englishman was absent too, so that the lecture was delivered (with all the academic formality characteristic of a German lecture-room) for my sole benefit.[12]

Machen attended lectures on systematic theology given by Wilhelm Herrmann, the most prominent theologian at Marburg and one of the leading liberal theologians in the world. William Park Armstrong, who had studied earlier under Herrmann, encouraged Machen to attend his lectures "if for no other reason than to come into contact with his vigorous, earnest and devout spirit." Armstrong wrote to Machen that when he heard Herrmann teach he was reminded "more of Dr. Purves" than anyone else with whom he had studied. The first time Machen heard Herrmann, he wrote to his mother, "may almost be described as an epoch in my life—so much deeper is his devotion to Christ than anything I have known in myself during the past few years."[13]

Albrecht Ritschl's most influential and consistent follower, Herrmann struggled with the problem of maintaining the Christian faith in the modern scientific world. Rejecting as a basis for truth reliance on Scripture, the teachings of Jesus, and doctrine, he separated the domains of science and faith. Herrmann regarded the Christian faith as the way in which the Christian thinks about God and Christ—as a result of the impression that the inner life of Jesus makes on the soul. Theology is simply a purely individual and subjective matter—an experience unassailable by history or science. Herrmann's liberalism was new and unsettling to Machen, but his devotion to Christ deeply impressed the student as he listened to the German professor lecturing with tears in his eyes on the anti-Christian attacks of materialistic science. Machen wrote to his mother, "Herrmann affirms very little of that which I have been accustomed to regard as essential to Christianity; yet there is no doubt in my mind but that he is a Christian, and a Christian of a peculiarly earnest type." Machen found Herrmann's *Communion of the Christian with God* one of the greatest religious books he had ever read. He believed that, although he may not have given the whole truth, Herrmann had "gotten hold of something that has been sadly neglected in the church and in the orthodox theology."[14]

Machen's dedication to intellectual honesty made a thorough and sympathetic investigation of liberalism necessary for him. He wrote to his mother, "As long as [one] feels that he has not *fully* learned to appreciate the arguments on both sides (and particularly the side to which he is inclined to be opposed)—just so long must he continue to be a doubter." Although he never came to the point of substituting Herrmann's views for his own orthodox position, for a time he was profoundly shaken, and even overwhelmed, by his encounter with this man whose fervor and moral earnestness were so impressive. In a letter to his father Machen described the appeal of Herrmann's teaching: "It is the faith that is a real experience, a real experience of God that saves us, not the faith that consists in accepting as true a lot of dogmas on the basis merely of what others have said. Every Christian is conscious of having experienced a miracle, but it is a miracle in his own inner life." Later, Machen would refer on rare occasions to his struggle at Marburg. One of his students recalled his saying that

the great Dr. Herrmann presented his position with such power I would sometimes leave his presence wondering how I could ever retain my confidence in the historical accuracy of the Gospel narratives. Then I'd go to my room, take out the Gospel of Mark and read it from beginning to end at one sitting—and my doubts would fade. I realized that the document could not possibly be the invention of the mind of a mere man.[15]

Machen came to see that Herrmann's position was fallacious for two reasons. First, the picture of the "liberal Jesus," which called forth Herrmann's unbounded reverence, was a fictitious creation. Secondly, the type of religious experience that Ritschlian liberalism endeavored to conserve was hardly true Christian experience. It knew nothing of the biblical view of sin and redemption through the death of Christ. Machen wrote, "If Herrmann was a Christian, he was a Christian not because of but despite those things which were most distinctive of his teachings. At the heart of Christianity is a view of sin whose profundities were a sealed book to Herrmann and to all his school. A man under true conviction of sin will never be satisfied with the Ritschlian Jesus, but will seek his way into the presence of that Jesus who redeemed us by His precious blood and is ever living to make intercession for us at the throne of God."[16]

Machen followed his work at Marburg with a summer term at Göttingen. There he studied with Emil Schürer, head of the New Testament department and author of the monumental and massive work *The History of the Jewish People in the*

Time of Jesus. Some found him a rather dry lecturer, but Machen appreciated his solid biblical scholarship. Machen also heard Wilhelm Bousset—a brilliant teacher and advocate of the "history of religions" method of New Testament study. He saw Bousset's aim to liberate Christianity from the dead forms of orthodoxy—so that it might ring out once more with its old power—as a "noble" one; but he doubted that it was being attained. He wrote to his brother Arthur, "What Bousset has left after he has stripped off the form is certainly well worth keeping; but whether it is the Christian faith that has been found to overcome the world is very doubtful."[17]

The young American student appreciated the caution, tact, and good sense Wilhelm Heitmüller displayed in his course on John, despite Heitmüller's low opinion of the historical value of the gospel. Machen's brother wrote to ask why he did not study under the great conservative scholar Theodor Zahn. Machen replied, "It is a mistake, I think, to suppose that any of the Princeton faculty would be inclined to advise a student in my circumstances to seek out a conservative university just because it is conservative; for Princeton Seminary differs from some other conservative institutions in that it does not hide from itself the real state of affairs in Biblical study at the present day, and makes an honest effort to come to an understanding with the ruling tendency."[18]

Machen continued to express some doubts as to "where the truth lies"; but "that Bousset and Heitmüller have gotten hold of it is something," he wrote, "that I should be sorry to think." Although appreciating the earnest religious life of the liberals, Machen, still struggling, continued to stand on the side of historic orthodox Christianity. He was prepared to give up his highly esteemed membership in *Germania* if it meant that he could not wear its uniform to a Baptist church, which he found much more evangelical than the state church. Machen was troubled, however, that conservative scholarship could not match the impressive attainments of the German liberals. He feared hypocrisy and longed to have "a real Christian faith and resulting Christian life." He shunned the idea of going into the ministry because he felt that this would be simply falling "back into the old rut" of doing what was expected of him. His brother suggested that a job as a teacher of New Testament might be more suitable for him than preaching, but Machen sharply replied, "In the field of the New Testament, there is no place for the weakling. Decisiveness, moral and intellectual, is absolutely required. Any other kind of work is not merely useless . . . but is even perhaps harmful." Machen saw in Germany that, unlike America where Christian leaders were often popular preachers who had little contact with the universities, there was "impressive scholarship which rooted liberal religion in sophisticated academic training."[19]

Gresham Machen's study in Germany gave him a deep impression of the power of liberalism. Years later he wrote, "I was not insensible of the attractiveness of that solution when I sat in Herrmann's classroom, and I am not insensible of it now. How happy we might seem to be if we could only avoid the debate about the existence of a personal God—if we could only relegate all that to a sphere of metaphysics with which the Christian man need have nothing to do!" Machen could not ignore the scholarship and influence of liberalism and was never able to dismiss the "'higher critics' *en masse* with a few words of summary condemnation. Much deeper, it seems to me, lies the real refutation of this mighty attack upon the truth of our religion," he wrote; "and we are not really doing our cause service by underestimating the power of the adversaries in the debate."[20]

In March 1906 Machen received a letter from William Park Armstrong asking if he could present his name to the Princeton trustees to be his assistant in New Testament. Machen declined. A few weeks later Ethelbert Warfield, president of Lafayette College, wrote to Machen inviting him to become instructor in Greek and German at Lafayette. When Ethelbert asked his brother, Benjamin, for Machen's address, Benjamin Warfield said that Lafayette could not have Machen because Armstrong was going to take him for Princeton. Armstrong persisted—writing back thoughtful answers to all Machen's objections. He explained that Machen did not have to come under care of a presbytery nor take any theological exam. He stated, "Only in your teaching you will be expected to stand on the broad principles of the Reformed Theology and in particular on the authority of the Scriptures in religious matters." A few years earlier Armstrong, in responding to Dr. Purves about teaching at the seminary, had told Purves that he had not settled everything. Dr. Purves had replied with the same words that Armstrong now wrote to Machen.

Still undecided, Gresham Machen decided to sail for home to consult with his parents and Dr. Armstrong and to try to reach a final decision. He arrived in August and immediately set out for his parents' summer home in Seal Harbor, Maine. In September he went to Princeton to meet with Armstrong and surprised even himself by agreeing to undertake the work for one year. Fearful that he had made the wrong decision, he anticipated the most trying year of his life. He longed to return to Germany and prepare for a career in teaching classics. He reminded his mother, "I am *not* a minister, or anything more than a mere layman."[21]

In the fall of 1906 Gresham Machen moved back into Alexander Hall and resumed his place in the Benham Club. He delighted the students with his pranks and his generosity. He would labor, or pretend to labor, up the three long flights of steps to his rooms on the fourth floor, murmuring loudly so that any student within earshot could hear, "Poor old Dassie, poor old Dassie." One of Machen's famous sayings was "Boys, there are two things wrong with this institution: you're not working hard enough and you're not having enough fun." On Saturday evenings he would fling his bedroom door open and shout, "All right, men, don't be tightwads!" That was his signal for the seminarians to gather in his rooms for apples, oranges, candy, dried fruits, nuts, cookies, soft drinks—and checkers and chess. Machen loved the games—apparently never losing, as his keen mind anticipated the moves of his opponents. He enjoyed tennis, walking, and bicycling. He was an enthusiastic spectator at Princeton football games and, although not as great a fan of baseball, he thought Ty Cobb and, later, Babe Ruth were "worth going to see." Machen often gave out tickets to Ivy League football games—usually seats on the fifty-yard line— with the characteristic question "Would you do me the favor of taking these tickets off my hands?"

Although he complained that his first faculty meeting was

[233]

"long and stupid," he again found the friendship and scholarship of the Princeton faculty a stabilizing force. Dr. Patton was his "spiritual father." Dr. Warfield, with his brilliant and comprehensive understanding of the Christian faith, strengthened Machen doctrinally. Dr. Armstrong, Machen's "most intimate friend," provided a model for Machen's teaching with his ability "to exhibit the connection between the supernaturalistic view of the New Testament and the theistic view of God and the world upon which the Christian religion depends." Machen socialized frequently with the Armstrong family, taking them to Princeton football games in return for the service "Army" rendered to Machen's car. Machen often had Sunday dinner with the Armstrongs and a late Sunday afternoon supper with "Wis" Hodge and his family.[22]

Before long Machen abandoned his plans to return to Germany and gave up thoughts of a career in classics. He gained the reputation of being one of the best teachers at the seminary. He abandoned his earlier method of closely following a manuscript for a more extemporaneous manner of teaching. He was a master of precise, lucid speech and attractive diction and style. The students could not help drawing a parallel between his skill in chess and checkers and the marvelous way he demolished the arguments of critical scholars. Ned B. Stonehouse, as he sat in Machen's course on Galatians, "felt not merely that Luther had been reborn, but that Paul himself had become alive, and was teaching and proclaiming as a fresh message the evangel that stands in irreconcilable opposition to 'another gospel which is not another.'"[23]

Machen made his classes exciting and unpredictable by humorous little gestures and expressions. Sometimes when a student was answering a question the professor would rise from his chair and, with utmost solemnity, balance a book on his head. At other times he would climb up on a chair and bend forward as though experimenting with the law of gravity. Again, he would take his stand about two feet from the classroom wall and lean forward slowly, hands at his sides, until his forehead touched the wall. He would remain in this strange position for several minutes, staring at the floor. Rituals like these endeared him to his students and always produced roars of laughter.

Machen also had a reputation for exacting standards and hard grading. He was disappointed that some students had little interest in New Testament Greek and avoided his rigorous elective courses. He threatened to fail three quarters of those enrolled in his class on the Pauline epistles. He fretted over "the extremely low intellectual standard among the future ministers of the Presbyterian Church," finally comforting himself with the thought that in the apostolic church "not many wise according to the flesh were called." Still, he believed that there should be "a place at least for *some* who would be able to cope with the problems of modern life and make modern culture subservient to the gospel."[24]

13

Zealous for the Gospel

We all know in the midst of what dangers, in the midst of what deaths, those who have gone before us have fulfilled this trust [to bear witness of the truth]. "Martyrs," we call them; and we call them such truly. For "martyrs" means "witnesses"; and they bore their witness despite cross and sword, fire and raging beasts. So constant was their witness, so undismayed, that this proverb has enshrined their eulogy for all time, that "the blood of the martyrs was the seed of the Church." They were our fathers: have we inherited their spirit? If we be Christians at all, must not we too be "martyrs," "witnesses"? Must not we too steadfastly bear our witness to the truth assailed in our time? There may be no more fires lighted for our quivering flesh: are there no more temptations to a guilty silence or a weak evasion?

BENJAMIN BRECKINRIDGE WARFIELD

WHILE Gresham Machen was studying in Germany his fellow Princeton Seminary student John Rogers Peale had gone as a missionary to China. There he and his wife were killed, joining the number of the Princeton missionary martyrs. The students placed in the classroom building a bronze tablet that read:

Of these the world was not worthy

WALTER MACON LOWRIE
class of 1840,
thrown overboard by pirates in the China Sea, 1847

JOHN EDGAR FREEMAN
class of 1838,
ROBERT McMULLEN
class of 1853,
who, with their wives, were shot by the order
of Nanasahib, 1857, at Cawnpore, India

LEVI JANVIER
class of 1840,
stabbed by a Sikh fanatic at Lodiana, India, 1864

ISIDOR LOEWENTHAL
class of 1854,
shot accidentally or by design at Peshawur, India, 1864

JOHN ROGERS PEALE
class of 1905,
killed with his wife by a mob at Lien Chow, China, 1905

FAITHFUL UNTO DEATH

The Princeton commitment to the evangelization of the world lived on in the new century and would soon bring forth another generation of missionaries to take the places of their fallen colleagues in obedience to "the last command" of the risen Savior.

*　　*　　*

In 1905 Charles Rosenbury Erdman was elected to the Princeton faculty as professor in the newly created chair of practical theology. Charles Erdman was born in Fayetteville, New York, in 1866, the son of Presbyterian minister William J. Erdman and his wife, Henrietta. William was raised in the Dutch Reformed Church but attended Union Theological Seminary in New York and was ordained by the New School Presbyterian Church in 1860. He served pastorates in New York, Michigan, Indiana, Massachusetts, North Carolina, and, from 1875 to 1878, at D. L. Moody's Chicago Avenue Church in Chicago. He was one of the founders of what became the Moody Bible Institute and was a frequent speaker at Moody's Northfield summer conferences.

Charles Erdman graduated from Princeton College and, after taking a year off for travel, entered Princeton Seminary. He interrupted his seminary program to spend a year studying the Bible under his father's guidance. He later explained:

Seminary authorities in those days felt that extensive Bible study was unnecessary. They took the position that all who enrolled to study for the ministry were thoroughly schooled already in the Bible. This was fallacious. I, for one, wasn't—at least not to the extent necessary—even though my father was a clergyman. The emphasis back in my seminary days was given to Latin, Greek, and Hebrew.[1]

Erdman graduated from Princeton Seminary in 1891 and accepted a call to organize a church in Overbrook, Pennsylvania. There he met and, on June 1, 1892, married Mary Estelle Pardee, daughter of wealthy coal magnate Calvin Pardee. After six years at Overbrook Charles accepted a call to the First Presbyterian Church of Germantown, Pennsylvania. Princeton Seminary offered him the chair of homiletics in 1902. He declined but accepted the call three years later to teach homiletics, church polity, pastoral care, Christian education, evangelism, and English Bible! Since Dr. Paxton's retirement in 1902 homiletics had been taught by visiting preachers and by seminary faculty of other departments. Although some directors and faculty were concerned that Dr. Erdman's appointment, the greater emphasis on practical courses, and the addition of English Bible could threaten the old curriculum, most were supportive. Gresham Machen believed that Erdman was of "the right stuff." Director James S. Dickson wrote to Erdman,

I believe that the most urgent need before the Seminary is the need for instruction in the best methods of reaching men for Jesus Christ, and in an evangelistic way, by the power of the Word of God that they have in their own hands. I am the last man in the world to depreciate the usefulness of classical training or of the years that students spend upon the original languages of the Scripture, but I *do* know that we must teach seminary students how to take up the Word of God that they will use in their pulpits and prayer-meeting rooms and expound the Scriptures in a definitely evangelistic way with the one purpose of saving souls. I hope that your coming to Princeton will begin a new era there, whose main characteristic will be the prominence of just this sort of teaching.[2]

Charles Erdman undertook his new role as seminary professor with enthusiasm and diligence. He was an experienced pastor and a winsome, witty man who valued friendliness and a sense of humor in others and constantly warned his students against a belligerent spirit. "A Christian minister," he wrote, "must be 'gentle,' sweetly reasonable, eager to show forbearance and kindly consideration; he must not be 'contentious' or quarrelsome, even as to matters of doctrine." In his teaching Erdman aimed, as he said, "at such a special, practical, spiritual, and evangelistic interpretation of the Bible as will directly equip the 'preacher for his pulpit and the pastor for all his personal work.'" Dr. Erdman became advisor to the seminary student association. He wrote books and articles, including two essays for *The Fundamentals,* and served as an editorial consultant to the *Scofield Reference Bible.* He was a popular preacher and frequent speaker at Bible conferences. In 1910 he attended the International Missionary Conference in Edinburgh. He was elected to the

Board of Foreign Missions of the Presbyterian Church and later became its president.[3]

*   *   *

Princeton Seminary provided the basic courses for the bachelor of divinity degree and offered its students many electives. During the 1907–8 school year the Old Testament department offered a course called "Belief in the Future Life among the Ancient Semites and its Bearing on the Interpretation of the Scriptures" taught by Dr. Davis. Dr. Vos taught a class in "Eighth-Century Prophets," and Dr. Boyd offered courses in "Criticism of Modern Theories of the Pentateuch" and "History of the Period after the Exile." In the New Testament field Dr. Vos taught "Pauline Eschatology" and "The Theology of the Epistle to the Hebrews." Dr. Armstrong taught "Studies in the Passion History" and "The Apostolic Fathers." Dr. Machen offered "Exegesis of II Corinthians" and "The Gospel Infancy Narratives." Dr. Wilson taught several courses in Semitic languages. Dr. DeWitt taught "History of Doctrine," "History of the Doctrine of the Atonement," and "American Church History." Dr. Greene offered "Philosophical Apologetics," "The Metaphysics of Christian Apologetics," "The Idealistic or Hegelian Theory of the Christian Religion," "The Ten Commandments with Special Reference to Modern Problems," and "The Ethics of the Old Testament." Dr. Warfield taught "Augustine and the Latin Patristic Theology" and the "Theology of John Calvin." Dr. Hodge offered courses in "The Person of Christ" and "The Doctrine of Justification." Dr. Erdman conducted classes in "The Pauline Epistles," "The General Epistles," "Acts," and "Methods of Christian Work."

The Princeton students also had the opportunity to hear prominent lecturers and preachers, such as those who visited the seminary during the 1907–8 school year. James Orr of the Glasgow College of the United Free Church of Scotland lectured on "Some of the Greater Movements in Theology and Philosophy in Germany in the Nineteenth Century." In October the L. P. Stone Lectures were given by D. Hay Fleming, the honorary secretary of the Scottish Historical

Society, on "The Causes, Characteristics and Consequences of the Reformation in Scotland." The Students' Lecturer on Missions, Charles R. Watson, long-time missionary in Egypt and secretary of the Board of Foreign Missions of the United Presbyterian Church, spoke on "Missions in the Nile Valley." A second series of missionary lectures—on "Korea's Challenge to the Christian Church"—was given in March by Horace Grant Underwood, one of the pioneer missionaries to Korea. A. T. Pierson, editor of *The Missionary Review of the World*, served as one of the lecturers in the regular curriculum course on missions. He discussed "The Pastor and Missions" under the headings "Missions as a Science," "Missions as an Art," "Missions as a Vocation," and "Missions as an Experience." T. H. P. Sailer, secretary of the Presbyterian Board of Foreign Missions, lectured on "The Responsibility of the Pastor for the Missionary Training of the Church." "The most inspiring event of the year," according to the *Princeton Seminary Bulletin*, was the visit of G. Campbell Morgan, the pastor of Westminster Chapel in London. In three addresses given on March 17 and 18, 1908—one at the First Presbyterian Church, one in Alexander Hall at the university, and the third in Miller Chapel at the seminary—the great English Bible teacher spoke to the whole Princeton community.

*　　　*　　　*

By the fall of 1908 the seminary's new coal-fired heating and electric plant was in operation, and the old coal stoves and oil lamps disappeared from the dormitories. Andrew Blackwood described how "each room was lighted by a small bulb, in-geniously put into sockets by a locking mechanism that prevented bulb-snatching." "When lighted," he said, "the bulb looked like a hot nail in a bottle." In 1910 the former refectory, which for a few years had been used as a dormitory, was converted into a gymnasium, with facilities for basketball, boxing, gymnastics, and wrestling—and also a music and social room. The *Princeton Seminary Bulletin* expressed the hope "that this finely equipped gymnasium will attract not only the strong, robust men in the Seminary, but that it will prove to be a blessing to students who are inclined to be weak, anaemic or nervous, and by whom gymnasium work should be regarded not only as a privilege, but a sacred duty." The seminary students, sometimes joined by students from the university, played baseball, cricket, rugby, and soccer. A tennis enthusiast, Dr. Machen financed and supervised the construction of new tennis courts at the seminary, but he had trouble convincing the groundskeeper to take an active interest in their maintenance.[4]

*   *   *

By the early twentieth century, liberal theology had moved beyond attack on biblical inspiration to challenge other major tenets of historic Christianity. In his introduction to a collection of B. B. Warfield's writings Martyn Lloyd-Jones has described the time as

the age of the "liberal Jesus" and "the Jesus of history," who was contrasted with "the Christ of Paul." The Bible had been subjected to such drastic criticism that not only was its divine inspiration and unique authority denied but the whole idea of revelation was in question. The Lord Jesus Christ was but a man, "the greatest religious genius of all time," miracles had never happened because miracles cannot happen, our Lord's mission was a failure, and His death on the cross but a tragedy. The great truths proclaimed in the historic Creeds of the Church, and especially in the great Confessions of Faith drawn up after the Protestant Reformation, concerning the Bible as the Word of God and the person and work of the Lord Jesus Christ were being questioned and rejected by the vast majority of "scholars."

B. B. Warfield led the Princeton defense of the historic Christian faith. "Warfield's method," Dr. Lloyd-Jones wrote,

was not to meet criticisms of the traditional theology with mere general philosophical and theological arguments, though he could and did do that also. It was rather along the following lines. He would first state the case as presented by the critic in a fair and clear manner. Then he would proceed to analyse it and deal with it clause by clause and word by word. He was thoroughly familiar with all the literature, but for him the test always was "to the law and to the testimony." For him the question was, Was this a true exegesis and interpretation of what the Scripture said? Was it consistent and compatible with what the Scripture said elsewhere? What were the implications of this statement? and so on. It was really the method of the advocate in the law courts who obtains his verdict, not by passionate and emotional appeals to an unlearned jury, but rather as the result of a masterly analysis and patient dissection and refutation of the case of the opponent, followed by a crystal clear and positive exposition of the truth addressed to the "learned judge on the bench."[5]

Dr. Warfield saw "the general indefiniteness in doctrinal construction which seems to be coming in upon us like a flood" as a weakening of all "external authority." The "sustained effort" to deny systematized truth in the form of doctrines and to deny an external authority to the Bible as the basis for belief was, Dr. Warfield said, a chief characteristic of "the newer religious thinking." Putting forth human reason under such descriptions as "the Christian consciousness" and "the indwelling Spirit which is the common endowment of Christians," and still clinging to fragments of the Bible, modern theology was "building out of them a foundationless house for their spiritual home." "Instead of stating Christian belief in terms of modern thought," as it claimed, Warfield asserted that it was attempting "to state modern thought in terms of Christian belief."

Against these views Warfield insisted that Christianity is constituted by facts and by "dogmas," that is, by the facts understood in one specific manner. The Bible, he argued, is both the record of the great deeds God has wrought for the salvation of the world and the authoritative interpretation of those deeds. Warfield did not deny "the rights of criticism," for he believed that the existence of truth demanded criticism. The crisis in biblical studies had arisen, he believed, not because of criticism itself but because of an "ineradicable tendency of man to confound the right of criticism with the rightness of his own criticism." Neither did Warfield ignore the gradual progression of doctrinal knowledge that characterizes the study of historical theology. Even though the church's understanding of the message of the Bible as set forth in its theology has been uneven and at times erroneous, its witness in its whole life over the ages has led to greater and greater clarity, Warfield believed. It was clear to him that orthodoxy and not liberalism has best represented that historic faith as it was won through hard study and courageous commitment to God's truth. Indeed, the history of the church itself was to Dr. Warfield one of the greatest testimonies to evangelical Christianity.[6]

Dr. Warfield defended "the three pillars" on which he believed the structure of Christianity rested: "the supernatural, the incarnation, [and] redemption." "In an important sense," he wrote, "these three things constitute the Christianity of the New Testament; proceeding from the more general to the more specific, they sum up in themselves its essence."[7]

Warfield held, as he told the students in his opening address of September 18, 1896, that "the supernatural is the very breath of Christianity's nostrils, and an anti-supernaturalistic atmosphere is to it the deadliest miasma." Modern theologians were seeking to "curb the supernatural, to bring it into the full service of reason," he claimed, stating that "the real question with them seems to be, not what kind and measure of supernaturalism does the Christianity of Christ and His apostles recognize and require; but, how little of the supernatural may be admitted and yet men continue to call themselves Christians." Warfield set forth five points at which Christians must recognize, he said, "the intrusion of pure supernaturalism into our conception of things." These he reviewed in a single sentence: "The confession of a supernatural God, who may and does act in a supernatural mode, and who acting in a supernatural mode has wrought out for us a supernatural redemption, interpreted in a supernatural revelation, and applied by the supernatural operations of His Spirit—this confession constitutes the core of the Christian profession." Warfield ended his address with the words:

Only he who holds this faith whole and entire has a full right to the Christian name: only he can hope to conserve the fullness of Christian truth. Let us see to it that under whatever pressure and amid whatever difficulties, we make it heartily and frankly our confession, and think and live alike in its strength and by its light. So doing, we shall find ourselves intrenched against the assaults of the world's anti-supernaturalism, and able by God's grace to witness a good confession in the midst of its most insidious attacks.[8]

With articles such as "How to Get Rid of Christianity," "Evading the Supernatural," and "Christianity and our Times," and scores of book reviews, Warfield showed how liberal theologians were allied in their denial of the supernatural. In reviewing Henry F. Henderson's *Religious Controversies of Scotland,* he stated that "under the assault of recent scientific and critical belief," the Presbyterian church in Scotland "seems in danger of losing her clear sense of the Supernatural, which is only another way of saying she is in danger of losing the vision of God. And when that is lost, everything is lost." Dr. Warfield constantly reminded the Princeton students and, through his writings, the Christian church that "anti-supernaturalism" is "the very principle of the presently prevalent criticism: and as supernaturalism is the very principle of Christianity, this criticism and Christianity can live together in harmony just as little as can fire and water."[9]

Dr. Warfield zealously defended the second "pillar" of Christianity, the incarnation of Christ. "One of the most portentous symptoms of the decay of vital sympathy with historical Christianity which is observable in present-day academic circles is the widespread tendency in recent Christological discussion to revolt from the doctrine of the Two Natures in the Person of Christ," he noted. "The significance of this revolt becomes at once apparent," Warfield said, "when we reflect that the doctrine of the Two Natures is only another way of stating the doctrine of the Incarnation; and the doctrine of the Incarnation is the hinge on which the Christian system turns." Although the doctrine of the two natures of Christ received its definitive statement at Chalcedon, Warfield believed that "there never was a time when it was not the universal presupposition of the whole attitude, intellectual and devotional alike, of Christians to their Lord." It is "the assertion concerning their Lord of all the primary witnesses of the Christian faith," Warfield asserted. "It is, indeed, the self-testimony of our Lord Himself, disclosing to us the mystery of His being." "We may reject it if we will," Warfield wrote, "but in rejecting it we reject the only real Jesus in favor of another Jesus—who is not another, but is the creature of pure fantasy. The alternatives which we are really face to face with are, either the two-natured Christ of history, or—a strong delusion." The Jesus the critics offered, he stated, is "a Jesus who thought as a man of his day, who lived as a man of his day, and who ceases to be a trustworthy guide to us in either what he said or what he did."[10]

Against modern attacks upon it, Warfield emphasized the doctrine of the substitutionary atonement of Christ, the third "pillar" upon which Christianity rests. In an address at Princeton Seminary on October 13, 1902, Warfield reviewed "Modern Theories of the Atonement." He showed how "the revolt from the conceptions of satisfaction, propitiation, expiation, sacrifice, reinforced continually by tendencies adverse to evangelical doctrine peculiar to our times, has grown steadily more and more widespread, and in some quarters more and more extreme, until it has issued in an immense confusion on this central doctrine of the gospel." The orthodox doctrine of substitutionary atonement, however, had not been lost "from the consciousness of the Church," Warfield said.

It has not been lost from the hearts of the Christian community. It is in its terms that the humble Christian everywhere still expresses the grounds of his hope of salvation. It is in its terms that the earnest evangelist everywhere still presses the claims of Christ upon the awakened hearer. It has not even been lost from the forum of theological discussion. It still commands powerful advocates wherever a vital Christianity enters academical circles: and, as a rule, the more profound the thinker, the more clear is the note he strikes in its proclamation and defense.[11]

Dr. Warfield defended the historic doctrine of the bodily resurrection of Christ, once viewed as "the very citadel of the Christian position." "If Christianity is entirely indifferent to the reality of [the fact of the resurrection of Jesus], then 'Christianity' is something wholly different from what it was conceived to be by its founders, and from what it is still believed to be by its adherents." Warfield showed how Christ

[248]

"deliberately staked his whole claim upon his resurrection" and how "the earliest proclaimers of the gospel conceived witnessing to the resurrection of their Master as their primary function." He argued that for "a Christianity which will meet the needs of sinful man, a Christianity which does not offer him merely the impression of a holy life, but provides him with salvation by a divine Redeemer, a resurrected Lord is indispensable. A 'Christianity' which can dispense with the immediately supernatural, to which the pre-existence and the proper deity of Christ are unknown, which discards the expiatory work of Christ, and which looks for no resurrection of the body," Warfield wrote, "may readily enough do without the fact of the resurrection of Christ. But when it comes to that, may we not also do very well without such a 'Christianity'? What has it to offer to the sin-stricken human soul?"[12]

In 1907 *The Lord of Glory* appeared, in which Dr. Warfield examined in detail the titles of Christ as used by the writers of the New Testament. These titles, Warfield concluded, "give endlessly repeated and endlessly varied expression" to three specific convictions—"Christ is the Messiah; Christ is our Redeemer; Christ is God." Warfield stated that

if Christ were not God, we should have a very different Jesus and a very different Christianity. And that is the reason that modern unbelief bends all its energies in a vain effort to abolish the historical Jesus and to destroy historical Christianity. Its instinct is right: but its task is hopeless. We need the Jesus of history to account for the Christianity of history. And we need both the Jesus of history and the Christianity of history to account for the history of the world.[13]

In 1910 Warfield's article "Jesus Christ" was published in *The New Schaff-Herzog Encyclopedia of Religious Knowledge*. The New Testament clearly presents Jesus as the Messiah, Warfield wrote, "definitely represented as a divine being who has entered the world on a mission of mercy to sinful man, in the prosecution of which He has given Himself up as a sacrifice for sin, but has risen again from the dead and ascended to the right hand of God, henceforth to rule as Lord of all." "The intense supernaturalism" of the Bible's portrait of Jesus, Warfield noted, is "of course, an offense to

[249]

our anti-supernaturalistic age." For a century and a half, he wrote, scholars have been working "to construct a historical sieve" that would strain out the miraculous and let "Jesus" through. Such attempts, Warfield judged, are complete failures because "Jesus is Himself the greatest miracle of all."[14]

Warfield's article "Christless Christianity" was published in 1912 in the *Harvard Theological Review*. The effort to eliminate the supernatural element from the Gospels has led not to a historical Jesus but to a "Christless Christianity," Warfield argued. He noted that even those liberals who accept the historicity of Jesus place little importance on him. They hold, Warfield stated, that "whether Jesus existed or not, is for our religious and Christian life, in the last analysis, a matter of indifference, if only this life be really religious and Christian." Such a religion, however, Dr. Warfield asserted, is no longer redemptive and so provides no hope for human need.[15]

*   *   *

Following the confessional revision of 1903, reunion talks had been taking place between the Presbyterian Church in the United States of America and the Cumberland Presbyterian Church, a denomination that had broken away almost a hundred years earlier over the requirement for an educated clergy and the "fatalistic" doctrine of election. B. B. Warfield wrote a series of articles for *The Presbyterian* in April and May of 1904, and for *The Cumberland Presbyterian* during the same year, in which he expressed his "misgivings" concerning the union. He argued that the Cumberland Confession of 1814 and 1883 was undeniably Arminian, although he admitted that the church espoused an "Evangelical Arminianism." Warfield claimed that it had not been a protest against Calvinistic "fatalism" that motivated the separation of the Cumberland church, but that a close examination of their 1814 revisions of the Westminster Confession of Faith demonstrated that it was plain Calvinism that had been removed from the Confession. None of the five points of Calvinism remained in it, Warfield stated, except for the perseverance of the saints, and that "inconsistently." Francis Patton said that reunion with the Cumberland Presbyterian

Church would be "more important than revision [of the Westminster Confession], far more important, for it is, in effect, not necessarily in intention, an indirect way of revising the Confession of Faith on radical grounds."

At a conference at Princeton Seminary on October 10, 1905, William Brenton Greene addressed the issue of church union in a paper entitled "Broad Churchism and the Christian Life." "Broad Churchism," he said, is "characterized by more or less of indifference to truth." He pointed to the decline of interest in doctrine. "It is on Christian doctrine that the fewest books are now being read. . . . The preaching of today is anything and everything but doctrinal. . . . Creeds are commonly laid on the shelf as having only an historical interest. . . . Even among us it is not generally thought worth while to teach our children our matchless 'Shorter Catechism.'"

Greene acknowledged the sincerity of "the Broad Church movement" in its desire to emphasize Christian living rather than Christian thinking in an effort to produce greater results. To Dr. Greene, however, "Broad Churchism" was not a friend but a foe of Christian living. An attitude that ignores or minimizes doctrinal thinking is "essentially sinful," stated Greene. It expresses "indifference to God." Ethics supplants dogmatics. "What is the duty which God requires of man? becomes the question. The inquiry, What are we to believe concerning God? loses all but a merely academic interest." The great doctrinal truths are never "mere abstract propositions," Greene said. "Every one of the doctrines of Christianity has practical applications." "Devotion to the truth of Christ has issued in effective activity in His cause," the Princeton professor proclaimed. He reminded his hearers of "the Huguenots of France, of the Dutch Republic, of the Covenanters of Scotland, of the English Puritans" and asserted that "their uniquely grand characters were the expression of their uniquely grand belief." "Brethren," said Dr. Greene, "we may not look for a revival of religion until there has been a revival of doctrinal instruction. True religion is impossible when Broad Churchism is weaning us from its only nourishment."[16]

Because of its steady allegiance to historic Christian doctrine, Princeton Seminary—now almost a hundred years old—was viewed by many as hopelessly old-fashioned. When a writer criticized Princeton for being "excessively zealous for the Gospel," Dr. Warfield answered, "The Gospel is a good thing to be 'excessively zealous' for."[17]

14

Incarnate Truth

We must not, as Christians, assume an attitude of antagonism toward the truths of reason, or the truths of philosophy, or the truths of science, or the truths of history, or the truths of criticism. As children of the light, we must be careful to keep ourselves open to every ray of light. If it is light, its source must be sought in Him who is the true Light; if it is truth, it belongs of right to Him who is the plentitude of truth.

BENJAMIN BRECKINRIDGE WARFIELD

DURING the 1891–92 school year B. B. Warfield preached a sermon entitled "Incarnate Truth" on the text John 1:14—"And the Word was made flesh, and dwelt among us . . . full of . . . truth." He is "still the true Light that lighteth every man that cometh into the world," Dr. Warfield told the seminary community; "and all the truth that is in the world comes from him and must seek its strength in him." "We may confide wholly in him," Warfield said, "because he is the Truth. Nor let us do this timidly. Trust is never timid." He continued:

Just because Jesus is the Truth, while we without reserve accept, proclaim, and live by every word which he has spoken, not fearing that after all it may prove to be false, we may with equal confidence accept, proclaim, and live by every other truth that may be made known to us, not fearing that after a while it may prove to contradict the Truth himself. . . . There is no truth in the world which does not come from him. It matters not through what channel it finds its struggling way into our consciousness or to our recognition—whether our darkened eyes are enabled to catch their glimpse of it by the light of nature, as we say, by the light of reason, by the light of history, or by the light of criticism. These may be but broken lights; but they are broken lights of that one Light which lighteth every man that cometh into the world. Every fragment of truth which they reveal to us comes from him who is the Truth, and is rendered great and holy as a revelation from and of him.[1]

In his teaching and writing Dr. Warfield continued Princeton's commitment to seek for every truth "that may be made known to us." Like his predecessors he followed with interest and discernment the scholarship of his day, particularly in the area of science. In his article on "The Antiquity and the Unity of the Human Race"—described by a modern scholar as "one of the most scientifically literate reflections on the religious implications of the subject by a theologian"— Warfield argued that the question of the antiquity of the human race had "of itself no theological significance. It is to theology, as such, a matter of entire indifference how long man has existed on earth." He then turned to the question of mankind's unity as an issue of grave theological importance. On both biblical and scientific grounds he attacked polygenism —the theory, held by some leading scientists, that the human race derived from multiple sources (with the assumption, often, that the different races were totally different biological species).[2]

Even before his student days at Princeton College Warfield had a keen interest in evolutionary theory. Dr. McCosh "did not make me a Darwinian, as it was his pride to believe he ordinarily made his pupils," Warfield wrote. "But that was doubtless because I was already a Darwinian of the purest water before I came into his hands, and knew my *Origin of Species* and *Animals and Plants under Domestication,* almost from A to Izard." Warfield acknowledged, however, that in "later years" he fell away from McCosh's "orthodoxy." Writing in 1916, Warfield related that McCosh

was a little nettled about it and used to inform me with some vigor —I am speaking of a time thirty years agone!—that all biologists under thirty years of age were Darwinians. I was never quite sure that he understood what I was driving at when I replied that I was the last man in the world to wonder at that, since I was about that old myself before I outgrew it.[3]

Warfield told the Princeton students that there were three general positions that were held with respect to the theory of evolution. Some saw it as a claim to furnish "a complete account of the origin and present state of the universe" and thus as a denial of God's design and providence. In this interpretation evolution was, as Charles Hodge once stated, "tantamount to atheism."[4] There have been many evolutionists, however, Warfield insisted, "who have been and have remained theists and Christians." Like James McCosh, they held to "the Christian doctrine of God" while considering the evolutionary hypothesis "a discovery of science of the order and conditions under which the various living forms have as a matter of fact come into existence." McCosh harnessed evolution "to his theistic conceptions," Warfield wrote, "and made it subservient to, and indeed give way before," his Christian supernaturalism. Warfield believed, however, that McCosh had gone too far in saying that evolution is a fact—"completely made out," "proved," "demonstrated." A third possibility, the one Warfield recommended, was to view evolution as merely "a working hypothesis"—"a more or less probable, or a more or less improbable conjecture of scientific workers as to the method of creation."[5]

In concluding his lectures on the subject of evolution Warfield told the Princeton students:

The upshot of the whole matter is that there is no *necessary* antagonism of Christianity to evolution, *provided that* we do not hold to too extreme a form of evolution. To adopt any form that does not permit God freely to work apart from law and which does not allow *miraculous* interventions (in the giving of the soul, in creating Eve, etc.) will entail a great reconstruction of Christian doctrine and a very great lowering of the detailed authority of the Bible.

He went on to say that "if we condition the theory by allowing the constant oversight of God in the whole process, and his occasional supernatural interference for the production of *new* beginnings by an actual output of creative force, producing something *new*, i.e., something not included even *in posse* in preceding conditions—we may hold to the modified theory of evolution and be Christians in the ordinary orthodox sense." Even so, Dr. Warfield was not inclined to urge this position. "I say we may do this," he told the students. "Whether we ought to accept it, even in this modified sense is another matter, and I leave it purposely an open question."[6]

During the fall term of 1903 James Orr, professor in the United Free Church College in Glasgow, delivered the seminary's L. P. Stone Lectures, published two years later as *God's*

Image in Man and Its Defacement in the Light of Modern Denials.
Orr argued that the Christian world view was antithetical to
the "ably constructed and defended" naturalistic world views
with which many Christians were seeking an alliance. On the
matter of evolution, however, Orr stated that when it was
viewed simply as a scientific theory, and "certain conditions
. . . fulfilled, and certain limits observed," it imperiled "no
religious interest." On the origin of man he believed that
according to "the pure data of science, apart from . . .
theories of development, . . . the balance of probability is in
favor of man's exceptional origin." He pointed out that some
evolutionists agreed with him that "a special supernatural
cause" was required to account not only for man's mind but
also for his body. He was convinced that any theory of
humanity's gradual evolution from animal forms was "fatal"
to the belief that humanity possessed a spiritual nature and
immortality. A decisive "leap" in the process must have
occurred—in which a supernatural initiative or cause came
into play.[7]

Warfield praised Orr's book as a "distinct contribution to
the settlement of the questions with which it deals, and to
their settlement in a sane and stable manner." He disagreed,
however, with the Scottish professor's contention that it was
inconsistent to postulate a special divine origin for man's
mind while denying it for his body. Warfield suggested that
an evolutionary development of the human body was
possible, with the gulf between the physical aspects of man
and those of his brutish parents bridged by "providential
guidance apart from a divine intervention." Still, man
became man only when God directly and supernaturally
created his soul. Warfield admitted that "the very detailed
account of the creation of Eve" presented a serious problem
in attempting to harmonize the Bible and evolution. Except
for that passage, however, Warfield told his students that he
did not think there was "any general statement in the Bible or
any part of the account of creation, either as given in Genesis
1 and 2 or elsewhere alluded to, that need be opposed to
evolution."[8]

Charles Hodge had argued that evolution of the Darwinian
type was incompatible with Christian theism. Warfield agreed

but held that there was considerable promise in a properly framed theory of evolution as a possible explanation of development by divine providence. He often used the idea of *concursus*—the simultaneous activity of divine and natural agency, neither replacing the other nor excluding the other —to show how it was possible to "examine one and the same phenomenon from very different but coherent perspectives."[9]

Both Hodge and Warfield championed the true progress of scientific discovery. Hodge would have cordially agreed with his student and successor that "we would not willingly drag behind the evidence indeed—nor would we willingly run ahead of it." Both Hodge and Warfield were convinced that although truly established scientific fact may illuminate the meaning of Scripture, science must not determine the content of faith. Warfield warned that "a 'Christianity' which is to be kept in harmony with a growing 'science, philosophy, and scholarship,' beating their way onward by a process of trial and correction, must be a veritable nose of wax, which may be twisted in every direction as it may serve our purpose."[10]

*   *   *

In 1903 the Presbyterian church called Charles Stelzle to a "special mission to workingmen." Under his dynamic leadership the Department of Church and Labor became an outstanding success. The Federal Council of Churches was organized in 1908 and turned its attention immediately to the church's responsibility for extending and applying "the principles of the new social order." Conservative Presbyterians supported efforts to improve working conditions, provide employment, build better housing, and ensure Sabbath rest but objected to an emphasis on social reform that threatened to lead to a neglect of evangelism and Christian nurture.[11]

The Princetonians had not been unmindful of the escalating social crisis in America. In 1886 A. A. Hodge told a Philadelphia audience that "for a free republic like ours there is no salvation except in obedience to the principles of the kingdom of God." He explained:

That kingdom rests ultimately upon the Fatherhood of God, the Elder Brotherhood and the redeeming blood of Christ, and the

[259]

universal brotherhood of men. . . . This human brotherhood is essential; it is eternal. The earthly conditions which separate us are accidental and transient. There is no gulf of ignorance, or poverty, or vice which should cut off or modify our expressions of tender love and sympathy. Even the very least of these humble ones Christ calls brethren. We must not keep them at arm's length; we must not neglect their interests; we must not, in the competitions of trade, push them to the wall. We must love them, and make them know we love them, and help them in their struggles with poverty and sin.

The kingdom of God embraces all classes, but it recognizes no class distinctions. We know neither capitalists nor labourers, neither rich nor poor, as such, but only men as men, men as brothers in Christ Jesus. If the rich operator, under the pressure of competition, obeying the so-called "laws of trade," pays starvation wages, we warn him, not as a rich man, but as a brother, that he is sinning against the law of the kingdom. Our brothers should, in spite of all the laws and competitions of trade, be enabled to live as becomes our brethren while they do our work. Charity degrades the lazy receiver. So the withholding a full share in the profit of the common business degrades the man hastening to get rich.

Hodge warned that "if capitalists combine to fight labour, labourers will combine to fight capital." "But if all will open their hearts to the love of Christ, and submit their wills absolutely to the reign of righteousness, and devote themselves to the performance of duty instead of the vindication of rights," Hodge said, "then the strong will bear the burden of the weak, and we will all together enjoy a common prosperity, in which the sympathy of all multiplies the happiness of each."[12]

Princeton's professor of apologetics and Christian ethics, William Brenton Greene, taught the required senior course in Christian sociology and offered a number of electives in this area. He contributed over one hundred book reviews and several major articles on social issues to *The Princeton Theological Review*.[13] Dr. Greene believed that "few subjects could be more important, and certainly none could be more pertinent," than the question of the duty of the church in the problems of "the family, philanthropy, industrial life, racial divisions and collisions." Greene never minimized the extent of these social problems, which, he said, had created "an atmosphere most adverse to both civic and personal righteousness." When he reviewed Walter Rauschenbusch's *Christianity and the Social Crisis*, Greene wrote, "The chapter on 'The Present Crisis' is a terrible indictment of our boasted modern and Christian civilization. Yet it is not unnatural that our author should make it. Anyone who could be a pastor for eleven years among the working people on the West Side of New York City, as he was, and could write of social evils less earnestly than he has, would be indeed hardhearted." Dr. Greene wrote that the volume *The Social Creed of the Churches* authorized by the Commission on the Church and Social Service of the Federal Council of the Churches of Christ in America "must be admitted by all to be a work of exceeding value. . . . It will, no doubt, do more than has been effected by almost any other one agency to overcome the indifference of society to social ills. These evils it sets forth clearly, exactly, and, therefore, appallingly."[14]

"For the church . . . to be indifferent to the great questions which concern society is inconceivable," Dr. Greene wrote. "Her mission is the redemption of society. The kingdoms of this world she must transform into the kingdom of her Lord and of his Christ. She could lose interest in the social question, therefore, only by becoming untrue to her mission and so to her Head. To save society for Christ is the church's work."[15]

The family, the state, and the church all have important roles in this task, Dr. Greene maintained, with the church being "the most potent agent in social regeneration." Since "the demand for social evangelism, for preaching the social truths of the Bible," was "a just one," Greene stated that the church must teach Christian people "the kind of life, both individual and social, which they were saved to live." The church must shape the "character, principles and motives" of those called to serve God in "the home, in the work-shop, in the study, in the senate-chamber, in every legitimate sphere of human life." "Therefore, 'Believe on the Lord Jesus Christ' is not the sum of the preacher's message. Or rather, it is this only when it is conceived to mean not merely, Come to Jesus as your Saviour from sin, but Come to Him as your Lord." Preaching, Greene said, must include social reform, directly where "God has pronounced on these questions" and by proclaiming and illustrating the "principles" of Scripture when the issue is not referred to in the Bible.[16]

Dr. Greene insisted, however, that the church must not "as an institution" undertake "to solve the social problem." She must not "preach sociology rather than theology." She must not "turn her preaching stations into social settlements." She must not "go into" and "control" politics. Ministers should remember that "the political sermon commonly hinders religion more than it helps politics." They must guard "against becoming only or chiefly" reformers or agitators and dedicate themselves unstintingly to their "unique and more urgent business" of preaching "the everlasting Gospel of the grace of God."[17]

The mission of the church is not "fundamentally or even chiefly social," Dr. Greene said. "It is primarily and characteristically individual, and it is above all religious. It contemplates saving men from sin rather than society from poverty." Greene warned that when the church attempts to create social policies "it is likely to miss the mark. Nay, it is worse; for it is likely to be as poison rather than medicine, as the wrong medicine which, however good the intention with which it is given, is often more harmful than poison." Dr. Greene believed that the church of the first three centuries "transformed all departments of human life." "The church regenerated society," he wrote, "just because she as an institute would have nothing to do with the reformation of it." He continued:

With the accession of Constantine a radical change took place. He elevated the church, and the church was willing to be elevated, to the throne of the empire. The church, then, became the reformer of society and ceased to be its regenerator. She added the methods of politics and of economics to those of the Spirit, but before she was aware of it the Spirit was grieved away. Instead of continuing to reform society, therefore, society transformed and degraded her.[18]

The principal ills of society, Dr. Greene believed, resulted from human sin and selfishness; the chief remedy was the "grace of God" rather than "social reorganization." "The most extreme social distress does but emphasize society's need of the Gospel," he maintained. "If . . . we would know how Christ's Gospel ought to control social life, it will be the Gospel rather than sociology that we should consider." Greene said that the Bible was as "truly the authority in sociology" as it was in "dogmatics and ethics." It contained much information and instruction that was "directly sociological," he wrote, and was "the final revelation of the will of God for man in his present state of existence." Even in those areas in which the Bible was silent, it contained "principles and limitations of universal and perpetual obligation" that guided Christians in combating the social problems of their time.[19]

In his reviews of books on social issues Dr. Greene forthrightly criticized what he believed to be unbiblical and destructive social ideas and programs, gently corrected theological mistakes, and elaborated his own views. The problem with "the social gospel," Greene believed, was that in making Christ into merely a social reformer, it had neglected his role as redeemer. It portrayed the kingdom of God as primarily "material and social rather than spiritual and individual." The "social gospel" assumed that "the wisdom of modern sociology" could be used to cure social problems and failed to recognize the problem of sin, the power of the Holy Spirit, and the importance of regeneration of individuals for the reforming of society. Dr. Greene reiterated that the surest way for the church to accomplish its task was by faithfulness to "our Lord's conception. His last and great commission to his church was to 'go into all the world and preach the Gospel to the whole creation.'" Because the church had "to a considerable degree turned aside from this her uniquely high and indispensable vocation, to 'social ministry'—this is *the* reason why as a social force there are now many who are counting her out." Again and again Greene returned to his central point: "It is in human sin and particularly in human selfishness that we discover the cause of the chief ills of society, and therefore it is in the grace of God rather than in social reorganization that we would find the one remedy that will strike at the root of the evil."[20]

Living in their pleasant town with its culture and academic aura, the Princeton faculty did not forget the human misery in the large cities near them. William Greene was their voice and conscience. Far from being a reactionary conservative on social issues, he probed, rebuked, encouraged, and labored to set forth in his teaching at the seminary and in his writings in *The Princeton Theological Review* the urgency of the crisis. Again and again he insisted that "the church of our day needs to hear the social gospel and ought to preach it." However, this must be, he would always add, "in accordance with the principles of Christ." "Even love must be according to truth," Greene wrote. "This is unpopular and unfashionable doctrine, but it was never more needed."[21]

*　　*　　*

In *The Princeton Review* of May 1883 Charles W. Eliot, president of Harvard, presented a challenge to traditional seminary education in which he called for the abandonment of outmoded theological ideas, openness to fresh approaches, and greater academic freedom. Francis Patton replied to Eliot in the July issue. Patton pointed out that ministerial training implies the existence of a church, which necessarily limits the freedom of the teacher. He objected to Eliot's proposal that students should elect more of their courses, since this would allow "a young man to be graduated from a theological seminary," Patton stated, "without having studied Old or New Testament exegesis, ecclesiastical history, or systematic theology."[22]

By the end of the century some seminaries had dropped the Hebrew requirement and were moving toward the elective system. Princeton, however, held to the traditional curriculum with its concentration on both biblical languages. Dr. Warfield argued that the curriculum for a Presbyterian seminary is determined by three facts. First, the seminaries (unlike departments of religion in a university) exist for the training of men for the ministry. "They do not exist primarily in order to advance theological learning," he said, "but in order to impart theological instruction; their first object is not investigation, but communication." Secondly, Presbyterian seminaries do not train men for "Christian ministry in general" but for the ministry of the Presbyterian church.

Consequently, Presbyterian seminaries have the right and obligation to require studies that promote the identity and position of that church. Thirdly, Presbyterian seminaries serve a church that holds to "a high ideal of ministerial education," and the seminary curriculum and requirements must reflect that ideal. Although recognizing that many studies could be beneficial to a seminary student, Warfield insisted that the curriculum "should be made to contain all that is needed to train men for an adequate ministry and nothing that is not needed for this one purpose." This meant seven areas of study, according to Dr. Warfield: apologetics, Old Testament, New Testament, church history, theology, ecclesiastics, and actual practice in ministry—each making "about equal claim upon our time and effort." Electives should be made available, but he acknowledged that in the full required curriculum there would be little room for them. These courses perhaps could be taught in a fourth year, Warfield suggested.[23]

In 1903 a student petition to the seminary directors and faculty called for the addition of instruction in English Bible to the Princeton curriculum. Dr. Warfield addressed the board in a report adopted by the entire faculty, stating that the students needed to be trained in "a comprehensive and exact study of the Biblical text" but added that to substitute English Bible for Old Testament and New Testament exegesis in the original languages "would be a fatal mistake." The mastery of English Bible, the faculty thought, should take place in "the family and school and college" and through personal Bible study. The directors, however, created a department of English Bible and secured temporary lecturers until the seminary was able to add Charles Erdman as professor of English Bible and practical theology in 1905.[24]

In 1909 students again complained to the trustees about the curriculum and criticized the teaching in the seminary, especially the courses of Patton, Davis, and Armstrong. They pointed out that whereas several Presbyterian seminaries had admitted some newer courses into their curricula, the Princeton faculty had resisted all changes. The directors, concerned about the seminary's reputation and slightly diminished enrollment (the junior class in 1908 was the smallest since 1876), appointed a subcommittee "to consider the question of the modification of the curriculum." This committee recommended that the curriculum be altered to allow for studies "covering the practical duties of the Christian minister in their relation to the concrete conditions of the present time."[25]

Dr. Warfield answered that it was the place of the faculty, not the directors, to implement the curriculum of the seminary's "Plan." Furthermore, he thought that the "requirements of 'the Plan' [did] not need amending; they need[ed] only be carried out more fully." The "Plan" provided, in Warfield's view, for the training of "well-rounded minister[s]"—"equal to the functions which belong to a minister of the New Testament order." "A comprehensive and thorough theological training," Warfield said, "is the condition of a really qualified ministry. When we satisfy ourselves with a less comprehensive and thorough theological training, we are only condemning ourselves to a less qualified ministry." Dr. Warfield was not opposed to the teaching of English Bible but believed that it should not be the basis for the seminary's instruction. He saw the value, and the necessity, of practical teaching. Theology, he stated, could not even exist without a "practical aim." "As long as we remain in the region of the pure intellect," he added, "we remain out of the proper region of theology." But Warfield insisted that Princeton Seminary already stressed the practical aspects of the theological disciplines. It was through the mastery of these, Warfield believed, that a person was enabled to minister effectively.[26]

The curriculum debate was widely publicized in the newspapers, and Princeton Seminary was pictured as being sadly behind the times. Gresham Machen believed that the student "rebellion" was directed against teaching methods rather than theological conservatism; but "pure 'cussedness,'" he said, described it better still. Machen was disturbed especially by the attack on Armstrong, whom he regarded as one of the most brilliant men of the faculty. When Dr. Patton heard that the students were complaining about Armstrong's teaching— claiming that they had difficulty hearing him and that the little they could hear they could not understand—he replied,

"The trouble with the students is that they sit too far back—
intellectually speaking!" Machen characterized the students'
dissatisfaction as a desire for "a little course in the English
Bible. . . . They want to be pumped full of material, which
without any real assimilation or any intellectual work of any
kind they can pump out again upon their unfortunate
congregations." He deplored "the incessant clamor for the
'practical'" and hoped that Princeton Seminary would have
the courage to keep its standard "high" and "wait for better
times." Machen hoped that Princeton Seminary might
conserve "a spark of learning for some future awakening in
the Church's intellectual life."[27]

Machen set forth his views in *The Presbyterian* of May 12,
1909. The difference of opinion at Princeton, he wrote,

arises out of the deeper difference as to the purpose of a theological seminary. If its primary purpose is to give young men a clear and
systematized understanding of the truth of God revealed in His
Word, and the history and life of His Church, one course of study
will be readily outlined. If the purpose is, in some haste, to prepare
young men to study the varying thought and attempt the regulation
of the social order of the present time, a very different method of
instruction will be necessary.

Patton, like Warfield and Machen, believed that the best
way to achieve the practical training of ministers was to
ensure that they were well taught in the traditional disciplines.
He wrote:

A Theological Seminary is, first of all, a school for the training of
men to preach the Gospel. The claims of theological learning
should never supersede or relegate to a subordinate position the
practical aims which were contemplated by those who founded this
Seminary; and if we magnify these claims, it is only because we
believe that the minister who would most effectively discharge the
duties of his high calling is he who, other things being equal, is best
equipped in his knowledge of the Disciplines that enter into the
theological curriculum.[28]

Although the directors were not entirely in agreement, the
required curriculum was continued. The Princeton faculty
was disturbed by criticism of its program and concerned

about its enrollment. In 1908 the faculty reported to the directors that "Princeton's reputation for conservatism in Theology does not help her in this eastern region in these days when the predilection is for freer lines of thought, [but] in the west Princeton's well-known Evangelical position is probably one of her best assets."

To set forth its case Princeton produced a promotional booklet—titled *A Modern School of the Prophets.* "For almost one hundred years," it read, "this seminary has tried to be faithful to its trust and has furnished to the Church that established it men of missionary zeal, evangelistic fervor, pastoral loyalty and scholarly ability." Noting that great agitation had been carried on recently in the secular as well as the religious press for a widening of the scope of theological training, the booklet stated that the Princeton curriculum would "not be spread to shallowness," but it would be made "as comprehensive as the time of the course [would] permit." It cited the appointment of Charles Erdman as professor of practical theology ("in answer to the call [the directors] felt the Church was making for a masterly presentation of the English Bible") and to the seminary's advantageous location between New York and Philadelphia for "the practical study of our present and urgent social needs" as evidence that Princeton was "in touch with the world of today." John H. Converse, a trustee of the seminary, paid for the students to visit the churches and missions of Philadelphia to study and engage in evangelistic work. This was so successful that the board of directors "provided for a continuation of such work, including with Philadelphia, Greater New York and the million-souled cities of New Jersey."[29]

The postgraduate department of the seminary operated to make the seminary "a producer not only of Christian preachers but also of Christian scholars." Graduate study at Princeton was "of particular value to graduates of other seminaries where the Calvinistic system [had] not been presented at all or presented in an unfavorable way." Princeton Seminary was confident that with its strong emphasis on study of the Bible and theology, its outstanding faculty trained in the practical work of the pastorate and as specialists in the great universities, and its abundance of visiting lecturers, it was "a modern school of the prophets"—well able to prepare "young men for the Christian ministry."[30]

The faculty made a strong case for the maintenance of Princeton's traditional approach to ministerial training. The unrest among the students, however, should have been taken more seriously. Some of it was probably "pure cussedness," as Machen said, but it pointed to an underlying problem at the seminary. Princeton had maintained faithfully the founders' priorities in promoting "solid learning" and "piety of heart," but it had lost something of Alexander's and Miller's ability to teach and model for the students the skills of ministry. The serious erosion of orthodox views in the church understandably focused the attention of the Princeton faculty on the defense of the faith, but it may have caused them to neglect other equally important matters. In his address for the opening of the ninety-first session of the seminary in the fall of 1902, Robert Dick Wilson, to answer critical attacks, made "a complete comparison of the vocabularies of the Hebrew and Babylonian" and compared them "in all important particulars with the vocabularies of the Syriac and Arabic languages." Wilson's lecture was a scholarly presentation that demonstrated the professor's considerable linguistic ability, but it was far better suited for the classroom than for the introductory address. Much more appropriate for these occasions were the solid but spiritual and pastoral themes of Archibald Alexander, Samuel Miller, and Charles Hodge. That Princeton still treasured that emphasis was splendidly demonstrated by B. B. Warfield's opening address for September 20, 1903, on "Spiritual Culture in the Theological Seminary."[31]

*   *   *

On May 4, 1909, Princeton Seminary celebrated the 400th anniversary of the birth of John Calvin. Dr. Warfield's address, "The Theology of John Calvin," Gresham Machen wrote his mother, was "the feature" of the day. "Not only did it exhibit Dr. Warfield's well-known mastery of the subject," he wrote, "but also it was really eloquent—certainly the finest thing of the kind that I have ever heard from Dr. Warfield."

"Of all the services which Calvin has rendered to humanity—and they are neither few nor small—the greatest was undoubtedly his gift to it afresh" of the "system of religious thought" now called Calvinism, Warfield told the Princeton community. "Calvinism is his greatest and most significant monument, and he who adequately understands it will best understand him." Warfield stated that the "formative principle of Calvinism" is not the doctrine of predestination; "it is only its logical implication. It is not the root from which Calvinism springs, it is one of the branches which it has inevitably thrown out." Neither are the "five points" the "formative principle of Calvinism." Like the doctrine of predestination, they "conduct us back to that formative principle, as the only root out of which just this body of doctrine could grow." "It is *the vision of God and His majesty,*" the Princeton professor of theology stated, "which lies at the foundation of the entirety of Calvinistic thinking." Thus Calvinism "begins . . . centres and . . . ends with the vision of God in His glory and it sets itself, before all things, to render to God His rights in every sphere of life-activity."[32]

* * *

Woodrow Wilson, Princeton University's president since 1902, strengthened the school academically with new professors and higher standards, prompting the New York *Evening Post* to comment wryly that he had "ruined what was universally admitted to be the most agreeable and aristocratic country club in America by transforming it into an institution of learning." Dreaming of a new library and a law school, Wilson encouraged wealthy philanthropists to think of Princeton. He appealed to his classmate Cyrus McCormick and reminded Andrew Carnegie that Princeton had been largely "made by Scotsmen" and is "thoroughly Scottish in all her history and traditions." "Being myself of pure Scots blood," Wilson said, "it heartens me to emphasize [that] fact." Wilson's successes, however, were balanced by disappointments and controversy. When he attempted to end the influence of the lavishly endowed eating clubs, with their closed memberships and social elitism, many wealthy alumni were outraged. He clashed with Dean Andrew West—who had become Wilson's opponent on most issues—over the location for the new graduate college. The president wanted it to be part of the central campus where it would add to the quality of undergraduate life. Enamored with the style of Oxford and Cambridge, the dean campaigned for a self-contained graduate college with sumptuous social amenities, a mile away on the "Golf Links." Wilson was dramatically defeated when William Cooper Procter (a member of the class of 1883 and president of Procter and Gamble soap manufacturers) left a large bequest for the graduate college, naming West, a long-time friend, as executor of his will. The board voted to accept Procter's money and West's plans. A few months later Wilson—having been for some time intrigued with the possibility of a political career—resigned to run for governor of New Jersey.[33]

The son of a Southern Presbyterian pastor, Woodrow Wilson revered the Bible as the rule for life and faith. He believed that people were basically defective, having disobeyed the God-ordained moral law, and that Christ was necessary for salvation. In opposition to the currently fashionable social gospel, Wilson believed that society could be changed only by changing individuals. In 1908 he wrote to John R. Mott, the leader of the student missionary movement:

I have had the fear in recent years that the ministers of our churches, by becoming involved in all sorts of social activities . . . have too much diverted their attention from the effectual preaching of the Word. The danger seems to be that individual churches will become great philanthropic societies instead of being what it seems to me they ought to be, organizations from which go forth the spiritual stimulation which should guide all philanthropic effort.[34]

Wilson essentially filled the role of "university pastor" and preached often—at the student Philadelphian Society, at chapel, at Sunday services, and at baccalaureates. His sermons, however, emphasized transformation in moral character that would lead to right action (with little mention of his own beliefs concerning human sinfulness and the necessity of the atoning work of Christ).

Woodrow Wilson kept his Presbyterian views and his professional and academic life in more or less separate categories and promoted the same dichotomy at the university. "Princeton," he insisted, "is a Presbyterian college only because the Presbyterians of New Jersey were wise and progressive enough to found it." "Religion cannot be handled like learning," he wrote. "It is a matter of individual conviction and its source is the heart. . . . That religion lies at the heart of Princeton's life is shown, not in the teachings of the classroom and of the chapel pulpit, but in the widespread, spontaneous, unflagging religious activity of the under-graduates themselves." To promote a Princeton University that was both nonsectarian and in some sense Christian, Wilson adopted "a broad religious-moral base that was functionally no different from liberal Protestantism." To "eliminate Presbyterian dogmatism from the curriculum," Wilson dropped all required biblical instruction and appointed new board and faculty members with little or no commitment to Presbyterianism—or even Protestant Christianity. The first Jew was added to the faculty in 1904 and the first Roman Catholic in 1909. In 1890 two thirds of the students were Presbyterians. By the end of the Wilson administration that number was down to a little over one third. The university's connection with the seminary, for many years a major factor in its life, became far less important. The decisive steps had been taken that would lead Princeton from "Protestant establishment to established nonbelief."[35]

15

The Centennial and the
New President

A BALLADE OF PRINCETON SEMINARY

At the Opening of its One Hundredth Session

A hundred years have sped them by
And brought their gifts to land and sea,
Wars, peace, emprise, achievements high,
Delights men scarce had hoped could be,
And with it all some vanity:
Deep, deep, the gulf 'twixt now and then!
What are these hundred years to thee,
O Princeton, loved of God and men?

Upon thy hill, serene of eye,
Thou sit'st in calm; and joyously
Thou call'st the years as by they fly,
That they may lay upon thy knee
Tribute from their fecundity:
The balance strike 'twixt now and then!
What are these hundred years to thee,
O Princeton, loved of God and men?

A hundred years of thinking high,
Of reverence and of loyalty:
Of open heart to every cry
Of human need and misery:
Each year more true, each year more free,
Well hast thou wrought 'twixt now and then,
Much are these hundred years to thee,
O Princeton, loved of God and men!

Envoy

Men, mark the years as past they flee,
And mark their tale 'twixt now and then:
And mark the waxing ministry
Of Princeton, loved of God and men!

BENJAMIN BRECKINRIDGE WARFIELD
September 21, 1911

ON May 7, 1912, the hundredth school year of Princeton Theological Seminary closed. In its first century Princeton had enrolled almost six thousand students—over a thousand more than any other seminary in the United States. First they came from the Middle States, the South, and New England, then from all areas of the growing country and from abroad. Beginning in the 1870s foreign-born students—mostly from Canada and Great Britain, especially Northern Ireland—composed about a quarter of the total enrollment. Near the turn of the century students from the Asian countries of Japan, China, India, and Korea began to come to Princeton Seminary in significant numbers. The seminary's denominational diversity, significant even in its earlier history, became more pronounced as Methodists, Baptists, Scottish United Presbyterians, Dutch Christian Reformed, Lutherans, and Brethren enrolled. Forty-three moderators of the General Assembly of the Presbyterian Church had studied at Princeton Seminary, as had half of the leaders of the church's missionary and benevolent work. Scores of church leaders for other denominations—including theologians, college presidents, and five bishops of the Protestant Episcopal church—were Princeton Seminary graduates.

*   *   *

Princeton Seminary's centennial celebration was held on May 5–7, 1912, with services on Sunday at the First Presbyterian

Church and at Miller Chapel, and meetings on Monday and Tuesday in Alexander Hall on the university campus. Representatives from a hundred theological seminaries and forty colleges and universities in the United States and around the world were present, as well as delegates from American, Canadian, Scottish, and Irish churches.

On Sunday Dr. Patton preached the sermon "Princeton Seminary and the Faith." Although paying tribute to the nineteenth-century New England theologians as men of brilliance and skill, Patton rejoiced that Princeton never "contributed anything to these modifications of the Calvinistic system." "There has been a New Haven theology and an Andover theology," he said, "but there never was a distinctively Princeton theology. Princeton's boast, if she have reason to boast at all, is her unswerving fidelity to the theology of the Reformation." Patton praised the early faculty's clear and warm-hearted commitment to the gospel. "I am not ashamed," he said, "to admit that our Princeton theologians have to a great extent been advocates. They have felt that their function was forensic as well as didactic. They have spoken and written in the warm glow of enthusiasm."[1]

Gresham Machen described the celebration ceremonies in a letter to his parents:

The academic processions on Monday and Tuesday mornings were exceedingly brilliant. The Scotch moderators were a show. They had knee trousers, buckles on their shoes, lace cuffs, three-cornered hats, and I forget what kind of colored gowns. . . .

Tuesday was the big day, Alexander Hall at the University was filled with a magnificent assemblage. The stage and the central part of the lower floor were brilliant with many-colored gowns, and the rest of the hall was occupied by ordinary folk. The singing of the first hymn, "Ein' Feste Burg," was one of the most inspiring things in the whole celebration. I never heard any hymn-singing like that. The speeches were by Dr. Stewart, moderator of the Church of Scotland, Dr. James Wells, moderator of the United Free Church of Scotland, and Dr. MacMillan, moderator of the Presbyterian Church of Ireland. Dr. Stewart was very poor. He seems to believe very little, and what he does believe, he is unable to express. Dr. MacMillan had only half a chance on account of the lateness of the hour. But James Wells was glorious. He believes in the Gospel and doesn't mind saying so. I don't know when I have seen such a combination of deep religious feeling and perfect dignity as was exhibited by his address. And his cordiality and respect towards Princeton Seminary was evidently unfeigned. His speech and Dr. Patton's were the great things of the celebration.[2]

Despite Machen's low opinion of his speech, Alexander Stewart—though not in full accord with the Princeton point of view—was nonetheless appreciative. He said, "In Britain and especially in Scotland the theological teaching of Princeton is regarded as one of the noblest examples of adherence to a clear and definite expression of the Christian faith." James Wells called for efforts to promote both world peace and evangelization, expressed his great hope for revival in Scotland, and closed with the words:

It is our heart's desire and prayer that your School of the Prophets may be the generous mother of a growing band of consecrated and gifted men who, by the grace of God, shall do exploits in establishing and extending the Kingdom of our Lord and Saviour Jesus Christ.

John MacMillan noted that Ireland gave to Princeton Seminary "the men who sat at her cradle and nursed her to strength—the Alexanders and the Hodges." He continued:

If there is one Church of the Presbyterian order which more than any other loves Princeton, it is the Irish Presbyterian Church, called to maintain an immovable position between ritualism and Romanism on the one hand, and rationalism on the other, to uphold the supremacy of Scriptural revelation, and to be loyal to the doctrines of Grace.[3]

A number of speeches were given at the alumni luncheon on Tuesday afternoon. Machen wrote to his parents that the best besides Dr. Patton's were given by an Episcopal bishop and by E. Y. Mullins, president of the Southern Baptist Theological Seminary in Louisville, Kentucky, who had studied with James P. Boyce, a graduate of the Princeton Seminary class of 1852 and founder of the Southern Baptist Seminary. In his remarks, which Machen described as "brilliant", Dr. Mullins set forth the three conditions that are the essence, he said, of triumphant Christianity—conditions that Princeton

Seminary had fulfilled. First, Christianity is "a message rather than an inquiry." "With you," Mullins said, "Christianity has been a voice, and not a scientific echo of a voice." It has not been "an echo of an echo of a voice." "Christianity with you is first a message," Mullins repeated; "second, it is an experience." Thirdly, the Baptist seminary president declared, "Princeton has also stood for the conviction that there must be messengers who embody the message and the experience." He described the source of Princeton's great influence:

As Mont Blanc enriches the valleys so Princeton Seminary has stood like Mont Blanc among the seminaries in this country. In a thousand ways you have not known, she has sent down her largess of blessing into the valleys, and we rejoice in what she has done. And the reason Mont Blanc can thus bless the valleys is because she lifts her head to the very skies where, from the inexhaustible heavens themselves, she draws her supply, and so Princeton has drawn her supplies from the eternal sources.[4]

Francis Patton responded to the congratulatory addresses. Machen wrote that "although Dr. Patton was very hoarse, his five-minute closing speech was one of the most eloquent things that I have ever heard from him." Patton said: "I think the world owes a great deal to theological controversy. Creed-statements, it is true, have been monuments built upon the battlefields of faith. They commemorate victories; but they also serve to promote peace; for they indicate the points in which Christians agree as well as the matters in which they differ." Dr. Patton noted that messages of congratulations had come even from Roman Catholic institutions. He expressed the wish that they could have been present; "for if they had been," he added, "I would have said, 'Now, my friends, you know that I differ with you a great deal, but I want to tell you that as between the present Pope of Rome and the Modernists, I would vote for the Pope of Rome every time.'"[5]

In one of the most memorable speeches of the days of centennial celebration Charles Beatty Alexander, grandson of Archibald Alexander, reviewed the early history of the seminary. The memory of its first professors, Alexander said, is not preserved on any stone or monument, nor is it best kept alive even in the Seminary so beloved by them, but in the truth which they implanted in ministers' lives and handed on by them to homes widely scattered, to burdened, toiling, sinning men and women, to whom it meant pardon, peace and eternal hope, to children whose plastic lives were moulded; to the heathen world, to whom it came as the shining of the Star of Bethlehem. In these things are indelibly written the testimony of the Church and of the world to the founders of this Seminary.

Charles Alexander went on to say that no one who has studied the history of Princeton Seminary can fail to be impressed "by the sincere fidelity to the principles of its founders" that has characterized their successors. He then stated that

one does not have to be a professional theologian to be aware that the kind of thought for which Princeton Seminary has always stood most firmly is now attacked persistently from many quarters. Voices come to us from across the sea and are raised here at home telling us that the sun is fast setting upon the old faith, and that the doctrines taught here will pass away like those of the Athenian and Roman schools. It may be said that in our own country the seminary stands in a somewhat isolated position. Isolation has been the portion of the exponents of truth in all ages. Although not an expert in these things, I venture to predict that if the sort of theology which is taught here should die, and if its enemies should grant it decent burial, like the Lord of Life Himself, it will have a triumphant resurrection.

Yet even if these sinister prophecies of the foes of Princeton theology should be fulfilled to the uttermost, if this Seminary should perish amid the ruins of its great traditions, I should wish that its remains might be marked and made memorable by a Cross. For it is the Cross which has been the inspiration of its founders and their successors, even as it is the hope and the glory of this passing world. For the Gospel which it teaches is an unconquerable force. The Cross which it uplifts is the world's greatest power. And by the Gospel of the Cross, this Seminary will stand in spite of attack, in spite of any storm of criticism or unbelief until its work is done, and God comes to take the talent given to our fathers, from whom we have received it with its increase, to the praise of His eternal glory.[6]

*　　*　　*

To commemorate the first hundred years of its history, the Princeton faculty published a volume of *Biblical and Theological Studies*. Francis Patton wrote on "Theological Encyclopedia," and B. B. Warfield contributed an essay "On the Emotional Life of our Lord." Gresham Machen wrote on "Jesus and Paul"; and the other faculty presented articles ranging from Old Testament studies, such as John D. Davis's "Child whose Name is Wonderful," to church history, with John DeWitt's "Jonathan Edwards: A Study." Another book, comprising essays on the deity of Christ by nine Princeton graduates, marked the centennial.[7]

Many people were glad that Princeton Seminary after a hundred years was still holding to the views of its founders, but others saw it as sadly behind the times. Although they acknowledged that Princeton had produced "the best conservative scholarship of the country," professors at the University of Chicago criticized the Presbyterian seminary for its old-fashioned views.[8]

* * *

After teaching church history at Princeton for twenty years, John DeWitt retired in May 1912. He was "a Presbyterian by birth, education, and conviction; he was conservative by temperament and by the influence of his professional work as a student and teacher of history." He found "the communion of the faithful of all lands and of all the centuries . . . a reality not only for the mind but also for the heart." DeWitt set forth Princeton's dual commitment to "piety" and "solid learning" not only in his teaching but also in his life. It was his custom every morning to read from the Bible and spend time, often a full hour, in prayer. At Dr. DeWitt's retirement, Frederick Loetscher, who had served as professor of homiletics from 1910 to 1913, returned to church history.[9]

* * *

In 1912 Gresham Machen began to teach Sunday school classes for teenagers at Princeton's First Presbyterian Church and agreed to become the Sunday school superintendent—as long as he would not have to lead singing! On September 20 Machen delivered the seminary's opening address on "Christianity and Culture." "One of the greatest problems that [has] agitated the church," he began, "is the problem of the relation between knowledge and piety, between culture and Christianity." In his six years as a teacher at Princeton Machen had become painfully aware of a tendency in the church, as well as among the seminary students, to set up a sharp disjunction between knowledge and culture on the one hand and piety and ministry on the other. The academic tendency expresses itself in those "who have devoted themselves chiefly to the task of forming right conceptions as to Christianity and its foundations," he said. The practical tendency answers, "While we are discussing the exact location of the churches of Galatia, men are perishing under the curse of the law; while we are setting the date of Jesus' birth, the world is doing without its Christmas message." Machen believed that the tremendous crisis facing the church lay chiefly "in the intellectual sphere." "The Church," he said, "is perishing today through the lack of thinking, not through an excess of it." He argued, as had the Princetonians before him, that "the Christian . . . cannot be indifferent to any branch of earnest human endeavor. It must be brought into *some* relation to the gospel. It must be studied either in order to be demonstrated as false, or else in order to be made useful in advancing the Kingdom of God." Christianity, Machen said, "must pervade not merely all nations, but also all human thought."[10]

"We may preach with all the fervor of a reformer," Machen told the students, "and yet succeed only in winning a straggler here and there, if we permit the whole collective thought of the nation or of the world to be controlled by ideas which, by the resistless force of logic, prevent Christianity from being regarded as anything more than a harmless delusion." In Machen's view, academic debates ultimately had profound practical consequences. "What is today a matter of academic speculation," he warned, "begins tomorrow to move armies and pull down empires."[11]

For Dr. Machen, the question of the proper relationship between culture and Christianity was an urgent one. Rejecting as unthinkable the liberal subordination of Christianity to culture and the attitude of many conservatives who rejected, or at least ignored, culture in the interest of "pure" Christianity, Machen defined the true relationship between the two as "consecration" of culture. He concluded his address with a strong appeal and challenge to the contemporary church:

Instead of stifling the pleasures afforded by the acquisition of knowledge or by the appreciation of what is beautiful, let us accept these pleasures as the gifts of a heavenly Father. Instead of obliterating the distinction between the Kingdom and the world, or on the other hand withdrawing from the world into a sort of modernized intellectual monasticism, let us go forth joyfully, enthusiastically to make the world subject to God. . . .

The Church is puzzled by the world's indifference. She is trying to overcome it by adapting her message to the fashions of the day. But if, instead, before the conflict, she would descend into the secret place of meditation, if by the clear light of the gospel she would seek an answer not merely to the questions of the hour but, first of all, to the eternal problems of the spiritual world, then perhaps, by God's grace, through His good Spirit, in His good time, she might issue forth once more with power, and an age of doubt might be followed by the dawn of an era of faith.[12]

Gresham Machen's address appeared in the January 1913 issue of *The Princeton Theological Review*. It foreshadowed the role the Princeton professor soon was to assume as a leader of the conservative forces in the church. He had already attracted attention at home and abroad. His articles on the birth of Christ were reviewed by Adolph Harnack in the *Theologische Literaturzeitung* of January 4, 1913. Harnack disagreed with Machen's conclusions but declared that his "admirable study was deserving of every attention."[13]

*   *   *

Woodrow Wilson, who had been elected governor of New Jersey on November 8, 1910—a month after he had resigned as president of Princeton University—received the Democratic nomination for president of the United States on the forty-sixth ballot. He spent election day, November 5, 1912, at home in Princeton. After dinner he read some of Robert

Browning's poetry to his family. Shortly before ten o'clock the bell in Nassau Hall began to ring in muffled tones that intensified until it tolled like "a thing possessed." Woodrow Wilson was elected! Armed with flags and torches the Princeton students marched to the Wilsons' house on Cleveland Lane, singing and cheering. Wilson, bareheaded, went out on a small porch to greet the crowd. As inaugural day approached Ellen and Woodrow Wilson found their "hearts very heavy" at the thought of leaving Princeton where they had spent most of their married life. On Sunday morning, March 2, 1913, the family attended worship services at the First Presbyterian Church and sat together for the last time in "Pew 57." The sermon that day was given by Dr. John DeWitt, retired professor of church history at the seminary. On Monday morning the Wilsons walked the few blocks from their home—saying goodbye to many friends who were standing along the way—to the town's little train station. The next president of the United States and Mrs. Wilson, with their three daughters, stood on the back platform of the train, smiling and waving as the Gothic towers of Princeton faded from sight.

*   *   *

On April 18, 1913, the seminary community sadly gathered in Miller Chapel for a memorial service for William Borden. During his freshman year at Yale William had attended the Student Volunteer Movement's national convention, at which he heard Samuel Zwemer plead for the Muslim world. The young student committed himself to seek God's will about missions. He graduated from Yale, where he excelled in scholarship and athletics, and applied to the China Inland Mission for service among the Muslims. The mission board recommended that he first study at Princeton Seminary. William Borden joined the Benham Club and quickly established a reputation as a good student and fine tennis player. Professor William Greene, who from his study window often watched Borden dashing down Library Place on his bicycle to an early morning class, thought to himself, "That man is so strong, and is so sane, that his prospect of life on

[283]

earth is better than that of any student in our Seminary."
Borden was a leader of the Princeton Student Volunteers for
Missions and was always present at the early Wednesday
morning missionary prayer service. While he was still a
student he became a trustee of the Moody Bible Institute in
Chicago and was appointed by the China Inland Mission as a
delegate to the 1910 Edinburgh Missionary Conference. The
very day that William Borden took his last examination at
Princeton he was in New York City with John R. Mott, deeply
absorbed in plans for the work he was to take up with the
Student Volunteer Movement. For three months he visited
colleges, speaking especially on the need of the Muslim
world. He arranged for his considerable inheritance from his
father, an attorney who was active in real estate after the
Chicago fire, to be given to Christian schools and missions
(including Princeton Seminary). Borden sailed for Egypt,
where he planned to study Arabic and the Koran before
going on to Kansu, a lonely, forbidden province in northwest
China with eight million Muslims. In Cairo he died of
cerebral meningitis.

Dr. Patton led the memorial service for William Borden in
Miller Chapel. After the hymn "For all the Saints who from
their Labors Rest" and the scripture reading from II Corin-
thians 5:1–10 there were four addresses and a sermon by
Dr. Erdman. The congregation sang the hymn "Immanuel's
Land," and the benediction was pronounced. A sister of
William's mother described the service:

The day was ideal—Princeton in its first spring beauty; the hour,
five o'clock, was perfect. Dr. Patton himself conducted the service
in a way so dignified, reverent and affectionate that nothing more
seemed needed. The chapel was nearly filled with students who had
known William, and the service throughout was simple, strong,
solemn, tender and triumphant. . . . As I listened, the whole of
William's life seemed to sweep before me. There was not one word
too much, nor undeserved. I marvelled that they had understood so
truly and loved so deeply in the space of but three years.[14]

Among the other memorial services for William Borden
one had a significance all its own. It was held in the little
Princeton African Methodist Church, where he had taught

Sunday school for two years. The children and adults of that church loved him and sorrowed for the loss of their friend.

*   *   *

Francis Landey Patton retired from the presidency of Princeton Seminary in 1913 to return to Carberry Hill in Bermuda, the home where he was born.[15] Princeton was the largest seminary in the country, with an enrollment of between 150 and 192. Even though financial deficits continued to plague the seminary at the time of Patton's retirement, Princeton's total assets, including investments and property, amounted to nearly $4 million, making it the most heavily endowed theological seminary in the United States. Dr. Patton was loved at Princeton and appreciated throughout the church as a teacher at the university, a professor at the seminary, and a preacher, lecturer, and defender of evangelical Christianity. The university awarded its former president the doctor of laws degree. Dean Andrew West described Patton as "theologian in the school of Augustine; philosopher in the house of Anselm; vindicator of the historic Christian faith—his kinship, in all humility of soul, is with the communion of saints intellectual and spiritual." A large congregation gathered nightly to hear Dr. Patton's final series of lectures, given at the request of students and faculty.[16]

*   *   *

Dr. Warfield served briefly as acting president while the directors looked for Patton's successor. Some favored William L. McEwan, Princeton graduate of 1885 and pastor of the Third Presbyterian Church of Pittsburgh. Others suggested Professor Charles Erdman. Finally Joseph Ross Stevenson—a member of the seminary's board of directors since 1902—was elected. The forty-eight-year-old Presbyterian minister from the Scotch-Irish area of western Pennsylvania had studied at Washington and Jefferson College, McCormick Seminary, and the University of Berlin. He served as pastor of a church in Sedalia, Missouri, taught church history at McCormick Seminary, and in 1902 became the minister at the Fifth

Avenue Presbyterian Church in New York City—a church that had many associations with Princeton Seminary. Seven of its former pastors had served as directors, and two—J. W. Alexander and George T. Purves—had also been teachers at the seminary. In 1909 Dr. Stevenson was called to the Brown Memorial Church in Baltimore—named for Isabella Brown, the donor of Brown Hall at Princeton Seminary.

Some Presbyterian leaders were pleased with the choice of Dr. Stevenson. Sylvester W. Beach, pastor of the First Presbyterian Church in Princeton and a member of the seminary's board of directors, wrote to Stevenson that he was delighted that the seminary had called a president "who knows and understands the practical problems of our day not less than the theological issues." Most of the faculty, however, were deeply disappointed. Dr. Machen appreciated Stevenson's "genuineness" and "the reality of his faith," but he distrusted his views on seminary education and wanted "a somewhat broader man"—with a greater commitment to theology as well as skill in leadership. Machen, however, grew to like Stevenson; he admired his fervor and frankness.[17]

The directors chose Jonathan Ritchie Smith for the chair of homiletics. A graduate of Princeton Seminary, Smith for a time was attracted by the critical views of Charles Briggs on the question of biblical inspiration but soon returned to the conservative outlook. He served churches in Peekskill, New York, and Harrisburg, Pennsylvania, and was known as an effective preacher and successful pastor. B. B. Warfield praised Smith's book *The Teaching of the Gospel of John* as an "excellent study," and Machen admired Smith's scholarly and attractive preaching and believed that he was "a man worth having." The sixty-three-year-old Smith was the third member of the seminary class of 1876—with Dr. Warfield and Dr. Purves—to serve on the faculty.

*   *   *

Directors and trustees, faculty and students, alumni and friends, and official delegates from nearly eighty institutions of higher learning (including Harvard University and Moody Bible Institute) filled Princeton's historic First Presbyterian

Church on the morning of October 13, 1914, for the inauguration of J. Ross Stevenson and J. Ritchie Smith. Dr. Smith
subscribed to the required formula, listened to the charge
from William L. McEwan, and delivered his inaugural address
on the "Place of Homiletics in the Training of Ministers." Dr.
Stevenson promised to adhere fully to the Westminster
Confession of Faith; and Dr. Patton, now president emeritus,
cordially welcomed him to his new post and reminded him
that "this Theological Seminary is a training camp for soldiers
of the cross." To accomplish its purpose, Dr. Patton said, the
seminary must have "a very generous theological curriculum,"
which would preserve the study of Greek and Hebrew and
the other elements of the seminary's "Plan" and also give the
students "a great deal of sound advice, good counsel and
plain, practical directions." Patton praised the seminary
teachers of the past who gave him his ideals and made him
say, "That is the way I should like to do my work." He added,
"I am an old man now and it is too late for me to take up a
new branch of study, but there are young men in this faculty
who, when I hear them talk upon the subjects to which they
are devoting their lives, make me wish that I was young again
that I might sit at their feet and take up these studies under
their leadership."

Dr. Patton continued:

This Theological Seminary . . . is also a fortress. By this I mean, of
course, that it is committed to the defense of Christianity as a supernatural religion. . . . When we affirm . . . that we are committed to
the defense of a definite theological position we shall be exposed to
criticism. "You claim," they will say, "to be searching for truth, but
you are really defending a foregone conclusion." . . . I can well
understand the position of those who say "We have here no continuing conviction but we seek one to come and we need all our
learning and logical power in order that we may find it." Our
position, I confess, is somewhat different from this. We are in
possession of certain definite convictions which are exposed to
hostile attack and we feel that the ripest scholarship and the most
searching inquiry can be employed in no better way than in the
defense of these convictions. Of course, if it is a fault to believe that
Christianity contains a certain definite body of knowledge we admit
that we are justly open to criticism, but I do not believe that to be
ever learning and never able to come to a knowledge of the truth is

a sign of theological supremacy. The greatest issue at the present time is that which deals with supernatural Christianity. . . . Princeton Seminary, in the Providence of God, is called to occupy a conspicuous place of honor in the defense of the faith once delivered to the saints.

Dr. Patton addressed his closing words directly to Stevenson:

May you have a long, happy and successful career, Mr. President, as the head of this institution and, under your guiding hand, may you see this seat of learning with an ever-increasing body of students, an enlarged curriculum and an adequate material equipment so far surpassing the glory of her former days that the friends and foes alike of historic Christianity, as they survey the great centers of theological learning and realize what this institution has done and will continue to do in defense of fundamental truths, may feel constrained to say—"There, there, in Princeton Theological Seminary, is to be seen the Gibraltar of the Christian faith."[18]

In his inaugural address on "Theological Education in the Light of Present Day Demands," Dr. Stevenson looked more to the future than to the past for the seminary's direction. "The modern age, which is considered as being altogether unique and which is making radical demands along every line of thought," he declared, "insists that in theological education there should be a complete readjustment, if not a sweeping revolution."[19]

John Grier Hibben—who had succeeded Woodrow Wilson as Princeton University's fourteenth president—pledged that the representatives of the university attending the seminary celebration "will endeavor, so far as lies within us, to preserve the faith and hope of our fathers and to remain true to the gospel which they professed." Hibben, a graduate of both Princeton University and Princeton Seminary, called for a "spirit of tolerance and helpful cooperation." "The need of the world," he said, "so urgent and so desperate, places upon all of our universities, theological seminaries, and churches alike, a heavy burden of responsibility, to minimize our differences of opinion and emphasize our common faith and common purpose."[20]

Before the speeches of the day had ended, it must have been obvious to all that Princeton Seminary was no longer unified as it had been for over a hundred years. Although most of the faculty and directors held to the old "Plan" and to the example of the seminary's founders, others—notably the new president—looked more to present issues and future challenges to shape theological education at Princeton.

*   *   *

Shortly after Dr. Stevenson's inauguration there was another move to change the curriculum by introducing more courses with a practical emphasis. Two proposals came from the curriculum committee of the board to the faculty in December 1914. The first outlined a reduction in the number of hours in the required curriculum, and the second introduced some electives in the seminary course. The first proposal was amended by the faculty to state that it would take further action concerning reduction of hours "only when definite concrete schedules designed to secure this result have been submitted for consideration." The second proposal also was amended to give the faculty supervision over the students in making their choice of electives. Both proposals, as amended, then passed the faculty—the first, eight to four and the second, seven to five. Voting against both, even as amended, were Warfield, Greene, Vos, and Hodge. (Robert Dick Wilson voted for the first and against the second.)

On January 9, 1915, the faculty again considered the matter of a reduced number of required hours. Voting for the curriculum committee majority report—recommending a reduction of required hours—were Stevenson, Davis, Wilson, Erdman, Loetscher, and Smith. Voting against the proposal were Warfield, Greene, Vos, Armstrong, Hodge, and Machen. With a tie vote, the issue remained unresolved. A week later the faculty met again to consider the matter. A decision was reached when Armstrong and Machen—having won their case for keeping the hours in Greek—decided to vote for the proposal as the best way to preserve as much as possible of the traditional curriculum. The others—Warfield,

Greene, Vos, and Hodge—recorded their opposition, stating that the reduction of hours in required courses would tend to make it more difficult to effectively teach the material and therefore "make the whole instruction of the seminary fatally superficial." Dr. Warfield made one last plea for the old curriculum. The directors expressed their great esteem for Warfield and "his long and eminent services to the Seminary" but voted nonetheless to make the changes.[21]

During the curriculum debate the faculty, for the most part, had divided between the "practical men" who supported some limited change and the "theological men" who wanted Princeton to stay as it was. Dr. Warfield and the others who stood with him would not have so vehemently resisted changes leading to a greater emphasis on practical courses if they had not been concerned that this direction could significantly alter the theological stance of the seminary. Machen was afraid that the emphasis on the "practical" by President Stevenson might lead to the appointment of a "pious liberal" or "some 'intensely practical' incompetent" to the faculty. If some of the faculty did not fully appreciate the practical needs of the church, the others failed to understand the legitimate theological concerns of their colleagues.[22]

* * *

A sincere and intelligent man with many good leadership qualities, J. Ross Stevenson saw the need to move beyond the old "head of the faculty" position—which had defined the role of Francis Patton—to that of a more active president. He wanted Princeton to have a greater influence in the entire Presbyterian church and to see it adapt to new ideas in preparing men to minister in the modern context. Dr. Stevenson, however, was basically theologically conservative, often claiming that his position was like that which "the fathers of the seminary" had held during the Old School–New School controversy a hundred years earlier. He did not want Princeton to "include Modernists, Liberals, or those of whatever name, who are disloyal to the Standards of the Presbyterian Church." Union Seminary in New York he described as a "seminary for destructive liberalism." But

Stevenson refused to directly and firmly oppose the rising tide of liberalism in the church. Though he was "very far indeed from asserting that Dr. Stevenson [was] a modernist," Gresham Machen was convinced that if Stevenson's policy prevailed, "Princeton Seminary [would] be in a very few years a modernist institution." Director Sylvester Beach had predicted that Stevenson's election would mean "a new and great epoch in our Seminary's history." Gresham Machen and others feared that it would lead to unacceptable changes. Soon it would become clear to all that Dr. Stevenson's election to the presidency was indeed "the dividing line" in the history of Princeton Seminary.[23]

16

The War Years

Christ does not yield to men: He triumphs over men. And this is the commission He gives to us: Let your light shine! Do not think you are imitating Him when you quench your light; when you permit the clamours of men to drown your voice of teaching. You imitate Him only when, despite men's opposition, you find a way to make your voice heard and the truth with which you are charged a power among them.

BENJAMIN BRECKINRIDGE WARFIELD

GRESHAM Machen made his sixth trip to Europe during the summer of 1913, taking, as he put it, some of his "mountain medicine" in the Tyrols of Austria and the Dolomites of Italy.[1] A year later, on June 23, Machen, now thirty-three years old, was ordained to the Christian ministry by the Presbytery of New Brunswick. Dr. Machen—who had been shaken by profound doubts as to the truth of orthodox Christianity during his study in Germany—did not take the constitutionally prescribed vows lightly. He affirmed solemnly that he believed "the Scriptures of the Old and New Testaments to be the Word of God, the only infallible rule of faith and practice" and that he received and adopted the Westminster Confession of Faith and Catechisms as "containing the system of doctrine taught in the Holy Scriptures."

At his ordination Machen preached on the text "Rejoice with trembling" (Psalm 2:11). He stated that most Christians were joyful but added that it was a joy stemming almost entirely from membership in the "happy, contented, respectable classes." This kind of joy, he said, was not the joy of which the Psalm spoke. True joy comes when "despairing, hoping, trembling, half-doubting, half-believing, staking all upon Jesus, we venture into the presence of the very God." Only the God of the old theology, Machen insisted, could restore the sense of guilt and forgiveness that modern religion lacked and thus enable Christians to "rejoice with trembling."[2]

Machen taught his seminary classes, preached often in churches, and worked hard at the grueling task of preparing the adult Sunday school lessons for the Presbyterian Board of Education series entitled "A Rapid Survey of the Literature and History of the New Testament." The editor often "punched up" his style and revised the lessons to make them more practical, much to the dismay of Machen, who wanted to deal with substantive issues. Machen accommodated the changes, however, and was praised for his gracious attitude. Dr. Warfield read the installments as they appeared—"greedily at once," he said. He declared that Machen had done "a very difficult piece of work admirably" and that he and his colleagues were "proud to have these lesson-helps emanate from Princeton."[3]

* * *

Dr. Warfield gave five lectures at the Princeton Summer School of Theology in June 1914 on the "Plan of Salvation."[4] With his clear and concise style, biblical astuteness, and grasp of historical theology, Warfield described and defended supernaturalism over against naturalism, evangelicalism over against sacerdotalism, particularism over against universalism, and biblical Calvinism over against what he called "reduced forms of Calvinism."

Warfield pointed out that there can be fundamentally only two doctrines of salvation—"that salvation is from God, and that salvation is from ourselves." Pelagianism, he said, was "the first organized system of self-salvation taught in the Church." "In the triumph of Augustinianism it was once for all settled that Christianity was to remain a religion, and a religion for sinful men, needing salvation, and not rot down into a mere ethical system, fitted only for the righteous who need no salvation." Pelagianism "died hard," however, "or rather it did not die at all" but emerged again as semi-Pelagianism; "and when the controversy with semi-Pelagianism had been fought and won, into the place of semi-Pelagianism there stepped that semi-semi-Pelagianism which the Council of Orange betrayed the church into, the genius of an Aquinas systematized for her, and the Council of

Trent finally fastened with rivets of iron upon that portion of the church which obeyed it." "Autosoterism" also characterizes modern liberal theology ("our Harnacks and Boussets and their innumerable disciples and imitators"), Warfield claimed. In fact, it "out-pelagianizes Pelagius" when, "with no real sense of guilt, and without the least feeling for the disabilities which come from sin, it complacently puts God's forgiveness at the disposal of whosoever will deign to take it from his hands." Warfield maintained that the Pelagian systems provided no real hope. He said,

It is only in almighty grace that a sinner can hope; for it is only almighty grace that can raise the dead. What boots it to send the trumpeter crying amid the serried ranks of the dead: "The gates of heaven stand open: whosoever will may enter in"? The real question which presses is, "Who will make these dry bones live?" As over against all teaching that would tempt man to trust in himself for any, even the smallest part, of his salvation, Christianity vests him utterly on God. It is God and God alone who saves, and that in every element of the saving process. "If there be but one stitch," says Spurgeon aptly, "in the celestial garment of our righteousness which we ourselves are to put in, we are lost."[5]

Moving to supernaturalistic views of the plan of salvation, Dr. Warfield criticized the "sacerdotalism" of the Roman Catholic and Greek Orthodox churches (and the Anglo-Catholic party within the Church of England) as a system according to which "God the Lord does nothing looking to the salvation of men directly and immediately: all that he does for the salvation of men he does through the mediation of the Church." "The question which is raised in sacerdotalism," Warfield said, "is just whether it is God the Lord who saves us, or is it men, acting in the name and clothed with the powers of God, to whom we look for salvation." Evangelicalism "refuses to have anything to do with sacerdotalism," Warfield asserted, "and turns from all instrumentalities of salvation to put its sole trust in the personal Saviour of the soul."[6]

Warfield then dealt with the "universalism" of "Evangelical Arminianism" and "Evangelical Lutheranism"—"that all that God does looking toward the salvation of sinful man, he does not to or for individual men but to or for all men alike, making no distinctions." These systems attempt to solve the ("let us say it frankly, insoluble") problem "of how it is God and God alone who saves the soul, and all that God does looking towards the saving of the soul he does to and for all men alike, and yet all men are not saved."[7]

Finally, Dr. Warfield came to Calvinism. He said,

As supernaturalism is the mark of Christianity, at large, and evangelicalism is the mark of Protestantism, so particularism is the mark of Calvinism. The Calvinist is he who holds with full consciousness that God the Lord, in his saving operations, deals not generally with mankind at large, but particularly with the individuals who are actually saved.

Calvinism, however, Warfield insisted, has "as important a mission in preserving the true universalism of the gospel (for there is a true universalism of the gospel) as it has in preserving the true particularism of grace." "In his own good time and way [God] will bring the world in its entirety to the feet of him whom he has not hesitated to present to our adoring love not merely as the Saviour of our souls, but as the Saviour of the world," Warfield proclaimed. "The Biblical doctrine of the salvation of the world is not 'universalism' in the common sense of that term," he added; "it does not mean that all men without exception are saved." It is, Warfield said, "an eschatological universalism," not "an each-and-every universalism."[8]

Dr. Warfield ended his lectures on the "Plan of Salvation" by stating that "the salvation of the world is absolutely dependent (as is the salvation of the individual soul) on its salvation being the sole work of the Lord Christ himself, in his irresistible might. It is only the Calvinist that has warrant to believe in the salvation . . . of the individual or of the world. Both alike rest utterly on the sovereign grace of God. All other ground is shifting sand."[9]

* * *

The seminary faculty had divided during the curriculum debate, but they were firmly united in their support of Billy Sunday. Sunday had abandoned a successful career as a

J. Ross Stevenson

William Park Armstrong c. 1929-30

J. Gresham Machen, 1929

AERIAL VIEW OF CAMPUS, 1934 AND KEY

1. New Lenox Library, 1879. Gift of James Lenox of New York. Removed for a parking lot in 1960.

2. Lenox Library, 1843. Gift of James Lenox of New York. Removed for Speer Library in 1955.

3. 80 Mercer Street. Faculty house. Home of Caspar Wistar Hodge Jr.

4. 74 Mercer Street. Faculty house. Home of Charles Hodge, built by him in 1823. Later home of his son, A. A. Hodge. B. B. Warfield and W. P. Armstrong later made their homes here.

5. Alexander Hall. The Seminary's first building, completed in 1818. Named for Archibald Alexander in 1893. The "Oratory," where the daily prayers and all early meetings were held, including the Sabbath Afternoon Conference, is on the second floor. J. G. Machen lived on the fourth floor throughout his Princeton career.

6. 58 Mercer Street. Faculty house. Home of Archibald Alexander, built for him in 1819. J. A. Alexander, J. C. Moffat and J. D. Davis later lived here.

7. 52 Mercer Street. Faculty house. G. Vos and A.W. Blackwood made their home here.

8. 44 Mercer Street. The Calvin Club, a student eating club which flourished from 1903 until 1952 made its home here. The eating clubs were dissolved in 1952 in favor of the Seminary's new dining facility, the Campus Center.

9. 20 Alexander Street. The Canterbury Club, a student eating club, 1907–1919.

10. 29 Alexander Street. The Seminary Club, a student eating club renamed the Warfield Club in 1927, flourished here from 1920 until 1952.

11. 44 Alexander Street. Payne Hall, an apartment complex built for visiting missionaries and their families in 1922.

12. 22 Dickinson Street. The Friar Club, a strong eating club, 1892–1952.

13. Stuart Hall, 1876. The classroom building, a gift of Robert and Alexander Stuart of New York City.

14. Miller Chapel, 1834. Named for Samuel Miller in 1893. Originally built between Alexander Hall and the Alexander House facing Mercer Street, it was moved to its present site in 1933.

15. Built in 1847, this building was originally a refectory and infirmary. In the 1890s it became a student gymnasium. In 1945 it was remodeled as the administration building.

16. Brown Hall, 1864. A student dormitory given by Isabella M. Brown of Baltimore.

17. Hodge Hall, 1893. A student dormitory named in memory of Charles Hodge and given by Mary M. Stuart (Mrs. Robert) of New York.

18. The Power House. Built in 1909 and replaced in 1967.

19. 86 Mercer Street. "Springdale," built in 1846, the residence of the Seminary presidents since 1903. Presidents F. L. Patton and J. R. Stevenson lived here.

20. 81 Mercer Street. Faculty house. Home of William M. Paxton.

View of Alexander Hall from the porch of Miller Chapel in early spring c. 1940

major league baseball player to devote his full time to Christian ministry. Licensed and ordained by the Presbyterian church, the Iowa native first held campaigns in small Midwestern towns, but by the eve of World War I he was receiving invitations from larger cities all over the United States. Crowding his way with 20,000 others into a Philadelphia tabernacle on a rainy January 24, 1915, Gresham Machen heard Billy Sunday preach. Machen was impressed by the huge crowd and by the earnestness of the personal workers, but he found the sermon rather commonplace. "The big argument for Billy Sunday is the result of his preaching," he decided. During a second visit about a week later Machen was far more impressed with the evangelist despite his showmanship. The "sermon was old-fashioned evangelism of the most powerful and elemental kind," he wrote; "in the last five or ten minutes of that sermon, I got a new realization of the power of the gospel." Noting the Unitarian opposition to Sunday, Machen commented, "I like Billy Sunday for the enemies he has." Professor J. Ritchie Smith and the seminary middlers also visited Sunday's meetings in Philadelphia and New York.

The Princeton Seminary faculty unanimously invited Billy Sunday to speak in Princeton on Monday, March 8, 1915, setting off great furor at the university and in the town. President Hibben refused the use of the university's Alexander Hall, and Dean West criticized the evangelist's "travesties of the teaching of Christ," as well as his "vulgarity" and "downright bad taste." Many university professors and some of the Princeton clergy were outraged by Sunday's comments about liberal theologians and unbelieving preachers. The town paper was bitterly hostile. The commotion made Machen even more enthusiastic for Billy Sunday. He was glad "that the Seminary in this public way is giving the right hand of fellowship to a man who is doing the Lord's work." Machen wrote, "His methods are as different as could possibly be imagined from ours, but we support him to a man simply because, in an age of general defection, he is preaching *the gospel*. We are not ashamed of his 'antiquated theology'; it is nothing in the world but the message of the cross, long neglected, which is manifesting its old power."

[299]

In a seminary prayer meeting Machen talked to the students about Billy Sunday's evangelism and its "very close" relationship to Princeton theology. He told the young men that "there is going to be an increasing need for pastors who are really able to teach the people; in Philadelphia for example the ground has been broken in a wonderful way, and the question is whether the seed is to be planted. My trip to Pittsburgh last year gave me a vivid impression of the intellectual interests which are awakened—though of course not satisfied—by the Sunday campaigns."[10]

The Billy Sunday meeting was held in the First Presbyterian Church, a much smaller place than the desired university building. Admission was by ticket only, and a packed house listened to the evangelist preach. Later in the day he spoke at Miller Chapel on I Kings 22. He appealed to the seminarians to follow the example of Micaiah—a man who was devoted to God, he told them, and fearless in preaching God's message. The *Princeton Seminary Bulletin* reported that "this was one of the best addresses of the year."[11]

*   *   *

On May 3, 1915, Dr. Machen was inaugurated as assistant professor of New Testament literature and exegesis. He had declined an invitation from Virginia's Union Theological Seminary so that he could remain at Princeton and continue there the "apologetic treatment of the problems of the New Testament" that had been his chief concern for the past twelve years. The charge was given by his old friend Dr. Patton. Machen then spoke, paying generous tribute to the seminary faculty, most of them his teachers, and especially praising Patton, his "spiritual father." He said of his colleague in New Testament, William Park Armstrong, "I shall never be able to acquire one tenth part of his learning, but to his constant guidance and example I shall owe at least whatever breadth of outlook and loyalty to the truth I may ever be able to attain."

In his inaugural address, entitled "History and Faith," Machen was concerned to send forth a clear note for the gospel. He focused on what he saw as the chief intellectual struggle of the day—that the Bible as historical narrative is not disposable, as the liberals taught, but is absolutely essential for the Christian faith. Machen began:

> The student of the New Testament should be primarily an historian. The centre and core of all the Bible is history. Everything else that the Bible contains is fitted into an historical framework and leads up to an historical climax. . . .
> Give up history, and you can retain some things. You can retain belief in God. . . . You can retain a lofty ethical ideal. But be perfectly clear about one point—you can never retain a gospel. For gospel means "good news," tidings, information about something that has happened.

That "good news," Machen asserted, is "the life and death and resurrection of Jesus Christ." He defended the Bible's view of Jesus—"a Saviour come from outside the world"— against modern substitutes that have been "tried and found wanting." The facts of the gospel are "confirmed by experience" that "adds to history that directness, that immediateness, that intimacy of conviction which delivers us from fear." But "Christian experience cannot do without history" as found in the Bible, Machen said. "Undermine that foundation, and the Church will fall. It will fall, and great will be the fall of it."[12]

*   *   *

Most of the Princetonians were deeply disturbed that the 1915 General Assembly did nothing to check the situation in New York and Brooklyn presbyteries, in which "virtual unbelievers" were being received into the ministry of the Presbyterian church. Dr. Machen believed that the church was still "fundamentally evangelical" but sadly indifferent to "the big questions." He hoped that the Southern Presbyterian Church—a more conservative denomination—would "keep quite separate" from the church in the North.[13]

*   *   *

At the beginning of the new school term, on September 17, 1915, Dr. Warfield gave the opening address in Miller

Chapel. "There is no one of the titles of Christ which is more precious to Christian hearts than 'Redeemer,'" he said. With obvious learning and devotion, Warfield summed up the significance and historic meaning of the word "Redeemer" in a breathtaking survey of the language of Christian worship and theology. He showed how modern liberal theology had evacuated the word "Redeemer" of all meaning, even as it threatened the word "Christianity." "Does the word 'Christianity' any longer bear a definite meaning?" Warfield asked. "We hear of Christianity without dogma, Christianity without miracle, Christianity without Christ." "People set upon calling un-Christian things Christian are simply washing all meaning out of the name," he said. "If everything that is called Christianity in these days is Christianity, then there is no such thing as Christianity."

"I think you will agree with me that it is a sad thing to see words like these die like this," Dr. Warfield said to the students. "And I hope you will determine that, God helping you, you will not let them die thus, if any care on your part can preserve them in life and vigor. But the dying of the words is not the saddest thing which we see here." Warfield went on to say:

The saddest thing is the dying out of the hearts of men of the things for which the words stand. As ministers of Christ it will be your function to keep the things alive. If you can do that, the words which express the things will take care of themselves. Either they will abide in vigor; or other good words and true will press in to take the place left vacant by them. The real thing for you to settle in your minds, therefore, is whether Christ is truly a Redeemer to you, and whether you find an actual Redemption in Him—or are you ready to deny the Master that bought you, and to count His blood an unholy thing? Do you realize that Christ is your Ransomer and has actually shed His blood for you as your ransom? Do you realize that your salvation has been bought, bought at a tremendous price, at the price of nothing less precious than blood, and that the blood of Christ, the Holy One of God? Or, to go a step further: do you realize that this Christ who has thus shed His blood for you is Himself your God?[14]

*   *   *

As Europe went to war during the summer of 1914 Gresham Machen applauded President Woodrow Wilson's efforts to maintain neutrality and was delighted with his Senate speech in which he pled for "peace without victory." But growing sympathy for the Allies and shock over Germany's sinking of the *Lusitania* in 1915 brought the nation closer to war. Princeton University's president, John Hibben, fervently promoted "preparedness" and began courses in military training. B. B. Warfield, lamenting the slow response of the United States, wrote two poems —"Awake, America!" and "The Coward Boy"—for the *New York Tribune.* "I wish with all my heart that America were with you in this struggle," he wrote to Charles Salmond—a Scot who had studied at Princeton in 1877–78 and was now pastor at the South Morningside United Free Church in Edinburgh.[15] Machen, however, was not yet convinced. "Princeton is a hot-bed of patriotic enthusiasm and military ardor, which makes me feel like a man without a country," he lamented. Machen feared "militarism" more than "unpreparedness" and condemned imperialism as satanic, "whether it is German or English." Finally, on a raw, rainy April 2, 1917, President Wilson went before Congress to declare that a state of war existed between the United States and Germany. Almost all of the nation, including the religious leaders, was solidly behind the war. The Federal Council of Churches enthusiastically announced, "The war for righteousness will be won! Let the Church do her part."[16]

J. Ross Stevenson was placed in charge of religious work at the military camps under the auspices of the International YMCA. Despite his lack of enthusiasm for the war, Machen was determined to serve his country in his capacity as a minister of the gospel. He debated as to whether he should become a chaplain or a YMCA worker, finally deciding that the latter would allow him to be "at the front right with the men" and offer him greater opportunities for ministry than "the severely official position of the chaplains." During the fall of 1917 he preached at various military camps in the United States. He had a few days in Princeton at the end of the year before sailing for Europe early in January. He preached in the seminary chapel to a large gathering, which,

Rebekah Purves Armstrong wrote to Machen's mother, was moved by the sermon and "the earnestness and beauty of his prayers." "We shall miss Gresham more than I can tell you," she added, "not only in the Seminary but also in our own household where I think you know the place he holds."[17]

*   *   *

Some thirty students left the seminary to enter war service, and enrollment declined from 187 in 1916–17 to 155 the following year and 114 during 1918–19. Because Dr. Stevenson was in Europe working with the YMCA, Dr. Warfield again became the leader of the faculty.

In October 1917 Warfield made a rare trip away from Princeton to deliver the Thomas Smyth Lectures at Columbia Theological Seminary in Columbia, South Carolina. Speaking on the topic of "miracles," Dr. Warfield described the great number of miracles wrought by Christ during his earthly life and the "extraordinary capacities produced in the early Christian communities by direct gift of the Holy Spirit." The apostolic church, Warfield said, "was marked out as itself a gift from God, by showing forth the possession of the Spirit in appropriate works of the Spirit—miracles of healing and miracles of power; miracles of knowledge, whether in the form of prophecy or of the discerning of spirits; [and] miracles of speech, whether of the gift of tongues or of their interpretation." Warfield argued that this state of things was "the characterizing peculiarity of specifically the Apostolic Church, and it belonged therefore exclusively to the Apostolic age." These supernatural gifts were "part of the credentials of the Apostles as the authoritative agents of God in founding the church." "Their function thus confined them distinctively to the Apostolic Church," Warfield claimed, "and they necessarily passed away with it." He stated that this conclusion was proven by investigation of the New Testament teaching as to the origin and nature of the supernatural signs and by the testimony of later ages as to their cessation.

In his lectures Dr. Warfield examined in detail "the chief views which have been held favorable to the continuance of the charismata beyond the Apostolic age." Beginning with the "patristic and medieval marvels," moving through "Roman Catholic miracles," the "Irvingite gifts," accounts of modern "faith-healing" and "mind-cure," and ending in a discussion of why Mary Baker Eddy found it necessary to visit a dentist, Warfield carefully set forth the reasons why he was convinced that they were "counterfeit miracles."[18]

*   *   *

"Keswick" or "Victorious Life" conferences were held in Princeton for several years "to lead Christians into a life of victory through moment-by-moment faith in Christ." Developed in England during the 1870s, popularized by its famous annual convention at Keswick in the lovely Lake District, and promoted in America by conferences, books, the *Scofield Reference Bible,* and especially by *The Sunday School Times,* "the Keswick message" gained wide acceptance by the early twentieth century. Although he admitted that earlier Keswick teachers may have presented "a stereotyped form of experience," Charles Erdman stated that the teaching was now "most careful and conservative and scriptural." It helps people "to appreciate and appropriate the riches of grace in Christ Jesus which are offered in common to all believers," Dr. Erdman claimed, adding that "such a message the church needs today."[19] In 1917 the *Presbyterian* gave high praise to one of the Princeton Keswick conferences. The editors emphasized the similarities between Keswick and Reformed teaching and found Keswick's emphasis on "trust" and "surrender" a welcome alternative to the social ethics of liberalism.

Dr. Warfield also found positive things about Keswick teaching—"it exalts Christ and it exalts faith," he said. But he disliked its "crass separation of sanctification from justification," which, he believed, laid "the foundation . . . for that circle of ideas which are summed up in the phrase, 'the Second Blessing.'" Of this separation of sanctification and justification, Warfield wrote, "not only do the generality of Christians know nothing, but the Scriptures know nothing." Against the Keswick teaching that Christians may (by surrender and trust) live a life free from sinning (while remaining sinners at heart), Dr. Warfield asserted that the Holy Spirit cures our sinning precisely by curing our sinful nature. "He makes the tree good," Warfield stated, "that the fruit may be good." "The sanctifying action of the Spirit terminates on us, not merely on our activities; under it, not only our actions but we are made holy." "Only, this takes time," Warfield added, "and therefore at no point short of its completion are either our acts or we 'perfect.'"[20]

In solid theological essays first published in *The Princeton Theological Review* Dr. Warfield dealt with the various expressions of Keswick and related movements, giving careful attention to the teachings of W. E. Boardman, Mr. and Mrs. Pearsall Smith, Charles Trumbull and *The Sunday School Times*, and the "German Higher Life Movement" and its chief exponent, Theodore Jellinghaus (who in 1912 renounced his views and returned to the Reformed position). Warfield summarized what he called the "essential elements" of these holiness movements:

In all of them alike, justification and sanctification are divided from one another as two separate gifts of God. In all of them alike sanctification is represented as obtained, just like justification, by an act of simple faith, but not by the same act of faith by which justification is obtained, but by a new and separate act of faith, exercised for this specific purpose. In all of them alike the sanctification which comes on this act of faith, comes immediately on believing, and all at once, and in all of them alike this sanctification, thus received, is complete sanctification. In all of them alike, however, it is added that this complete sanctification does not bring freedom from all sin; but only, say, freedom from sinning; or only freedom from conscious sinning; or from the commission of "known sins." And in all of them alike this sanctification is not a stable condition into which we enter once for all by faith, but a momentary attainment, which must be maintained moment by moment, and which may readily be lost and often is lost, but may also be repeatedly instantaneously recovered.[21]

The whole range of perfectionist teachings in America and Europe came under Warfield's scrutiny in 1917 and the following several years.[22] He analyzed Albrecht Ritschl's doctrine of the Christian life in two articles, "Ritschl the Rationalist" and "Ritschl the Perfectionist." The teaching of

Albrecht Ritschl—that the Christian life is a matter merely of ethical activity in the kingdom of God—did not surprise Warfield. "It lies in the very nature of a naturalistic system that it should lay all its stress on the activities of the Christian life," he wrote; "there is nothing else on which it could lay its stress." Warfield followed his treatment of Ritschl with three articles entitled "'Miserable-Sinner Christianity' in the Hands of the Rationalists," in which he set forth the Reformation theology with its emphasis on sin and grace. "We are always unworthy, and all that we have or do of good is always of pure grace," Warfield stated. "Though blessed with every spiritual blessing in the heavenlies in Christ, we are still in ourselves just 'miserable sinners': 'miserable sinners' saved by grace to be sure, but 'miserable sinners' still, deserving in ourselves nothing but everlasting wrath."[23]

*   *   *

Gresham Machen had hoped to serve in a religious capacity with the YMCA but was assigned to duty in Belgium and France as a canteen director. He spent nine months near the front in drab, monotonous, and, at times, dangerous work. He lived with the constant noise of guns and the sinister buzz of aircraft; he battled rats and longed for some clean clothes and a regular bath. During the days of loneliness, rain, mud, death, and destruction, Machen tried to stay as close to the front as he could to render real service to the men. Any doubts as to the justice of the Allied cause disappeared, and he prayed for "their righteous victory."[24]

The Princeton professor spoke words of comfort and encouragement to weary soldiers and shared the gospel with lost ones. He relished the work as a "glorious opportunity to render service" and did not regret the interruption of his studies. He wrote to his mother that "a preacher who is preaching *all the time* is apt to run dry." He found satisfaction in doing useful work, and he found peace in reading the Psalms in his French Bible—"the best reading imaginable for army life." Separated from his Greek New Testament for a while, he read in the evenings from the King James Version.

"The grandeur of our old English Bible" appealed to him as never before.[25]

Machen, who only reluctantly supported American involvement in Europe, now intensely hated war. He wrote:

If this war is ever concluded in a really satisfactory way, I am going to be an active worker for peace. And the kind of work that I believe might be really effective is the work of moral education in all languages of the world. War is righteous when it is conducted as in France for the delivery of women and children and the repelling of an invader. But how any human being can have the heart or the utter absence of heart to continue this war for one moment merely for conquest reveals to my mind as nothing else in the world the abyss of sin.[26]

Armistice finally came on November 11, 1918, and in the place of the familiar roar of war was "the *silence* of that misty morning." On November 14 Machen wrote a long letter to his mother. He began: "The Lord's name be praised! Hardly before have I known what true thanksgiving is. Nothing but the exuberance of the psalms of David accompanied with the psaltery and an instrument of ten strings could begin to do justice to the joy of this hour." He was thankful to God for preserving his life. He had "somehow gained the conviction" that he was in God's care, he wrote, "and that He would not try me beyond my strength; that courage would keep pace with danger, or rather that danger . . . would keep within the limits of courage." He added that in the last two weeks he had come to a better understanding of the eighth chapter of Romans—"Who shall separate us from the love of Christ? Shall tribulation, or distress, or persecution, or famine, or nakedness, or peril, or sword?"[27]

Now that the war was over his mother wanted him to come home quickly, and he was longing to return to normal life with its mountain climbing and study of the New Testament. He felt compelled, however, to remain in Europe to reach the soldiers, now relieved from the stress of war, with the message of the gospel. Armstrong wrote to Machen on December 18, expressing both his willingness to have him stay in Europe and an earnest desire to have him back in Princeton. Machen's mind was put at ease. "If there is or ever was on this earth a better fellow than Army," he wrote, "I have yet to hear of him." For the next three months—in shacks with dirt floors, dimly lit candles, and just the edge taken off the chill by wood stoves—Machen preached his "barrel of six talks" with enthusiasm. "I never before knew what the preaching of the gospel is," he wrote.[28]

Gresham Machen returned home in the spring of 1919. On May 6 he gave a brief address to the seminary alumni on the "Church in the War." He said:

In many cases the church has done nobly in the war. There have no doubt been many chaplains, many YMCA secretaries, and many soldiers in the ranks who have proclaimed the gospel of Christ faithfully and humbly and effectively to dying men. Any discouraging estimate of the situation is subject to many noble exceptions. But, in general, in view of the manifest estrangement between the church and large bodies of men, there is at least some plausibility for the common opinion that the church has failed.

"Fortunately, if the church has failed, it is at least perfectly clear why she has failed," Machen declared. "She has failed because men have been unwilling to receive, and the church has been unwilling to preach, the gospel of Christ crucified."[29]

*   *   *

A large number of Princeton Seminary students were going overseas as missionaries; the class of 1918 sent one fifth of its graduates to the foreign mission field.[30] Samuel Zwemer of Hope College in Holland, Michigan, and missionary to the Muslims in Cairo, taught at Princeton for one term during 1918. William E. Miller was stirred to give his life to mission work in Iran by Zwemer's lectures. "He told us the Moslem people had become neglected by us Christians," Miller later explained, "and he called us to respond. I had already decided to become a missionary, but this was God's call for me to go to the Moslem world."[31] During the first decades of the twentieth century, a growing number of international students studied at Princeton. Many came from Asia, especially Japan, from South Africa, and, after the war ended, from Europe.[32]

In the fall of 1921 the cornerstone was laid for Payne Hall—a residence for missionaries and their families studying at Princeton during furlough. The land on the corner of Alexander and Dickinson Streets—the site of the old Slayback store patronized by many generations of students—was purchased and donated by Dr. and Mrs. Charles Erdman. Mr. and Mrs. Calvin Payne of Titusville, Pennsylvania, contributed over $140,000 for the handsome apartment building.[33]

*   *   *

In January 1921 Dr. Machen gave the James Sprunt Lectures at Union Theological Seminary in Virginia. He had worked hard to survey the recent scholarship on the topic of "Paul and his Environment," fretting repeatedly about his incomplete preparation. The lectures, however, were well received at Union Seminary, as was Gresham Machen himself. President W. W. Moore, a long-time friend of the Machen family, said that Machen "came right into the current of the life of the seminary and community in a way that no preceding lecturer on this foundation has done."

The lectures were published in October as *The Origin of Paul's Religion*.[34] At first Machen did not like the title, which had been suggested by Dr. Moore, because the word "religion" was at odds with his understanding of Christianity's uniqueness. He was finally reconciled to it by reflecting on the fact that he was "trying to meet the modern historian on his own ground" in taking "the religious life of Paul first of all as a phenomenon of history that requires explanation."

The history-of-religions approach taught a radical discontinuity between Jesus and Paul; whereas Machen argued that the religion of Paul, as reflected in the Epistles, was at its heart a religion of faith in the Jesus Christ who lived and died in Palestine as the divine Redeemer. Machen stressed that Paul did not derive his understanding of Christianity from his Jewish heritage or Hellenistic environment, nor from contemporary religious movements such as the mystery religions of Egypt or Persia. Paul's religion was based fully on the accounts he had received of the life, death, and resurrection of Jesus. Paul's theology, Machen asserted, was based "either upon the Son of God who came to earth for men's salvation" or else "upon a colossal error." Machen wrote:

The religion of Paul was not founded upon a complex of ideas derived from Judaism or from paganism. It was founded upon the historical Jesus. But the historical Jesus upon whom it was founded was not the Jesus of modern reconstruction, but the Jesus of the whole New Testament and of the Christian faith; not a teacher who survived only in the memory of His disciples, but the Saviour who after His redeeming work was done still lived and could still be loved.

Machen showed how Paul's Hellenistic background prepared him perfectly to preach the gospel among the Gentiles. He argued that "to almost as great an extent as any great historical movement can be ascribed to one man," the establishment of Christianity as a world religion was the work of Paul. It was "the epoch-making work of Paul," who understood the meaning of the life and death of Christ, which established the theological and ethical lines of the Christian movement and made explicit the universal mission of the church.[35]

Machen's attack on the critical theories and his forceful restatement of Pauline theology had great appeal to conservatives. *The Presbyterian* praised Machen's book and rejoiced that at Princeton Seminary another outstanding champion of Reformed theology had emerged. Even Machen's critics admired the scholarship, fairness, and clarity in his "strong defence of old-fashioned supernaturalism." B. W. Bacon, whose *Jesus and Paul* had been subjected to Machen's particular criticism, pointed out that people

have learned to look to Princeton Seminary as the headquarters of apologetic and polemic theology; and in seeking here a strong, clear, and logical defence of the traditional supernaturalistic viewpoint they will not be disappointed. Professor Machen upholds the best standards of his school. He does not profess to write without bias; but he has read thoroughly, presents clearly and fairly his opponent's view, and answers it logically. The work is a good example of sound American scholarship in the field of apologetics.[36]

Rudolph Bultmann commended Machen for his fairness in representing liberal views and his analysis of Paulinism. He stated that Machen had correctly described many shortcomings in the other theories but had not advanced his own. Machen had gone too far in denying the influence of other religions and cultures on Paul and had decided complicated questions, Bultmann charged, "by means of a logic which [looked] at things from the outside."[37]

Although *The Origin of Paul's Religion* was regarded as "an intelligent curiosity" by most liberal scholars, it "made a substantial contribution to the discussion of first-century Christian history." In the fall of 1938 Carl F. H. Henry found in the Northern Baptist Theological Seminary library a copy of Machen's *Origin of Paul's Religion.* "I could not put [it] down until I had completed all but the last chapter," Henry wrote. New Testament scholar Floyd V. Filson commented in 1951 that Machen's "book, *The Origin of Paul's Religion,* and his contention that classic Christian theology is the necessary outcome of faithfulness to the New Testament, were far truer to fact than much shallow theology which often marked the social gospel."[38]

17

Warfield of Princeton

HYMN FOR THE OPENING OF THE SEMINARY

Great God the Giver, Thou hast faithful been,
Here Thou hast set Thy name, and we have seen
Thy mercies grow from year to year more green,
    Lord, we thank Thee.

'Twas Thou didst raise these walls: and Thou didst give
Thy saints Thy truth to teach, Thy truth to live;
They wrought their work, and Thou didst it receive,
    Lord, we thank Thee.

Unto their feet Thou gatheredst of Thy Sons,
The love of Thee waxed fire within their bones,
The world has heard their voice, its huts, its thrones,
    Lord, we thank Thee.

God of our fathers, still pour out Thy grace
In plenteous streams upon this hallowed place,
Still show it all Thy glorious faithfulness,
    Lord, we thank Thee.

And as the flood of years rolls ever by,
Build here Thy holy house each year more high,
Establish here Thy truth unchangeably,
    Lord, we pray Thee.

And every year send forth a sacred host,
Taught of thy Christ, filled with the Holy Ghost,
The cross their only theme, their only boast,
    Lord, we pray Thee.

BENJAMIN BRECKINRIDGE WARFIELD

BENJAMIN Breckinridge Warfield was internationally recognized as a scholar of great ability. His fifth honorary degree was awarded in 1913—*sacrae theologiae* doctor —by the University of Utrecht in the Netherlands.[1] One member of Utrecht's faculty senate had opposed bestowing the honor on a foreigner on the occasion of the centenary of the restoration of the university after its repression by the French during the Napoleonic Wars. But the minutes recorded that his motion "found no support." Abraham Kuyper wrote to congratulate Warfield on the honor. With charming humility Dr. Warfield replied, "I am, of course, very deeply sensible of the honor done me by the University of Utrecht in conferring this degree upon me. But I am not sure I am not even more honored still by the pleasure you express in it. I would almost rather you be pleased than I were honored."[2]

*   *   *

Annie Kinkead Warfield died on November 18, 1915. Almost forty years earlier Annie had suffered a nervous breakdown when she and her husband were caught in a terrible thunderstorm while walking in Germany's Harz Mountains. She never recovered. Through all the years of their married life Dr. Warfield faithfully cared for his invalid wife. He guarded, protected, and stood by her while carrying his full teaching load and pursuing demanding writing assignments. The seminary students often noted his gentle and loving care for

Mrs. Warfield as they walked together on Princeton streets and, later, back and forth on the porch of their campus home. Finally she was bedridden and saw few people besides her husband. By his own choice Dr. Warfield became almost confined to his house; he was never away from her for more than an hour or two at a time. He set aside time to read to her every day. They left Princeton only once in the ten years before her death, for a vacation that he hoped would help her. With his excellent health and varied interests Dr. Warfield must have felt this restriction, but he never complained. He wonderfully demonstrated "the ineffable quality in time of trouble when someone promises to be 'with us' as we walk through the valley of the shadow."[3]

Gresham Machen believed that despite his constant care for his wife, Dr. Warfield had "done about as much work as ten ordinary men." He wondered what the effect of her death would be upon him. In a letter to his mother Machen wrote:

I think . . . that he will feel dreadfully lost without her. As Mrs. Armstrong said, he has had only two interests in life—his work, and Mrs. Warfield, and now that she is gone there may be danger of his using himself up rather quickly. If so, I do not know who is to take his place. I am more and more impressed with him; he is certainly one of the very biggest men in the Church either in this country or in any other.[4]

The Warfields had no children but loved those of the seminary community. While R. B. Kuiper was a graduate student at Princeton in 1912 he and his wife, Marie, became parents. The baby received a gift with a note that read "Doctor and Mrs. Warfield present their compliments to little Miss Kuiper, and beg to congratulate her on being born, and to thank her for being born in Princeton. Will she kindly accept these little pins as a souvenir of her birthplace? April 9, 1912." Dr. Warfield wrote several sensitive and loving articles on children—in which he eloquently described how "it is only from Jesus that the world has learned properly to appreciate and wholesomely to deal with childhood and all that childhood stands for."[5]

*   *   *

[316]

On Christmas Eve of 1920 Dr. Warfield suffered a heart attack. Until the Christmas vacation he had been actively at work and had met all of his classes with his usual punctuality. After a period of slow recovery he taught his afternoon class on a crisp February 16. Because of his weakness he asked to be excused from his usual custom of standing to lead the opening prayer. He then "plunged into a glowing exposition of the third chapter of First John. The discourse quickly gathered about the sixteenth verse as a center"—"Hereby perceive we the love of God, because he laid down his life for us: and we ought to lay down our lives for the brethren." "All the eloquence of Dr. Warfield's Christian heart, all the wisdom of his ripened scholarship focused on the interpretation of that text." "The laying down of His life in our stead was a great thing," he said, "but the wonder of the text is that He being all that He was, the Lord of glory, laid down His life for us, being what we are, mere creatures of His hand, guilty sinners deserving His wrath." The more fully we realize his glory and his gift and our sinfulness, Dr. Warfield continued, the deeper becomes "our wonder at His grace and our wish to glorify His name."[6]

"The lecture was over; Dr. Warfield returned to his lonely dwelling: there came a few sharp shocks of pain—and he left the work that had been his joy, to be with the Saviour whom he loved."[7] Preaching in the seminary chapel after the death of Charles Aiken in 1892, Dr. Warfield had described "the innumerable throng" that "have laid aside the trials and labors of earth, well-pleasing to their Lord, and entered into their rest with him." "While yet our farewell to them on this side of the separating gulf was sounding in their ears," Warfield said, "the glad 'Hail!' of their Lord was welcoming them there." He concluded with the words "May God grant to each of us to follow them. May he give us his Holy Spirit to sanctify us wholly and enable us when we close our eyes in our long sleep to open them at once, not in terrified pain in torment, but in the soft, sweet light of Paradise, safe in the arms of Jesus!"[8]

In a letter to his mother Gresham Machen spoke of "the great loss which we have just sustained in the death of Dr. Warfield. Princeton will seem to be a very insipid place without him. He was really a great man. There is no one living in the Church capable of occupying one quarter of his place." A few days later Machen wrote again:

Dr. Warfield's funeral took place yesterday afternoon at the First Church of Princeton. . . . It seemed to me that the old Princeton—a great institution it was—died when Dr. Warfield was carried out.

I am thankful for one last conversation I had with Dr. Warfield some weeks ago. He was quite himself that afternoon. And somehow I cannot believe that the faith which he represented will ever really die. In the course of the conversation I expressed my hope that to end the present intolerable condition there might be a great split in the Church, in order to separate the Christians from the anti-Christian propagandists. "No," he said, "you can't split rotten wood." His expectation seemed to be that the organized Church, dominated by naturalism, would become so cold and dead, that people would come to see that spiritual life could be found only outside of it, and that thus there might be a new beginning.

Nearly everything that I have done has been done with the inspiring hope that Dr. Warfield would think well of it. . . . I feel very blank without him. . . . He was the greatest man I have known.[9]

*   *   *

On October 11, 1921, Caspar Wistar Hodge Jr. was inducted into the chair of systematic theology that had been held in succession by his grandfather Charles Hodge, his uncle A. A. Hodge, and his teacher B. B. Warfield. The charge to the new professor was given by Dr. Maitland Alexander, who was the grandson of Archibald Alexander, president of the seminary board of directors, and pastor of Pittsburgh's First Presbyterian Church. "I am glad to have been chosen" to give the charge, Dr. Alexander said, "because the names of Alexander and Hodge have been associated through all the years of this Seminary's history. The friendships, between your grandfather and mine, between my father and yours, and again between us in the third generation, make the links in a chain of ancestral and life-long friendship which I am sure will never be broken." Alexander was confident that Caspar Wistar Hodge, like his predecessors, would base his teaching on the authority found in the Word of God and would present the Reformed Faith "undiluted and unweakened—the great System which believes in the Deity of our Lord, Atonement through his blood and absolute dependence of the sinner on Divine grace." He called on the grandson of Charles Hodge to be faithful and zealous in training men for the ministry and in maintaining and defending the position of Princeton—which, he said, is "the Apostolic position; it is the position of the Lord Jesus Christ." He told Hodge that he could be "a great and inspiring leader" to hundreds of ministers "as they strive to exalt Christ the Son of God, uplift His precious Cross and stand with the doctrine of Grace in the path of the hopeless sinner." Dr. Alexander concluded:

I therefore pray that the Holy Spirit may . . . teach you, that as you review the past history of the Theological Department of this Seminary and its achievements, as you look forward to its administration in the most difficult days of its history, you may hear the voice of Him "whose mercy is from everlasting to everlasting upon them that fear Him and whose righteousness is unto children's children," even the Lord God of the Covenant, saying, "Be thou strong and very courageous that thou mayest observe to do according to all the law which my servant Moses commanded thee: turn not from it to the right hand or to the left . . . for then thou shalt make thy way prosperous and then thou shalt have good success."

Caspar Hodge was deeply aware of the significance of the role he was assuming as Princeton's professor of theology. He began his inaugural address:

I have a very profound sense of unworthiness in taking up the duties of the Chair to which you have called me—a Chair made famous by the illustrious men who have preceded me, and whose labours have helped to give Princeton Seminary a fame throughout the world for sound learning and true piety. We think today of Archibald Alexander, that man of God, the first Professor in this Seminary; of Charles Hodge, whose *Systematic Theology* today remains as probably the greatest exposition of the Reformed Theology in the English language; of Archibald Alexander Hodge, a man of rare popular gifts and of unusual metaphysical ability; and last, but not least, excelling them all in erudition, of Dr. Warfield, whose recent death has left us bereft of our leader and one of the greatest men who has ever taught in this Institution.

[319]

I would pause a moment to pay a tribute to his memory. He was my honoured teacher and friend. For twenty years I had the privilege of helping him in this department, and drew inspiration from his broad-minded scholarship. At the time of his death he was, I think, without an equal as a theologian in the English-speaking world. With Doctors Kuyper and Bavinck of Holland, he made up a great trio of outstanding exponents of the Reformed Faith. His loss is simply irreparable. But he has gone to his reward, to meet the Lord he loved and served, and we must seek to carry on the work he did so faithfully and well.[10]

*   *   *

By profound study and extensive reading in English, German, French, and Dutch, B. B. Warfield, to a degree that has rarely been equaled, excelled in the whole field of theological learning—exegetical, historical, and doctrinal.[11] Tributes to Warfield stress his great learning and scholarship. Francis Patton thought that Dr. Warfield "combined in rare degree the widely different attainments of Charles Hodge and Addison Alexander." John DeWitt said that he had known intimately the three great Reformed theologians of America in the preceding generation—Charles Hodge, William Shedd, and Henry B. Smith—and that he was certain not only that Warfield knew a great deal more than any one of them, but that he knew more than all three of them put together! Later Martyn Lloyd-Jones declared that B. B. Warfield was "the greatest exponent, expounder and defender of the classic Reformed faith in the 20th century." According to Hugh T. Kerr, Warfield—in Miller Chapel, Stuart Hall, and through the pages of religious magazines and journals—"brought scholarly distinction" to the Princeton Seminary campus.[12]

Bishop Butler, wrote Alexander Whyte, "has no biography. Butler's books are his whole biography." The same is true of Dr. Warfield. A biography of Warfield has not yet been written, but his "testimony" of mind and heart can be read in his books and in hundreds of essays and reviews, all written with precise, careful, wide-ranging scholarship and in simple, graceful English. Here we have "a theological authorship," Hugh Kerr has written, "on the order of Augustine, Aquinas,

Luther, Calvin, and Barth. Surely we must say that the astonishing quantity of the Warfield biblical and theological corpus issued from a constant and continuous intellectual life at a study desk surrounded on all sides by his books and inspired no doubt in his sequestered confinement by the great theological minds of all times, as he patiently scribed with his own hand page after page after page."[13]

Dr. Warfield's scholarly emphases shifted during the decades of his life. As a New Testament professor in the 1880s he dealt mostly with textual criticism and the apologetical foundations for revelation and inspiration. The historical origins of Christianity captured his attention during the 1890s. From 1900 to 1910 he focused on Christology, and from 1910 to 1921 he wrote on the application of redemption and the doctrine of sanctification. After his death about half of Dr. Warfield's written works were selected by Ethelbert Warfield, Caspar Wistar Hodge, and William Armstrong and published in ten substantial volumes by the American division of Oxford University Press. When Martyn Lloyd-Jones discovered these ten volumes in a Toronto library in 1932 his feelings were, he later wrote, like those of "stout Cortez," as described by Keats, when he first saw the Pacific. Dr. Lloyd-Jones "revelled in the ten volumes to a degree which he had done with no other modern writer. As in the older Reformed authors, here was theology anchored in Scripture, but with an exegetical precision more evident than in the older authors, and combined with a devotion which raised the whole above the level of scholarship alone."[14]

B. B. Warfield expounded and defended historic Christianity at a time when, especially in academic circles, its day was frequently and confidently declared to be done. In insisting on "primacy of Christian doctrine, and on the consequent right and duty to ascertain and accurately to state this doctrine," Warfield wrote, "we have the consciousness of being imitators of Paul even as he was of Christ."

How much the apostle made, not merely of the value of doctrine as the condition of life, but of the importance of sound doctrine! His boast, we will remember, is that he is not of the many who corrupt the truth, but that he, at least, has preached the whole counsel of God. He is not content that Jesus Christ should be preached, but insists on a special doctrine of Christ—Jesus Christ and him as crucified. He even pronounces those that preach any other gospel than that he preached accursed: and we should carefully note that this curse falls not on teachers of other religions, but on preachers of what we might speak of today as different forms of Christianity. In a word, in all his teaching and in all his practice alike, Paul impresses upon us the duty and the supreme importance of preserving that purity of doctrine which is the aim of Systematic Theology in its investigation into Christian truth to secure.[15]

Warfield was splendidly equipped to write a great systematic theology, but he was content to defend, update, and extend the Princeton theology as set forth in Charles Hodge's three volumes. "Forty and six years was this temple in building," Francis Patton explained, "and Dr. Warfield was not the man to turn the key in the door of that temple and leave it to the moles and bats." Warfield devoted himself instead to the exposition and defense of particular doctrines. He "was a dogmatic rather than a systematic theologian, and was less interested in the system of doctrine than in the doctrines of the system. It was to the discussion of particular doctrines in connection with the most recent phases of thought that he gave the greater part of his attention." Warfield's expositions of doctrinal points were all the more convincing because they were based on his considerable exegetical skills—especially in the Greek New Testament but also in the Hebrew.[16]

*　　*　　*

Dr. Warfield's conviction that the Christian faith and biblical truth should be interpreted with intellectual rigor and honesty continued and strengthened Princeton's tradition of "solid learning"; his commitment to the other half of the seminary's ideal—"piety of the heart"—was just as strong. One of the first articles that B. B. Warfield wrote—"The Bible's 'Summum Bonum,'"—addressed the question "What is the highest good which man can strive after?" Warfield showed how the Bible takes a person "out of himself, and bids him seek the highest good in the glory, not of his pitiful self, but of his all-glorious God."[17]

Warfield encouraged and helped the Princeton students in their endeavors for a true spirituality. His sermons to them were "the ripe result of religious experience and minute exegetical knowledge," said Francis Patton, "and in their meditative simplicity reminded us of some of the best Puritan divines."[18] Speaking in the oratory in Stuart Hall on "Spiritual Culture in the Theological Seminary," Dr. Warfield, in his opening address in September 1903, said,

It is natural that at the opening of a new session the minds of both professors and students, especially of those students who are with us for the first time, should be bent somewhat anxiously upon the matter which has brought us together. How are we who teach best to fulfill the trust committed to us, of guiding others in their preparation for the high office of minister of grace? How are you who are here to make this preparation, so to employ your time and opportunities as to become in the highest sense true stewards of the mysteries of Christ? Standing as you do at the close of your university work and at the beginning of three years more of mental labor . . . it would not be strange if your thoughts as they busy themselves with the preparation you require for your ministerial work should be predominately occupied with intellectual training. It is the more important that we should pause to remind ourselves that intellectual training alone will never make a true minister; that the heart has rights which the head must respect; and that it behooves us above everything to remember that the ministry is a spiritual office.

Dr. Warfield outlined in a practical way how the spiritual training of the students could be advanced during their time in the seminary. He stressed the "diligent use of the public means of grace"—the Sunday morning service in the chapel, the Sunday Afternoon Conference, and the daily prayer meetings for faculty and students. He urged the students to take every part of their seminary work as "a religious duty." Warfield explained:

If you learn a Hebrew word, let not the merely philological interest absorb your attention: remember that it is a word which occurs in God's Holy Book, recall the passages in which it stands, remind yourselves what great religious truths it has been given to have a part in recording for the saving health of men. Every Biblical text whose meaning you investigate treat as a Biblical text, a part of God's Holy Word, before which you stand in awe. It is wonderful how even the strictest grammatical study can be informed with reverence. . . . And the doctrines—need I beg you to consider these doctrines not as so many propositions to be analyzed by your logical understanding, but as rather so many precious truths revealing to you your God and God's modes of dealing with sinful man?

Treat, I beg you, the whole work of the seminary as a unique opportunity offered you to learn about God, or rather, to put it at the height of its significance, to learn God—to come to know him whom to know is life everlasting. If the work of the seminary shall be so prosecuted, it will prove itself to be the chief means of grace in all your lives.

Theological training, Dr. Warfield told the students, is composed of *lectio, meditatio, oratio*—study, meditation, prayer. He suggested a dozen devotional classics that he looked upon as "indispensable":

Augustine's *Confessions*; *The Imitation of Christ*; the *Theologia Germanica*; Bishop Andrewes' *Private Devotions*; Jeremy Taylor's *Life of Christ*; Richard Baxter's *The Saints' Everlasting Rest*; Samuel Rutherford's *Letters*; John Bunyan's *Pilgrim's Progress*; Sir Thomas Browne's *Religio Medici*; William Law's *Serious Call*; John Newton's *Cardiphonia*; Bishop Thomas Wilson's *Sacra Privata*.

"To these twelve I should add two or three others which have peculiar interest to us as Princetonians," Warfield continued, "and which I am sure are worthy of association with them—Jonathan Edwards' *Treatise Concerning Religious Affections*, Archibald Alexander's *Thoughts on Religious Experience*, and Charles Hodge's *Way of Life*." Dr. Warfield urged the students to become familiar with books of hymns and prayers, religious biography, the best of religious fiction, and "the great Creeds of the Church." "I do not think I go astray," he told them, "when I say to you in all seriousness that the second and third volumes of Dr. Schaff's *Creeds of Christendom* have in them more food for your spiritual life—are 'more directly, richly and evangelically devotional'—than any other book, apart from the Bible, in existence."[19]

Addressing the opening session of the seminary in October 1911, Dr. Warfield again took as his theme the "Religious Life of Theological Students"—"the most important subject which can engage our thought," he said. He reviewed the historic Princeton connection between faith and learning and called on the students to be diligent in their studies and faithful in their performance of public worship and in the exercise of private devotion. He ended his address with a reference to "old Cotton Mather" and "a great little book" that he wrote to serve as a guide to ministerial students:

The not very happy title which he gave it is *Manductio ad Ministerium.* But by a stroke of genius he added a sub-title which is more significant. And this is the sub-title he added: *The angels preparing to sound the trumpets.* That is what Cotton Mather calls you, students for the ministry: the angels, preparing to sound the trumpets! Take the name to yourselves, and live up to it. Give your days and nights to living up to it! And then, perhaps, when you come to sound the trumpets the note will be pure and clear and strong, and perchance may pierce even to the grave and wake the dead.[20]

The Princetonians—Warfield's colleagues and his students —respected Dr. Warfield as a master thinker and teacher and loved him as a humble Christian who helped them live more Christ-like lives. Twenty years after he studied at Princeton, F. T. McGill wrote that B. B. Warfield "possessed the most perfect combination of faculties of mind and heart that I have ever known in any person." "If Dr. Warfield was great in intellectuality, he was just as great in goodness," McGill continued. "Over a long period of years this man stands out in my mind as the most Christ-like man I have ever known."[21]

*   *   *

Although Dr. Warfield was marked, according to his brother, by "a loftiness and aloofness," he had a genuine love for people and "a heart open to every appeal." He strongly supported missions, both at home and overseas. He concluded one of his chapel sermons with the words:

Need we pause further to enforce that the highest form of the love of truth, the love of the Gospel of God's grace, which braves all things for the pure joy of making known the riches of his love to fallen man? The missionary spirit is the noblest fruit of the love of truth; the missionary's simple proclamation the highest form of witness-bearing to the truth. This spirit is no stranger among you. And I am persuaded that your hearts are burning within you as you think that to you this grace has been given, to preach unto the Gentiles the unsearchable riches of Christ.[22]

Dr. Warfield had a particular sympathy and concern for African Americans. Warfield wrote that since Christians know "that God has made of one blood all the nations of the earth," their task is to "serve as the hand of the Most High in elevating the lowly and rescuing the oppressed." He questioned whether it was "good public policy" ("apart from all question of religion and the kingdom of God") to continue a social system that allowed a class of people to have heaped upon it "year after year, petty injustices and insults, to beget undying hatred in its heart and to perpetuate all the evils of race alienation into an indefinite future, if not even to treasure up for ourselves wrath against a day of wrath?" As a Southerner—"in birth, training, and affiliations" he said—Warfield admitted sorrowfully that "the Southern people are not thoroughly awake either to the necessity of, or to their duty in this matter." In a brief poem entitled "Wanted—A Samaritan" Warfield wrote:

> Prone in the road he lay,
> Wounded and sore bested;
> Priests, Levites, passed that way,
> And turned aside the head.
>
> They were not hardened men
> In human service slack:
> His need was great: but then,
> His face, you see, was black.[23]

Dr. Warfield taught his students that it was the love of God in Christ that changed the world and it must lead his followers to serve and love others. In a chapel sermon he said, "If we would follow Christ, we must, every one of us, not in pride but in humility . . . forget ourselves, and seek every man not his own things but those of others." Dr. Warfield challenged the students to "imitate the incarnation."

Self-sacrifice brought Christ into the world. And self-sacrifice will lead us, His followers, not away from but into the midst of men. Wherever men suffer, there will we be to comfort. Wherever men strive, there will we be to help. Wherever men fail, there will we be to uplift. Wherever men succeed, there will we be to rejoice. Self-sacrifice means not indifference to our times and our fellows: it means absorption in them. It means forgetfulness of self in others. It means entering into every man's hopes and fears, longings and despairs: it means manysidedness of spirit, multiform activity, multiplicity of sympathies. It means richness of development. It means not that we should live one life, but a thousand lives— binding ourselves to a thousand souls by the filaments of so loving a sympathy that their lives become ours. It means that all the experiences of men shall smite our souls and shall beat and batter these stubborn hearts of ours into fitness for their heavenly home.[24]

*   *   *

At the invitation of the faculty of Princeton Seminary Francis Patton gave a memorial address in honor of B. B. Warfield on May 2, 1921, in the First Presbyterian Church of Princeton. "Princeton Theological Seminary is walking today in the shadow of an eclipse which in various degrees of visibility has been observed, I doubt not, throughout the greater part of the Christian world," Patton told the congregation. "A prince and a great man has fallen in Israel." As Princeton's professor of theology from 1887 to 1920, Dr. Warfield taught 2,750 students. Through them and through his many writings his influence in the Presbyterian church and beyond, in the United States and overseas, was massive.[25]

18

Christianity and Liberalism

The Church is puzzled by the world's indifference. She is trying to overcome it by adapting her message to the fashions of the day. But if, instead, before the conflict, she would descend into the secret place of meditation, if by the clear light of the gospel she would seek an answer not merely to the questions of the hour but, first of all, to the eternal problems of the spiritual world, then perhaps, by God's grace, through His good Spirit, in His good time, she might issue forth once more with power, and an age of doubt might be followed by the dawn of an era of faith.

J. GRESHAM MACHEN

ON February 16, 1846, Archibald Alexander wrote a letter of thanks to Mrs. Phebe Robinson, who had sent a generous gift of twenty dollars for some needy seminary student. Dr. Alexander commented that he sincerely joined Mrs. Robinson "in praying that this fountain of divine truth may never be poisoned or adulterated with error." He added: "My time of service, which is going on thirty-four years, must be nearly ended; and I bless God for the continual favor which He has manifested to the institution; and I entertain a strong confidence that this Seminary will continue to teach the pure doctrines of the grace of God to the end of the world. It can hardly become corrupt in doctrine as long as the General Assembly continues sound in the faith."[1]

*   *   *

What Dr. Alexander could not imagine, his successors at Princeton Seminary observed with great distress. By the end of the World War theological liberalism had become entrenched in almost all of the leading seminaries. Guided by the "conscious, intended adaptation of religious ideas to modern culture," it was slowly altering the theological convictions of most of the major Protestant denominations.[2]

The 1920s—"the most sharply defined decade in American history"—brought "ten restless years roaring from jubilation to despair amid international and domestic dislocation." The

United States experienced strikes and bomb throwings, the "Red Scare" and the rise of world communism, racial unrest, and a great depression. Secular ideas began to dominate in most universities. Antisupernaturalistic relativism became for many "a world view" that functioned as "a virtual religion." A "revolution in morals" threatened to sweep away traditional Christian standards of personal behavior. Church attendance declined. The United States was no longer in any significant sense a bastion of "Christendom."[3]

Responding to these radical changes in American life, religious liberals—or "modernists" they were often called—attempted to save the Christian faith by "deifying the historical process," "stressing the ethical," and elevating the "centrality of religious feelings." Their ideas gained a wide hearing through popular books like *The Man Nobody Knows* by Bruce Barton and the inspirational sermons of preachers such as Harry Emerson Fosdick. Conservatives viewed the rise of modernist theology with growing alarm and vigorously countered that the only hope was a return to historic Christian orthodoxy.[4]

The General Assembly of the Presbyterian Church had rejected the tenets of modernism in the Portland Deliverance of 1892, in its doctrinal declarations of 1910 and 1916, and in the trials of Charles Briggs and Henry P. Smith. Some presbyteries, however, were ordaining men who accepted the higher critical method and other assumptions of liberalism. The movement from evangelicalism that had been proceeding more or less quietly for half a century was far more general than had been thought, and by the second decade of the twentieth century liberal sentiment in the church was widespread. Doctrinal issues were avoided, heresy prosecutions disappeared, and theological liberals gained leadership positions in the church.

In 1920 the American Council on Organic Union proposed a federation of nineteen denominations. The Philadelphia Plan, as it was called, was presented to the General Assembly of the Presbyterian Church by Princeton Seminary's president, J. Ross Stevenson, vice chairman of the General Assembly's Committee on Church Cooperation and Union. It was sent by the assembly for a vote in the presbyteries.

In one of his last writings Dr. Warfield stated that the "Philadelphia Plan" contained nothing that was not believed by evangelicals—or Roman Catholics or even Unitarians. "The creed on the basis of which we are invited to form a union . . . contains nothing distinctively evangelical at all," Warfield wrote, "nothing at all of that body of saving truth for the possession of which the Church of Christ has striven and suffered through two thousand years." Rather it contained "only 'a few starved and hunger-bitten dogmas' of purely general character—of infinite importance in the context of evangelical truth, but of themselves of no saving sufficiency. So far as the conservation and propagation of evangelical religion is concerned, we might as well form a union on our common acceptance of the law of gravitation."[5]

Dr. Warfield was not opposed to "true church unity." Although its "complete expression" would not be realized "until the Church is presented to the Bridegroom without spot or blemish," he believed that meanwhile "it is ours to advance toward this ideal." The "true pathway" to our present duty, Warfield maintained, leads us to:

(1) Hearty recognition of all Christians as members of the body of Christ, and of all denominations which preach the gospel of Christ as sections of this one body; (2) Hearty and unwavering testimony to all God's truth known to us, as the truth of God to be confessed by all his people; (3) Cooperation in all good works as brethren; and (4) Formal federation of denominations for prosecuting tasks common to the federated bodies, so far as such federation involves no sacrifice of principle or testimony.

The last clause was crucial for Warfield. "Unity in Christ," he wrote, "is not founded on disloyalty to the truth that is in Christ."[6]

In three articles published during 1921 Dr. Machen put forth his objections to the "Philadelphia Plan." The plan contained some "great Christian truths," according to Machen, but omitted "not some, but practically all, of the great essentials of the Christian faith"—including "the transcendence and omnipotence of God, the deity of Christ, the virgin birth, the resurrection, the atoning death." The plan's "preamble couched in the vague language of modern

[333]

naturalism," Machen wrote, "clearly relegated to the realm of the nonessential our historic Confession of Faith." On this basis union would be achieved, he explained, not because Protestants had come to a common understanding of the gospel and the mission of the church but because they agreed that such matters were no longer important. Machen asserted that the Christian church's primary task was to set forth in its life and preaching the gospel of Christ and that the Presbyterian church was bound by its creedal commitment to do so in faithfulness to the Westminster Confession of Faith.[7]

Machen was particularly unhappy with Dr. Stevenson's support for the "Philadelphia Plan." He wrote to Stevenson, "One of the very greatest arguments that we had to face was the argument that the president of Princeton Seminary was in favor of the Plan and that therefore it must be perfectly safe." Dr. Erdman also came out in support of the federation, making known his position in an address to the students on the eve of Dr. Warfield's funeral. Machen was invited by the students to present the other side. Professors Greene, Hodge, Armstrong, and Allis all published articles supporting Machen's position. "It is splendid to see the way my Princeton fathers and brethren have stood by me," Machen wrote to his mother.[8]

*   *   *

With tumultuous changes threatening American life and major shifts taking place in the Christian churches, Princeton Seminary entered the decade of the 1920s. Archibald Alexander's grandson Maitland Alexander, who in 1904 had succeeded Ethelbert Warfield as president of Princeton's board of directors, provided steady leadership.[9] Princeton Seminary, considered by many to possess the ablest faculty of Reformed ministers in the world, was attracting students from about thirty American states and twenty foreign countries. Pennsylvania was home to the largest number of Princeton's students, although fewer now came from the Eastern states than formerly. The South, from Virginia to Texas, was represented, and the Midwest now sent significant numbers of students. More came from Iowa than from either New Jersey or New York. By the early 1920s forty per cent of the students were members of non-Presbyterian denominations. Internationals added to the diversity of the Princeton classrooms as Japanese, British, and South African students, along with others, prepared for service in their homelands.

The 1921 catalogue listed eighty-six courses offered in eight departments: Old Testament, New Testament, Semitic philology, church history, apologetics and Christian ethics, systematic theology, practical theology and homiletics, and history of religion and missions. Classes were held in the mornings, including Saturdays, starting at 8:10, as well as in the late afternoons and three evenings each week. The seminary awarded the bachelor of theology degree to students completing the three-year curriculum, and a course of study leading to a master's degree was available.[10] The seminary chorus was established in 1923 with twenty-eight singers under the direction of Finley D. Jenkins, a graduate of 1919. An addition to the new Lenox Library was completed in 1925 to help house the library's more than 100,000 volumes. Joseph H. Dulles and William B. Sheddan, both graduates of the seminary, were the librarians.

In 1922 Oswald T. Allis, who had been instructor in Semitic philology since 1910, became assistant professor. Allis was a graduate of the University of Pennsylvania and of Princeton Seminary. He earned the Ph.D. degree from the University of Berlin (with a concentration in archaeology and Assyriology). At his inauguration as assistant professor in 1922 Allis was charged to teach his students that the Old Testament was "plenarily inspired of God" and was therefore "absolutely authentic" and "worthy of all acceptation, as the beginning of the revelation completed in Jesus Christ." He responded that the liberals' "errors and inconsistencies" had been "exposed again and again" and called for many new scholars to "stand in the breach and defend the faith once for all committed to the saints." In his work at Princeton Dr. Allis carried on, as he put it, "the heritage of unfeigned faith in the Holy Scriptures which dwelt in that noble succession of teachers, among whom Joseph Addison Alexander, William Henry Green and Robert Dick Wilson were so eminent."[11]

[335]

*   *   *

Dr. Machen was the most exciting and popular professor at Princeton. "He was a vigorous teacher who stated his positions with force and clarity," one of his students said. Students flocked to his elective courses on the "Birth of Christ Narratives" and "Paul and his Environment." Pulling his Greek Testament out of his side pocket, Machen lectured without notes. One day the students, who were expected to follow him in the Greek text, left an open English Bible on the desk. When Dr. Machen came in he picked it up, looked it over carefully, and said, with a wide grin, "Why, I believe it's a Bible!" Machen's students often were surprised, then grateful, to see his genial face at their doors—offering his help to explain and drill them in Greek just when they needed it. When he lacked time he would pay a tutor to assist those who needed extra help.[12]

Machen, who had written that "Old Princeton died when Dr. Warfield was carried out," believed that the Princeton tradition—though severely threatened by liberal forces in the Presbyterian church—was still alive. Although he loved the quiet of the study and the library, he believed that the Reformed faith should be preached as well as taught in the seminary classrooms, and he gave himself unstintingly to both tasks. During the 1922–23 school year he taught his classes at Princeton and maintained a grueling schedule of ministry. On October 8, 1922, he spoke at Union College on the "Bible and its Meaning to Us." The next weekend he addressed the Synod of Iowa and spoke to the students of Parsons College. On October 23 he preached to the Methodist ministers of the Camden, New Jersey, district on the "Fundamentals of the Christian Faith" and on October 27 gave the same talk at the Marble Collegiate Church under the auspices of the National Bible Institute. He addressed the monthly meeting of the Philadelphia Ministers' Association on December 18. During January 1923 he gave four lectures on the "Christian Faith" at the YMCA in Easton, Pennsylvania, addressed the students at Lafayette College three times, and spoke at the annual dinner of the officers and teachers of the Sunday school of the Second Presbyterian Church of

Elizabeth, New Jersey. February 5 and 6 found him in Chicago, where he spoke at Founders' Week at Moody Bible Institute. From February 11 to April 8 he gave nine Sunday afternoon lectures at the Marble Collegiate Church on such topics as "Is Christianity True?" "Basic Facts of Christianity," "The Living Christ," and "What is Salvation?" On February 22 he spoke at a Baptist conference in Philadelphia on "The Fundamentals" and on March 26 delivered an address at the Central Presbyterian Church of Montclair, New Jersey. In April he gave three talks before the Pennsylvania State YMCA Convention and spoke in Newark, New Jersey, for the Evangelistic Committee of Newark. On May 3 he was in Columbus, Ohio, to preach at a Union Bible Conference sponsored by Moody Bible Institute. When he was not engaged elsewhere he preached almost every Sunday in New Jersey and surrounding states, including six sermons at Marble Collegiate Church in New York City.[13]

* * *

In 1922 Clarence Edward Macartney was elected to the board of directors of Princeton Seminary. His father, a pastor in the Reformed Presbyterian Church, had been brought up, Macartney wrote, "in that splendid training school of psalm-singing, oath-refusing, secret society-abominating, non-voting and Bible-believing Covenanters." His mother, Catherine Robertson, a Scot from Rothesay on the Isle of Bute, was a woman of "high intellect, profound spirituality, and broad learning." After serving a church in Ohio the Macartneys moved to Beaver Falls, Pennsylvania, a center of Covenanter people and the location of the church's Geneva College. There Clarence was born in 1879. He spent fourteen happy years in Beaver Falls and then moved with his parents to California, Colorado, and finally Wisconsin.[14]

Clarence graduated from the University of Wisconsin in 1901 with a major in English literature and serious doubts about orthodox Christianity. He planned to pursue graduate work at Harvard, but on his arrival in Cambridge decided rather to travel in Europe. He boarded a steamer to Liverpool and spent the rest of the year wandering through Scotland, England, and France. Now inclined to explore the ministry as a vocation, he enrolled at Yale Divinity School in the fall of 1902. But after spending a few days there and attending only one class, he packed his bags and, as he put it, "retreated to Princeton." "Princeton Theological Seminary, with its grand and ancient tradition of a stalwart defense of the truth, and of the glory of the Christian revelation, was the right thing for me," he later explained. "I had found my true place. Henceforth, there was no wavering; no halting between two opinions, but straight forward towards the goal."[15] Macartney finished a master's degree at Princeton University in 1904 and the next year graduated from Princeton Seminary. He became pastor of the First Presbyterian Church of Paterson, New Jersey, where he served until 1914 when he was called to the Arch Street Presbyterian Church of Philadelphia.

*　　*　　*

To the dismay of Presbyterian conservatives, the popular liberal Baptist minister, Harry Emerson Fosdick, had served for several years as regular "guest preacher" at the First Presbyterian Church in New York City. Machen described Fosdick's "undogmatic Christianity" as "dreadful!" On May 21, 1922, Fosdick preached a sermon entitled "Shall the Fundamentalists Win?" in which he contended that belief in the inerrancy of Scripture, the virgin birth, and the physical return of Christ was not essential to the Christian faith. "All theology tentatively phrases in current thought and language the best that, up to date, thinkers on religion have achieved," Fosdick said; "and the most hopeful thing about any system of theology is that it will not last."[16]

In a sermon entitled "Shall Unbelief Win?" Clarence Macartney, courteously but forcefully, asserted that Fosdick's naturalistic views were "a direct assault upon cardinal Christian truth" and called upon evangelical Christians to fight for the faith "earnestly and intelligently and in a Christian spirit." Macartney warned that liberalism would lead the church to a new type of Christianity—"a Christianity of opinions and principles and good purposes, but a Christianity without worship, without God, and without Jesus Christ."

[338]

With Macartney's leadership the Presbytery of Philadelphia overtured the General Assembly to condemn the teachings expressed in Fosdick's sermon and to instruct the Presbytery of New York to see that further preaching at the First Presbyterian Church conformed to the doctrines of the Confession of Faith. Presbytery's action caused "a mighty stir," as newspapers gave the matter wide publicity and the debate raged in all parts of the church. Macartney was surprised by "the intemperate and bitter abuse which poured forth" from "the so-called Liberals and Modernists" and was disappointed that some conservatives tried to avoid the issue lest they be labeled "fundamentalists." He was especially distressed with the cool response of some of the Princeton Seminary faculty—since "the Philadelphia overture was only defending what Princeton had taught us," he stated. The majority of the faculty, however, was on his side. "Dr. Machen," he wrote, "came out like a lion at the very beginning of the battle."[17]

*   *   *

On November 3, 1921, Dr. Machen addressed the Twenty-Eighth Annual Convention of the Ruling Elders' Association of Chester (Pennsylvania) Presbytery on the "Present Attack against the Fundamentals of our Christian Faith, from the Point of View of Colleges and Seminaries." Machen's address was published in *The Princeton Theological Review* with the title "Liberalism or Christianity?" Encouraged by many, Machen expanded the essay into "a landmark volume," *Christianity and Liberalism.*[18]

Christianity and Liberalism began with the sentence, "The purpose of this book is not to decide the religious issue of the present day, but merely to present the issue as sharply and clearly as possible, in order that the reader may be aided in deciding it for himself." For Machen the issue was clear. One had to choose between two mutually incompatible religions —the religion of modern liberalism and the Christian religion. "The great redemptive religion which has always been known as Christianity," he wrote, "is battling against a totally diverse type of religious belief . . . called 'modernism' or 'liberalism.'"[19]

Liberalism, Machen wrote, is a religion of "human morality and goodness," whereas Christianity proclaims God's redemption of sinful mankind through Christ. "Here is found the most fundamental difference between liberalism and Christianity," according to Machen; "liberalism is altogether in the imperative mood, while Christianity begins with a triumphant indicative; liberalism appeals to man's will, while Christianity announces, first, a gracious act of God." Machen carefully described the representative ideas of liberalism, showing how they differed fundamentally from traditional Christianity in basic conceptions of God, man, the Bible, Christ, salvation, and the church.[20]

Liberalism neglects "the awful transcendence of God" and ignores the sinfulness of man, Machen claimed. It rejects the authority of the Bible, substituting instead a foundation of "the shifting emotions of sinful men." Whereas liberalism regards Jesus Christ "as an Example and Guide," Christianity accepts him as a Savior; "liberalism makes Him an example for faith; Christianity, the object of faith." The "modern liberal," Machen wrote, tries to have faith in God like the faith that he supposes Jesus had in God; but he does not have faith in Jesus. Christianity teaches that Jesus was no mere prophet or inspired teacher but rather a supernatural person, a heavenly redeemer who came to earth for the salvation of sinners. "The Jesus of the New Testament has at least one advantage over the Jesus of modern reconstruction," Machen wrote; "He is real."[21]

Liberalism finds salvation in man; Christianity finds it in an act of God. The "salvation" of the liberals is actually a form of legalism, obeying the commands of God rather than trusting in the death of Christ who is God. The modern liberal teachers, Machen declared, "persist in speaking of the sacrifice of Christ as though it were a sacrifice made by someone other than God. . . . [But] the fundamental thing [in the Christian doctrine of the cross] is that God Himself, and not another, makes the sacrifice for sin—God Himself in the person of the Son who assumed our nature and died for us, God Himself in the person of the Father who spared not His own Son but offered Him up for us all."[22]

The church, Machen charged, "has been unfaithful to her

Lord by admitting great companies of non-Christian persons, not only into her membership, but into her teaching agencies" so that "the greatest menace to the Christian Church today comes not from the enemies outside, but from the enemies within." Dr. Machen maintained that the Presbyterian church was composed of people who agreed upon a "certain message about Christ" and who united "in the propagation of that message." The church's constitution bound its ministers to teach and defend the Westminster Confession of Faith. After solemnly subscribing to the Bible as "the only infallible rule of faith and practice" and the Westminster Confession as containing "the system of doctrine taught in the Holy Scriptures," it was dishonest, he believed, for a Presbyterian minister to view the Bible as a collection of inspirational writings and the Confession as outdated theories. It was time, Machen argued, for the Presbyterian church to reaffirm "the absolute exclusiveness of the Christian religion" and for those ministers who did not hold to this conviction to withdraw from its jurisdiction.[23]

The pungency, clarity, and burning conviction of *Christianity and Liberalism* captured the attention of both friends and foes. "Charlie Erdman," who, Machen noted, "next to Army [William Armstrong] . . . seems to have been the first man in Princeton to read my book through," sent a "very nice" note but regretted Machen's implied criticism of Presbyterian missionaries. Dr. Stevenson wrote a long letter praising the book but maintaining that conservatives should not stir up trouble by attempting to remove liberals from the church. *The Princeton Seminary Bulletin* stated that Machen was "animated by no merely polemic purpose"; he hoped "to help laymen as well as ministers to obtain a clearer and more orderly acquaintance with the Christian faith."[24]

The New York *Herald Tribune* advised liberals to read *Christianity and Liberalism* before undertaking any further reconstruction of Christianity. The Toronto *Globe* praised Machen as a writer "of ample erudition" and "compelling force." *Christian Century*, the leading voice of liberalism, conceded that the issues Machen raised were not unimportant and that they involved, as Machen claimed, the clash between "two religions." Even Unitarians praised *Christianity and*

Liberalism, saying that Dr. Machen had done them the great service of putting the issues in a clear-cut and definite form. As one reviewer put it, "You must be either a believer or an unbeliever, an evangelical or a liberal, you cannot be both at the same time."[25]

The volatile and colorful H. L. Mencken, who did "as much as any other writer to identify fundamentalism with obscurantism and charlatanism," wrote:

Dr. Machen is no mere soap-box orator of God, alarming bucolic sinners for a percentage of the plate. On the contrary, he is a man of great learning and dignity—a former student at European universities, the author of various valuable books, including a Greek grammar, and a member of several societies of savants. . . . I confess that as a life-long fan of theology, I can find no defect in his defence of his position. Is Christianity actually a revealed religion? If not, then it is nothing: if so, then we must accept the Bible as an inspired statement of its principles. . . . If Christianity is really true, as he believes, and if the Bible is true, then it is true from cover to cover. So answering, he defies the hosts of Beelzebub to shake him. As I have hinted, I think that, given his faith, his position is completely impregnable. There is absolutely no flaw in the argument with which he supports it. If he is wrong, then the science of logic is hollow vanity, signifying nothing.[26]

In his *Preface to Morals* Walter Lippman, one of the outstanding journalists of the day, wrote that much of the fundamentalist movement had "become entangled with all sorts of bizarre and barbarous agitations" so that "the central truth" that "the fundamentalists have grasped" no longer appealed "to the best brains and the good sense of a modern community." He went on to state, however, that there was also "a reasoned case" against modernism:

Fortunately this case has been stated in a little book called *Christianity and Liberalism* by a man who is both a scholar and a gentleman. The author is Professor J. Gresham Machen of the Princeton Theological Seminary. It is an admirable book. For its acumen, for its saliency, and for its wit this cool and stringent defense of orthodox Protestantism is, I think, the best popular argument produced by either side in the current controversy. We shall do well to listen to Dr. Machen.[27]

*   *   *

Machen was often called a fundamentalist. Although he appreciated much of what the fundamentalist movement stood for, he disliked the word. Machen said:

If, indeed, I am asked whether I am a Fundamentalist or a Modernist, I do not say, "Neither." I do not quibble. . . . I have very definitely taken sides. But I do not apply the term "Fundamentalist" to myself. I stand, indeed, in the very warmest Christian fellowship with those who do designate themselves by that term. But, for my part, I cannot see why the Christian religion, which has had a rather long and honorable history, should suddenly become an "-ism" and be called by a strange new name.[28]

Machen was a conservative, but he suggested that the word "radical" might be more appropriate. He wrote in 1925:

In one sense, indeed, we are traditionalists; we do maintain that any institution that is really great has its roots in the past; we do not therefore desire to substitute modern sects for the historic Christian Church. But on the whole, in view of the conditions that now exist, it would perhaps be more correct to call us "radicals" than to call us "conservatives." We look not for a mere continuation of spiritual conditions that now exist, but for an outburst of new power; we are seeking in particular to arouse youth from its present uncritical repetition of current phrases into some genuine examination of the basis of life.[29]

Machen preferred, however, to call himself a Christian because he believed "the historic Christian faith." And he was grateful to be a Calvinist, "standing in the great central current of the Church's life—the current which flows down from the Word of God through Augustine and Calvin, and which has found noteworthy expression in America in the great tradition represented by Charles Hodge and Benjamin Breckinridge Warfield and the other representatives of the "Princeton School."[30]

19

A Mighty Battle

TO J. GRESHAM MACHEN

"This is the month and this is the happy morn
Wherein the Son of Heaven's eternal King,
Of Wedded maid and Virgin mother born,
Our great redemption from above did bring."

To you who have so well defended
The faith which Milton sings,
Whose thought has far transcended
The look of "earthly things,"
I send these lines
Which are the signs
And tokens of my love
(Confusions wild
Of trochee and iambic
Which have beguiled
An hour with my alembic).
I pray that coming from above
Strength may be yours to fight
For truth, until life's night
Has curtained you in rest;
Till taught by you to seek the true
Men find the Highest and the Best.
And those who doubt and those who scorn,
With those to false views leaning,
Shall learn the joyous meaning
Of this bright Christmas morn.

Bermuda
25 Dec. 1923

Affectionately,
FRANCIS L. PATTON

ONE day just before the meeting of the General Assembly Mrs. Stevenson, the wife of the seminary president, met B. B. Warfield on the street and said, "Dr. Warfield, I hear there is going to be trouble at the Assembly. Do let us pray for peace." "I am praying," replied Warfield, "that if they do not do what is right, there may be a mighty battle."[1]

* * *

At the General Assembly of 1923 in Indianapolis the Committee on Bills and Overtures brought in its report. "It was a weak and meaningless evasion," according to Clarence Macartney, "and tantamount to a whitewash of Dr. Fosdick and the Presbytery of New York." The minority report (signed by only one of the twenty-three committee members) was then presented. William Jennings Bryan, who had been narrowly defeated in the vote to choose a moderator, demanded a roll call "so that the folks back home will know how we voted." "In the gathering gloom," Macartney reported, "the dramatic roll took place." With overwhelming support from the ruling elders, the minority report—the Philadelphia overture—was carried 439 to 359; and the Presbytery of New York was directed to take such action "as will require the preaching and teaching in the First Presbyterian Church of New York to conform to the system of doctrines taught in the Confession of Faith." Eighty-five commissioners filed an official protest against the assembly's action. The General Assembly reiterated that "the five fundamentals" were "essential and necessary articles" for those serving as ministers. It was now clear to all that the Presbyterian church was seriously divided.

*   *   *

Beginning in October 1923 Dr. Machen served as stated supply of the First Presbyterian Church of Princeton. On December 30 he preached on the "Issue in the Church." Machen asserted that

> two mutually exclusive religions are contending for the control of the Church today. One is the great redemptive religion known as Christianity; the other is the naturalistic or agnostic Christianity. . . . A separation between the two is the crying need of the hour; that separation alone can bring Christian unity. That does not mean that we are without sympathy for those who differ from us with regard to this great concern of the soul; on the contrary, many of us, in the years of struggle, have faced only too clearly the possibility that we, too, might be forced to go with the current age and relinquish the Christian faith. We are certainly not without admiration for the many high qualities of that type of thought and life which the non-doctrinal religion of the present day, at its best, is able to show. But we are also not without admiration for Socrates and Plato; yet Christian they certainly were not. Christianity is a peculiar type of life which is founded upon a distinctive message; and where it loses its sense of its separateness it ceases to exist.[2]

Machen's sermons angered Henry Van Dyke, professor of English literature at the university.[3] He wrote to the session that he was giving up his pew as long as Machen preached because he would no longer listen to "such a dismal, bilious travesty of the Gospel." "We want to hear about Christ, not about Fundamentalists and Modernists," he said. Van Dyke's letter was released to the newspapers, and the matter attracted wide attention.[4] Dr. Machen continued to preach at the church through the spring of 1924. In expressing its appreciation for Machen's sermons, the session paid "an especial tribute to his able and logical defense of the doctrines with which the 'Old First' has always been identified." They assured him "that as he led the congregation in the Apostles' Creed they said it with and like him—without mental reservations."[5]

*   *   *

"An Affirmation Designed to Safeguard the Unity and Liberty of the Presbyterian Church in the United States of America" (commonly called the Auburn Affirmation) was signed by over twelve hundred Presbyterian ministers during the spring of 1924.[6] It declared that the five-point doctrinal statement of 1910, 1916, and 1923 "attempts to commit our church to certain theories concerning the inspiration of the Bible, and the Incarnation, the Atonement, the Resurrection, and the Continuing Life and Supernatural Power of our Lord Jesus Christ." "We are opposed to any attempt to elevate these five doctrinal statements, or any of them, to the position of tests for ordination or for good standing in our church," the document continued. It explained that "some of us regard the particular theories contained in the deliverance of the General Assembly of 1923 as satisfactory explanations of these facts and doctrines. But we are united in believing that these are not the only theories allowed by the Scriptures and our standards as explanations of these facts and doctrines of our religion, and that all who hold to these facts and doctrines, whatever theories they may employ to explain them, are worthy of all confidence and fellowship."[7]

"To a great host of Presbyterians," Clarence Macartney wrote, "this affirmation was a Christ-dishonoring proclamation, if ever there was one. Imagine the Christian Church establishing itself in the pagan world in the first century on the ground of such affirmations!" Gresham Machen stated that the doctrines that the Auburn Affirmation called "theories" were "facts upon which Christianity is based and without which Christianity would fall." The affirmation really advocates "the destruction of the confessional witness of the Church," he wrote. "To allow interpretations which reverse the meaning of a confession is exactly the same thing as to have no confession at all."[8]

The General Assembly of 1924 met in Grand Rapids, Michigan, with a great array of newspaper correspondents present. Nominating Dr. Macartney to be moderator, William Jennings Bryan said, "It was his vigilance that detected the insidious attack made upon the historic doctrines of the Presbyterian Church; it was his courage that raised the standard of protest about which the Church rallied; it was his leadership that won a decisive victory for evangelical Christianity and historical Presbyterianism." Dr. Erdman also was nominated and supported by those conservatives who wished to avoid controversy and by liberals who appreciated Erdman's tolerance of theological diversity in the church. Dr. Macartney won by a close vote of 464 to 446. When he took the gavel from the retiring moderator, Macartney told the commissioners that he had dreamed that he had been elected moderator of the General Assembly of the Presbyterian Church and on the following night had been sentenced to be "hanged by the neck until dead." "The first part of the dream," he said, "has come true. No doubt there are some here who may wish that the second part also would come true!"[9]

Dr. Mark Matthews, pastor of First Presbyterian Church of Seattle, moved that Dr. Fosdick immediately cease preaching at the First Presbyterian Church of New York City.[10] The General Assembly, however, took a more moderate position, requiring Fosdick to seek membership in the Presbyterian church and so become "subject to the jurisdiction and authority of the Church."[11] Although the assembly did act on the Fosdick issue, it took no action in response to the Auburn Affirmation or its signers and declared the five-point doctrinal statement of 1923 unconstitutional. Even with Macartney as moderator and Machen, Matthews, Bryan, and many other conservative leaders in attendance, the General Assembly failed to slow the liberal advance. Dr. Machen wrote to a friend, "We did suffer a great defeat at the end of the Assembly; and I think that if we represent it as a victory, or if we give the impression that we regard the battle as over, we are traitors to our cause."[12]

*　　*　　*

Princeton Seminary was now sharply divided. A majority of the directors and the faculty, with Dr. Machen their most effective spokesman, and most of the students were on one side. A minority of the directors, most of the trustees, President Stevenson, Charles Erdman, Frederick Loetscher, J. Ritchie Smith of the faculty, and some of the students were on the other side, with Dr. Erdman their most influential advocate. "It has been a hard thing to be a Christian in Princeton Seminary under the present conditions," Machen sadly wrote to Ethelbert Warfield.[13]

Both parties at Princeton were conservative in their theology. Dr. Erdman even described himself as a fundamentalist in his doctrinal beliefs. But Stevenson and Erdman placed the unity of the church above strict doctrinal orthodoxy and promoted peace and tolerance in the interest of the church's mission. Machen stood for strict adherence to Christian orthodoxy as set forth in the Confession of Faith. Whereas Stevenson and Erdman reflected "the non-confessional character of American evangelicalism and the Victorian tendency to sentimentalize faith," Machen stood in the Old Princeton doctrinal tradition of Charles Hodge and B. B. Warfield. Without an uncompromising belief in the true gospel, Machen insisted, the Presbyterian church would have no message to preach and could offer no hope to a lost world.[14]

*   *   *

The long-standing tensions between Dr. Machen and Dr. Erdman deepened in the summer of 1924. When Erdman followed Machen as pulpit supply at Princeton's First Presbyterian Church Henry Van Dyke returned to his pew. An editorial in *The Presbyterian* suggested that this indicated that there were "two parties" developing at Princeton Seminary. Erdman angrily responded that no division existed at Princeton "on points of doctrine." "The only division I have observed," he added, "is as to spirit, methods, or policies." He then mentioned "the unkindness, suspicion, bitterness and intolerance of those members of the [seminary] faculty, who are also editors of *The Presbyterian*." Only Dr. Machen fitted the description, for no other faculty member was an editor of *The Presbyterian*.

Machen, who agreed "to some extent" with the content of *The Presbyterian* editorial, "disapproved most heartily of the style of it and its appearance in just the way and place in which it did appear." In his answer to Dr. Erdman's charge Machen attempted "to take the matter from the personal plane upon which Dr. Erdman had put it and to place it upon the ground of principle." Even though he differed from Erdman "profoundly," he had tried never to allow their differences to prevent him from holding Dr. Erdman "in high personal esteem." Machen insisted, however, that there was indeed "a very serious doctrinal difference" between Erdman and himself—not a difference over specific doctrines but "the importance which is to be attributed to doctrine as such." "Dr. Erdman does not indeed reject the doctrinal system of our church," Machen wrote, "but he is perfectly willing to make common cause with those who reject it, and he is perfectly willing on many occasions to keep it in the background." "I on the other hand," Machen stated, "can never consent to keep it in the background. Christian doctrine, I hold, is not merely connected with the gospel, but it is identical with the gospel, and if I did not preach it at all times, and especially in those places where it subjects me to personal abuse, I should regard myself as guilty of sheer unfaithfulness to Christ."

Eager to restore a better relationship with his colleague, Machen wrote to Erdman:

I have been just a little afraid lest what I said on the campus the other night, or rather my failure to say all that I ought to have said, may have seemed to indicate lack of appreciation for your assurance of continued friendship despite the disagreements which have risen. May I now say how earnestly I hope that your feeling toward me is still that which you so graciously expressed. I should be distressed beyond measure if there should ever be any break in the personal relationship which has been such a privilege to me all these years.

Dr. Erdman responded that "nothing which has occurred can alter our friendly relations." "I am sure I have made many mistakes," he wrote, "but I hope to be forgiven—and shall try to forget—and face the future with new zeal for Christ and his cause." He added that he recognized Machen's "superior equipment for apologetics" and that each of them "in his own way must strive to defend and declare the truth in the face of widespread defection and unbelief."[15]

*   *   *

John Murray came from Scotland to study at Princeton in the fall of 1924.[16] He joined the Benham Club, where his fellows appreciated "his subtle Scottish wit" and his "lively jousts with Irish fellow members." His prayers impressed his fellow students. One wrote, "I think I . . . never heard praying quite like that before, with its awesome sense of God's holiness and man's sinfulness and creaturehood, combined with full assurance of His love and grace." John Murray wrote home, "My session's work at Princeton I enjoyed very much. It is a great matter to have an institution with such scholarship still faithful to the truth and faith once and for all delivered to the saints." Already steeped in the Puritan divines from his study in Scotland, Murray "found [at Princeton] the theology of the Westminster Confession in living embodiment, and taught from the original languages of the Scriptures with a freshness and an exactness of exegesis which was new to him. Before he crossed the Atlantic he had known little Greek; it was [Princeton] Seminary . . . which instilled in him the conviction that doctrine must be arrived at through a painstaking examination of the Scriptures in their original languages." Murray especially appreciated the teaching of Gresham Machen and Geerhardus Vos (whom he later described as "the most penetrating exegete it has been my privilege to know").[17]

*   *   *

In November 1924 Francis Landey Patton returned to Princeton, where he had lived and taught for thirty-two years, to deliver a series of five lectures on the theme of "Fundamental Christianity." "Though having passed his eighty-second birthday, Dr. Patton spoke with great vigor and maintained the deepest interest throughout, by his brilliant reasoning, his personal fervor and his scintillating metaphors," reported *The Princeton Seminary Bulletin.*[18]

Patton began his lecture on the "Theistic View of the World" by saying that "if a man should drift of an evening in an open boat and find himself out of sight of land, he might have some trouble to know where he was. This is very much the difficulty of a great many men in the present day. They have drifted, and are out at sea." In his second lecture Patton spoke on the "three claimants" for the "seat of authority in religion"—reason, the church, and the Bible. Dr. Patton illustrated: "After all, like the telegram you receive at the hands of the messenger, you need your reason to interpret the message, you need the Church to bring it to you, but there must be a message. The Bible is your message; your authority."

Speaking on the "New Christianity," Patton said that it takes but "limited experience and observation to note that the religious thought and activity of the present day are different from that of fifty years ago. No matter which is better, it is evident there is a difference. As Postum is different from coffee, and no honest grocer will give me the former for the latter, just so, the licensed vendor of spiritual food is under the same sort of obligation." "It is high time," said Dr. Patton, "we were asking ourselves, what is Christianity?"

"Is there a body of belief in which it originated, with which it is identified, without which that which claims to be Christianity, is no Christianity at all; or is Christianity a label which you can tack onto any man's system of thinking?" "The journey of doubt is a very long one," Patton warned. "Many may be highly distressed when they hear the roar of the wheels under their plush-seated Pullman and the conductor puts his head in the doorway and calls out, 'This train makes no stops. The next station is agnosticism.'"

After giving "the reasons for believing in the divinity of Christ," Dr. Patton concluded the fourth lecture by saying, "A chain may be as strong as its weakest link, but this is no chain; it is a cable made up of twisted strands; it is a hawser, that will hold through wind and tide." Patton's last lecture, "Way of Salvation," set forth the teaching of the Apostle Paul. "Paul must always be estimated in cubic measure," Patton said, "for

he was great in three dimensions—intellect, feeling and will."
Dr. Patton closed his Princeton lectures by telling the many
friends that had gathered to hear him:

This eternal purpose, how majestic the conception is. And then this
eternal hope, how glorious. . . . I like to think of one of those prayer
meetings up there where they sing, O, how they do sing. And the
great orchestra leads them; the great white-robed throng.

And yet I am glad of the other side too. I am glad we have a
religion that is not simply a series of make-believe propositions,
something where the worm of Hegelianism has eaten the substance
out of the leaves of the tree of life. I am glad we have a religion that
is not reduced to a nerveless, jelly-fish simplicity. I rejoice that it is a
system so co-ordinated, whose doctrines are so concatenated, which
has been so logically constructed that if discovered in some future
age by an excavating paleontologist he would be forced to remark:
"Gentlemen, this belonged to the order of vertebrates."[19]

*   *   *

The Princeton Seminary students found themselves sharply
at odds with the liberal doctrinal position and policies of
the Students' Association of Middle-Atlantic Theological
Seminaries, an interseminary movement to which Princeton
belonged. On October 24, 1924, the president of the
Princeton Students' Association reported that the organization had "so far departed from the central message of
evangelical Christianity" as to make its purpose—to promote
fellowship among member seminaries—"impossible of
attainment and practically undesirable."[20]

A new League of Evangelical Students was founded with
Princeton leadership in the spring of 1925. Dr. Machen
believed that the establishment of the League of Evangelical
Students was a proper action; its creed, he said, was a statement of "simple evangelical principles" held in common by
Christians of different denominations. Dr. Stevenson,
however, regretted the new league's "doctrinal test" as compared with the "broad catholicity" of the old organization,
and he complained to the board of directors that the
activities of those students on the seminary campus supporting the League of Evangelical Students was "threatening the

order and discipline of the Seminary." Dr. Erdman, who had served as student adviser since 1907, asked the student leaders to make it clear that he had no responsibility in the matter. When the students requested the faculty to elect a new student adviser, Robert Dick Wilson (on Machen's motion) was chosen. Erdman deeply resented "this humiliation." The *New York Times* portrayed the incident as a continuation of the feud between Machen and Erdman. On May 14, 1925, Machen explained the matter in *The Presbyterian*: "The student request and the faculty's response to it were due, not at all to any personal criticism of Dr. Erdman, but, primarily, at least, to his negative attitude with regard to the new League of Evangelical Students into which the majority of the students desired to enter."[21]

*　　*　　*

Dr. Machen preached in Miller Chapel on March 8, 1925, on the "Separateness of the Church." He stated that "the really serious attack upon Christianity has not been the attack carried on by fire and sword" but "the attack from within." He traced the history of efforts to change and compromise the Christian message from the Gnostics of the second century to the gradual permeation of Protestant churches during the past one hundred years "by the spirit of the world." "The forces of unbelief have not yet been checked," Machen told the Princeton students and faculty,

and none can say whether our own American Presbyterian Church, which we love so dearly, will be preserved. It may be that paganism will finally control, and that Christian men and women may have to withdraw from a church that has lost its distinctness from the world. Once in the course of history, at the beginning of the sixteenth century, that method of withdrawal was God's method of preserving the precious salt. But it may be also that our Church in its corporate capacity, in its historic grandeur, may yet stand for Christ. God grant that it may be so!

Machen put the issue clearly before the students. "What are you going to do, my brothers," he asked, "in this great time of crisis?"

[356]

Will you stand with the world, will you shrink from controversy, will you witness for Christ only where witnessing costs nothing, will you pass through these stirring days without coming to any real decision? Or will you learn the lesson of Christian history; will you penetrate, by your study and your meditation, beneath the surface; will you recognize in that which prides itself on being modern an enemy that is as old as the hills; will you hope, and pray, not for a mere continuance of what now is, but for a rediscovery of the gospel that can make all things new; will you have recourse to the charter of Christian liberty in the Word of God? God grant that some of you may do that![22]

*   *   *

On April 4 Machen wrote to Clarence Macartney, "If the Lord had given us about three or four men like you instead of only one, the Presbyterian Church would be safe. . . . Your coming to Princeton next Tuesday night will mean much to us who are trying to carry the battle against such handicaps in the Seminary." Machen expressed his appreciation for Macartney's article "The Gospel or Not," which had just appeared in the *Ladies Home Journal.* It "is one of your finest utterances," he wrote, "which is saying a great deal."[23]

In "The Gospel or Not" Macartney stated that it was indeed sad "that Christians and Churches should be in conflict and contention one with another, but what is far sadder is the fact that this division and contention is produced by a teaching and a preaching within the Church which is subversive of the principles of revealed Christianity." Macartney acknowledged that "evangelical Christians oppose the modernist on every front" but stated that we are not "the foes of knowledge" nor are we opposed to "scholarly research as to the documents of the Bible." He denied that liberals were the only scholars. "The truth is that 'all scholars' do not agree," he wrote. "Great and devout scholars repudiate nearly all the theories and conclusions of the radical critics." He added, "One would hardly like to say, for example, that Dr. Robert Dick Wilson, of Princeton, was not a master in the field of Old Testament, or that his distinguished colleague, Dr. J. Gresham Machen, was not a scholar in the language and history of the New Testament." Nor do evangelical Christians oppose modernists,

Macartney stated, "because they are not in agreement with Church unity." "When the evangelical speaks of church unity," he wrote, "he does not refer to the ramshackle unity of federations and resolutions and other popular devices, but to the real unity of faith in the Lord Jesus Christ."

Dr. Macartney listed reasons why evangelicals do oppose modernists. First, he wrote, we oppose them "because of their methods of propagation." He explained: "There is today, undoubtedly, both an unorganized and an organized attempt to lift Christianity from its supernatural foundation and place it on the basis of purely natural laws, forces and facts. Men have a perfect right to carry on such a crusade if they so desire and are so convinced. But we deny that they have the right to carry on such a campaign in the pulpit of churches pledged in the most unmistakable terms to supernatural and evangelical Christianity, or from theological seminaries founded to propagate such a faith." If "our liberal friends . . . wish to attack historic and evangelical Christianity," Macartney added, "let them take off its uniform and withdraw from its fortress." "Because of the attitude [modernism] takes toward Christ, and toward the Bible, and toward human sin, it cannot call sinners to repentance," he claimed, and therefore "it can do nothing to save the world." Evangelicals, Macartney concluded, "know their own weaknesses, their limitations, and that they carry the heavenly treasure in earthen vessels. But they also know him in whom they have believed, and to him they will witness and for him they will contend! Their song shall be the noble chant of Isaac Watts:

> I'm not ashamed to own my Lord,
> Or to defend his cause,
> Maintain the honor of his Word,
> The glory of his cross."

*　　　*　　　*

"Something like an awakening" occurred at Princeton Seminary during the 1924-25 school year, according to Gresham Machen. The morale of the student body had been "rather low." "There was marked indifference to the central things of the faith; and religious experience was of the most superficial kind." Machen believed that "genuine spiritual advance" had occurred among the students, at least in part, because of controversy at the seminary. Students had begun to think for themselves, and "true and independent convictions" had been formed. "The evil of compromising associations" had been discovered, and "Christian heroism in the face of opposition" had "come again to its rights." Machen said:

Some of us discern in all this the work of the Spirit of God. And God grant that His fire be not quenched! God save us from any smoothing over of these questions in the interests of a hollow pleasantness; God grant that great questions of principle may never rest until they are settled right! It is out of such times of questioning that great revivals come. God grant that it may be so today! Controversy of the right sort is good; for out of such controversy, as Church history and Scripture alike teach, there comes the salvation of souls.[24]

*   *   *

Charles Erdman, a candidate for the office of moderator of the General Assembly, declared that he ran on the platform of "old-fashioned orthodoxy and Christian spirit and constitutional procedure." Some conservatives opposed Erdman because he would not clearly separate himself from the "modernist and indifferentist party" that was supporting his candidacy. Erdman's defenders attacked the "deliberate misrepresentation of his position by the extreme Fundamentalist faction of the Presbyterian Church headed by William J. Bryan, Dr. Clarence Macartney of Philadelphia . . . and Professor J. Gresham Machen." The 1925 General Assembly elected Erdman moderator.[25] When some liberals threatened to leave the church because the assembly upheld a complaint against two ministers who would not affirm the virgin birth of Christ, Dr. Erdman proposed that a special commission of fifteen members be appointed "to study the present spiritual condition of our Church and the causes making for unrest, and to report to the next General Assembly, to the end that the purity, peace, unity and progress of the Church may be assured." The motion passed unanimously. Dr. Macartney believed that the conservative cause had been strengthened by the actions of the 1925 General Assembly, but Machen feared that "the evangelical movement" had been stopped and that "the Modernists" were "in even more complete control" than before.[26]

*   *   *

In July 1925 John T. Scopes was put on trial in Dayton, Tennessee, for teaching evolution in public school. The famous trial lawyer and religious skeptic, Clarence Darrow, and William Jennings Bryan clashed in furious debate, as a multitude of reporters churned out stories about the small-town setting, the carnival atmosphere, and the ignorance of fundamentalism.

Dr. Machen had declined William Jennings Bryan's invitation to testify at the Scopes trial "with the very greatest regret," insisting on his "incompetence to help." He wrote that he was "deeply interested" in Bryan's fight against "the naturalistic doctrine of evolution" and was "morally certain as to the debasing character of much of the teaching with regard to this subject that has been going on in the public schools," but he admitted that he had not engaged in the kind of study that would qualify him "to give expert testimony." A few weeks earlier Machen had declined an invitation from the *New York Times* to state the case against evolution. Machen instead wrote an article on "What Fundamentalism Stands For Now," which was published on June 21 along with the article "What Evolution Stands For Now" by zoologist Vernon Kellogg.[27]

Despite his reluctance to be drawn into the debate over evolution, Machen did accept the possibility of a providentially guided evolution "as God's way of working in certain spheres . . . through nature," but he insisted that the first two chapters of Genesis and the Christian doctrine of sin and the fall required the creative power of God in sharp distinction from evolution "at the origin of the present race of man." Without going deeply into the matter, Machen believed that he was following the views of Warfield and "what Princeton has stood for all through its history."[28]

Machen's colleague Caspar Wistar Hodge Jr. stressed the "largely hypothetical character of the evolution theories" but held in principle that evolution could be "conceived in harmony with Christian Supernaturalism" if evolution was viewed as a divinely guided process and if divine intervention was allowed. Hodge taught that "the Scripture does *not* represent man as the product of *mere* second causes acting under God's providential control." There is something in man "which is new and is not contained even potentially in the preceding forms of life." But the grandson of Charles Hodge was willing to grant that the body of man, as far as the Bible is concerned, could have a genetic connection with the lower animals; it could have been made by God through providential activity rather than direct creation.[29]

Princeton's professor of apologetics, William Brenton Greene, believed that the theory of evolution had become a "world-view" that, if accepted, determined a person's "conception of God and of man and of duty and of sin and of destiny." Since evolution teaches that "the world has been gradually unfolded through immeasurable past time by natural causes alone," the hypothesis is "a godless one; it enthrones evolution in the room of God." Because of the humanistic presuppositions of its advocates, Dr. Greene opposed the theory of evolution. He also pointed to its serious scientific problems. He believed that the theory was "embarrassed by complexity and inconsistency" and that its most influential school, that is, Darwinism, was "in collapse."[30]

*   *   *

In November 1925 Machen's *What is Faith?* appeared, dedicated to Francis Landey Patton "as an inadequate but heartfelt expression of gratitude and respect." The book contained the material of a course of lectures that Dr. Machen gave at the Grove City Bible School in the summer of 1925. "We shall endeavor," Machen said, "to arrive at an answer to the question, 'What is Faith?' If that question were rightly answered, the Church, we believe, would soon emerge from its present perplexities and would go forth with a new joy to the conquest of the world." One of Machen's chief purposes in the lectures was to "defend the primacy of the intellect and in particular to try to break down the false and disastrous opposition which has been set up between knowledge and faith." Machen treated, in a popular but theologically responsible manner, the themes of "Faith in God," "Faith in Christ," "Faith Born of Need," "Faith and the Gospel," "Faith and Salvation," "Faith and Works," and "Faith and Hope."[31]

A British edition of *What is Faith?* was published in 1926. The *Anglican Theological Review* judged it one of the five best books of the year. The *British Weekly,* during the spring and summer of 1926, published eight articles on Machen's book, written by theologians teaching in British universities. The editor, John Hutton, had heard Machen's lectures at Grove City. He was "deeply moved," he wrote, "by the spoken word, delivered as it was with that firmness and passion and conviction which are the very constitution of Dr. Machen's personality." Machen's *What is Faith?* Hutton declared, is "a book of controversy in the highest and most honourable sense of that word. It will do us all an immense service, in the way of helping us to state to ourselves what it is we have come to mean. For these are bad days for the Church when we avoid the deepest questions, when we content ourselves with saying that there is truth everywhere, on one side perhaps as much as on the other."[32]

20

The Banner of Truth

Let us not fear the opposition of men; every great movement in the Church from Paul down to modern times has been criticized on the ground that it promoted censoriousness and intolerance and disputing. Of course the gospel of Christ, in a world of sin and doubt, will cause disputing; and if it does not cause disputing and arouse bitter opposition, that is a fairly sure sign that it is not being faithfully proclaimed.

J. GRESHAM MACHEN

A T their fall meeting in 1925 the seminary directors elected Clarence Edward Macartney to succeed William Brenton Greene as professor of apologetics and Christian ethics (with the possibility of transferring him later to homiletics). One of the most eloquent and effective preachers in the Presbyterian church, Macartney had for several years taught at Princeton, coming regularly from Philadelphia to assist Dr. Smith in homiletics. Macartney, who had preached without notes from the second Sunday of his ministry, urged the Princeton students to do the same. "If you can trust the Lord for your salvation, for eternity," he told them, "surely you can trust him for twenty-five minutes for your sermon the next time you preach!"[1]

In January 1926 Dr. Macartney preached at Princeton. Gresham Machen wrote to congratulate him on his sermon and to urge him to accept the faculty appointment:

I hear great reports of your sermon in the Seminary Chapel last Sunday. It must have been very eloquent, and very good for the souls of men. There was, I understand, an extraordinarily large congregation, but it was unfortunate that so many of the faculty for one reason or another had to be out of town. I was preaching for one of the members of the brave minority in New York Presbytery. But I do wish I could have heard your wonderful sermon. The students, I am told, listened with rapt attention, and were much impressed. All three of the older of Dr. Armstrong's children— one of them being a Smith College girl—were greatly impressed. And that is a great triumph—to get hold of young people of just that age, in addition to getting hold of the older people. Mrs. Armstrong, who is a great admirer of your preaching, gave an interesting report of the occasion.

The situation here at Princeton is such that we simply have to have you: and I do not see how we are going to get along till we do have you. Really I feel that we cannot continue the battle much longer without reinforcements. It is not worthwhile to go into details, but if I did so I think you would feel that the Faculty of Princeton Seminary offers the most important critical position in the whole world to be kept for the evangelical faith.

I wish your decision could be announced. It would put new heart into us. We need sorely new blood on the evangelical side here at Princeton. Sometimes I feel as though I should like simply to fly from the battle. It is such an uphill fight and those who stand for the right are physically weak, strong though they are in spirit.[2]

Dr. Macartney, however, decided not to join the Princeton faculty. "There was, of course, a certain appeal in the cloistered walks and venerable halls of Princeton," Macartney later wrote, "but I have never doubted that I made the right decision when I declined the chair to which I had been elected. When the time came for the final decision, I felt that I would rather preach myself than try to tell others how to preach."[3]

*   *   *

On June 21, 1926, John D. Davis died. For thirty-eight years Dr. Davis had been "a fine teacher of Semitic languages and Old Testament history, a reputable scholar" and a faithful representative of the Princeton Old Testament school.[4] He focused all of his energy on his teaching at the seminary, where he lived out his motto "This one thing I do." Older alumni remembered him as their teacher of Hebrew. Later graduates appreciated his courses in Old Testament history, poetic literature of the Old Testament, and introduction and exegesis of the prophets. Davis published his *Dictionary of the Bible* in 1898; it went through four editions by 1924, becoming the most influential and widely used one-volume Bible dictionary. Dr. Davis was the writer of critical notes in the *Westminster Teacher* from 1899 until 1907 and contributed frequently to biblical and archaeological journals. Frederick

Loetscher, a student and later colleague of Dr. Davis's, wrote, "His publications are more than a guide for the perplexed: they are a shield for faith, an arsenal for the unarmed, a storehouse of biblical scholarship and spiritual wisdom fitted to sustain and comfort all those who . . . still believe in the written and the Incarnate Word of God."[5]

"Modest, reserved, self-repressing, diffident at times to the point of shyness," Davis often sat in a faculty meeting without speaking a word although he was the senior professor and most of the little group were his former students. He had "no desire to be conspicuous in moulding events by direct personal influence upon them: rather would he spend himself, quite unseen of the world, in training a succession of men" to be leaders in the church. Davis knew he was not at his best on the conference platform or in the arena of theological debate. He took no public part in the debate concerning the revision of the Confession of Faith and avoided most of the ecclesiastical controversies of his time. During the meeting of the New Brunswick Presbytery in January 1921, however, he spoke out against the "Philadelphia Plan" of church federation. Dr. Machen wrote a few days later, "I had been a little afraid about Dr. Davis, but he came out magnificently for the Christian faith."[6]

*   *   *

When Dr. Warfield died in 1921 the Princeton board of directors had wanted to move Gresham Machen to systematic theology. Machen knew theology well and presented it compellingly in his sermons and books, but he declined this "magnificent opportunity" so that he could continue his work in New Testament. After Dr. Macartney turned down the professorship of apologetics the directors, by a vote of nineteen to nine, elected Dr. Machen to the chair of apologetics.[7]

Machen was reluctant to make the major move from New Testament, in which he had been trained in the United States and Germany, to apologetics. Moreover, he preferred having another conservative voice added to the faculty. He decided, however, to accept the appointment as a way to further the evangelical cause at Princeton and in the Presbyterian church. Caspar Wistar Hodge wrote, "You will make a great professor of apologetics and fill the place better than any one I know." But Hodge expressed sadness at Machen's leaving what he regarded as "the most important department in the Seminary. . . . To 'open the Scripture,' to expound its truths, I consider the highest of all tasks, and even of greater 'apologetic' value in the long run than its 'defense.'" Machen knew that his election had to be confirmed by the General Assembly, but he wrote to his mother that "hated though I am, I hardly think that the unprecedented step will be taken of contesting the confirmation of a professor's election by a Seminary Board of Directors."[8]

*   *   *

The special commission appointed by the 1925 General Assembly met with Dr. Machen on December 2, 1925. Machen stated forthrightly that the "one great underlying cause" of unrest in the church was

the widespread and in many quarters dominant position in the ministry of the Church as well as among its lay membership of a type of thought and experience, commonly called Modernism, which is diametrically opposed to the Constitution of our Church and to the Christian religion. All the disturbances which have agitated the Church in our day, all the controversies which have been so much regretted, are necessary consequences of that one cause; and it is as unreasonable to blame those who call attention to that cause as it would be to regard as disturbers of the peace those who raise an alarm of fire when a building is threatened by the flames. The real cause of the disturbance is not the ringing of fire alarms or the clatter of fire apparatus, but the fire and only that. So the real cause of disturbance in our Church today is Modernism and Modernism alone.[9]

The special commission reported to the 1926 General Assembly meeting in Baltimore. It recognized that there were serious differences within the Presbyterian church but repudiated Machen's view that there were two mutually exclusive religions. The commission urged that "the Christian principle of toleration" be practiced by all "without endangering the basic positions of the church." It did not identify those basic positions, however, and played down the importance of doctrinal agreement. It stated that "Presbyterianism is a great body of belief, but it is more than a belief; it is also a tradition, a controlling sentiment." Toleration of diverse doctrinal views for the sake of evangelical unity, not concern for precise orthodoxy, it asserted, had been the dominant, and successful, tendency in the church. The report was greeted by applause and carried with only one negative vote. "Instead of telling what is really the matter with the Church," Machen charged, the report engaged "in abuse of the evangelical party" and made "all smooth for the destructive forces."[10]

Despite its emphasis on good will and mutual toleration, the General Assembly of 1926 refused to confirm Dr. Machen's election to the chair of apologetics at Princeton. The assembly's advisory committee recommended that no action be taken on Machen's election and that a committee be appointed to make "a sympathetic study of the conditions affecting the welfare of Princeton Seminary." Several members of the Princeton board of directors and O. T. Allis of the faculty spoke for Machen; but the General Assembly voted by a large majority to delay his appointment and to establish a Committee of Five—"a purely partisan committee," in Machen's view—to conduct an investigation of the situation at Princeton Seminary.

In the debate about Dr. Machen two issues were raised frequently. For most American Protestants, liberal as well as conservative, prohibition was a great Christian crusade, and it was well known that Machen had voted against a resolution in New Brunswick Presbytery that endorsed the eighteenth amendment to the United States Constitution. Slanderous and malicious reports circulated that Machen held "a loose and evil attitude toward temperance and even drunkenness itself."[11] "One would have thought that the real issue"—in the debate about Machen's election to the Princeton chair—"was not the truth of the Bible, the vicarious atonement, the virgin birth and the resurrection," said Clarence Macartney, "but prohibition."[12]

Not only was Machen faulted for his views on prohibition, he was judged to be "temperamentally defective, bitter and harsh in his judgment of others." Those who knew Dr. Machen best, however, were charmed by his courteous manners, his warmth, and his gentleness. One of his Princeton students described Machen as "a man of nobility, magnanimity, gentility and tender considerateness." Another student found Machen one day pulling the covers from his bed after it had been made. He said to the embarrassed professor, "Sir, why don't you show the maid how you want it fixed? I'm sure she'd be glad to oblige." "Oh, I couldn't do that," Machen replied. "I'm afraid she'd lose face." A colleague who served with him on a board that experienced many difficult meetings said that he "never heard Dr. Machen in all those hours of committee, harshly raise his voice or speak bitterly of anyone, even those who most vigorously opposed him."[13]

Clarence Macartney, in reviewing Machen's book *The Christian Faith in the Modern World*, wrote: "Those who have thought of Dr. Machen only as a severe Calvinistic, dogmatic theologian and controversialist may be surprised to discover through reading this book that its author, as his close friends have always known, is a man of the widest human interests and culture, a delightful companion, a lover of nature." Machen was concerned to pass on to the Princeton students an appreciation for friendship, courtesy, and respect for one another. In a talk on the "Christian and Human Relationships," he brought out "two sides to the life of Paul: a supreme devotion to Christ and the things of the other world in which all outward conditions are held to be comparatively valueless; and a delicate tact in the various relationships of this life; in union with a wonderful intensity in affections for other men."[14]

In matters of principle, however, Dr. Machen was single-minded and determined. One of his students, R. B. Kuiper, said, "If any one word describes the man, it is the word *integrity*. He could not tolerate any falsity or ambiguity in his beliefs or commitments." Kuiper added that "a certain character has gone down in the history of our country as 'the Great Compromiser.' Dr. Machen may well go down in the history of our church as the great non-compromiser." Ned Stonehouse stated that "political expediency and craft were entirely foreign" to him. John Murray wrote that Machen's "devotion to Christ and his profound jealousy for Christ's honour in the church made it utterly impossible for him to stand aside and be a spectator in the areas of practical life in the church." Such strong conviction was seen by some, however, as stubbornness; and Machen's insistence that the Presbyterian church was to be an exclusive institution committed to the preservation of the orthodox Christian faith was interpreted as harsh and narrow-minded.[15]

Machen never shunned controversy, but he insisted that, first of all, controversy must be "perfectly open and above board." "In controversy," he wrote, "I do try to observe the Golden Rule; I do try to do unto others as I would have others do unto me. And the kind of controversy that pleases me in an opponent is a controversy that is altogether frank." Secondly, "the defence of the faith should be of a scholarly kind," Machen stated. "Mere denunciation does not constitute an argument; and before a man can refute successfully an argument of an opponent, he must understand the argument that he is endeavouring to refute. Personalities, in such debate, should be kept in the background; and analysis of the motives of one's opponents has little place."[16]

"Both Dr. Machen's friends and his enemies knew that no one in the whole country was better qualified for the Chair of Apologetics," commented Clarence Macartney; "but he was the target of abuse because of his uncompromising stand on the great issue before the church." Following the action of the General Assembly to delay Machen's appointment to the Princeton chair many messages of shock and sorrow—and encouragement—reached Dr. Machen from his family and friends, ministers of the Presbyterian church and other denominations, and students in the seminary. Macartney wired, "Be of good courage. The happenings of this day will greatly increase your influence and will serve to awaken a sleeping church. The reproach of Christ is your honor and reward." The gentle William Brenton Greene was incensed with "the brutal insult" inflicted on Machen on the floor of the assembly. "But it is not an insult to you alone," he wrote. "'In all their afflictions *He* was afflicted, and the angel of his presence saved them.' Keep thinking on that, and eternity itself will not exhaust its comfort."[17]

The overseers of Knox College at the University of Toronto, the theological college of the Canadian Presbyterian Church, invited Machen to be its principal. Columbia Theological Seminary asked him to join its faculty as professor of New Testament. Other invitations came, but Dr. Machen was committed to Princeton Seminary, although he was distressed that the opposition to him could bring "great danger upon Princeton." He wrote: "No doubt I have been at fault in many ways in the manner in which I have tried to maintain what I believe to be right; but I earnestly hope that my faults may not be allowed to bring harm upon the institution that I love—an institution which is performing today, to a degree attained perhaps never before in its history, a worldwide service in the defence of the Reformed or Calvinistic Faith."[18]

*   *   *

The attention of the Presbyterian church focused on Princeton Seminary as the Committee of Five began its work. It held meetings in Princeton in November 1926 and interviewed seminary alumni, faculty, members of the boards, and students. The 125 alumni who traveled to Princeton to testify were divided in their assessment of the cause of the problems at the seminary. The majority of the faculty expressed its support for Machen and stated that a strong stand should be taken at Princeton—an institution "historically affiliated with the doctrinal point of view in the Church known as the Old School"—against the liberalism that was troubling the Presbyterian church. The differences in the church, the faculty majority maintained, were "concerned not with two forms of the Reformed Faith but with the very nature of evangelical Christianity itself." Dr. Stevenson, however, advocated a spirit of inclusivism that would make the seminary representative of the whole church. He saw the problem at the seminary as caused by "suspicion, distrust, dissension and division" in the faculty. Dr. Smith said that the seminary faculty should "deal with truth not in the controversial way but in the way of a direct presentation of the truth and leaving the truth to make its own application and appeal." He favored a broader seminary, he told the committee, but not one with "liberal or modernistic elements." Dr. Loetscher, while not taking sides, deplored the tension in the faculty. But Dr. Machen insisted that the real issue was doctrinal —"the maintenance of the historic position of Princeton Seminary in the defense of the faith."[19]

Individual faculty members voiced their appreciation for Machen. Dr. Armstrong, his colleague in the New Testament department, said:

We have labored together not only in the work of our Department but in the Faculty and in the Church, holding as we do similar views concerning the purpose of the Seminary and concerning the public policy of the Church. Ever sensitive to the high obligations of his calling, [Dr. Machen] has never been willing to sacrifice principle to expediency; but while devotion to principle has brought him into debate with those from whom he differs, he has been mindful always of the proprieties, as his writings will testify. Thinking clearly and of strong convictions, he has not hesitated to state issues with precision; but though his methods of presenting his opinions have seemed to some to be severe, and have been characterized as harsh, they have never descended to the level of personalities. And the dominant motive in all his activity has been no other than zeal for the Gospel as it is set forth in the Scriptures and expounded in our Confession of Faith.[20]

Caspar Wistar Hodge stated that he had known Dr. Machen "intimately for some twenty years. His love and zeal for the truth of the Gospel, his high-mindedness, and his scrupulous fairness toward those holding opposing views have won my admiration." Hodge went on to praise Machen for his "spirit of Christian patience and forbearance in the midst of the most bitter attacks and unfounded slanders." He added, "If the time has come when a man cannot make a bold and noble defense of the Truth without being subjected to abuse, then indeed the darkness of medieval intolerance threatens to overwhelm the Presbyterian Church, and to stifle its witness to the Truth of God."[21]

Dr. Machen and Dr. Erdman again attempted a personal reconciliation. Both men acknowledged their faults. Dr. Erdman regretted the "bitter, intolerant spirit" that had divided them. "I have no doubt shown it and regret it," Erdman said. "I do want to get it out of my heart." Dr. Machen desired to resume "friendly relations" with Erdman but reserved, he added, the right to differ with him.[22]

The directors of the seminary passed, by an overwhelming majority, a statement praising Machen for "his scholarship, his reputation here and in other countries, his ability as a teacher, and his inspiring work in his classes." They asked that Princeton Seminary be allowed to continue, according to its "Plan," to represent the conservatives in the Presbyterian church. Dr. Maitland Alexander, president of the board of directors, blamed the wide divergence of views between the seminary's directors and its president for the trouble at Princeton. Princeton's student association passed without a dissenting vote a resolution that expressed "unbounded confidence in Dr. J. Gresham Machen as a scholar, as a teacher, as a gentleman, and as a Christian." A minority of students were sympathetic to the views of Stevenson and Erdman, but even they agreed as to the injustice of the attacks upon Dr. Machen.

*   *   *

In the spring of 1927 Machen gave the Thomas Smyth Lectures at Columbia Theological Seminary. Speaking on the subject of the virgin birth of Christ, he demonstrated through intricate literary and historical analysis that the traditional supernaturalistic biblical claims better explain the evidence than the competing naturalistic accounts.[23] He showed that the virgin birth did not appear as a late addition in the New Testament but had an original place in Matthew and Luke, which presented independent but not contradictory accounts. He argued that there was no gradual formation of the tradition in the early patristic period; it was just as firmly established at the beginning of the second century as at its close. He claimed that denials of the virgin birth—arising from antisupernatural dogmatic presuppositions—failed to explain the origin of the doctrine. He showed how it could not have come from Jewish or pagan ideas.

Dr. Machen criticized the liberal practice of separating religion and history to try to save some Christian ideals while

[374]

abandoning biblical accounts such as the virgin birth that do not fit modern understanding of science. Machen argued that "there can scarcely be a greater error" than to regard religious truth "as in some way distinct" from scientific truth. "On the contrary," Machen continued, "all such distinctions are at best merely provisional and temporary; all truth, ultimately, is one. And we must continue to insist, even in the face of widespread opposition, that if the virgin birth is a fact at all, it belongs truly to the realm of history."

"The story of the virgin birth is the story of a stupendous miracle," Machen said, "and against any such thing there is an enormous presumption drawn from the long experience of the race." But that presumption can be overcome, he argued, "when the tradition of the virgin birth is removed from its isolation and taken in connection with the whole glorious picture of the One who in this tradition is said to be virgin-born." When we come to see Christ as He is—to view him "in the light of God and against the dark background of sin . . . as the satisfaction of man's deepest need, as the One who alone can lead into all glory and all truth"—we will come, despite all, Machen insisted, "to the stupendous conviction that the New Testament is true, that God walked here upon the earth, that the eternal Son, because He loved us, came into this world to die for our sins upon the cross." "When you have arrived at that conviction," he said, "you will turn with very different eyes to the story of the virgin and her child. Wonders will no longer repel you."

Dr. Machen believed that the doctrine of the virgin birth is important because the New Testament teaches it and so the authority of the Bible is at stake. "The Bible contains . . . history," Machen insisted, "and unless that history is true the authority of the Bible is gone and we who have put our trust in the Bible are without hope." An "integral part" of the good news of the Bible, he said, "was the fact that Jesus Christ was conceived by the Holy Ghost and born of the virgin Mary." The doctrine of the virgin birth is also important, Machen stated, "as a test for a man to apply to himself or to others to determine whether one holds a naturalistic or a supernaturalistic view regarding Jesus Christ." "If a man affirms that Jesus was born without human father, being conceived by the Holy Ghost in the virgin's womb," Machen argued, "he has taken the momentous step of affirming the entrance of the supernatural into the course of this world."

"A man is not saved by good works, but by faith; and saving faith is acceptance of Jesus Christ 'as He is offered to us in the gospel,'" Machen said as he closed his lectures. He added, "Part of that gospel in which Jesus is offered to our souls is the blessed story of the miracle in the virgin's womb. . . . The New Testament presentation of Jesus is not an agglomeration, but an organism, and of that organism the virgin birth is an integral part. Remove the part, and the whole becomes harder and not easier to accept; the New Testament account of Jesus is most convincing when it is taken as a whole. Only one Jesus is presented in the Word of God; and that Jesus did not come into the world by ordinary generation, but was conceived in the womb of the virgin by the Holy Ghost."[24]

When Dr. Machen's lectures on the virgin birth appeared in book form in 1930 *The Times Literary Supplement* described it as "elaborate, learned, and full." The New York *Herald Tribune* praised Machen for his "extensive and profound scholarship" and called the book a credit "to the reputation of American theological learning." Conservatives were encouraged, as one reviewer put it, that "modernists [did] not have all the scholarship on their side." Dr. Machen was pleased that even those reviewers who disagreed sharply with his position were generous in viewing the book as a valuable source of information, and he was greatly encouraged by the book's positive reception by Roman Catholics.[25]

*   *   *

Dr. Machen had little opportunity to continue with scholarly projects as the struggle at Princeton and in the Presbyterian church demanded his time and attention. He declined an invitation to become president of the new Bryan University in Tennessee, citing his lack of administrative experience and his desire to remain at Princeton Seminary. He wrote that he sympathized fully in the effort "to promote an education that shall be genuinely Christian" and prayed that "those who, like you, wherever they may be, cherish such a desire may not be discouraged by the opposition of the world." "You represent a cause which cannot ultimately fail," he continued. "And even now, despite all the forces of unbelief, despite hostile actions even of the organized church, the Gospel of Jesus Christ still shines out from the Word of God and is still enshrined in Christian hearts." Dr. Machen, no doubt, encouraged himself with those words.[26]

*   *   *

The General Assembly's committee for the investigation of Princeton Seminary finished its work and published its findings in April 1927. It stated that the president and all the professors were "loyal to the standards of the Church, and to the task of teaching and defending the conservative interpretation of the Reformed Faith in its purity and integrity." It criticized Dr. Machen's unwillingness "to trust the doctrinal loyalties of his colleagues." The committee reported that in its opinion, "the root and source of the serious difficulties at Princeton and the greatest obstacle to the removal of these difficulties" was "the plan of government by two boards."

Since 1824 a board of directors and a board of trustees had shared responsibility for the seminary's management. From the establishment of the school in 1812 the directors had governed the seminary, subject to the power of the General Assembly. The assembly elected the directors and professors until 1870, when it gave the authority to the board of directors to elect its own members and to appoint professors, subject to the veto of the assembly. In 1822 the seminary was incorporated by the legislature of New Jersey with a board of trustees appointed as custodians of the property. This self-perpetuating board reported annually to the General Assembly. Although the possibility of problems arising from the existence of two boards was recognized, the Princetonians believed that it was a sound arrangement, reflecting Presbyterian polity—one body in charge of spiritual matters and another responsible for property and the investment of funds.

The General Assembly of 1927 unanimously elected

Robert E. Speer, secretary of the Board of Foreign Missions, as moderator and, after long and heated debate, adopted the report of the special committee on Princeton by a decisive majority of 503 to 323. The special committee was expanded to eleven members and given authority to create a new structure for the seminary—a single board of control to replace the old boards. The report also recommended that approval of the election of Machen to the chair of apologetics and O. T. Allis to the chair of Semitics— appointments that strengthened the conservative cause at Princeton—be deferred pending the reorganization.

The 1927 General Assembly rejected the Five-Point Deliverance of 1910, 1916, and 1923—ruling that the assembly did not have the right to establish "essential and necessary articles" as requirements for ordination. It could declare an article of faith essential and necessary only by quoting "the exact language of the article as it appears in the Confession of Faith." This action, in effect, repudiated the previously exercised power of the General Assembly to define, clarify, and thus preserve the church's doctrine. The position of the Auburn Affirmation was in effect adopted; and tolerance for liberals was now guaranteed. It was clear that the Presbyterian church was ready to move to suppress Princeton and its specific Calvinistic orthodoxy.[27]

* * *

Dr. Machen was on a speaking trip in Great Britain during the 1927 General Assembly. On May 30 he addressed the General Assembly of the Free Church of Scotland on the topic "What is Christianity?" "You—the Free Church of Scotland—have stood for two things," he said. "You have stood for liberty of conscience; and you have stood for the Reformed Faith, the system of doctrine which is taught in the Scriptures, which are the Word of God. You are a city set on a hill which cannot be hid. Your example has been an encouragement to those all over the world who are facing the same issue which you, by the grace of God, were enabled to face so nobly."[28]

Heartened by "the warmth of Christian fellowship" that he

had experienced in Scotland, Machen went on to London, where on June 10 he gave three lectures (under the auspices of the Bible League of Great Britain) on the topic "Is the Bible Right About Jesus?" He concluded the lectures with these words:

What I think we ought to be opposed to is a partial view of the evidences of Christianity. Let us not appeal to experience as over against the Bible; let us take along with the documentary evidence in the Gospels the great wealth of evidence that comes to us in other spheres, the evidence provided by the consciousness of sin, of the need of salvation, the need of a Saviour. Then we can come to the wonderful message of the Gospel. It has then evidencing value enough. Accept it, and come to the feet of Jesus, and hear Him say to you, as you contemplate Him upon the cross: "Thy faith hath saved thee. Go in peace."[29]

While in Britain Machen received a letter from William Park Armstrong, who wrote, "The Assembly proved to be against us on every issue. I am distressed for the Seminary and for you and Allis. I cannot see how good can come . . . until the wrong is righted. We shall have to be patient and continue to fight." Machen described the 1927 assembly as "probably the most disastrous meeting, from the point of view of evangelical Christianity, that has been held in the whole history of our Church." If the proposed reorganization succeeded, he believed, Princeton would "be destroyed" and a "new institution of an entirely different type would replace it." Princeton Seminary would no longer continue as it had for over a hundred years and the "one remaining strong centre of evangelical influence in the Presbyterian Church U.S.A." would be crushed.[30]

* * *

On October 1 the seminary faculty passed a resolution stating that the report of the special committee adopted by the General Assembly was manifestly a "party document supporting the administrative policy of the President against the policy of the Board of Directors and of the Faculty." The faculty majority expressed its conviction that the proposal to establish a single board of control for the seminary would be "fatal to the maintenance of the historic doctrinal position" of Princeton. Many in the church agreed. The editor of *The Presbyterian* wrote, "All this talk about the alleged benefits of a one-board control is but a 'smoke screen' to conceal the real objective of its advocates. . . . They want to get rid of the present Board of Directors because they know that as long as this Board directs the affairs of the Seminary, it will not become an inclusive institution."[31]

Dr. Machen hoped that "the right of thoroughgoing conservatives in the Presbyterian Church to have at least one Seminary that clearly and unequivocally represent[ed] their view [might] still be recognized and Princeton [might] still be saved." Believing that "the sense of fair play in the rank and file of the Church" would be brought to bear upon the decision of the next assembly, Machen prepared and published a forty-eight-page booklet entitled *The Attack upon Princeton Seminary: A Plea for Fair Play*, in which he cited legal, administrative, and historical points that favored maintaining control by the board of directors. "Princeton Seminary, as a conservative institution, can be saved only by . . . leaving the control of the institution (in spiritual matters) in the hands of the Board that has made it what it is," he argued. Reorganization, Machen maintained, was "an effort to crush [Princeton's] 'noble tradition' of piety and learning." He clearly set forth the doctrinal nature of the controversy. Three major emphases in the Princeton tradition were in jeopardy: Princeton's adherence to "the complete truthfulness of the Bible as the Word of God," its commitment to "the Reformed or Calvinistic faith as being the system of doctrine that the Bible contains," and its insistence on a scholarly defense of the Bible and the Westminster Standards. "As over against . . . a reduced Christianity," he insisted, "we at Princeton stand for the full, glorious gospel of divine grace that God has given us in his Word and that is summarized in the Confession of Faith in our Church." The seminary under the new policy, Machen believed, would be "inclusive of those who obscure the great issue of the day; but it will be exclusive of those who have determined to warn the church of her danger and to contend earnestly for the faith."[32]

Dr. Machen pled that the conservatives of the church be allowed to have "at least one theological institution, not that *others* think is sound, but that *they* think is sound." He admitted that the "solitary position" of Princeton would seem to many to be explained simply by "the fact that we are the supporters of a hopelessly discredited cause"; but, he added, there was another possible way of looking at the matter. "Instead of holding that we have been left behind in the march of progress, one might also conceivably hold that in a time of general intellectual as well as moral decadence we are striving to hold aloft the banner of truth until the dawn of a better day."[33]

Dr. Machen and the faculty majority maintained that according to the seminary's charter and the terms of the 1870 reunion, Princeton was obligated to teach "Old School theology." The *Presbyterian Banner* remarked sharply, "If Princeton is standing where the church stood in 1870 it is time that it should move forward and stand where the church stands today." Many, however, stood with Machen. From Scotland John Murray wrote, "It was with pleasure that I read your pamphlet, 'A Plea for Fair Play.' I suppose that if Princeton's historic identity should be undermined and destroyed there are sufficient in America loyal enough to the Reformed faith who would do their utmost to found and build another to take its place." Murray added sadly, "But the library could not possibly be duplicated." In a letter to *The Presbyterian*, Francis Patton opposed "the present attempt to disrupt the government of Princeton Theological Seminary." Princeton, he stated, had "always stood for the unmodified Calvinism of the Westminster Confession. It has a right to remain so."[34]

21

The End of an Epoch

The old Princeton Seminary may have been good or it may have been bad—opinions differ about that—but at least it was distinctive and at least it was a power in the affairs of men. It was known throughout the world as the chief stronghold of a really learned and really thorough-going "Calvinism" in the English-speaking peoples. Even its opponents, if they were scholars, spoke of it with respect.

J. Gresham Machen

T HE state of New Jersey had rapidly become urbanized,
but "around Princeton, shielding her, is a ring of
silence—certified milk dairies, great estates with
peacocks and deer parks, pleasant farms and woodlands," F.
Scott Fitzgerald wrote. "The busy East has already dropped
away when the branch train rattles familiarly from the
junction. Two tall spires and then suddenly all around
you spreads out the loveliest riot of Gothic architecture in
America, battlement linked on to battlement, hall to hall,
arch-broken, vine-covered—luxuriant and lovely over two
square miles of green grass."[1] The beauty of the seminary
campus blended toward the southeast with the broad green
stretches of the golf course and the impressive buildings of
the Princeton University Graduate College. Cleveland Tower
—rising 173 feet above the surrounding landscape—was the
nation's memorial to Grover Cleveland, who, after leaving
the White House, retired to Princeton and became a trustee
of the university.

The old Marquand Chapel was destroyed by fire in 1920
and replaced by a magnificent Gothic structure modeled
after the chapel of King's College, Cambridge. On Memorial
Day of 1928, at the opening of the new chapel, the choir
entered the nave to lead the people in singing the ninetieth
Psalm in the English metre of Isaac Watts: "O God, our help
in ages past, Our hope for years to come, Our shelter from
the stormy blast, And our eternal home." The high medieval
French pulpit looked down on pews made from army-surplus

wood originally designated for Civil War gun carriages. The chancel's oak paneling was carved in England from Sherwood Forest trees. The stained-glass windows depicted scenes from Bunyan's *Pilgrim's Progress,* Dante's *Divina Commedia,* Malory's *Le Morte D'Arthur,* and Milton's *Paradise Lost.* The four great windows visible from the transept symbolized endurance, love, truth, and hope. The Princeton shield with its open Bible was carved in stone over the main entrance of the chapel. Below the shield were the words *Dei Sub Numine Viget* ("Under God's power she flourishes").

*   *   *

The 1928 General Assembly, meeting at Tulsa, Oklahoma, faced the issue of Princeton Seminary and Gresham Machen's appointment. A petition containing over 10,000 signatures (including those of more than 2,850 ministers) was presented. It read:

The undersigned, ministers and elders of the Presbyterian Church in the United States of America, contemplate with alarm the possibility of any change in the Plan of Princeton Theological Seminary which would interfere in any way with the control of its spiritual and educational policies by the Board of Directors.

The noble conservatism of the institution, its valiant and trenchant blows in defense of Evangelical Christianity as understood by us and our fathers, and its steadfast adherence, in the midst of a world of doubt, skepticism and mysticism, to the full truthfulness of Holy Scripture and the simple faith through which alone men can be saved—these qualities have been due solely to the wise conservation of the Board of Directors in selecting a faculty which would not lapse into modern vagaries, but with learning and ability would defend and propagate the faith clearly expressed in our Confession.

The present Faculty carries on the best traditions of the Alexanders and the Hodges, of Green, Warfield and Patton. The only offense laid to the charge either of the Faculty or of the Board of Directors is excess of zeal for the purity of the faith. Is this a time when such a charge can safely be entertained by the Church? When there is rampant everywhere in the world, and even in some parts of our Presbyterian Church, denial, doubt, or disparagement of the virgin birth of our Lord, the miracles which He and His apostles wrought, the reality of His resurrection and the veracity of the Scriptures as a whole—when such things are found, is it a time for the Church to abolish the Board of Directors for strongly and earnestly believing in and defending the truth of the Bible and the gospel that the Bible contains?

Shall the control of Princeton Seminary be disturbed at such a time as this? We believe that it is dangerous, and injurious to the best interests of the Church and of Evangelical Christianity.

We, therefore, the signers of this Petition, earnestly pray you to reject the reorganization of the Seminary recommended to the General Assembly of 1927 by the Special Committee to visit Princeton, and thus to leave the control of this great institution where it now resides.[2]

The General Assembly took no specific action in response to the petition but received the majority report of the Committee of Eleven. The report recommended a consolidated board and enlarged powers for the president of the seminary, making him "the final authority" in all faculty matters. A minority report was filed by Ethelbert Warfield, who acquiesced to the one-board proposal but objected to the expanded office of the president at the expense of faculty "independence of thought and speech." The assembly chose to postpone final action on Princeton for another year, instructing the directors "to proceed immediately to compose the differences at the Seminary" and to report to the next assembly. Machen's election to the chair of apologetics by the seminary directors was once again tabled, but the opponents of reorganization had purchased another year of time. "The Assembly is against us doctrinally," Machen wrote on May 31, "and if we can get them to tolerate us for the present, perhaps that is all that we can expect." On June 20 Machen asked the directors to allow him to withdraw his acceptance of the position of professor of apologetics. Two years had passed since his election by the directors and Machen did not want to prolong the controversy. He would remain an assistant professor of New Testament, the position he had filled with distinction since 1914.

*　　*　　*

The influential Swiss theologian, Emil Brunner, visited Princeton in the spring of 1928 and expressed "a special desire" to meet Dr. Machen.[3] On April 23 Machen addressed a meeting of Presbyterian ministers in the Philadelphia area on the topic "Karl Barth and 'The Theology of Crisis.'" Machen pointed out the "profoundly Christian elements" in the thinking of Barth and Brunner and their associates. "The world, they hold, has been estranged from God by the awful fact of sin," he said. "Man can never bridge that chasm, but God has bridged it." God has come to us "not in a feeling or in an experience, but in his *Word.*" That Word is

not something that grows out of the life of man; psychology can never reveal it; it has come . . . directly from above. It is not an idea, but "revelation." . . . By this revelation from God the helplessness, the sinfulness, the awful guilt of man are made clear; in fact a man never truly knows the guilt of sin until the message of salvation is already knocking at the door of his soul. . . . And that word is not only a word of condemnation; it is also a word of grace. The wonder has been accomplished. God has bridged the impassible chasm; we could never go to him, but he has come to us. He has come to us, say these writers, in the person of Jesus Christ. . . . The living and Holy God, man lost in sin, God's grace in the gift of Jesus Christ his Son, faith as itself the gift of God—it sounds like John Bunyan and John Calvin and the Shorter Catechism and the Reformed Faith.

Although Machen found "a large measure of agreement" between those "who are not ashamed of being 'orthodox'" and Barth and Brunner, he had "an uneasy feeling" about "their attitude toward the plain historical information that the Bible contains." "Does [Barth] do away with the objectivity of truth; does he fall back at last into that subjectivity against which his whole teaching starts out to be a mighty protest?" Machen asked. He feared that Barth's "real meaning is that we can hear the Word of God in the New Testament, as addressed to our own soul, no matter what the facts about Jesus of Nazareth were." Machen concluded that "the truth is that the radicalism of Barth and Brunner errs by not being radical enough." They have broken with "the whole development of theology since Schleiermacher and with the entire immanence philosophy upon which it is based," but they must go on to break with "the application of that immanence philosophy to the historical problem that the

New Testament presents." "What we need is a more consistent Barthian than Barth," Machen said; "we need a man who will approach the New Testament documents with presuppositions that are true instead of false, with presuppositions that will enable him to accept at its face value the testimony of salvation that the New Testament contains."[4]

Much of what Machen had said about modern Christianity —its surrender of the Word of God for religious experience, and its abandonment of traditional theology for the standards of twentieth-century culture—was now heard again in the stern accents of "the theology of crisis." As Machen did, Emil Brunner, Karl Barth, and Reinhold and H. Richard Niebuhr "subjected twentieth-century modernism to the light of Scripture and found modernism wanting." It was, wrote Richard Niebuhr, a religion in which "a God without wrath brought men without sin into a kingdom without judgment through the ministrations of a Christ without a cross."[5]

*   *   *

Dr. Machen was delighted when in the fall of 1928 the directors, despite Dr. Stevenson's opposition, invited Cornelius Van Til to become instructor in apologetics for the 1928–29 school year. Machen wrote to his mother, "It is the first real forward step that has been taken in some time. Van Til is excellent material from which a professor might ultimately be made." Cornelius Van Til had come to Princeton Seminary as a student in 1922. He wrote prizewinning papers at the seminary and established a reputation as a competent philosopher in courses that he took at the university. A member of the Christian Reformed Church, he was reluctant to get involved in the Presbyterian issues being passionately discussed at Princeton. He asked Geerhardus Vos, "Why should I, an outsider, get mixed up in a denominational skirmish when I'm not in the denomination?" His fellow Dutchman replied:

Look, this is going to be a much broader matter than a single denominational issue. Princeton may be a Presbyterian seminary under the direction of the General Assembly, but don't forget that

[389]

it's a rallying point for many, many wonderful Christian people all over the world—people who love Reformed doctrine and life. For years it's been used by God as a breakwater against the tides of unbelief and a sounding board for the faith of our fathers. You cannot, you dare not, stand by and look on like an indifferent spectator when a conflict is being fought in the arena.[6]

William Brenton Greene died on November 16, 1928. Princeton mourned his death. Gresham Machen wrote, "I loved Dr. Greene. He was absolutely true, when so many were not. He was always at Faculty and Presbytery, no matter how feeble he was. He was one of the best Christians I have ever known."[7]

*   *   *

On March 10, 1929, Dr. Machen preached for the last time in the Princeton Seminary chapel. His text was I Timothy 6:12—"Fight the good fight of faith." He said that "the Apostle Paul was a great fighter" and that he was followed by others who fought faithfully and courageously for the truth.

Tertullian fought a mighty battle against Marcion; Athanasius fought against the Arians; Augustine fought against Pelagius; and as for Luther, he fought a brave battle against kings and princes and popes for the liberty of the people of God. Luther was a great fighter; and we love him for it. So was Calvin; so were John Knox and all the rest. It is impossible to be a true soldier of Jesus Christ and not fight.

Machen's words rang out clearly in the old Princeton chapel, "God grant that you—students in this seminary—may be fighters, too! . . . You will have a battle when you go forth as ministers into the church. The church is now in a period of deadly conflict. The redemptive religion known as Christianity is contending, in our own church and in all the larger churches of the world, against a totally alien type of religion." Machen stressed that "this battle is a battle of love; and nothing ruins a man's service in it so much as a spirit of hate." We must fight, he said, like Paul, who knew the peace of God, and so possessed "an inner sanctuary in his life that no enemy could disturb." "If you are at peace with [God]," Machen told the students, "then you can care little what men may do. You can say with the apostles: 'We must obey God rather than men'; you can say with Luther: 'Here I stand, I cannot do otherwise, God help me. Amen.'"

With compelling questions Machen drove home his point:

Where are you going to stand in the great battle which now rages in the church? Are you going to curry favor with the world by standing aloof; are you going to be "conservative liberals" or "liberal conservatives" or "Christians who do not believe in controversy," or anything else so self-contradictory and absurd? Are you going to be Christians, but not Christians overmuch? Are you going to stand coldly aloof when God's people fight against ecclesiastical tyranny at home and abroad?

He continued:

There are many hopes that I cherish for you men, with whom I am united by such ties of affection. I hope you may be gifted preachers; I hope that you may have happy lives; I hope that you may have adequate support for yourselves and for your families; I hope that you may have good churches. But I hope something for you far more than all that. I hope above all that, wherever you are and however your preaching may be received, you may be true witnesses for the Lord Jesus Christ; I hope that there may never be any doubt where *you* stand, but that always you may stand squarely for Jesus Christ, as He is offered to us, not in the experiences of men, but in the blessed written Word of God.

Machen closed his sermon with calm but intense words:

God grant . . . that in all humility, but also in all boldness, in reliance upon God, you may fight the good fight of faith. Peace is indeed yours, the peace of God which passeth all understanding. But that peace is given you, not that you may be onlookers or neutrals in love's battle, but that you may be good soldiers of Jesus Christ.[8]

*   *   *

As the 1929 General Assembly approached, the *Christian Century* noted, "It looks as though the [Princeton] issue [can] no longer be evaded. The Presbyterians will have to stand

and be counted, and the result of the counting will go far toward fixing the dogmatic complexion of the denomination." When the assembly met in St. Paul, Minnesota, Dr. Machen was present as a commissioner from New Brunswick Presbytery. There were six different reports concerning Princeton Seminary. Debate was limited, and Machen was allowed five minutes. "Mr. Moderator," he said,

We at Princeton Seminary have been proclaiming an unpopular gospel, which runs counter to the whole current of the age; yet it is a gospel of which we are not ashamed. We have proclaimed it in great human weakness, and we are conscious of our unworthiness to be entrusted with a treasure so great. Of some charges, indeed, our hearts acquit us; many things have been said about us that are not true. Yet weak and faulty enough we are, and we confess our weakness freely in the presence of the General Assembly and of Almighty God. But who of you, my brethren, is sufficient unto these things?

We have derived our authority to preach this unpopular gospel not from any wisdom of our own, but from the blessed pages of God's Word. But from this gospel that the Scriptures contain, the world has gradually been drifting away. Countless colleges and universities and theological seminaries throughout the world, formerly evangelical, have become hostile or indifferent to that which formerly they maintained. They have done so, often with many protestations of orthodoxy, and often with true evangelical intentions too, on the part of those who were unwitting instruments in the change. So it is with Princeton Seminary. We impugn no man's motives today; many of those who are lending themselves to this reorganization movement no doubt themselves believe in the Bible and are unaware of what is really being done. But no one who has the example of other institutions in mind, who knows the trend of the times, and who knows the facts about the present movement, can doubt but that we have here only a typical example of the same old story, so often repeated, of an institution formerly evangelical that is being made to drift away by insensible degrees from the gospel that it was founded by godly donors to maintain.

I cannot show you how that is true; for I have but a few minutes to speak; but there are many throughout the world who well know that it is true. I cannot show you how unjust it is; but there are many of Christ's little ones whom the injustice of it grieves to the very heart. With these grieved and burdened souls, who are perplexed by the uncertainty of the age, and who are looking to Princeton

Seminary for something to be said against modern unbelief and in favor of the full truthfulness of God's Word—with these we are united today in a blessed fellowship of sympathy and prayer. To that fellowship I believe that most of you would belong if you only knew the facts. It is hard for me to look into your faces and see many of you ready to do that ruthless thing which, if you only knew its meaning, you would be the first to deplore. I cannot reach your minds, for the time does not suffice for that; and God has granted me no gift of eloquence that I might reach your hearts. I can only hope that a greater and more mysterious persuasion may prevent you from doing unwittingly that which is so irrevocable and so wrong. One thing at least is clear—there are many Christians in many lands who will feel that if the old Princeton goes, a light will have gone out of their lives. Many are praying today that you may be kept from putting out that light. If you destroy the old Princeton today, by destroying the Board of Directors which has made it what it is, there are many, I admit, who will rejoice; for there are many who think that the old gospel and the old Book are out of date. But if there are many who will rejoice, there are also those, Mr. Moderator, who will grieve.[9]

Unmoved by Machen's words, a decisive majority of the commissioners voted to adopt the majority report of the Committee of Eleven that Princeton Seminary be reorganized by the merging of the two boards—the trustees, who directed the financial affairs of the seminary, and the directors, who were responsible for curriculum and faculty. The seminary was placed under a new thirty-three-member board, made up of eleven members from each of the two existing Princeton boards plus eleven new members. The hiring and dismissal of faculty was to be left entirely to the judgment of the board, and the approval of the General Assembly was no longer required.

*   *   *

Dr. Machen did not want to leave Princeton. Sadly he wrote to his mother in the middle of June that he wanted to "*live* at Princeton, say what I please, and write big, thick books." But he did resign within a month after the reorganization became official. The passing of the old Princeton Seminary, he felt, marked the "end of an epoch in the history of the

[393]

modern church." Princeton had "resisted bravely the current of the age," but now, Machen wrote, it "has been made to conform to the general drift" and is "lost to the evangelical cause." Three other faculty members—Robert Dick Wilson, Oswald T. Allis, and Cornelius Van Til (who had been offered the chair of apologetics)—also resigned.[10]

The Princeton Theological Review abruptly ceased publication. Since 1918 Dr. Allis had been its editor, and Machen and Wilson were major contributors. For a hundred years, under the leadership of distinguished editors from Charles Hodge to O. T. Allis, and under a variety of names, the Princeton journal had been a powerful force in setting forth historic Christianity and Reformed theology as a true and relevant message for the church and the world.[11]

The new seminary board met on June 14, 1929, and stated that it intended "to continue unchanged the historic policy of the Seminary."[12] It announced that the following faculty members, "in loyalty to the action of the highest court of our Church," would continue at Princeton: J. Ross Stevenson, Geerhardus Vos, William Park Armstrong, Charles R. Erdman, Frederick Loetscher, J. Ritchie Smith, and Caspar Wistar Hodge. Hodge, Vos, and Armstrong never wavered in their outspoken loyalty to Machen but, to his great disappointment, decided to remain at Princeton. They had not been subjected to the hostility and personal abuse that Machen had faced for the last three years. Furthermore, Vos was ill, Armstrong faced financial problems, and Hodge wanted to maintain the family tradition at Princeton. Several new professors and instructors were added to the seminary faculty, including John Murray, who came to assist Dr. Hodge in systematic theology. Murray had graduated from Princeton in 1927 with the degrees of bachelor and master of theology. According to the *Princeton Seminary Bulletin* "few students have maintained as high a level of scholarship as did Mr. Murray during his seminary course." Awarded the Gelston-Winthrop Scholarship, Murray did postgraduate study in New College, Edinburgh.[13]

Those who supported the reorganization of Princeton Seminary in 1929 claimed that it was simply administrative streamlining; it was not, they argued, doctrinally motivated.

John W. Hart, however, correctly asserts that "in retrospect, the conservatives were right. Princeton was reorganized not for administrative or even ecclesiastical but for theological reasons. The Presbyterian Church in the United States of America did not want to preserve the old Princeton because the church had abandoned its commitment to the Princeton Theology of Hodge, Warfield, and Machen." Despite the pledge of the new board that there would be "no departure from the conservative doctrinal position maintained for more than a hundred years" at Princeton, change did come. Lefferts A. Loetscher, professor of church history at Princeton and the son of the earlier Princeton professor, described the reorganization of 1929 as the passing of the rigid theology of the past and the beginning of "a new start and a very different perspective. The historical-critical approach is now dominant and assured," he wrote.[14]

*   *   *

For several years conservative Presbyterians had discussed the possibility of founding a new seminary that would carry on the old Princeton tradition. The idea appealed to Machen, who believed that "a really evangelical seminary might be the beginning of a really evangelical Presbyterian church." On July 18, 1929, a meeting of over seventy persons—including former directors, faculty, and students of Princeton—resolved to establish a new seminary to continue "the policy of unswerving loyalty to the Word of God and to the Westminster Standards for which Princeton Seminary has been so long and so honorably known." In the language of the old Princeton "Plan," the new seminary declared that one of its goals was "to develop in those who shall aspire to the ministerial office, both that piety of the heart, which is the fruit of the renewing and sanctifying grace of God, and solid learning."[15]

On September 25, 1929—just a month before the stock market crash intensified the Great Depression—Westminster Theological Seminary was formally opened in the Witherspoon Building in Philadelphia. There were fifty-two students, most of whom had come from Princeton. One was

Harold John Ockenga, a Methodist who transferred to Westminster "to finish his theological training under the men whose reputation had been responsible for his going to Princeton."[16]

After a brief welcome from Robert Dick Wilson, Gresham Machen gave the main address on "Westminster Theological Seminary: Its Purpose and Plan." Westminster Seminary would endeavor by God's grace to hold "the same principles that the Old Princeton maintained," Dr. Machen told the congregation. He went on to say:

We believe, first, that the Christian religion, as it is set forth in the Confession of Faith of the Presbyterian Church, is true; we believe, second, that the Christian religion welcomes and is capable of scholarly defense; and we believe, third, that the Christian religion should be proclaimed without fear or favor, and in clear opposition to whatever opposes it, whether within or without the church, as the only way of salvation for lost mankind.[17]

The former Princeton teachers—Machen, Wilson, Allis, and Van Til—were joined by four others. Paul Wooley, graduate of Princeton University and Princeton Seminary, was appointed instructor in church history. Allan MacRae, who had studied under Robert Dick Wilson at Princeton and was doing graduate work in Berlin, came to assist Dr. Wilson, now well past seventy. Ned Stonehouse, 1927 graduate of Princeton Seminary who had completed a doctorate at the Free University of Amsterdam, joined Dr. Machen in teaching New Testament. R. B. Kuiper of the Christian Reformed Church, a student who had made a great impression during a year of study at Princeton following his graduation from Calvin Theological Seminary, taught systematic theology the first year. In 1930 Caspar Wistar Hodge's assistant, John Murray, who was unhappy with the new outlook at Princeton, moved to Westminster to teach theology. Dr. Machen gave himself to the demanding task of building a new seminary that would unashamedly hold forth the majestic testimony that had been the witness of Princeton for one hundred and seventeen years.[18]

*   *   *

When Erasmus censured Luther for "obstinate assertiveness," the great reformer replied that "it is not the mark of a Christian mind to take no delight in assertions; on the contrary a man must delight in assertions or he will be no Christian. And by assertion . . . I mean a constant adhering, affirming, confessing, maintaining, and an invincible persevering."[19] The history of old Princeton Seminary is a testimony to "an invincible persevering." Archibald Alexander, Samuel Miller, and Charles Hodge affirmed and confessed the doctrines of the Reformed faith against those who would deny or weaken them. A. A. Hodge and B. B. Warfield maintained biblical authority against the attacks of higher criticism. Warfield, Machen, and their colleagues battled for historic Christianity against an unbelieving liberalism. Archibald Alexander and Charles Hodge were called "moderates" in the 1830s, whereas B. B. Warfield and Gresham Machen were often described as "ultraconservatives" in the 1920s. It was not that the later Princetonians were more bellicose or theologically rigid than their predecessors, as is sometimes suggested. The nineteenth-century debates of Alexander, Miller, and Hodge usually had to do with differences within traditional Christianity; but the twentieth-century battle of Machen against liberalism was, as he saw it, a struggle for the very existence of the Christian faith. Machen's "controversialism was not unlike theirs," George Marsden writes; "not unlike Hodge's in helping to exclude the mildly innovative New School Presbyterian Party from the Presbyterian Church in 1837, not unlike Warfield's militant opposition to Charles Briggs's questioning of the inerrancy of Scripture in the 1890s. This was a venerable heritage, and Machen owned it entirely. His predecessors presumably would have done much the same."[20] Alexander, Miller, and Hodge defended the Reformed faith. Warfield fought for the Bible. Machen made a "grand and heroic stand for the Everlasting Gospel" —as his friend Clarence Edward Macartney put it.

The 1920s was a period of siege for the conservatives of Princeton Seminary. Divided from within and attacked from without, they concentrated their energies on fighting to maintain the legacy that they had inherited from Archibald Alexander, Samuel Miller, and Charles Hodge. However, in

Old Princeton's desperate struggle, attention to some very good things was lessened. Sturdy biblical exposition, great preaching, and more evangelistic and missionary zeal—along with its stalwart defense of the faith—would have strengthened the Princeton cause.

* * *

When the Presbyterian church rejected the Old Princeton message and chose institutional unity above doctrinal integrity, it undermined not only its own history but also its witness. Opening its doors to the influences of a secularizing society, it became more and more difficult for the church to sustain its Christianity and to pass it on to the following generations. Most of the baby boomers surveyed in a recent study of Presbyterians who have left the church said they knew little about what their parents believed—a finding that led the authors to conclude that in passing on their faith to the next generation, parents have to teach their children about doctrine. A second conclusion from the study was that children of the church were more likely to maintain their Christian identity if they were taught that Christianity is the only way of salvation. In the words of the sociologists themselves, "the single best predictor of church participation turned out to be *belief*—orthodox Christian belief, especially the teaching that a person can be saved only through Jesus Christ."[21] It was the message that Princeton—from Archibald Alexander to J. Gresham Machen—sought to preserve and preach.

22

The Princeton Theology

"The Kingdom of Jersey," as Americans pleasantly call the state to which the little town [of Princeton] belongs, is noted for three things: its fruit, its legislation, and its theology. The last it gets from Princeton: and throughout the United States "Princeton theology" has long been regarded as a synonym for orthodoxy.

Princetoniana

Oh, for more Princeton theology, for it is the teaching of the Word of God.

CHARLES HADDON SPURGEON

OLD Princeton "retained a remarkable consistency over the course of its remarkable life." Archibald Alexander, the first professor, was one of the most learned clergymen of his time. He exemplified the Princeton ideal and was followed by a succession of able, dedicated teachers who shared his vision and elaborated, sharpened, and deepened his work. They joyfully took what they received, studied it, ascertained its biblical foundations, and faithfully passed it on in their teaching and writing with "clearness and dignity" and "not infrequent eloquence." The result, as Moisés Silva has written, was a seminary characterized by "warm devotion to the Reformed faith. Noble aggressiveness in the defense of historical orthodoxy. Emphasis on the exegesis of the original languages of Scripture. Commitment to the blending of piety and intellect. Willingness to engage opposing viewpoints with scholarly courtesy and integrity."[1]

*   *   *

When Princeton Seminary was established in 1812 its founders promised to create a school where "piety of the heart" would be joined with "solid learning," thus putting into practice an emphasis of the Reformed faith. "Learning joined with piety" is required in ministers, wrote John Calvin. John Sturm, Reformed scholar and teacher at Strasbourg, set forth his objective as the formation of men who were "pious, learned, and capable of expressing themselves well." John

[401]

Witherspoon urged his Princeton College students "to keep clear views of the importance of both piety and literature, and never suffer them to be divided." "Religion without learning, or learning without religion, in the ministers of the gospel," stated Princeton Seminary's "Plan," "must ultimately prove injurious to the Church."[2]

*   *   *

In 1812, at his inauguration as Princeton Seminary's first professor, Archibald Alexander preached on John 5:39— "Search the scriptures; for in them ye think ye have eternal life: and they are they which testify of me." He set forth the reasons for believing that the Bible was indeed the very Word of God and emphasized the importance of thorough knowledge of the Bible, with Greek and Hebrew required for accurate exegesis, as the basis of ministerial training. Divine authority and careful study of the Bible became the theme of Princeton Seminary's history. In 1915 B. B. Warfield summed up a century of Princeton theology when he stated that "the Scriptures are throughout a Divine book, created by the Divine energy and speaking in their every part with Divine authority directly to the heart of the readers." "Princeton's fidelity to the plenary inspiration of the Bible was consistent," Mark Noll writes; "each generation refined the position that it had received. The effort throughout was painstaking, careful, scholarly, and learned."[3]

From Archibald Alexander to Gresham Machen, the Princetonians held that the text of Scripture as originally inspired by the Holy Spirit was absolutely true and without error and falsehood. They believed that this was the Bible's own view of itself; it was Christ's view of the Bible; and it was the position of the mainstream of the Christian church until the time of the Enlightenment. Furthermore, they believed that such a view of the Bible was necessary for the health of the church. Gresham Machen told the Princeton students in a chapel message in 1926:

You may not say with the prophets of old: "God has spoken directly and independently to me; I appeal to no external authority; when I speak it is 'Thus saith the Lord.'" But you can do something else.

You can mount your pulpit stairs; open reverently the Bible on the desk; pray to the gracious Spirit to make plain the words that He has spoken; and so unfold to needy people the Word of God.

Do you think that is a low function? Do you think that involves a slavish dependence on a book? Do you think that it means that advance and freedom are to be checked? The history of the Church should be the answer. Again and again history has shown that the Bible, when accepted in the very highest sense as the Word of God, does not stifle life but gives life birth; does not enslave men, but sets them free. Those who talk about emancipating themselves from the slavish doctrine of what they call "verbal" inspiration are not really emancipating themselves from a tyranny, but they are tearing up the charter upon which all human liberty depends.

And so, after all, you can say in a high, true sense, as you draw upon the rich store of revelation in the Bible: "Thus saith the Lord." If you accept the Bible as the Word of God you will have one qualification of a preacher. Whatever be the limitations of your gifts, you will at least have a message.[4]

Princeton did not hold to a mechanical dictation view of inspiration; its formulations concerning the Bible were carefully nuanced statements that emphasized the divine truth communicated and the unique personality of each writer. The 1881 article by A. A. Hodge and B. B. Warfield on "Inspiration" not only drew criticism from liberals who denied the inerrant character of the autographs, but also from some conservatives who believed that the authors' lively presentation of the integrity of the human writers of Scripture had compromised divine authorship.[5]

Careful study of the Bible accompanied Princeton's defense of it as the Word of God. Generations of Princetonians gave themselves to the ongoing task of a reverent and scholarly investigation of the biblical text as the basis for their theology. Here, as in so many other areas, Archibald Alexander set the Princeton pattern. The seminary's two greatest systematic theologians, Charles Hodge and B. B. Warfield, came to their discipline from training and teaching in the Old and New Testaments. Geerhardus Vos, professor of biblical theology, was a noted exegete. Gresham Machen, who epitomized Old Princeton's theological commitments during its last generation, was an outstanding New Testament scholar. In reviewing Reuben A. Torrey's *What the Bible Teaches,* B. B. Warfield commended the Moody Bible Institute teacher for his presentation of many of the Bible's great doctrines but questioned his approach to biblical interpretation. Warfield believed that Torrey's method embodied "a tendency . . . to formulate doctrine on the basis of a general impression derived from a cursory survey of the Scriptural material or on the basis of the specific study of a few outstanding texts isolated from their contexts, and then to seek support for it in more or less detached passages." Far better, in Warfield's view, was "the thorough understanding" to be found in truly "inductive" exegesis.[6]

Impressed with the Baconian method of scientific induction, the Princetonians often compared the work of the theologian with that of the scientist. J. W. Alexander wrote that the theologian should proceed in his investigation precisely as do the chemist and the botanist—that is, by careful examination of the data, from which results cautious conclusions. Charles Hodge believed that Scripture contains the "facts which God has revealed concerning himself and our relation to Him." As the scientist gathers the facts of nature and uses them to formulate laws, "we must take the facts of the Bible as they are, and construct our system so as to embrace them in all their integrity." B. B. Warfield said that we are to exercise all the faculties God has given us and exhaust all the tests at our command to assure ourselves of the facts. "Criticism consists in careful scrutiny of the facts," he added, "and is good or bad in proportion to the accuracy and completeness with which the facts are apprehended and collected, and the skill and soundness with which they are marshaled and their meaning read." Theology is "just as much a science as is chemistry," Gresham Machen wrote. "The two sciences, it is true, differ widely in their subject matter; they differ widely in the character of the evidence upon which their conclusions are based; in particular they differ widely in the qualifications required of the investigator: but they are both sciences, because they are both concerned with the acquisition and orderly arrangement of a body of truth." Like scientists in their pursuit of the laws of the natural world, the Princeton theologians were committed to the equally rigorous theological task of the investigation and organization of the teaching of the fully accurate and authoritative facts of the Bible.[7]

With all their emphasis on the objective truthfulness of Scripture and the scientific nature of biblical interpretation, the Princetonians did not slight the doctrine of the testimony of the Holy Spirit. In his inaugural address Archibald Alexander said that in times of perplexity

a lively impression made by the Spirit of truth banishes all doubt and hesitation; and then the same texts or arguments which were before unavailing to our conviction and satisfaction exhibit the truth in a light as clear as demonstration. This may appear to some to savour of enthusiasm. Be it so. It is, however, an enthusiasm essential to the very nature of our holy religion, without which it would be a mere dry system of speculation, of ethics and ceremonies.[8]

In his *Systematic Theology* Charles Hodge gave great importance to the inward teaching of the Holy Spirit, not as a substitute for external revelation but as a guide in determining what the Bible teaches. He wrote:

The question is not first and mainly, What is true to the understanding, but what is true to the renewed heart? The effort is not to make the assertions of the Bible harmonize with speculative reason, but to subject our feeble reason to the mind of God as revealed in his Word, and by his Spirit in our inner life. . . . The true method in theology requires that the facts of religious experience should be accepted as facts, and when duly authenticated by Scripture, be allowed to interpret the doctrinal statements of the Word of God.[9]

The doctrine of "the witness of the Spirit" was used by some theologians and preachers to "make us independent of the Bible," as Gresham Machen put it. In a chapel message Machen told the Princeton students that "just the opposite is the case."

The Holy Spirit is the Spirit of truth. He does not contradict in one generation what He has said in another. He does not contradict the Scriptures that He himself has given. On the contrary, what He really does is to make the words of Scripture glow with a heavenly light and burn in the hearts of men.[10]

*   *   *

In an article on the "Use and Abuse of Systematic Theology" J. W. Alexander defended the arranging of the teachings of the Bible into a system of theology as necessary and good, warned that such efforts must be careful and wise, and compared them "to the map of a country over which a geographer travels, and which offers convenient direction, while at the same time the traveller does not hold it to be perfect, but proceeds to amend it by actual survey." "The true light in which a system of theology should be viewed by one who uses it as an aid in scriptural study," wrote Alexander, "is as a simple *hypothesis*, an approximation to the truth, and a directory for future inquiries."[11]

Although not equating the inerrant truth of the Bible with the fallible work of theologians, and not viewing the work of theology as complete, the Princetonians did greatly value the theological achievements of the Christian church. In his review of J. A. W. Neander's *History of the Planting of the Christian Church* Charles Hodge wrote:

"I cannot agree," says Neander, "with the conviction of those who think that [modern theology] will be only a repetition of what took place in the sixteenth or seventeenth century, and that the whole dogmatic system, and the entire mode of contemplating divine and human things, must return as it then existed." Neither can we [continued Hodge]; but at the same time we must protest against those who would sweep away as rubbish the whole of that glorious structure with cries of *Rase it, rase it, even to the foundation thereof.* We have no respect for speculations which refuse all aid from those great spirits whom God raised up. . . . We . . . do not believe that every race is to lay a new foundation.[12]

A. A. Hodge held that just as "revelation itself was brought forth gradually through a historic process," so "by another process, no less historical, since the close of revelation, its contents have been gradually more and more perfectly apprehended in the thought and life of the Church." The younger Hodge explained:

All true development, while it unfolds and perfects, also preserves the essential identity of the things developed, from the ovum to the accomplished end. Substitution is not development, and to put one thing for another is the trick of the magician, not the *experimentum crucis* of the philosopher.[13]

B. B. Warfield believed that progress is made in theology not by destroying old systems and starting from scratch again, but by receiving, correcting, and assimilating the impulses given. Warfield asserted that our understanding of Christianity would advance as our understanding of both natural and special revelation is corrected and enlarged. The task of the modern theologian, however, is to perfect an existing structure rather than to construct a wholly new one. Warfield wrote:

If the temple of God's truth is ever to be completely built, we must not spend our efforts in digging at the foundations which have been securely laid in the distant past, but must rather give our best efforts to rounding the arches, carving the capitals, and fitting in the fretted roof. What if it is not ours to lay foundations? Let us rejoice that that work has been done! Happy are we if our God will permit us to bring a single capstone into place.[14]

Warfield taught the Princeton students that epochal doctrinal constructions had been made throughout church history—especially in the early church and by the sixteenth-century reformers—leaving the modern church the joyous task of building on that good foundation. He agreed with the plan of James Orr's *Progress of Dogma*, in which the Scottish theologian defined doctrine as "simply the system of theology spread out through the centuries." Warfield described this "organic growth" as "the ripened fruit of the ages," the result of which is "the system which we all inherit." The context for the working out of Christian doctrine is human history, and it is the Holy Spirit, Warfield explained, who leads the church into fuller and deeper understanding of the truth. Heresies challenge the church to respond with a more definitive expression of truth already implicitly or partially held. Christian life and worship moves the church toward a more perfect understanding of the truth that lies at the heart of all its experience. Theological truth had come, in Warfield's view, not entirely or even mainly through intellectual activity, but also through the practical and everyday life of the church. He wrote:

Throughout all the ages every advance in the scientific statement of theological truth has been made in response to a practical demand, and has been made in a distinctly practical interest. We wholly misconceive the facts if we imagine that the development of systematic theology has been the work of cold, scholastic recluses, intent only upon intellectual subtleties. It has been the work of the best heart of the whole Church driving on and utilizing in its practical interests, the best brain.[15]

Carefully and slowly, not infallibly but sometimes in great achievement, the church carried on its task. After nearly two thousand years of doctrinal development and church life, the superstructure—and much of the interior—of the theological enterprise was "virtually complete." Accordingly, the Princeton teachers saw their major task as conserving the truth that had already been achieved through nineteen centuries of struggle, challenge, and theological ferment.[16]

In an often quoted statement, Charles Hodge wrote: "Whether it be a ground of reproach or of approbation, it is believed to be true that an original idea in theology is not to be found in the pages of the *Biblical Repertory and Princeton Review* from the beginning until now. The phrase 'Princeton Theology,' therefore, is without distinctive meaning." Frank Hugh Foster has commented that Hodge "may be safely left by the historian of a progressive school of theology to the natural consequence of his own remark that during the many years of his predominance at Princeton that institution had never brought forward a single original thought." The Princetonians, however, considered their lack of originality a mark of honor. Archibald Alexander stated that "until men (and above all men, professors in theological seminaries) shall consent to come to the Word of God, and receive its doctrines simply as they are revealed, and not strive to be wise above what is written, we shall make no real progress in divine knowledge." A. A. Hodge once said to a Yale teacher who was making fun of the "fossilized" theology of Princeton: "The trouble with you Yale theological professors is that you only teach your students to think. . . . In Princeton we let God do the thinking, and teach the students to believe."[17] The Princetonians were right in claiming that their theology was not new. When they said new things, or expressed old things in a new way, or advocated new methods, it was always in an effort to conserve the old truth. Their determination to be faithful witnesses enabled them to succeed. The Reformed faith was safe in their hands.

Although Princeton Seminary took its stand against "new ideas," it was committed to "new discoveries." In his 1831 address to the students at the close of the semiannual examination, Ashbel Green told them that they should make "improvements" in theology by means of

an increase of clear perception and deep feeling, in relation to the beauty, glory, excellence, consistency and sweetness of evangelical truth—and increase, too, in a knowledge of the manner in which revealed truth may best be taught, inculcated and defended—an increase, also, of discernment, as to the errors to which the truth is opposed, and the consequent correction of some minor errors in your own minds—an increase, in a word, of your acquaintance and understanding of the Bible in all its parts, and of the glorious scope and tendency of the whole: if only this, or chiefly this, be intended by an improvement in theology, then, I say, I hope you will make great improvements; for I believe that such improvements will always be made by every minister of the gospel, just in proportion as he grows in grace, and persists in studious habits.

In 1835 Dr. Green returned to the same theme, urging the students to make "new discoveries in divine revelation"— "discoveries of no new doctrines, but new discoveries of the spiritual import and the 'riches of glory' of the old doctrines."[18]

The Princetonians agreed that progress should be made in theology, but they rejected as extremely questionable and dangerous the liberal idea that a temporary scholarly consensus disproves previous results and leads more or less automatically to a future higher consensus. Their conviction that the old truth—the fruit of the church's hard-won theology—must be preserved as well as perfected brought them into direct conflict with the modern view that the past represented more an obstacle to truth than a guide. Gresham Machen wrote that we believers in historic Christianity maintain the objectivity of truth; and in doing so we and not the modernists become advocates of progress. Theology, we hold, is not an attempt to express in merely symbolic terms an inner experience which must be expressed in different terms in subsequent generations; but it is a setting forth of those facts upon which experience is based. It is not indeed a complete setting forth of those facts, and therefore progress in theology becomes possible; but it may be true so far as it goes; and only because there is that possibility of attaining truth and of setting it forth ever more completely can there be progress.[19]

There would not be a perfect theology, however, before the consummation of history. The knowledge of God, B. B. Warfield wrote, "will be perfected only in the minds and hearts of the perfected saints who at the end, being at last like God, shall see Him as He is. Then, the God who has revealed Himself to His people shall be known by them in all the fullness of His revelation of Himself. Now we know in part; but when that which is perfect is come, that which is in part shall be done away."[20]

Despite their high view of the importance of theology and their persistent work to preserve and perfect the church's theological heritage, the Princetonians did not place theology above the Bible. Gresham Machen spoke for the Princeton tradition when he said,

How infinitely superior is God's Word to all human attempts to summarize its teaching! Those attempts are necessary; we could not do without them; everyone who is really true to the Bible will engage in them. But it is the very words of the Bible that touch the heart, and everything that we—or for that matter even the greatest theologians—say in summary of the Bible must be compared ever anew with the Bible itself.[21]

*   *   *

Princeton College professor Lyman Atwater stated that the "Princeton theology" was not "a special body of dogmas peculiar to Old School Presbyterians" but a faithful presentation of "the doctrines of catholic Calvinism of the Reformed and Puritan churches, as shown by their symbols [and] the writings of their great theologians." In his "Retrospect of the

[410]

History of the Princeton Review" Charles Hodge summarized the Princeton theology:

> The conductors of the *Princeton Review* . . . firmly believed that the system of doctrine contained in the Westminster Confession of Faith, the system of the Reformed Church and of Augustinians in all ages, is the truth of God revealed for His glory and the salvation of men. They believed that the upholding of that system in its integrity, bearing witness to it as the truth of God, and its extension through the world, was the great duty of all those who had experienced its power.[22]

A. A. Hodge described the Princeton theology as a "close and persistent adherence to the type of Calvinism taught in the Westminster Standards as these are interpreted in the light of the classical literature of the Swiss and Dutch and English Puritan theologians, who wrote after the date of the synod of Dort, especially Francis Turretin of Geneva and John Owen of England." Princeton's careful study of the old Reformed writers committed generations of Presbyterian ministers to "solid learning" in theology, guided by some of the greatest theological minds of the past—men who showed, Karl Barth has written, that "Protestant dogmatics was once a careful, orderly business."[23]

Of the American theologians, the Princetonians were most impressed by Jonathan Edwards. When John DeWitt contributed an article on Edwards for *Biblical and Theological Studies*, he wrote that it was "peculiarly appropriate . . . in a volume celebrating the Century of Princeton Theological Seminary" because Jonathan Edwards "was the earliest of the great theologians who have lived at Princeton." During his short eight weeks in Princeton his only teaching was "in divinity" and "from the chair which may be said to have been transferred from the College to the Theological Seminary when the Seminary was opened in 1812." Unitarian Oliver Wendel Holmes recognized the affinity between Princeton and Edwards when, in criticizing Edwards's theology as foreign to the civilized history of New England, he stated that "his whole system" belonged more to Scotland or New Jersey, "where the Scotch theological thistle has always flourished."[24]

Although rejecting some of Edwards's philosophical ideas and recognizing his "individualisms," the Princetonians stood firmly with him in his Calvinistic theology and evangelical spirituality. "The peculiarity of Edwards's theological work is due to the union in it of the richest religious sentiment with the highest intellectual powers," wrote B. B. Warfield. In September 1870, at a gathering of the descendants of Jonathan Edwards at Stockbridge, Massachusetts, Samuel Irenaeus Prime, the editor of the *New York Observer* and a graduate from Princeton Seminary's class of 1833, gave a short address. Prime "startled his hearers by declaring that to remember Edwards meant far more than a mere bow to history," for, he said, the message he preached was the truth of the Bible, and so it is relevant to every age. "It has the life of Christ in it," he explained; "it subordinates the reason to divine authority, and adores the Holy Ghost. . . . His *theology* had revivals and repentance, and salvation from hell, in it; and this made it, and makes it, and will keep it divine theology till Christ is all in all." A student at Princeton Seminary, Prime declared, hears that same theology and, as he visits the graves of Edwards and his fellow laborers of an earlier age, "something of their fire kindles in his soul."[25]

The Princetonians gloried in the work of the great Reformed theologians of the past, but they did not ignore those thinkers with whom they disagreed. J. W. Alexander wrote that "those who were privy to his [father's] daily studies were astonished at the time which he bestowed on the most dangerous writers." Although Archibald Alexander deplored the skepticism that the German works engendered concerning the "canonical integrity, the authenticity, and the inspiration of the Bible," he was persuaded

that if the Church consents to close her eyes upon the increasing facilities for biblical investigation which are now possessed in Germany, and to turn away from the controversies there waged, she will find herself in a field of battle without armour, or, if armed, with the mail and greaves and heavy weapons of a former age, wholly unsuited to the emergency and the new modes of attack.[26]

Charles Hodge, J. A. Alexander, B. B. Warfield, Geerhardus Vos, Gresham Machen, and other Princetonians studied in

Europe, not avoiding the scholars who took different positions from those they had been taught at Princeton. The Princeton professors worked hard to teach their students not only the true theology as they understood it; they also presented, fairly and competently, opposing views. What Robert Dick Wilson said at the close of a lecture was true of the whole Princeton tradition: he had "not shirked the difficult questions."[27]

*   *   *

At Princeton—as in much of early-nineteenth-century Protestantism—Scottish Common Sense Philosophy reigned. Congregationalists at Yale and Unitarians at Harvard embraced it nearly as enthusiastically as did Presbyterian Princeton.[28] Against the skepticism of philosophers such as David Hume, the Scottish philosophy affirmed that the human mind is structured by God in such a way as to have access to knowledge of the real world. The dictates of common sense—such as reality of the self, the law of non-contradiction, reliability of sense perception, and basic cause-and-effect connections—provide people with considerable knowledge about nature and human nature. The Princetonians were right, George Marsden has written, in insisting that we must "build our accounts of reality around premises that include the affirmation that God has created both our minds and the rest of the world." Furthermore, as John Stewart points out, Scottish Common Sense Philosophy held that "a person of simple common sense could rightly discern the essence of the Scripture's message. Such a conviction was a natural extension of the Protestant principle of *sola Scriptura.*"[29]

Just as the Princetonians believed that Baconianism was practiced "by the wise in every age," they saw Scottish Common Sense Philosophy as setting forth universal and permanent truths. B. B. Warfield claimed that one of the main features of Augustine's philosophy of knowledge was the assertion "that the objects of sensible and intellectual perception alike have indubitable objectivity." For Augustine "man no more creates the world of ideas he perceives within him, than the world of sense he perceives without him." In a footnote Warfield cited Nourrison, who wrote concerning Augustine's philosophical views, "No Scotchman of our day could express it better."[30]

Living in a far different intellectual climate from that of his predecessors, Gresham Machen summed up his own view and reflected what was really essential to the Princeton philosophical tradition:

I am not altogether unaware of the difficulties that beset what may be called the common-sense view of truth; epistemology presents many interesting problems and some puzzling antinomies. But the antinomies of epistemology are like other antinomies which puzzle the human mind; they indicate the limitations of our intellect, but they do not prove that the intellect is not reliable so far as it goes. I for my part at least am not ready to give up the struggle; I am not ready to rest in a pragmatic skepticism; I am not ready to say that truth can never be attained.[31]

The Princetonians never allowed Scottish Common Sense Philosophy to stand by itself or to determine their theological outlook. Far more important than their philosophical views were their biblical and confessional commitments. They made their philosophy serve their theology, and not the other way around. They criticized various points of the Scottish thinking when necessary and used it when they could to communicate with a culture in which, until the late nineteenth century, it was generally persuasive.[32]

"The Princeton Theology established itself as an important voice in America," writes Mark Noll. "Although it stood by its Calvinism while the rest of America swarmed for democracy, it nonetheless spoke the language of the American intellectual marketplace so effectively that the marketplace could not but pay attention." Charles Hodge and J. A. Alexander wrote in 1848 that "one of the strongest proofs that the gospel is of God may be derived from the co-existence of immutable constancy in that which is essential, with indefinite flexibility in that which is dependent on change of time and circumstances." "No one will doubt that Christians of today must state their Christian belief in terms of modern thought," B. B. Warfield wrote. "Every age has a language of its own and can speak no other. Mischief comes only when, instead of stating Christian belief in terms of modern thought, an effort is made, rather, to state modern thought in terms of Christian belief."[33]

* * *

Some scholars have maintained that Princeton, with its strong emphasis on objective truth, underestimated the importance of the subjective dimension of human knowledge. The Princetonians, however, recognized that many factors influenced beliefs. In his last article in the *Biblical Repertory and Princeton Review,* a year before his death, Archibald Alexander wrote:

As the Bible is a spiritual book, it demands, as a prerequisite to any just appreciation of it, a peculiar moral and spiritual culture. A bad man stands scarcely any chance of reaching the full truth. For even if he should sincerely strive after it, as an intellectual exercise, his views must necessarily be warped and modified by his own internal state.[34]

In his 1822 inaugural address Charles Hodge argued that "every unrenewed man has many erroneous principles and opinions" that greatly influence his interpretation of the Bible. Piety, Hodge stated, is required for "the perception of divine truth." A. A. Hodge pointed out that all human knowledge is imperfect—"whether in science or in theology, because we know things only in parts, and can never comprehend the absolute whole." "All things go out into mystery," he said; "all our knowledge is conditioned upon the essential unknowableness of God. In all our knowing and in all our worship, the infinite God is always beyond." "This tremendous fact," Hodge taught, "conditions all human knowledge in every stage of it."[35]

In his study of "Augustine's Doctrine of Knowledge" B. B. Warfield pointed out that Augustine taught that whereas "ideas [that] shine into the souls of man are, as it were, divine and unchangeable, men's perceptions to those ideas vary and change." Augustine cites several reasons for this, Warfield added, "including age, maturity, life's circumstances, in other words, the varying factors in both humanity and in the individual human's life. Human nature qualifies the reception of the ideas, and one need only observe the varying degrees in which men hold truth to see that this is so."[36]

In their battle with the critics the Princetonians described their own position as "believing criticism." William Henry Green argued that the higher critical view of the Bible was based on the critics' presuppositions and was not, as they liked to claim, the result of impartial investigation. Dr. Green countered with the Princeton presupposition of the divine origin of the Bible. Such a conviction, he maintained, was required for an appreciation of the Scriptures "even as a literary phenomenon." Dr. Green assured his students, however, that belief in the Bible's inspiration was "not blindly held" but was rather "confirmed afresh by critical study."[37]

In commenting on B. B. Warfield's *Counterfeit Miracles,* Colin Brown states that Warfield at times appears to be "a hard evidentialist, arguing that miracles can be recognized as objective, supernaturally caused events by anyone who takes the trouble to look fairly at the evidence." Brown points out, however, that Warfield actually approached "the New Testament miracles from the standpoint of prior belief-commitments," as evidenced by his insistence on "taking the New Testament at face value, and his desire to see miracles within the context of creation, the incarnation, and the resurrection of Christ." Brown concludes that "Warfield's approach to the New Testament miracles is by no means the straightforward, objective evidentialism that it has been imagined to be and that he himself perhaps thought it to be. . . . For belief-commitments of various kinds were built into the very fabric of Warfield's position."[38]

In his criticism of the theory of evolution William Brenton Greene argued that it is impossible to separate natural history and supernatural revelation. "The facts of nature are so vitally related to the Supernatural that they cannot be fairly considered out of relation to [God] any more than one science can be presented in absolute isolation from the other sciences," he wrote. "Facts cannot be studied justly in independence of the great fact which both constitutes and supports them. Now that fact is God."[39]

Gresham Machen was true to the Princeton tradition when he told the students, "We have in the Bible an account of the great presuppositions that should underlie all our thinking—the righteousness and holiness of God and the sinfulness of man." George Marsden has commented that "although [Machen] himself did not often put it this way, his common sense affirmations were in fact based on presuppositions concerning the Triune God revealed in Scripture. In fact, Machen took a Biblically founded view of reality as basic and derived an epistemology from it. His great insight was that the prevailing view of 'truth' in modern thought was in conflict with the view of truth assumed in Scripture."[40]

*　　*　　*

Sometimes it is stated that the Princeton apologetics over-estimated the power of rational argument and neglected the Calvinistic doctrine that unregenerate people simply cannot accept the evidence because they are blinded by sin. The Princetonians did believe that a good case could be made for Christianity. At his address at the opening of Westminster Theological Seminary on September 25, 1929, Gresham Machen summed up a century of Princeton teaching by saying that the question "Is Christianity true?" should not "be evaded; what is more it need not be evaded by any Christian. To be a Christian is a truly reasonable thing; Christianity flourishes not in obscurantist darkness, where objections are ignored, but in the full light of day."[41] At the same time, how-ever, the Princeton professors firmly believed that the power and presence of sin blinds the eyes, distorts the vision, and fills unbelievers with illusions. They recognized that people come to Christ without being first convinced by rational arguments that Christianity is true.

Archibald Alexander received a letter from a West Point cadet who had rejected the gospel and had, as he wrote, "denied all." Then one of his friends, "noted for his brightness of intellect," told him that he had been reading Alexander's *Evidences of the Christian Religion* and was "almost persuaded" to become a Christian. The cadet also obtained a copy of the book and went to his room to read it.

I opened to the introduction, the most blind of unbelievers; all around me was perfect clouds and darkness. I began to read, I had proceeded half way through the introduction, and was suddenly impressed that the religion of Christ was of God. I did not doubt its truth more than I did my life: yet I was entirely without argument. At that time I could have given no reason, yet I did not doubt. I felt a perfect belief that an Omnipotent Spirit did it.

Dr. Alexander commented that to some, this young man's conversion experience "may seem to savour of enthusiasm" but, he added, we "cannot prescribe limits to the Holy Spirit, in his ways of leading benighted souls into the path of life." Still, it may be asked, wrote Alexander, "how could there be a rational conviction of the truth of Christianity, when the individual knew no reasons or arguments in favour of it?" "To which it may be answered," continued Alexander, "that Christianity has a light of its own, independent of all external evidences; and if the Spirit of God cause one ray of this divine light to irradiate the mind, the truth becomes manifest."[42]

Charles Hodge frequently put forth rational arguments for the truthfulness of Christianity, but a greater emphasis impressed his students. William Paxton, who studied under Hodge from 1845 to 1848 and later served on the seminary faculty, wrote after Charles Hodge's death: "Every student remembers . . . with what a simple confidence he rested upon the Word of God for every proof, and that he never asked us to accept any one point of doctrine simply on the ground of rational demonstration. He was not a rationalist in any sense of the word. His sole authority for everything was the teaching of Scriptures."[43]

Dr. Hodge wrote that "every Christian" knows that rational arguments are "not the foundation of his faith: he has firmer ground on which to rest the destiny of his soul. He does not believe Grotius or Paley; he believes God himself, speaking in his Word. The evidence of the truth is in the truth itself." In his *Systematic Theology* Charles Hodge stated that we are "not to make the assertions of the Bible harmonize with the speculative reason, but to subject our feeble reason to the mind of God as revealed in his Word, and by his Spirit in our inner life."[44]

Hodge summed up the Princeton approach to faith when he wrote:

We believe in Christ, for the same reason that we believe in God. His character and his claims have been exhibited to us, and we assent to them; we see his glory and we recognize it as the glory of God. This exhibition is made in the gospel; it is made to every reader of the Word. And when such a reader, though he had never before heard of the Bible, finds this glorious personage, ratifying all those truths which were latent in his own consciousness, and needed only to be stated to be recognized as truths; and when he hears him say that he came to give his life a ransom for many, that whosoever believeth on him shall never perish, but have eternal life, he confides in him with humble and entire confidence. . . . Such a man believes the gospel on the highest possible evidence; the testimony of God himself with and by the truth to his own heart; making him see and feel that it is truth.[45]

In an essay on the "Deity of Christ" B. B. Warfield stated, "The supreme proof to every Christian of the deity of his Lord is . . . his own inner experience of the transforming power of his Lord upon the heart and life. Not more surely does he who feels the present warmth of the sun know that the sun exists, than he who has experienced the re-creative power of the Lord knows him to be his Lord and his God." Warfield, who held that Christianity was destined to reason itself to victory, believed that one's "logical capacity can scarcely be made the condition" of salvation. He wrote that "evidence cannot produce belief, faith, except in a mind open to this evidence, and capable of receiving, weighing, and responding to it." Therefore, wrote Warfield, "the sinful heart—which is enmity towards God—is incapable of that supreme act of trust in God" until "the creation by God the Holy Spirit of a capacity for faith under the evidence submitted."[46]

Even though the arguments for the truthfulness of Christianity could not give birth to a faith that establishes the heart, God, the Princetonians believed, was pleased to use them to open blind eyes. B. B. Warfield wrote:

It certainly is not in the power of all the demonstrations in the world to make a Christian. Paul may plant and Apollos water; it is

God alone who gives the increase. But it does not seem to follow that Paul would as well, therefore, not plant, and Apollos as well not water. Faith is the gift of God; but it does not in the least follow that the faith that God gives is an irrational faith, that is, a faith without grounds in right reason. It is beyond all question only the prepared heart that can fitly respond to the "reasons," but how can even a prepared heart respond, when there are no "reasons" to draw out its action? . . . The Holy Spirit does not work a blind, an ungrounded faith in the heart. What is supplied by his creative energy in working faith is not a ready-made faith, rooted in nothing, and clinging without reason to its object; nor yet new grounds of belief in the object presented; but just a new ability of the heart to respond to the grounds, sufficient in themselves, already present to the understanding. We believe in Christ because it is rational to believe in him, not though it be irrational.[47]

Warfield's successor, Caspar Wistar Hodge Jr., wrote, "Because you cannot make a man a Christian by merely presenting him with arguments addressed to his intellect, it does not by any means follow that he can be made a Christian apart from all evidence of the truth of Christianity." "The ultimate source of faith," continued Hodge, "is the power of the Spirit. But faith is not blind, and rational grounds may enter into the grounds of even saving faith." All the arguments in the world, however, do not "in the least minimize the absolute necessity of the Witness of the Holy Spirit, without whose light in our hearts we would grope in darkness, unable to be convinced by any evidence, and too blind to see the glory of God as it shines in the face of Jesus Christ and in the pages of the Word of God."[48]

"If you take account of all the facts, you will be convinced of the truth of Christianity," Gresham Machen wrote; "but you cannot take account of all the facts if you ignore the fact of sin. You cannot take account of all the facts if, while searching the heavens above and the earth beneath, you neglect the facts of your own soul." "It is impossible to prove first that Christianity is true, and then proceed on the basis of its truth to become conscious of one's sin," he continued; "for the fact of sin is itself one of the chief foundations upon which the proof is based." In Machen's view, "When that fact of sin is recognized, and when to the recognition of it is added a fair scrutiny of the historical evidence, then it seems thoroughly reasonable to believe that Christianity is true." But Machen was convinced that "an intellectual conviction of the truth of Christianity is always accompanied by a change of heart and a new direction for the will." "In order that Christianity may be recognized as true by men upon this earth the blinding effects of sin must be removed. The blinding effects of sin are removed by the Spirit of God; and the Spirit chooses to do that only for those whom He brings by the new birth into the Kingdom of God." Machen asserted:

Regeneration, or the new birth, therefore, does not stand in opposition to a truly scientific attitude toward the evidence, but on the contrary it is necessary in order that that truly scientific attitude may be attained; it is not a substitute for the intellect, but on the contrary by it the intellect is made to be a trustworthy instrument for apprehending truth. The true state of the case appears in the comprehensive answer of the *Westminster Shorter Catechism* to the question, "What is effectual calling?" "Effectual calling," says the Catechism, "is the work of God's Spirit, whereby, convincing us of our sin and misery, enlightening our minds in the knowledge of Christ, and renewing our wills, He doth persuade and enable us to embrace Jesus Christ, freely offered to us in the gospel." That does justice to all aspects of the matter; conviction of sin and misery as the prerequisite of faith, the enlightening of a mind blinded by sin, the renewing of the will; and all these things produced by the Spirit of God.[49]

*　　*　　*

The theology of A. A. Hodge was "conservative" without being "narrow," according to C. A. Salmond.[50] This aptly describes the whole of Old Princeton. From Archibald Alexander to Gresham Machen there was an unvarying allegiance to the traditional doctrines of Christianity and to "the system of faith" as taught in the Westminster Confession. In their effort to base their theology on a truly inductive study of the whole Bible, the Princetonians were guided by the mainstream of doctrinal development—historic Christianity they called it—particularly as it took the shape of Reformed theology in the sixteenth century and gained definitive statement in the Westminster Confession in the seventeenth century. The Princeton professors believed that this theological heritage must be preserved while it was furthered and deepened by continual and thorough study of the Scriptures. It was this combination of "detailed scholarship and an understanding of great principles" that was, according to Gresham Machen, "characteristic of the old Princeton Seminary."[51]

*   *   *

Old Princeton's reputation for scholarship is so strong that its commitment to spiritual life has often been overlooked. The Princeton "Plan" of 1812 stressed "piety of the heart" equally with "solid learning." The "Plan"—in the section entitled "Of Devotion and Improvement in Practical Piety"—required the students to "spend a portion of every morning and evening in devout meditation, in reading the holy Scriptures solely with a view to a personal and practical application to the passage read, and in humble fervent prayer, and praise to God." It charged the professors with the responsibility "to encourage, cherish, and promote devotion and personal piety" among the students. In chapel, conference, and classroom, in conversation and correspondence, in articles and books, the Princeton faculty stressed the joys and responsibilities of Christian living. Archibald Alexander's *Thoughts on Religious Experience* and *Log College*, Samuel Miller's *Letters to a Seminary Student*, Charles Hodge's *Way of Life*, and B. B. Warfield's *Faith and Life* are just a few of the Princeton writings that have as their major purpose the building up of Christians' lives. Dr. Warfield's statement about the Sunday Afternoon Conferences could be applied to all the work of the Princeton professors—"They kept the fire burning on the altar for a hundred years."[52]

*   *   *

Some scholars have presented the Princeton tradition as having two strands—a scholastic doctrinal mentality, and a warm spiritual and evangelistic impulse—that pulled apart and went their separate ways by the 1920s. "Running all the way through the history of the old Princeton theology,"

[422]

Lefferts Loetscher writes, "you have this antithesis" between objective truth and spiritual experience; the Princetonians "never quite brought the act together. More and more though, this 'objective' method gained ground." The history of Princeton Seminary indicates, however, that both learning and spiritual growth were simultaneous and united goals. The Princetonians insisted on the inseparable relationship between right doctrine and right living. They believed that the objective and subjective dimensions of the Christian faith must never be separated and, indeed rightly, cannot be separated.[53]

"Truth is in order to holiness," Archibald Alexander wrote, "and between truth and holiness there is an indissoluble connexion." He described how the Christian "experiences new views of divine truth," discerning "in the truth of God, a beauty and excellence, of which [the soul] had no conception until now." "There is a new perception of truth; whether you ascribe it to the head or heart," Alexander wrote, "I care not."[54]

Charles Hodge also sought to combine the objectivity of truth revealed in the Bible and the subjectivity of lived religious experience. He wrote:

It is true that Christianity is a life, but it is untrue that it is not a doctrine. It is true that Christ as a person is the object of faith, but it is untrue that the proposition, "Jesus is the Son of God," and others of like kind, are not the objects of faith. . . . Christianity, objectively considered, is the testimony of God concerning his Son, it is the whole revelation of truth contained in the Scriptures, concerning the redemption of man through Jesus Christ our Lord. Subjectively considered, it is the life of Christ in the soul, or, that form of spiritual life which has its origin in Christ, is determined by the revelation concerning his person and work, and which is due to the indwelling of his Spirit. In one sense, therefore, we may affirm that Christianity is a doctrine, and in another sense we may with equal truth affirm that Christianity is a life.[55]

At times Charles Hodge gave priority to religious feelings —as when he told the students on his return from Europe in 1829 that "opinions on moral and religious subjects depend mainly on the state of the moral and religious feelings."

Francis Patton stated that in Hodge's sermons in the Sunday Afternoon Conference, "the theology of the intellect" became "the theology of the feelings." At other times Hodge insisted that piety grows out of correct doctrine. In one of his last articles, "Christianity without Christ," he wrote that "the inward religious life of men, as well as their character and conduct, is determined by their doctrinal opinions." He added, however, that it is equally true that "the religious life of men is often determined more by the plain teaching of the Scriptures and by the common faith of the church than by their theological theories. Hence, men have often more of Christ in their religion than in their theology. It is, however, of the last importance to remember that sound doctrine is, under God, our only security for true religion and pure morals."[56]

B. B. Warfield chided Harnack for failing to set forth "a just appreciation of the intimate relation which subsists between Augustine's peculiar type of piety and his distinctive type of doctrine." Harnack, Warfield wrote, "speaks almost as if it were conceivable that one of these could have come into existence apart from the other." Warfield added, "The truth is, of course, that they are but the joint products in the two spheres of life and thought, but the joint products of the same body of conceptions, and neither could possibly have arisen without the other." In his treatment of theological themes Warfield frequently turned to Christian devotion and worship to demonstrate the indissoluble link between the church's belief and practice.[57]

* * *

Like Alexander and Hodge and the other Princetonians before him, B. B. Warfield emphasized the importance of a true spirituality for the seminary student and the minister. At the close of a defense of systematic theology in his inaugural address Warfield added:

If such be the value and use of doctrine, the systematic theologian is preeminently a preacher of the gospel; and the end of his work is obviously not merely the logical arrangement of the truths which come under his hand, but the moving of men, through their power,

[424]

to love God with all their hearts and their neighbors as themselves; to choose their portion with the Savior of their souls; to find and hold Him precious; and to recognize and yield to the sweet influences of the Holy Spirit whom He has sent. With such truth as this he will not dare to deal in a cold and merely scientific spirit, but will justly and necessarily permit its preciousness and its practical destination to determine the spirit in which he handles it, and to awaken the reverential love with which alone he should investigate its reciprocal relations. For this he needs to be suffused at all times with a sense of the unspeakable worth of the revelation which lies before him as the source of his material, and with the personal bearings of its separate truths on his heart and life; he needs to have had and to be having a full, rich, and deep religious experience of the great doctrines with which he deals; he needs to be living close to his God, to be resting always on the bosom of his Redeemer, to be filled at all times with the manifest influences of the Holy Spirit. The student of systematic theology needs a very sensitive religious nature, a most thoroughly consecrated heart, and an outpouring of the Holy Ghost upon him, such as will fill him with that spiritual discernment without which all native intellect is in vain. He needs to be not merely a student, not merely a thinker, not merely a systematizer, not merely a teacher—he needs to be like the beloved disciple himself in the highest, truest, and holiest sense, a divine.[58]

On another occasion Dr. Warfield told the Princeton students that "any proper preparation for the ministry must include these three chief parts—a training of the heart, a training of the hand, a training of the head—a devotional, a practical, and an intellectual training." "The three must be twisted together in a single three-ply cord," Warfield explained. "We are not to ask whether we will cultivate the one or the other; or whether we will give our chief attention to the one or the other. We must simultaneously push our forces over all three lines of approach, if we are to capture the stronghold of a successful ministry at all." "How are we to obtain . . . spiritual culture in the seminary?" Warfield asked. He answered, "There is but one way, brethren, to become strong in the Lord. That way is to feed on the Bread of Life!" Warfield pointed out that "public means of grace" abounded at Princeton Seminary—the Sunday morning services in the chapel, the weekly conference on Sunday afternoon, the prayers that opened every class, and the daily meeting of faculty and students "to listen to a fragment of God's Word, mingle their voices in praise to God, and ask his blessing on the labor of the day." In addition, said Warfield, "the entire work of the seminary deserves to be classed in the category of the means of grace; and the whole routine of work done here may be made a very powerful means of grace if we will only prosecute it in a right spirit and with due regard to its religious value." "I beseech you, brethren," Dr. Warfield said,

take every item of your seminary work as a religious duty. I am emphasizing the adjective in this. I mean do all your work religiously—that is, with a religious end in view, in a religious spirit, and with the religious side of it dominant in your mind. Do not lose such an opportunity as this to enlighten, deepen, and strengthen your devotion. Let nothing pass by you without sucking the honey from it. [59]

Writing in *The Presbyterian Messenger,* Warfield stated that religious experience is not the product of theology, and theology is not the product of religious experience, but "both are products of religious truth, operative in the two spheres of life and thought." Three "channels of communication"—authority, intellect, and heart—must relate harmoniously as the bases of both religion and theology. Exaggeration of authority yields to traditionalistic dogmatism that renders mute the heart and the intellect. An improper stress on intellect results in rationalistic system-building that precludes any authoritative claims of God's word or of human conscience. Following only the heart renders one susceptible to mysticism that will bow to no authoritative word or rational thought. According to Warfield,

authority, intellect, and the heart are the three sides of the triangle of truth. How they interact is observable in any concrete instance of their operation. Authority, in the Scriptures, furnishes the matter which is received in the intellect and operates on the heart. The revelations of the Scriptures do not terminate upon the intellect. They were not given merely to enlighten the mind. They were given through the intellect to beautify the life. They terminate on the heart. Again, they do not, in affecting the heart, leave the intellect untouched. They cannot be fully understood by the intellect, acting alone. The natural man cannot receive the things of the Spirit of God. They must first convert the soul before they are fully comprehended by the intellect. Only as they are lived are they understood. Hence the phrase, "Believe that you may understand," has its fullest validity. No man can intellectually grasp the full meaning of the revelations of authority, save as the result of an experience of their power in life. Hence, that the truths concerning divine things may be so comprehended that they may unite with a true system of divine truth, they must be: first, revealed in an authoritative word; second, experienced in a holy heart; and third, formulated by a sanctified intellect. Only as these three unite, then, can we have a true theology. And equally, that these same truths may be so received that they beget in us a living religion, they must be: first, revealed in an authoritative word; second, apprehended by a sound intellect; and third, experienced in an instructed heart. Only as the three unite, then, can we have a vital religion.[60]

With these words B. B. Warfield aptly summarized and exemplified the long Princeton effort to contain both "solid learning" and "piety of the heart" within the life of the seminary. In their personal examples, their teaching, and their writings, the Princeton professors committed themselves to instilling in the students in balanced measure the two parts of Princeton Seminary's goal.

*   *   *

For over a hundred years the men of Old Princeton represented —competently, consistently, and powerfully—the mainstream of the historic Christian faith. During their school's early years the Princetonians were the spokesmen for most American Presbyterians and for others who favored their orthodox Calvinism. Later, Princeton became the primary voice of Old School Presbyterianism, and then, in the latter part of the nineteenth century, of the large conservative wing of the Presbyterian church. In the early twentieth century, as many Presbyterians abandoned the old theology and American Protestantism was wracked with controversy, Princeton Seminary remained a center of orthodoxy to which Christians of different denominations looked for hope and direction.

Old Princeton ceased to exist in 1929, but through its history and literature it still inspires, instructs, and encourages. Its influence is felt in the Presbyterian Church (United States of America) and at Princeton Theological Seminary. It is strong within the Orthodox Presbyterian Church, the Presbyterian Church in America, other Presbyterian denominations, and at theological seminaries, such as Westminster, Covenant, and Reformed. Princeton's influence continues as well in the wider evangelical community. George Marsden comments: "Although the Princetonians were unhappy with many of the emphases of . . . broader evangelicalism, they nonetheless were allied with it and eventually became the intellectually most influential group in the conservative, or Bible-believing, evangelicalism that survived and now flourishes in the twentieth century. In fact, the Princetonians have been more influential in twentieth-century evangelicalism than they were among their nineteenth-century contemporaries." Oxford University theologian Alister McGrath has written: "There is new interest in the writings and ideas of the Old Princeton School, which gave nineteenth-century American evangelicalism an intellectual resilience that persisted until the rise of modernism in the 1920s diverted evangelicalism into countercultural measures of an often anti-intellectual nature."[61]

*　　*　　*

It is appropriate to end this story of Old Princeton Seminary with words of Charles Hodge's grandson Caspar Wistar Hodge Jr. On the occasion of his induction into the chair of theology in 1921 he spoke these words—as relevant today as they were then:

We are being told that the Reformed Faith or Calvinism is dead today or at least about to pass away. Doubtless it has not many representatives among the leaders of religious thought, nor does it court a place alongside the wisdom of this world. But wherever humble souls catch the vision of God in His glory, and bow in adoration and humility before Him, trusting for salvation only in His grace and power, there you have the essence of the Reformed

Faith. Once let this life blood of pure religion flow from the heart to nourish the anaemic brain and work itself out in thought, and it will wash away many a cobweb spun by a dogmatic naturalism claiming to be modern, but in reality as old as Christianity itself.

And if amongst professed theologians we find not many who accept this faith, let us thank God that here in America and in our Church, the influence of Charles Hodge, Robert Breckinridge, James Thornwell, Robert Dabney, William G. T. Shedd, and Benjamin Warfield, still lives on.

What other hope have we than that which this Reformed Faith gives us? The forces of evil are powerful in the world today in the sphere of human life. In the realm of religious thought sinister shapes arise before us, threatening our most sacred possessions. And if we look within our own hearts, often we find there treachery from the lust of the flesh and the pride of life, when we would fain keep our eye single for the glory of God. With foes on every hand around us and within; with dark clouds of yet unknown potency for harm forming on the horizon; we dare not put our trust in human help or in the human will, but only in the grace and power of God. We must take the standpoint of the Reformed Faith, and say with the Psalmist: "My soul, wait thou only upon God; for my expectation is from Him. He only is my rock and my salvation; He is my defense; I shall not be moved. In God is my salvation and glory: the rock of my strength and my refuge is in God."[62]

APPENDICES

B. B. Warfield, 1890.

1

Bibliographical Note

For bibliographical information on the earlier history of Princeton Seminary see volume 1, 431–34.

The history of the closing decades of Old Princeton is best found in *The Presbyterian Controversy: Fundamentalists, Modernists, and Moderates* (New York: Oxford University Press, 1991) by Bradley J. Longfield; *Defending the Faith: J. Gresham Machen and the Crisis of Conservative Protestantism in Modern America* (Baltimore: The Johns Hopkins University Press, 1994) by D. G. Hart; and in the dissertation by Ronald Thomas Clutter, "The Reorientation of Princeton Theological Seminary, 1900–1929" (Dallas Theological Seminary, 1982).

Numerous articles and books on specific aspects or periods of the Princeton history are indicated in the footnotes of this book.

Data on the faculty and students of Princeton Seminary (1812–1929) can be found in the footnotes of the book and in the *Biographical Catalogue of the Princeton Theological Seminary, 1815–1932*, compiled by Edward Howell Roberts (Princeton: Trustees of the Theological Seminary of the Presbyterian Church, 1933). The biographical summaries of faculty in appendix 2 are adapted from the *Biographical Catalogue*. For a statistical analysis of Princeton Seminary students, which summarizes some of the data of the seminary's biographical catalogues, see Peter Wallace and Mark Noll, "The Students of Princeton Seminary, 1812–1929: A Research Note," in *American Presbyterians* 72 (1994): 203–15. The authors comment, "To understand American elite religious life for a century or more after 1812 . . . it is difficult to think of a better place to begin than with the students who attended Princeton Seminary" (214).

[433]

For the life of Charles Hodge see A. A. Hodge, *The Life of Charles Hodge, D.D. LL.D., Professor in the Theological Seminary, Princeton, N.J.* (New York: Charles Scribner's Sons, 1880). Half of this volume is comprised of Charles Hodge's diary and letters. Of the numerous books and dissertations on Charles Hodge's theology, two have especially good treatments of his life—Charles A. Jones, "Charles Hodge, The Keeper of Orthodoxy: The Method, Purpose and Meaning of His Apologetic" (Ph.D. diss., Drew University, 1989); and John W. Stewart, "The Tethered Theology: Biblical Criticism, Common Sense Philosophy, and the Princeton Theologians, 1812–1860" (Ph.D. diss., University of Michigan, 1990).

William Henry Green's life is sketched in John D. Davis's "William Henry Green" in *The Presbyterian and Reformed Review* 11 (1900): 377–96. See also "The Jubilee of Prof. William Henry Green," in *The Presbyterian and Reformed Review* 7 (1896): 507–21. Dwayne Davis Cox's M.A. thesis (University of Louisville, 1976), "William Henry Green: Princeton Theologian," and dissertations by John W. Stewart and Marion A. Taylor provide valuable information about Green, as well as his Princeton contemporaries. See John W. Stewart, "The Tethered Theology", and Marion A. Taylor, "The Old Testament in the Old Princeton School" (Ph.D. dissertation, Yale University, 1986).

There is little published material on A. A. Hodge's life. The most valuable sources are William M. Paxton's *Address Delivered at the Funeral of Archibald Alexander Hodge* (New York: Anson D. F. Randolph, 1886) and Francis Landey Patton's *Discourse in Memory of Archibald Alexander Hodge* (Philadelphia: Tomes Printing House, 1887). An interesting volume that sheds some light on the personality of A. A. Hodge is C. A. Salmond's *Princetoniana. Charles & A. A. Hodge: with Class and Table Talk of Hodge the Younger* (Edinburgh: Oliphant, Anderson & Ferrier, 1888).

For Benjamin Breckinridge Warfield's life see the biographical sketch by Ethelbert D. Warfield in *Revelation and Inspiration* (New York: Oxford University Press, 1927); Francis L. Patton's "Benjamin B. Warfield, A Memorial Address," in *The Princeton Theological Review* (July 1921): 369–91; and Samuel G. Craig's "Benjamin B. Warfield" in *Biblical and*

Theological Studies (Philadelphia: Presbyterian and Reformed Publishing Company, 1952). Craig notes the great need for a full-length biography of Warfield. "Believing as we do that he labored within the main stream of Christianity as it makes its way across the centuries from the Proto-evangelium to the Consummation at a time when its progress, humanly speaking, was being seriously impeded—as is still the case—we are confident that such a volume would have more than a passing value" (vi). Additional valuable resources are the "Warfield Commemorative Issue, 1921–1971" of the *Banner of Truth* 89 (1971); Wilbur B. Wallis, "Benjamin B. Warfield: Didactic and Polemical Theologian," *Presbyterion: Covenant Seminary Review* 3 (1977): 73–94; Stanley W. Bamberg, "Our Image of Warfield Must Go," *Journal of the Evangelical Theological Society* 34 (1991): 229–41; Hugh T. Kerr, "Warfield: The Person Behind the Theology," paper presented at the Annie Kinkead Warfield Lectures, Princeton Seminary, February 1982.

For J. Gresham Machen's life see the biography by Ned B. Stonehouse, *J. Gresham Machen: A Biographical Memoir* (Grand Rapids: William B. Eerdmans, 1954); reprinted in 1978 by Westminster Theological Seminary and in 1987 by Banner of Truth Trust; Darryl G. Hart, "'Doctor Fundamentalis': An Intellectual Biography of J. Gresham Machen, 1881–1937" (Ph.D. diss., The Johns Hopkins University, 1988) and *Defending the Faith: J. Gresham Machen and the Crisis of Conservative Protestantism in Modern America* (Baltimore: The Johns Hopkins University Press, 1994). See also the section on Machen in Bradley J. Longfield, *The Presbyterian Controversy: Fundamentalists, Modernists, and Moderates* (New York: Oxford University Press, 1991). Additional sketches of Machen's life appear in Paul Woolley, *The Significance of J. Gresham Machen Today* (Nutley, N.J.: Presbyterian and Reformed Publishing Company, 1977); Henry W. Coray, *J. Gresham Machen: A Silhouette* (Grand Rapids: Kregel Publications, 1981); and George Marsden, "Understanding J. Gresham Machen," *Princeton Seminary Bulletin* 11 (1990): 46–60; and also in *Understanding Fundamentalism and Evangelicalism* (Grand Rapids: William B. Eerdmans Publishing Company, 1991). See also Machen's brief autobiographical sketch, "Christianity in

Conflict," in *Contemporary American Theology: Theological Auto-biographies,* ed. Vergilius Ferm (New York: Round Table Press, 1932), 245–74. A chronological bibliography of Machen's published and unpublished writings can be found in *Pressing toward the Mark: Essays Commemorating Fifty Years of the Orthodox Presbyterian Church,* eds. Charles G. Dennison and Richard C. Gamble (Philadelphia: The Committee for the Historian of the Orthodox Presbyterian Church, 1986), 461–85.

2

Biographical Summaries of Faculty

PROFESSORS

Dates refer to periods in office and names are given in chronological order of appointment.

For Archibald Alexander, Samuel Miller, Charles Hodge, John Breckinridge, Joseph Addison Alexander, James Waddel Alexander, William Henry Green, Alexander Taggart McGill, Caspar Wistar Hodge, and James Clement Moffat, see volume 1, 435–38.

CHARLES AUGUSTUS AIKEN, Ph.D., D.D.   1871–1892

Born, Manchester, Vermont, October 30, 1827; Dartmouth College, 1846; teacher, Lawrence Academy, Groton, Massachusetts, 1846–47; teacher, Phillips Academy, Andover, 1847–49; Andover Theological Seminary, 1849–50, 1852–53; University of Halle, University of Berlin and University of Leipzig, 1850–52; ordained, Congregational Church, October 19, 1854; pastor, Yarmouth, Maine, 1854–59; professor, Latin Language and Literature, Dartmouth College, 1859–66; professor, Latin Language and Literature, College of New Jersey, 1866–69; president, Union College, 1869–71; professor, Christian Ethics and Apologetics, Princeton Theological Seminary, 1871–82, Oriental and Old Testament Literature and Christian Ethics, 1882–88, Oriental and Old Testament Literature, also the Relations of Philosophy and Science to the Christian Religion, 1888–92; died, Princeton, New Jersey, January 14, 1892. Ph.D., College of New Jersey, 1866; D.D., College of New Jersey, 1870.

[437]

ARCHIBALD ALEXANDER HODGE, D.D., LL.D. 1877–1886

Born, Princeton, New Jersey, July 18, 1823; College of New Jersey, 1841; Princeton Theological Seminary, 1843–47; ordained, New Brunswick Presbytery, May 1847; missionary, Allahabad, India, 1847–50; pastor, Lower West Nottingham, Maryland, 1851–55; pastor, Fredericksburg, Virginia, 1855–61; pastor, First Church, Wilkes-Barre, Pennsylvania, 1861–64; professor, Didactic and Polemic Theology, Western Theological Seminary, 1864–77; stated supply, First Church, Pittsburgh, 1865; pastor, North Church, Allegheny City, 1866–77; associate professor, Exegetical, Didactic and Polemic Theology, Princeton Theological Seminary, 1877–79, professor, Didactic and Polemic Theology, 1879–86; died, Princeton, New Jersey, November 11, 1886. D.D., College of New Jersey, 1862; LL.D., Wooster College, 1876.

FRANCIS LANDEY PATTON, D.D., LL.D. 1881–1913

Born, Warwick, Bermuda, January 22, 1843; Knox College, Toronto; University of Toronto; Princeton Theological Seminary, 1863–65; ordained, New York Presbytery, June 1, 1865; pastor, Eighty-fourth Street Church, New York City, 1865–67; pastor, Nyack, New York, 1867–70; pastor, South Church, Brooklyn, 1871; pastor, Jefferson Park Church, Chicago, Illinois, 1874–81; professor, Theology, Theological Seminary of the Northwest, 1871–81; professor, Relations of Philosophy and Science to Christian Religion, Princeton Theological Seminary, 1881–88; president, Princeton University, 1888–1902, professor, Ethics, 1886–1913; president, Princeton Theological Seminary, 1902–13, lecturer, Theism, 1888–1903, professor, Philosophy of Religion, 1903–13, president emeritus, 1913–32; residence, Warwick, Bermuda, 1913–32; died, Warwick, November 25, 1932. D.D., Hanover College, 1872, Yale University, 1888; LL.D., Wooster College, 1878, Harvard University, 1889, University of Toronto, 1894, Yale University, 1901, Johns Hopkins University, 1902, University of Maryland, 1907, Princeton University, 1913; honorary M.A, Princeton University, 1896; Moderator, General Assembly, 1878.

WILLIAM MILLER PAXTON, D.D., LL.D.   1883–1902

Born, Adams County, Pennsylvania, June 7, 1824; Pennsylvania College, Gettysburg, 1843; Princeton Theological Seminary, 1845–48; ordained, Carlisle Presbytery, October 4, 1848; pastor, Greencastle, Pennsylvania, 1848–50; pastor, First Church, Pittsburgh, 1851–65; professor, Sacred Rhetoric, Western Theological Seminary, 1860–67; lecturer, Union Theological Seminary (New York), 1872–75; pastor, First Church, New York City, 1866–83; professor, Ecclesiastical, Homiletical and Pastoral Theology, Princeton Theological Seminary, 1883–1902, professor emeritus, 1902–4; died, Princeton, New Jersey, November 28, 1904. D.D., Jefferson College, 1860; LL.D., Washington and Jefferson College, 1883; Moderator, General Assembly, 1880.

BENJAMIN BRECKINRIDGE WARFIELD, D.D., LL.D., Litt.D. S.T.D.   1887–1921

Born, Lexington, Kentucky, November 5, 1851; College of New Jersey, 1871; Europe; editor; Princeton Theological Seminary, 1873–76; University of Leipzig, 1876–77; stated supply, Concord Church, Kentucky, 1875; stated supply, First Church, Dayton, Ohio, 1876; stated supply, First Church, Baltimore, Maryland, 1877–78; ordained evangelist, Ebenezer Presbytery, April 26, 1879; instructor, New Testament Literature and Exegesis, Western Theological Seminary, 1878, professor, 1879–87; professor, Didactic and Polemic Theology, Princeton Theological Seminary, 1887–1921; died, Princeton, New Jersey, February 16, 1921. D.D., College of New Jersey, 1880; LL.D., College of New Jersey and Davidson College, 1892; Litt.D., Lafayette College, 1911; S.T.D., University of Utrecht, 1913.

JOHN D. DAVIS, Ph.D., D.D., LL.D.   1888–1926

Born, Pittsburgh, Pennsylvania, March 5, 1854; College of New Jersey, 1879; University of Bonn, 1879–80; Europe, 1880–81; Princeton Theological Seminary, 1881–83; instructor, Hebrew, Princeton Theological Seminary, 1883–84; Hebrew Fellowship, University of Leipzig, 1884–86;

instructor, Hebrew, Princeton Theological Seminary, 1886–88; ordained, Pittsburgh Presbytery, April 26, 1887; professor, Hebrew and Cognate Languages, Princeton Theological Seminary, 1888–92, Semitic Philology and Old Testament History, 1892–1900, Oriental and Old Testament Literature, 1900–26; died, Philadelphia, Pennsylvania, June 21, 1926. Ph.D., College of New Jersey, 1886; D.D., Princeton University, 1898; LL.D., Washington and Jefferson College, 1902.

GEORGE TYBOUT PURVES, D.D., LL.D. 1892–1900

Born, Philadelphia, Pennsylvania, September 27, 1852; University of Pennsylvania, 1872; Princeton Theological Seminary, 1873–77; ordained, Chester Presbytery, April 27, 1877; pastor, Wayne, Pennsylvania, 1877–80; pastor, Boundary Avenue Church, Baltimore, Maryland, 1880–86; pastor, First Church, Pittsburgh, Pennsylvania, 1886–92; professor, New Testament Literature and Exegesis, Princeton Theological Seminary, 1892–1900; stated supply, First Church, Princeton, 1895–99, pastor, 1899–1900; pastor, Fifth Avenue Church, New York City, 1900–1; died, New York City, September 24, 1901. D.D., Washington and Jefferson College, 1888, University of Pennsylvania, 1894; LL.D., Lafayette College, 1895.

JOHN DeWITT, D.D., LL.D. 1892–1912

Born, Harrisburg, Pennsylvania, October 10, 1842; College of New Jersey, 1861; law student; Princeton Theological Seminary, 1861–63; Union Theological Seminary (New York); ordained, New York Presbytery, June 9, 1865; pastor, Irvington, New York, 1865–69; pastor, Centennial Congregational Church, Boston, Massachusetts, 1869–76; pastor, Tenth Presbyterian Church, Philadelphia, 1876–82; professor, Ecclesiastical History, Lane Theological Seminary, 1882–88; professor, Apologetics, McCormick Theological Seminary, 1888–92; professor, Church History, Princeton Theological Seminary, 1892–1912, professor emeritus; died, Princeton, New Jersey, November 19, 1923. D.D., College of New Jersey, 1877; LL.D., Hanover College, 1888.

WILLIAM BRENTON GREENE JR., D.D.   1892–1928

Born, Providence, Rhode Island, August 16, 1854; College of New Jersey, 1876; teacher; Princeton Theological Seminary, 1877–80; ordained, Boston Presbytery, June 3, 1880; pastor, First Church, Boston, Massachusetts, 1880–83; pastor, Tenth Church, Philadelphia, Pennsylvania, 1883–92; Stuart professor, Relation of Philosophy and Science to the Christian Religion, Princeton Theological Seminary, 1892–1903, Apologetics and Christian Ethics, 1903–28; died, Princeton, New Jersey, November 16, 1928. D.D., College of New Jersey, 1891.

GEERHARDUS VOS, Ph.D., D.D.   1893–1932

Born, Heerenveen, Netherlands, March 14, 1862; Amsterdam Gymnasium, 1881; Calvin Theological Seminary, 1881–83; Princeton Theological Seminary, 1883–85; Fellowship, Hebrew, University of Berlin, 1885–86; University of Strasbourg, 1886–88, Ph.D.; professor, Theology, Calvin Theological Seminary, 1888–93; ordained evangelist, New Brunswick Presbytery, April 24, 1894; professor, Biblical Theology, Princeton Theological Seminary, 1893–1932, professor emeritus, 1932–49; residence, Roaring Branch, Pennsylvania, 1932–33; Santa Ana, California, 1933–41; Grand Rapids, Michigan, 1941–49; died, Grand Rapids, August 13, 1949. D.D., Lafayette College, 1893.

WILLIAM PARK ARMSTRONG, D.D.   1899–1944

Born, Selma, Alabama, January 10, 1874; College of New Jersey, 1894, 1896, M.A.; Princeton Theological Seminary, 1894–97, 1899; University of Marburg, 1897; University of Berlin, 1897–98; University of Erlangen, 1898; ordained, New Brunswick Presbytery, July 2, 1900; instructor, New Testament Literature, Princeton Theological Seminary, 1899–1903, professor, New Testament Literature and Exegesis, 1903–40, graduate professor, New Testament Exegesis, 1940–44; died, Princeton, March 25, 1944. D.D., Temple University, 1915.

ROBERT DICK WILSON, Ph.D., D.D., LL.D.   1900–1929

Born, Indiana, Pennsylvania, February 4, 1856; College of New Jersey, 1876, 1879, M.A., 1886, Ph.D.; Western Theological Seminary, 1880–81; University of Berlin, 1881–83; instructor, Old Testament, Western Theological Seminary, 1883–85, professor, 1885–1900; professor, Semitic Philology and Old Testament Introduction, Princeton Theological Seminary, 1900–29; professor, Semitic Philology and Old Testament Criticism, Westminster Theological Seminary, 1929–30; died, Philadelphia, Pennsylvania, October 11, 1930. D.D., Lafayette College, 1894; LL.D., Wooster College, 1921.

CASPAR WISTAR HODGE, Ph.D., LL.D., D.D.   1901–1937

Born, Princeton, New Jersey, September 22, 1870; College of New Jersey, 1892, 1894, Ph.D.; Heidelberg University; University of Berlin; instructor, Philosophy, Princeton University, 1895–97; associate professor, Ethics, Lafayette College, 1897–98; Princeton Theological Seminary, 1898–1901; ordained, New Brunswick Presbytery, September 18, 1902; instructor, New Testament, Princeton Theological Seminary, 1901–2, assistant, Dogmatic Theology, 1901–7, assistant professor, Didactic and Polemic Theology, 1907–15, professor, Dogmatic Theology, 1915–21, professor, Systematic Theology, 1921–37; died, Princeton, February 26, 1937. D.D., Grove City College, 1935.

CHARLES ROSENBURY ERDMAN, D.D., LL.D.   1905–1936

Born, Fayetteville, New York, July 20, 1866; College of New Jersey, 1886; teacher; Princeton Theological Seminary, 1887–89, 1890–91; ordained, Philadelphia North Presbytery, May 8, 1891; stated supply, Overbrook Church, Philadelphia, Pennsylvania, 1890–91, pastor, 1891–97; pastor, First Church, Germantown, 1897–1906; professor, Practical Theology, Princeton Theological Seminary, 1905–36, professor emeritus, 1936–60; pastor, First Church, Princeton, New Jersey, 1924–34; died, 1960. D.D., Wooster College, 1912, Princeton University, 1925; LL.D., Davidson College, 1924; Moderator, General Assembly, 1925.

FREDERICK WILLIAM LOETSCHER, Ph.D., D.D., LL.D.
1910–1945

Born, Dubuque, Iowa, May 15, 1875; Princeton University, 1896, 1901, M.A., 1906, Ph.D.; teacher, Lawrenceville School, New Jersey; Princeton Theological Seminary, 1897–1901; Newberry Scholar; University of Berlin, 1901–2; University of Strasbourg, 1902–3; ordained, New Brunswick Presbytery, December 19, 1903; instructor, Church History, Princeton Theological Seminary, 1903–7; pastor, Oxford Church, Philadelphia, Pennsylvania, 1907–10; professor, Homiletics, Princeton Theological Seminary, 1910–13, Church History, 1913–45; professor, Church History, Temple University, 1945–51; died, Princeton, July 31, 1966. D.D., Lafayette College, 1914; LL.D., University of Dubuque, 1918.

JOSEPH ROSS STEVENSON, D.D., LL.D. 1914–1936

Born, Ligonier, Pennsylvania, March 1, 1866; Washington and Jefferson College, 1886, 1889, M.A.; McCormick Theological Seminary, 1886–89; University of Berlin, 1889–90; ordained, Kansas City Presbytery, December 31, 1890; pastor, Broadway Church, Sedalia, Missouri, 1890–94; adjunct professor, Ecclesiastical History, McCormick Theological Seminary, 1894–97, professor, 1897–1902; pastor, Fifth Avenue Church, New York City, 1902–9; pastor, Brown Memorial Church, Baltimore, Maryland, 1909–14; president, Princeton Theological Seminary, 1914–36, president emeritus, 1936–39, professor, History of Religion and Christian Missions, 1914–29, acting professor, Homiletics, 1929–30; died, Princeton, August 13, 1939. D.D., Washington and Jefferson College, 1897, University of Edinburgh, 1919, Presbyterian Theological College (Halifax, Nova Scotia), 1920; LL.D., Ursinus College, 1908, Lafayette College, 1915; Moderator, General Assembly, 1915.

JONATHAN RITCHIE SMITH, D.D. 1914–1929

Born, Baltimore, Maryland, June 23, 1852; College of New Jersey, 1872; law study; Princeton Theological Seminary, 1873–76; ordained, Westchester Presbytery, June 26, 1876;

pastor, First Church, Peekskill, New York, 1876–98; pastor, Market Square Church, Harrisburg, Pennsylvania, 1900–14; professor, Homiletics, Princeton Theological Seminary, 1914–29; professor emeritus; residence, Englewood, New Jersey; died, Englewood, February 23, 1936. D.D., Franklin and Marshall College, 1903.

Associate and Assistant Professors

ANDREW CAMPBELL ARMSTRONG JR., Ph.D., L.H.D.
1886–1887

Born, New York City, August 22, 1860; College of New Jersey, 1881, Fellow, 1881–82, M.A.; Princeton Theological Seminary, 1882–85; University of Berlin, 1885–86; associate professor, Church History, Princeton Theological Seminary, 1886–87; ordained, New York Presbytery, February 7, 1887; instructor, College of New Jersey, 1887–88; professor, Philosophy, Wesleyan University (Connecticut), 1888–1930, professor emeritus, 1930–35; died, Cromwell, Connecticut, February 21, 1935. Ph.D., College of New Jersey, 1896; L.H.D., Wesleyan University, 1930.

JAMES OSCAR BOYD, Ph.D., D.D.
1900–1915

Born, Rahway, New Jersey, October 17, 1874; New York University, 1895; Butler Fellow, New York University, University of Erlangen, 1895–96; Princeton Theological Seminary, 1896–99, B.D., GS Green Fellow, 1899–1900; Princeton University, 1905, Ph.D.; ordained, New York Presbytery, June 3, 1900; instructor, Old Testament Literature, Princeton Theological Seminary, 1900–7, assistant professor, Oriental and Old Testament Literature, 1907–15; pastor, Church of the Redeemer, Paterson, New Jersey, 1915–21; YMCA, war service, 1918–19; secretary, Arabic-Levant Agency, American Bible Society, 1921–26; secretary, Levant Agency, 1926–44; died, Oneida, New York, August 14, 1947. D.D., New York University, 1915.

JOHN GRESHAM MACHEN, D.D., Litt.D.   1906–1929

Born, Baltimore, Maryland, July 28, 1881; Johns Hopkins University, 1901, graduate study, 1901–2; Princeton Theological Seminary, 1902–5, B.D.; Princeton University, 1904, M.A.; New Testament Fellow, University of Marburg and University of Göttingen, 1905–6; instructor, New Testament, Princeton Theological Seminary, 1906–14, assistant professor, New Testament Literature and Exegesis, 1914–29; ordained, New Brunswick Presbytery, June 23, 1914; YMCA, war service, 1918–19; professor, New Testament, Westminster Theological Seminary, 1929–37; died, Bismark, North Dakota, January 1, 1937. D.D., Hampden-Sydney College, 1921; Litt.D., Wheaton College (Illinois), 1928.

OSWALD THOMPSON ALLIS, Ph.D., D.D.   1910–1929

Born, Wallingford, Pennsylvania, September 9, 1880; University of Pennsylvania, 1901; Princeton Theological Seminary, 1902–5, B.D.; GS Green Fellow, Hebrew, 1905–7; Princeton University, 1907, M.A.; University of Berlin, 1907–10, 1913, Ph.D.; ordained, Philadelphia Presbytery, May 31, 1914; instructor, Semitic Philology, Princeton Theological Seminary, 1910–22, assistant professor, 1922–29; professor, Old Testament History and Exegesis, Westminster Theological Seminary, 1929–30, Old Testament 1930–49; died, Wayne, Pennsylvania, January 12, 1973. D.D., Hampden-Sydney College, 1927.

NOTES

NOTES

Preface

1. John Oliver Nelson, "The Rise of the Princeton Theology: A Genetic Study of American Presbyterianism until 1850" (Ph.D. diss., Yale University, 1935), 298–99.

1. Faith and Learning

1. *PRR* 8 (1897): 662.
2. Until the late nineteenth century, theological seminaries offered the most advanced scholarship in the humanities and social sciences. See W. Bruce Leslie, *Gentlemen and Scholars: College and Community in the "Age of the University," 1865–1917* (University Park: Pennsylvania State University Press, 1992).
3. *Memorial Book of the Sesquicentennial Celebration of the Founding of the College of New Jersey and of the Ceremonies Inaugurating Princeton University* (New York: Charles Scribners, 1898), 82. A. A. Hodge later wrote: "Professor Guyot lived in Princeton then; a man of great genius, as highly educated a man of science as I ever saw. He was for many years professor of history in the University of Lausanne, before he gave himself up to material science. He was one of the most devout Christians who ever kindled the flame of holy love from the light of nature and revelation; he was absolutely a believer in the Bible as it stood in every way." A. A. Hodge, *Popular Lectures on Theological Themes* (Philadelphia: Presbyterian Board of Publications, 1887; repr., as *Evangelical Theology: Lectures on Doctrine,* Edinburgh: The Banner of Truth Trust, 1976), 150–51.
4. Professor Charles West of Princeton College wrote: "Rarely has academic history repeated itself with such precision and emphasis as in the person of James McCosh, who, though unique in his own generation, had a real prototype in the person of one, though only one, of his predecessors, President John Witherspoon, the ruler of Princeton a century ago. Each of them was in point of ancestry a Covenanter, by birth a Lowland Scotchman, in his youth a student in the University of Edinburgh, in his manhood a minister of the Church of Scotland at a crisis in its history, and in that crisis an important

[449]

figure, Witherspoon heading the opposition to moderatism and Dr. McCosh helping to form the Free Church." *Sesquicentennial Celebration of the College of New Jersey*, 665–66. Witherspoon arrived at Princeton in 1768, McCosh in 1868. Each lived in Princeton the last twenty-six years of his life, dying a century apart almost to the day—Witherspoon on November 15, 1794, and McCosh on November 16, 1894.

5. *Sesquicentennial Celebration of the College of New Jersey*, 440; J. David Hoeveler Jr., *James McCosh and the Scottish Intellectual Tradition: from Glasgow to Princeton* (Princeton: Princeton University Press, 1981), 226.

6. *Inauguration of James McCosh, D.D., LL.D. as President of the College of New Jersey* (New York: Robert Carter and Brothers, 1868), 94; Hoeveler, *James McCosh*, 93. Thomas Chalmers (1780–1847) was Scotland's greatest nineteenth-century churchman and leader in the Free Church, ending his days as principal and professor of theology in New College, Edinburgh. William Hamilton (1788–1856) was distinguished professor of philosophy and one of the last major representatives of Scottish Realism. Thomas Guthrie (1803–73) was an important social reformer and noted preacher. McCosh described Guthrie as "the pictorial preacher of the age." D. K. and C. J. Guthrie, *Autobiography of Thomas Guthrie, D.D. and Memoir* (London, 1877), 266.

7. *PRR* 6 (1895): 651; *PTR* 1 (1903): 340. The quotations are from Francis L. Patton and Alexander T. Ormond, a student and then teacher in the department of philosophy at Princeton College. According to David N. Livingstone, McCosh's book attempted "to temper Scottish philosophy's rationalistic tendencies with the evangelical sense of sin and belief in an omnipotent deity." David N. Livingstone, *Darwin's Forgotten Defenders: the Encounter between Evangelical Theology and Evolutionary Thought* (Grand Rapids: Wm. B. Eerdmans; Edinburgh: Scottish Academic Press, 1987), 107.

8. *PRR* 6 (1895): 652.

9. *PRR* 8 (1897): 663.

10. James McCosh, *The Life of James McCosh: A Record Chiefly Autobiographical,* ed. William Milligan Sloane (Edinburgh: T. & T. Clark, 1896), 184.

11. *Inauguration of James McCosh,* vi, 11.

12. *Inauguration of James McCosh,* 93–94.

13. Hoeveler, *James McCosh,* 265.

14. *Sesquicentennial Celebration of the College of New Jersey,* 440;

Leslie, *Gentlemen and Scholars*, 107.

15. John Calvin, *Institutes of the Christian Religion* 1, 5, 1–2.

16. Thomas Jefferson Wertenbaker, *Princeton, 1746–1896* (Princeton: Princeton University Press, 1946), 285. Charles W. Shields, *Philosophia Ultima; or, Science of the Sciences*, 2 vols. (London: Sampson Low, Marston, Searle & Rivington, 1889). Shields is described in the *Dictionary of American Biography* as "one of the last of that venerable band of clerical professors in the Eastern endowed colleges who regarded themselves and were regarded by others as no less defenders of Christian orthodoxy than teachers of literature, philosophy, and science." He became an advocate of reunion of the Protestant churches and entered the Episcopal ministry in 1898.

17. Archibald Alexander, "Inaugural Address," in Mark A. Noll, ed., *The Princeton Theology, 1812–1921: Scripture, Science and Theological Method from Archibald Alexander to Benjamin Breckinridge Warfield* (Grand Rapids: Baker Book House, 1983), 84.

18. *BRTR* 1 (1829): 101–20; Anita Schorsch, "Samuel Miller, Renaissance Man: His Legacy of 'True Taste,'" *JPH* 66 (1988): 85–86; Charles Hodge, *Sermon before the Board of Foreign Missions in the Church in University Place, May 7, 1848, on the Teaching Office of the Church* (New York: Board of Foreign Missions, 1882), 15; *BRPR* 31 (1859): 106; Jonathan Wells, "Charles Hodge on the Bible and Science," *AP* 66 (1988): 158.

19. Charles Hodge, *Systematic Theology*, 3 vols. (New York: Charles Scribner and Company, 1871–73; repr., Grand Rapids: William B. Eerdmans Publishing Company, 1979) 1: 1, 57, 171, 573.

20. Hodge, *Evangelical Theology*, 150. See William Henry Green's article on the genealogies of Genesis, "Primeval Chronology," *Bibliotheca Sacra* 47 (1890): 285–303. Although Charles Hodge believed that the Bible did not teach the date of the creation of man, he felt that 10,000 years was sufficient. A. A. Hodge increased that time to 16,000, but he did not seem concerned if science should go beyond that. B. B. Warfield speculated that 200,000 years may have elapsed between Adam and Abraham. Caspar W. Hodge reduced Warfield's span to 20,000 years for the same period. Deryl Freeman Johnson, "The Attitudes of the Princeton Theologians Toward Darwinism and Evolution from 1859–1929" (Ph.D. diss., University of Iowa, 1968), 287.

21. *AP* 66 (1988): 160.
22. In his *Systematic Theology* Hodge mentions the "interval" theory but defends the "era" theory as the best method of reconciling the Mosaic account with the scientific facts, *Systematic Theology* 1: 570–74.
23. *BRPR* 31 (1859): 115; *BRPR* 34 (1862): 461. For Princeton and evolution see Johnson, "The Attitudes of the Princeton Theologians Toward Darwinism"; and Charles Hodge, *What is Darwinism? And Other Writings on Science and Religion*, eds. Mark A. Noll and David N. Livingstone (Grand Rapids: Baker Books, 1994). This volume contains a valuable "Introduction: Charles Hodge and the Definition of 'Darwinism.'" I am especially indebted to W. Brian Aucker, "Hodge and Warfield on Evolution," *Presbyterion: Covenant Seminary Review* 20 (1994): 131–42.
24. David N. Livingstone, "The Idea of Design: The Vicissitudes of a Key Concept in the Princeton Response to Darwin," *Scottish Journal of Theology* 37 (1984), 330. Livingstone wrote: "Hodge's scientifically literate ruminations on the subject . . . demonstrate just how genuine was his concern to marry theological reflection to scientific research." In his discussion of theologians in *Darwin's Forgotten Defenders*, Livingstone concentrates on the Princeton school "because its faculty were in many ways the classical theological architects of modern conservative evangelicalism" (xii). Livingstone, *Darwin's Forgotten Defenders*, 102–3. Jonathan Wells argues that Charles Hodge, "the most prominent anti-Darwinian theologian in America," based his objection to Darwinism on the argument *to* not *from* design, that is, belief in a designed world is the outcome of a prior belief in God and the Scripture. "Charles Hodge believed in design because he believed in God, not in a God because he saw design," writes Wells. Jonathan Wells, *Charles Hodge's Critique of Darwinism: An Historical-Critical Analysis of Concepts Basic to the 19th Century Debate* (Lewiston, New York: Edwin Mellen Press, 1988), 215. Hodge, *Systematic Theology* 2: 12–33.
25. Hodge, *What is Darwinism?* eds. Noll and Livingstone, "Introduction," 26.
26. Charles Hodge, *What is Darwinism?* (New York: Scribners, Armstrong and Company, 1874); Hodge, *What is Darwinism?* eds. Noll and Livingstone, 78, 89, 155–57.
27. Hodge, *What is Darwinism?* eds. Noll and Livingstone, 157.
28. "Asa Gray's Review of *What is Darwinism?*" in Hodge, *What is*

Darwinism? eds. Noll and Livingstone, 169. Several modern historians of science regard Hodge's *What is Darwinism?* as one of the most perceptive works of its period precisely because it defines Darwinism as an ateleological cosmology. See Neal C. Gillespie, *Charles Darwin and the Problem of Creation* (Chicago: University of Chicago Press, 1979), 112; and Walter J. Wilkins, *Science and Religious Thought: A Darwinian Case Study* (Ann Arbor: UMI Research Press, 1987), 44.

29. Charles A. Jones, "Charles Hodge, The Keeper of Orthodoxy: The Method, Purpose and Meaning of His Apologetic" (Ph.D. diss., Drew University, 1989), 132; Hodge, *What is Darwinism?* eds. Noll and Livingstone, "Introduction," 33. Jonathan Wells concludes that Christianity and Darwinism "cannot be regarded as compatible . . . unless the former is taken to mean something other than what the mainstream theological tradition has meant by Christianity, or the latter is taken to mean something other than what Charles Darwin meant by Darwinism." Wells, *Charles Hodge's Critique of Darwinism*, 223.

30. Hodge, *What is Darwinism?* eds. Noll and Livingstone, "Introduction," 38, 138, 149. See also David N. Livingstone, "Darwinism and Calvinism: The Belfast-Princeton Connection," *Isis* (1992): 408–28. Hodge's sense of humor, which so endeared him to his students, appears in his footnote to the above quotation. Hodge wrote: "We have heard a story of a gentleman who gave an artist a commission for a historical painting, and suggested as the subject the passage of the Israelites over the Red Sea. In due time he was informed that his picture was finished, and was shown by the artist a large canvas painted red. 'What is that?' he asked. 'Why,' says the artist, 'that is the Red Sea.' 'But where are the Israelites?' 'Oh, they have passed over.' 'And where are the Egyptians?' 'They are under the sea.'"

31. George M. Marsden, *The Soul of the American University: From Protestant Establishment to Established Nonbelief* (New York: Oxford University Press, 1994), 203; Wertenbaker, *Princeton*, 312; James McCosh, *The Religious Aspect of Evolution* (New York: Charles Scribner's Sons, 1890), 58; Livingstone, *Darwin's Forgotten Defenders*, 106; *PTR* 1 (1903): 345; James McCosh, *Christianity and Positivism: A Series of Lectures to the Times on Natural Theology and Christian Apologetics* (London, 1871), 90–92. Francis L. Patton summed up McCosh's view on evolution by stating that "he undertook to show that

evolution can do some things and that there are some things it cannot do: and that so far as it claimed to be a theory explanatory of the origin of species it was a mistake to regard it as atheistic or in irreconcilable hostility to the Bible." *PRR* 6 (1895): 658.

32. David Starr Jordan, *The Days of a Man, being memories of a naturalist, teacher, and minor prophet of democracy* (Yonkers-on-Hudson, N.Y.: World, 1922) 1: 150–51; McCosh, *Christianity and Positivism*, 43.

33. *PR* 8 (1887): 617, 622, 624–25; *PR* 10 (1889): 220.

34. Arnold Guyot, *Creation; or, The Biblical Cosmogony in the Light of Modern Science* (New York: C. Scribner's Sons, 1884), 118.

35. Hoeveler, *James McCosh*, 253; Theodore Ledyard Cuyler, *Recollections of a Long Life: An Autobiography* (New York: Baker and Taylor Company, 1902), 239.

36. C. A. Salmond, who studied at Princeton Seminary in 1877–78, wrote that "the atmosphere of American colleges is still, at least in certain instances, including Princeton, to a noteworthy extent a *religious* atmosphere." C. A. Salmond, *Princetoniana: Charles and A. A. Hodge; with Class and Table Talk of Hodge the Younger* (New York: Scribner and Welford, 1888), 18. David Riddle Williams, *James H. Brookes: A Memoir* (St. Louis: Presbyterian Board of Publication, 1897), 275. *The Princeton Alumni Weekly* 16 (April 19, 1916): 653. Warfield wrote: "With nearly a fourth of the students in the College looking towards the Seminary and nearly a third of the students in the Seminary looking back to the College, the path between the two institutions was naturally beaten very smooth." During the 1872–73 academic year, 51 out of the 117 students in the seminary were graduates of Princeton College.

37. *Autobiography of the Rev. William Arnot and Memoir* (London: James Nisbet and Company, 1878), 436.

38. Cuyler, *Recollections*, 238.

39. Greville MacDonald, *George MacDonald and His Wife* (London: George Allen and Unwin, 1924), 441. The 500 students who came to hear George MacDonald composed nearly the entire college and seminary.

40. E. J. Goodspeed, *Moody and Sankey in Great Britain and America* (St. Louis and Chicago: N. D. Thompson and Co., 1876), 407, 415.

41. Mark A. Noll, *A History of Christianity in the United States and Canada* (Grand Rapids: William B. Eerdmans Publishing Company, 1992), 289; Stanley N. Gundry, *Love Them In: The*

Life and Theology of D. L. Moody (Grand Rapids: Baker Book House, 1976), 82, 84, 123, 137–38, 201–2.

42. *PQPR* 5 (1876): 716–17. For an account of Moody's reception by British Calvinists, see Iain H. Murray, *Revival and Revivalism: The Making and Marring of American Evangelicalism, 1750–1858* (Edinburgh: The Banner of Truth Trust, 1994), appendix 1, "Revivalism in Britain," 391–414.

2. Jubilee!

1. Stephen Colwell, *New Themes for the Protestant Clergy: Creeds Without Charity, Theology Without Humanity, and Protestantism Without Christianity* (Philadelphia: Lippincott, Grambo and Company, 1851), 115.
2. Charles A. Aiken, *Addresses and Essays* (New York, 1871), 3.
3. *PQPR* 1 (1872): 26–29.
4. For a summary of Atwater's views see Lyman H. Atwater, "The Doctrinal Attitude of Old School Presbyterians," *Bibliotheca Sacra* 21 (1864): 65–126.
5. Nelson, "The Princeton Theology," 298–99. A collection of some of Charles Hodge's most important essays appeared in 1857 as *Essays and Reviews: Selected from the Princeton Review* (New York: Robert Carter, 1857), and has been recently republished by Garland Publishing in its series "American Religious Thought of the 18th and 19th Centuries."
6. *LCH*, 390–91.
7. E. David Willis-Watkins, "Systematic Theology by Charles Hodge," *AP* 66 (1988): 269.
8. *AP* 66 (1988): 270; Hodge, *Systematic Theology* 1: 17; *LCH*, 516.
9. G. F. Barbour, *The Life of Alexander Whyte D.D.* (New York: George H. Doran, 1924), 172.
10. *Sword and Trowel* (1872): 141.
11. David F. Wells, "The Stout and Persistent 'Theology' of Charles Hodge," *Christianity Today*, August 30, 1974, 12. Hodge's *Systematic Theology* has remained in print, and for decades it was used as the basic theology text in many seminaries. In 1950 Martyn Lloyd-Jones answered a letter requesting advice on theology books with the following recommendations: Charles Hodge's *Systematic Theology*, B. B. Warfield's *Revelation and Inspiration*, and John Calvin's *Institutes of the Christian Religion*. Lloyd-Jones added, "If you master these you really need no more, but of course there are many lesser books which are of great value." Iain H. Murray, *David*

Martyn Lloyd-Jones: The Fight of Faith, 1939–1981 (Edinburgh: The Banner of Truth Trust, 1990), 421. In 1995 it was reported that Hodge's *Systematic Theology* was "still the primary textbook for theology in the one remaining seminary in North Korea." The Pulitzer Prize-winning writer Annie Dillard is said to have "read Charles Hodge's *Systematic Theology* aloud"! Philip Yancey, "A Pilgrim's Progress," *Books & Culture: A Christian Review* (September/October 1995): 12. An abridged edition, of 565 pages, edited by Edward N. Gross, was published in 1988 by Baker Book House.

12. Salmond, *Princetoniana*, 48; Charles Hodge, *The Church and Its Polity* (London: Thomas Nelson and Sons, 1879). The quotations in the above paragraph are from A. A. Hodge's preface to his father's volume (iii, iv). James Moffatt's *Presbyterian Churches* (London: Methuen & Co., 1928) refers to Charles Hodge as "one of the soundest Presbyterian churchmen" (98–99).

13. *Henry Boynton Smith: His Life and Work*, ed. Elizabeth L. Smith (New York: A. C. Armstrong, 1881), 362.

14. *LCH*, 515–17.

15. *LCH*, 259. A. A. Hodge judged Krauth's *Conservative Theology* as "the best book on Lutheran theology in the English language." Salmond, *Princetoniana*, 195. One who did not speak was William G. T. Shedd, since Union Seminary in New York was represented by Shedd's colleague Henry B. Smith. During the day Shedd and a friend were walking under the shade of the old trees on the campus of Princeton College. The conversation turned to the occasion that had brought them to Princeton. Dr. Shedd looked at the buildings and grounds of the college and said, "Yes, colleges like this *cost*. They take time; they call for self-denial; they demand lives consecrated to their service. But they pay—sometimes pay largely, and pay all at once. Princeton College gave back to the Church and the State a fine interest on all that is invested here when it produced such a man, as Charles Hodge." *The Presbyterian*, April 29, 1896.

16. *LCH*, 518–19.

17. *LCH*, 528, 530.

18. *SSW* 1: 437.

19. *LCH*, 236, 536. A gynecologist, Hugh Lenox Hodge was professor of obstetrics at the University of Pennsylvania from 1835 to 1863 and author of a number of respected medical texts. He was a lifelong member of Second Presbyterian

Church in Philadelphia. When, in 1868, the congregation decided to move from Seventh and Arch streets to a new building on the corner of Walnut and Twenty-first streets, Dr. Hodge was chosen as chairman of the building committee. He lived to see the beautiful building completed and was present at its dedication. Hugh Hodge had seven sons, five of whom survived him. Four entered the ministry, and one became a noted Philadelphia surgeon.

20. *LCH*, 547; *History, Essays, Orations, and Other Documents of the Sixth General Conference of the Evangelical Alliance Held in New York, October 2–12, 1873* (New York, 1874), 11. I am indebted to Dr. John William Stewart, Associate Professor of Ministry and Evangelism at Princeton Seminary, for calling my attention to this prayer.

21. *LCH*, 548–50. One foreign delegate said, "It paid me for crossing the ocean just to see Dr. Hodge during that glorious speech." When a Baptist paper expressed its disapproval of the catholicity of his address, Charles Hodge wrote a courteous reply in which he defended his views and signed the letter "Your brother in the bonds which no difference between Baptists and Pedo-baptists can sunder." *LCH*, 550.

22. Charles Hodge, *A Discourse delivered at the Re-opening of the Chapel, September 27, 1874* (Princeton: Chas. S. Robinson, 1874), 36. In 1893 the chapel was named in honor of Samuel Miller. In 1933 Miller Chapel was moved to its present site, enlarged, and restored. Most of the present interior represents restoration work, although the carving of the gallery parapet and the columns supporting the gallery are original.

23. *Encyclopedia of the Presbyterian Church in the United States of America* (1884), 724.

24. The land and the three buildings donated by James Lenox cost $100,000. The generosity of the Lenox family toward Princeton Seminary continued when James Lenox's sister, Henrietta Lenox, donated an additional $100,000 after her brother's death in 1880 and, on her own death a decade later, left a bequest for an equal amount.

3. *The Hodges: Father and Sons*

1. *LCH*, 573.

2. *Addresses at the Inauguration of Rev. Archibald Alex. Hodge, D.D., LL.D. as Associate Professor of Didactic and Polemic Theology in the*

Theological Seminary at Princeton, N.J., Nov. 8, 1877 (Philadelphia: Sherman and Co., 1877), 8, 10–11, 15–16.

3. *Inauguration of Archibald Alex. Hodge,* 17–21, 25, 38; Salmond, *Princetoniana,* 85.

4. *LCH,* 574.

5. Francis L. Patton, *Archibald Alexander Hodge: A Memorial Discourse* (Philadelphia: Times Printing House, 1887). Patton's tribute to A. A. Hodge was reprinted in the Banner of Truth edition of Hodge's *Evangelical Theology,* ix–xli. Patton, "Discourse," in Hodge, *Evangelical Theology,* xiii–xiv.

6. A. A. Hodge, *Outlines of Theology* (New York: R. Carter & Brothers, 1860), 8; Patton, "Discourse," in Hodge, *Evangelical Theology,* xv–xvi. In his memorial discourse for A. A. Hodge, Francis Patton used Hodge's call to Lower West Nottingham as a rebuke to ministers who would not take small, poor churches. They "seem to have the impression," Patton stated, "that if they bury themselves in small places remote from cities and away from railroads, God will not know how to find them when the great work is ready which he has for them to do." Patton, "Discourse," in Hodge, *Evangelical Theology,* xv.

7. In reviewing a book by Samuel G. Craig, minister of the North Presbyterian Church, William Brenton Greene wrote: "Mr. Craig, in the preface of his volume, speaks of these discourses as 'Sermon-Lectures,' and they deserve the title. Their solid substance and attractive literary form will recall to some of the older members of the congregation the angelic Doctor, A. A. Hodge, who was the first pastor of the church, and gave many a course of Sermon-Lectures which attracted and fascinated the leading minds of all the region round about." *PTR* 13 (1915): 498.

8. Patton, "Discourse," in Hodge, *Evangelical Theology,* xviii.

9. Francis L. Patton, *Caspar Wistar Hodge: A Memorial Address* (New York: Anson D. F. Randolph and Company, 1891), 9, 29–30.

10. Salmond, *Princetoniana,* 88.

11. Patton, *Caspar Wistar Hodge,* 50, 56.

12. *PSB* 15 (1921): 12; *Centennial Celebration of the Theological Seminary of the Presbyterian Church in the United States of America at Princeton, New Jersey* (Princeton: at the Theological Seminary, 1912), 520; Charles Beatty Alexander, *Address Delivered, By Invitation of the Directors, on the Occasion of the One Hundredth Anniversary of the Seminary in Alexander Hall, Princeton, New Jersey, May 6, 1912* (Princeton: printed for the Seminary, 1912), 16.

13. Thomas Cary Johnson, *The Life and Letters of Robert Lewis Dabney* (Edinburgh: The Banner of Truth Trust, 1977), 368; *Centennial Celebration of the Theological Seminary*, 520. Thirteen per cent of the more than 3,000 students who attended the seminary between 1815 and 1889 were foreign born. Between 1815 and 1879, 220 Princeton Seminary students were born in Britain and Ireland and 100 in Canada.

14. William Berryman Scott, *Some Memories of a Palaeontologist* (Princeton: Princeton University Press, 1939), 75. Hodge may have read Darwin's *Journal of a Naturalist.* The title in Scott's account, *Voyage of a Naturalist,* seems to be a confusion of two of Darwin's books, *Journal of a Naturalist* and *Voyage of the Beagle.* Hodge, *What is Darwinism?* eds. Noll and Livingstone, "Introduction," 31.

15. Charles Hodge, *Conference Papers or Analyses of Discourses, Doctrinal and Practical; Delivered on Sabbath Afternoons to the Students of the Theological Seminary, Princeton, N.J.* (New York: Charles Scribner's Sons, 1879; repr. as *Princeton Sermons; Outlines of Discourses, Doctrinal and Practical* (London: The Banner of Truth Trust, 1958), 371–73.

16. Salmond, *Princetoniana*, 42.

17. Francis L. Patton, "Charles Hodge," *PR* 6 (1881): 377.

18. *LCH,* 251, 430.

19. Lyman H. Atwater, *A Discourse Commemorative of the Late Dr. Charles Hodge* (Princeton: Charles S. Robinson, 1878).

20. *LCH,* 253, 599, 613.

21. *LCH,* 585, 616.

22. Cuyler, *Recollections,* 219.

23. C. A. Salmond wrote that "apart from occasional bursts of eloquence," Charles Hodge "was never to become an eminent preacher." Salmond, *Princetoniana,* 20. Hodge's contention that the salvation of all infants dying in infancy is a doctrine which has been held by all evangelical Protestants is an example of Hodge's overstating the facts. See Hodge, *Systematic Theology* 1:26–27. *LCH,* 252.

24. Salmond, *Princetoniana,* 36; *LCH,* 257. Archibald Alexander also saw a connection between Calvin and Charles Hodge; he often said that Hodge's mind resembled Calvin's "without his severity." Salmond, *Princetoniana,* 34, 36.

25. Daniel A. Payne, *Recollections of Seventy Years* (New York: Arno Press, 1969), 248; B. B. Warfield, "The Beginning of Princeton Seminary," *The Presbyterian,* May 1, 1912, 6; John Macleod, *Some Favorite Books* (Edinburgh: The Banner of

Truth Trust, 1988), 98; *Charles Hodge: The Way of Life*, ed. Mark
A. Noll (New York: Paulist Press, 1987), 31; Sydney E. Ahlstrom,
"Theology in America: A Historical Survey," in *The Shaping of
American Religion*, eds. James Ward Smith and A. Leland
Jamison (Princeton: Princeton University Press, 1961), 264.
26. *LCH*, 535.
27. "Publisher's Introduction," in James Petigru Boyce, *Abstract of
Systematic Theology*, 1887 (reprinted by the den Dulk Christian
Foundation, Escondido, California), iv; *LCH*, 595; *Centennial
Celebration of the Theological Seminary*, 519; Charles A. Aiken,
*Discourses Commemorative of the Life and Work of Charles Hodge,
D.D., LL.D.* (Philadelphia: Henry B. Ashmead, 1879), 23; *The
New Schaff-Herzog Encyclopedia of Religious Knowledge* 5: 306.
Numerous modern historians have praised Charles Hodge.
Mark Noll describes Hodge's works as "forcefully Calvinistic,
eminently clear, determinedly logical, and yet infused with a
great deal of spiritual ardor" (*The Princeton Theology*, 14).
David Livingstone writes, "Forceful, transparent, lucid, and
zealous, Hodge still casts a long shadow over the theology of
evangelical Christianity" (*Darwin's Forgotten Defenders*, 101).
28. *LCH*, 608. C. A. Salmond wrote that Charles Hodge "did
more for the heathen abroad than the world knows."
Salmond, *Princetoniana*, 65. An important statement of
Charles Hodge's influence in missions is found in Richard
Gardiner's senior thesis (Princeton Theological Seminary,
1994), "Princeton and Paris: An Early Nineteenth Century
Bond of Mission. The Significance and Extent of the Relationship between Reformed Evangelicals in the United States
and France, 1810–1860: including a study of the associations
of Charles Hodge of Princeton Seminary with the Monod
brothers of France, and a sketch of the efforts of the
Princetonian in Paris, Robert Baird, which led to the formation of the 'World Evangelical Alliance.'" Gardiner writes:
"Not only did Hodge himself visit Paris and make intimate
friends" among the French evangelicals, "but almost all of the
early American missionaries to France were Hodge's
students: Baird, Proudfit, Kirk, Mines, and the Alexanders."
29. *LCH*, 392.

4. *Thy Word is Truth*

1. Salmond, *Princetoniana*, 52; Aiken, *Discourses Commemorative of
the Life and Work of Charles Hodge*, 23.

2. Joseph Fort Newton, *David Swing: Poet & Preacher* (Chicago: The Unity Publishing Co., 1909), 101–2. Newton stated: "Ill-advised as [Patton's] attack was, and somewhat ill-mannered, it was in behalf of the strict standards of his church. He held, and rightly so, that the church had a creed, and that until the creed was revised it should be maintained."

3. Salmond, *Princetoniana*, 120.

4. Francis L. Patton said: "He made use of his father's Systematic Theology; but that book in his hands was like an illuminated medieval manuscript, and from title-page to colophon, it was filled with the bright, beautiful, quaint and sometimes grotesque creations of his fancy." Patton, "Discourse," in Hodge, *Evangelical Theology*, xxxii. For a brief comparison of Charles Hodge's theology with that of A. A. Hodge, see Ralph J. Danhof, *Charles Hodge as a Dogmatician* (Goes, The Netherlands: Oosternaan & Le Cointre, 1929), 148–51. According to Mark Noll, A. A. Hodge had "the greatest capacity for precise and concise expression among the major Princetonians." *The Princeton Theology*, ed. Noll, 14. Patton, "Discourse," in Hodge, *Evangelical Theology*, xxxiii. Patton calls this book "a faithful mirror" of A. A. Hodge's "mental life." "The preacher and the professor are alike visible in these lectures" (xxxiv–xxxv). See Salmond, *Princetoniana*, 115–239, for a sample of the sayings and opinions of A. A. Hodge during the first session of his teaching at Princeton Seminary. Scottish student C. A. Salmond, after studying for a short time in Germany, spent the 1877–78 school year at Princeton. He "greatly relished the post-graduate course in contemporary philosophy taught by President McCosh in the college" and the classes at the seminary. Salmond had, as he put it, "the inestimable privilege of studying under both the Hodges during the one session in which Providence was to permit their joint services to the Church." Salmond, *Princetoniana*, 13, 81.

5. Hodge, *Evangelical Theology*, 389–90.

6. Hodge, *Evangelical Theology*, 140, 145.

7. Salmond, *Princetoniana*, 115, 119, 121; Hodge, *Evangelical Theology*, 191.

8. Hodge, *Evangelical Theology*, 64.

9. Hodge, *Evangelical Theology*, 27–28.

10. Hodge, *Evangelical Theology*, 106, 108.

11. Hodge, *Evangelical Theology*, 34–35.

12. Salmond, *Princetoniana*, 181.

13. Hodge, *Evangelical Theology*, 58–59; Salmond, *Princetoniana*, 185–86.
14. Hodge, *Evangelical Theology*, 23.
15. Salmond, *Princetoniana*, 205–6, 210–11.
16. Hodge, *Evangelical Theology*, 122–23.
17. Hodge, *Evangelical Theology*, 136–37.
18. Salmond, *Princetoniana*, 178.
19. Hodge, *Evangelical Theology*, 311–12.
20. Salmond, *Princetoniana*, 231.
21. Salmond, *Princetoniana*, 238–39.
22. Salmond, *Princetoniana*, 232, 239; Hodge, *Evangelical Theology*, 383. Nathaniel Rubinkam was a student of the class of 1878.
23. Patton, "Discourse," in Hodge, *Evangelical Theology*, xxiii; *PR* (1878): 304–21. Francis Patton thought that A. A. Hodge probably regarded this article "as the best piece of theological work he ever did." Patton, "Discourse," in Hodge, *Evangelical Theology*, xxvi. Hodge, *Outlines of Theology*, 16.
24. Hodge, *Evangelical Theology*, 181, 183, 263, 268.

5. *Evolution and Inspiration*

1. Hodge, *Evangelical Theology*, 39; Hodge, *Outlines of Theology*, 247–48.
2. A. A. Hodge, *A Commentary on the Confession of Faith. With questions for theological students and Bible classes* (Philadelphia: Presbyterian Board of Publication, 1869), 118; Hodge, *Evangelical Theology*, 41.
3. A. A. Hodge, "Introduction," in Joseph S. Van Dyke, *Theism and Evolution. An Examination of Modern Speculative Theories as Related to Theistic Conceptions of the Universe* (New York: A. C. Armstrong and Sons, 1886), xviii. Joseph Van Dyke was a graduate of Princeton College and Princeton Seminary. Salmond, *Princetoniana*, 189. A. A. Hodge's biography of his father almost entirely omits Charles Hodge's anti-Darwinian statements. There is one sentence on the debate at the Evangelical Alliance and another single sentence on his father's book on Darwinism—"In 1874 he published a small book entitled 'Darwinism,' in opposition to the prevailing doctrine of Atheistic Evolutionism." Hodge, *What is Darwinism?* eds. Noll and Livingstone, "Introduction," 29.
4. Archibald Alexander Hodge, *Outlines of Theology, rewritten and enlarged* (New York: Hodder & Stoughton, 1878; repr. London: The Banner of Truth Trust, 1972), 39; *PR* 1 (1880):

586–89. Hodge characterized Gray as "a thorough evolution-ist of the Darwinian variety, and at the same time a thoroughly loyal theist and Christian." Hodge saw "whatever is really true and significant" in the "scientific doctrine of evo-lution" as anticipated by "Augustinian theology"—"the fact that the universe in all its spheres and through all its history is the continuous logical evolution of one purpose, to one end, through the energies of one infallible and inexhaustible Will." Hodge, *Evangelical Theology*, 43.

5. Hodge, *Evangelical Theology*, 41, 148.

6. *Dr. James Woodrow as seen by his Friends*, ed. Marion W. Woodrow (Columbia, S.C.: R. L. Bryan Co., 1909), 824–25.

7. Hodge, "Introduction," in Van Dyke, *Theism and Evolution*, xviii; *PR* 1 (1880): 588; Hodge, *Evangelical Theology*, 145.

8. Mark S. Massa, *Charles Augustus Briggs and the Crisis of Historical Criticism* (Minneapolis: Fortress Press, 1990), 11. See Josef L. Altholz, "A Tale of Two Controversies: Darwinism in the Debate over 'Essays and Reviews,'" *Church History* 63 (1994): 50–59.

9. In 1886 *The Princeton Review* was followed by *The New Princeton Review*, a journal for Princeton College decorated with the re-cently chosen college colors of orange and black. It continued only until 1889.

10. Massa, *Briggs*, 28, 51–52.

11. Massa, *Briggs*, 55.

12. Massa, *Briggs*, 18, 57–58.

13. In May 1881 the long controversy came to an end when Smith was dismissed from his academic duties. His ministerial status in the Free Church remained unaffected, though he ceased to exercise it. He continued an academic career at Cambridge, leading to his appointment as professor of Arabic in 1889. He died in 1894 at the age of forty-seven.

14. Massa, *Briggs*, 178.

15. *PR* 2 (1881): 225–60. This article was reprinted in Philadel-phia in 1881 and again in Glasgow in 1891 in a volume of essays on *The Westminster Doctrine Anent Holy Scripture*. Baker Book House reprinted the Hodge-Warfield article in 1979 with an introduction by Roger Nicole and valuable appen-dixes. Archibald A. Hodge and Benjamin B. Warfield, *Inspiration*, ed. Roger R. Nicole (Grand Rapids: Baker Book House, 1979). James Samuel McClanahan, "Benjamin B. Warfield: Historian of Doctrine in Defense of Orthodoxy, 1881–1921" (Ph.D. diss., Union Theological Seminary in

Virginia, 1988), 58. In another letter (January 14, 1881) Hodge wrote to Warfield, "You are, with Prof. F. L. Patton, the future hope and strength of this Review." Massa, *Briggs,* 59; *PR* 2 (1881): 260. Ernest Sandeen, Jack Rogers, and Donald McKim have argued that A. A. Hodge and B. B. Warfield, buffeted by the findings of higher criticism and developmental science, abandoned the earlier, more flexible views of Scripture held by Archibald Alexander and Charles Hodge, as well as most of the Christian tradition, for a rigid doctrine of the inerrancy of the original autographs. See Ernest R. Sandeen, "The Princeton Theology: One Source of Biblical Literalism in American Protestantism," *Church History* 31 (1962): 307–21; and Jack B. Rogers and Donald K. McKim, *The Authority and Interpretation of the Bible: An Historical Approach* (San Francisco: Harper and Row 1979), 263–322. Their thesis, however, is contrary to the evidence that a number of scholars have provided. See Roger R. Nicole, "Charles Hodge's View of Inerrancy," in Hodge and Warfield, *Inspiration,* ed. Nicole, 93–95; Randall H. Balmer, "The Princetonians and Scripture: A Reconsideration," *Westminster Theological Journal* 44 (1982): 352–65; and "The Princetonians, Scripture, and Recent Scholarship," *JPH* 60 (1982): 267–70; John D. Woodbridge and Randall H. Balmer, "The Princetonians and Biblical Authority: An Assessment of the Ernest Sandeen Proposal," in *Scripture and Truth,* eds. D. A. Carson and John D. Woodbridge (Grand Rapids: Baker Book House, 1983); and *Inerrancy and the Church,* ed. John D. Hannah (Chicago: Moody Press, 1984). Randall Balmer argues that, like Warfield and the younger Hodge, the earlier Princetonians believed the Scriptures to be without error in their original form. For example, Archibald Alexander wrote in his *Evidences of the Authenticity, Inspiration, and Canonical Authority of the Holy Scriptures* (1836) that the Holy Spirit preserved the sacred writers "from all error and mistake," and stated that "the Scriptures . . . have come down to us in their original integrity, save those errors which arose from the carelessness or ignorance of transcribers" (229–30). Lefferts Loetscher contrasts Archibald Alexander, who, he states, avoided asserting literal inerrancy of the autographs, with A. A. Hodge and B. B. Warfield, who made such a claim. Lefferts A. Loetscher, *Facing the Enlightenment and Pietism: Archibald Alexander and the Founding of Princeton Theological Seminary* (Westport, Conn.: Greenwood, 1983), 228. Ronald Huggins argues that Loetscher misinterprets Alexander's views on the autographs. Indeed, as Huggins shows, Alexander shared the same understanding of inspiration as was set forth in the 1881 Hodge-Warfield article. Ronald V. Huggins, "A Note on Archibald Alexander's Apologetic Motive in Positing 'Errors' in the Autographs," *Westminster Theological Journal* 57 (1995): 463–70. Charles Hodge wrote in 1857: "Infallibility, or absolute freedom from error, is claimed for a book containing sixty-six distinct productions, on all subjects of history, of law, of religion, of morals; embracing poetry, prophecy, doctrinal and practical discourses, covering the whole of man's present necessities and future destiny, written by about forty different men, at intervals more or less distant, during fifteen hundred years." See Charles Hodge, "Inspiration," *BRPR* 29 (1857): 660–98. In his *Systematic Theology* Charles Hodge wrote that inspiration is "not confined to moral or religious truths," but extends to "statements of facts, whether scientific, historical, or geographical." He argued that the few discrepancies in the Bible—"which with our present means of knowledge, we are unable satisfactorily to explain"—furnish "no rational ground" for denying the Bible's infallibility. He stated that "the whole Bible was written under such an influence as preserved its human authors from all error," and ascribed mistakes in contemporary texts of the Bible to "errors of transcribers." Hodge, *Systematic Theology* 1: 163, 169–70, 182. Balmer points out the broad range of nineteenth-century theologians who shared the "Princeton" view of biblical inspiration. John D. Hannah writes in the introduction to *Inerrancy and the Church*: "The thesis of this book is that the position of the church, as it has been delineated by scholars, clerics, and teachers, is that of the absolute authority and inerrancy of the Scriptures. That was the view of Augustine, Luther, and Calvin, as well as of the entire church: inerrancy is the 'central church tradition.' The novel interpreters of the doctrine of Scripture were not Turretin, Hodge, and Warfield but Orr, Barth, Berkouwer, and [Jack] Rogers" (ix). The Hodge-Warfield position was construed by some evangelicals as presenting a lowered view of inspiration. Warfield published two clarifications, one in *The Presbyterian* for August 13, 1881, and the other in *The Truth* for February 1883. For a collection of Princeton writings on the Bible, see *The Princeton Defense of Plenary Verbal Inspiration*, ed. Mark A. Noll (London and New York: Garland Publishing Inc., 1988).

16. Massa, *Briggs*, 64.
17. Lefferts A. Loetscher, *The Broadening Church: A Study of Theological Issues in the Presbyterian Church since 1869* (Philadelphia: University of Pennsylvania Press, 1954), 33. Loetscher states that the letter of Caspar Wistar Hodge "contains about the best brief analysis which these years produced of the points at issue in the Presbyterian Biblical controversy."
18. Dwayne Davis Cox, "William Henry Green: Princeton Theologian" (M.A. thesis, University of Louisville, 1976), 67, 69.
19. *PR* 4 (1883): 410.

6. A Sacred Trust

1. *Report of Proceedings of the Second General Council of the Presbyterian Alliance Convened at Philadelphia, September, 1880*, eds. John B. Dales and R. M. Patterson (Philadelphia: Presbyterian Journal Company, 1880), 363.
2. Francis L. Patton, *The Inspiration of Scripture* (Philadelphia: Presbyterian Board of Publications, 1869). Patton's book repeated the views of Charles Hodge and anticipated the position that A. A. Hodge and B. B. Warfield put forth in 1881.
3. Paul C. Kemeny, "Francis Landey Patton: An Enigmatic Conclusion to a Career of Conflict," unpublished paper, 15.
4. William B. Greene, *The Function of Reason in Christianity. Inaugural Address of William Brenton Greene, Jr., D.D., as Stuart Professor of the Relations of Philosophy and Science to the Christian Religion* (New York: Anson D. F. Randolph & Company, 1893), 31–32.
5. William Henry Green, *Address at the Funeral of Rev. Alexander Taggart McGill, D.D., LL.D., in Princeton, January 16, 1889*, 12. After his retirement Dr. McGill remained professor emeritus at the seminary until his death on January 13, 1889.
6. Alexander T. McGill, *Church Government: A Treatise Compiled from His Lectures in Theological Seminaries* (Philadelphia: Presbyterian Board of Publication and Sabbath-School Work, 1888), 3–4.
7. *SSW* 1: 472.
8. *SSW* 1: 479.
9. *In Memoriam: William Miller Paxton* (New York, 1905), 74, 76, 85–87.
10. McCurdy moved from strict adherence to the Princeton views on the Old Testament to acceptance of the documentary

theory of the Pentateuch and other higher critical views, although he maintained strong ties with Princeton Seminary and always expressed great respect for his mentor Dr. Green. In 1885 he began a long and successful career at the University of Toronto as professor and then head of the Oriental languages department.

11. *PSB* 30 (1936): 11.

12. Patton, "Discourse," in Hodge, *Evangelical Theology*, xxix–xxx.

13. C.H. Spurgeon wrote in *The Sword and the Trowel*: "We commend the *Outlines of Theology* to all who would be well instructed in the faith. It is the standard text book of our college. We differ from its teachings upon baptism, but in almost everything else we endorse Hodge to the letter." A. A. Hodge visited Spurgeon in London in 1877. Spurgeon's copy of Hodge's *Outlines of Theology* contains A. A. Hodge's autograph and this entry in Mr. Spurgeon's handwriting: "Autograph written in my study, Aug. 8, 1877—C. H. S." *C. H. Spurgeon Autobiography, Vol. 2: The Full Harvest 1860–1892* (Edinburgh: The Banner of Truth Trust, 1973), 341. Hodge revised his *Outlines of Theology* for a new edition published in 1878. There were nine editions of Hodge's *Outlines* between 1860 and 1876 and seven editions of the enlarged book between 1878 and 1949. Hodge's *Outlines of Theology* was reprinted by the Banner of Truth Trust in 1972. The introduction to the Banner of Truth reprint of Hodge's *Confession of Faith* (1958) states: "This book provides probably the finest concise exposition of the greatest systematic Confession of Faith in the English language" (xii–xiii). *Popular Lectures on Theological Themes* was published in England in 1890 as *Evangelical Theology*. The Banner of Truth Trust reprinted Hodge's *Evangelical Theology* in 1976.

14. Patton, "Discourse," in Hodge, *Evangelical Theology*, xxvi; *PR* 5 (1884): 269.

15. John Aspinwall Hodge was born in Philadelphia in 1831. He graduated from the University of Pennsylvania and Princeton Theological Seminary. He was pastor of the Presbyterian church in Mauch Chunk, Pennsylvania (1856–65), and the First Presbyterian Church of Hartford, Connecticut (1866–92). From 1893 until his death in 1901 he served as professor of English Bible at Lincoln University in Pennsylvania.

16. Hodge, *Evangelical Theology*, 402. Hodge's lectures given in Philadelphia early in 1886 are found in *Evangelical Theology*.

17. William M. Paxton, *Address Delivered at the Funeral of Archibald Alexander Hodge, D.D., LL.D.* (New York: Anson D. F. Randolph and Company, 1886); Salmond, *Princetoniana*, 55, 103.

18. Preface (by C. A. Salmond) in Hodge, *Evangelical Theology*, (iii), 97; Patton, "Discourse," in Hodge, *Evangelical Theology*, xxi, xxxiii.

19. Patton, "Discourse," in Hodge, *Evangelical Theology*, x, xix, xxxiii; Alexander, *Address . . . 1912*, 16. The student quoted above was Paul van Dyke, who was appointed instructor in church history at Princeton Seminary from 1889 to 1892. He served as pastor of Edwards Congregational Church in Northampton, Massachusetts, from 1892 to 1898, when he became professor of history at Princeton University.

20. Salmond, *Princetoniana*, 34; Hodge, *Evangelical Theology*, 401. A. A. Hodge, with his father and B. B. Warfield, held that "the whole body of those dying in infancy" are saved and thus "constitute the vast majority of the essential Church" (259). Hodge, *Evangelical Theology*, 257.

21. David M. Howard, *Student Power in World Missions* (Downers Grove, Ill.: InterVarsity Press, 1970), 86–87.

22. *Addresses and Papers of John R. Mott, The Student Volunteer Movement for Foreign Missions* (New York: Association Press, 1946) 1: 12.

23. Robert Speer served as a lay secretary of the Presbyterian Board of Foreign Missions for forty-six years. His mature thought moved toward the themes of the theology of Horace Bushnell. An ecumenist, Speer was elected president of the Federal Council of Churches in 1920. He supported the reorganization of Princeton Seminary under broader theological control and clashed with J. Gresham Machen over policies and practices of the Presbyterian board.

24. *Addresses delivered at the Celebration of the Centennial of the General Assembly of the Presbyterian Church* (Philadelphia: MacCalla & Company), 10–11, 16, 22–23.

7. *The Majestic Testimony*

1. B. B. Warfield, "Introductory Essay on Augustine and the Pelagian Controversy," in *Nicene and Post-Nicene Fathers of the Christian Church, St. Augustine: Anti-Pelagian Writings*, ed. Philip Schaff, (New York: Christian Literature Company, 1887; repr. Grand Rapids: Wm. B. Eerdmans Publishing Company, 1956), xi–lxxi; B. B. Warfield, *Studies in Tertullian and*

Augustine (New York: Oxford University Press, 1930), 289–412.

2. *PR* 3 (1882): 325–56; D. Clair Davis, "Princeton and Inerrancy: The Nineteenth Century Philosophical Background of Contemporary Concerns," in *Inerrancy and the Church*, ed. Hannah, 361. Warfield's *Introduction to the Textual Criticism of the New Testament* went through nine editions by 1907 and became a popular seminary text in the United States and in Europe, where it was praised by Joseph Henry Thayer and William Robertson Nicoll. A. T. Robertson's *Introduction to the Textual Criticism of the New Testament* (Nashville: Sunday School Board of the Southern Baptist Convention, 1925) was dedicated "to the memory of B. B. Warfield." Until it passed out of print Robertson had used Warfield's *Introduction* in his classes at Southern Baptist Theological Seminary in Louisville. "No one else outside of [F. J. A.] Hort . . . had so clearly and so fully set forth the principles of textual criticism that the student could readily grasp the science and apply it," Robertson stated. Robertson had tried to get Dr. Warfield to revise his book, but he "declined on the ground that his interest had come to be chiefly in the sphere of dogmatic theology since his removal to Princeton" (viii). Theodore P. Letis has argued that Warfield was the first professor at Princeton to advocate the reconstruction of the text according to the canons of German criticism. Theodore P. Letis, "B. B. Warfield, Common-Sense Philosophy and Biblical Criticism," *AP* 69 (1991): 175–90. But for proof of agreement of the earlier Princetonians with Warfield's view see Marion Ann Taylor, *The Old Testament in the Old Princeton School (1812–1929)* (San Francisco: Mellen Research University Press, 1992). Taylor writes: "[Archibald] Alexander was willing to acknowledge that the received text contained human errors and he confidently expected that the tools of text criticism could restore the received text to its more pristine form" (24–25). Charles Hodge also taught the "means of restoring the purity of the text," commending to his students principles of criticism that were "conservative and yet generally informed by critical scholarship of his day" (62). Although William Henry Green recognized errors in the current text of the Bible, he stated that they were few in number and held that no other work of antiquity had been so accurately transmitted. He believed that a judicious use of the tools of textual criticism would offer solutions to most of these problems (191).

3. *Inauguration of the Rev. Benjamin B. Warfield, D.D. as Professor of Didactic and Polemic Theology* (New York: Anson D. F. Randolph and Co., 1888), 5.

4. William Warfield wrote two books on this topic, *The History of Short Horn Cattle in America* (1849) and *The Theory and Practice of Cattle Breeding* (1888). The Warfields of Maryland were a distinguished family, one of whom was Bessie Wallis Warfield who became the Duchess of Windsor.

5. Robert J. Breckinridge clashed with Princeton Seminary over Old School strategy leading to the division of the church in 1837 and during the debate on the eldership and the nature of Presbyterian polity (in which Breckinridge and James Henley Thornwell opposed Charles Hodge). Another cause of tension was personal. Samuel Miller Breckinridge—the son of Robert's brother John—was left in the care of his grandfather Samuel Miller when John Breckinridge died in 1841. The boy caused Dr. Miller much anxiety. Finally, Robert Breckinridge removed Samuel from Dr. Miller's care and sent him to Union College. Samuel Breckinridge later studied law and moved to St. Louis to set up practice there. Despite his theological affinity for Southern Presbyterian thought, Robert J. Breckinridge was an uncompromising Union supporter during the Civil War. Two of his sons, however, became officers in the Confederate army, one of whom was John Cabell Breckinridge, the famous Confederate general. Robert J. Breckinridge's nephew, John C. Breckinridge, served as vice-president under James Buchanan and then ran as a Southern Democrat against Abraham Lincoln in 1860. He was a first cousin once removed of B. B. Warfield. See James C. Klotter, *The Breckinridges of Kentucky, 1760–1981* (Lexington: University Press of Kentucky, 1986).

6. In 1869 Robert Brank became pastor of Central Presbyterian Church in St. Louis and served there until his death in 1895.

7. *Princeton Alumni Weekly*, April 12, 1916, 623.

8. *Princeton Alumni Weekly*, April 12, 1916, 624.

9. *Princeton Alumni Weekly*, April 12, 1916, 623, 625; *Princeton Alumni Weekly*, April 19, 1916, 652. Warfield later wrote: "I used to remark to Dr. McCosh on all fitting (perhaps I would better say, on all possible) occasions, that he and I ought to feel very close to one another, as we had entered College together. The remark seemed invariably to cause him some surprise. And this surprise did not wholly pass away when I remarked further, with becoming modesty, that we had both

entered to advanced standing, although our standing was, of course, not quite the same. He usually said, Huh! with some energy, and we let it go at that." *Princeton Alumni Weekly*, April 12, 1916, 623.

10. Benjamin's younger brother, Ethelbert Dudley Warfield (1861–1936), also became a minister. Ethelbert followed Benjamin to the College of New Jersey, then studied a year at Oxford. He took a law degree at Columbia and practiced law in Lexington before moving through a succession of academic positions at Miami (Ohio) University (1887–90), Lafayette College (1890–1914), and Wilson College (1915–35). He was a member of the board of directors of Princeton Seminary from 1894 to 1929 and served as president of the board from 1904 to 1915.

11. Professor Bruce M. Metzger of Princeton Seminary has stated (in a private conversation with James McClanahan) that in illustrating the transmission of the New Testament text, Warfield would compare the different families of New Testament manuscripts with different breeds of cattle. McClanahan, "Warfield," 55.

12. *PSB* 15 (1921): 10–11. Charles Barrett served Presbyterian churches in New York, Maryland, Colorado, and New Jersey. He died in 1925.

13. Luthardt (1823–1902) was a conservative Lutheran scholar, well known in the English-speaking world. Delitszch (1813–90) was from a pietistic background and of Jewish descent; he was an Old Testament scholar who adopted moderately critical views.

14. B. B. Warfield, *The Inspiration and Authority of the Bible* (Philadelphia: Presbyterian & Reformed Publishing Co., 1948), 419. Warfield's quotation in this paragraph is from Peter Bayne, *The Chief Actors in the Puritan Revolution* (London: J. Clarke & Co., 1878).

15. Warfield, *Inspiration and Authority of the Bible*, 419–20, 441–42.

16. Dr. Warfield would live in that house (74 Mercer Street) for thirty-five years, the rest of his life.

17. Ethelbert D. Warfield, "Biographical Sketch of Benjamin Breckinridge Warfield," in B. B. Warfield, *Revelation and Inspiration* (New York: Oxford University Press, 1927), viii.

18. Massa, *Briggs*, 77–78. Henry Van Dyke was a pastor in Brooklyn, New York, and father of the better-known Henry Van Dyke who was pastor of the prestigious Brick Presbyterian Church in New York City and professor of English literature at Princeton University.

19. Charles A. Briggs, *Whither? A Theological Question for the Times* (New York: Charles Scribner's Sons, 1889), ix, x, 7–8, 16. Chapter headings give the drift of his argument: "Drifting," "Orthodoxy," "Changes," "Shifting," "Excesses," "Failures," "Departures," "Perplexities," "Barriers." The final chapter is titled "Thither." Briggs stated, "The book is polemical. It is necessary to overcome that false orthodoxy which has obtruded itself in the place of Westminster orthodoxy. I regret, on many accounts, that it has been necessary for me to attack so often the elder and younger Hodge[s], divines for whom I have great respect and admiration. Their names will always rank among the highest on the roll of American theologians. It has also been necessary to expose the errors of my younger associates in the editorship of the *Presbyterian Review,* and other divines, my friends and colleagues." Dr. Briggs made it clear that he looked for the evolution of a higher or "ultimate" Christianity "that will suit our race" and that will be "as much higher than Protestantism as Protestantism is higher than Romanism."

20. *PR* 10 (1889): 552. The next year Schaff wrote: "Let us be honest, and confess that old Calvinism is fast dying out. It has done a great work, and has done it well, but cannot satisfy the demands of the present age. We live in the nineteenth, and not in the seventeenth century." Philip Schaff, *Creed Revision in the Presbyterian Churches* (New York: Charles Scribner's Sons, 1890), 40. B. B. Warfield described Schaff as representing a position "in which not only Arminianism, Lutheranism, and Calvinism, but also Rationalism and Supranaturalism, are reconciled." B. B. Warfield, *Studies in Theology* (New York: Oxford University Press, 1932), 588.

21. *PR* 10 (1889): 588–89.

22. William G. T. Shedd, *Calvinism: Pure and Mixed; A Defence of the Westminster Standards* (New York: C. Scribner's Sons, 1893; repr., Edinburgh: The Banner of Truth Trust, 1986), x. This book contains a number of Shedd's writings on the revision controversy. See also William G. T. Shedd, *The Proposed Revision of the Westminster Standards* (New York: Charles Scribner's Sons, 1890).

23. Philip Schaff, *Creed Revision in the Presbyterian Churches*, 11–14, 42. In a letter to B. B. Warfield dated February 17, 1887, Schaff wrote: "I think Am[erican] Presbyterianism can afford to be liberal in the right direction on the basis of funda-

mental orthodoxy. The Hodges, father and son of blessed memory, have taken a very important step beyond the boundary of narrow Calvinism as regards the salvation of infants. We must take another step as regards the freedom of will. The success of Arminianism and evang[elical] Methodism teaches us a lesson which should not be lost." McClanahan, "Warfield," 445.

24. Charles Briggs, "The Advance Towards Revision," in *How Shall We Revise the Westminster Confession of Faith?* (New York: Charles Scribner's Sons, 1890): 1–33; *Ought the Confession of Faith Be Revised? A Series of Papers by John DeWitt, Henry J. Van Dyke, Benjamin B. Warfield, W.G.T. Shedd* (New York: Anson D. F. Randolph and Company, 1890), 121.

25. *Ought the Confession of Faith Be Revised?* 39–41. Warfield wrote concerning subscription to the Confession of Faith, "Overstrictness encouraged laxity in performance, while a truly liberal, but conservative formula bound all essentially sound men together against laxity." This is exactly what the American formula provided, Warfield believed. Warfield, *On the Revision of the Confession of Faith* (New York: Randolph, 1890), 66, 70.

26. *PRR* 3 (1892): 329–30. The Princeton Seminary professors were of one mind with Dr. Warfield. It was said that Caspar Wistar Hodge opposed revision "not because he felt that in minor statements [the Westminster Confession] was incapable of improvement, but because he knew that our terms of subscription were liberal enough to remove every burden from the conscience of any man who heartily believed in generic Calvinism. He also felt, as others did, that it would be hard to arrest a movement after it had begun; and, moreover, that while older men might be satisfied with a softening of the harder lines of Calvinism, there would be no inconsiderable number of younger men who would be willing to see the Calvinistic elements eliminated." Patton, *Caspar Wistar Hodge:*

27. Material in this section is taken from Lois A. Boyd and R. Douglas Brackenridge, *Presbyterian Women in America: Two Centuries of a Quest for Status* (Westport, Conn.: Greenwood Press, 1983), 110–11. See Alexander T. McGill, "Deaconesses," *PR* 1 (1880): 268–90; and B. B. Warfield, "Presbyterian Deaconesses," *PR* 10 (1889): 287–88, and "The Deaconess as Part of the Church," *Presbyterian Deaconess Quarterly* 1 (1905): 1–3. Warfield later opposed a 1920 move to "admit properly

qualified and elected women to ordination as Ruling Elders," arguing "forcefully that passage of the overture would represent a defection from biblical standards and would create havoc in church courts." Boyd and Brackenridge, *Presbyterian Women*, 120–21. Although 139 presbyteries favored ordination of women as ruling elders, the proposal failed because 152 presbyteries were required for passage.

28. William Henry Green, *A Discourse Commemorative of James Clement Moffat, D.D., June 7, 1890*, 10–11. See James C. Moffat, *Song and Scenery; or, A Summer Ramble in Scotland* (New York: L. D. Robertson, 1874).

29. On May 7, 1901, a tablet of antique brass on a foundation of oak wood was placed on the right side of the seminary chapel overlooking the pews occupied by the Hodges. It read: "Archibald Alexander Hodge, 1823–1886, Professor of Systematic Theology, 1877–1886"; and "Caspar Wistar Hodge, 1830–1891, Professor of New Testament Literature and Exegesis, 1860–1891"; "Thanks be to God, which giveth us the victory through our Lord Jesus Christ."

30. *SSW* 1: 460.

31. *Inauguration of George Tybout Purves, D.D., as Professor of New Testament Literature and Exegesis* (New York: Anson D. F. Randolph & Company, 1892), 56–57.

8. Cloud of Witnesses

1. Massa, *Briggs*, 87–89; Bradley J. Longfield, *The Presbyterian Controversy: Fundamentalists, Modernists, and Moderates* (New York: Oxford University Press, 1991), 23.

2. Since the reunion in 1870 the General Assembly had had veto power over the appointment of Union Seminary professors.

3. Massa, *Briggs*, 98.

4. William Henry Green, "Heresy Hunters," in *The Presbyterian*, February 15, 1893, 12.

5. *SSW* 1: 443–44; B. B. Warfield, *The Saviour of the World: Sermons Preached in the Chapel of Princeton Theological Seminary* (New York: Hodder and Stoughton, 1914?; repr. Cherry Hill, N.J.: Mack Publishing Company, 1972; repr. Edinburgh: The Banner of Truth Trust, 1991), 206.

6. *PTR* 22 (1924): 205; *PR* 10 (1889): 553–89. See John DeWitt, *Sermons on the Christian Life* (New York: Charles Scribner's, 1885).

7. Greene, *The Function of Reason in Christianity*, 10–11, 55, 68.

8. Massa, *Briggs*, 103–4.
9. Massa, *Briggs*, 108–9. On May 14, 1899, Dr. Briggs was ordained in the Episcopal church.
10. A. A. Hodge, "Preface," in Charles Hodge, *Commentary on the Epistle to the Romans* (New York: A. C. Armstrong and Son, 1900), iv; *Discourses at the Inauguration of the Rev. William Henry Green as Professor of Biblical and Oriental Literature in the Theological Seminary at Princeton, N.J.* (Philadelphia, 1851), 47, 56–57, 63.
11. *SSW* 2: 12.
12. *Redemptive History and Biblical Interpretation: The Shorter Writings of Geerhardus Vos*, ed. Richard B. Gaffin, Jr. (Phillipsburg: Presbyterian and Reformed Publishing Company, 1948), xi.
13. For brief accounts of Vos's life see Ransom Lewis Webster, "Geerhardus Vos (1862–1949): A Biographical Sketch," *Westminster Theological Journal* 40 (1978): 304–17; and "Introduction," in *Redemptive History and Biblical Interpretation*, ed. Gaffin, ix–xiv.
14. Geerhardus Vos, *The Idea of Biblical Theology as a Science and as a Theological Discipline* (New York: Anson D. F. Randolph and Co., 1894); *Redemptive History and Biblical Interpretation*, ed. Gaffin, 3–24. Vos preferred the name "history of special revelation" to that of "biblical theology" but found it impossible to change "a name which has the sanction of usage." "Introduction," in *Redemptive History and Biblical Interpretation*, ed. Gaffin, xiv.
15. *PTR* 14 (1916): 60. For brief summaries of Vos's teaching, see J. F. Jansen, "The Biblical Theology of Geerhardus Vos," *PSB* 66 (1974): 22–34; Gaffin, "Introduction," in *Redemptive History and Biblical Interpretation*, xiv–xxiii; and Richard Lints, "Two Theologies or One? Warfield and Vos on the Nature of Theology," *Westminster Theological Journal* 54 (1992): 235–53. Gaffin considers Vos to be "the first in the Reformed tradition, perhaps even the first orthodox theologian, to give pointed, systematic attention to the *doctrinal* or *positive* theological significance of the fact that redemptive revelation comes as an organically unfolding historical process and to begin working out the methodological consequences of this insight" (xv). Vos anticipated by decades many of the theological conclusions later reached by Oscar Cullman, Joachim Jeremias, C. H. Dodd, and Herman Ridderbos.
16. *The Princeton Theology*, ed. Noll, 26; *SSW* 2: 546–47. Roger Nicole lists eighty-three articles on the doctrine of the

Scripture produced by Warfield between 1880 and 1915. Hodge and Warfield, *Inspiration*, ed. Nicole, 83–90.

17. B. B. Warfield, "Professor Henry Preserved Smith on Inspiration," *PRR* 5 (1894): 600–53; reissued as *Limited Inspiration* (Philadelphia: Presbyterian and Reformed Publishing Company, 1962).

18. *SSW* 2: 582–84.

19. Warfield, *Revelation and Inspiration*, 229–391.

20. *SSW* 2: 579, 581.

21. B.B. Warfield, *The Westminster Assembly and its Work* (New York: Oxford University Press, 1931), 277, 332–33. For a competent comparison of Warfield and the Princeton view of Scripture with the view of the Westminster Confession and its writers see John D. Woodbridge, "Biblical Authority: Towards an Evaluation of the Rogers and McKim Proposal," *Trinity Journal* 1 (1980): 165–236. For a brief statement see Roger R. Nicole, "The Westminster Confession and Inerrancy," in Hodge and Warfield, *Inspiration*, ed. Nicole, 97–100. John Allen Delivuk concludes that "Edward Reynolds and the other authors of the *WCF* believed that the Bible was inerrant. This was shown . . . by the seventeenth-century meaning of the word *infallible*, the confession writers' use of *infallible* in contexts where it could be used interchangeably with *inerrant*, and by their view of Scripture as the product of a perfect God, who had given some of his attributes, such as truth and perfection, to his word." John Allen Delivuk, "Inerrancy, Infallibility, and Scripture in the *Westminster Confession of Faith*," *Westminster Theological Journal* 54 (1992): 349–55. For Warfield's evaluation of the teaching of the Westminster divines on inerrancy of the original autographs see his articles "The Westminster Doctrine of Holy Scripture" and "The Doctrine of Inspiration of the Westminster Divines" in Warfield, *The Westminster Assembly and its Work*, 155–333; and "The Westminster Doctrine of Holy Scripture," "The Inerrancy of the Original Autographs," and "The Westminster Confession and the Original Autographs" in *SSW* 2: 560–94.

22. *PTR* 8 (1910): 167; *PRR* 4 (1893): 177–221; Warfield, *Revelation and Inspiration*, 169–226; *SSW* 2: 581–82.

23. *PTR* 19 (1921): 372. Dr. Warfield continued his defense of the orthodox doctrine of the Bible when, in 1915, he contributed the article "Inspiration" to the *International Standard Bible Encyclopedia*. According to Wilbur B. Wallis, it was a "compact,

powerful, comprehensive treatment" that combined all of Warfield's "hard-won exegesis and theological power." Wilbur B. Wallis, "Benjamin B. Warfield: Didactic and Polemic Theologian," *Presbyterion: Covenant Seminary Review* 3 (1977): 15. Even opponents of the doctrine of plenary verbal inspiration have acknowledged the importance of the writings of Warfield on this subject. Robertson Nicoll, in a letter to James Denney written in 1894, suggested that "the only *respectable* defenders of verbal inspiration" were the Princeton school of Warfield and William Henry Green. Thomas H. Darlow, *William Robertson Nicoll, Life and Letters* (London: Hodder and Stoughton, 1925), 341.

9. *The Seminary and the College*

1. Marion Ann Taylor comments, "Through his teaching and writing, [Archibald Alexander] . . . widely disseminated recent Old Testament critical scholarship . . . , effectively communicated the importance of subjects related to the Old Testament and encouraged several of his students . . . to get . . . specialized training in Old Testament studies." Taylor, *The Old Testament in the Old Princeton School,* 46, 85–86, 101.
2. *Professor William Henry Green's Semi-Centennial Celebration, 1846–1896* (New York: Charles Scribner's Sons, 1896), 35–36. The student was J. F. McCurdy. Taylor, *The Old Testament in the Old Princeton School,* 176. The first of many editions of Green's Hebrew grammar appeared in 1861. In 1888 Green published a new and thoroughly revised edition, considered by some to be "the most serviceable book for reference now in English."
3. Taylor, *The Old Testament in the Old Princeton School,* 202; William Henry Green, *The Argument of the Book of Job Unfolded* (New York: Robert Carter and Brothers, 1874), 9, 326, 342.
4. *PR* 1 (1878): 147.
5. *SSW* 2: 500; William Henry Green, *The Pentateuch Vindicated from the Aspersions of Bishop Colenso* (New York: John Wiley, 1863), 9, 15.
6. Taylor, *The Old Testament in the Old Princeton School,* 227–28.
7. Taylor, *The Old Testament in the Old Princeton School,* 238–39.
8. Taylor, *The Old Testament in the Old Princeton School,* 229.
9. William Henry Green, *The Hebrew Feasts in their Relation to Recent Critical Hypotheses Concerning the Pentateuch* (New York: Robert Carter and Brothers, 1885), 28; Taylor, *The Old Testa-*

ment in the Old Princeton School, 244; John D. Davis, *The Life and Work of William Henry Green: A Commemorative Address. Delivered in the Chapel of Princeton Theological Seminary. Tuesday, March 27, 1900* (Philadelphia: MacCalla and Company, 1900), 26.

10. Taylor states that "Green's arguments for the unity of the book based on his sensitive observations about the present shape and meaning of the book of Genesis are most important for they adumbrate an approach to the study of Genesis which has only recently been 'discovered' by post-critical Old Testament scholars." Green, *Prophets and Prophecy: A Compilation from Notes of the Lectures before the Senior Class (1877–1895)*. See Taylor, *The Old Testament in the Old Princeton School,* 208, 212, 214, 225, 250.

11. Taylor, *The Old Testament in the Old Princeton School,* 167.

12. *William Henry Green's Semi-Centennial Celebration,* 21–22, 36, 41.

13. *William Henry Green's Semi-Centennial Celebration,* 33, 35–36.

14. *William Henry Green's Semi-Centennial Celebration,* 45.

15. *William Henry Green's Semi-Centennial Celebration,* 45–46.

16. *William Henry Green's Semi-Centennial Celebration,* 52–53.

17. *William Henry Green's Semi-Centennial Celebration,* 177.

18. Leslie, *Gentlemen and Scholars,* 65. For a scholarly evaluation of the McCosh presidency see George M. Marsden, *The Soul of the American University,* chapter 12, "Holding the Line at Princeton," 196–218.

19. *Sesquicentennial Celebration of the College of New Jersey,* 70; Hoeveler, *James McCosh,* 270–71. "The noted philanthropist admitted it was a fair exchange, a case of Scot against Scot."

20. Hoeveler, *James McCosh,* 269.

21. Hoeveler, *James McCosh,* 270. When the trustees built an infirmary in 1892 they named it the Isabella McCosh Infirmary—"with the striking picture of the tireless bearer of its name in the waiting room . . . a fitting monument."

22. Hoeveler, *James McCosh,* 270.

23. *Princeton Alumni Weekly,* April 19, 1916, 652; *PRR* 6 (1895): 657. The quotations are from B. B. Warfield, who studied under McCosh at Princeton from 1868 to 1871, and Francis L. Patton.

24. *PR* 3 (1882): 326. McCosh summarized the Scottish Philosophy under three main ideas: it proceeds throughout by observation; it observes the operations of the mind by the inner sense—that is, consciousness; by observation principles are discovered which are above observation, universal and eternal.

25. Marsden, *The Soul of the American University*, 202. James McCosh, *First and Fundamental Truths: Being a Treatise on Metaphysics* (New York, 1889). McCosh regarded this book as "the cope-stone" of what he had been "able to do in philosophy" (i). *PRR* 6 (1895): 660; *PTR* 1 (1903): 353; *Sesquicentennial Celebration of the College of New Jersey*, 76. The quotations are from Francis L. Patton and Alexander T. Ormond.

26. Leslie, *Gentlemen and Scholars*, 66.

27. James McCosh raised $3 million in twenty years, mainly from wealthy donors (mostly with Scottish roots) in New York, Philadelphia, and Pittsburgh. Leslie, *Gentlemen and Scholars*, 243.

28. F. Scott Fitzgerald, *Afternoon of an Author: A Selection of Uncollected Stories and Essays* (New York: Charles Scribner's Sons, 1957), 72; Hoeveler, *James McCosh*, 338.

29. Paul C. Kemeny, "Keeping Princeton a 'Christian College,' 1888–1902," unpublished paper, 1. Mark Twain said that he considered Dr. Patton "the best after-dinner speaker he ever heard."

30. Kemeny, "Keeping Princeton a 'Christian College,'" 2.

31. *Sesquicentennial Celebration of the College of New Jersey*, 440, 450–51.

32. *PRR* 6 (1895): 661–62.

33. *The Princeton Theology*, ed. Noll, 20–21. Of the twenty seminary professors up to 1900, ten graduated from the college, four taught at the college, eleven were college trustees, and ten were awarded honorary degrees by the college. College personnel, such as James Carnahan, John Maclean, James McCosh, and Lyman Atwater, served on the seminary boards. Seminary professors who were members of the college board included J. W. Alexander (1851–59), Charles Hodge (1850–78), and William Henry Green (1868–1900). *PRR* 8 (1897): 663–64; Cuyler, *Recollections*, 237–38.

34. *PRR* 6 (1895): 123–24.

35. *Sesquicentennial Celebration of the College of New Jersey*, 55.

10. *Princeton* Contra Mundum

1. This bequest was the culmination of the generosity of the Stuart family, which gave more than a million dollars to Princeton Seminary for a professorship, faculty houses, a classroom and a dormitory, and general endowment and operating expenses.

2. After graduation William Byrd served rural churches in North Carolina and then became principal of a secondary school for black students in Arkansas. In 1905 he was called to Trinity Presbyterian Church in Rochester, New York, and in 1917 to Lafayette Presbyterian Church of Jersey City, New Jersey. The last years of his life were spent as pastor of the nondenominational Community Church in Jersey City. One of the founders of the National Association for the Advancement of Colored People, Byrd always felt a deep loyalty to Princeton and the students and faculty he knew there. His son Franz said that his father's "experience at Princeton Seminary taught him that there were good people of different races who didn't look down upon people because of the color of their skin."

3. William K. Selden, *Princeton Theological Seminary: A Narrative History, 1812–1992* (Princeton: Princeton University Press, 1992), 65.

4. B. B. Warfield, "Christian Supernaturalism," in *Studies in Theology*, 25–46.

5. B. B. Warfield, *The Significance of the Westminster Standards as a Creed: An Address* (New York: Charles Scribner's Sons, 1898), 2, 13, 22, 26–29, 32.

6. *SSW* 2: 441. Abraham Kuyper served as prime minister of the Netherlands from 1901 to 1905. In 1907, on the occasion of his seventieth birthday, it was said of him: "The history of the Netherlands, in Church, in State, in Society, in Press, in School, and in the Sciences of the last forty years, can not be written without the mention of his name on almost every page, for during this period the biography of Dr. Kuyper is to a considerable extent the history of the Netherlands." Kuyper died on November 8, 1920. He was the author of many books, including *Encyclopedia of Sacred Theology* and *The Work of the Holy Spirit*. He wrote more than 2,000 devotional meditations, 110 of which are found in the book *To Be Near Unto God*. For biographical information see John Hendrik De Vries, "Biographical Note," in Abraham Kuyper, *To Be Near Unto God* (New York: Macmillan Company, 1925), 10–12; Frank Vanden Berg, *Abraham Kuyper* (St. Catharines, Ontario; Paideia Press, 1978), 17, 21, 24, 27, 33–35; and James D. Bratt, "Abraham Kuyper," *Encyclopedia of the Reformed Faith*, ed. Donald K. McKim (Louisville, Kentucky: Westminster/John Knox Press; Edinburgh: Saint Andrew Press, 1992), 213.

7. Abraham Kuyper, *Calvinism* (New York: Fleming H. Revell Company, 1899), 27–31, 297–98.

8. *SSW* 1: 204, 206; Warfield, "Introductory Note," in Abraham Kuyper, *Encyclopedia of Sacred Theology* (New York: C. Scribner's Sons, 1898; reprinted as *Principles of Sacred Theology*, Grand Rapids: Baker Book House, 1980). Dr. Warfield assisted Kuyper's daughter when she visited the United States in 1917 and served as her host in Princeton. Dr. Kuyper sent Warfield a copy of his *Encyclopedia of Sacred Theology* with a handwritten note in Dutch reading, "To Professor Doctor Benj. Warfield at Princeton. Cordially given with grateful acknowledgment of what you did for my daughter Catherine two years ago while she was journeying in America—The Hague 17 September 1919—Dr. A. Kuyper." Donald Fuller and Richard Gardiner, "Reformed Theology at Princeton and Amsterdam in the Late Nineteenth Century: A Reappraisal," unpublished paper, 24.

9. George M. Marsden, *Understanding Fundamentalism and Evangelicalism* (Grand Rapids: William B. Eerdmans Publishing Company, 1991), 127; Vanden Berg, *Abraham Kuyper*, 255; *SSW* 2: 109–10; *PTR* 10 (1912): 379.

10. Kuyper, *Calvinism*, 30; *SSW* 2: 95. For Kuyper's views see *Principles of Sacred Theology*, 150–59.

11. *PTR* 11 (1913): 82.

12. *The Princeton Theology*, ed. Noll, 242; *SSW* 2: 115; B. B. Warfield, "Introductory Note," in Francis R. Beattie, *Apologetics or the Rational Vindication of Christianity*, 3 vols. (Richmond: Presbyterian Committee of Publication, 1903) 1: 26; *SSW* 2: 99–100. A Canadian, Francis Beattie studied at Knox College, Toronto, and at the Presbyterian College in Montreal. He was a pastor in Canada and the United States and served as professor in Columbia Theological Seminary from 1888 to 1893 and then at the Presbyterian Seminary of Louisville.

13. *SSW* 2: 99. Mark Noll has written that study of Warfield's work will demonstrate, even to those who side with Kuyper, "how exhaustively thorough and unremittingly plausible were the arguments Warfield marshaled both for the truth of classic Christianity and for the power of reason." Mark Noll, "B. B. Warfield," in *Handbook of Evangelical Theologians*, ed. Walter A. Elwell (Grand Rapids: Baker Book House, 1993), 36.

14. Hodge, *Systematic Theology* 3: 790–868; Hodge, *Outlines of Theology*, 568; B. B. Warfield, *Biblical Doctrines* (New York: Oxford University Press, 1929), 52, 647.

15. See Paul C. Kemeny, "Princeton and the Premillennialists:

The Roots of the *mariage de convenance*," *AP* 71 (1993): 19; Hodge, *Systematic Theology* 3: 791, 862; *PRR* 8 (1897): 818–20; Samuel H. Kellogg, "Is the Advent Pre-Millennial?" *PR* 3 (1882): 475–502. Kemeny demonstrates convincingly that Ernest Sandeen's thesis—that "fundamentalism of the late nineteenth and early twentieth centuries in America was comprised of an alliance between dispensationalists and Princeton-oriented Calvinists"—is faulty. Kemeny shows that "the relationship was more of an informal friendship, marked with rare instances of cooperation, than a purposeful coalition" (17). Charles R. Eerdman, who joined the Princeton faculty in 1905, was a premillennialist. He addressed the doctrine of the end times most fully in an essay he wrote for *The Fundamentals* entitled "The Coming of Christ" and in a 1922 volume, *The Return of Christ.*

16. *PRR* 13 (1902): 180; Davis, *William Henry Green*, 23–24.

17. Davis, *William Henry Green*, 29. Marion Ann Taylor summarized Green's life work: "Although greatly revered as an apologist and teacher, Green also was an outstanding OT scholar. His early works in Hebrew grammar in the early sixties represented a major contribution to the field of Hebrew studies in America. His more practical contributions to the Revised Version of the OT exhibited his philological expertise in a different way. His publications on the Song of Songs, Job, the OT canon and text, together with his more distinctively polemical writings on the work of Bishop Colenso, the Hebrew feasts, the book of Genesis and the higher criticism of the Pentateuch and his hundreds of articles constitute an impressive publishing record. While Green directed some of his writing to the academic community, he most often had a popular yet well-educated Christian audience in mind. Accordingly, though most of Green's writings failed to have a lasting impact on the academic community, especially the continental community, they certainly were well received by the American public who looked to Green for assistance in the task of understanding the OT and for guidance in a perplexing time of change and unrest." Taylor also notes that "the post-critical phase of twentieth-century OT scholarship with its emphasis on such issues as canon, text, authority and the Bible as literature and scripture has in many ways vindicated the scholarly work of W. H. Green. For besides his work as an apologist, Green correctly focused his scholarly energies on issues which have proven to be of fundamental

importance to the study of the OT. Moreover, he correctly identified fundamental weaknesses in the critical approach. However, because of the conservative theological stance of the Old Princeton School with which Green was associated, his genuine insights were lost to his contemporaries and to the next generation of OT scholars. OT scholarship has only recently begun to shift its focus to the issues which Green realized were of fundamental importance." Taylor, *The Old Testament in the Old Princeton School,* 249, 251.

18. *SSW* 1: 462. For examples of Purves's sermons see *Faith and Life: Sermons* (Philadelphia: Presbyterian Board of Publication, 1902).

19. *PTR* 4 (1906): 316; *SSW* 1: 460, 464.

20. *SSW* 1: 480, 489.

21. *SSW* 1: 493; *In Memoriam: William Miller Paxton,* 111.

22. Loetscher, *The Broadening Church,* 83.

23. *SSW* 1: 93, 102; Warfield, *Studies in Theology,* 117–231; *SSW* 1: 402. Thirty-two separate articles by Warfield on confessional revision are listed in *A Bibliography of Benjamin Breckinridge Warfield 1851–1921,* eds. John E. Meeter and Roger Nicole (Nutley, N.J.: Presbyterian and Reformed Publishing Company, 1974).

24. McClanahan, "Warfield," 420; *PRR* 13 (1902): 2, 36–37.

25. See "The Confession of Faith as Revised in 1903," *SSW* 2: 370–410. This writing first appeared as a pamphlet published in Richmond, Virginia, in 1904.

26. *SSW* 2: 377, 380–82. C. A. Salmond wrote that "the salvation, through the merit of the Redeemer, of all children dying in infancy was one of the 'recurring fervours' of Dr. [Charles] Hodge in his theological teaching." Salmond, *Princetoniana,* 34.

27. *SSW* 2: 384–86, 388, 390.

28. *SSW* 2: 392–93.

29. *SSW* 2: 398.

30. Loetscher, *The Broadening Church,* 89. In 1936 Gresham Machen asked Caspar Wistar Hodge Jr. for his opinion of B. B. Warfield's evaluation of the revisions of 1903. (The occasion for Machen's query was the debate on doctrinal standards in the newly forming Presbyterian Church of America, later called the Orthodox Presbyterian Church.) Hodge replied that he was unable to decide "whether or not the Confession as revised is self-contradictory or whether it destroys the Reformed system of doctrine." After reading

John Murray's article in *The Presbyterian Guardian* for September 1936 ("Shall We Include the Revision of 1903 in Our Creed?"), Hodge wrote to Machen again: "I can't help feeling that Dr. Warfield's article was too apologetic altogether, but I think it exceedingly plausible, and were he alive and arguing with John Murray, whose fine article in the *Guardian* I have just read, I imagine B.B.W. would unearth authorities to get the better of John. However that may be, what Murray says about the purpose of creed making at the time of the Westminster Confession and that of ecclesiastics of modern days, has my approval and admiration of the way he has said it. Also I agree with his statements about infant salvation, though B.B.W. followed Chas. Hodge and wrote at length to prove that the best Refd. thought in America and elsewhere was on his side." Iain H. Murray, "Life of John Murray," in *Collected Writings of John Murray* (Edinburgh: The Banner of Truth Trust, 1982) 3: 62–63.

31. Taylor, *The Old Testament in the Old Princeton School*, 224; Sydney E. Ahlstrom, *A Religious History of the American People* (New Haven: Yale University Press, 1972), 783.

32. A. C. McGiffert, "The Progress of Theological Thought During the Past Fifty Years," *The American Journal of Theology* 20 (1916): 324–27; Darryl G. Hart, "'Doctor Fundamentalis': An Intellectual Biography of J. Gresham Machen, 1881–1937," (Ph.D. diss., The Johns Hopkins University, 1988), 78.

33. William R. Hutchison, *The Modernist Impulse in American Protestantism* (Cambridge: Harvard University Press, 1976), 199–200. Hutchison quotes Francis Patton's son, George S. Patton: "The theory of writers . . . who seek to fit Christianity into the general scheme of the evolution of religion is fascinating; we feel its force. But let us be honest with ourselves. Let us face the question whether Christianity is a supernatural religion or not, whether it is from heaven or of men, whether it is the absolute religion or simply the purest form of religion that has yet appeared in the developmental history. If the former be true, then there is still need, as there always has been need, of a Christian apologetic. But if we believe the latter, let us give up the old terminology and the old method of defending the faith. And when we have given up the God-Man Christ Jesus, and the miracles He wrought, and His resurrection from the dead, and His atonement for sin, then at least, if not before, let us pause and ask, as Strauss asked long ago, whether we are still Christians—for surely these be-

liefs are of the essence of Christianity." *PRR* 8 (1897): 540.

34. Ahlstrom, *Religious History of the American People*, 813; William Childs Robinson, *Columbia Seminary and the Southern Presbyterian Church: A Study in Church History, Presbyterian Polity, Missionary Enterprise, and Religious Thought* (Decatur, Ga.: Dennis Lindsey Printing Company, 1931), 151.

35. *The Congregationalist*, February 15, 1900; Mark A. Noll, *Between Faith and Criticism: Evangelicals, Scholarship, and the Bible in America* (San Francisco: Harper & Row, 1986), 47.

11. The Faculty of 1902

1. For Patton's presidency at Princeton University see Marsden, *The Soul of the American University*, chapter 13, "Making the World Safe from the Traditionalist Establishment," 219–35; and Paul C. Kemeny, "President Francis Landey Patton, Princeton University, and Faculty Ferment," *AP* 69 (1991): 111–21.

2. *The Inauguration of the Rev. Francis Landey Patton* (New York: Gray Brothers, 1888), 43; *PRR* 6 (1895): 655; Marsden, *The Soul of the American University*, 220.

3. Paul C. Kemeny, "He Could 'Not Be Depended On For Anything At All'; Francis Landey Patton's Presidency at Princeton University, 1888–1902," unpublished paper, 18; Marsden, *The Soul of the American University*, 221. Some of the seminary faculty also joined in the petition for the liquor license. The Old School heritage of Princeton Seminary held that since drinking of alcoholic beverages was not forbidden in Scripture, it was a matter of Christian liberty.

4. Kemeny, "Keeping Princeton a 'Christian College,'" 7.

5. Marsden, *The Soul of the American University*, 221; Frances Wright Saunders, *Ellen Axson Wilson: First Lady Between Two Worlds* (Chapel Hill: University of North Carolina Press, 1985), 115.

6. C. Osgood, *Lights in Nassau Hall: A Book of the Bicentennial Princeton, 1746–1946* (Princeton: Princeton University Press, 1951), 30; Hoeveler, *James McCosh*, 341; Clarence E. Macartney, *The Making of a Minister: The Autobiography of Clarence E. Macartney* (Great Neck, N. Y.: Channel Press, 1961), 122; Kemeny, "Patton's Presidency," 20.

7. Only 30 percent of entering students in 1915 were Presbyterians. In the 1920s Episcopalians and Presbyterians each constituted about one third of each class.

8. Marsden, *The Soul of the American University*, 201; Kemeny, "Keeping Princeton a 'Christian College,'" 11–12.

9. Marsden, *The Soul of the American University*, 222; Kemeny, "Patton's Presidency," 24.

10. Marsden, *The Soul of the American University*, 223.

11. David Chalmers, "Woodrow Wilson," in *Encyclopedia of Religion in the South*, ed. Samuel S. Hill (Mercer University Press, 1984), 842. One of Wilson's earlier reforms was the honor system. Princeton graduate and novelist F. Scott Fitzgerald wrote: "Princeton's sacred tradition is the honor system, a method of pledging that to the amazement of outsiders actually works, with consequent elimination of suspicion and supervision. It is handed over as something humanly precious to the freshmen within a week of their entrance. Personally I have never seen or heard of a Princeton man cheating in an examination." Fitzgerald, *Afternoon of an Author*, 75–76. Much of the credit for the establishment of the honor system belongs to Ellen Axson Wilson, who worked with a group of students concerned about cheating. She prodded her husband to press for the reform at faculty meetings. The plan was inaugurated at midyear examinations in February 1893. Saunders, *Ellen Axson Wilson*, 89–90.

12. Kemeny, "Keeping Princeton a 'Christian College,'" 15; Selden, *Princeton Theological Seminary*, 84; *PSB* 58 (1965): 51.

13. O. T. Allis, "Personal Impressions of Dr. Warfield," *Banner of Truth* 89 (1971): 10; *PTR* 19 (1921): 370. In 1965 Gwilym O. Griffith, a Welshman who studied at Princeton from 1906 to 1909, described his recollections of Dr. Warfield: "With his noble head, his impressive profile, his patriarchal beard, he exhaled authority. Perhaps he was more impressive when sitting, for his stature was not commanding; but, gowned and seated at his lecture-desk, he inspired something akin to awe. His utterance was marked by a slight—very slight—lisp, which was by no means an impediment; oddly enough, it lent character and distinction to his speech." *PSB* 58 (February 1965): 50.

14. J. Gresham Machen, *The Christian View of Man* (New York: MacMillan, 1937; repr., The Banner of Truth Trust, 1965), 273; Warfield, *Studies in Theology*, 104–5.

15. Jay E. Adams, *Studies in Preaching: the Homiletical Innovations of Andrew W. Blackwood* (Presbyterian and Reformed Publishing Company, 1976), 41; John E. Meeter, "Foreword," *SSW* 2: ix. After teaching at Knox College, Toronto, for two years,

Robinson became professor at McCormick Theological Seminary in 1898, where he served until 1939.

16. Adams, *Blackwood*, 35, 40.

17. Machen, "Christianity in Conflict," 264; letter from C. D. Brokenshire to John E. Meeter, June 25, 1942; *Banner of Truth* 89 (1971): 13. Warfield contributed an article on "Singing and Believing" to *The Presbyterian* and signed it "O. L. D. Fogy" (*SSW* 1: 379–80).

18. O. T. Allis, "Personal Impressions of Dr. Warfield," *The Banner of Truth* 89 (February 1971): 11. Allis wrote that "this *obiter dictum* impressed itself on my memory more than anything else in the discussion."

19. *PSB* 58 (1965): 50–51.

20. *SSW* 1: 395–96.

21. *SSW* 1: 383–84.

22. For a bibliography of Vos's writings see *Redemptive History and Biblical Interpretation*, ed. Gaffin, 547–59. His major works include: *The Idea of Biblical Theology as a Science and as a Theological Discipline* (1894), *The Teaching of Jesus Concerning the Kingdom of God and the Church* (1903), *The Self-Disclosures of Jesus: The Modern Debate about the Messianic Consciousness* (1926), and *Biblical Theology: Old and New Testaments* (1948).

23. The *Princeton Seminary Bulletin* 43 (1950), noting Vos's death, states that "his dry wit was the delight of his friends" and "his published writings were the despair of his contemporaries" (42).

24. Ned B. Stonehouse, *J. Gresham Machen: A Biographical Memoir* (Grand Rapids: Wm. B. Eerdmans, 1954; repr., Edinburgh: The Banner of Truth Trust, 1987), 72; Geerhardus Vos, *Grace and Glory: Sermons Preached in the Chapel of Princeton Theological Seminary* (Grand Rapids: The Reformed Press, 1922), 104.

25. Catherine F. Vos, *Child's Story Bible* (Grand Rapids: Wm. B. Eerdmans Publishing Company, 1935–36; repr., The Banner of Truth Trust, 1969).

26. Taylor, *The Old Testament in the Old Princeton School*, 254.

27. *PSB* 58 (1965): 50.

28. Taylor, *The Old Testament in the Old Princeton School*, 268; William White Jr., *Van Til: Defender of the Faith* (Nashville: Thomas Nelson Publishers, 1979), 100.

29. Taylor, *The Old Testament in the Old Princeton School*, 270. Taylor states that Wilson "applied his scientific approach most rigorously to his studies on the book of Daniel which earned him the reputation of being America's last great

defender of the traditional position regarding Daniel's authorship and dating" (269).

30. J. Gresham Machen, "Christianity in Conflict," in *Contemporary American Theology: Theological Autobiographies,* ed. Vergilius Ferm (New York: Round Table Press, Inc., 1932) 1: 253.

31. *PTR* 22 (1924): 200, 218; Macartney, *The Making of a Minister,* 124. See John DeWitt, "The Relations of Church History to Preaching," *PTR* 5 (1907): 98–112.

32. W. B. Greene's major work was *The Metaphysics of Christian Apologetics.*

33. *PSB* 58 (February 1965): 50. As a student Gresham Machen described Greene's lectures in apologetics as "hopelessly weak," but he later came to appreciate Dr. Greene's teaching. Hart, "Doctor Fundamentalis," 51.

34. Stonehouse, *Machen,* 391; *PSB* 58 (1965): 49–50.

35. See David J. Burrell, *The Sermon: Its Construction and Delivery* (New York: Fleming H. Revell Company, 1913); Adams, *Blackwood,* 36–37. Years later Blackwood, after successful pastorates, returned to Princeton to teach homiletics, no doubt in part motivated by his own youthful disappointment at not finding good teaching methods in the practical theology courses of the seminary during his time as a student there.

36. Salmond, *Princetoniana,* 14; *A Modern School of the Prophets* (Princeton Theological Seminary), 8.

37. B. B. Warfield, "The Princeton Seminary of the Future," *New York Observer,* May 10, 1906.

12. J. Gresham Machen

1. Later Sidney and Mary Lanier spent a few happy years in Baltimore—sometimes called "the last refuge of the Confederate spirit in exile"—where Sidney won fame as a musician, poet, and writer, and where they enjoyed the pleasant company, good wine, and wonderful food of the Machen home. One of Gresham Machen's favorite poems was Sidney Lanier's "Marshes of Glynn."

2. Machen, "Christianity in Conflict," 248. In a review of Machen's *Christian Faith in the Modern World* (New York: Macmillan, 1936) Clarence Edward Macartney wrote: "In the chapter, 'How God May Be Known,' he thus speaks of his impressions when he stood on the Matterhorn: 'I saw the vastness of the Italian plain which was like a symbol of infinity.

I saw the snows of distant mountains. I saw the sweet green valleys, far, far below at my feet. I saw the whole glorious round of glittering peaks, bathed in an unearthly light; and as I see that glorious vision again before me now, I am thankful from the bottom of my heart that from my Mother's knee I have known to whom all that glory is due.' (Those who have heard Dr. Machen speak of his mother will not wonder that he writes the word with a capital M)." Macartney Archives, Geneva College, Beaver Falls, Pennsylvania.

3. Machen, "Christianity in Conflict," 248–49; Longfield, *The Presbyterian Controversy*, 32. See also Bradley James Longfield, "The Presbyterian Controversy, 1922–1936: Christianity, Culture, and Ecclesiastical Conflict" (Ph.D. diss., Duke University, 1988).

4. Machen, "Christianity in Conflict," 246–48.

5. J. Gresham Machen, *What is Faith?* (New York: Macmillan Company, 1927), 22, 43. Machen added, "And I will venture to say that although my mental ability was certainly of no extraordinary kind I had a better knowledge of the Bible at fourteen years of age than is possessed by many students in the theological Seminaries of the present day." See Donald G. Miller, *The Scent of Eternity: A Life of Harris Elliott Kirk of Baltimore* (Macon, Ga., 1989). In 1909 the Princeton Seminary board of directors considered Harris Kirk, one of the Southern church's most popular preachers, for the vacant chair of homiletics. When Kirk refused the offer Machen was relieved, because, according to D. G. Hart, Machen believed that Kirk "was too much beholden to the standard pieties of Victorian Protestantism and not aware of the issues that were dividing the American churches." Kirk knew nothing of Machen's reaction and later preached at Machen's ordination. D. G. Hart, *Defending the Faith: J. Gresham Machen and the Crisis of Conservative Protestantism in Modern America* (Baltimore: The Johns Hopkins University Press, 1994), 29.

6. Machen, "Christianity in Conflict," 251; Hart, "Doctor Fundamentalis," 23; Hart, *Defending the Faith*, 19.

7. Hart, "Doctor Fundamentalis," 43. In about 1900 an arrangement was made with Princeton University to permit Princeton Seminary students to enroll concurrently as graduate students in the university and after four terms to receive the master of arts degree. Over twenty per cent of the seminary students pursued further work at Princeton University during the decades of the 1900s and 1910s. Selden,

Princeton Theological Seminary, 69. During his time at the seminary Machen earned a master's degree from the university.

8. Selden, *Princeton Theological Seminary*, 66. Other clubs—such as Adelphian, Benedict, Boors, Canterbury, Epicurean, and Irish—came and went, but the four "great" clubs were Benham, Friars, Calvin, and Warfield, which replaced the Seminary Club in the early 1930s.

9. Machen, "Christianity in Conflict," 252, 254, 264. Patton had been a frequent guest in the Machen home in Baltimore. "I admired him then greatly, and I came afterwards to love him with all my heart," Machen wrote.

10. Hart, "Doctor Fundamentalis," 51; *PTR* 3 (1905): 641–70; *PTR* 4 (1906): 37–81; Machen, "Christianity in Conflict," 264.

11. Stonehouse, *Machen*, 85, 97; Hart, *Defending the Faith*, 14–15; Machen, "Christianity in Conflict," 258–59. If Machen had been in Princeton that fall he would have seen the eleventh annual football game between Army and Navy played on the neutral ground of University Field. President and Mrs. Theodore Roosevelt had lunch with the Woodrow Wilsons at Prospect and attended the game. Following the custom that the president of the United States, as the commander in chief, view one half of an Army-Navy game from the Army side and the other half from the Navy side, Roosevelt crossed the field at halftime—exuberant, smiling, waving his hat, and tugging along the dignified university president.

12. Machen, "Christianity in Conflict," 258.

13. Longfield, *The Presbyterian Controversy*, 41.

14. Stonehouse, *Machen*, 107–8.

15. Stonehouse, *Machen*, 140; Henry W. Coray, *J. Gresham Machen: A Silhouette* (Grand Rapids: Kregel Publications, 1981), 19.

16. Machen, "Christianity in Conflict," 257.

17. Stonehouse, *Machen*, 125.

18. Stonehouse, *Machen*, 126.

19. Stonehouse, *Machen*, 117, 122, 128; Hart, "Doctor Fundamantalis," 50.

20. Machen, "Christianity in Conflict," 256, 258.

21. Stonehouse, *Machen*, 139.

22. Stonehouse, *Machen*, 209; Machen, "Christianity in Conflict," 252–53; Hart, *Defending the Faith*, 130.

23. Stonehouse, *Machen*, 171.

24. Hart, "Doctor Fundamantalis," 57.

13. Zealous for the Gospel

1. Longfield, *The Presbyterian Controversy*, 137.
2. Stonehouse, *Machen*, 215; Longfield, *The Presbyterian Controversy*, 228.
3. Longfield, *The Presbyterian Controversy*, 138.
4. *Princeton Theological Seminary Alumni News*, Summer 1980, 2–5.
5. B. B. Warfield, *Biblical Foundations*, (London: Tyndale Press, 1958), 8–9.
6. *SSW* 2: 291, 294, 596; B. B. Warfield, *Critical Reviews* (New York: Oxford University Press, 1932), 322; Warfield, *Studies in Theology*, 587. In seven articles published in the *Presbyterian and Reformed Review* between October 1896 and October 1900 Warfield reviewed the seven volumes of Adolf Harnack's *History of Dogma*. He much appreciated James Orr's *Progress of Dogma* (published in 1897), which paralleled Warfield's own view of doctrinal development.
7. B. B. Warfield, *Christology and Criticism* (New York: Oxford University Press, 1929), 450–51.
8. B. B. Warfield, "Christian Supernaturalism," in *Biblical and Theological Studies* (Philadelphia: Presbyterian and Reformed Publishing Company, 1952), 5, 7, 21.
9. *PTR* 4 (1906): 132; McClanahan, "Warfield," 467–68.
10. Warfield, *Christology and Criticism*, 259, 261–62, 310; *SSW* 2: 296.
11. B. B. Warfield, *The Person and Work of Christ* (Philadelphia: Presbyterian and Reformed Publishing Company, 1950), 376–77.
12. *SSW* 1: 193, 195, 202.
13. B. B. Warfield, *The Lord of Glory: A Study of the Designations of our Lord in the New Testament with Especial Reference to His Deity* (New York: American Tract Society, 1907), 298, 303–4. The book was dedicated to William Park Armstrong Jr. and Caspar Wistar Hodge Jr. with a statement in Greek meaning "To two disciples; to two fellow workers; to two teachers; to two fellow bondslaves; to two men of the same mind, I give thanks."
14. Warfield, *Christology and Criticism*, 151, 163.
15. B. B. Warfield, "Christless Christianity," *Harvard Theological Review* 5 (1912): 423–73; *Christology and Criticism*, 313–67. Ethelbert Warfield considered this one of B. B. Warfield's finest writings.
16. *PTR* 4 (1906): 306–16.

17. B. B. Warfield, "The Princeton Seminary of the Future," *New York Observer*, May 10, 1906.

14. Incarnate Truth

1. *Princeton Sermons: Chiefly by the Professors in Princeton Theological Seminary* (New York: Fleming H. Revell Company, 1893), 99, 107–8.
2. B. B. Warfield, "On the Antiquity and the Unity of the Human Race," *PTR* 9 (1911): 1–25; and Warfield, *Studies in Theology*, 235–58; David N. Livingstone, "B. B. Warfield, the Theory of Evolution and Early Fundamentalism," *The Evangelical Quarterly* 58 (1986): 79–80.
3. *Princeton Alumni Weekly*, April 6, 1916, 652. Warfield was thirty years old in 1881, three years after he began to teach at Western Seminary.
4. Walter Lowrie, the Kierkegaard scholar who studied at Princeton Seminary from 1890–93, wrote in 1938 a footnote in one of his volumes of Kierkegaard's works: "Brandes conjectured that if S. K. had lived in his time he might have been perverse enough to reject Darwin's celebrated theory of evolution. In fact, he did emphatically reject it in advance . . . Exactly the same argument was urged by Benjamin Warfield, who was my teacher of theology in 1890. In those days it was scoffed at or ignored, but in the end it brought *that* theory of evolution into disrepute." Soren Kierkegaard, *Training in Christianity*, trans. and ed. Walter Lowrie (Princeton: Princeton University Press, 1941), 30.
5. Manuscript notes for lectures on "Anthropology" (1888), Speer Library, Princeton Theological Seminary; quoted in Johnson, "Attitudes of Princeton Theologians Toward Darwinism," 197–98. In his 1888 lectures on the "Religious Aspect of Evolution," McCosh stated that evolution was supported by scientific evidence and that Christians should look upon it "simply as the method by which God works." McCosh, *The Religious Aspect of Evolution*, 7.
6. Lectures on "Anthropology"; quoted in Johnson, "Attitudes of Princeton Theologians Toward Darwinism," 246.
7. James Orr, *God's Image in Man and Its Defacement in the Light of Modern Denials* (London: Hodder and Stoughton, 1905), 95, 125–26, 151–52.
8. B. B. Warfield, "Review of *God's Image in Man* by James Orr," *PTR* 4 (1906): 555–58; B. B. Warfield, *Critical Reviews*, 136–41.

Although Warfield saw greater possibility of divinely guided development in the forming of the human body than did James Orr, he was uncomfortable with Orr's view that some higher notion was needed to synthesize "evolution" and "special creation." Warfield believed that such an idea would blur the distinction between evolution (or development by divine providence) and mediate creation (or divine intervention). It would play into the hands of the antisupernaturalists, Warfield warned, who seek to rule out any divine intervention, at least, after the origin of matter. Warfield, "Review of *God's Image in Man* by James Orr,": 555–58. Lectures on "Anthropology"; quoted in Johnson, "Attitudes of Princeton Theologians Toward Darwinism," 239.

9. Mark Noll has emphasized aptly this characteristic element of Warfield's theology, pointing out that "the conception of *concursus* enabled Warfield to study without fear the humanity of Scripture while retaining belief in its divine origin and character. It was this conception that allowed him to focus on authorial intent when discussing the doctrine of Scripture, and that allowed him to approve a providential form of evolution. To Warfield, *concursus* was grounded in general considerations of both God's immanence and his transcendence, and it was a conception that Warfield linked to doctrines of both providence and grace. It was, in other words, an interpretive device growing out of mature theological reflection." Mark A. Noll, "Evangelicals and the Study of the Bible," *The Reformed Journal* 34 (April 1984): 19.

10. *PRR* 6 (1895): 366. Warfield, *Critical Reviews*, 322. In 1908 Warfield expressed a more negative assessment of the theory of evolution when he wrote that the scientific difficulties were actually "destructive" of the theory—not of its "plausibility" but its "actual working power." "For ourselves," Warfield wrote, "we confess frankly that the whole body of evolutionary constructions prevalent today impresses us simply as a vast mass of speculation, which may or may not prove to have a kernel of truth in it." Warfield, *Critical Reviews*, 182, 186. The issue continued to be discussed at Princeton and in the pages of *The Princeton Theological Review*. Ministers such as John Duffield, theologians such as George Frederick Wright (professor at Oberlin), and various scientists put forth their views in the *Review*'s pages.

11. Ahlstrom, *Religious History of the American People*, 803. Charles Stelzle (1869–1941) was born in poverty in New York City's

famous Bowery. He attended Moody Bible Institute for two years and was ordained a Presbyterian minister in 1900. He combined a liberal political agenda with a conservative theology and a warmly evangelical spirituality.

12. Hodge, *Evangelical Theology*, 285–86.
13. See Earl William Kennedy, "William Brenton Greene's Treatment of Social Issues," *JPH* 40 (1962): 92–112; and Gary Scott Smith, "Conservative Presbyterians: The Gospel, Social Reform, and the Church in the Progressive Era," *AP* 70 (1992): 93–110. For a brief summary of Greene's views see his article on "The Church and the Social Question." *PTR* 10 (1912): 377–98.
14. *PTR* 10 (1912): 377; *PTR* 5 (1907): 700–1; *PTR* 11 (1913): 166.
15. *PTR* 10 (1912): 379.
16. *PTR* 10 (1912): 385.
17. *PTR* 10 (1912): 379–80, 396–97; *PTR* 11 (1913): 168.
18. *PTR* 10 (1912): 389, 393.
19. *PTR* 10 (1912): 385; *PTR* 14 (1916): 512. See *PTR* 11 (1913): 119–22.
20. *PTR* 10 (1912): 515–16; *PTR* 5 (1907): 701.
21. *PTR* 14 (1916): 512; *PTR* 12 (1914): 521. The loosely organized Christian Socialist Fellowship, founded in 1906, affiliated itself with the Socialist party, which in the election of 1912 drew almost a million votes. Charles Erdman, who contributed the article "The Church and Socialism" for *The Fundamentals*, stated that there was so little biblical teaching on political and social issues that the church had "no right to ally itself with any political party, or to commit itself to any one form of social or industrial organization." William Brenton Greene wrote that even if it could be established "that socialism is the cure-all for social ills, it would still be an open question whether the church is as well qualified to lecture on socialism as she is to preach the Gospel and whether failure in the former might not lead to failure in the latter." Charles R. Erdman, "The Church and Socialism," in *The Fundamentals: A Testimony to the Truth* (Chicago: Testimony Publishing Company) 12: 108–19; *PTR* 5 (1907): 701.
22. Francis L. Patton, "On the Education of Ministers: A Reply to President Eliot," *PR* (July 1883): 49–59. B. B. Warfield wrote in 1909: "For a hundred years, now, our Unitarian friends have been urging upon us this secularized conception of the ministerial functions and of the minister's training. Ex-

president Charles W. Eliot, of Harvard, for example, winningly commended it to us a quarter of a century ago in a much-talked-of article in *The Princeton Review,* but was happily set right by Dr. F. L. Patton in the next number." *SSW* 1: 370.

23. B. B. Warfield, "The Constitution of the Seminary Curriculum," *The Presbyterian Quarterly* 38 (1896): 413–15, 426, 430.

24. B. B. Warfield and John D. Davis, "Report of the Faculty of Princeton Theological Seminary to the Board of Directors on the Study of the Bible," Princeton, New Jersey, 1 May 1903, 1, 3–4.

25. Ronald Thomas Clutter, "The Reorientation of Princeton Theological Seminary 1900–1929" (Th.D. diss., Dallas Theological Seminary, 1982), 79, 83.

26. B. B. Warfield, *The Fundamental Curriculum of the Seminary,* 9; *SSW* 1: 373; *SSW* 2: 212.

27. Stonehouse, *Machen,* 150–52.

28. Francis L. Patton, in *Biblical and Theological Studies by the Members of the Faculty of Princeton Theological Seminary, published in commemoration of the one hundredth anniversary of the founding of the seminary* (New York: Charles Scribner's Sons, 1912), 3.

29. Selden, *Princeton Theological Seminary,* 97–98.

30. *A Modern School of the Prophets,* 4–6, 9, 14.

31. *PTR* 1 (1903): 239; *SSW* 2: 468–96.

32. B. B. Warfield, *Calvin and Augustine* (Philadelphia: Presbyterian and Reformed Publishing Company, 1974), 488–91. The articles in *The Princeton Theological Review* for 1909 were devoted largely to Calvin and Calvinism: "Calvin, an Epigone of the Middle Ages or an Initiator of Modern Times?" and "Music in the Work of Calvin," by E. Doumergue; "Calvin and Common Grace," by Herman Bavinck; "Calvin's Doctrine of God," "Calvin's Doctrine of the Knowledge of God," and "Calvin's Doctrine of the Trinity," by B. B. Warfield; "John Calvin—the Man," by John DeWitt; and "The Reformation and Natural Law," by A. Lang.

33. Marsden, *The Soul of the American University,* 228; Leslie, *Gentlemen and Scholars,* 121; John M. Mulder, *Woodrow Wilson: The Years of Preparation* (Princeton: Princeton University Press, 1978), 163.

34. Marsden, *The Soul of the American University,* 224.

35. James T. Burtchaell, "The Decline and Fall of the Christian College," in *First Things* 12 (1991): 27; Mulder, *Woodrow Wilson,* 178; Marsden, *The Soul of the American University:* , 227, 231.The attempt of Princeton College to combine academic

learning and evangelical Christianity has been noted throughout these two volumes of the history of Princeton Seminary. During its early history the college was dominated by the piety and Calvinism of its first presidents. John Witherspoon's goal was for a college equally dedicated to evangelical piety and academic endeavor. After a dangerous tilt toward enlightenment learning during the Samuel Stanhope Smith years, the college swung back to a greater emphasis on Bible study and spiritual life in Ashbel Green's administration. An appealing combination of scholarship and piety marked the administrations of Presidents Carnahan and Maclean. Princeton attempted to move toward greater academic standing without jettisoning its evangelical convictions and practices during the time of James McCosh. Francis Patton tried to keep Princeton Christian in some distinctive, doctrinal sense while accepting changes over which he had no control. By the time of Wilson's presidency, forces long at work in American university life pushed Princeton toward nonsectarian and even secular academic ideals. George Marsden has demonstrated that the secularization of the American universities was not a sharp discontinuity with their evangelical pasts, demanded by militant secularists, but a gradual modification introduced by professing Christians, intended to enhance rather than annul the Christian culture of their institutions.

15. The Centennial and the New President

1. Stonehouse, *Machen*, 61–62; *Centennial Celebration of the Theological Seminary*, 346.
2. Stonehouse, *Machen*, 183–84.
3. *Centennial Celebration of the Theological Seminary*, 469, 498, 517.
4. *Centennial Celebration of the Theological Seminary*, 557.
5. Stonehouse, *Machen*, 184; *Centennial Celebration of the Theological Seminary*, 565.
6. Alexander, *Address . . . 1912*, 18–20. Charles Beatty Alexander (1849–1927) was a distinguished lawyer and trustee of Princeton University. The university's Alexander Hall was named in his honor in 1892.
7. *Is Jesus God?—an Argument by graduates of Princeton Seminary* (New York: American Tract Society, 1912).
8. Hart, "Doctor Fundamentalis," 100.
9. *PTR* 22 (1924): 230, 232. John DeWitt died on November 19,

1923, singing softly the first lines of his favorite hymn, "Rock of ages, cleft for me, let me hide myself in thee. . . ."

10. *PTR* 11 (1913): 1, 6.

11. *PTR* 11 (1913): 7. George Marsden comments: "This insight—which I think is a profound one—does not seem to have been compelling to many American Protestant leaders, either liberal, moderate, or conservative, in the first half of the twentieth century." Marsden, *Fundamentalism and Evangelicalism*, 200.

12. *PTR* 11 (1913): 14–15.

13. *PTR* 11 (1913): 14–15; J. Gresham Machen, *What is Christianity? and other Addresses*, ed. Ned B. Stonehouse (Grand Rapids: William B. Eerdmans, 1951), 156–69; Stonehouse, *Machen*, 179–80.

14. Mrs. Howard Taylor, *Borden of Yale '09: "The Life that Counts"* (Philadelphia: China Inland Mission, 1926), 270.

15. In 1886 Francis Patton, commenting on A. A. Hodge's love for Princeton, said, "Sometimes, when my own heart yearns for the scenes of my childhood and the blue waters of my island-home, I can appreciate his affection for Princeton: it was home." Patton, "Discourse," in Hodge, *Evangelical Theology*, xix.

16. Selden, *Princeton Theological Seminary*, 103; Stonehouse, *Machen*, 66.

17. Clutter, "Reorientation of Princeton Theological Seminary," 91. Writing to his mother on February 24, 1916, Machen commented, "Fortunately, I *like* Dr. Stevenson much better than I did at first." Stonehouse, *Machen*, 221. Added to Stevenson's duties as president was that of professor of the history of religion and Christian missions.

18. *PSB* 9 (1915): 18.

19. *PSB* 9 (1915): 6.

20. *PSB* 9 (1915): 21. After considerable agonizing, the trustees in 1911 had elected John Hibben (by a 17-to-9 vote) as president of the bitterly divided university.

21. Clutter, "Reorientation of Princeton Theological Seminary," 100, 103. In his dismay over the curriculum change, Dr. Warfield stopped attending faculty meetings until Dr. Stevenson took a leave of absence for six months to serve as a chaplain during World War I. Then, Warfield—as the senior member of the faculty—was present at every faculty meeting. When Stevenson returned to the seminary in April 1919 Warfield once again was conspicuously absent. He attended

only two meetings from that day until his death in February 1921.

22. Stonehouse, *Machen*, 220–21.

23. Clutter, "Reorientation of Princeton Theological Seminary," 91, 128, 130–31; Stonehouse, *Machen*, 212.

16. *The War Years*

1. See Machen's essays "Mountains and Why We Love Them" and "The Benefits of Walking" in *What is Christianity?* 304–17. During his final months in Europe following World War I Machen wrote to his mother, "Sometimes a longing for the mountains comes over me that is almost like a passion. I hate to see the best mountaineering years of my life slipping by unused. The passion grows on me, instead of diminishing, as physical vigor declines. Sometimes I imagine that I am just starting up for some great peak on one of those frosty Alpine mornings. I tremble with delight at the thought of the joys alone. But the subsequent plunge into the humdrum of mere lowland life is a cruel deception. The air of the heights is to me more intoxicating than wine." Stonehouse, *Machen*, 289.

2. Hart, *Defending the Faith*, 32. Hart writes that Machen "expressed discomfort with Victorian Protestantism" in this sermon and put forth "a definition of Christian joy that broke with the optimism that then prevailed widely in American Protestantism."

3. Hart, *Defending the Faith*, 44. Machen's lessons were published in book form under the title *The New Testament: An Introduction to its Literature and History*, ed. W. John Cook (Edinburgh: The Banner of Truth Trust, 1976).

4. Benjamin B. Warfield, *The Plan of Salvation* (Philadelphia: Presbyterian Board of Publication, 1915; repr., Grand Rapids: Wm. B. Eerdmans Publishing Company, 1970). Warfield dedicated this book to "John DeWitt, Emeritus Professor of Church History in Princeton Seminary—Lover of Letters, Lover of Men, Lover of God."

5. Warfield, *The Plan of Salvation*, 33, 36, 47–48, 50–51.

6. Warfield, *The Plan of Salvation*, 53, 55–56, 68.

7. Warfield, *The Plan of Salvation*, 69, 75.

8. Warfield, *The Plan of Salvation*, 87, 98–99, 102. Warfield wrote that "it is a mere caricature of Calvinistic particularism to represent it as finding its center in the proclamation that there are few that are saved." Warfield, *The Plan of Salvation*, 97.

9. Warfield, *The Plan of Salvation*, 104.
10. Stonehouse, *Machen*, 226–28.
11. *PSB* 10 (1916): 18.
12. Machen, *What is Christianity?* 170–72, 182–84. "Though not billed as such, the lecture was clearly Machen's response to his former teacher, Wilhelm Herrmann," writes Bradley Longfield. Longfield, *The Presbyterian Controversy*, 48.
13. Stonehouse, *Machen*, 221.
14. Warfield, *Biblical Doctrines*, 375, 396–97.
15. Salmond had Warfield's letter to him published in *The Scotsman*, April 25, 1916, with the comment "Were I at liberty to give the writer's name, he would be recognized by many as one of the acutest and sanest thinkers in America."
16. Ahlstrom, *Religious History of the American People*, 884.
17. Hart, *Defending the Faith*, 45; Stonehouse, *Machen*, 255.
18. B. B. Warfield, *Counterfeit Miracles* (New York: C. Scribner's Sons, 1918; repr., as *Miracles: Yesterday and Today, True and False*, Grand Rapids: Wm. B. Eerdmans Publishing Company, 1954; repr., as *Counterfeit Miracles*, Edinburgh: The Banner of Truth Trust, 1972), 3, 5–6. Colin Brown writes that "Warfield's book was marked by the solid erudition and commitment to Reformed evangelicalism that characterized his other writings." He also notes that "a certain poignancy attaches to Warfield's work in view of the debilitating illness of his wife throughout their married life." Colin Brown, *Miracles and the Critical Mind* (Grand Rapids: Eerdmans Publishing Company, 1984), 199.
19. Charles R. Erdman, "Modern Spiritual Movements," in *Biblical and Theological Studies*, 365, 385.
20. B. B. Warfield, *Perfectionism* (New York: Oxford University Press, 1931) 2: 568–70, 580, 584.
21. Warfield, *Perfectionism* 2: 563. Marsden describes Warfield's criticism of Keswick as a "quarrel between allies," soon overshadowed by the controversy with modernism. George M. Marsden, *Fundamentalism and American Culture: The Shaping of Twentieth-Century Evangelicalism: 1870–1925* (New York: Oxford University Press, 1980), 99.
22. Wilbur B. Wallis writes that in the thousand pages of the two volumes on "Perfectionism," Warfield "deals with two major lines of development. The one is the unbelieving, critical attack on the Reformed conception of the Christian life. The work of Albrecht Ritschl came under review in two studies, 'Albrecht Ritschl and his Doctrine of Christian Perfection.'

This rationalistic treatment of the Christian life was further reviewed by Warfield in the three articles, '"Miserable Sinner" Christianity in the Hands of the Rationalists.' On the Bible-believing side was the holiness movement flowing from the work of Robert Pearsall Smith. This led to the Keswick movement in Britain and linked onto the Pentecostal development in America. Warfield's review of these 19th and early 20th century developments give important perspectives for understanding the problems of our own day." Wilber B. Wallis, "Benjamin B. Warfield: Didactic and Polemic Theologian," *Presbyterion: Covenant Seminary Review* 3 (1977): 79. Warfield also produced articles on the "Oberlin" perfectionism (with a treatment of the theology of Charles Finney), John Humphrey Noyes and his "Bible Communists," and the "Mystical Perfectionism" of Thomas Cogswell Upham.

23. Warfield, *Perfectionism* 1: 55, 113–14.
24. Stonehouse, *Machen*, 264.
25. Stonehouse, *Machen*, 257, 260, 274.
26. Stonehouse, *Machen*, 261.
27. Stonehouse, *Machen*, 283–84, 287.
28. Stonehouse, *Machen*, 291–93.
29. Machen, *What is Christianity?* 211.
30. During the 1910s and 1920s a higher percentage of Princeton Seminary students than ever before became foreign missionaries. Restricting totals to primary occupations in a life, the percentage ranges from a low of 1.4 % of students attending from 1815 to 1829 to a high of 8.2 % of students from the 1910s and 1920s. Peter Wallace and Mark Noll, "The Students of Princeton Seminary, 1812–1929: A Research Note," *AP* 72 (1994): 212.
31. *Princeton Theological Seminary Alumni/ae News* 27 (1989), 7. Zwemer gave another series of lectures in 1920 and joined the Princeton faculty in 1929. When he was installed as Professor of the History of Religion and Christian Missions on October 1, 1930, he said: "It is a far call from the camel's saddle in Oman or a seat in a coffee shop in the bazaars of Cairo to a Professor's chair. I count myself happy, however, henceforth to have a small part in promoting those high ideals of the Christian ministry as a world-wide mission, for which Princeton has always stood." J. Christy Wilson, *Apostle to Islam: A Biography of Samuel M. Zwemer* (Grand Rapids: Baker Book House, 1952), 210.
32. The first Japanese to receive a degree from the seminary was

Chojuro Aoki (1901), who devoted his life to teaching in his native land. Toyohiko Kagawa graduated in 1915 and became an internationally famous evangelist and social worker. Of the 37 South African students who attended during the first three decades of the twentieth century, every one returned home after finishing studies in the United States.

33. Mr. Payne was engaged in the petroleum business in Titusville, Pennsylvania, where the first oil well had been drilled in 1859.

34. J. Gresham Machen, *The Origin of Paul's Religion* (New York: Macmillan, 1921; repr., Grand Rapids: Wm. B. Eerdmans Publishing Company, 1947). The book was dedicated to "William Park Armstrong—My Guide in the Study of the New Testament and in all Good Things."

35. Machen, *The Origin of Paul's Religion*, 169, 317.

36. Stonehouse, *Machen*, 331–32.

37. Hart, "Doctor Fundamentalis," 118.

38. Hart, "Doctor Fundamentalis," 122. Mark Noll writes that in *The Origin of Paul's Religion* and his other works Machen "largely succeeded in blending concern for theological principle with scholarly care in historical reconstruction." Noll, *Between Faith and Criticism*, 54. George Marsden describes *The Origin of Paul's Religion* as a monument to "careful historical research and argumentation." *PSB* 11 (1990): 51. Carl F. H. Henry, *Confessions of a Theologian: An Autobiography* (Waco, Texas: Word Books, 1986), 93. Floyd V. Filson, "The Study of the New Testament," in *Protestant Thought in the Twentieth Century: Whence and Where?* ed. Arnold S. Nash (New York, 1951), 60.

17. Warfield of Princeton

1. From Princeton College Warfield received the doctor of divinity degree in 1880 and the doctor of laws degree in 1892. He also received honorary doctorates from Davidson College in 1892 and Lafayette College in 1911.

2. Warfield's humility was noted often by his contemporaries. The Princeton University class historian wrote in 1901 that "the Reverend Dr. Warfield says that there is nothing for him to tell of himself during the past five years, as his is an uneventful life." A few years later the historian reported, "Having received no communication, Warfield is known to be alive because he was seen by several of the class walking on

the campus at Reunion." McClanahan, "Warfield," 18.

3. Hugh T. Kerr, "Warfield: The Person Behind the Theology," paper presented at the Annie Kinkead Warfield lectures at Princeton Seminary, February 1982. In his will B. B. Warfield endowed a lectureship at Princeton Seminary to include at least six lectures on some topic of Reformed theology and to carry not his name but that of his wife—Annie Kinkead Warfield. Dr. Kerr was the Benjamin Breckinridge Warfield Professor of Systematic Theology at Princeton Seminary.

4. Stonehouse, *Machen,* 220.

5. Edward Heerema, *R. B.: A Prophet in the Land* (Jordan Station, Ontario: Paideia Press, 1986), 44; *SSW* 1: 233.

6. William Childs Robinson, *Our Lord: An Affirmation of the Deity of Christ* (Grand Rapids: Wm. B. Eerdmans Publishing Company, 1949), 123–24. Robinson was a graduate student at Princeton in 1920–21 and was present for Dr. Warfield's last lecture. After serving for a time as pastor in the Presbyterian Church in the United States of America he became professor at Columbia Seminary in 1926, where he taught until his retirement in 1967. Beloved as "Doctor Robbie," he championed the orthodox Calvinism of Warfield and Princeton.

7. *PTR* 19 (1921): 381. This statement is from Francis L. Patton's "Memorial Address."

8. Warfield, *The Saviour of the World,* 215–17.

9. Stonehouse, *Machen,* 309–10. The omission indicated by the ellipsis points before the final sentence of Machen's letter is "with all his glaring faults." Exactly what Machen meant by Warfield's "glaring faults" is difficult to determine, when his comments about his teacher and colleague are always, as above, so strongly favorable. Machen may have found him opinionated and strongly committed to his own point of view, but so was Machen himself. Machen, always sociable and affable, may have found Warfield too aloof and austere in his personality, but there is no hint of this in Machen's correspondence. He may have felt that Warfield could have been more involved in presbytery and denominational matters, as Machen himself was, but surely he appreciated Dr. Warfield's limitations in this area because of his wife's illness.

10. *Addresses Delivered at the Inauguration of Reverend Caspar Wistar Hodge, Ph.D. as Charles Hodge Professor of Didactic and Polemic Theology in Princeton Theological Seminary, October 11, 1921,* 3–7. Within the space of nine months the three great Reformed

leaders died—Abraham Kuyper on November 12, 1920; B. B. Warfield on February 16, 1921; and Herman Bavinck on July 29, 1921.

11. Warfield's reading was as broad as it was deep. Ethelbert Warfield wrote, "Always a diligent student, he also read widely over an unusual range of general literature, including poetry, fiction and drama, and often drew illustrations from the most unexpected sources." Warfield, *Revelation and Inspiration*, viii. Warfield loved poetry. He prefaced his *Lord of Glory* with these lines from Robert Browning:

> "This man so cured regards the curer, then,
> as—God forgive me!—who but God Himself,
> Creator and sustainer of the world,
> That came and dwelt on it awhile! . . .
> And must have so avouched himself in fact . . .
> The very God! think Ahib; dost thou think?"

12. *PTR* 19 (1921): 386. Warfield, *Biblical Foundations*, 10. It was Dr. Lloyd-Jones who did most to reintroduce Warfield's writings in England with the testimony that, for evangelicals, probably no works have "proved to be of greater practical help and a greater stimulus" than those of Dr. Warfield (7). Kerr, "Warfield."

13. Barbour, *Alexander Whyte*, 1. Francis Patton said, "[Dr. Warfield's] writings impress me as the fluent, easy, offhand expression of himself. He wrote with a running pen, in simple, unaffected English, but with graceful diction, and only a moderate display of documented erudition." *PTR* 19 (1921): 371. Kerr, "Warfield." Dr. Kerr summarized Warfield's contribution as follows: "He brought scholarly distinction and theological controversy and excitement to this campus. Not everyone, then or now, could agree with Warfield's austere and overly persuasive apologetic theology, but no one could decry or minimize his intellectual integrity or the sheer vastness of his theological grasp. Among the best of the religious leaders of his day, he stood out as a theological renaissance figure."

14. Iain H. Murray, *David Martyn Lloyd-Jones: the First Forty Years, 1899–1939* (Edinburgh: The Banner of Truth Trust, 1982), 286. The ten volumes were published by the Oxford University Press (New York) between 1927 and 1932. They are *Revelation and Inspiration, Biblical Doctrines, Christology and Criticism, Studies in Tertullian and Augustine, Calvin and Calvinism, The Westminster Assembly and its Work, Studies in Perfectionism,*

volumes 1 and 2, *Studies in Theology,* and *Critical Reviews.* More than half of the Oxford edition, rearranged with some different titles, was reprinted by the Presbyterian and Reformed Publishing Company between 1948 and 1958: *The Inspiration and Authority of the Bible, The Person and Work of Christ, Biblical and Theological Studies, Calvin and Augustine,* and *Perfectionism.* In 1970 John E. Meeter wrote that the five-volume set of Warfield, still in constant demand, had more than ten times as many copies in print as the original collection, "indicating that today there is even more interest in the writings of Benjamin B. Warfield than at the time of his death some fifty years ago." The entire Oxford University Press edition was reprinted by Baker Book House in 1981. Presbyterian and Reformed Publishing Company published (in 1970 and 1973) two volumes of *Selected Shorter Writings of B. B. Warfield,* edited by John E. Meeter. For a complete list of Warfield's writings see *A Bibliography of Benjamin Breckinridge Warfield, 1851–1921,* eds. Meeter and Nicole.

15. *SSW* 2: 279.
16. *PTR* 19 (1921): 387. Francis Patton continued: "The day will come when the times will call not for a new theology but for a new systematic theology. New forms of philosophy must be dealt with, new phases of historical controversy must be considered, new witnesses for the truth from archaeology, from science, from history, must be heard. And some one with architectonic gifts must levy contributions from all departments of theology for the new structure. Who that new architect will be we do not know, but I venture the prediction that some of the choicest stones in that new building will be those which have been hewn and shaped in the Warfield quarry" (389–90). Warfield's writings on the discipline of systematic theology include: "The Idea of Systematic Theology" (1896), "The Right of Systematic Theology" (1896), "The Indispensableness of Systematic Theology to the Preacher" (1897), "Recent Reconstructions of Theology" (1898), and "Theology as a Science" (1900). *PRR* 7 (1896): 417–58. Warfield's article on "The Right of Systematic Theology" was published in book form in Scotland, with a commendatory preface by James Orr and endorsements by leading theologians of all three branches of Scottish Presbyterianism.
17. Warfield, *SSW* 1: 131–32.
18. Some of Warfield's sermons have been collected in *The Gospel of the Incarnation* (New York: Anson D. F. Randolph, 1893),

The Power of God unto Salvation (Philadelphia: Presbyterian Board of Publication, 1903), *The Saviour of the World,* and *Faith and Life* (London: Longmans, Green, 1916; repr. The Banner of Truth Trust, 1974). *The Gospel of the Incarnation* was "affectionately" dedicated "to the students of Princeton Seminary, for whom they were prepared, to whom they were preached, and on whose request they are now printed." *Faith and Life* contains some of Warfield's Sunday Afternoon Conference addresses given at the seminary. One reviewer of *The Power of God unto Salvation* wrote, "Dr. Warfield is one of our most accomplished and honored scholars. He is also a devout and sweet-spirited Christian preacher. The very marrow of the gospel is condensed into these living pages." Another stated that Warfield's sermons "are full of doctrine, yet are alive with a rich experience and a practical bearing. They are meant for the heart as well as for the brain." *SSW* 2: 718.

19. *SSW* 2: 468–69, 476, 478–80, 488–90, 493. In his article "The Indispensableness of Systematic Theology to the Preacher," Warfield wrote: "Readers of Dr. Palmer's *Life of Thornwell* will recall a . . . testimony to what the reading of the Westminster Confession did for Thornwell's soul; and we can ourselves testify from experience to the power of the Westminster Confession to quicken religious emotion, and to form and guide a deeply devotional life." *SSW* 2: 286.

20. *SSW* 1: 411, 425. Abraham Kuyper's daughter, Catherine M. E. Kuyper, translated Warfield's address into Dutch and published it in *De Heraut,* May 4–25, 1913.

21. *The Banner of Truth* 89 (February 1971): 18.

22. Ethelbert D. Warfield, "Biographical Sketch of Benjamin Breckinridge Warfield," in Warfield, *Revelation and Inspiration,* viii; *Princeton Sermons,* 113–14.

23. *SSW* 2: 739–41; B. B. Warfield, *Four Hymns and Some Religious Verses* (Philadelphia: Westminster Press, 1910). See B. B. Warfield, "A Calm View of the Freedmen's Case" and "Drawing the Color Line," *SSW* 2: 735–50. Warfield offended Gresham Machen in 1913 by vigorously supporting the seminary's decision to allow a black student to live in Alexander Hall. Although Machen affirmed that blacks could represent "the best part of human nature," he insisted that blacks and whites remain socially separated. In 1922 President Lowell of Harvard refused to allow black students to live in Harvard's dorms. From its early period, Princeton Seminary admitted African-American students and later provided them with the

opportunity to take graduate courses at the college. When in 1876 some college students protested to James McCosh about a black student enrolled in his course, McCosh suggested that they were perfectly free to drop the course. But even McCosh was not able to change the undergraduate admissions policy. Princeton University did not have an African American graduate until 1947. Between 1900 and 1929 Witherspoon Presbyterian Church in Princeton was served by three African-American graduates of Princeton Seminary, who later attained positions of wide influence. Leonard Z. Johnson became a professor at Howard University. George S. Stark was for many years pastor of the Siloam Church in Brooklyn. Augustus E. Bennett held several pastorates, including Grace Church in Chicago.

24. Warfield, *The Saviour of the World,* 178–79, 182–83.

25. *PTR* 19 (1921): 369. In his more than half century of teaching at Princeton Seminary Professor of New Testament (1940—) Bruce M. Metzger has taught more students than any Princeton professor, possibly more than any other seminary teacher in United States history.

18. Christianity and Liberalism

1. "Some Hitherto Unpublished Letters of Prof. Archibald Alexander, D.D.," *JPHS* 7 (1914): 349.

2. Hutchison, *The Modernist Impulse,* 2.

3. Ahlstrom, *Religious History of the American People,* 895; Marsden, *Fundamentalism and Evangelicalism,* 180.

4. Marsden, *Fundamentalism and Evangelicalism,* 34–35.

5. *SSW* 1: 386.

6. *SSW* 1: 305–7.

7. Stonehouse, *Machen,* 306, 312; Clutter, "Reorientation of Princeton Theological Seminary," 111; Machen, "The Proposed Plan of Union," *Presbyterian* 90 (June 10, 1920): 9.

8. Clutter, "Reorientation of Princeton Theological Seminary," 112; The "Philadelphia Plan" was defeated, 100 presbyteries in favor and 150 opposed.

9. Maitland Alexander's commitment to Old Princeton theology was expressed in the charge that he gave to the congregation at First Presbyterian Church in Pittsburgh at the dedication of the Mary McMasters Jones preaching pulpit: "I charge you, the members of this Church, to see to it

that when my work has been finished in this Church, that no man shall ever stand here as its minister who does not believe in and preach an inspired and infallible Bible, a living Christ who is God, and the Cross and shed Blood, the only way of everlasting life. Let no graces of speech, executive ability or power, charm of diction or literary equipment, obscure the paramount qualification for a minister of this Church, namely that he shall be true to the Bible, to all the standards of the Presbyterian Church, to the Deity of God's only Begotten Son, and Salvation through His Precious Blood alone." Macartney, *The Making of a Minister*, 205.

10. During the previous two decades degrees had been awarded only to those few students who completed undergraduate and required seminary studies plus an additional year.

11. *PSB* 16 (1922): 14; *PTR* 11 (1923): 113; Oswald T. Allis, *The Old Testament: Its Claims and Its Critics* (Nutley, N.J.: Presbyterian and Reformed Publishing Company, 1972), viii. Allis produced nine books—three on issues related to Bible revisions and translations, one concerning dispensationalism, and five on the Old Testament. Although critics scoffed at Allis's position on such issues as the Mosaic authorship of the Pentateuch and the unity of Isaiah, conservatives appreciated his defense of traditional views and his forthright criticism of the errors of modernism. Clarence Macartney, Allis's classmate at Princeton Seminary, wrote concerning *The Unity of Isaiah*, "All those who believe that the Book of Isaiah predicts the birth, the resurrection and the grand and final triumph of Christ will find solid ground for their belief and their hope in this timely and most notable book by Dr. Allis." Taylor, *The Old Testament in the Old Princeton School*, 277.

12. *Princeton Theological Seminary: In the Biblical Tradition for over a Century* (Princeton: Princeton Theological Seminary, 1980), 11. The quotation is from Lefferts A. Loetscher, who added that the seminarians took delight in asking Machen questions in class that would provoke him to become polemical. *Presbyterian Journal*, November 27, 1985, 8. The story about Machen and the Bible is from R. Laird Harris, professor-emeritus, Covenant Theological Seminary. Machen's *New Testament Greek for Beginners* (New York: Macmillan Company, 1923) had astonishing success. By 1955 the work was in its twenty-eighth printing.

13. Machen was an effective preacher. He wrote in the preface to his *Christian View of Man* that "the author believes that the

Reformed Faith should be preached, as well as taught in the classroom, and that the need for the preaching of it is particularly apparent at the present time. The author is trying to preach it in this little book, and preach it very specifically to the people of our generation." J. Gresham Machen, *The Christian View of Man* (London: The Banner of Truth Trust, 1965), 11.

14. Macartney, *The Making of a Minister*, 32; Longfield, *The Presbyterian Controversy*, 105.

15. Macartney, *The Making of a Minister*, 120. Clarence's sister wrote that "the study of the Scriptures under wise guidance restored the faith which the University had nearly wrecked." Longfield, "The Presbyterian Controversy," 270.

16. Longfield, *The Presbyterian Controversy*, 10; Harry E. Fosdick, *As I See Religion* (New York: Harper & Brothers, 1932), 5.

17. Longfield, *The Presbyterian Controversy*, 11; Macartney, *The Making of a Minister*, 184–86.

18. J. Gresham Machen, "Liberalism or Christianity?" *PTR* 20 (1922): 93–117; *Christianity and Liberalism* (New York: Macmillan Co., 1923). Longfield, *The Presbyterian Controversy*, 28. *Christianity and Liberalism* sold only about 1,000 copies in 1923, but sales jumped to over 4,000 in 1924 (due in large part to the publicity surrounding Henry Van Dyke's attack on Machen's preaching at Princeton's First Church). *Christianity and Liberalism* has been in steady, at times strong, demand ever since.

19. *The Christian View of God and the World* (1893) by James Orr had put forth the same thesis—"the Christian view" and the plethora of opinions that could be lumped together as "the modern view" are in cosmic struggle. Warfield described Orr's book as "noble" and John DeWitt called it "exceptionally able, suggestive and useful." *PRR* 9 (1898): 510.

20. Machen, *Christianity and Liberalism*, 47.

21. Machen, *Christianity and Liberalism*, 62, 79, 96, 116.

22. Machen, *Christianity and Liberalism*, 132.

23. Machen, *Christianity and Liberalism*, 159–60.

24. Stonehouse, *Machen*, 346; *PSB* 17 (1923): 19.

25. Hart, "Doctor Fundamentalis," 156; Stonehouse, *Machen*, 347.

26. Hart, *Defending the Faith*, 61; H. L. Mencken, *The Forum and Century*, March 31, 1930; see Coray, *Machen*, 40–41.

27. Walter Lippman, *A Preface to Morals* (New York: Macmillan, 1929), 31–32. Jack Rogers describes *Christianity and Liberalism* as "a model of scholarship and openness." *AP* 66 (1988): 306.

D. G. Hart states that *"Christianity and Liberalism* is still very relevant to us as Reformed believers because Dr. Machen's struggle is still central to the development of the Reformed faith in North America." D. G. Hart, *"Christianity and Liberalism* in a Postliberal Age," *Westminster Theological Journal* 56 (1994): 329–44 (330). A recent comment on Machen's book comes from Harold Bloom: "Real Fundamentalists would find their archetype in the formidable J. Gresham Machen, a remarkable Presbyterian New Testament scholar at Princeton, who published a vehement defense of traditional Christianity in 1923, with the aggressive title *Christianity and Liberalism.* I have just read my way through this, with distaste and discomfort but with reluctant and growing admiration for Machen's mind. I have never seen a stronger case made for the argument that institutional Christianity must regard cultural liberalism as an enemy to faith." Harold Bloom, *The American Religion: the Emergence of the Post-Christian Nation* (New York: Simon and Schuster, 1992), 228.

28. Ahlstrom, *Religious History of the American People,* 816; Hart, "Doctor Fundamentalis," 127. Machen declined to join the World's Christian Fundamentals Association (which began in 1919) because its commitment to dispensationalism and premillennialism caused him "serious concern." Hart, "Doctor Fundamentalis," 132. Machen, "Christianity in Conflict," 270.

29. Machen, *What is Faith?,* 18.

30. Stonehouse, *Machen,* 428.

19. A Mighty Battle

1. W. J. Grier, "Benjamin Breckinridge Warfield, D.D., LL.D., Litt.D.," *Evangelical Quarterly* 22 (1950): 121. This article was reprinted with slight revisions in *The Banner of Truth* 89 (February 1971): 3–9.

2. J. Gresham Machen, *God Transcendent and other Selected Sermons* (Grand Rapids: Wm. B. Eerdmans Publishing Company, 1949; repr., The Banner of Truth Trust, 1982), 47–48. The first eight sermons in this volume were preached while Machen was stated supply at First Presbyterian Church in Princeton.

3. Henry Van Dyke graduated from Princeton University in 1873 and from Princeton Seminary in 1877. He served as pastor of a Congregational church in Newport, Rhode Island,

and later of Brick Presbyterian Church in New York City. In 1899 he came to Princeton University as professor of English literature. He was ambassador to the Netherlands and Luxembourg during the Wilson administration. Van Dyke was a popular writer of outdoor essays, travel sketches, literary criticism, and inspirational stories—including *The Story of the Other Wise Man* and *The First Christmas Tree*. Henry Van Dyke and Gresham Machen were distantly related.

4. Allan A. MacRae wrote: "My first knowledge of J. Gresham Machen came when I read on the front page of a Los Angeles newspaper that Dr. Henry Van Dyke had walked out of a service at First Presbyterian Church in Princeton where Dr. Machen had preached, declaring his preaching was 'a bilious travesty of the gospel.' About that time Dr. Machen's book, *Christianity and Liberalism*, appeared, and I found that I could not lay it down until I had completed reading it. . . . His clear style and convincing logic made me long to know him personally. The next fall I entered Princeton Seminary and was privileged to become a friend of Dr. Machen." *Presbyterian Journal*, November 27, 1985, 7, 8. Enrollment figures at Princeton Seminary show a marked increase after the publication of *Christianity and Liberalism* and the Van Dyke incident—from 156 in 1919–20, and 224 in 1923–24, to 255 in 1928–29.

5. Hart, *Defending the Faith*, 60.

6. The affirmation was drawn up in Auburn, New York, with one of the professors at Auburn Seminary, Robert H. Hastings, a leader in the movement. Auburn and Union (New York) graduates were specially solicited and accounted for more than half of the signers. The 1,293 signatures represented more than one tenth of the ministers of the PCUSA.

7. Longfield, *The Presbyterian Controversy*, 78–79. The second printing of the Auburn Affirmation (May 5, 1924) included a note concerning "some important utterances of one of our church's greatest leaders, Dr. Charles Hodge, for more than half a century professor in Princeton Theological Seminary." This attempt to pacify conservatives and separate Machen from the older Princeton deals with Hodge's contention that the 1861 General Assembly erred in passing the Gardiner Spring Resolutions. The note quotes from Hodge's articles in the *Biblical Repertory and Princeton Review* for July and October 1861 and comments: "His discussion was occasioned by an action of the General Assembly of 1865 concerning matters of

civil right and duty; but from his words it will be seen that he held that the authority of the deliverances of General Assemblies 'on all points of truth and duty,' to use his own language, is constitutionally limited." Hodge, however, protested the General Assembly's action in adding new and unconstitutional (political) requirements for church membership. That is quite a different matter from the doctrinal deliverance of 1910, 1916, and 1923, when the General Assembly required acceptance of five specific doctrines (found in the Confession of Faith) as necessary for ordination. Machen wrote that the five-point statement "contained nothing distinctive of the Reformed Faith, and certainly did not err on the side of too great detail." It did nevertheless enunciate "certain great facts and doctrines about which all the great branches of the historic church are agreed." *Christianity Today*, May 1930, 6.

8. Macartney, *The Making of a Minister*, 191; Hart, "Doctor Fundamentalis," 239. Machen wrote: "But might not God have revealed the 'theory' of a thing just as truly as the thing itself; might He not Himself have given the explanation when He gave the thing? In that case the explanation just as much as the thing itself comes to us with a divine authority, and it is impossible to accept one without accepting the other." Machen, *What is Faith?* 145.

9. C. Allyn Russell, "Clarence E. Macartney—Fundamentalist Prince of the Pulpit," *JPH* 52 (1974): 54; Macartney, *The Making of a Minister*, 193.

10. A native of Calhoun, Georgia, Matthews served churches in Georgia and Tennessee before becoming pastor of the First Presbyterian Church in Seattle in 1901. A conservative Presbyterian, colorful preacher, and strong-minded civic leader, Matthews saw his church become the largest Presbyterian church in the country (with 9,000 members).

11. Despite the pleadings of Henry Sloan Coffin and other liberals, Fosdick refused to join the Presbyterian church. On October 22, 1924, First Presbyterian Church accepted Fosdick's resignation and on March 1, 1925, he preached his farewell sermon. He became pastor of Park Avenue Baptist Church, which by 1930 occupied a new building and was named Riverside Church.

12. Stonehouse, *Machen*, 369. Machen would later say that it was "a fearful sin of omission" that "an effort was not made in 1924, in every single presbytery in which any of us stood, to

bring the Auburn Affirmationists to trial!" Stonehouse, *Machen*, 501.

13. Clutter, "The Reorientation of Princeton Theological Seminary," 149. It is difficult to use accurate labels for the two groups at Princeton Seminary. "Moderates" and "conservatives," and "conservatives" and "ultra-conservatives" have been suggested, but each pair presents problems. Hart suggests "sentimental evangelicals" (for the Stevenson-Erdman group) and "doctrinal evangelicals" (for the Machen group). Hart tabulates the "conservative" and "moderate" division at Princeton as faculty: seven to four; directors: nineteen to nine; and trustees: five to seventeen. Hart, "Doctor Fundamentalis," 253. Frederick Loetscher was "perhaps the closest of the four [Stevenson, Erdman, Loetscher, and Smith] to the viewpoint of the faculty 'majority.'" Loetscher, *The Broadening Church*, 139. Machen did not see Frederick Loetscher in all respects "in the same category" as Stevenson and Erdman. *JPH* 51 (1973): 61.

14. Hart, "Doctor Fundamentalis," 269–70. Longfield writes that "Erdman represented the broad segment of the church that was conservative in theology, tolerant in spirit, and evangelistic in purpose; that is to say, Erdman, perhaps more than any other member of the Princeton faculty, epitomized the values and beliefs of late-nineteenth-century Protestant evangelicalism." Longfield, *The Presbyterian Controversy*, 132.

15. Clutter, "The Reorientation of Princeton Theological Seminary," 148–151. Hart has stated that as the facts about the editorial in *The Presbyterian* came to light before the Princeton committee, "Erdman became evasive and defensive about the specifics of the incident. His responses to questions even suggested that he had wanted to damage Machen's reputation." Hart, *Defending the Faith*, 122. On January 27, 1925, Machen wrote to Clarence Macartney that there were "many things to admire" about Dr. Erdman, but that "the disagreement is now extremely deep." Longfield, "The Presbyterian Controversy," 317–18.

16. John Murray was born on October 14, 1898, and reared on a croft near Bonar Bridge in the Highlands of Scotland. He grew up in the Free Presbyterian Church of Scotland, served with the Royal Highlanders (Black Watch) in World War I, and graduated from the University of Glasgow with an M.A. degree in 1923. To prepare for ministry he studied with tutor Donald Beaton of Wick, who suggested that he go to

Princeton Seminary with a view to future service as a theological tutor in the Free Presbyterian Church.

17. Iain H. Murray, "Life of John Murray," *Collected Writings of John Murray* 3: 22, 25, 28–29,

18. *PSB* 18 (1924): 10.

19. *PSB* 18 (1924): 10–14. Patton gave the same lectures at Union Seminary in Virginia. The lectures were published as *Fundamental Christianity* (New York: Macmillan Company, 1926). Dr. Patton disappointed some of his closest friends when his published lectures appeared to approve of a greater theological tolerance in the Presbyterian church. Apparently Patton's personal views had not changed but he believed that the adoption of the 1903 amendments and the union with the Cumberland Presbyterian Church had in effect given the church a broader theological base. Also in *Fundamental Christianity* Patton declared that "it is a hazardous thing to say that being inspired the Bible must be free from error; for then the discovery of a single error would destroy its inspiration. Nor have we any right to substitute the word 'inerrancy' for 'inspiration' in our discussion of the Bible unless we are prepared to show from the teaching of the Bible that inspiration means inerrancy—and that, I think, would be a difficult thing to do." Patton had abandoned his own earlier view that the inerrancy of the Bible is essential to its inspiration, as set forth in his *Summary of Christian Doctrine.* He now believed, he wrote, that "differences of opinion on this point must be allowed to exist, as they have always existed, among Christians." Patton, *Fundamental Christianity*, 163–64. Stonehouse aptly comments: "It remains true, if one takes account of the basic thrust of Patton's book rather than merely of certain isolated statements, that Patton was no doubt in full agreement that the Liberalism or Modernism of their day had no rightful place within the household of the Presbyterian Church." Stonehouse, *Machen*, 412.

20. Clutter, "The Reorientation of Princeton Theological Seminary," 135. When a Unitarian seminary was admitted to membership, one Princeton student stated that "there was [no longer] agreement even as to John 3:16 in its reference to the only begotten Son." Students from several seminaries argued that Buddha was as much a savior as Christ. Stonehouse, *Machen*, 377.

21. Clutter, "The Reorientation of Princeton Theological Seminary," 141. The Princeton students voted 140 to 70 to enter

the new league but failed to get the three-fourths vote necessary.

22. Machen, *God Transcendent*, 106–7. In the introduction to this volume of Machen's sermons editor Ned B. Stonehouse wrote, "Soon [after it was preached] thousands of copies [of the sermon] in pamphlet form were circulated throughout the world."

23. Macartney Archives, Geneva College, Beaver Falls, Pennsylvania.

24. Machen, *What is Faith?* 42–43.

25. Charles Erdman was the ninth Princeton Seminary professor to serve as moderator (either before or during their Princeton periods). The others were Samuel Miller (1806), Archibald Alexander (1807), Charles Hodge (1846), Alexander T. McGill (1848), Francis L. Patton (1878), William M. Paxton (1880), William Henry Green (1891), and J. Ross Stevenson (1915).

26. Longfield, *The Presbyterian Controversy*, 148.

27. Longfield, "The Presbyterian Controversy," 370; Machen, "What Fundamentalism Stands For Now" in *What is Christianity?* 253–60. In explaining his hesitancy to discuss the question of evolution in public, Machen once wrote, "I have some objection to discussing subjects that I know little or nothing about." Longfield, *The Presbyterian Controversy*, 69.

28. Letter to G. S. Duncan, February 18, 1924; Hart, "Doctor Fundamentalis," 214; Longfield, "The Presbyterian Controversy," 169. Machen's father had supported the theistic evolutionist James Woodrow of the Southern Presbyterian Church. Machen's niece said that when the General Assembly of the Presbyterian Church in the United States met in Baltimore in 1881, the Machen residence became the meeting place for those who defended James Woodrow. See Machen, *The Christian View of Man*, 114–24, for a later, more forthright discussion of evolution. There Machen stated, "I hold that the immense gaps which admittedly exist in the evidence for continuity between the lower animals and man are highly significant and I do not believe that they will ever be filled up" (123).

29. Lectures on "Anthropology," Speer Library, Princeton Theological Seminary; quoted in Johnson, "Attitudes of the Princeton Theologians Toward Darwinism," 259, 271.

30. *PTR* 20 (1922): 537, 541. A brief statement of Greene's views

are found in his *Christian Doctrine*: "The work of creation is twofold: (1) Immediate creation, or the origination of the material—i. e., the principles and causes of all things (Gen. 1:1). (2) Mediate creation, or the origination of the different forms of things, and especially of different species of living beings, out of the already created material (Gen. 1:2–31). The former, of course, was instantaneous and due solely to the act of God; the latter was gradual and the result of the co-operation of God with what He had called into being. The distinctive agent in the whole work of creation is the second person of the Godhead, the Son or Word of God (John 1:3). The process of creation, from the nature of the case, is and must be incomprehensible to all save God. The basal fact is that the material of the universe was called into being 'out of nothing' by the command of the Son of God (Ps. 33:6; Heb. 11:3). The mediate creation, or the formation of the material thus brought into being, took place in six stages or in six 'days.' These, as the scriptural usage of the word permits and as science establishes, were periods of indefinite length." On the origin of man Greene wrote: "The soul of Adam, the first man, was created immediately by God out of nothing (Gen. 2:7; Eccl. 12:7). Adam's body, however, was formed out of pre-existing material but also by the intervention of God. It did not grow of itself; nor was it wholly produced by any process of providential but natural evolution: God Himself, in cooperation with nature, worked it up (Gen. 2:7). When we inquire the date, or the precise method of His creation of man we meet the unknown." W. Brenton Greene, Jr., *Christian Doctrine* (Philadelphia: Westminster Press, 1910), 19, 23. For recent scholarly criticisms of the theory of evolution, see Michael Denton, *Evolution: A Theory in Crisis* (Bethesda, Md.: Adler & Adler, 1986) and Phillip E. Johnson's careful examination of grand-scale "Darwinism" in his *Darwin on Trial* (Downers Grove, Illinois: InterVarsity Press, 1991). Early-twentieth-century contributors to *The Princeton Theological Review* generally supported assimilation of at least some form of evolution. By the 1920s, however, there was an increasing number of anti-evolution articles by such authors as George McCready Price, Floyd E. Hamilton, and Ambrose J. Wilson.

31. Machen, *What is Faith?* 26, 40.
32. Stonehouse, *Machen*, 397–98.

20. The Banner of Truth

1. *JPH* 52 (1974): 40.
2. Macartney Archives, Geneva College, Beaver Falls, Pennsylvania.
3. Macartney, *The Making of a Minister*, 197–98.
4. Taylor, *The Old Testament in the Old Princeton School*, 253.
5. *PTR* 24 (1926): 561.
6. *PTR* 24 (1926): 538. As the Princeton faculty divided, Davis generally voted with the minority of Stevenson, Erdman, Loetscher, and J. Ritchie Smith. Henry W. Smith died in 1926. Henry Smith had taught speech at Princeton Seminary for nearly forty-eight years. The *Princeton Seminary Bulletin* noted that "he had as a teacher been in association with all those who have taught in the seminary in the hundred and fourteen years of its history except five professors—the three Alexanders, Dr. Miller and Dr. Breckinridge." *PSB* 20 (1926): 10.
7. Francis Patton, who was not present, had written to urge the directors to vote for Machen for the position because he was the most able scholar effectively defending historic Christianity. Patton's support was especially important for Machen, since their relationship had been strained. When the Auburn Affirmation was signed, Patton wrote to Machen that he intended to keep out of the controversy, wishing to avoid "the ungenerous criticism" that it would bring, and asked Machen not to quote him on the issues. Machen wrote on July 11, 1926, "In this desperate situation you are found fighting with the enemy! That, I think, is one of the hardest things to bear in this whole situation." Kemeny, "Keeping Princeton a 'Christian College,'" 22–23.
8. Stonehouse, *Machen*, 386–87.
9. Clutter, "The Reorientation of Princeton Theological Seminary," 159.
10. Clutter, "The Reorientation of Princeton Theological Seminary," 164.
11. Stonehouse, *Machen*, 391. Machen believed that the amendment was unwise (in that it would give the federal government more power at the expense of local and state governments) and that the church should not involve itself directly in what he saw as a political issue. In social and political issues Machen consistently defended religious liberty and cultural pluralism, stressed the importance of personal

freedoms, and opposed almost any extension of state power. Machen's civil libertarianism and his Southern perspective kept him from identifying America and Christianity as many twentieth-century evangelicals have. D. G. Hart has written: "Machen's views on the relation between church and society alienated most Presbyterians and were an important factor in the Presbyterian controversies. His conception of the church meant that rather than being a dominant institution, it was to represent only one viewpoint within the marketplace of ideas in America. Indeed, Machen blamed the privileged position of Protestantism within America for the demise of conservative Christian beliefs. In order to maintain their established position within a culture growing increasingly pluralistic, mainstream Protestant churches, he thought, had accommodated viewpoints that undermined the gospel. For Machen, the church had to be intolerant to retain its identity; and if intolerant, it could not provide leadership for a culture that encouraged religious pluralism. To be sure, Machen hoped that the church would grow and that Christians would someday outnumber unbelievers in America. Still, he held that the church's authority extended only to the faithful; it could not set the cultural norms for non-Christians." Hart, "J. Gresham Machen," in *Handbook of Evangelical Theologians*, 143.

12. Stonehouse, *Machen*, 388; Macartney, *The Making of a Minister*, 187. Macartney added, "I myself lamented Dr. Machen's stand on that issue; but I did not permit this to blind me to his magnificent witness to the great truths of the Gospel." The earlier Princetonians refused to condemn moderate drinking. Charles Hodge wrote in 1835: "We regard the attempt now making to prove from the word of God the use of wine to be a sin, as one of the most ominous of the indications of fanaticism which our country has ever witnessed. The advocates of this doctrine . . . have assumed another and a higher standard of truth and duty than the word of God, and virtually proclaim themselves wiser than their Maker, and better than their Saviour." *BRTR* 7 (1835): 622.

13. Hart, "Doctor Fundamentalis," 248; Stonehouse, *Machen*, 327; *Presbyterian Journal*, November 27, 1985, 7; Wilbur M. Smith, *Before I Forget* (Chicago: Moody Press, 1971), 114; Macartney Archives, Geneva College, Beaver Falls, Pennsylvania; Machen, *What is Christianity?* 203. The only criticism of Machen by his friends and associates was that he was not a skillful leader. Samuel D. Craig stated that as a tactician

Machen was "about the world's worst." Machen, Craig, said, should be on the All-American team, but not the quarterback. Wilbur Smith wrote that Machen "did not consult with his disciples and followers and co-workers as he ought to have done." Smith, *Before I Forget*, 122.

14. In a sermon Machen asked: "What sweet and lovely thing in human living may not be included in that one great business of living unto Christ? Art, you say? Is that excluded? No, indeed. Christ made the beauty of the world, and He made men that they might enjoy that beauty and celebrate it unto His praise. Science? All the wonders of the universe are His. He made all, and the true man of science has the privilege of looking just a little way into His glorious works. Every high and worthy human pursuit may be ennobled and enlarged by being consecrated unto Christ." Machen, *God Transcendent*, 139.

15. R. B. Kuiper, *New Horizons*, April 1991, 16; Heerema, *R.B.: A Prophet in the Land*, 122; Stonehouse, *Machen*, 499; John Murray, "Foreword to British Edition" of *The Christian View of Man*, 9.

16. Machen, *What is Christianity?* 133–34.

17. Macartney, *The Making of a Minister*, 187. After Machen's death Pearl S. Buck, noted author and former Presbyterian missionary whom Machen had vigorously criticized because of her liberal views, wrote a tribute to her opponent: "We have lost a man whom our times can ill spare, a man who had convictions which were real to him and who fought for those convictions and held to them through every change in time and human thought. There was power in him which was positive in its very negations. He was worth a hundred of his fellows who, as princes of the church, occupy easy places and play their church politics and trim their sails to every wind, who in their smug observance of the convictions of life and religion offend all honest and searching spirits. No forthright mind can live among them, neither the honest skeptic nor the honest dogmatist. I wish Dr. Machen had lived to go on fighting them." *The New Republic*, January 30, 1937.

18. Stonehouse, *Machen*, 388, 391. Both Union Seminary in Virginia and Louisville Seminary earlier had invited Machen to join their faculties. Machen felt "most deeply distressed at rejecting any proposal" that came to him from "the Southern Church." Stonehouse, *Machen*, 235.

19. Clutter, "The Reorientation of Princeton Theological Semi-

nary," 178, 183; Longfield, "The Princeton Controversy," 398. Smith's attitude is seen in the comment of Alexander MacLeod, a student from 1924 to 1928. In a practice sermon "The Bible or Babel," MacLeod said that the only alternative to accepting the Bible of Christ and the apostles as the standard of truth was theological chaos, an idea the students heard frequently from Dr. Machen. MacLeod wrote, "Professor Smith who was in charge, in his critique after the sermon, severely took me to task for painting such a gloomy picture of the state of the Church." *Collected Writings of John Murray* 3: 24.

20. Stonehouse, *Machen*, 415.
21. Stonehouse, *Machen*, 416–17.
22. Hart, "Doctor Fundamentalis," 260.
23. The substance, though not the form, of the lectures appeared in Machen's book *The Virgin Birth of Christ* (New York: Harper and Brothers, 1930; repr., Grand Rapids: Baker Book House, 1965). Machen had long studied this topic. His senior thesis at Princeton Seminary was on the birth narratives of Jesus. See also his review of James Orr's *Virgin Birth of Christ* in *PTR* 6 (1908): 505–8.
24. Machen, *The Virgin Birth of Christ*, 219, 381, 385–87, 390–91, 396–97.
25. Hart, "Doctor Fundamentalis," 189. According to George Marsden, Machen provided conservative evangelicals with "the major counterexample" against the accusation that evangelicalism was incompatible with serious scholarship and served as an inspiration for the rise of evangelical scholarship in the 1950s (*Fundamentalism and Evangelicalism*, 183).
26. Longfield, "The Presbyterian Controversy," 374.
27. Acknowledging the potential for doctrinal confusion left by the General Assembly's decision to eliminate the "fundamentals" as an ordination requirement, Lefferts Loetscher wrote: "But in sweeping away by a stroke of interpretation much of the previously exercised power of the General Assembly to define and thus to preserve the Church's doctrine, the commission established a principle which has much broader implications than the Church has yet had occasion to draw from it. If the Church now has no means of authoritatively defining its faith short of the amending process—which could hardly function in the midst of sharp controversy—ecclesiastical power is seriously hindered for the future from preventing more radical theological innovations than those

discussed in the 'five points.'" Loetscher, *The Broadening Church*, 135.

28. Machen, *What is Christianity?* 17.
29. Machen, *What is Christianity?* 65.
30. Stonehouse, *Machen*, 423; Longfield, "The Presbyterian Controversy," 403; Clutter, "The Reorientation of Princeton Theological Seminary," 196–97.
31. Loetscher, *The Broadening Church*, 145.
32. Stonehouse, *Machen*, 427.
33. J. Gresham Machen, *The Attack Upon Princeton Seminary: A Plea for Fair Play* (Princeton: By the Author, 1927), 34–35.
34. Loetscher, *The Broadening Church*, 144; *Collected Writings of John Murray* 3: 29; Kemeny, "Keeping Princeton a 'Christian College,'" 24–25.

21. The End of an Epoch

1. Fitzgerald, *Afternoon of an Author*, 71–72. F. Scott Fitzgerald was a student at Princeton University from 1913 to 1917. Looking back at the Princeton of his students days, he wrote that one seeks in vain "for any corner of the republic that preserves so much of what is fair, gracious, charming and honorable in American life" (79). Fitzgerald's novel *This Side of Paradise*—set partly in Princeton—was upsetting to faculty and alumni. President Hibben wrote "a kind but reproachful letter" to Fitzgerald, who for the next seven years did not return to Princeton. Finally in 1927 he visited the school. He wrote: "We went up to Princeton. There was a new colonial inn, but the campus offered the same worn grassy parade ground for the romantic spectres of Light-Horse Harry Lee and Aaron Burr. We loved the temperate shapes of Nassau Hall's old brick, and the way it seems still a tribunal of early American ideals, the elm walks and meadows, the college windows open to the spring. . . ." F. Scott Fitzgerald, *The Crack-Up* (New York: New Directions Books, 1993), 48, 88.
2. Stonehouse, *Machen*, 434.
3. According to Douglas Horton, the man responsible for the first English translation of Karl Barth, Brunner spoke of Machen's work "in the highest terms." D. G. Hart, "Machen on Barth: Introduction to a Recently Uncovered Paper," *Westminster Theological Journal* 53 (1991): 189. Machen and Barth had studied at Marburg just two years apart, where they were both thoroughly captivated for a time by the piety and teach-

ing of Wilhelm Herrmann.

4. J. Gresham Machen, "Karl Barth and 'The Theology of Crisis,'" *Westminster Theological Journal* 53 (1991): 197–205.

5. Marsden, *Fundamentalism and Evangelicalism*, 201; H. Richard Niebuhr, *The Kingdom of God in America* (New York: Harper, 1937), 193. William Hutchison has written: "Echoing Machen, and in fact announcing a triumph of which Machen himself was quite unsure," Walter Lowrie, "a convert to Episcopalianism but a Princetonian in background and training . . . rejoiced that in the high places of German and American liberal religion, it had now been conceded 'that Liberalism . . . is *not* Christianity.' That concession, he said, had put an end to 'a vast deal of hypocrisy.' Perhaps people would now, all along the line, face the choices truly before them." Hutchison, *The Modernist Impulse*, 292. In 1932 *The Expository Times* commented editorially on the similarities between the teachings of B. B. Warfield and Karl Barth: "No doubt Dr. Warfield and the Barthians show a common adherence to the Pauline-Evangelical theology of sin and grace. . . . Both Warfield and Barth recall to us the theocentric standpoint of the Protestant Reformation. They would remind us that theology is not theistic philosophy. In Christianity it is God who speaks and man who listens, and the function of Christian theology is to hear and expound God's authentic Word, not to set forth man's thoughts about God. It is a religious or theocentric rather than a philosophical or anthropocentric emphasis. That is why the name of a traditional Calvinist like Dr. Warfield may be associated with those of Neo-Calvinists like Karl Barth and Brunner." Cited in McClanahan, "Warfield," 629. George Marsden states that in the field of religion "the closest counterparts" to J. Gresham Machen may be Reinhold and H. Richard Niebuhr. As a Southerner, Machen had an outsider's view of contemporary (Northern) American culture; the Niebuhrs, who were reared in the German-speaking Evangelical Synod, were alert to issues of Christianity and culture that persons raised within the establishment were less likely to see. Marsden, *Fundamentalism and Evangelicalism*, 200.

6. Stonehouse, *Machen*, 437; White, *Van Til*, 48.

7. Stonehouse, *Machen*, 439.

8. Machen, *God Transcendent*, 118–29. Charles Hodge's last talk at the Sabbath Afternoon Conference, April 14, 1878, was also on "Fight the Good Fight of Faith."

9. Stonehouse, *Machen*, 439–40.

10. Hart, *Defending the Faith*, 128; Hart, "Doctor Fundamentalis," 278; Longfield, "The Presbyterian Controversy," 421.

11. Leslie W. Sloat wrote: "There is one particular body of American Calvinistic literature which, we think, stands head and shoulders above any other, both in the consistency of its adherence to historic Reformed thought, and in the clarity of its application of that thought to the problems of contemporary living. We refer to the body of literature which, in the form of a series of periodicals, issued from Princeton Theological Seminary, beginning in 1825 and continuing practically without interruption down to 1929." Leslie W. Sloat, "American Calvinism Speaks," *Westminster Theological Journal* 7 (1944): 1–2.

12. Clarence Macartney, now pastor of the First Presbyterian Church of Pittsburgh, resigned from the Princeton board. Macartney gave the 1928–29 Stone Lectures at Princeton Seminary on John Bunyan. The "Pilgrim's Progress" stained-glass window (designed by Henry Lee Willet of Philadelphia in 1931) in the Geneva College Library was inspired by Macartney's lectures. Francis Patton continued as a member of the new board but took no active part. On July 18, 1932, he wrote to Machen that his hopes had been disappointed but that he had "acquiesced" to the decision of the General Assembly. On Patton's eighty-fifth birthday, January 22, 1928, the city of Hamilton unveiled an official portrait of Patton— "Bermuda's Grand Old Man," according to *The Royal Gazette*. On November 25, 1932, Dr. Patton died.

13. Ned B. Stonehouse stated that the decisions of Vos, Armstrong, and Hodge to remain at Princeton were "not fully explicable." Machen sympathized with his friends "in the peculiar predicament in which they were placed" but grieved for months over their decision to remain at Princeton. Stonehouse added: "It is . . . clear that these decisions were not made with enthusiasm; rather it appears that the spirit manifested was one of sorrowful resignation. The wife of one of those concerned once told me, following the establishment of Westminster, that it was very difficult to work for one institution and pray for another." Stonehouse, *Machen*, 450. Vos retired from Princeton in 1932, at the age of seventy, and moved to Pennsylvania and then to California. At the death of his wife in 1937, Dr. Vos moved to Grand Rapids, Michigan, to live with his daughter and her husband. On August 13,

1949, he died and was buried beside his wife at Roaring Branch, Pennsylvania. Armstrong continued at Princeton until his death in 1944. Machen wrote in 1932 that Dr. Armstrong "has remained . . . at the new Princeton Seminary, after the recent reorganization, but he certainly belongs spiritually to the old." Machen, "Christianity in Conflict," 253. Armstrong's successor at Princeton, Otto A. Piper, paid tribute to Dr. Armstrong in his inaugural address on February 9, 1942: "It was my special privilege to work in the New Testament field under the splendid leadership of my predecessor, Professor William Park Armstrong, D.D." Piper said that "Dr. Armstrong's study at 74 Mercer Street, where he meets with his graduate students in an informal way, has become a sanctuary of learning and one of the foci of intellectual life on the campus." *PSB* 36 (August 1942): 5. Caspar Wistar Hodge taught at Princeton as professor of systematic theology until his death in 1937—one hundred and seventeen years after his grandfather began to teach at Princeton. During this period, except for the years 1891 through 1901, there was at least one Hodge on the Princeton faculty. Caspar Wistar Hodge regularly supported Westminster Seminary with financial gifts. He wrote to Machen on September 22, 1936: "Dear Das, I was glad to see you once more. Classes are coming on me and I am so old that I have to prepare for each one, as I did not use to do. . . . My time is largely spent in somewhat heated defense of you." *Collected Writings of John Murray* 3: 62–63.

14. John W. Hart, "Princeton Theological Seminary: The Reorganization of 1929," *JPH* 58 (1980): 137; Loetscher, *Princeton Theological Seminary*, 10.

15. Stonehouse, *Machen*, 442, 448.

16. Harold Lindsell, *Park Street Prophet: A Life of Harold John Ockenga* (Wheaton: Van Kampen Press, 1951), 31. Ockenga estimated that one fourth of Westminster's students were Methodists. The Arminian students were attracted to the Calvinist seminary because the issues of the day, explained Ockenga, were the truthfulness of the Bible and "Christ vs. Paganism."

17. Stonehouse, *Machen*, 458.

18. After Machen refused to sever his connections with the Independent Board for Presbyterian Foreign Missions (which he helped form in 1933), he was brought to trial by the Presbytery of New Brunswick. Clarence Macartney wrote: "Whatever

happens to Dr. Machen ecclesiastically, it is, of course, well known that his name will be honored and revered by true followers of the Lord Jesus Christ, of all churches, long after the names of his persecutors and detractors have been forgotten. Let us pray that our Presbyterian Church in the United States of America shall not dishonor and humiliate itself by expelling from its communion such a mind, such a personality, and such a true follower of our Lord." Macartney, Review of Machen's book *The Christian Faith in the Modern World.* Machen was suspended from the ministry of the Presbyterian Church in the United States of America in 1935. He played a central role in founding a new denomination, the Presbyterian Church of America (later the Orthodox Presbyterian Church). On a trip to Bismarck, North Dakota, to present the new denomination to a small group of Presbyterians, Machen developed pneumonia and died on January 1, 1937. Clarence Macartney wrote: "When I heard of the passing of Dr. Machen the words of King David over Abner came to my mind: 'Know ye not that there is a prince and a great man fallen this day in Israel?' Dr. Machen was my classmate at Princeton and a firm friend through all the years that have passed since then. I am glad in this public way to testify to my affection for him, my admiration for his superb intellect, his prominent scholarship, his magnificent courage, and his clear discernment of the spread of apostasy in the Christian Church. He was the greatest theologian and defender of the Christian faith that the Church of our day has produced. . . . We shall see him no more in the flesh. His eloquent voice will not be heard again in the pulpits of the land. Yet, he being dead yet speaketh. Like Paul, he kept the faith delivered unto the saints, and like Paul's noble companion, Barnabas, he was a good man and full of the Holy Ghost." "Dr. Macartney's Comment on the Death of Dr. Machen," Macartney Archives, Geneva College, Beaver Falls, Pennsylvania. Caspar Wistar Hodge declared that Machen was "the greatest theologian in the English-speaking world" and said that evangelical Christianity had lost "its greatest leader." Hart, "Doctor Fundamentalis," 339.

19. *Luther's Works* (Philadelphia: Fortress Press, 1972) 33: 19–20. In a sermon "Justified by Faith," Gresham Machen commented on Erasmus: "Froude's *Life and Letters of Erasmus* is rather a convincing book. It pictures the great scholar of the Reformation period as being at heart, though of course not

consciously or explicitly, a precursor of the non-doctrinal Christianity so popular at the present day. And whatever may finally be thought of the picture, it has a certain amount of *prima facie* evidence in its favor. Erasmus will always be known to history as the man who would not take sides. There was in his day a great spiritual conflict, the greatest that the world had known for fifteen centuries. Erasmus certainly contributed to the outbreak of it, but he would not accept the final consequences of his own work; he would not fight in the van of the battle, and finally he retired to an inglorious life in the rear. . . . The choice between Luther and Erasmus had to be made in the sixteenth century and the same choice has to be made today." Machen, *God Transcendent*, 82–83.

20. Marsden, *Fundamentalism and Evangelicalism*, 185.
21. Benton Johnson, Dean R. Hoge, and Donald A. Luidens, "Mainline Churches: The Real Reason for Decline," *First Things* 31 (March 1993): 13–18.

22. *The Princeton Theology*

1. *The Princeton Theology*, ed. Noll, 40. John Oliver Nelson comments concerning the *Biblical Repertory and Princeton Review* that its "clearness and dignity, and even its not infrequent eloquence, are characteristic of the Princeton Theology itself." Nelson, "The Princeton Theology," 298–99. Moisés Silva, "Old Princeton, Westminster, and Inerrancy," *Westminster Theological Journal* 50 (1988): 65.
2. Calvin, *Institutes* 4, 3, 11; John T. McNeill, *The History and Character of Calvinism* (London: Oxford University Press, 1954), 146.
3. Mark A. Noll, "The Princeton Theology," in *Reformed Theology in America: A History of Its Modern Development*, ed. David F. Wells (Grand Rapids: William B. Eerdmans Publishing Company, 1985), 19–20.
4. Machen, *God Transcendent*, 111–12. George Marsden has written, "This doctrine of 'inerrancy,' as it came to be known, was no invention of the late nineteenth century. Many Christians in the past had said or assumed much the same thing" (*Fundamentalism and Evangelicalism*, 37).
5. *PR* 2 (1881): 225–60.
6. *PRR* 39 (1899): 562–64.
7. *BRTR* 4 (1832): 174–75. J. W. Alexander wrote, "This is the method which bears the name of Bacon, though practiced

. . . by the wise in every age." Hodge, *Systematic Theology* 1: 11, 13; *SSW* 2: 596; Machen, *What is Faith?* 33.

8. Alexander, "Inaugural Address (1812)," in *The Princeton Theology*, ed. Noll, 86.
9. Hodge, *Systematic Theology* 1: 16.
10. Machen, *God Transcendent*, 111.
11. *BRTR* 4 (1832): 171–90.
12. *BRPR* 16 (1844): 181–82.
13. Salmond, *Princetoniana*, 95–96.
14. Warfield, "The Idea of Systematic Theology," in *Studies in Theology*, 77.
15. McClanahan, "Warfield," 131–32; Warfield, *Studies in Theology*, 80–81.
16. For a statement of Gresham Machen's views on this subject—and a good summary of the Princeton position—see "The Creeds and Doctrinal Advance," in *God Transcendent*, 144–53.
17. *LCH*, 256–57; Frank Hugh Foster, *A Genetic History of the New England Theology* (Chicago: University of Chicago Press, 1907),432; *William Henry Green's Semi-Centennial Celebration*, 70.
18. *BRTR* 3 (1831): 352; *BRTR* 7 (1835): 545.
19. Machen, *What is Faith?* 32–33.
20. Warfield, "The Task and Method of Systematic Theology," in *Studies in Theology*, 105.
21. Machen, *God Transcendent*, 176.
22. Lyman H. Atwater, "The Doctrinal Attitude of Old School Presbyterians," *Bibliotheca Sacra* 21 (1864): 65–66; *LCH*, 255.
23. *Schaff-Herzog Encyclopedia* (1891), 1929; Karl Barth, "Foreword" to Heinrich Heppe, *Reformed Dogmatics: Set Out and Illustrated from the Sources* (London: George Allen & Unwin, 1950), vi.
24. John DeWitt, "Jonathan Edwards: A Study," *Biblical and Theological Studies*, 111, 128. DeWitt's article was an address delivered in the Meeting House of the Parish Church of Stockbridge, Massachusetts, October 5, 1903, at the celebration of the 200th anniversary of the birth of Jonathan Edwards. It was repeated in Miller Chapel on October 16, 1903, and published in the seminary's centennial volume in 1912. Hoeveler, *James McCosh*, 268.
25. A. A. Hodge stated, "President Edwards was always brimming over with ideas of his own, which stood in need of regulating." Salmond, *Princetoniana*, 179. Warfield, "Edwards and the New England Theology," in *Studies in Theology*, 527–28. Iain

H. Murray, *Jonathan Edwards: A New Biography* (Edinburgh: The Banner of Truth Trust, 1987), xxx, xxxi. Prime's speech, writes Murray, was "the most memorable of the whole assembly."

26. *LAA*, 372–73; *BRTR* 5 (1833): 16–18.

27. *PTR* 1 (1903): 254. Machen wrote, "Many criticisms have been brought against the old Princeton Seminary; but whoever brings against it the charge that it substituted passionate dogmatism for fair and scholarly treatment of the opposing views can be set down as either violently prejudiced or completely ignorant about that of which he is venturing to speak." Machen, "Christianity in Conflict," 258–59.

28. See Ligon Duncan III, "Common Sense and American Presbyterianism: An Evaluation of the Impact of Scottish Realism on Princeton and the South," (M.A. thesis, Covenant Theological Seminary, 1987.)

29. Marsden, *Fundamentalism and Evangelicalism*, 198; John W. Stewart, "The Tethered Theology: Biblical Criticism, Common Sense Philosophy, and the Princeton Theologians" (Ph.D. diss., University of Michigan, 1990), 290. George Marsden has commented that Scottish Common Sense Realism "affirmed, as Scripture took for granted, that the human mind is structured by God in such a way as to have access to knowledge of the real world. Most importantly, consistent with a Biblical view, it affirmed that we can know about historical events in such a way that we can rest our faith on them. Common Sense insisted, as Scripture took for granted, that if the events did not really take place, then there was no basis for our faith. Furthermore, it said that we can trust reliable testimony as to the occurrence of such events. This testimony was guaranteed by the revelation of God himself in Scripture." George M. Marsden, "J. Gresham Machen, History and Truth," *Westminster Theological Journal* 42 (1979): 175.

30. Warfield, "Augustine's Doctrine of Knowledge," *Calvin and Augustine*, 393.

31. Machen, *What is Faith?* 27–28. Marsden states that this viewpoint enabled Gresham Machen and his associates at Princeton to recognize trends that few other mainline Protestant thinkers seemed concerned about. Modern hermeneutics was on a track leading toward radical deconstruction—which "asserts as an absolute that we cannot get beyond our own interpretations and therefore there are no absolutes." This is the result of assuming "a purely natural-

istic chance universe," Marsden writes, but it is "incompatible with anything like a traditional Christian view." Marsden, *Fundamentalism and Evangelicalism*, 198.

32. James McClanahan states, "Princeton stood . . . where Calvin and the Reformers stood, indeed perhaps all pre-enlightenment theologians, although Scottish Common Sense Realism is an attempt to *deal* with the Enlightenment." McClanahan, "Warfield," 631.

33. *The Princeton Theology*, ed. Noll, 37–38; *BRPR* 20 (1848): 467.

34. *BRPR* 22 (1850): 250.

35. Stewart, "The Tethered Theology," 129. See also Hodge, *Systematic Theology* 1: 187–88; Hodge, *Evangelical Theology*, 16.

36. Warfield, "Augustine's Doctrine of Knowledge," *Calvin and Augustine*, 143, 149–52.

37. Taylor, *The Old Testament in the Old Princeton School*, 194. William Hutchison has noted that unlike much fundamentalism, which merely fumed at liberal scholarship, "Princeton appeared to acknowledge scholarly inconclusiveness on both sides, but then drive to a deeper level and demand a choice, as a matter of faith, between differing premises of scholarship." Hutchison, *The Modernist Impulse*, 201.

38. Brown, *Miracles*, 200–3.

39. *PTR* 20 (1922): 560–61. Earlier Greene wrote: "Science has her investigators in almost every village, and she conducts her researches with instruments of precision hitherto unrivalled and even unconceived: but while she explores the poles of the earth and uncovers the depths of the oceans and resolves the mysteries of the stars and discovers how to utilize for human interests one after another of nature's forces, she is failing more and more to grasp the meaning of the universe, and so is missing the real worth of her achievements; and the reason is that we wait for such a baptism of the Spirit of God as shall constrain us to see and to adore Him in all his works." *PTR* 10 (1912): 383.

40. Machen, *God Transcendent*, 111; Marsden, "J. Gresham Machen, History, and Truth," *Westminster Theological Journal* 42 (1979): 174–75. Michael Sudduth writes, "Reformed evidentialists (such as Jonathan Edwards, Charles Hodge, and B. B. Warfield) . . . have generally not questioned the plausibility of taking theistic belief as a first principle, but they have questioned the inference from this that such principles should *never* be argued for." Michael L. Czapkay Sudduth, "Bi-level Evidentialism and Reformed Apologetics," *Faith and*

Philosophy 11 (1994): 382.

41. *Bulletin of Westminster Theological Seminary* 28 (1989).
42. Archibald Alexander, *Thoughts on Religious Experience*, (Philadelphia: Presbyterian Board of Publications, 1841: repr. London: The Banner of Truth Trust, 1967), 167, 169.
43. *LCH*, 595.
44. *BRPR* 12 (1840): 33; Hodge, *Systematic Theology* 1: 16.
45. *BRPR* 17 (1845): 274.
46. *SSW* 1: 156. McClanahan writes that Charles Hodge spoke of the Christian faith as essentially "right knowledge" and yet gave much more material on the experience of the believer than Warfield, who spoke of the Christian faith as essentially "dependence upon God," yet wrote much more on knowledge and authority. This only proves, McClanahan concludes, "that both Princetonians were equally concerned about doctrine and experience, but the *times* necessitated certain emphases." McClanahan, "Warfield," 241–42. Warfield, *Christology and Criticism*, 457. Warfield added, "But, on the other hand, it will scarcely do to represent ignorance or error as advantageous to salvation" (458). Warfield, "On Faith in its Psychological Aspects," in *Biblical and Theological Studies*, 397–98.
47. B. B. Warfield, "Introduction," in Beattie, *Apologetics* 1: 24–25.
48. *PTR* 11 (1913): 78, 83–84.
49. Machen, *What is Faith?* 130–31, 134–36. Greg Bahnsen argues that Machen's views were not opposed to the "presuppositional" thinking of Cornelius Van Til, but what Bahnsen puts forth as Machen's views are in line with the Old Princeton tradition as a whole. Greg L. Bahnsen, "Machen, Van Til, and the Apologetical Tradition of the OPC," in *Pressing Toward the Mark: Essays Commemorating Fifty Years of the OPC*, eds. Charles G. Dennison and Richard C. Gamble (Philadelphia: The Committee for the Historian of the OPC, 1986), 279.
50. Hodge, *Evangelical Theology*, v.
51. Machen, "Christianity in Conflict," 253.
52. For "The Plan of a Theological Seminary," see David B. Calhoun, *Princeton Seminary: Faith & Learning (1812–1868)* (Edinburgh: The Banner of Truth Trust, 1994), Appendix 1, 413–30. For a competent study of this often neglected side of the Princeton tradition, see W. Andrew Hoffecker, *Piety and the Princeton Theologians: Archibald Alexander, Charles Hodge, and Benjamin Warfield* (Grand Rapids: Baker Book House, 1981).

53. Loetscher in *Princeton Theological Seminary*, 3.

54. Alexander, *Religious Experience*, 44, 84.

55. *BRPR* 32 (1860): 119. See also Hodge, *Conference Papers*, 308, in which he says that "Christianity is . . . a system of doctrine, it is an inward life, and it is a rule of action."

56. In his *Systematic Theology* Hodge wrote that the "inward teaching of the Spirit" is "so legitimate and powerful" that it is "no uncommon thing to find men having two theologies—one of the intellect, and another of the heart. The one may find expression in creeds and systems of divinity, the other in their prayers and hymns. It would be safe for a man to resolve to admit into his theology nothing which is not sustained by the devotional writings of true Christians of every denomination. It would be easy to construct from such writings, received and sanctioned by Romanists, Lutherans, Reformed, and Remonstrants, a system of Pauline or Augustinian theology, such as would satisfy any intelligent and devout Calvinist in the world." Hodge, *Systematic Theology* 1: 16–17; *PQPR* 5 (1876): 361–62; Hodge, *Systematic Theology* 3: 41–113.

57. Warfield, *Studies in Tertullian and Augustine*, 251. McClanahan states that "here is seen the consistent view of Warfield and Princeton that truth is prior to and produces both theology and piety/experience." McClanahan, "Warfield," 221.

58. *PRR* 7 (1896): 271.

59. *SSW* 2: 471–72, 475–76, 478–79.

60. *SSW* 2: 671.

61. Marsden, *Fundamentalism and Evangelicalism*, 125–26; Alister E. McGrath, "Why Evangelicalism is the Future of Protestantism," *Christianity Today*, June 19, 1995, 21. A remarkably large number of books from Old Princeton remain in print. The Banner of Truth Trust has reprinted twenty-nine titles of Princeton Theological Seminary authors. See the list in Calhoun, *Princeton Seminary: Faith & Learning*.

62. *PTR* 20 (1922): 13–14.

GENERAL INDEX

GENERAL INDEX

Volume numbers are indicated by bold type, **1** and **2**; page numbers by plain type. A small n followed by a number indicates a footnote.

Barnes, Albert (*continued*)
commentary on Romans **1** 196;
sermon on "The Way of
Salvation" **1** 242; charge of
heresy **1** 242, 248; tribute to J.
W. Alexander **1** 380; views on
slavery **1** 483, n22
Barth, Karl, theologian **2** 388–89,
520–21, n3, 521, n5
Bavinck, Herman, theologian **2**
180–81, 320, 502–3, n10
Beatty, Francis R., professor,
Columbia and Louisville
seminaries **2** 182, 481, n12
Beecher, Lyman, pastor, Second
Presbyterian Church,
Cincinnati; president of Lane
Seminary **1** 194, 220–21, 247–
48, 293–94, 305
Benham Club. *See* Eating clubs at
Princeton Seminary
Biblical and Theological Studies
2 280
Biblical Repertory
–founding by Charles Hodge **1**
116–17
–supervision by Robert Patton
during Hodge's study in
Europe **1** 117
–"Association of Gentlemen"
1 193–94
–name changes **1** 194
–*Theological Essays* **1** 318
–Patrick Fairbairn's comments **1**
318–19
–Lyman Atwater as co-editor **2** 32
–Charles Hodge's retirement **2**
32
–Charles Hodge's contribution **2**
32, 57–58
–tribute of the *British Quarterly
Review* **2** 60
–changes after Hodge's retirement **2** 83
–"American Calvinism Speaks" **2**
522, n11
–"clearness and dignity" **2** 525,
n1

*Biblical Repertory and Princeton
Review.* See *Biblical Repertory*
*Biblical Repertory and Theological
Review.* See *Biblical Repertory*
Biblical theology at Princeton
Seminary **2** 137–41, 208
Blackwood, Andrew, pastor;
professor at Princeton Semi-
nary: study at Harvard and
Princeton Seminary **2** 205; on
homiletics at Princeton Semi-
nary **2** 215–16; Princeton
Seminary student **2** 243;
Princeton Seminary professor **2**
488, n35
Blair, John, professor at Princeton
College **1** 12
Blair, Samuel, minister; educator **1**
5, 9, 66
Board of directors of Princeton
Seminary **1** 31–32, **2** 377, 380
Board of trustees of Princeton
Seminary **1** 99–100, **2** 377
Boardman, Henry A., pastor,
Tenth Presbyterian Church,
Philadelphia: J. A. Alexander's
sermons at Tenth Church **1** 284;
tribute to Archibald Alexander
1 346; election to Princeton
Seminary faculty **1** 361–62;
address at Princeton Seminary's
semicentennial celebration **1**
404–5; address at Charles
Hodge's jubilee **2** 37; conversation with Charles Hodge **2** 62;
death **2** 93
Borden, William, missionary
volunteer **2** 283–85
Boyce, James Petigru, pastor;
founder of the Southern Baptist
Theological Seminary,
Louisville: reading biographies
at Princeton Seminary **1** 129;
tribute to Charles Hodge **1** 263,
2 61; on J. W. Alexander as a
lecturer **1** 287; biographical
note **1** 484, n4; teacher of E. Y.
Mullins **2** 277

Green, William Henry (*continued*)
genealogies **2** 12, 451, n20
–librarian **2** 43
–article in *The Presbyterian Review*
series on Scripture **2** 87–88
–sermon at the funeral of James
Moffat **2** 125–26
–Briggs trial **2** 132
–appeal to Geerhardus Vos **2** 138
–Princeton professor **2** 149–55
–*The Pentateuch Vindicated* **2** 151
–debate with William Rainey
Harper **2** 152–53
–*Moses and the Prophets* **2** 152
–*The Higher Criticism of the
Pentateuch* **2** 153
–*The Unity of the Book of Genesis* **2**
153
–lectures on the Hebrew feasts **2**
153
–semicentennial **2** 155–59
–death **2** 184
–John D. Davis's commemorative
address **2** 184–85
–comment in *The
Congregationalist* **2** 194
–summary of his work **2** 482–83,
n17
Greene, William Brenton,
Princeton Seminary professor
–call to Princeton Seminary **2**
134
–biographical sketch **2** 134
–inaugural address **2** 134–35
–teaching **2** 214–15
–"broad churchism" **2** 251
–writings on social issues **2** 260–
64
–views on evolution **2** 361, 514–
15, n30
–death **2** 390
Guthrie, Thomas, preacher and
social reformer **1** 118, **2** 5, 450,
n6
Guyot, Arnold, Princeton College
professor **2** 3–4, 20, 116, 449, n3
Gymnasium, Princeton Seminary **2**
243–44

Hall, Robert and Marian, supporters of Princeton Seminary **1** 319
Halyburton, Thomas, professor of
divinity, University of St.
Andrews **1** 46, 128–30, 227–28,
457, n9
Hamilton, William, professor of
philosophy, Edinburgh University **2** 5, 450, n6
Hampden-Sydney College:
founding **1** 21; John Blair Smith
1 47; Archibald Alexander's
presidency **1** 51–52, 54, 446,
n17; missionary society **1** 148;
seminary **1** 163–64; John Holt
Rice **1** 166
Henry, Joseph, Princeton College
professor; director of the
Smithsonian Institute:
Princeton College professor
and scientist **1** 167–68; teacher
of A. A. Hodge **1** 268, **2** 79; and
Charles Hodge's lameness **1**
277; and Caspar Wistar Hodge
1 385; Smithsonian Institute
1 459–60, n10; desire for
William Henry Green to accept
Princeton College presidency **2**
4; on Charles Hodge's meteorological record **2** 39; funeral **2** 56
Herrmann, Wilhelm, theologian **2**
228–30, 232, 499, n12
Hibben, John Grier, Princeton
University president: comments
at J. Ross Stevenson's inauguration **2** 288; refusal of use of
Alexander Hall to Billy Sunday
2 299; promotion of military
preparedness **2** 303; election as
president of Princeton University **2** 497, n20; letter to F. Scott
Fitzgerald **2** 520, n1
Hodge, Archibald Alexander, son
of Charles Hodge; Princeton
Seminary professor
–birth **1** 113
–first "abiding image" of his
father **1** 122

Lenox, James (*continued*)
Library **2** 43; gifts to Princeton
Seminary 457, n24
Liberty Hall **1** 44, 47–48, 269
Librarians, Princeton Seminary
–Archibald Alexander **2** 43
–William Henry Green **2** 43
–Charles Aiken **2** 43
–William H. Roberts **2** 43
–Joseph H. Dulles **2** 100, 335
–William B. Sheddan **2** 335
Library, Princeton Seminary: use
of Princeton College library **1**
78; library in seminary building
1 83; Society of Inquiry library **1**
146; Lenox Library **1** 270–71,
473, n35; new Lenox Library **2**
43; funds **2** 173; addition to the
new Lenox Library **2** 335; John
Murray's comment **2** 381
Lindsley, Philip, Princeton College
professor; president of
Cumberland College, Tennessee **1** 107, 115, 166
Lippman, Walter, journalist **2** 342
Lloyd-Jones, David Martyn, pastor,
Westminster Chapel, London **1**
442, n11, **2** 244–45, 320–21,
455–56, n11, 503, n12
Loetscher, Frederick, Princeton
Seminary professor: instructor
in church history **2** 214;
successor to John DeWitt **2** 280;
continuation at Princeton
Seminary after the reorganization **2** 394; position during
controversy **2** 512, n13, 516, n6
Loetscher, Lefferts A., son of
Frederick Loetscher; Princeton
Seminary professor: on the
reorganization **2** 395; statement
on the Princeton tradition **2**
422–23; comment on Machen **2**
507, n12; comment on the
General Assembly's elimination
of the "fundamentals" **2** 519–20,
n27
Log College: founding by William

Tennent **1** 4; visit of George
Whitefield **1** 4; closing in 1742,
and graduates **1** 4–5; and
Samuel Finley **1** 9; and George
Whitefield **1** 14; role of the Log
College in American theologi-
cal education **1** 27, **2** 109;
Archibald Alexander's *Log
College* **1** 254–55
Louisville (Presbyterian) Seminary
2 193, 518, n18
Lovejoy, Elijah, minister; newspa-
per editor **1** 327, 346–47
Lowrie, John C., missionary;
secretary, Board for Foreign
Missions **1** 140, 164
Lowrie, Walter, Kierkegaard
scholar **2** 492, n4, 521, n5
Lowrie, Walter Macon, missionary:
Princeton Seminary student **1**
143; "missionary brethren" at
Princeton **1** 143; letter to
Princeton **1** 159; letter from
Archibald Alexander **1** 184, 272;
and J. A. Alexander's commen-
tary on Isaiah **1** 279; monument
in China **1** 407; Charles
Hodge's tribute **1** 494, n29
L. P. Stone Lectures, Princeton
Seminary **2** 173: George Purves
(1887–88) **2** 127; Abraham
Kuyper (1898–99) **2** 177–79; D.
Hay Fleming (1907–8) **2** 242–
43; James Orr (1903–4) **2**
257–58; Clarence Macartney
(1928–29) **2** 522, n12

Macartney, Clarence, pastor, Arch
Street Presbyterian Church,
Philadelphia, First Presbyterian
Church, Pittsburgh
–student at Princeton Seminary,
comment on Frederick
Loetscher **2** 214
–election to Princeton Seminary
board of directors **2** 337
–biographical sketch **2** 337–38,
508, n15

–"Shall Unbelief Win?" **2** 338–39
–1923 General Assembly **2** 347
–election as moderator of the 1924 General Assembly **2** 350
–"The Gospel or Not" **2** 357–58
–appointment to Princeton Seminary faculty declined **2** 365–66
–review of Machen's *Christian Faith in the Modern World* **2** 370
–1928–1929 Stone Lectures **2** 522, n12
–resignation from Princeton Seminary's board of directors **2** 522, n12
McCheyne, Robert Murray, pastor, St. Peter's Church, Dundee **1** 128–29, 149–50
McCormick, Cyrus, Presbyterian layman and philanthropist **1** 399, **2** 94–95, 270
McCormick Seminary **2** 94–95, 119, 134, 285
McCosh, Isabella Guthrie, wife of James McCosh **2** 5, 160–61, 478, n21
McCosh, James, president of Princeton College
–visit to the United States in 1866 **2** 4–5
–biographical sketch **2** 5–6
–election to presidency of Princeton College **2** 7
–inauguration **2** 7–8
–president of Princeton College **2** 8–10, 21–22, 159–61, 163–64
–on evolution **2** 15, 18–19, 256–57, 453–54, n31, 492, n5
–address at the Presbyterian Alliance **2** 93
–on the Student Volunteer Movement **2** 107
–Warfield's view of McCosh **2** 116
–*Whither?* **2** 122
–philosophy **2** 5–6, 161–62, 478, n24

–*First and Fundamental Truths* **2** 162
–debate with Charles Eliot of Harvard **2** 163–64
–retirement **2** 165–66
–death **2** 166
–tributes to McCosh **2** 166–67
–compared with John Witherspoon **2** 449–50, n4
McCurdy, James Frederick, instructor at Princeton Seminary; professor, University of Toronto **2** 99, 156, 466–67, n10
MacDonald, George, novelist **2** 23
McGill, Alexander Taggart, Princeton Seminary professor
–biographical sketch **1** 362–63
–teaching **1** 362–63, 377, 384, 387, **2** 95–96
–on deaconesses **2** 125
–retirement and death **2** 466, n5
Maclean, John, son of John Maclean (Princeton College's first professor of chemistry); Princeton College president
–on Charles Hodge's conversion **1** 108
–New England trip with Hodge **1** 111–12
–comment on Ashbel Green **1** 166
–teacher **1** 167
–"pastor" to students **1** 169
–"Association of Gentlemen" **1** 193
–Princeton College president **1** 364–65
–and James C. Moffat **1** 387
–Civil War **1** 391–92
–resignation **2** 3
–as A. A. Hodge's illustration **2** 71–72
–B. B. Warfield's college memories of Maclean **2** 116
Macloskie, George, Princeton College professor **2** 19–20
MacRae, Allan A., professor, Westminster Seminary;

MacRae, Allan A. (*continued*)
president, Faith Seminary **2**
396, 510, n4
Machen, Arthur Webster, father of
J. Gresham Machen; lawyer **2**
221–23
Machen, J. Gresham, Princeton
Seminary professor
–early life **2** 221–24
–student at Princeton Seminary **2**
224–27
–study in Germany **2** 227–33
–instructor at Princeton Seminary **2** 233–35
–financing new tennis courts **2**
244
–on ministerial training **2** 266–67
–Sunday school teaching **2** 280–
81
–"Christianity and Culture" **2**
281–82
–articles on the birth of Christ **2**
282
–ordination **2** 295
–adult Sunday school lessons **2**
296
–and Billy Sunday **2** 299–300
–inauguration as assistant
professor; "History and Faith"
2 300–1, 499, n12
–on World War I **2** 303
–YMCA worker **2** 303–4, 307–
9
–"The Church in the War" **2** 309
–James Sprunt Lectures **2** 310
–*The Origin of Paul's Religion* **2**
310–12
–comments on Warfield **2** 317–18
–opposition to the Philadelphia
Plan **2** 333–34
–teaching **2** 336
–speaking schedule for the 1922–
23 school year **2** 336–37
–*Christianity and Liberalism* **2** 339–
42, 508, n18, 508–9, n27,
510, n4
–on fundamentalism **2** 343, 509,
n28

–stated supply, First Presbyterian
Church, Princeton **2** 348–49,
508, n18, 509, n2, 510, n4
–tensions with Charles Erdman **2**
351–53, 373–74, 512, n15
–League of Evangelical Students
2 355–56
–sermon on the "Separateness of
the Church" **2** 356–57
–and the 1924–25 "Awakening" **2**
358–59
–on evolution **2** 360, 514, n28
–*What is Faith?* **2** 361–62
–election to the chair of
apologetics **2** 367–68
–statement to the Special
Commission **2** 368
–on prohibition **2** 369, 517, n12
–temperament and integrity **2**
369–71
–*The Christian Faith in the Modern
World* **2** 370
–invitations to other schools **2**
372, 518, n18
–Thomas Smyth Lectures **2** 374–
76
–*The Virgin Birth of Christ* **2** 374–
76, 519, n23
–letter to Bryan University **2** 376–
77
–1927 speaking trip to Great
Britain **2** 378–79
–*The Attack upon Princeton
Seminary: A Plea for Fair Play* **2**
380–81
–withdrawal of acceptance of the
chair of apologetics **2** 387
–"Karl Barth and 'The Theology
of Crisis'" **2** 387–89
–sermon, "Fight the Good Fight
of Faith" **2** 390–91
–speech at the 1929 General
Assembly **2** 392–93
–resignation from Princeton
Seminary **2** 393–94
–"Westminster Theological
Seminary: Its Purpose and
Plan" **2** 396

Confession **2** 505, n19
Trustees, Princeton Seminary. *See*
Board of trustees
Turretin, Francis, theologian: read
by Archibald Alexander at
Liberty Hall **1** 48; Princeton
Seminary text **1** 90–91, 149,
262, **2** 33, 411; publication
history **1** 452, n29; relevance **1**
452, n31; J. W. Alexander's
evaluation **1** 471, n6

Union Seminary (New York City):
invitation to J. A. Alexander **1**
205; founding in 1836 **1** 259;
termination of relationship with
the General Assembly of the
Presbyterian Church **2** 135–36,
474, n2
Union Seminary (Virginia):
Samuel B. Wilson **1** 94; Society
of Inquiry **1** 149; John Holt Rice
1 163–64,172, 446, n18, **2** 193;
Southern seminary **1** 259–60;
Robert L. Dabney **1** 386;
orthodox Calvinism **2** 193;
invitation to J. Gresham
Machen **2** 300, 518, n18;
Machen's James Sprunt
Lectures **2** 310–12
Unitarianism **1** 293–95

Van Dyke, Henry (father), pastor:
support for confessional
revision **2** 123; Briggs case **2**
132; pastor in Brooklyn **2** 471,
n18
Van Dyke, Henry (son), pastor,
Brick Presbyterian Church, New
York City; Princeton University
professor: anniversary ode at
Princeton College's sesquicentennial **2** 169; Machen in
Van Dyke's classes **2** 224;
attack on Machen **2** 348, 508,
n18, 510, n4; return to First
Presbyterian Church **2** 351;
pastor and professor **2** 471, n18;

biographical note **2** 509–10, n3
Van Dyke, Paul, instructor,
Princeton Seminary; pastor;
professor at Princeton University **2** 468, n19
Van Til, Cornelius, instructor,
Princeton Seminary; professor
at Westminster Seminary **2** 389–
90, 394
Voluntary associations **1** 239–41
Vos, Catherine Francis, wife of
Geerhardus Vos **2** 139, 210
Vos, Geerhardus, Princeton
Seminary professor
–biographical sketch **2** 138–39
–call to Princeton Seminary **2**
138
–inauguration **2** 139–40
–on biblical theology **2** 140–41,
208, 475, n15
–on confessional revision **2** 188
–"The Scriptural Doctrine of the
Love of God" **2** 188
–teaching **2** 205, 208–10
–advice to Van Til **2** 389–90
–remaining at Princeton Seminary after the reorganization
2 522–23, n13
–death **2** 522–23, n13

Waddel, James, "the blind
preacher of Virginia"; father-in-
law of Archibald Alexander:
biographical sketch **1** 54–55;
and William Wirt's *British Spy* **1**
446–47, n22; description by
Clarence Macartney of
Waddel's preaching **1** 447, n23
War with Mexico **1** 324
Ward, William, missionary **1** 140
Warfield, Annie Kinkead, wife of
B. B. Warfield: marriage and
travels in Europe **2** 118; illness
and death **2** 315–16, 499, n18;
Annie Kinkead Warfield
Lectures **2** 502, n3
Warfield, Benjamin Breckinridge,
Princeton Seminary professor

Witherspoon, John (*continued*)
  –leader of the Presbyterian
    church **1** 16
  –influence **1** 16–18
  –later life and death **1** 20–21
  –Lafayette's honorary diploma **1**
    100
  –influence on Princeton Semi-
    nary **1** 127
  –John A. Mackay's comment
    on Witherspoon **1** 443–44,
    n32
  –A. A. Hodge's illustration **2** 70–
    71
  –"Piety and Literature" **2** 401–2

  –McCosh and Witherspoon
    compared **2** 449–50, n4
Woodrow, James, theologian and
    professor **2** 81, 514, n28
Woodward, Henry, missionary **1**
    100–1, 151
Wooley, Paul, professor, Westmin-
    ster Seminary **2** 396
Woolsey, Theodore, president of
    Yale **1** 101, 194–95, **2** 37–38, 39
World War I **2** 303–4, 307–9

Zwemer, Samuel, missionary
    statesman, Princeton Seminary
    professor **2** 309, 500, n31